WORLD
MYTHOLOGY

GENERAL EDITOR: ROY WILLIS

DUNCAN BAIRD PUBLISHERS

LONDON

World Mythology
General Editor: Roy Willis

First published in the United Kingdom and Ireland in 1993.
This revised edition published in 2006 by
Duncan Baird Publishers Ltd
Sixth Floor
Castle House
75–76 Wells Street
London W1T 3QH

Conceived, created and designed by Duncan Baird Publishers

Editor: Peter Bently
Designers: Bob Gordon and Gail Jones
Picture research: Jan Croot
Maps and illustrations: Sue Sharples

British Library Cataloguing-in-Publication Data:
A CIP record for this book is available from the British Library

10 9 8 7 6 5 4 3 2 1

ISBN-10: 1-84483-166-3
ISBN-13: 9-781844-831661

Typeset in Sabon and Albertus
Colour reproduction by Scanhouse, Malaysia
Printed by Imago, Thailand

Captions to illustrations on pages 1–3:
Page 1: Aztec featherwork disc depicting running water encircling
a fanged god, early 16th century.
Page 2: Melanesian totemic carving.
Page 3: Exuberant carving of a demon from a stone wall-panel
adorning a temple in Bali, Indonesia.

CONTENTS

Foreword by Robert Walter 8

INTRODUCTION 10
Dr Roy Willis

GREAT THEMES OF MYTH 17
Dr Roy Willis

A WORLD MYTHOGRAPHY 35

Egypt 36
PROFESSOR JOHN BAINES AND DR GERALDINE PINCH

The Middle East 56
PROFESSOR THE REVEREND CANON J.R. PORTER

India 68
DR JOHN BROCKINGTON

China 88
DR JOHN CHINNERY

FOREWORD

by Robert Walter,
President, Joseph Campbell Foundation

"How about this one, C.J.?" I asked, handing my seven-year-old son the storybook I had pulled from the library shelf. He studied the cover. "Do you want to try to read it?"

"I already know how it starts," he asserted, not opening the book.

"You do? How?"

" 'Once upon a time ...' They all start like that. Why?"

"Because they're stories about things that happened long ago."

"Yes. But the same things happen now, too."

"Sometimes."

"Oh, all right," he said, flipping through the pages. "But you know what else, Bob?"

"What's that?"

"Sometimes ... I mean, some stories ... I don't think they really happened at all."

"Probably not."

"But that's all right," he added quickly. "They're still good stories."

•   •   •

Nearly everybody loves a good story. Certainly every child does. Our sense of self – our notion of who we are, from whence we came, and whither we are going – is defined by the tales we tell. We are, in essence, who we tell ourselves we are. The narrator of a recent novel has exactly that revelation:

Standing on the rock, looking out, I understood what the story was.

Here's the story: life is a dream.

It's all a story we're telling ourselves. Things are dreams, just dreams, when they're not in front of your eyes. What is in front of your eyes now, what you can reach out and touch, now, will become a dream.

The only thing that keeps us from floating off with the wind is our stories. They give us a name and put us in a place, allow us to keep on touching.[1]

Stories do enable us "to keep on touching" one another. They are, as it were, windows, each framing a particular view of a distinct landscape we might otherwise have never known; and, paradoxically, no matter how unique the perspective, how foreign the vista, if we observe carefully, we can learn something about ourselves. My friend and mentor, Joseph Campbell, a skilled raconteur who appreciated a well-told tale, explains:

The retelling of age-old tales for the sheer delight of their "once-upon-a-time" is an art little practiced in our day, at least in the Western world; and yet, when ... a colorful sample of the art ... is brought to us, the enchantment works and we are carried in imagination to a Never-Never-Land that we, somehow, have long known. ... Their fascination is of ways of life fundamentally different from our own, which yet speak, somehow, to some part of us to which, perhaps, we have not been paying attention: the part of fantasy and dream, which may lead to vision and from vision on to a revelation of some kind – if not about the universe, then at least about ourselves.

For in the past, and today throughout the primitive world that is so fast disappearing even from the hidden corners of the earth, people lived largely out of the visions, either of great teachers, such as the Buddha, Moses, Zarathustra, Jesus, and Muhammad, or, in less developed lands, of their own village seers and shamans. The fabrics and art works of their hands, consequently, were shaped by the visions that had shaped their lives, and these speak subliminally to our own possibilities of vision, telling of qualities of life either lost to us or waiting to be realized.[2]

Implicit in Campbell's remarks is a critical distinction: almost any good story will enchant and can teach us something, but only certain beguiling visions, stories with the power to shape and control our lives, can inspire and, far too often, destroy us. Such potent timeless tales, he would insist, are the only ones that can properly be called "myths." By extension, mythology is, for Campbell, the study of all stories imbued with this puissance.

Not everyone, however, would agree; many, arguably most, are far more comfortable with Robert Graves' circumscribed definition:

Mythology is the study of whatever religious or heroic legends are so foreign to a student's experience that he cannot believe them to be true. Hence the English adjective "mythical", meaning "incredible"; and hence the omission from standard European mythologies, such as this, of all Biblical narratives even when closely paralleled by myths from Persia, Babylonia, Egypt and Greece; and of all hagiological legends.[3]

These observations warrant consideration, especially here in a book where similar omissions have been made; but from Campbell's unprejudiced perspective, no hagiology – including the Bible – is the divine revelation of incontrovertible Truth, for all are, in actuality, fabulous human constructs, wondrous tales of "once upon a time," marvelous myths:

From the point of view of any orthodoxy, myth might be defined simply as "other people's religion," to which an equivalent definition of religion would be "misunderstood mythology," the misunderstanding consisting in the interpretation of mythic metaphors as references to hard fact. ...

Like dreams, myths are productions of the human imagination. Their images, consequently, though derived from the material world and its supposed history, are, like dreams, revelations of the deepest hopes, desires and fears, potentialities and conflicts, of the human will – which in turn is moved by the energies of the organs of the body operating variously against each other and in concert. Every myth, that is to say, whether or not by intention, is *psychologically* symbolic. Its narratives and images are to be read, therefore, not literally, but as metaphors.[4]

For Campbell, then, all myths are "transparent to transcendence:" that is, they are psychic metaphors revelatory of universal axioms; but for many, their own myths are literal facts, while everybody else's are imaginative constructs. Lest you think this distinction is merely academic, simply switch on the evening news or scan the headlines in any daily paper. We think ourselves an intelligent species, and yet, on the eve of the twenty-first century, we are still ravaged by ancient tribal enmities, most of which are fueled by reductive interpretations of exemplary tales and heroic sagas, of myths that have been handed down from generation to generation. Moreover, as Campbell has noted again and again, such mayhem is, and always has been, the inevitable, tragic consequence of literal readings of mythological images, of metaphors:

In the popular nightmare of history, where local mythic images are interpreted, not as metaphors, but as facts, there have been ferocious wars waged between the parties of such contrary manners of metaphoric representation. ...

One cannot but ask: What can such tribal literalism possibly contribute but agony to such a world of intercultural, global prospects as that of our present century? It all comes of misreading metaphors, taking denotation for connotation, the messenger for the message; overloading the carrier, consequently, with sentimentalized significance and throwing both life and thought thereby off balance. To which the only generally recognized correction as yet proposed has been the no less wrongheaded one of dismissing the metaphors as lies (which indeed they are, when so construed), thus scrapping the whole dictionary of the language of the soul (this is a metaphor) by which mankind has been elevated to interests beyond procreation, economics, and "the greatest good of the greatest number."[5]

You hold in your hands a book about myths, which is to say, a book about metaphors, the tools of poets and artists. Its pages are alive with the voices and visions of the artists/mythmakers who have gone before us, with mythological narratives and images, with the "language of the soul." Read these pages as you would read a dream journal, for the task of the modern human being is to interiorize mythic symbology; to realize that all the gods and demons are within; to understand that heaven, hell, and other such realms are not places somewhere "out there" to which you go when you die, but psychological states within us all; to comprehend, in short, that all mythological images are aspects of your own immediate experience.

Accordingly, if you approach this book with an open mind, with the innocence of the child for whom the world is inherently magical, you will explore exotic landscapes and discover untold wonders; you will become reacquainted with the gods of old, with the ancestral demiurges that live within us still; you will learn much about your forbears and neighbors, and even more about yourself; and, of course, you will hear many delightful stories of "once upon a time."

Bob Walter

ROBERT WALTER

---

[1] Tom Spanbauer, *The Man Who Fell in Love with the Moon* (New York: Atlantic Monthly Press, 1991), p.190.

[2] Joseph Campbell, "Myths from West to East," an essay in Alexander Eliot's *Myths* (New York: McGraw-Hill, 1976), p.31.

[3] *New Larousse Encyclopedia of Mythology* (London: Hamlyn Publishing, part of Reed International Books, first published 1959), p.v.

[4] Joseph Campbell, *The Inner Reaches of Outer Space: Metaphor as Myth and as Religion* (New York: Van der Marck Editions, 1985; Harper Perennial, 1988), p.55.

[5] *The Inner Reaches of Outer Space*, op.cit., p.58.

INTRODUCTION

The Greek word *mythos* from which the English term myth is derived originally meant simply "word", "saying" or "story". It was only after the work of the Greek writer Herodotus in the 4th century bc, particularly his history of the war between the Greeks and the Persians, that the concept of historical fact became established in ancient Greek thought. In contrast, *mythos* then came to mean "fiction" and even "falsehood", as distinct from *logos*, the "word of truth". From that time on it was also recognized that *logos* always has an identifiable author, who in the Judaic, Christian and Islamic traditions may be God himself; whereas *mythos* comes down to us anonymously, from some remote source and time beyond calculation.

Theories of myth

Despite the contemptuous dismissal of *mythos* by Herodotus, mythical stories have continued to grip the imagination through the centuries, and there have been numerous attempts by scientists and philosophers to discover the secret of their lasting appeal. In the early modern era, the Italian Giambattista Vico in his *Scienza Nuova* (New Science) of 1725 argued that myths were not distorted versions of Biblical narratives, as was generally accepted in Europe at that time; rather, they were imaginative attempts to solve the mysteries of life and the universe, and as such they were comparable, at an earlier stage of human development, with modern scientific theories.

Later theorists tried to find a single cause for myth-making. A famous 19th-century exponent of such an approach was the German folklorist Friedrich Max Müller, for whom all myths produced by the Indo-European peoples could be understood as originating in symbolic stories, or allegories, about natural phenomena such as the sun, moon, sky or dawn, overlaid with human characters. An example was the ancient Greek myth of Persephone, a girl who was abducted by Hades, king of the underworld, but allowed to return to the upper world for two-thirds of every year (that is, not winter). Müller suggested (it

seems an obvious point now) that this story had originally symbolized the seasonal alternation of winter and summer in the northern hemisphere.

Another influential theorist was the British anthropologist J.G.Frazer, whose 12-volume work *The Golden Bough* (1911-15) brought together mythical stories from all over the world on the subject of divine kingship and the ritual sacrifice of kings, killed by their successors as soon as they were too old to rule effectively. A similar hypothesis has more recently been presented by Walter Burkert, a German folklorist who in 1979 interpreted "scapegoat" myths as relics of primitive mankind's supposedly frequent experience of being compelled to sacrifice a weaker member of the group to pursuing carnivores so that the rest might escape.

Mind and society

Others have looked inward to explain the continuing appeal of particular myths, or of myth in general, claiming that they resonate with permanent features of the human mind or psyche. An example is Sigmund Freud's reading of the Greek myth of Oedipus, in which the hero unknowingly kills his own father and marries his mother. According to Freud, this ancient story portrays the unconscious feelings of all young males about their parents. A general theory of myth was propounded by Freud's collaborator and later opponent Carl Gustav Jung. For this Swiss psychoanalyst, myths draw their mysterious power from the fact that the principal characters in them embody primitive archetypes which have exercised great influence over the human psyche, such as the Wise Old Man or the Mother.

J.G.Frazer worked entirely in the library, but a century ago anthropologists had already begun to study tribal societies at first hand. This approach brought them into touch for the first time with "live" myths and myth-making, and has greatly added to our understanding of the subject in its many-sided complexity. A major contribution was Bronislaw Malinowski's demonstration that the origin myth of the Melanesian inhabitants of

EVIDENCE FOR MYTH

Our knowledge of tribal myth comes mainly second-hand from travellers, missionaries, colonial administrators, and more recently from the field research of anthropologists. Some tribal peoples have produced writers who have set down ancient stories for a Western readership, but obviously we have to rely on what these authors choose to tell us.

The literate civilizations of antiquity have bequeathed a legacy of writings and inscriptions bearing witness to their mythological heritage. However, here too

we are dealing with the end-results of a long process of selection and ordering of what were in the first place oral narratives.

Antique texts have presented archaeologists with formidable problems of interpretation. Understanding of the hieroglyphs of ancient Egypt became possible after 1799 with the discovery near Alexandria of the trilingual Rosetta Stone. Without that advance in knowledge, the riches of the tomb of Tutankhamun, unearthed in 1922, would have lost much of their importance for our understanding

A wall painting from the tomb of Horemheb (ruler of Egypt 1319-1292BC), Thebes: he is between the falcon-headed god Horus and the cow goddess Hathor.

of Egyptian thought. Decipherment of the so-called Linear B script in the 1950s gave us access to the myths of the ancient Mycenaean culture of Crete. But the script of the Indus Valley civilization, in what is now Pakistan and India, still remains undeciphered.

*The Gandhara region
of India was a cultural crossroads, as reflected by a sculptural
style that mixes Buddhist iconography with Graeco-Roman
motifs – here, Herakles (Hercules) with his club.*

TRANSMISSION OF MYTH

Mythical narratives, like folk stories, generally "travel" easily from one group of people to another. Of course, the myths may change in the process, and even within the same group changes may occur as myths are told and retold.

A well-known example of the mobility of myth is the "Great Flood" motif, which is found all over the Middle East and eastern Mediterranean, including Greece, as well as south and east Asia and the Americas. Throughout Africa the Semitic (and Biblical) motifs of a tower being built to heaven and of the "parting of the waters" by a priestly or royal leader occur in numerous local versions. And the stories of Prometheus and of Jason and the Golden Fleece are part of the local mythology of the Caucasus cultures of Georgia and Armenia.

It is often impossible to discover the place of origin of a widely distributed mythical motif. There is more certainty where records suggest the incorporation of a local body of myth into an introduced literate tradition. This happened, for example, in Tibet, where official Buddhism absorbed shamanistic elements from the indigenous culture.

*Bacchus (shown here, left, in a mosaic of
the 1st-2nd century AD) replaced Dionysos
as god of wine and ecstasy in the
mythology which the Romans adopted
from the Greeks.*

the Trobriand Islands, while apparently referring to the remote past, drew its meaning from its direct relevance to the present social order. In this story the ancestors of the four Trobriand clans were said to be certain animals which emerged from a hole in the ground at the beginning of time. The mythical beasts did not appear simultaneously, however, but in an order which was always the same in all versions of the myth. Malinowski showed that this order corresponded precisely with the existing social status of the four clans in relation to each other: the animal ancestor of the highest-status clan emerged first from the primeval earth, the second animal was ancestor of the clan next in rank, and so on.

Oppositions and contradictions

The fact that seemingly archaic tales can relate directly to the way society is organized in the present does not, of course, imply that myths cannot contain a variety of other meanings, perhaps equally or more important. In the latter half of the 20th century no scholar has done more for the profound understanding of myth than the French anthropologist Claude Lévi-Strauss. In his exhaustive analyses of the myths of the native peoples of North and South America, Lévi-Strauss has sought to show how the narratives aim to resolve perceived contradictions in human experience. These may be immediate and sensory (such as the conflict between life and death, hunger and satiation) or extremely abstract (such as the philosophical problem of the One and the Many). Lévi-Strauss argues that myth-makers seek to resolve all manner of contradictions by relating, or trying to relate, one aspect of life to its opposite in a chain of "binary oppositions" – for example, youth and age, wet season and dry season, male and female, human and animal, culture and nature, life and death.

In Lévi-Straussian analysis, a myth "raises as many questions as it answers". In his interpretations of more than eight hundred myths, most of them with several variants, from the peoples of North and South America, Lévi-Strauss has shown in massive detail how the "questions" posed by myths are taken up by other myths in an unending process that ceaselessly crosses and re-crosses geographical and tribal boundaries.

Lévi-Strauss's theory and method have been successfully applied to the myths of India, Africa, Australia and Oceania, as well as ancient Greece (including a pioneering analysis of the Oedipus myth by Lévi-Strauss himself in 1955). But still many questions remain. One avenue of research neglected by Lévi-Strauss in his preoccupation with "binary oppositions" is the question of narrative structure, the way in which episodes are put together to make a "story". In his Oedipus analysis, Lévi-Strauss asserts that the ordering of such episodes is a matter of no consequence for understanding the meaning of the narrative. But can that really be the case?

The work of the Russian folklorist Vladimir Propp and his followers suggests on the contrary that narrative structure is of fundamental importance to the meaning of all traditional stories, including "myths". Propp identified a total of thirty-one episodes or "functions" as constituting the basic building-blocks of all Russian folktales: these include Interdiction, Violation of Interdiction, Villainy, Departure from Home on Quest, Dialogue with Magical Helpers, Appearance of Villain, Flight, Pursuit, and Deliverance from Pursuit. Moreover, although few of the one hundred traditional stories analysed by Propp contain all thirty-one of these "functions", those episodes that appear in any particular tale *always do so in the same order*. The work of the American folklorist Alan Dundes on Native North American stories suggests that here too, although the list of basic episodes is much shorter, they again occur in a fixed sequence. Similar results have been obtained from research in Africa, where Dundes' student Lee Haring has identified a sequence of six episodes in a characteristic story from the Kamba people of Kenya.

Myth and folktale

On the distinction between "myth" and "folktale" the experts tend to become not only divided but surprisingly uninformative. There is general agreement that the two modes of narrative have much in common: they are both communal products, meaning that they lack identifiable authors, and exist in multiple versions. But what, if anything, is the difference between them? Although the two forms shade into each other in complicated ways, one approach is to apply the label "myth" to those anonymous stories that seek to explain the origins of the world, including human society and culture. Since these are matters of universal human concern, it is not surprising to find that everyone can immediately recognize a myth as so defined, no matter how distant or foreign the culture from which it emanates.

Arthur and the thirty kingdoms, illustrated in the medieval Chronicle of Peter Langtoft.

MYTH, HISTORY AND LITERATURE

Myth and history are intricately interwoven in the documentary records of literate civilizations. One famous example of deliberately fabricated historical myth is the Roman poet Virgil's epic elaboration in the *Aeneid* of a pre-existing story linking the foundation of what became the Roman empire with the Trojan exile Aeneas (see pp.172-3). Myths of origin have commonly been used in similar ways, in a variety of cultures, to assert a sense of communal prestige.

At the beginning of the modern era, the relative ease with which the Spanish adventurer Hernán Cortés destroyed the powerful Aztec empire in 1521 is usually related to a contemporary Aztec myth which foretold the coming of bearded white strangers with godlike attributes. Similar myths are said to have existed among the Incas of South America and could have influenced the 16th-century collapse of the Inca empire.

Just as myth may reinforce history, history may conversely become part of the the raw material of the mythic imagination. Often probability is stretched to fabulous limits. The chronicler William of Newburgh (*c*.1198) points out that Geoffrey of Monmouth, in his *History of the Kings of Britain*, makes the little finger of King Arthur thicker than the loins of Alexander the Great. Hard facts about the real Arthur are singularly lacking, although it is possible that he was the leader whom Nennius credits with the decisive battle of Mount Badon against the Saxons (*c*.AD500).

What sort of social conditions produce "myth" in this cosmic sense? It appears that such stories are most prominent in pre-scientific societies with either the simplest or the most sophisticated type of social organization. We find them on the one hand in unstratified societies reliant on hunting and gathering, which of all human communities are the most intimately dependent on nature. (Examples here come from the hunter-gatherer peoples of North and South America, Southeast Asia, Australia and Africa, as well as the Polar Inuit.) On the other hand, we find some of the most complex mythologies in pre-scientific societies which have sufficiently freed themselves from dependence on their environment to develop a hierarchy which includes a privileged intellectual priesthood. (Examples include ancient India and Greece, China and Japan, the Dogon, Bambara and Yoruba peoples of West Africa, the Incas of South America and the Mayan and Aztec peoples of Central America, as well as the Celtic and Germanic peoples of northern Europe.)

"Folktale" is the product of societies which are based on agriculture and are also intermediate in complexity between the simple hunter-gatherer communities and the class-specialized states. The content of the folktale characteristically has to do with social conflict and problems rather than the cosmic issues addressed in myth. (The anonymous and orally transmitted "folktales" must be carefully distinguished from "fairytales", the literary creations of 19th-century Romanticism.)

Typically, a folktale conveys a social message: for example, it may focus on the conflict between youthful enterprise and elderly authority. Often, however, such tales also carry "echoes" of earlier phases of social evolution. For example, in Slav folktales (many of which date from a time long before Russian-speakers became a distinct ethnic group seven or eight centuries ago, and even before the first appearance of the Slavs in the 5th century AD), the presence of the ogress the Baba Iaga may reflect a goddess cult associated with death and the underworld. Similarly, myths concerning golden apples, also found in Slav tales, may be connected with a long-vanished solar cult as well as, quite possibly, even more ancient beliefs linked with journeys to the underworld undertaken by the tribal shaman. Ancient associations with shamanism can be found too in the frequent occurrence in the folktales of Russia and other European countries of the metamorphosis of human beings into animals, and vice versa (as in the case of the werewolf).

In simple terms, one can say that folktales are domesticated myths: stories put together from mythic elements with the dual purpose of entertaining and pointing some moral about human society.

The making of myths

An advantage of the modern immersion of anthropologists and folklorists in field studies is that we no longer think of myths and folktales, as we did in the 19th century, as the primitive equivalents of printed texts. Instead, research in the many rural and tribal societies around the world where myths are still "alive" has made us aware of the dynamic and ever-changing nature of oral narrative. In a sense, every retelling of a myth or folktale is a new creation. The moment of composition is the telling: an oral poem is composed not for but in performance.

This does not mean that the poem, tale or myth is created whole, out of nothing. It is made from a store of ideas and images, generated in countless previous performances that exist in the memory of the narrator, and also in the memories of all those who not only hear, but participate in, the performance, since the performative production of myth and folktale is typically the work not just of an individual but of a whole group.

The participation of the "audience" in story-making typically takes the form of questions and comments which stimulate both the memory and the imagination of the story-teller. This is something I came to appreciate in story-telling sessions in which I participated with a group of Fipa people in southwest Tanzania, East Africa.

Myth and legend

But what of legend, another concept frequently opposed to myth? Scholars are generally agreed that a "legend" is an originally literary story based on a supposedly historical figure or event, a story which contains elements or themes from earlier, mythical narrative transmitted by oral tradition. Legendary stories are found worldwide in cultures with ancient literary traditions, such as China, Japan, India, Mesopotamia, Egypt, Greece, Rome, and Celtic Britain. An example from the Celtic tradition of Ireland is the national epic called *Táin Bó Cuailgne*, "The Cattle Raid of Cooley", an early literary masterpiece replete with mythical motifs. Another and more famous example of this genre is the cycle of Arthurian legends, which was originated by the 12th-century English scholar Geoffrey of Monmouth and based on the exploits of Arthur, an early leader of the Britons in the wars against Saxon invaders. The stories of King Arthur and the Knights of the Round Table, as they have become known in English, contain many allusions to prehistoric Celtic mythology, such as Arthur's visits to the realm of the dead in search of a magic cauldron (the Holy Grail). There are even suggestions that the tale of the king and his following of knights may go back a great deal further than the first appearance of the Celts in history: remarkably similar stories have been recorded in the traditions of ancient Scythia (present-day Romania) and in the accounts of the exploits of Jimmu-tenno, the mythical first emperor of Japan (see p.122).

The three categories – myth, folktale and legend – overlap and shade into each other, as we have seen: both folktale and legend may be grounded in, or punctuated by, mythical elements, and this book, while concentrating on myth, makes no apologies for excursions into folktale (especially that of Central and Eastern Europe) and legend (especially that of Japan, Rome and the Celtic Regions).

The lasting appeal of myth

We can now return to the question raised at the beginning of this Introduction: what accounts for the attraction that myth continues to exert?

A fertile ground for myth-making is the type of small-scale society where people are more or less equal and where there is little occupational specialization or class structure. Typically, the nearest thing to a specialist found in such a society is the shaman, the expert in exploring the invisible worlds above and below the human domain and in bringing back, for the benefit of all, knowledge and wisdom from these realms. The shaman's work resembles in some ways that of the modern scientist, in that it is based on the accumulation of experience gained at first hand by experiment; it is also, like that of the priest, concerned with the domain of spirit. Yet the shaman also possesses a kind of creative freedom which is characteristic of neither scientist nor priest in our society, but rather belongs to the artist. The world of myth originates in the scientific and religious artistry of the shaman, and its most conspicuous aspect is that of *play*.

Stories of shape-shifting (one example is the Inuit tales of men who become polar bears) exemplify this playful spirit. As mythologies developed a cast of divine actors with specialized functions, the mischievous transformation could either become a generalized character trait (as with the various members of the ancient Greek pantheon), or could be specialized in the role of the Trickster – the Coyote or Raven among the North American Indians, Loki among the Nordic divinities, Eshu or Elegba among the peoples of West Africa. Elsewhere in Africa the trickster has been domesticated as the folktale character of the cunning Hare, a figure which reappears in the Brer Rabbit of Black American oral tradition.

Creative play, I would suggest, is the essence of myth-making. Although myth ceaselessly changes and develops, it somehow never loses touch with its roots in tribal shamanic experience. Because this experience is about the interconnections between all aspects of life – visible and invisible, terrestrial and celestial, human, animal, vegetable and mineral – myth cannot but be all-embracing, cosmic in its range. Thus, myth registers and conveys meaning in the deepest sense. But coming from a worldwide human tradition which is irrevocably egalitarian (non-hierarchic, non-authoritarian), it is a meaning that plays with its hearer or reader rather than imposing itself. This, I would suggest, is the secret of its universal and continuing appeal.

GREAT THEMES
OF MYTH

CREATION

The origins of the world

DIVINE INTENTION

Before the universe came into being it already existed as a thought in the mind of Amma (God), the supreme creator divinity, say the Dogon people of West Africa. They attribute the appearance of all things to the deliberate intention of God, and there is a similar implication in the Hindu myth of Brahma imagining the universe in meditation, his divine thoughts then taking on material form.

The idea of God as supreme artist occurs throughout the African continent. For example, the Tiv people of northern Nigeria, who are well known for their woodwork, think of God as the Carpenter, who "carved" the world in accordance with his vision of a perfect place.

Other accounts are less explicit, some seeming to imply that the beginning of things was an accident. Thus, in Norse creation myths the world began through the apparently fortuitous commingling of two contrary elements, fire and ice, within the great abyss of chaos called Ginnungagap.

The riddle of how the world came to be in the first place is a central problem for all mythologies. Sometimes the beginning of all things is described as a total emptiness or void, or alternatively as a limitless expanse of water, an undifferentiated waste clothed in darkness – an idea common to the mythical narratives of the Middle East, the Khoisan peoples of southern Africa and many traditions of North America and Southeast Asia. However, the most widely distributed creation image depicts the primal universe in the form of an egg, containing the potentiality of everything within its all-enveloping shell.

The usual pattern is for some kind of action to occur, initiating a process of change and development. For the Dogon people of West Africa, a vibration set up by Amma the creator god burst the confines of the cosmic egg and liberated the opposed divinities of order and chaos. The watery waste pictured by the Cheyenne of North America was redeemed through the efforts of the humble watercoot in salvaging from the depths a beakful of mud which was then transformed by the All Spirit into dry land. A similar story of a helpful bird, the swallow, in making the first land is told in the islands of Southeast Asia. And in Egyptian myth, the primordial act of creation was the raising of a mound of land out of the watery abyss called Nun.

Duality

In all mythologies the initial meaning of creation is the appearance of separation and plurality in place of oneness and undifferentiation. Typically, the first stage is the most elementary form of distinction – that is, duality. In the Chinese cosmic egg story, when the divine ancestor Pan Gu had grown inside the shell for 18,000 years, the egg exploded into two parts, the light half forming the heavens, the dark half forming the earth. In the Maori creation myth, the world began when the two creator beings, Rangi the male sky and Papa the female earth, broke apart from their immobile embrace in the void and assumed their opposed and complementary positions in the cosmos. The notion occurs too in the beliefs of ancient Mexico:

The theme of the primeval cosmic egg is illustrated in this rock painting found on Easter Island in the South Pacific (Polynesia). The image apparently shows a composite "birdman" figure holding the egg which contains the world.

creation began when Ometecuhtli, self-created Lord of Duality, separated into his male and female aspects as Ometeotl and Omecihuatl, the parents of the gods. An interesting variation is the creation myth of the Bambara people of West Africa, according to which the cosmic egg emitted a voice which then produced its own opposite-sex double, thus bringing into being the primordial twins and divine parents of the world.

The same theme of a primal duality is also found in some versions of the Greek creation story, in which the first gods to appear were Uranos, the male sky, and Gaia, the female earth.

Life out of death

In many traditions, creation is brought about by sacrificial death. In the Chinese account it is the cosmic giant Pan Gu who gives up his life to bring the world into being. Exhausted by the long labour of separating earth and sky, Pan Gu lies down and dies. The various parts of his immense body then become transformed into the manifold features of the heavens and the landscape.

This story resembles a Vedic hymn of the Indian tradition which tells how Purusha, a primordial being, is sacrificed: his bodily parts then become the many components of the universe, including gods, man and animals. In Saharan Africa the world was originally made out of the numerous segments of the sacrificed cosmic serpent Minia, God's first creation – an event remembered in animal sacrifice in the region to this day. There is a similar cosmic drama in Assyro-Babylonian myth when the celestial king Marduk slaughters the serpent Tiamat, the feminine principle of chaos, and divides her enormous corpse: from one half Marduk constructs the vault of heaven, from the other the solid earth. In Norse mythology the three creator gods slaughter the bisexual primeval giant Ymir, forming the earth from his body, the sea from his blood and the sky from his skull.

Cyclical worlds

Some mythologies formalize the struggle between creative order and destructive chaos in terms of a perpetual cycle of creation and destruction, by which worlds are unendingly brought into existence, destroyed and remade. In North America the myth-making imagination of the Hopi people portrays a series of worlds, the first of which was destroyed by fire, the second by freezing, the third by flood; we are now in the fourth world, which is also due to come to an end soon. This scheme resembles that of the Aztecs of Central America, whose mythology tells of the successive creation and destruction of five worlds, brought about by conflicts between the various divine offspring of the Lord of Duality. However, the most philosophically elaborate of all such schemes is perhaps that of Hindu India. This tells how the great god Vishnu, resting on the coils of the cosmic serpent Ananta in the waters of chaos, emits a lotus from his navel which opens to reveal the creator god Brahma. From Brahma's meditation the world is created, lasting an immense expanse of time before dissolving back into chaos, from which a new universe eventually emerges in exactly the same way. Each of the four successive eras within a world cycle is inferior to the previous one. Egyptian myth also anticipates that the universe will eventually dissolve back into chaos, after which a new cycle of creation will begin.

The Graeco-Roman tradition contains nothing about the destruction of the world, but does describe five successive ages, each associated with a different race of men. This cycle began with the Golden Age when human beings enjoyed eternal youth and freedom from toil, and concludes with the present era, the Age of Iron, which is destined to end in humanity's self-destruction. It seems possible that the Celtic tradition of the five successive invasions of Ireland is a version of the Mediterranean myth of the five ages.

CROSS-REFERENCES

Accounts of creation: pp.38, 62, 90, 104, 112-13, 128-9, 194, 222, 237-8, 266-7, 280-81, 290-91, 302-3

Order out of chaos: 38, 70-71, 90-91, 104, 129, 194, 230, 266-7, 280-81

The primeval sea: 62, 70-71, 112, 222

The cosmic egg: 38, 39, 70, 90, 104, 266, 302

The cosmic serpent: 62, 70, 72-3, 74, 199, 266, 277, 280, 302-3

The primal duality: 112-13, 223, 237-8

Creation out of destruction: 62, 70, 90, 194, 277, 290, 294

Cycles of creation: 41, 74, 85, 237-8

Ages of man: 131

COSMIC ARCHITECTURE

The structure of the universe

SUN AND MOON

Throughout the Americas, a common myth explains the relationship between a female sun and a masculine moon as that of sister and brother who are also illicit lovers. Their incestuous and clandestine meetings take place at night when the sun secretly creeps into her lover's bed. But being unable to see him in the dark, she paints dark patches on his cheeks so that she will be able to recognize him later. That, the myth says, explains the discoloured face of the moon. In other North American myths the sun is male, having come from the decapitated head of a man, while the female moon is believed to be the severed head of a woman.

In Africa the cyclical changes in the apparent shape of the moon are said to go back to a time when Moon unwisely began to boast about his loveliness, which he claimed exceeded that of Sun. In anger, Sun broke Moon into small pieces. Ever since, Moon has been scared of Sun and only rarely does he dare to show his whole self in the sky.

In myth the visible world of everyday life is always part of a larger whole. Most traditions describe the normally invisible components of the universe as a world above, or heaven, which is the abode of superior beings, gods or divine ancestors; and an underworld, peopled by the dead and by subterranean spirits.

This image is common to the various Indo-European traditions, to the tribal peoples of Asia, Oceania and the Americas, and to the northern polar peoples. Often the worlds above and below are pictured as mirror images or replicas of the middle world where human beings live, each with its own sky and earth. In many mythologies there is a central pillar or axis which unites the three worlds constituting the cosmos. Sometimes this central axis takes the form of a World Tree. The best-known World Tree is Yggdrasil of Norse tradition. Other notable examples are those of the Ngaju Dayak people of Kalemantan (Indonesian Borneo), the Mayan peoples of Central America, and the peoples of the Sahara region. The idea also occurs in the creation stories of the aboriginal peoples of North and South America. A similar concept is the Tree of Life which occupies a central position in the Kaballah, the Hebrew mystical tradition.

More complex versions of this three-world cosmos describe seven, eight or nine levels of both upper and lower worlds. Seven is the figure given in the Indian tradition, and versions of this cosmic model are found all over southern Asia. A Norse tradition describes nine worlds set one above the other, between which there is constant traffic.

This gilded sun disc, from Trundholm, Denmark, has been dated to the 13th century BC. It is believed to have been associated with a Germanic cult of the sky and seasonal fertility. The sun chariot motif also occurs in prehistoric Celtic art.

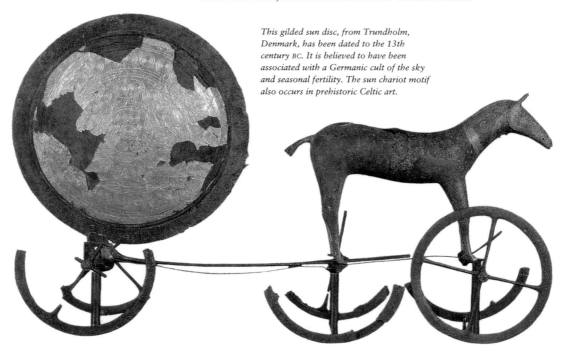

The four directions and the elements

The mythical universe has a lateral as well as a vertical structure. Throughout the world, ancient traditions describe the four quarters that correspond to the cardinal directions (east, west, north and south) as the fundamental divisions of horizontal space. The Tibetan *mandala* (see illustration, right) is a pictorial representation of the same idea. A further "direction" – the centre, or "here" – is sometimes added, making five parts in all, as in China, Celtic Ireland, and North and Central America. In these traditions also, the "centre" was sometimes thought of as comprising the two vertical directions, "up" and "down", so making a universe with six spatial dimensions.

In the mythology of the eastern Mediterranean and North and West Africa, the universe was thought to be constructed out of four elemental substances: air, fire, earth and water. In most of the Saharan and West African traditions each of the four cardinal directions is associated with one of these elements: east with fire, west with water, south with air, north with earth. The eastern Mediterranean traditions, along with those of the Dogon of Mali, West Africa, allocate the elements somewhat differently, air being linked with east and fire with south. A theory of elements is also part of ancient Chinese cosmology. This theory names five elements (wood, fire, soil, metal and water), each associated with one of the five recognized directions ("centre", north, south, east and west).

The heavenly bodies

The celestial bodies commonly appear in myth as living beings, variously divine, human or animal. The sun appears most often as a male divinity, as in the ancient Egyptian cult of the sun god. However, the sun can also be female (the goddess Amaterasu in Japan) and the moon male: see margin, opposite. The male moon appears in myths of southern Africa, where it commonly features as the husband of the planet Venus. Elsewhere, sun and moon are marital partners or, as in some North American myths, brother and sister in the role of incestuous lovers.

Certain groupings of stars are also personalized. In the southern hemisphere, the constellation of the Pleiades is regarded in the myths of South America, Southeast Asia and Australia as a group of sisters whose appearance in the night sky heralds the onset of the rains. Throughout southern Africa, the constellation Orion is seen as a hunter with his dog in pursuit of a game animal. The Greeks identified the constellation Ursa Major (the Great Bear) with the nymph Callisto, whom Zeus placed in the heavens as a bear, together with her son Arcas, the "bear keeper". The part of this constellation which we call the Plough or Big Dipper is known to Native North Americans as the heavenly bear.

The house as cosmic model

In many parts of the world, houses or dwelling-places are consciously modelled on a mythological picture of the universe. This is characteristic of the cultures of the island peoples of Southeast Asia. Typically, the left side of the house represents the underworld, the right side the world above, or heaven. For the Ngaju Dayak people, who recognize the four "cosmic directions", the centre of the house represents the Tree of Life, the vertical axis that unites the three worlds. Among the peoples of the Amazon forests of South America, houses are similarly constructed on a cosmic model, and the same is true of the round tents and centre poles of the nomadic tribes of Siberia.

The houses of the Dogon people of Mali are built to represent the creator god Nommo in human form, but the villages are either square, representing the four-directional earth, or oval, to represent heaven and the cosmic egg. These two versions are always paired, to denote the divine twinship of Heaven and Earth.

Tantric Buddhism (which was eradicated from its Indian homeland by invading Moslems during the 13th century, but remained strong in Tibet) uses a cosmic diagram, the mandala, *as a focus for meditation. The* mandala *represents a palace of the gods. Categorized as either "peaceful" or "wrathful", the palace is formed of radiant light of five colours, or of skulls from the orifices of which issue black smoke, violent sparks and stench. Within the four courtyards of the* mandala *are to be performed the rites of pacification (white, in the east), enrichment (yellow, in the south), control (red, in the west) and destruction (green, in the north). Within the central area of the palace, as blue as deepest space, the supreme rites of enlightenment are achieved.*

MYTHS OF HUMANITY

Causes of life and death

Surprisingly, many mythologies around the world have comparatively little to say about the creation of human beings. The Hebraic tradition represented in the Biblical Book of Genesis says merely that God "created man in His own image". According to one Greek myth, the first man was created from clay and the first woman from earth. Commonly, a more elaborate account is given of cosmic creation than of the origins of humankind.

In North America, a Hopi myth describes the first human beings as formed from earth by Spider Woman, the creator divinity. In Africa, myths usually speak of the Creator as making humans in some place apart, from which they are then introduced into the world. Some stories have them falling from the sky at the beginning of time, while the Herero of southwest Africa say that the first people emerged from a "tree of life" in the underworld. Another African motif is the idea of God making a vessel from which human beings later came out. The Azande version of this story relates that men were originally sealed inside a canoe, together with the sun, moon, stars, night and cold; the sun managed to melt the seal and humanity emerged.

The origins of misfortune

Whether the world came into existence by accident or design, once created it is seen in all mythologies as subject to arbitrary change. The cause of unpredictable events is often put down to the whim of divinities motivated by such apparently human emotions as sexual desire, anger or jealousy. In Egyptian myth the violent god Seth created havoc on earth by murdering his brother Osiris, of whose high reputation he seems to have been jealous. The spite of the Greek goddess Eris ("strife"), insulted because Zeus had not invited her to the wedding of the sea-nymph Thetis to the mortal Peleus, leads indirectly to the Trojan war. In the story of the war, a complicated series of events in which the primary players are divine beings impelled by low motives leads to great human suffering and loss of life.

Greek mythology delivers a similar message in its account of how evil, in the form of sickness and death, came into the world in the first place. Here again, this disaster for humanity is seen as the outcome of a long struggle between supernatural beings (in this case, Prometheus and Zeus). The myth also explains, as a device by Zeus to even the score against Prometheus, the creation of the first woman, Pandora. Sent with a sealed jar (or "box") to Prometheus's brother Epimetheus, who introduces her into human society, she opens the fatal jar out of curiosity, releasing into the world its dire contents of evils, including every kind of sickness; only hope remains inside. Throughout this myth, Prometheus appears as the promoter of human civilization.

Incest and death

The introduction of evils through Pandora is echoed in many other mythological traditions. Polynesian myth, for example, connects the origin of death with the creation of the first woman. A Maori version of the story tells how Tane, god of forests and trees, fashioned the first woman from the sand of Hawaiki island. She bore him a daughter called Hine-titama or Dawn Maiden, whom the god then married also. But Dawn Maiden had not known that Tane was her father. When she discovered the shocking fact, she fled to the underworld. Tane pursued her there, but Dawn

The idea of the first woman as a physical offshoot of the first man is seen in the Biblical story of God making Eve out of Adam's rib (a variant is shown here in a medieval illustration). The many parallels include a Central African myth which has the first woman created from the left knee of the first man.

Maiden told him that he had "severed the cord of the world", and from that time on she would remain in the underworld and pull Tane's human children down to the realm of darkness. That is how both death and the prohibition of incest came to humanity.

A Shoshoni story from North America describes the origin of death in a casual discussion between Wolf the creator divinity and Coyote the trickster. When Wolf says that anyone who dies might be brought back to life by shooting an arrow under them, Coyote argues that if everyone lived there would soon be no space on earth. Wolf sees the point, and contrives that Coyote's son should be the first to die. His own logic working against him, Coyote has to accept that the loss cannot be reversed.

The ecological necessity of death (whose advent is again associated with a woman) is conveyed in an Inuit (Eskimo) myth. For a long time, according to this story, there was no death: people were periodically rejuvenated. But eventually the population became dangerously large, threatening to tip up the land and plunge everyone into the sea. Then an old woman, seeing the danger, used magical words to summon death and war. So the world was lightened, and universal catastrophe averted.

The causes of disease
In the medical philosophy of the Yoruba people of Nigeria, which was brought to earth by the god Ifa, everyone has in his or her body the causative agents which give rise to disease. These agents are various kinds of "worms", and a number of each kind are normally contained in "bags" located in different parts of the body. Their presence is said to be necessary for the maintenance of health: disease occurs only when "worms" multiply excessively and burst out of their "bags". To prevent this from happening, it is necessary to observe moderation in eating, drinking and sex. On the other side of Africa, the Mandari people of the southern Sudan attribute the main causes of disease to invasion of the sufferer's body by spirits, or sorcery by an enemy. Sickness caused by a sky spirit manifests itself as pain in the head or the upper part of the body. The cure is ritual sacrifice to persuade the spirits to withdraw. Similar ideas of illness caused by invasion or capture by spirits occur in shamanism in the Arctic regions, North America and elsewhere.

SUPERNATURAL BEINGS

God, spirits and demons

DEMONS AND AMBIVALENT SPIRITS
Malevolent beings in myth and folklore
are a projection of humanity's deepest
fears. The range of forms is enormous,
embracing semi-human and non-human
creatures, dragons and monsters, giants
and giantesses, demons and dwarves
ranged against the gods in perpetual
cosmic struggle, and specialized figures
such as the invisible *oni* of Japan who
attend the gods of the underworld. In
Western myth spiritual beings are usually
either positive or negative, but in other
cultures there is a greater preponderance
of ambivalent or neutral beings. In Islam,
for example, the *djinni* (genies) can be
either benevolent or malevolent: they were
created out of fire 2,000 years before the
creation of Adam, the first man.

In all mythologies the principal actors in the drama of cosmic creation
begin as spirit beings so fundamental or so awe-inspiring, or both, as to be
describable only as generalities. Native North Americans refer to the All
Spirit or Great Mystery (for example, Wakan Tanka, the supreme deity of
the Lakota). The Hindu creator divinity is Brahma, whose name means
The Absolute. Amma, the original creator god of Dogon myth, is said to
mean The One Who Holds. God is a word of disputed etymology, but
probably derives from a term meaning The Worshipped One.

Destroyer and preserver

The abstract and immaterial supreme being is in many creation stories
provided with a material and animated counterpart in the form of a
gigantic snake. This supernatural creature, associated with water or the
rainbow or both in creation myths as diverse as those of Australia, India,
Southeast Asia, Mesopotamia, Egypt, Africa, Scandinavia and the
Americas, symbolizes a primal chaos which is also the source of all energy
and materiality. The cosmic serpent may be seen as the foundation of
created life (as in Asia, Australia and Africa) or the preserver of creation
(for the Fon people of West Africa the cosmic serpent has the eternal task
of holding the world together); however, it can also be the ultimate
destroyer of creation, as in Norse and southern Asian myth.

Composite beings

After the enormous snake, the next actor to appear on the mythological
scene is often another gigantic being, though this time with recognizably
human characteristics. An example is the Chinese creator god Pan Gu,
who became so huge that he could span the distance between earth and
heaven. Other early members of the Chinese pantheon appear as partly
animal and partly human – for example, the creator couple Fu Xi and Nü
Gua may be portrayed with combined human and serpentine bodies.

   Another frequent theme in early creation mythology is the appearance
of humanoid beings combining both male and female characteristics. In
Egypt the creator divinity Atum is represented as androgynous. One Greek
(Orphic) account of creation describes a bisexual first being, Phanes. In
Norse creation myths the primeval giant Ymir, who was both male and
female, was formed from the union of fire and ice at the beginning of time.

Divine specialization

As the world takes shape through divine activities, the beings who embody
spiritual forces tend to lose their monstrous qualities and, while still
retaining supernatural powers and status, fall into the familiar categories
of animal and human, male and female.

   Thus, in Greek mythology, after the first cosmic upheavals and the
defeat of the Titans, the Olympian gods and goddesses lead lives not
totally removed from those of human beings. Like aristocratic humans in
civilized societies, they take on such specialized functions as patrons of the
arts and crafts, of love and of war. This attribution of social functions to
the gods becomes even more emphatic in Roman mythology, which to a
large extent is a rationalized version of the Greek.

   In Norse myth, the period after the death of the androgynous giant
Ymir saw the appearance of gods of war, music and crafts and goddesses
of fertility. In Mayan religion the supreme creator deity Itzamna was the

*Lilith, the demonic female deity of
Hebraic folklore, appears to have been
derived from a Mesopotamian being of
similar name. She is sometimes said to
have borne demonic offspring by Adam.*

patron of writing and scholarship, and Ix Chel or Lady Rainbow was the divine patroness of medicine, weaving and childbirth. Divinities with such functions can be found in a broad range of cultures.

In some cultures, divine specialization was a matter of locality rather than of role. Spirits peculiar to specific places played an important part in the life of the community. In ancient Japan every region, village and house had its resident spirit, with powers that had to be respected. In addition, unusual natural features such as large or oddly shaped rocks, old trees and springs were also associated with spirits. This is also true over much of Africa, Oceania and Australia, and in pre-Buddhist Tibet and Mongolia.

A vast number of gods and, more especially goddesses, are connected with fertility, ranging from generalized earth mothers to complex figures such as Tlaloc and his female parallels in Mesoamerica.

Lords of the four quarters and the three realms

Particular supernatural beings also took charge of different regions of the cosmos. In China the creator divinity Fu Xi came to be portrayed as possessing four faces, each overseeing one of the four cosmic directions (north, south, east and west). In pre-hispanic Central America each of the four quarters of the universe had its own spiritual lord: the east was overseen by the Red Tezcatlipoca (otherwise Xipe Topec, the flayed god), the south by his blue counterpart, the west by the white lord (or Quetzalcoatl, the Feathered Serpent), and the north by the Black Tezcatlipoca (Lord of the Night Sky). There is a parallel arrangement in the Hebraic tradition that associates the archangel Raphael with the east, Gabriel with the west, Michael with the south and Uriel with the north.

The tripartite division of the cosmos into upper, middle and lower regions also required particular divinities to take responsibility for them. In Egyptian myth Osiris was ruler of the underworld, Geb of the earth, and the goddess Nut of the sky. In ancient Greece the equivalent of Osiris was Hades; Pan, appropriately provided with horns and cloven hooves, ruled over the earthly realm of wild nature; Zeus was the king of heaven, associated with the summit of Mount Olympus.

Rama, the seventh avatar of the god Vishnu in Hindu mythology, is depicted here in an illustration of the epic of which he is the hero, the Ramayana *(see p.77). The image shows multiple episodes in one setting. Rama appears tending a fire (to the left of the hut), and with his brother Lakshmana (right), sitting in front of Sita, his wife. An avatar (the word means "descent") is an incarnation of a deity in human or animal form to combat a specific evil in the world. The Christian notion of God's incarnation as Christ differs from the idea of the avatar in being a unique intervention in earthly history, rather than one stage of a world cycle.*

COSMIC DISASTERS

The end of the world

CYCLES OF DESTRUCTION

The greatest emphasis on global catastrophe is probably to be found in Mesoamerica. According to Aztec traditions, the continuing conflict between the deities associated with each of the four quarters of the universe has entailed a series of cataclysms. The first era ended with the world being consumed by jaguars, the second was destroyed by a great hurricane, the third by fire and the fourth by flood: we are now in the fifth world, which is destined to be devastated by earthquakes.

Another version of this myth told by the Hopi people says that the first world was destroyed, as punishment for human misdemeanours, by an all-consuming fire that came from above and below. The second world ended when the terrestrial globe toppled from its axis and everything was covered with ice. The third world ended in a universal flood. The present world is the fourth; its fate will depend on whether or not its inhabitants behave in accordance with the Creator's plans.

Global catastrophe is sometimes seen in myth as a deserved punishment inflicted by the gods for the folly or wickedness of humankind. The Hebraic story of Noah and the Ark is a familiar version of this idea: Noah and his wife, with the animals they save, are the only survivors of a great flood brought on by God as a punishment for the world's sinfulness. The story echoes an Assyro-Babylonian account (from which it is probably derived) of a cosmic deluge, with Utnapishtim as the Noah figure, who after his adventure becomes immortal. In Greek myth, Zeus sends a great inundation to punish humanity for the misdeeds of the Titan Prometheus. Deucalion, the son of Prometheus, builds an ark and survives with his wife Pyrrha to re-establish the human race.

Indian mythology contains an echo of the Middle Eastern "ark" theme. Manu, the first man, earns the gratitude of a little fish which he saves from being eaten by larger ones. Later, the fish, which has grown to enormous size, warns Manu of a coming cosmic deluge and instructs him on how to build a ship and stock it with "the seed of all things". The gigantic fish then tows the laden vessel to safety.

In some stories of the great flood, the world that emerges from the catastrophe turns out to be better than the one before. For example, in the Andean culture of South America, the sun god, after sending a devastating flood to the earth, causes his son Manco Capac and his daughter Mama Ocllo to teach the arts of civilization to the survivors.

A version of the great flood motif told by the Yao people of southern China focusses on a man who catches the Thunder God responsible for a global inundation. The captive escapes by appealing to the man's children, a boy and a girl, whom he rewards by giving them a tooth which grows into an enormous gourd. Now that the god is free again, the flood returns, soon covering the whole earth. The man floats up to the sky in a specially constructed boat and persuades the Lord of Heaven to order the Thunder God to stop the inundation. This happens so suddenly that the man is killed when his boat hits the ground, whereas his two children survive inside their gourd. This pair are the only survivors of the global flood. They marry, and the girl gives birth to a "ball of flesh". They slice this ball into pieces and mount the ladder leading up to heaven. A gust of wind carries the pieces of flesh to the four corners of the earth, where they become people and the world is repopulated.

The interest of this story for comparative mythology is that it picks up on some of the major creation themes worldwide. A limitless expanse of water is one of the commonest images of a world about to come into being. The enormous gourd reminds us of the widely occurring cosmic egg motif and the brother and sister of the primal parents. The tree that brings them together is reminiscent of the *axis mundi* or Tree of Life that in many mythologies unites the three worlds. Finally, the partition of the "ball of flesh" (which again refers back to the "cosmic egg" image) echoes the primal sacrifice which in so many cultures signals the creation of a recognizable world.

The Chewong people of the Malayan tropical forest, who like others in Southeast Asia subscribe to the idea of a multi-layered universe, believe that every so often their own world, which they call Earth Seven, turns upside down, so that everything on it is drowned or destroyed. However, through the agency of the creator god Tohan, the flat new surface of what had previously been the underside of Earth Seven is moulded into

ARCHA NOE E

mountains, valleys and plains. New trees are planted, and new humans brought into being.

The overturning of the world is not the only story of cosmic disaster related among the Chewong. Catastrophe can also occur through floods caused when someone commits the cardinal sin of laughing at animals. This misdeed annoys the Original Snake whose home is beneath the human world, and the angry movment of this creature causes the primeval waters to inundate the offenders.

Punishment for sexual transgression

In northern Australia an Aboriginal myth describes a catastrophic flood caused by the error of two young sisters in having sex with two men who belonged to the same moiety (clan division) as themselves. A half-human python called Yurlunggur swallows the sisters and brings down a flood which covers the earth. After the waters have subsided, Yurlunggur regurgitates the two women, together with the two sons they have borne from their wrongful unions. The place where Yurlunggur landed becomes the first male initiation ground, where young men learn to distinguish between women they are allowed to mate with and marry, and those they are not.

The theme of forbidden sexual union is also linked with cosmic catastrophe in a myth of the Kuba people of Central Africa. In this story Woot, the founder of the tribe, commits incest with his sister Mweel and then abandons her, causing unending darkness to descend on the earth. Mweel then sends messengers in the form of the birds of morning to her brother, who eventually returns and establishes a social order in which men exchange their sisters in marriage in an orderly system. The sun then rises again. (The catastrophe of the sun's withdrawal is also found in a Japanese myth about a struggle between two divinities, the storm god Susano and the sun goddess Amaterasu.)

An illustration from the Nuremberg Bible of 1483, showing Noah and his family with the animals in the ark which saved them from the Great Flood. The importance of the flood story has been related to the situation of Babylon between two powerful rivers, the Tigris and Euphrates. Both were subject to disastrous inundations, which covered a vast area.

HEROES AND TRICKSTERS

Agents of change

THE THEME OF INGENUITY
Combat by deception is a common trickster theme. In one Oceanic tale, a girl puts coconut oil on the trunk of a banana plant to prevent an ogre from climbing up to seize her. He catches her by imitating her sister's voice, and swallows her. The sister then puts two barnacle shells under her tongue, and every time the ogre who has been holding her captive speaks to her, she answers word for word in a mocking fashion. Enraged, he seizes and swallows her too, but this is just what she had planned. Using the shells, the two sisters cut through the ogre's belly to freedom.

This Maori carving shows Kupe, the culture hero to whom, in Maori myth, the discovery of New Zealand is attributed.

The mythological traditions of all cultures feature heroic figures who perform extraordinary feats in the course of laying the foundations of human society. Usually, though not invariably, these "culture heroes" are male, are possessed of supernatural abilities, and may indeed be gods. In Greek myth, for example, the culture hero was the Titan Prometheus, who stole fire from heaven for the benefit of humankind and was savagely punished by Zeus for his crime. A typical story from Oceania tells of a primordial hero called Sida, Sido, Sosom or Souw who journeyed through the communities of Papua New Guinea, teaching people to speak, stocking the seas with fish and providing vegetables for cultivation. Related to the culture hero is the trickster figure, found all over the world, who may be either creative (a form of culture hero) or subversive. Mischievous, cunning and humorous, tricksters are often seen as possessing the ability to switch between animal and human personae.

Another important type of hero is that represented in human form by Odysseus, whose epic voyages and encounters with supernatural beings intent on his destruction became a model of manly enterprise, courage and endurance in a hostile world. In many hero stories the protagonist is aided by a strong protector: Perseus is helped by Athene, Theseus by Poseidon. Heroic figures associated with the foundation or early history of a tribe or state have been used to strengthen a sense of collective identity, notable examples being Aeneas, Beowulf, Cú Chulainn and Finn.

The theft of fire

In the tribal societies of the Amazon forests of South America a common myth describes the first human beings as living without fire and eating raw meat. One day a young man or boy becomes marooned up a tree in a forest. He is rescued by a jaguar, who takes him to its lair, where he sees fire and smells and eats cooked meat for the first time. The boy steals a burning ember from the fire, and thus introduces fire and cooking to human society. This theme of stolen fire as a key event in the development of society is widespead in myth.

In the Gilbert Islands of the western Pacific, the source of fire is the sun itself: the culture hero Bue snares the sun, and thereby brings fire to humans. Elsewhere in Oceania, Maui is credited with stealing fire from humankind for its keeper in the underworld, the enchantress Mahui-ike.

Beneficent and mischievous tricksters

In North America the culture heroes, like the early creator divinities, are commonly represented in myth as animals. In a story related by the Cherokee people, a number of birds and snakes unsuccessfully attempt to obtain fire that has been lodged by the gods in a hollow sycamore tree on an island. Finally, the female Water Spider manages to obtain a precious live coal from the fire and bring it back for humanity. Another story, from the Lakota people, concerns a mysterious female culture heroine who introduces the people to the complex symbolism of the sacred pipe; then she transforms herself into a black buffalo before disappearing for ever.

Along the Pacific coast of North America the Raven is presented as discoverer of fire. He is also the trickster who outwits the enemies of humankind, a role played in other parts of the continent by the coyote, the hare and the spider, and among the Plains peoples by a figure called The Old Man or Old Man Coyote. These cosmic jokers have the important task of staking a claim for the freedom of the human spirit. They work for the right of humanity to assume the godlike role of re-making the world, even if the attempt on behalf of humanity involves a tendency toward ludicrous and sometimes disastrous mistakes.

This ambiguous potential of the trickster is evident in numerous Oceanic myths. Maui, for example, comes to grief when he tries to enter the sleeping goddess of the underworld and gain mastery over death: a bird who accompanies Maui on his enterprise bursts out laughing at the comical sight, awakening the goddess, who puts the intruder to death.

Unlike these cosmic transformers and jokers, the personalized animal tricksters of African folklore (for example, the hare, the spider and the tortoise) often deploy their inventive faculties, usually with success, to discomfort and confound the rich and powerful in their imaginary societies. Their intention is to subvert the social rather than the cosmic order.

In Africa the task of subversion is most famously discharged by the trickster god Eshu (or Elegba), the African counterpart of Loki in Norse myth (and paralleled also in Japan in the shape-shifter Kitsune). Eshu is a joker who delights in frustrating the will of gods and people alike. In the ancient Greek pantheon the type is represented by Hermes, who is a trickster, liar and thief. Like Eshu, Hermes was also messenger of the gods.

Bhima fights the Rakshasa (demon) Alambusha in an episode from the Mahabharata, *the great Indian epic. Bhima is the great strong man among the Pandava brothers, and is designated "son of the wind".*

ANIMALS AND PLANTS

Energy, transformation and kinship

Creatures of cosmic dimensions figure in myth all over the world. Commonly, certain birds symbolize the upper world of spirits, while immense serpents represent the chaotic energy contained in the underworld. In North America the awesome Thunderbird, said in the northwest to be large enough to carry off whales, engages in continual battle with the water-dwelling serpents for mastery of the earth. Another idea found all through North America is that of the enormous turtle who bears the world upon his back, itself an image of the tripartite universe: its upper shell represents heaven, its lower shell the underworld, its body the middle realm of earth. The same image, sometimes featuring a tortoise, occurs throughout southern Asia and in China.

A motif strikingly similar to that of the Thunderbird against the water serpents pervades the mythology of southern Africa. Here the fabulous Lightning Bird dominates the sky, just as the cosmic serpent, known in Central Africa (as in Australia) as the Rainbow Serpent, rules the watery underworld. A stone sculpture depicting a mighty bird of prey with a snake coiling around its feet adorns the citadel of Great Zimbabwe, and the motif also occurs in the art of the West African Yoruba people. Another example is to be found in the mythology of ancient Egypt, where, during his night voyage, the sun constantly battles against the chaos serpent Apep.

Creatures of the tree
The vegetable kingdom has provided myth with the widespread image of the Tree of Life or World Tree, its roots in the underworld and its branches reaching up to heaven. This idea is epitomized in the World Ash, known as Yggdrasil, of Norse tradition. Interestingly, this ancient Nordic symbol also incorporates the idea of the opposed bird and snake also found in

In Greek myth the winged horse Pegasus sprang from the blood of Medusa after she had been beheaded by Perseus. Another hero, Bellerophon, captured Pegasus and attempted to ride him to heaven. Bellerophon was thrown off, and Pegasus ended up as a constellation. In late antiquity, the flight of Pegasus was regarded as an image of the immortal soul.

North American and African myth, for it bears an eagle in its topmost branches and has a serpent gnawing at its roots. A squirrel runs up and down its enormous trunk, carrying messages between the symbolic animals of the upper and nether regions of the universe. A Southeast Asian example of similar imagery is the Tree of Life of the Ngaju Dayak of Borneo, with a hornbill nesting in its uppermost boughs and a watersnake coiled beneath.

Animal and human kinship
Many systems of belief explicitly affirm the kinship between human beings and other life-forms. Native American traditions typically invest animals with equal status to humans as children of the paternal Sky and maternal Earth. It is often said that in ancient times people and animals were spiritually indistinguishable, and readily assumed each other's forms. The ancestors of tribes on the American northwest coast are thought to have been animals who, after landing on the beaches, transformed themselves into human beings. The idea of animals as precursors and creators of human beings is also found in Africa. According to Khoisan traditions, the first living thing on earth was the tiny praying mantis, and it was he who created the earliest races of beings, including humanity. An ancient Egyptian myth describes how the world is brought into being by the cry of a heron, a manifestation of the creator sun god.

In Mesoamerica it is said that every human being participates in a mystical co-existence with an animal "double" or *nahual*, an idea also found in parts of West Africa. In South America, entire family or clan groups similarly share a mystical identity with certain animal species.

The traditions of the circumpolar Inuit, like those of the Native North Americans, describe an early period when all animals and humans lived in the same community, speaking the same language, frequently changing appearance, and intermarrying. The polar bear was said to be the closest to human beings of all the animals, though detectable in his human form by his oversized canine teeth and huge appetite for fat.

Transformations
Metamorphosis, the theme of the Roman poet Ovid's verse narratives, is a subject of universal fascination that has filtered through into all aspects of modern popular culture. Among many Southeast Asian myths that describe human beings changing into animals and plants is a story from the forest peoples of Malaysia telling how the creator god solved a problem of overpopulation by transforming half the people into trees.

The imagination of modern Western societies is still gripped by the werewolf, which figures in the folklore of many peoples of Europe and elsewhere. Such wolfman stories have a parallel in a widespread African tradition whereby some men and women had the ability to change themselves into predatory beasts such as lions, leopards or hyenas. A similar power is attributed in South and Central America to the tribal shamans, who are said to transform themselves into jaguars – a feat described in numerous myths.

The animal consort
Another commonly occurring motif is the animal consort. The Gaelic folktales of Scotland abound in stories of men and women who are really seals and marry human husbands, often leaving them in due course and returning to the sea. A widespread myth in southern Africa is that of the python-god who marries a human wife, sometimes dragging her down with him to his watery underworld home. Similarly, there is a Native North American myth of a youth who finds himself in the kingdom of the deer (an animal believed to be capable of taking on human form): the youth transforms himself into a deer, and takes a deer for a wife.

PLANTS IN MYTH AND RELIGION
Trees are believed in many cultures to be a connection between heaven and earth, and are sometimes perceived as the home of spirits. The most important supernatural figures associated with plantlife, however, are the deities of cultivated plants, especially numerous in Mesoamerican myth. Gods of the vine, which connects agriculture with the state of ecstasy, also play a prominent role.

Throughout Southeast Asia the sowing, cultivation and harvesting of rice is accompanied by rituals honouring the "spirit" of this staple cereal. Many peoples of the regions have a divinity of rice, usually female (the Rice Mother). The mountain-dwelling Lamet of northern Laos are among the societies which recognize a "vital principle", called *klpu*, which belongs only to human beings and to the rice plant.

The parasitic sandalwood and its close relatives are used in religious practices in many parts of the Eastern world.

This 10th-century Indian bronze depicts the youthful Krishna dancing on the head of the snake demon Kaliya, shown with five hoods around a tiny human torso. Snakes (typically seen as cobras) play a major part in Indian myth.

BODY AND SOUL

Spirit and the afterlife

*This Alaskan mask probably represents
the shaman's journey to the spirit
realm. The face in the centre is the
shaman's soul.*

The mythological imagination everywhere tends to see the visible world of daily life as containing, or in some way associated with, an invisible essence which could be called "soul" or "spirit". In the case of powerful objects such as the sun, the soul or spirit essence is easily envisaged as an especially potent deity. Soul is similarly attributed to the moon, the earth, and spectacular features of the landscape such as mountains, lakes or even large trees.

Sometimes the invisible spirit counterpart of the everyday world is thought of as a place apart. Melanesian myths often feature events in a mirror world located underground. Celtic tradition tells of an Otherworld, a place of magic, mystery and danger which can be entered through caves or lakes, and is sometimes located in the west. Despite the perils entailed for ordinary mortals in venturing into the hidden world, it is described as a place of unending happiness and eternal youth.

The human soul is often thought of as a normally invisible duplicate of the visible body, and is sometimes called a "shadow". Germanic folklore makes frequent mention of this eerie "double", or *doppelgänger*, which has the disconcerting habit of suddenly manifesting itself, often far away from its material counterpart. Throughout Africa it is supposed that witches inflict injury and death by invisibly attacking their victims' souls or shadow selves, thereby causing parallel damage in the physical body.

The soul's journey

Many traditions picture the journey of the human soul after death as a descent into the underworld, the realm of the dead. In many parts of Africa it is believed that the souls of the departed spend a certain amount of time in this underworld before deciding to be born again in the upper world of human life. Other traditions tell of a fearful ordeal of judgment that awaits the newly departed soul. In Japanese myth those found guilty of grievous sin are consigned to one of sixteen regions of an infernal domain called Jigoku. The myths of ancient Egypt paint a vivid picture of the soul being examined by forty-two judges in the throne room of Osiris, lord of the underworld. Those who fail to prove that they have lived virtuous lives are devoured by a monster; whereas the fortunate souls who pass the test when their hearts or consciences are weighed against the feather of the goddess Maat, deity of justice and truth, join the gods in their eternal battle against the serpent of chaos, Apep.

Greek tradition places the underworld beyond the great river called Ocean which surrounds the world, or deep inside the earth. To reach the domain called Hades (which was also the name of its divine ruler, a brother of Zeus), the newly departed souls have to be ferried across the infernal river Styx by Charon the boatman. Once there, as in Egypt, the souls were judged and then punished or rewarded accordingly.

The soul's journey is often provisioned by the living. For example, the Greek and Roman dead were given not only money to be ferried across the Styx, but also confectionery for Cerberus, the terrifying three-headed dog which guarded the entrance to Hades.

Reincarnation

In many mythical systems some form of rejuvenation followed the soul's sojourn in the realm of the dead. In Africa it is usually supposed that souls are reborn into the kin group or clan to which they had belonged in the previous life. In the Oriental civilizations influenced by Hindu and Buddhist philosophy it is commonly believed that reincarnational destiny depends on the person's conduct in earlier lives: the good are rewarded with incarnation in higher social castes or groups, the wicked in low-status groups, or as animals. Conversely, it is held that particularly virtuous animals can be reincarnated as human beings.

Soul capture
Among the forest peoples of South America and the islands of Southeast Asia it is commonly held that the soul resides in the human head, and another person's soul can be captured by cutting off and ritually processing this part of his anatomy. Hence the custom of head-hunting in these regions, and the abundance of myths on the topic. Cannibalism in South America may be similarly aggressive, but can also be used as a means to absorb the vital spiritual qualities of deceased relatives.

Shamans and shape-shifters
In tribal societies worldwide there are acknowledged experts in the exploration of the invisible world of spirit. These adepts, who generally use their discoveries for the benefit of their fellows, are termed "shamans" – a word derived from the Tungus people of Siberia. Many myths derive from shamanistic journeys into the spirit world, during which the shamans typically meet and converse with spirit beings, which are often encountered in animal form. The shaman is said to leave his or her body while in a trance state induced either by pyschotropic drugs or by the rhythmic sound of a drum or rattle. Shamans all over the world tell similar stories of moving up or down a mystical pillar or axis to explore the upper and lower regions of the cosmos. Often this pillar or axis is imagined in the form of a tree, stretching from the underworld up to the sky. In those invisible realms above and below the visible world of daily life the shaman is free of the limitations of time, space and personal identity. He or she can assume the attributes of powerful animals: the eagle or bear in North America and northern Asia, the jaguar in Central and South America, the lion and leopard in Africa.

Dream journeys
Many tribal peoples believe that the human soul temporarily leaves the body during the dream-state, wandering in other worlds and meeting other souls, including those of the dead. These nocturnal journeys have provided a great deal of material for myth-making. In North America and Southeast Asia such voyages are thought to expose the errant soul to the danger of abduction by a sorcerer or malevolent spirit; when this happens, local shamans are customarily employed to search for and retrieve the lost soul.

The afterlife
The geography of paradise varies widely from culture to culture. In Japanese myth, Amer lies above the earth, watered by a tranquil river, which is the Milky Way; otherwise the scenery resembles that on earth, though on a more extensive scale. Valhalla, heavenly abode of the bravest Norse warriors, was also of vast extent. It consisted of an enormous hall with no fewer than 540 doors. Every morning the warriors issued from the hall fully armed and spent the morning in playful combat with each other. In the evening they returned to the great hall and refreshed themselves by feasting and drinking cups of heavenly mead presented to them by the celestial maidens, the Valkyries. In some traditions the heavenly realm is situated on the same plane as the earth. Slavonic myth tells of a blissful land of the dead located in the east, beyond the sunrise; while the Celtic islands of the blessed were located to the west. Frequently a perilous voyage over water must be undertaken before paradise is reached.

Osiris was king of the underworld in ancient Egyptian myth, and kings were thought to become Osiris when they died. Certain cults believed that immortality could be attained by following this god. He is depicted as a royal mummy with crossed arms, a crook and a flail.

THE LIVING AND THE DEAD
In Celtic belief the world of the living is closer to the world of the dead during the hours of darkness. A person born at night could see ghosts and phantoms. In rural Ireland anyone venturing out at night might see the "little people", and find their own dead relatives among them.

The dead can disturb the living at certain specific times of year. In Scotland Hallow'een is traditionally celebrated by boys called "guysers" who go about with blackened faces, impersonating the spirits of the dead and demanding gifts.

Chinese Buddhists celebrate a Feast of Wandering Souls, intended to relieve the sufferings of the restless dead.

MARRIAGE AND KINSHIP
Myths of the social order

A Yoruba mask, from Nigeria, used on ceremonial occasions. The mask represents ancestor spirits, and the dancing celebrant who wore it in a ritual parade was believed to become possessed by the spirits for as long as the parade lasted. Both the mask and its wearer become the spirits they evoke.

Myths are often concerned with validating fundamental social distinctions, such as those between the rulers and the ruled in societies with hereditary kingship; between social classes or castes; between old and young; and between male and female, particularly in the relationship of marriage.

Male and female
One of the principal tasks of the "culture hero" (see p.28) is to establish the order of society. In Australia and Papua Guinea one of the achievements of the hero is to establish the ritual of male initiation, which legitimizes the superior social status of men as against women, and defines categories of potential marriage partners. Myths of these regions and of South America frequently assert that originally women ruled society but lost this privilege through some fault they had committed.

Supernatural authority for the superior social status of males is a common motif in creation myths. Eve in the Hebraic myth of Genesis, and Pandora in Greek mythology, were seen as bringing their sex into disrepute. The Japanese creation story underscores the inherent inequality of male and female marriage partners by describing the unfortunate consequences of failing to observe the principle of male precedence. When Izanami, the female member of the primal pair, presumptuously greets her male consort Izanagi without waiting humbly for him to address her first, the result is the birth of a monstrous first child, which they abandon to the sea. Apprised through divination of the cause of their misfortune, the couple thereafter take care to observe the rule of male primacy, and they are duly rewarded with fine progeny.

Ancestry, rank and kingship
Myths of ancestry frequently imply a hierarchy of status, reflected by the order in which the ancestors of different groups or peoples first appeared on earth. It is not always the oldest, but sometimes the most recent, emergence that claims the most superior rank: for example, in the pre-colonial African state of Bunyoro (now Uganda) the royal dynasty descended from the most recent arrivals in the country, while the peasant class were long-established. This hierarchy is mirrored in a myth by which the creator god Ruhanga uses a cunning test to chose a different social rank for each of his three sons.

Unsurprisingly, kingship tends be validated, in cultures all over the world, by claims to the most prestigious of all possible ancestry: descent from divinity itself. Traditionally, the imperial line of Japan traced its ancestry back to the sun goddess Amaterasu. Solar descent was also part of the title to legitimacy asserted by the Polynesian kings of Hawaii and the Inca kings of South America. The divine king of the Shilluk people of Africa is believed to be an incarnation of Nyikang, the first Shilluk king and founder of the nation, who was born of a sky god and a river goddess.

In ancient times, the pharaohs of Egypt claimed descent from the divine couple Isis and Osiris. Some of the Roman emperors, such as Gaius (Caligula) went further and claimed to be gods in their own right, and after death it was customary for the pre-Christian emperors to be declared gods and worshipped. Aeneas, the mythical Trojan hero who was revered as the founder of the city of Rome, was claimed to be the son of the goddess Aphrodite.

A WORLD
MYTHOGRAPHY

EGYPT

The interior of the spectacular temple built by the Egyptian
pharaoh Ramesses II (ruled 1279-1213BC) at Abu Simbel, on the
west bank of the Nile about 150 miles southwest of Philae.

Ancient Egypt is often seen as a land dominated by gods, kings and priests. Its temples are covered with images of gods, and religion looms large in the records recovered from the three thousand years of Egyptian civilization. Yet surprisingly little is known about the myths which embodied the Egyptian understanding of the world. Narratives were written down only after 2000BC, although there are much earlier pictorial representations and allusions: for example, kings of the Second Dynasty (*c.*2800BC) represented their struggles in terms of the conflict of Horus and Seth (see p.44).

Myths were less significant than the cult of the gods, an essential state activity conducted in temples accessible only to the king and priests. If the cult was performed properly, the land prospered.

Divine service centred around daily care for the cult images of the gods in their sanctuaries. Local people seldom took part in cults except as an audience for festivals when deities "visited" one another by being carried in procession or by river. Early temples were depicted as simple perishable structures enclosed by fences, but they grew in complexity and numbers, as their originally discrete gods became associated with one another.

Myths developed by elaborating on the relations between gods. No single version of a story was seen as correct, and the content could be adapted for different circumstances. Thus, the role of Seth (see pp.44-5) was transformed in the Late Period, when he became the enemy of the gods and was ritually annihilated.

UPPER AND LOWER EGYPT

The two regions which made up the Egyptian state, Upper and Lower Egypt (see map), were crucial to political life and religion. Egyptian thought was strongly dualistic: no true unity could exist without subdivision, and the world before creation was the time "before there were two things". The country had no single embracing name and was called "The Two Lands". The ancient gods Horus and Seth each came to be associated with a part of the country, Horus presiding over Lower Egypt, Seth over Upper Egypt. Nekhbet, the vulture goddess of Nekheb, and Wadjet, the cobra goddess of Buto, were Egypt's protective goddesses, and were strongly associated with kingship.

Upper Egypt, which included such important centres as Thebes (see below), has produced most of the surviving evidence for myths, but parts of Lower Egypt, such as the region around Memphis, were at least as important.

REGIONAL MYTHS

Many deities were important only in particular regions or were local variants of national gods. Some myths explained local features, such as the origin of a mountain or the associations of an old building. Others, the best known of which date to the Graeco-Roman period, were set throughout the country.

SOURCES FOR MYTH

Few narratives are preserved, and myths are reconstructed from indirect evidence. One source is the body of religious texts: funerary texts, rituals and hymns for divine cults, and magical texts. Pictorial representations provide much material, but few depict episodes of myths directly. Most date to 1500BC or later. They include reliefs in major temples, the decoration of tombs, coffins and other burial equipment, and objects dedicated in temples or used in magic. Central myths may occur in disguised form in literary texts.

TIME CHART

Dates of periods and kingdoms before 664BC are approximate.

Formative Period
3200-3000 BC
Early Dynastic Period
3000-2550 BC
Old Kingdom
2550-2150 BC
First Intermediate Period
2150-1980 BC
Middle Kingdom
1980-1640 BC
Second Intermediate Period
1640-1520 BC
New Kingdom
1540-1070 BC
Third Intermediate Period
1070-664 BC
Late Period
664-332 BC
Graeco-Roman Period
332 BC-AD 395

THEBES

Thebes (right), modern Luxor, was briefly the capital (c.2000BC and c.1520-1450BC). The prime religious centre for more than a millennium, it is the site of the largest surviving temple complexes in the ancient world, and of the royal tombs in the Valley of the Kings. Its principal god, Amon (see p.39), may have originated elsewhere and supplanted the falcon god Mont of Armant.

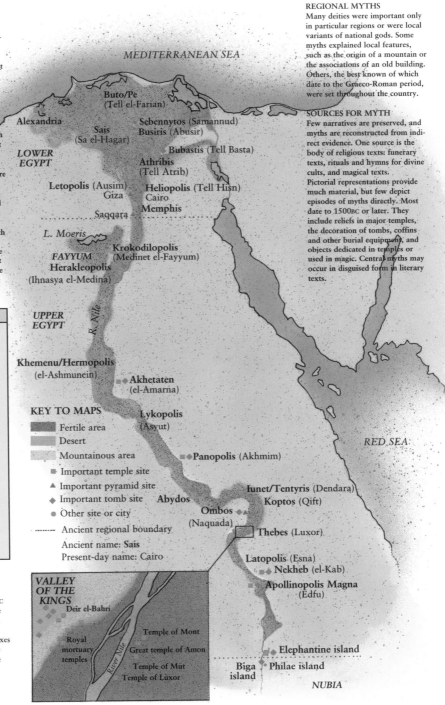

MEDITERRANEAN SEA

Buto/Pe (Tell el-Farian)
Alexandria
Sais (Sa el-Hagar)
Sebennytos (Samannud)
Busiris (Abusir)
Bubastis (Tell Basta)
LOWER EGYPT
Athribis (Tell Atrib)
Letopolis (Ausim)
Giza
Heliopolis (Tell Hisn)
Cairo
Memphis
Saqqara
L. Moeris
FAYYUM
Krokodilopolis (Medinet el-Fayyum)
Herakleopolis (Ihnasya el-Medina)
UPPER EGYPT
R. Nile
Khemenu/Hermopolis (el-Ashmunein)
Akhetaten (el-Amarna)

KEY TO MAPS

- Fertile area
- Desert
- Mountainous area
- ■ Important temple site
- ▲ Important pyramid site
- ◆ Important tomb site
- ● Other site or city
- ----- Ancient regional boundary
- Ancient name: **Sais**
- Present-day name: Cairo

Lykopolis (Asyut)
Panopolis (Akhmim)
RED SEA
Iunet/Tentyris (Dendara)
Koptos (Qift)
Abydos
Ombos (Naquada)
Thebes (Luxor)
Latopolis (Esna)
Nekheb (el-Kab)
Apollinopolis Magna (Edfu)
Elephantine island
Biga island
Philae island
NUBIA

VALLEY OF THE KINGS

Deir el-Bahri
Royal mortuary temples
River Nile
Temple of Mont
Great temple of Amon
Temple of Mut
Temple of Luxor

THE FIRST GODS

Order from chaos

The above detail, taken from a papyrus of the 13th century BC, shows the Benu bird, revered at Heliopolis as the first deity. The Greeks identified the Benu bird with the phoenix, which burnt itself to death every five hundred years and rose rejuvenated from the ashes.

Before the gods came into existence there was only a dark, watery abyss called the Nun, whose chaotic energies contained the potential forms of all living things. The spirit of the creator was present in these primeval waters but had no place in which to take shape. The destructive forces of chaos were embodied by the great serpent Apep or Apophis.

The event that marked the beginning of time was the rising of the first land out of the waters of the Nun. This primeval mound provided a place in which the first deity could come into existence. He sometimes took the form of a bird, a falcon, a heron, or a yellow wagtail, which perched on the mound. An alternative image of creation was the primeval lotus, which rose out of the waters and opened to reveal an infant god. The first deity was equipped with several divine powers, such as Hu ("Authoritative Utterance"), Sia ("Perception") and Heka ("Magic"). Using these powers, he created order out of chaos. This divine order was personified by a goddess, Maat, the daughter of the sun god. The word Maat also meant justice, truth and harmony. The divine order was constantly in danger of dissolving back into the chaos from which it had been formed.

The first deity became conscious of being alone and created gods and men in his own image and a world for them to inhabit. Deities were said to come from the sweat of the sun god and human beings from his tears. The power of creation was usually linked with the sun, but various deities are also named as the creator. At the temple of the sun god in Heliopolis, the Benu bird (see left, above) was said to be the first deity. Depicted as a heron, the shining bird was a manifestation of the creator sun god, and brought the first light into the darkness of chaos. When it landed on the primeval mound, it gave a cry that was the first sound.

The Ogdoad

*I*n ancient Egypt the forces of chaos could be personified as eight divinities, the Ogdoad.

The Ogdoad consisted of four couples, each pair of divinities representing an aspect of the primeval state. Nun and Naunet were the god and goddess of the primeval waters. Kek and Keket were the deities of darkness. Amon and Amaunet embodied an invisible power. Heh and Hehet were boundlessness. Other couples were sometimes included in the Ogdoad, but the total number of deities was always eight. These deities were imagined as snakes

Seven of the Ogdoad and the sun god Ra-Harakhty in falcon form. A papyrus of c.1350BC.

and frogs, creatures of the primeval slime. However, the Ogdoad are sometimes depicted as baboons greeting the first sunrise (see left).

The Ogdoad was worshipped principally at a place called Khemenu ("Eight Town") by the Egyptians and Hermopolis by the Greeks (see map on p.37), which claimed to be the site of the "Island of Flame", where the sun rose for the first time. The Ogdoad came together to form the cosmic egg from which the sun god was hatched. Part of the shell of the cosmic egg was said to be buried inside a temple at Hermopolis.

Divine creators

The Egyptians possessed four main creator deities, Amon-Ra, Atum, Khnum and Ptah, each of which was the focus of an important cult.

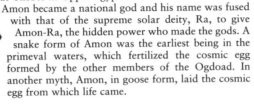

Amon-Ra One of the Ogdoad, Amon was worshipped as a fertility god at Thebes in Upper Egypt. In the 2nd millennium BC, Amon became a national god and his name was fused with that of the supreme solar deity, Ra, to give Amon-Ra, the hidden power who made the gods. A snake form of Amon was the earliest being in the primeval waters, which fertilized the cosmic egg formed by the other members of the Ogdoad. In another myth, Amon, in goose form, laid the cosmic egg from which life came.

Amon holding the symbols of life and power, on a Late Period bronze plaque.

Atum A creator deity worshipped at Heliopolis, who first emerged from the primeval chaos in the shape of a serpent, but was usually shown in human form. As Ra-Atum, he represented the evening sun who had to return to the womb of Nut to be renewed each night. Like other creator deities, Atum represented a totality which contained both male and female. In one early myth, Atum is lonely on the primeval mound, so he takes his phallus in his hand and produces semen, from which comes the first divine couple, Shu and Tefenet (see pp.40-41).

Khnum The principal cult centre of the god Khnum was on the southern island of Elephantine. Khnum was thought to control the annual rising of the Nile and embodied the life-giving power of this inundation. His sacred animal was the ram, a symbol of virility, and he was usually shown as a man with a ram's head. In his temple at Esna, Khnum is described as "father of fathers and mother of mothers". He shaped gods, humans and animals from clay on his potter's wheel and put the breath of life into their bodies.

Ptah Worshipped at Memphis, Ptah was the god of crafts, and was said to fashion the gods and kings out of precious metals. The intellectual power behind creation, he created all the other gods by thinking of them in his heart and speaking their names aloud.

A Late Period bronze statuette of the god Ptah, the divine craftsman-creator.

THE HAND OF ATUM
The myth of Atum was sometimes reinterpreted so that creation began with the sexual union of a god and goddess. The female partner was identified with the Hand of Atum. Of the various goddesses who can be called "The Hand", the most important were Hathor and Neith (see pp.50-51). The faience head (above) combines attributes of Hathor and Nut, another goddess who embodied female creative power.

THE ENNEAD

The Nine Gods of Heliopolis

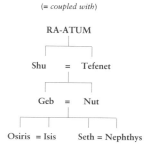

A faience figurine of the goddess Nut in the form of a sow, c.600BC. Sometimes it was claimed that Nut wanted to devour her offspring, as a sow will eat its farrow.

The most detailed Egyptian account of creation concerns the deities known as the Nine Gods of Heliopolis, or the Ennead (from the Greek ennea, nine). The first of these was Ra-Atum, who came into being on the primeval mound and planned the multiplicity of creation in his heart. He caused the first division into male and female when he took his semen in his mouth and spat or sneezed out Shu, the god of air, and Tefenet, the goddess of moisture. They explored the dark Nun and were lost to Ra-Atum, who sent his divine Eye, a fiery power regarded as the sun god's daughter, to look for them. The goddess returned with Shu and Tefenet, and the first human beings were formed from the tears wept by Ra-Atum on being reunited with his children.

From the sexual union of Shu and Tefenet came Geb, the earth god, and Nut, the sky goddess. These two embraced so closely that there was no room for anything to exist between them. Nut became pregnant by Geb, but it was impossible for her children to be born. Eventually, their father Shu, the air god, separated Geb and Nut. With the aid of eight beings known as the Heh gods, Shu held the sky goddess high above the earth, so that there was space for living creatures and air for them to breathe. There was thought to be a second sky below the earth.

The primeval waters continued to surround the cosmos of earth and sky. The sky goddess sometimes took the form of a naked woman arching over the earth (see illustration, opposite), and sometimes the form of a cow patterned with stars. She was said to swallow the sun every evening and was sometimes accused of wanting to swallow all her children. In such instances Nut was represented as a sow, a creature notorious for eating its own young.

The children of Nut were two pairs of twins, Osiris and Isis, and Seth and Nephthys (see pp.42-5). Osiris and Isis are said to have fallen in love in the womb, but Nephthys despised her brother Seth. As the eldest of the children of Geb and Nut, Osiris was destined to rule Egypt.

Family tree of the Ennead

(= *coupled with*)

RA-ATUM

Shu = Tefenet

Geb = Nut

Osiris = Isis   Seth = Nephthys

In this papyrus illustration of c.1100BC, Shu, the air god, separates his children Geb, the earth god, and Nut, the sky goddess. The solar barque, the boat in which the sun crosses the heavens, is shown above the starry body of Nut.

Ra and the punishment of humankind

A text inscribed on one of the golden shrines from the tomb of King Tutankhamun (who ruled c.1336BC-1327BC), and which also appears on the walls of later royal tombs, tells of a time when Ra, the creator sun god, lived on earth as the ruler of gods and people.

As the sun god aged, human beings began to plot against him. When Ra saw this, he summoned his divine Eye, in the form of the goddess Hathor. He also sent for Shu, Tefenet, Geb, Nut and the eight primeval gods of the Ogdoad (see p.38). Ra asked Nun, the oldest of these primeval gods, for advice as to what to do about the rebellious people. Nun and the other gods counselled the sun god to send his divine Eye to destroy humankind. Ra agreed, and the Eye goddess was transformed from Hathor into Sekhmet, the raging lioness (see p.50), who slaughtered some of the people and waded in their blood.

Ra decided to save the remainder of humanity. In order to distract Sekhmet from her orgy of killing, he ordered the high priest of his temple at Heliopolis to make 7,000 jars of beer and to dye it red. When this had been done, the beer was poured out on the ground so that it looked like a lake of blood. The Eye goddess saw the lake and her reflection in it. She lapped up the dyed beer and became so drunk that she forgot about slaughtering the rest of humankind. The Eye goddess was transformed from the savage Sekhmet back into the beautiful Hathor, but although humanity was now safe from the lion goddess's rage, plague and death had now come into existence.

Ra felt so weary and sad that he longed to put an end to creation and return to the watery abyss. Nun ordered Shu and Nut to help to protect the sun god. The sky goddess became a cow and carried Ra up into the firmament, where he created the stars and the fields of paradise. Nut began to shake because she was so high above the earth, but Shu and the eight Heh gods supported her.

Each day the sun god journeyed across the sky and each night he entered the underworld. When he did so, humanity became terrified by the darkness of night, so Ra decided to make the moon, to light the sky in his absence, and he appointed the moon god Thoth as his deputy. Ra warned the earth god, Geb, about the magical powers of the chaos serpents and chose Osiris to rule over humanity.

This cosmos would not last for ever, the Egyptians believed. The time would come when the creator would grow so weary that he and all his works would dissolve back into chaos. Then the cycle of creation would recommence.

OSIRIS

Upholder of order

This gold pendant (c.850BC) shows Osiris as a mummified king, flanked by Isis and his son Horus. After death Osiris ruled the underworld (Duat). Apparently seen in early times as the terrifying king of a realm of demons, he became the just judge who welcomed the virtuous dead to paradise.

Osiris became the first king, and his consort was his sister Isis (see family tree, p.40). He was revered as a god of agriculture who taught humanity the secrets of farming and civilization. His rule was threatened by the forces of chaos, which included his brother, Seth. One myth says that strife entered creation only when Seth violently broke out of his mother's womb.

The death of the good god Osiris was one of the central events of Egyptian myth, but the story was rarely set down in detail. Two stages in the episode are mentioned: his murder and his dismemberment. The earliest accounts simply say that Osiris was thrown down by his brother Seth on the river bank at Nedyet, a mythical place sometimes identified with part of Abydos, the sacred site where the mysteries of Osiris were celebrated. Later versions of the myth state that Osiris was drowned in the Nile, and Seth is often named as the murderer. He is said to have taken the form of a crocodile or a hippopotamus to attack his innocent brother, although in one version he turns himself into a bull and tramples Osiris to death. The foreleg which trampled Osiris was later cut off by the god Horus and thrown into the sky, where it became part of the constellation we call the Great Bear. Another late tradition states that Seth became a small insect, perhaps a mosquito, and gave Osiris a fatal bite on the foot.

Isis searched for her husband and used her magic powers to prevent or reverse the decay of his corpse. She summoned the jackal god Anubis who embalmed and bandaged the body of Osiris, making him the first mummy. In later versions of the myth, Seth found the divine body of Osiris and ripped it to pieces, and these pieces were said to be buried at sites all over Egypt: the head at Abydos, the heart at Athribis, a leg on Biga island, and so on. The dismemberment of Osiris was compared with the annual cutting down and threshing of wheat and barley. Osiris was thought to rise again with the growth of the new crops.

The mourning goddesses

*I*sis and her sister Nephthys, the consort of Seth, watched over the body of their brother Osiris in the form of sparrowhawks. At funerals it was the custom for two women to play the roles of Isis and Nephthys and lament over the mummified corpse.

Nephthys loved Osiris, and a late tradition even made the god Anubis their son. The two goddesses wept and lamented over Osiris, begging his spirit to return to them. In one

account, Isis avows: "While I can still see I will call to you, crying to heaven's height. You do not come to me, although I am your sister, whom you loved upon earth."

Osiris, the creator god Ptah and a funerary god, Sokar, are shown in this papyrus of c.1100BC as a single deity. Isis and Nephthys protect his throne. The animal skin hanging from a pole is one of the emblems of Anubis, the god of embalming.

ISIS

The devoted widow

From early times, Isis, consort of Osiris, played a major role in myth. She retrieved her husband's body and used her magic powers to revive Osiris for just long enough to conceive a son by him: hovering in the form of a sparrowhawk, she fanned the breath of life into him with her wings. In another version of the story, Isis was impregnated by divine fire.

Once she knew that she was pregnant, Isis fled to the marshlands of the Nile delta to hide from her brother Seth, who, she knew, would try to harm or even kill her child. Isis bore a divine son, Horus, at Chemmis near Buto. There she nursed him, protected by deities, such as the scorpion goddess Selqet, and waited until Horus was old enough to avenge his father.

The cult of Isis gradually spread beyond the borders of Egypt. In the late 1st or early 2nd century AD, the Greek writer Plutarch produced a version of the story of Isis and Osiris in which Osiris was a king of Egypt who travelled through the world teaching the skills of agriculture and crafts to all humanity. Seth was jealous of his brother and conspired with his followers to seize the throne. He had a beautiful chest made to the measurements of Osiris and announced at a feast that the painted chest would be given to the person who could fit exactly inside it. Osiris lay down in the chest and found that it fitted him. Seth and the other conspirators slammed the lid on the chest and sealed it with molten lead. Then the coffin was thrown in the Nile and drifted out into the Mediterranean, eventually coming ashore in the Lebanon (see below). Isis recovered the coffin and took it back to Egypt. She left it only when she went to visit Horus at Buto. One night, while Isis was away, Seth went hunting in the Delta and found the coffin. He opened it, tore the body of Osiris into fourteen pieces and scattered them across Egypt. Isis buried each piece where she found it, but the phallus could not be recovered because it had been eaten by a fish. Plutarch gives this as the main reason why Egyptian priests did not eat fish.

Isis suckles her son Horus: a Late Period gold and bronze votive statuette.

Isis in the Lebanon

The Greek writer Plutarch wrote a version of the story of Osiris and Isis in c.AD100. According to this account, when Isis heard of Seth's betrayal and murder of her husband she searched everwhere for the body of her husband. She travelled to Byblos in the Lebanon after hearing a rumour that Osiris might be there.

The coffin had been washed ashore at Byblos and had become entangled in the roots of a small tree. This tree quickly grew so tall and beautiful that it was cut down to form a pillar in the city's royal palace. Isis came to the palace and sat weeping in a courtyard. She impressed the royal handmaidens by braiding their hair and breathing perfume onto their skins, and the queen of Byblos appointed the goddess as nurse to her younger son. Isis nursed the prince by giving him her finger instead of her breast. She grew fond of the boy and decided to give him eternal life, so she laid him in a fire that would burn away his mortality.

As the prince lay in the fire, Isis transformed herself into a swallow and flew around the pillar that had been made from the tree. The queen of Byblos heard her lamenting and came into the room. She saw her child burning and screamed, stopping the spell before the magic was complete. Isis then revealed her identity and demanded that the pillar be cut open. When the coffin of Osiris was exposed, Isis gave a cry of grief so terrible that it killed the baby prince.

HORUS AND SETH

The struggle for the throne of Osiris

The sometimes violent quarrel between the
gods Horus and Seth was a central element in
Egyptian myth. In the earliest versions of the
story, Horus and Seth seem to be brothers, but
later they were usually regarded as nephew
and uncle. After the death of his brother Osiris,
the father of Horus (see p.42), Seth had seized his throne.
Horus therefore went before a divine tribunal presided
over by Geb or Ra and claimed that he, not Seth, should succeed to the
throne of his father. Shu and Thoth declared that Horus was in the right.
The sun god was angry that his opinion had not been asked first and
refused to accept the verdict. One of the gods insulted him and he went to
sulk in his tent. Later, restored to good humour, the sun god told Seth and
Horus to speak for themselves. Seth claimed that he deserved to be king
because he was the only one strong enough to defend the barque of the
sun. Some of the Ennead (see p.40) agreed with him, but Isis persuaded
them to change their minds.

Seth refused to go on with the trial with Isis present, and the sun
god agreed that the council should reconvene on an island. The divine
ferryman, Nemty, was told not take Isis across in his boat, so the goddess

*Horus, shown as a man with the head of a
falcon, leads the soul of the scribe Ani into
the presence of Osiris. Horus wears the
costume of a king and the double crown of
Upper and Lower Egypt. The image comes
from a papyrus of the 13th century* BC.

The followers of Seth

The Egyptians represented Seth as a mythical animal, part wild ass and part pig or anteater. His domain was the desert and most desert animals were associated with him, as were oxen and donkeys, because they were used to thresh barley and thus trod on the body of Seth's victim Osiris, the father of Horus, which was contained in the grain. Horus condemned these animals to perpetual beatings. A series of myths set in northern Upper Egypt concern conflicts between Seth's human followers and the allies of Horus.

Seth kept trying to disturb the body of Osiris, taking the guise

Seth, the strongest of the gods, defended the sun barque against the serpent Apep. In this papyrus of the 11th century BC, Seth stands in front of the sun god to spear Apep.

of various animals. On one occasion he turned himself into a panther, but Thoth recited magic spells against him, whereupon Seth fell to the ground. Anubis tied him up, branded his fur and then skinned him. Seth's followers tried to march to his rescue, but Anubis beheaded them all.

Seth recovered from his injuries and gathered new followers in the desert hills, but Isis came against him. Seth turned himself into a bull, but Isis took the form of a dog with a knife at the end of her tail and pursued him. The goddess Hathor turned into a venomous snake and bit Seth's followers. Their blood stained the hills red.

disguised herself as an old woman and bribed Nemty with a gold ring. On the island she turned herself into a beautiful girl, so that Seth would desire her. She asked the god to help her, explaining that she was the widow of a herdsman and that her only son had been robbed of their cattle by a brutal stranger. Seth declared that it was indeed wicked for a son to be robbed of his inheritance. Isis at once transformed herself into a sparrowhawk and flew up into a tree. She told Seth that he had condemned himself out of his own mouth.

Seth complained to the Ennead about this incident, and they punished Nemty by cutting off his toes. Seth then challenged Horus to a trial of strength, proposing that they each turn themselves into a hippopotamus and try to stay under water for three months. Horus agreed, but Isis was afraid that her son would lose, so she made a copper harpoon and threw it into the water. First she hit Horus by mistake, then she harpooned Seth, who pleaded for mercy. Isis felt sorry for him and let him go. Horus was so angry that he jumped out of the water, cut off his mother's head, and then fled to the desert hills with it. Isis turned herself into a stone statue as a disguise and returned to the assembly of the gods, but Thoth recognized her. The sun god ordered the Ennead to punish Horus for wounding his mother. Seth found him sleeping and tore out his eyes. However, the goddess Hathor restored the young god's sight with the milk of a gazelle.

Eventually, after Horus had appealed for justice again, the gods wrote to the dead Osiris. He wrote back demanding to know why his son had been defrauded of his inheritance, and threatened to send the demons of the underworld into the realm of the gods. The sun god finally agreed that Horus should be king. Seth was forced to accept the judgment and Isis rejoiced to see her son crowned at last. The sun god summoned Seth to live with him in the sky and become the god of storms.

SOLAR MYTHS

The eternal cycle of renewal

This unique stela of c.1000BC shows a woman adoring Ra-Harakhty while the rays of his disc radiate benefit toward her. Above is the hieroglyph for the sky, with another sun disc and two wedjat eyes. The sides are made up of the heraldic plants of Upper and Lower Egypt, while the heads of their inhabitants, or perhaps of the earth god Aker, protrude from the baseline.

This pectoral from the tomb of King Tutankhamun represents the name of the king, "The Lord of Manifestations of Ra", and uses the scarab in a composition symbolizing the rising of the sun.

In most periods the sun god was the principal god of Egypt. The world was organized according to two interlocking principles of the emergence and actions of the creator and the daily cycle of the sun through the cosmos. The cosmos was, essentially, Egypt.

Each day at dawn the sun god was born from the sky goddess. He attained maturity by midday, and aged by evening. At nightfall he entered the underworld (see opposite). Each day, month, and year, and the reign of every king, renewed the creation of the world. This constant renewal of the cosmos implied that it was perpetually under threat, a pessimistic view elaborated in rich cycles of hymns to the sun god and in compositions presenting his passage through the underworld, all designed to help ensure that the order of things would not fail. The god travelled in a barque, attended by countless beings, including the blessed dead. Only a few were depicted; these were either aspects of his being or deities who steered and defended the barque. The god's timeless enemies, led by the giant snake Apep, sought to bar his passage through the sky and underworld.

All of creation acclaimed the sunrise, and this welcome sustained the sun god's passage. Some traditions focussed on the god's essential benevolence. Texts presenting him in this light provided the point of departure for the monotheistic religious ideas of King Akhenaten (see p.52).

The sun god, his night voyage, and the stars

The sun god was thought to travel through the underworld on his nightly journey, which was illustrated in huge "underworld books". These were inscribed in New Kingdom royal tombs, so that the king could join in the solar cycle in the next world.

The underworld books are divided into the twelve hours of the night. Each hour centres on the sun god in his barque, and around him are the beings who inhabit that region. One entire composition shows about a thousand figures, consisting of the blessed dead, the demons and deities of the region, and the condemned who are tortured indefinitely. As the sun god passes, he addresses the beings of each hour, who respond in welcome and are revived by the light he sheds. The descriptions are very exact, giving the dimensions of the spaces through which he travels. His barque mostly sails along a watery path, but at one juncture he moves over endless sands, towed by a group of jackals.

Some compositions depict how, in the middle of the night, the sun god descends into the deepest regions of the underworld and is fused with its ruler Osiris. The resulting image is captioned both "Ra who rests in Osiris" and "Osiris who rests in Ra". But whereas Ra could be linked with Amon to produce a deity with a single name (Amon-Ra), Ra and Osiris were too fundamentally different. Their brief association brought daily renewal, but it could not be permanent.

Throughout the night, the sun god had to contend with his arch-enemy, the snake Apep (see p.45), but in the last hours he himself entered a great snake, from which he emerged rejuvenated, to be reborn at dawn. The sun's cycle was celebrated daily in many temples,

not just in solar sanctuaries. Priests performed the cult inside the building and it was poorly known outside. Vital parts of the cult were kept secret and are known only from evidence dating from 1100BC and later. The ultimate meaning of much of the solar cycle was concealed. A text describes how the king, as the principal priest, "knows" eight things about the sunrise, among them the "speech which the Eastern Souls pronounce". The Eastern Souls were baboons, animals which characteristically bark at sunrise. The hidden meaning of their barking was known only to the king.

The sun god had many forms during his daily cycle. As the morning god he could be a child, but typically he was a scarab known as Khepry. The scarab (see opposite), which pushes a ball of dung comparable in form with the sun, symbolized regeneration, rebirth and transformation. The sun god's midday form was Ra–Harakhty, "Ra, Horus of the Horizon", often depicted as a human figure with a falcon head crowned by a sun disc. Harakhty was an ancient god, and the idea of a falcon crossing the sky in a barque is known from the First Dynasty. Ra-Harakhty was the name most used in myths of the god's rule on earth. The evening sun was Atum or Ra-Atum, shown in human form with the double crown otherwise mostly worn by kings. His night form, with a ram's head, was a purely pictorial figure with no specific name. However, it was captioned "Flesh (of Ra)", implying that the image was a vehicle for the sun god's presence if not strictly identifiable with him.

Other gods were associated with the heavens. Some major deities were identified with stars or planets: the moon was Thoth, Mercury was Seth, and the constellation Orion was Osiris. The myths of the Ennead were enacted by the complex movements of the relevant heavenly bodies, especially those which cross the band of the heavens traversed by the sun, or which, like Venus, herald the sunrise.

This composition on a ceiling in the tomb of King Ramesses VI (c.1130BC) depicts the night voyage of the sun. The long snake may symbolize the solar barque, while the god in his ram-headed night form stands on the double figure of an adoring human. The recumbent figure with raised head is Osiris, united with Ra in the night, and the female figure on the right is the sky goddess Nut.

MYTH AND MAGIC

The secret name of Ra; the Book of Thoth

Bes was one of several monstrous-looking deities who protected people from misfortune. His image was incorporated into decoration of all kinds, especially on small objects that might be used as amulets or kept in the home. This miniature faience plaque dates from the Graeco-Roman period.

For the Egyptians, magic was valuable both in this world and the next, as a way to forestall and control misfortunes. Some magical spells give complete narratives of mythical episodes: these were recited while a prescription was ingested or applied to the body of a patient, who was identified with a protagonist of the myth. Magical hymns were addressed to the gods, whose true names were kept secret because they were a source of magic power. One story, part of a magical spell, relates how Isis found out the most secret of all divine names, that of the sun god, Ra. He was growing old and he sometimes drooled. Isis watched where his spittle fell, mixed it with clay and made a snake, which she brought to life and left beside a road where the sun god often walked.

When Ra came by, the snake bit him and disappeared. The sun god immediately felt a terrible burning pain as the poison spread through his body. Ra's cries brought the Nine Gods to his side, and he told them that he had been wounded by something that he had not created. Isis promised to heal him if he would reveal his true name. Ra told Isis that he was the creator whose name was Khepry at dawn, Ra at midday and Atum at evening (see p.47). Isis complained that the true name had still not been spoken. The pain became worse and Ra could bear it no longer. He opened his heart to Isis and told her his secret name. Isis summoned the poison out of Ra by speaking his true name and thus healed the sun god, promising not to pass the power of the secret name to anyone but Horus. The name itself is not revealed in the spell.

The magic of Thoth

*T*he moon god, Thoth, who could be shown as a baboon, an ibis or a man with the head of an ibis, was particularly associated with the secret knowledge involved in magic. His main cult centre was at Khemenu, called Hermopolis by the Greeks, who identified him with Hermes (see p.144). The following story was written down in Ptolemaic times.

A prince called Setna Khaemwese learns that a book of magic written by Thoth is buried in an ancient tomb near Memphis. He breaks into the tomb and is confronted by ghosts, who warn him that Thoth killed their living selves for stealing his magic book from a

This New Kingdom statue group shows Thoth as the patron deity of scribes. He recorded the gods' decisions and, it was believed, invented hieroglyphic script.

chest at the bottom of the Nile. Undeterred, Setna defeats the ghosts with powerful amulets and takes the Book of Thoth. He then encounters a beautiful woman called Tabubu and is captivated by her, but before she will let Setna make love, she demands that he settle all his wealth on her and have his own children killed. He agrees, but as soon as they embrace he finds himself lying naked and alone in the middle of a road.

However, Setna discovers that his children are alive and well and that the beautiful woman was just a phantom. He wisely decides to return the Book of Thoth.

SNAKES AND SCORPIONS

The agents of chaos

Snakes and scorpions were more than everyday hazards: they embodied the chaotic powers which threatened the ordered world. Like other creatures perceived as enemies, they typically inhabited the desert. Someone who was bitten or stung was exposed to preternatural dangers.

One literary text illustrates how snakes were associated with the margins of the cosmos. It tells of a government official who was shipwrecked in the Red Sea and came to a fabulous island of abundance. He heard a great commotion and an enormous snake, possibly with a human head, appeared before him. It was evidently a god, and the man fainted with shock. The snake picked up the official in its mouth and took him to a place of safety, where the man recounted how all his fellow voyagers had been lost in the shipwreck. The snake then told how it had once returned home to find that its own family of 74 snakes had been burned to ashes by a shooting star, so that it was completely alone. It drew the rather austere moral that one should bear a loss with fortitude. However, the number 74 points to a deeper meaning: these are the 74 manifestations of the sun god which were consumed in the final holocaust of creation. The snake form of the god lives in a world beyond creation. To encounter him, the traveller had moved outside time itself.

If snakes and scorpions could be mastered in this world, they were beneficial. Two early kings were named Scorpion and Snake, but later the powers of these creatures were associated mainly with goddesses, all of whom could be designated by a hieroglyph of a snake. The principal scorpion goddess was Selqet, who oversaw childbirth and protected mummified corpses during burial. Some snake goddesses were associated with places where snakes were especially common: the harvest goddess Renenutet with fields and granaries, and Meresger, the goddess of the Theban Peak, with the desert.

Many magical spells combated snake and scorpion wounds, which could not be treated medically. Some spells included narratives of myths involving snakes and scorpions. For example, one spell tells how Isis was fleeing from the workshop where Seth had confined her to weave a shroud for Osiris. She was going towards Chemmis, where she secretly raised her son Horus, accompanied by seven scorpions, whom she commanded to be discreet. As she approached a settlement, a rich woman saw the strange procession and closed her door. Isis was taken in by a fisherman's wife, but the scorpions took offence on behalf of Isis against the rich woman and one of them crept into the woman's house. It stung the woman's son and the venom set the house alight. The rich woman went through the streets wailing in anguish, and Isis summoned up a rainstorm to extinguish the fire. She then took pity on the woman's child, who, by implication, was identified with her own son Horus. The goddess pronounced a magical spell and cured the child, whose mother at once regretted having closed her door to Isis. In remorse and gratitude, the rich woman gave her possessions to the fisherman's wife.

This narrative has a strong moralizing flavour, emphasizing that generosity has its own reward and that it is found among the poor and outcast more readily than among the rich. The rainstorm, which is almost unnatural in a rainless country such as Egypt, shows how the order of things was disturbed by an untoward event. Some magical spells even threaten that the sun will cease to appear and that the seasons will not follow one another if the desired effect is not achieved.

The infant Horus, whose mother Isis protected him from Seth and from the dangers of the Delta marshes (see p.43), symbolized protection and success against adversity. Stelae (inscribed upright stone slabs) of the Late Period, such as the one above, show a nude Horus brandishing snakes and other symbols and standing on a pair of dangerous crocodiles. The surface of the above stela is covered with images of magically potent deities.

POWERFUL GODDESSES

Neith, Sekhmet and Bastet

The goddesses of Egyptian mythology are often more formidable than the male deities, visiting warfare or destruction on those who cross them. A notable example is Neith, the Great Mother, whose chief cult centre was Sais (see map, p.37). She was associated with war and hunting, and her symbol was a shield with two crossed arrows. Neith was also a creator deity, said to have emerged from the Nun to create gods and men. When she spat into the Nun, the chaos serpent Apep was born from her spittle. She was also the mother of the crocodile god, Sobek. In the quarrel of Horus and Seth (see p.44), the gods write to Neith for advice; she threatens to make the sky fall in if her recommendation is not accepted.

Sekhmet ("Powerful One") was a terrifying lioness goddess. The sun god sent her to slaughter rebellious humanity (see p.41), and criminals were sometimes sacrificed to her. Contagious diseases were said to be her messengers, and her priests served as doctors.

Other goddesses were less forbidding, although their influence was equally potent. They include another feline deity, Bastet, who was the goddess of love, sex and fertility. Originally a lioness goddess, from the middle of the 2nd millennium BC she began to be shown as a cat.

The cat and the lioness

In this myth, the Eye of Ra, identified with the goddess Hathor, goes to live in Nubia, south of Egypt. In the course of the story she appears in two contrasting feline manifestations: as Sekhmet, the lioness goddess, and Bastet, the cat goddess.

The Eye of Ra quarrelled with her father and retreated to the distant Nubian desert. Thoth disguised himself as a baboon and went south after the goddess. (Originally it was Shu, or a warrior god called Anhur, "He who brings back the Distant One", who pursued the goddess, but later this role was given to Thoth.) He found her in the form of the cat goddess and prevented her from attacking him by telling her a story. Then he talked about Egypt to make the goddess homesick, but she saw through his ploy and turned into a raging lioness goddess. Thoth soothed her with more stories and promises of offerings in all the temples of Egypt, and persuaded her to travel north with him.

When they reached the border, the goddess was greeted by joyful crowds. Near Thebes, a serpent of chaos tried to kill her while she slept, but Thoth woke her in time. At Heliopolis she was reunited with Ra and transformed herself into Hathor.

A gilded statuette of the lioness Sekhmet from the tomb of Tutankhamun. As a daughter of Ra, she wears a sun disc on her head. She was worshipped at Memphis as consort of Ptah.

A Late Period bronze figure of the cat goddess Bastet. The kittens symbolize Bastet's role as a fertility goddess. A great fertility festival was held each year at her temple in Bubastis.

OTHER GODDESSES

Anat, Astarte, Hathor and Taweret

In a letter to the council of gods during the quarrel of Horus and Seth (see p.44), Neith suggested that two foreign goddesses, Anat and Astarte, should be given to Seth to compensate him for ceding his right to the throne to Horus. This probably implies that Seth was unfit to marry an Egyptian goddess. Another story, in a magical text, tells how Seth came upon the goddess Hathor while she was bathing in the river, leapt on her like a ram and raped her. The fertile seed flew from the goddess to Seth's forehead and made him ill, because Hathor was the bride of the Night Sun and could only be made pregnant by divine fire. Seth's wife Anat hurried to ask Ra for his help. Isis retrieved the divine seed and cured Seth.

Seth's other foreign wife, Astarte, appears in a myth in which the gods of Egypt are in conflict with a sea god. Ptah and the Ennead were forced to pay tribute to the Sea. The harvest goddess Renenutet carried their tribute of silver, gold and lapis lazuli to the shore, but the insatiable Sea wanted more, and threatened to enslave the gods of Egypt if he did not receive it. Renenutet sent a bird as a messenger to Astarte's house to tell her to take tribute to the sea. Astarte wept when she heard this. She took the tribute to the shore, but on reaching her destination she sang and mocked the Sea. Then the Sea demanded Astarte herself. The beautiful goddess appeared before the Ennead (see p.40), who gave her a dowry of jewels, including the necklace of Nut and the signet ring of Geb. Astarte went down to the shore carrying the treasure, but Seth went with her to fight the Sea. The end of the story is missing, but it is most likely that the strength of Seth overcame the Sea and that Astarte was saved.

FOREIGN GODDESSES

Several goddesses from Syria and Palestine were incorporated into the Egyptian pantheon by the later 2nd millennium BC. The following are the most important:

ANAT The warrior goddess Anat was usually shown carrying a shield, a spear and an axe. In Syria, she was the sister and lover of Baal, who was worshipped in Egypt as a form of Seth. In Egyptian myth, Anat was a daughter of Ra. She was said to dress like a male warrior, but she was also a cow goddess.

ASTARTE Another warrior, whose Mesopotamian counterpart was Ishtar (see p.61). In Egypt, Astarte was a daughter of the sun god or of Ptah. She appeared as a naked woman carrying weapons and was often shown on a horse.

QUDSHU A consort of Min, an Egyptian fertility god, Qudshu was sometimes seen as a form of Hathor. She was depicted as a naked woman standing on a lion's back and holding snakes and lotus flowers.

Hathor and Taweret

Hathor, the patroness of lovers, was among the most complex of Egyptian deities. Her most famous temple was at Dendara. Like Taweret, she protected women and children and was connected with death and rebirth.

Hathor helped women to conceive and give birth. In cow form, she nursed the infant Horus at Chemmis. She welcomed souls to the underworld and refreshed them with food and drink. Taweret helped the dead to be reborn in the Nun (see p.38). She could appear as a fearsome beast, part hippopotamus, part lion and part crocodile. Since Seth could take hippopotamus form, Taweret was often regarded as his consort. When his leg was thrown into the sky (see p.42), she prevented it from doing further harm.

Hathor and Taweret, here identified with a divine cow called the Great Flood, stand before an entrance to the underworld in the mountains of western Thebes. A scene from the Book of the Dead.

KINGS AND THE GODS

The sacred role of the pharaohs

Hathor, mother of kings, welcomes King Sety I: a relief in his tomb at Thebes.

From the time of his accession, an Egyptian pharaoh (king) played the part of a god. He was a manifestation of the sky god Horus, and the son of the sun god Ra. Nekhbet and Wadjet, the goddesses of Upper and Lower Egypt respectively, were his protectors. A king's titles proclaimed these and other relationships. His throne-name, unique for each ruler, announced the way in which he manifested the sun god. Thus, Thutmose IV was Menkheprura "The Enduring One of the Manifestations of Ra".

The king could be the "son" of any major deity, but this description often meant little more than that the king ranked below the deity. The notion of the divine parent and offspring extended to depictions of the king suckling the breast of goddesses like a child. There were also numerous accounts of the king's descent from the sun god. In its basic form, the sun god appeared in the shape of the reigning king and had intercourse with the mother of his successor. She recognized the god from his aroma, welcomed him, and conceived after their night together. The creator god Khnum (see p.39) formed the child on his potter's wheel. Many deities assisted in the birth. The divine father blessed the baby, who was suckled by goddesses.

Some kings went beyond their traditional role and were deified in their own lifetimes; for example, Amenhotep III was depicted making offerings to his deified self. Other kings were deified after their deaths. Senwosret III, who pushed Egypt's southern boundary deep into Nubia in the 19th century BC, was worshipped on the frontier as a local deity, as was his son Amenemhat III in the Fayyum oasis, where he had undertaken many land reclamation projects.

Ruddjedet and Khufu

*T*he myth of the royal divine birth could be woven into an account of a real historical event. The following story from a papyrus tells how the first three kings of the Fifth Dynasty were born and survived.

Ruddjedet, the wife of a priest, became pregnant with triplets by the god Ra, Lord of Sakhebu (near Letopolis). The Fourth Dynasty king, Khufu (otherwise known as Cheops), who built the Great Pyramid, heard of this and wished to intervene, but was unable to reach Ruddjedet's home. Ra sent Isis and Nephthys, together with Meskhenet, Heqet (two goddesses of

Akhenaten (c.1350BC), here with his family, rejected most cults, but still claimed to be the son of the sun god.

birth) and Khnum, to protect Ruddjedet from Khufu. They arrived disguised as musicians, delivered and named the three babies, and departed, leaving three royal crowns concealed in a sack of barley as tokens of kingship. When the couple were about to use the barley, they heard the sound of festivities for a king, and realized that the triplets were destined to be kings.

Later, Ruddjedet quarrelled with her servant, who in revenge tried to betray her to Khufu, but was eaten by crocodiles on the way. Through this intervention – crocodiles were frequent agents of divine retribution – the children survived to succeed Khufu.

Gods and people

In Egyptian mythology, stories of encounters between deities and ordinary people are relatively rare. The following tale, dating to the late 2nd millennium BC, is seemingly about two human brothers in whom the gods take an interest. However, the brothers have the names of deities: Anubis (the jackal god) and Bata (a bull god who was an aspect of Seth). The story echoes many other myths.

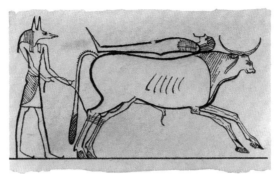

Anubis, shown as a jackal-headed man, forces the bull Bata to carry the mummy of Osiris. The image appears in an early Graeco-Roman period papyrus containing the local myths of Saka in Upper Egypt. In this version, Anubis and Bata are enemies.

Bata, who was exceptionally strong and understood the speech of animals, lived with his elder brother Anubis. He helped Anubis to farm his land and looked after the cattle. One day, when the brothers were ploughing the fields, they ran out of seed, so Anubis sent Bata back to the house to fetch some. Bata found his brother's wife sitting on the ground plaiting her hair and asked her to open the storeroom and get him some seed corn. She told him to go and fetch it himself, as she was busy.

When Bata came back from the storeroom he was carrying three sacks of wheat and two of barley. Anubis' wife saw how strong and handsome her brother-in-law was and tried to seduce him. Bata rejected her and angrily strode back to the fields. Afraid that Bata would tell his brother about her attempted seduction, she rubbed grease into her skin to make herself look bruised, and lay on her bed pretending to be sick. When her husband came home, she claimed that Bata had tried to rape her and had beaten her when she rejected him. Anubis was furious and sharpened a spear with which to kill his brother. A cow warned Bata of the danger and he prayed to the sun god, who put a river of crocodiles between the brothers. From his side of the river, Bata protested his innocence and castrated himself. Anubis believed him and killed his wife.

Bata went to live in the Valley of the Pine in Syria. He hid his heart at the top of the pine tree and built himself a mansion. One day, the Ennead (see p.40) visited Bata and pitied his loneliness. Ra ordered Khnum to make a wife for Bata. This new wife was a woman of divine beauty, but the seven goddesses who pronounced a person's fate predicted that she would die by the knife.

Bata was delighted with his wife. He warned her not to leave the house while he was out hunting in case the Sea should snatch her. The woman disobeyed him and the Sea nearly caught her, tearing a tress of hair from her head and carrying it to Egypt, where it was found by Pharaoh's washermen. They took it to the king, who was amazed by its beauty and fragrance. He sent envoys to every foreign land to search for the owner of the hair. Bata killed most of the envoys who came to his valley, but one escaped to tell of her whereabouts. Then Pharaoh sent soldiers and an old woman who tempted Bata's wife with jewelry. His wife revealed the secret of her husband's heart and the soldiers cut down the pine tree. Bata fell dead and his wife became Pharaoh's chief queen.

Anubis went to the valley and found the pine tree cut down and Bata lying dead. He searched for four years until he found his brother's shrivelled heart and placed it in a bowl of water. Bata came to life again, turned himself into a magnificent bull, and told Anubis to take him as a gift to Pharaoh. At court, Bata told the queen who he was. The next time Pharaoh was feasting with her, she asked him to grant her a wish. When he agreed, she asked to eat the bull's liver. Pharaoh was angry, but the bull was sacrificed and its liver given to the queen. As the bull died, two drops of its blood fell beside the palace gates and grew into two beautiful persea trees. Pharaoh was delighted, but the queen knew that the trees were Bata and demanded that they be made into furniture for her. As the trees were felled, she accidentally swallowed a splinter and became pregnant. She bore a son, who, after Pharaoh's death, announced that he was Bata and told his story. He had the queen executed and reigned for thirty years. He was succeeded by Anubis.

PRIEST-MAGICIANS

Setna Khaemwese and Imhotep

The ba was a spiritual aspect of an indi-vidual, usually shown as a bird with a human head. The ba of a deceased person was able to move through the underworld and revisit the earth by day. This detail (right) is taken from a papyrus of the 11th century BC.

The human heroes of Egyptian stories are usually not warriors but magicians, or lector-priests – men who had studied the books of magic kept in Egyptian temples. A papyrus dating to the mid-2nd millennium BC contains stories about their magical deeds. One lector-priest is said to have made a wax crocodile come alive to kill his wife's lover. Another magician, who was only a villager, was able to tame a lion and to re-attach the severed head of a goose to its body.

The much later cycle of stories about Prince Setna Khaemwese (see also panel, p.48) tells of rivalry between the priest-magicians of Egypt and the sorcerers of Nubia. The real Setna Khaemwese was a son of Ramesses II (*c*.1279-1213BC). As high priest of Ptah, he studied and restored some of the pyramids and tombs at Giza, and these antiquarian interests seem to have given rise to his later reputation as a magician. According to the cycle, a Nubian chief challenges Pharaoh to find a man who can read a let-ter without opening it. Setna's young son Siosire succeeds in this, and reads the letter aloud. Long ago, he reads, a Nubian king's sorcerer animated four wax figures which abducted the Egyptian king and gave him five hun-dred blows before returning him to his palace. This humiliation was avenged by an Egyptian called Horus son of Paneshe, who performed the same assault on the Nubian king. He then defeated the Nubian sorcerer in a contest of magic and banished him from Egypt for 1,500 years. After the letter is read, the Nubian chief declares that he is the sorcerer returned for vengeance. Siosire in turn reveals that he is Horus son of Paneshe. He van-quishes the Nubian and returns to the underworld.

Imhotep and the seven-year famine

*O*ne real person who featured in myth was Imhotep, minister and architect to King Djoser in the 27th century BC. Tradition made him the son of Ptah by a human mother. This story comes from an inscription near Aswan, which claims to be a decree of King Djoser, but was in fact written by the priests of Khnum around the 2nd century BC.

For seven years, the Nile had failed to rise high enough to irrigate the fields. King Djoser's peo-ple were near starvation, so he consulted the chief lector-priest Imhotep about the source of the inundation. Imhotep discovered that Hapy, the spirit of the inundation, lived in twin caverns under the island of Elephantine. When it was time for the Nile to rise, the flood waters were con-trolled by the ram god Khnum, who alone could unbolt the doors of the caverns. When Djoser heard this, he made lavish offerings to Khnum. That night, in a dream, Khnum promised Djoser that he would release Hapy. The famine was subsequently ended by a bountiful harvest.

Imhotep (left) was also credited with the invention of stone architecture and the authorship of books of wisdom. Long after his death, he was venerated as a god of medicine.

LIFE AFTER DEATH

The soul in the underworld

In an episode of the Setna cycle (see opposite), Siosire takes his father into the underworld to show him the fates of two men after they have died and been judged before Osiris. A cruel rich man has been condemned to eternal torment. A virtuous poor man has been given all the rich man's grave goods and has become a blessed spirit. This late text presents the judgment of the dead as central to Egyptian religion. In earlier times, it was just one of many dangers that the soul had to overcome before it could reach the paradise known as the Field of Reeds.

The Egyptian underworld was imagined as an elaborate landscape of rivers and islands, deserts and lakes of fire. To find a way through it, and to placate or overcome the gods and demons who inhabited it, the soul had to become a hero-magician. From the late 3rd millennium BC, people of rank and wealth had spells inscribed on their coffins. Later these spells were developed into the body of texts now known as the Book of the Dead, and papyrus rolls containing illustrated selections from the book were buried with wealthy Egyptians from the 16th century BC on. The deceased would be depicted overcoming such underworld dangers as the Four Crocodiles of the West.

On reaching the throne room of Osiris, a dead person had to declare himself or herself innocent of various crimes before the forty-two judges of the underworld. The heart (that is, the conscience) of the dead person was weighed on a pair of scales against the feather of the goddess Maat, who was the personification of justice and truth. A female monster called the Devourer of the Dead squatted by the scales, ready to consume the deceased if the heart weighed more than the feather. This fate could be avoided by use of a spell that stopped the heart from declaring its owner's crimes. Those who passed this test were judged pure and became spirits with the power to move among the gods. They might be invited to join the millions who travelled in the barque of the sun and battled against the chaos serpent, Apep (see pp.45 and 47).

In the above scene from a papyrus of the 14th century BC, Anubis leads the soul of the scribe Hunefer to be judged before Osiris. The heart of Hunefer is weighed against the symbol of justice and truth. Thoth records the result and Horus presents Hunefer to Osiris. The four sons of Horus stand on a lotus before Osiris, and Isis and Nephthys are shown behind his throne.

THE MIDDLE EAST

A stone relief from the Palace of Sargon II (721-705BC) at Khorsabad.
A winged protective genius of this kind is often depicted in Assyrian art.

The heart of the ancient Middle East was Mesopotamia, bounded on the west by the River Euphrates and on the east by the Tigris. A non-Semitic people, the Sumerians, penetrated *c.*3300BC into the southern part of this area, and were later conquered by Semitic invaders who had occupied Akkad to the north. The power centre of these invaders was the city of Babylon, and Sumer and Akkad became known as Babylonia. Later still the Assyrians, who had settled further north in the Tigris valley, conquered Babylon and eventually established a great empire. Peripheral to Mesopotamia proper were such areas as Asia Minor, Syria-Palestine and Persia, all influenced by Mesopotamian culture and religion.

The Sumerians developed a political system and body of religion which remained the basis for all Mesopotamian life thereafter. Society was organized around the city-state, each with its tutelary deity. Popular religion was animistic: the world was thought to be full of mysterious and unpredictable forces. There is a huge mass of texts consisting of spells to avert demons; there was also a considerable omen-literature, by which it was hoped to divine the future. Alongside this was the official religion, with its great temples, elaborate rituals and professional priesthoods, on which the welfare of state and society depended. The great gods were organized in a pantheon by the theological speculations of the priests. Kingship was a divine gift, lowered from heaven: the nation's welfare was bound up with that of the king, who was a sacral figure, taking the key role in the main religious festivals.

Most myths originated in scribal centres attached to the temples: they are found on the clay tablets (in the cuneiform script developed by the Sumerians) discovered in the archives of such cities as Ur, Babylon and Nineveh. The texts – sophisticated poetic compositions recounting the exploits of a limited number of deities, as well as folklore motifs and legends of semi-divine heroes – are often fragmentary and their precise interpretation is still disputed.

TIME CHART

c.2600-1850 BC	Sumerian city-states
	Third dynasty of Ur, c.2113-1991BC
c.1890-900 BC	Semitic rulers gain control in Mesopotamia
	First dynasty of Babylon, c.1894-1550BC
	Reign of Hammurabi of Babylon, c.1792-1750BC
c.1740-1200 BC	Hittites in Asia Minor
	Old Kingdom, c.1742-1460BC
	Hittite Empire, c.1460-1200BC
c.1500-1200 BC	Golden age of Ugarit
c.883-612 BC	Assyrian domination of Mesopotamia
	Sennacherib (c.705-681BC) makes Nineveh the imperial capital
	Reign of Asshurbanipal, c.669-627BC
	Fall of Nineveh, 612BC
c.625-539 BC	Neo-Babylonian empire
	Reign of Nebuchadrezzar, 605-562BC
c.539-331 BC	Persian empire in control of Mesopotamia
	Conquest of Babylon, 539BC, by Cyrus (539-530BC)
	Darius I (552-486BC) builds new capital at Persepolis
	Alexander the Great conquers Persian empire, 331BC

BABYLON

The town plan below shows Babylon as it was expanded and restored by Nebuchadrezzar. The city had more than fifty temples, but its heart was the great sanctuary complex sacred to Marduk, called Esagila, "the house of the exalted head". This contained Marduk's own temple and also E-temen-an-ki, "house of the foundations of heaven and earth": this was the ziggurat of Babylon, possibly the prototype of the Tower of Babel in Genesis. From Esagila, a processional way led to the Ishtar gate, lavishly decorated with glazed tiles and representations of mythical animals. This route saw the climax of the spring New Year festival, the supreme religious observance in Mesopotamia, when Marduk's triumph over the forces of chaos was celebrated in a great procession, led by the king, with the images of Marduk and Nabu, to a temple north of the city.

ZIGGURATS

The ziggurat was the distinctive type of Mesopotamian temple, and most major cities of the region had one. It was a great brick stepped tower up to 50 yards (45m) high. On its top stood a small temple, and there was generally another at its foot. It was possibly seen as a kind of ladder linking earth and heaven (like Jacob's ladder in Genesis). In the upper temple, the deity would come to communicate with his worshippers. If the Greek historian Herodotus is to be trusted, this was also a setting for the sacred marriage ceremony, which played an important role in Mesopotamian religion.

KEY TO INSET MAP

ⁿ⌐⌐ⁿ Fortified wall
= City gate
▲ Temple
○ Hanging Gardens

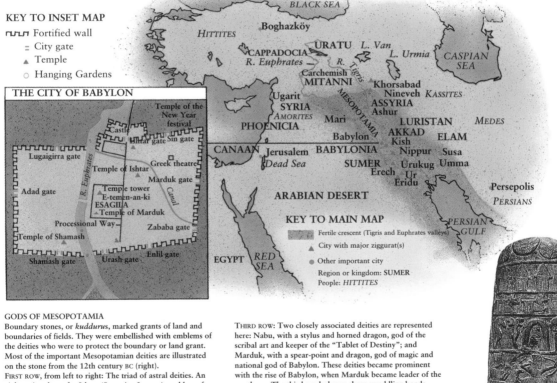

THE CITY OF BABYLON

Map labels: Temple of the New Year festival · Castle · Ishtar gate · Sin gate · Lugaigirra gate · Temple of Ishtar · Greek theatre · Marduk gate · Adad gate · Temple tower E-temen-an-ki · ESAGILA · Temple of Marduk · Canal · R. Euphrates · Processional Way · Zababa gate · Temple of Shamash · Shamash gate · Urash gate · Enlil gate

Main map labels: BLACK SEA · Boghazköy · HITTITES · CAPPADOCIA · R. Euphrates · URATU · L. Van · L. Urmia · CASPIAN SEA · Carchemish · R. Tigris · MITANNI · Khorsabad · Nineveh · KASSITES · Ugarit · SYRIA · ASSYRIA · Ashur · AMORITES · Mari · MESOPOTAMIA · LURISTAN · MEDES · PHOENICIA · Babylon · AKKAD · Kish · ELAM · CANAAN · Jerusalem · BABYLONIA · Nippur · Susa · Dead Sea · SUMER · Urukug · Umma · Erech · Ur · Eridu · Persepolis · PERSIANS · ARABIAN DESERT · PERSIAN GULF · EGYPT · RED SEA

KEY TO MAIN MAP

▒ Fertile crescent (Tigris and Euphrates valleys)
▲ City with major ziggurat(s)
● Other important city
  Region or kingdom: SUMER
  People: HITTITES

GODS OF MESOPOTAMIA

Boundary stones, or *kudduru*s, marked grants of land and boundaries of fields. They were embellished with emblems of the deities who were to protect the boundary or land grant. Most of the important Mesopotamian deities are illustrated on the stone from the 12th century BC (right).

FIRST ROW, from left to right: The triad of astral deities. An eight-pointed star for Ishtar (Sumerian Inanna), goddess of war and sex, identified with the planet Venus; a crescent for Sin (Nanna), the moon god, the greatest of the astral deities; a sun-disc for Shamash (Utu), the sun god.

SECOND ROW: Horned crowns on pedestals symbolize the "great gods" particularly prominent in the myths: Anu (An), the head of the pantheon; Entil, national god of Sumer; and Ea (Enki), god of wisdom and the waters.

THIRD ROW: Two closely associated deities are represented here: Nabu, with a stylus and horned dragon, god of the scribal art and keeper of the "Tablet of Destiny"; and Marduk, with a spear-point and dragon, god of magic and national god of Babylon. These deities became prominent with the rise of Babylon, when Marduk became leader of the pantheon. The third symbol may show swaddling bands, standing for one of the great mother goddesses.

Of the remaining deities shown, three in particular may be noted. On the fourth row, a two-headed lion mace indicates Nergal, the dreaded god of pestilence and the underworld. The fifth row shows the scorpion-man, important in much Mesopotamian myth. On the last row, the double lightning forks and the bull symbolize Adad, the weather god.

SUMER AND BABYLON

Myths from the first cities

A statue of the fertility goddess who in various forms, such as Inanna (Ishtar), was universal in the ancient Middle East.

It is only during the present century that the true significance of Sumerian civilization, religion and mythology has come to be appreciated. All the main aspects of Mesopotamian culture, such as the city-state, kingship, the pantheon, the temple and its cult, are the creation of the Sumerians, and their basic features remained essentially unchanged throughout all the vicissitudes of Mesopotamian history.

The cuneiform texts which contain the Sumerian myths were written during the age of the Third Dynasty of Ur, or in the following period, in different cities of the region. Especially important are those from the library of Nippur, the supreme religious centre of Sumer, but there can be little doubt that the myths themselves go back to a much earlier epoch. With the possible exception of Egypt, they may be claimed to represent the world's oldest mythology.

In these texts, the scribes and thinkers of the Third Dynasty of Ur produced a cosmological and theological system which became the fundamental creed and dogma of the whole of the Middle East. The documents often pose difficulties of interpretation; nor are the Sumerian myths entirely consistent, as the main religious centres developed independent cycles, with their own deities as the main actors. Nevertheless, the mythology evolved by the Sumerians was homogeneous, presenting a picture of an ultimately harmonious world-order in which

Dumuzi and Enkimdu

The Sumerian tale of Dumuzi and Enkimdu depicts in mythical form the age-old rivalry between the pastoral and agricultural modes of existence, a theme similar to that underlying the story of Cain and Abel in the Book of Genesis. However, the central concern of the myth is the wooing of Inanna the fertility goddess by Dumuzi and their eventual union.

The goddess Inanna is set to choose a husband, and the two rivals for her hand are Dumuzi the shepherd and Enkimdu the farmer. Utu, the sun god, Inanna's brother, urges her to accept Dumuzi, but at first Inanna expresses a firm preference for Enkimdu. However, Dumuzi continues to press his suit, claiming that he is able to offer far more valuable produce from his flocks and herds than Enkimdu can provide. The two rivals meet and quarrel on a river-bank, but Enkimdu quickly submits and agrees to allow Dumuzi's flocks to pasture anywhere in his land. Thereupon the shepherd invites the farmer to his wedding with the goddess, and the text ends with Enkimdu promising to bring various farm products as gifts to Dumuzi and Inanna.

Several other myths represent Dumuzi as Inanna's husband, and a considerable number of compositions, of a markedly erotic nature, celebrate the love of Inanna for him. As fertility goddess, Inanna renewed vegetation and prompted the birth of animals and human beings: Dumuzi was the incarnation of the creative forces of spring, and his marriage with Inanna symbolized and effected the renewal of life at the turn of the year. This event was regularly actualized in the Sacred Marriage rite, celebrated in various cities, in which the king assumed the role of Dumuzi or Tammuz (see p.61) and was believed to have sexual intercourse with the goddess, thus ensuring the fertility and prosperity of the land.

One Sumerian text tells how Shulgi, a king of the Third Dynasty of Ur, actually performed this ritual, entering the bridal chamber to be greeted by Inanna with a rapturous love song. After their union was consummated, the goddess pronounced a "good fate" for king and country for the coming year.

creation and the pantheon emerged peacefully from the primeval sea, man was made for the service of the gods, and the universe was controlled and sustained by immutable divine decrees, the *me*.

Babylonian myths reflect an unpredictable universe, which poses crucial questions for humanity: how can mankind deal with the unpredictable activities of the gods (the theme of the Flood myths)?; why does mankind not enjoy immortality, which the gods jealously reserve to themselves (the theme of the Gilgamesh epic)? These two concerns are the subject of the tale of Adapa.

One of the Seven Sages of prehistory (powerful beings evoked in magical rites), Adapa was a priest of Ea in the city of Eridu. On one occasion, the south wind overturned his fishing boat. Adapa cursed the wind and prevented it from blowing, so that the moisture it brought was denied to the land. The supreme god Anu summoned him to heaven to justify himself. His patron Ea advised him how to placate Anu, and told him not to eat or drink anything which the god offered him, as it would be the water and food of death. This, however, was deceptive counsel, for Anu in fact presented Adapa with what was really the water and food of life, which would cause him to become immortal, like the gods. When Adapa rejected the offer, Anu burst out laughing and sent him back to earth. The end of the story is missing, but it would seem that Anu granted special privileges to Eridu and its priesthood, but decreed disease and demons as the general lot of humankind; Adapa, however, would be able to combat these ills by his magical powers.

Another important (but again fragmentary) Babylonian myth is the story of Zu, an Akkadian adaptation of an earlier Sumerian myth. The bird-god Zu, whose home is the underworld, stole the Tablet of Destiny, which gave the wearer control of the universe, from the god Enlil. Anu then asked two gods in turn to volunteer to slay Zu, but they refused in the face of the supreme power Zu now possessed. Finally, a successful champion appears: Marduk in Babylonian sources, Lugalbanda in Sumerian. Details of Zu's defeat are lacking but a cylinder seal impression (see margin, above right) suggests that he was eventually brought before Ea, depicted as the water god, for judgment.

THE JUDGMENT OF ZU
This cylinder seal impression appears to show Zu being judged by Ea after stealing the Tablet of Destiny. Zu regularly appears as the enemy of the high gods, and this myth probably reflects a change in the religious pattern of Mesopotamia whereby, with the influx of fresh populations, ancient chthonic (underworld) deities were being subordinated to the newer sky gods.

Etana

The Akkadian myth of Etana reflects the central role of kingship in Mesopotamian society.

In the Sumerian King List, Etana is listed as the ruler of Kish, "a shepherd who ascended to heaven." He was appointed by the gods to bring to mankind the blessing of kingship. But he has no son to continue the dynasty (this is also the predicament of Keret in Ugaritic myth: see p.64), and knows that his only remedy is to ascend to heaven

The ascent of the shepherd-king, appropriately witnessed by two shepherds, with their flocks and sheepdogs, is shown on this cylinder seal.

to obtain the plant of birth from Ishtar, mistress of birth. Advised by the sun god Shamash, he enlists the aid of an eagle, whom he rescues from a pit to which the bird had been consigned for betraying his friend the serpent. Etana is carried on the eagle's back in a spectacular flight.

At this point the text breaks off. However, because the Sumerian King List records the name of Etana's son and heir, his quest for the plant of birth would appear to have been successful.

GILGAMESH

The great epic of mortality

A terracotta mask of the demon Humbaba (Sumerian Huwawa) from the city of Ur. Masks like this were used to ward off the many demons who were thought to people the Mesopotamian world.

The fullest version of the great Gilgamesh epic is an Akkadian text from Asshurbanipal's library at Nineveh. Gilgamesh, described as "two-thirds god and one third man", has been oppressing his subjects in Erech. When they appeal to the gods for a counterpart to keep their ruler in check, the gods create Enkidu, the archetypal savage, who is covered with hair and lives with the wild beasts. He loses his special nature when he has intercourse with a prostitute, who introduces him to civilization. He then engages Gilgamesh in combat, after which the two become close friends and embark on heroic exploits, such as the killing of Humbaba. On their return to Erech, the goddess Ishtar invites Gilgamesh to be her consort, but he scornfully rejects her advances. Enraged, she sends the "Bull of Heaven" against him, but Gilgamesh and Enkidu slay the creature.

The gods decide that Enkidu must die for his part in the slaying of Humbaba and the Bull. Enkidu's fate brings home to Gilgamesh the reality of death, and so he sets out to discover the secret of eternal life. Crossing the Waters of Death, he visits the one man who has gained immortality, Utnapishtim, who tells him of an immortalizing plant at the bottom of the sea. Accompanied by Utnapishtims's boatman, Gilgamesh recovers the plant, but it is stolen by a snake before he can use it (this is how the skin-sloughing snake acquires the gift of rejuvenation). Gilgamesh finally returns to Erech, and takes the boatman on a tour of his splendid city.

The Sumerian versions

There are five extant Sumerian texts about Gilgamesh, an early Sumerian king who was later deified: these were woven together and reinterpreted by Babylonian scribes to form a connected epic.

The third of the texts relates how the goddess Inanna send the huge Bull of Heaven to Gilgamesh after he has rejected her seduction attempts (see above).

In the fourth text, Inanna wishes to cut down a tree to make a bed and chair, but is unable to do so because the tree is guarded by various demonic creatures. However, at Inanna's request, Gilgamesh expels these monsters, and from the wood of the tree the goddess fashions two objects, called *pukku* and

The slaying of the demon Humbaba, recounted in both Sumerian and Akkadian texts. Gilgamesh stands on the left, wearing a crown.

mukku – perhaps a ritual drum and drum-stick. For some reason these fall down to the underworld, from which Enkidu undertakes to retrieve them. Once there, he is unable to return. However, the god Enki makes a hole in the ground, through which the shade of Enkidu emerges, to tell Gilgamesh of the gloomy state of those deported there.

The final composition of the sequence is usually entitled the Death of Gilgamesh, but the text may in fact refer to Enkidu's death: in any case, its theme is the inevitablity of death and the vanity of all hopes of immortality. This, indeed, is the message of the Gilgamesh epic as a whole as expressed in its most complete (that is, Babylonian) version.

ISHTAR AND TAMMUZ

The descent to the underworld

Inanna, or Ishtar in the Akkadian version, is the supreme goddess of sexual love and fertility, and also goddess of war, "the lady of battles". The most important myth in which she is the central figure is that of her descent to the underworld.

No reason is given for the goddess's descent to the nether world: possibly she wishes to extend her power there. Before setting out she instructs her vizier Ninshubur that he should go in turn to three gods for their help in the event of her not reappearing. In the underworld, she has to pass through seven gates, at each of which she must remove one item of clothing and jewelry, so that finally she is naked, denuded of all the powers her garments symbolized. She confronts the goddess Ereshkigal, ruler of the underworld and her own sister, and tries to seize her throne, but she is condemned to death and her corpse hung on a nail in a wall. Suspecting some disaster, Ninshubur goes to the god Enki who, from the dirt of his fingernails, creates two sexless beings and gives them the Plant and Water of Life. They penetrate to Ishtar and revive her, but she is allowed to leave only on condition that she will provide a substitute for herself. She leaves the underworld, accompanied by fierce demons, and nominates her husband Dumuzi as her substitute. The poem ends with a speech ordaining that Dumuzi will spend half a year in the underworld and his sister Geshtinanna, "Lady of the Grape Vine", the other half.

Inanna (Ishtar) appears on this stele in her aspect as goddess of war, riding on a lion, and armed with a quiver on each shoulder and a sword on her left side. Her descent and return from the underworld portray mythically the disruption and restoration of fertility.

Tammuz, the dying god

*D*umuzi, or Tammuz in Hebrew, has more than one aspect. Although not one of the great gods, he was held in high regard in popular religion and his cult was widespread.

Under one aspect Tammuz was the embodiment of vegetation: a relief shows him holding what appears to be bunches of grapes on which goats are feeding, and flanked by two goddesses whose flowing vases provide the moisture necessary for the crops. However, most significantly, he was the archetypal dying god, and thus became assimilated to other deities of the same type, such as Adonis in Greek myth.

The annual withering of vegetation during the hot season is symbolized by his death and captivity in the underworld. He is the object of many Mesopotamian liturgies which lament his disappearance and the consequent desolation of nature – rites celebrated particularly by women, even as far as Jerusalem, as is shown by a reference in the prophecy of Ezekiel in the Bible. It has often been supposed that his resurrection was also ritually celebrated: there is no clear evidence for this but the fact that this sojourn in the underworld is said to last for only half the year makes it probable that his return to life was the focus for a rite of spring. However, it is Inanna (Ishtar) who provides the only clear instance of a deity's death and resurrection in Mesopotamian literature.

MYTHS OF CREATION

Enki, Marduk and the divine decrees

This cylinder seal probably shows the slaying of Tiamat by Marduk. Tiamat is originally the salt-water ocean; in the myth she embodies primeval chaos, represented as a female dragon-like monster which must be overcome before the ordered universe can be created. One text mentions Marduk's weapons, shown here – the mace with which he crushes Tiamat's head, lightning to attack her, and, possibly, a net to ensnare her and her companions.

Sumerian cosmogony has to be pieced together from a variety of origin myths, involving a number of deities, whose activities are not easy to reconcile and seem to reflect the rivalry between the gods of different Sumerian cities. The ultimate origin of all things was the primeval sea, personified as the goddess Nammu. She gave birth to the male sky god, An, and the female earth goddess, Ki, whose union in turn produced the "great gods". Among these was Enlil, source of the ordered universe, responsible for vegetation, cattle, agricultural tools and the arts of civilization. Man was created to serve the gods and provide them with sustenance.

The same role is ascribed to Enki, whose home is Apsu, the underground water. Enki, as god of wisdom, is the possessor of *me*, a central concept of Sumerian religion. The *me* are the pre-ordained divine decrees (probably on tablets) which determine the development of all institutions of religion and society. Their possession conferred absolute power, so it is not surprising that gods were eager to acquire them. One myth tells of the goddess Inanna visiting Enki with this purpose. He receives her with a great banquet, and under the influence of wine gives her the *me*, of which more than a hundred are listed. After Inanna's departure, Enki tries to recover the *me* but Inanna repels his emissaries with magical spells and finally reaches her own city Erech. This myth accounts for the rise of both goddess and city to pre-eminence in Sumer.

The Babylonian creation myth

The Babylonian creation epic presents a coherent whole. Focussing on Marduk, god of Babylon, it reworks and transfers to him older myths originally concerning other deities. Its purpose was to justify Marduk's position as the greatest of all gods and the pre-eminence of his own city. The text is a liturgical poem of magical potency, the recitation of which was an integral part of the Spring New Year Festival, the principal religious celebration of Babylon, thought to effect the renewal of the creation.

In the beginning, nothing existed except Apsu, the sweet-water ocean, and Tiamat, the salt-water ocean. From their union springs a succession of gods, culminating in the great gods Anu and Ea, who begets Marduk. But conflict

Marduk, above a horned serpent and the primeval ocean. A Babylonian lapis lazuli seal.

arises between the younger gods and the primeval deities. Ea kills Apsu and Tiamat determines on revenge. She assembles a horde of ferocious monsters, such as the scorpion-man, with her son Kingu at its head, whom she invests with the "Tablet of Destiny", corresponding to the Sumerian *me*.

Various gods attempt to subdue Tiamat, but they fail and finally the pantheon choose Marduk as their champion. Marduk accepts on condition that he is recognized as king of the gods. He defeats and kills Tiamat: he divides her body in two, one half forming the sky, the other half the earth. From Kingu he takes the Tablet of Destiny. Next, Marduk kills Kingu and from his blood, mixed with earth, creates mankind. The gods build for Marduk in Babylon his own temple, Esagila, with its ziggurat.

THE FLOOD

Destruction and survival

The flood myth is a dramatic reflection of the unpredictable inundations of the Tigris and Euphrates rivers. The fullest story occurs in the epic of Atrahasis. Mankind is created to serve the gods and to relieve them of the necessity of labour. But within twelve hundred years, humanity multiplies so rapidly that their noise disturbs the gods' peace. Enlil seeks to reduce their numbers by sending first a plague and then a twice-repeated drought, but each time his plans are thwarted by the wise Enki, who reveals Enlil's intentions to Atrahasis, pious king of Shurupak, and instructs him in counteractive measures. Finally, Enlil compels the other deities to send a great flood, binding them with an oath of secrecy. Enki circumvents this by speaking not directly to Atrahasis but to the reed hut in which the king is living. Following Enki's counsel, Atrahasis builds a boat in which he takes refuge with his family and various animals when the flood is launched. The gods find that, without human beings, their sustenance is cut off and the need for them to labour returns: they lament what has happened. After seven days, the flood subsides and Atrahasis emerges to offer a sacrifice to the gods. Enlil is initially furious, but finally accepts the continuance of mankind. However, he proposes measures to limit population growth, instituting classes of priestesses debarred from having children and introducing infant mortality. Atrahasis is rewarded with eternal life and a position among the gods.

THE FLOOD IN THE GILGAMESH EPIC

Utnapishtim, the survivor of the flood in the Gilgamesh epic (see p.60), recounts in detail the building of a boat in the form of a perfect cube, and gives a vivid picture of the effects of the flood. He tells how, as the waters finally subsided, he sent out a dove, a swallow and a raven to reconnoitre the ground and how he then emerged to offer a sacrifice, around which all the gods clustered to "smell the sweet savour". These features link the Babylonian story closely to the Biblical flood narrative. Finally, Ea tells the angry Enlil that he should not seek entirely to wipe out the human race but should punish them, when necessary, by sending wild animals, famine or plague. Enlil accepts the advice and rewards Utnapishtim with the gift of immortality.

The Sumerian flood myth

The flood myth survives in three main versions, whose basic features show derivation from a common prototype. Humanity seriously offends the gods, and is punished at the instigation of the deity Enlil by a flood intended to wipe out the race. However, one man and his family are spared by the intervention of the god Enki or Ea to make a fresh start for humankind. The Sumerian deluge myth survives only in a fragmentary state but it is clearly the origin of all the later Mesopotamian versions. It describes the institution of Sumerian civilization, kingship, city-states and irrigation.

After a lacuna in the text, Enki is found speaking of the gods' decision to destroy mankind by a flood, in spite of the regrets of the mother goddess, Inanna. Enki resolves to save the pious

Utu, with other deities, in his barque. In this vessel, in which he was thought to traverse the sky daily, the sun god appeared to Ziusudra in the flood myth.

King Ziusudra and tells him of the gods' purpose by speaking through the reed-wall of the king's house. At this point the text is again broken, but presumably Ziusudra receives instructions to build a boat, for there follows a description of a seven-day flood, when "the storm-winds tossed the huge boat on the great waters". Then Utu, the sun god, appears in his barque, bringing back light, and Ziusudra emerges to offer a sacrifice to An and Enlil, who would appear to have been responsible for the flood. They are appeased and repopulate the earth and renew its vegetation and finally grant Ziusudra "eternal life, like a god".

The third version of the myth is that in the eleventh tablet of the Gilgamesh epic (see margin, above), in which the hero Utnapishtim tells how he and his family survived the flood.

UGARITIC MYTHS

Kingship and succession

UGARITIC DEITIES
At the head of the Ugaritic pantheon
stands El, the supreme authority in
all matters human and divine: he is the
creator, "the father of gods and men",
depicted as an aged and venerable figure.
However, the most active deity in the
myths is the young god Baal, identified
with the storm-god Hadad, and with
the deified principle of fertility; he dwells
on a mountain in the remote north.
Associated with them are two female
figures, Ashera or Astarte and Anath,
examples of the fertility goddesses found
throughout the ancient Middle East.
Ashera is the consort of El and mother
of the pantheon. Anath is Baal's sister,
chief helper in his vicissitudes and
distinguished by her violent and warlike
character. Other deities of lesser importance are Reshef and Horon, gods of
pestilence, and Athar, the Venus star,
parallel to Ishtar in Mesopotamia.
The myths also feature two adversaries
of Baal: Yam, the sea, and Mot, the
destructive power of drought and sterility.

*The god El on his throne, accepting an
offering from a crowned worshipper, who
may be the king of Ugarit. The deity
wears a crown with widespread bull's
horns: his left hand is raised in a gesture
of benediction. This stele from Ugarit
illustrates the characteristics of El which
the texts ascribe to him by the epithets
King, Bull, Kindly, Merciful and Holy.*

From 1928 onward, excavations at the North Syrian site of ancient Ugarit
(modern Ras Shamra) uncovered a number of tablets containing mythical
poetic texts, providing first-hand evidence of the religion of the
Canaanites, about which comparatively little had hitherto been known.
The texts date between *c*.1400BC and *c*.1350BC, but the myths they
contain are certainly much earlier: they are the creations of generations of
popular or official singers, and some of them had a place in temple
liturgies. The Ugaritic myths and legends display many features in
common with those of Mesopotamia, but also have distinctive
characteristics of their own.

Two texts are concerned with important aspects of Canaanite society.
The first is the legend of King Keret. The story opens with Keret bemoaning
the loss of seven successive wives, which blights his hopes of an heir. The
supreme god El appears to him in a dream and instructs him to invade a
neighbouring kingdom and take Huray, the daughter of its king, in
marriage. Keret sets out, promising to give several times Huray's weight in
silver and gold to the fertility goddess Ashera if he is successful. He achieves
his purpose and, on his return, El blesses him and promises that Huray will
bear him eight sons, the eldest of which will be suckled by Ashera and
Anath. Over a period of seven years, these children are duly born. But then
it appears that Keret has not kept his vow to Ashera. He falls gravely ill, so
that he can no longer administer justice and the fertility of the crops is
impaired. A ceremony is held in Baal's palace to bring the fructifying rains.
Afterwards Keret regains his health and his throne and is able to quell the
attempt of one of his sons to supplant him. The story says much about the
concept of kingship as it was understood in the ancient Middle East, the
king being held as a sacred figure, the channel of blessing who brings order
and fertility to his land and society: as he suffers or prospers, so do they.

Similar concerns underlie the legend of Aqhat. The patriarch Daniel (the
same name is found in the Bible) is childless but, at the instigation of Baal,
El grants him a son, Aqhat. When Aqhat grows up, a divine craftsman gives
him a bow and arrows. The goddess Anath covets these and tries to
persuade Aqhat to surrender them. When he refuses, she sends her
attendant Yatpan to murder Aqhat but the bow is destroyed in the struggle,
thus thwarting Anath's plan. As a result, Baal withholds the rain and the
crops fail. Daniel searches for Aqhat's remains and, when he finds them,
buries them in the family tomb and holds mourning rites for seven years.

The end of the myth is lost, but scholars are generally agreed that it told
of the resurrection of Aqhat, the return of fertility to the country, and
perhaps the recovery of the bow. Behind the story there may well lie an
original myth to account for the summer drought and its eventual breaking,
symbolized by Aqhat's death and resurrection, while the bow may
represent the constellation of Orion, whose setting and rising corresponded
to the beginning and end of the dry season.

Two other myths are essentially theogonies – accounts of the birth of
gods. One relates how El has intercourse with two women, probably
representing the goddesses Ashera and Anath, and fathers first two
divinities, Shachar ("Dawn") and Shalim ("Dusk"), and then apparently
the Ugaritic deities in general. The second myth recounts the arrangements
for the marriage of the moon god Yarikh to the moon goddess Nikkal, in
the course of which the Kotharat, the divine midwives, are summoned to
attend the birth of a son.

Baal, the storm god

The most important Ugaritic myths, forming a cycle of three interrelated episodes, are concerned with the young storm god Baal. The whole was probably intended to be recited at a great festival in the autumn, celebrating the end of the agricultural year and looking forward to the coming of the early rains (just as the Babylonian creation epic was recited during the New Year festival in Babylon).

The first text deals with Baal's defeat of Yam, or "sea". Also called Nahar ("river") and named as "dragon", "serpent" and "Leviathan" in other Ugaritic documents, Yam was the equivalent of the Mesopotamian Tiamat (see p.62).

At the beginning of the myth, Yam claims royal power, and the supreme god El decides to grant him this, but warns him that he will first have to overcome Baal. In this part of the story there is evidence of tension and rivalry between the old El and the young Baal, which appears several times in the texts. With the aid of magical weapons supplied by the divine craftsmen, Baal engages in a mighty battle with Yam, kills him and scatters the remains, and then proclaims himself king. Yam represents the unruly forces of chaos, which threaten men and nature. By defeating him, Baal shows that he is the one who can control the flow of water from the heavens, and so send the fructifying rains on which agriculture depended.

The second episode opens with a great banquet, celebrating Baal's victory over Yam. However, then Baal recedes into the background, and there follows an account of a bloodthirsty slaughter of Baal's worshippers at the hands of Anath, which may reflect the intense anxiety of the population at the end of the dry season. Baal seeks to control Anath by promising to reveal to her the secret of the lightning, which would bring the life-giving storms. Next Baal complains that he has no palace like the other gods. Anath goes to El to ask him to grant Baal a house, but El at first refuses. Eventually, El is persuaded to agree to this by his

Baal or Hadad as the storm god. Standing on the mountains, he holds a mace, representing thunder, and a lance, representing the lightning bolt.

consort Ashera. There follows a description of the building of the palace, after which Baal takes up residence, an event which is celebrated by a great feast. Behind the whole narrative lies a foundation myth of Baal's temple at Ugarit, paralleling the building of Esagila for Marduk after his defeat of Tiamat (see p. 62). Finally, as Baal sits in his palace, he asks whether anyone can resist his supreme power and issues a challenge to Mot, god of death, a primeval earth monster (parallel with Yam the primeval sea monster). This introduces the third section of the myth.

The theme of the final part is the attempt of Mot to usurp Baal's kingship, by means of two confrontations. First, Mot forces Baal to submit to his power and descend to the underworld, thus bringing the summer drought. In Baal's absence, Ashera, at El's request, nominates her son Ashtar to replace Baal as king, but he proves unequal to the task, Meanwhile, Anath searches for Baal. `She comes upon Mot, and kills him, threshing and burning him. However, it seems that only an earthly aspect of Mot is involved, because in an episode that recalls Ishtar's dangerous journey (see p. 61), Anath descends to the underworld to try and persuade Mot to release Baal. Eventually, largely by the intervention of the sun goddess Shapash, Baal returns and is restored to his former state.

Then Mot issues his second challenge. He leaves his underworld home and, for the first time, meets Baal face to face. A battle ensues which ends in a draw, when El appears and persuades the reluctant Mot to acknowledge Baal as king.

As the personification of man's last enemy, death, Mot cannot be vanquished, only kept in check by Baal with the help of the supreme head of the gods. Here the myth touches on the universal tragedy of death, a theme which is more poignantly treated in the Gilgamesh epic (see p. 60).

MYTHS OF THE HITTITES

Dragons and lost gods

The bas-relief (above) comes from the Hittite city of Malatya. The weather god (perhaps with his son) is attacking a great serpent and showering hail upon it. According to the texts, the god is at first defeated by the dragon Illuyankas, but is finally victorious. The myth was recited at the Hittite New Year festival.

A non-Semitic people, the Hittites settled in Asia Minor toward the beginning of the 3rd millennium BC and eventually created an empire which embraced much of the Middle East, enduring until *c*.1225 BC. The Hittites' pantheon was much larger than that of Mesopotamia, because their religion absorbed the cults of other peoples, such as the Hattians (the earlier inhabitants of Asia Minor) and the Hurrians (of northern Mesopotamia). It was also strongly influenced by Babylonian religion, and its pantheon included several Babylonian deities.

Hittite myths fall into two main categories: the slaying of the dragon, and the missing god. The best example of the latter is the myth of Telepinu, god of agriculture and son of the great weather god. For some unexplained reason, Telepinu goes into hiding and his absence blights nature and society. Barley and wheat fail, oxen, sheep and humans are unable to conceive, and those who are pregnant cannot give birth. Even the gods go hungry. The gods (especially the weather god) attempt to discover Telepinu. Finally they succeed and he flies home on the back of an eagle. Prosperity returns to the land, and there is a specific promise of life and vigour for the king and queen. This narrative may have been used as an invocation to induce a god to return to an alienated worshipper.

Ullikummi and Teshub

An especially important deity in the Hittite mythological texts is the weather god Teshub, the Hittite version of Hadad. How Teshub achieved his prominence is narrated in two texts, which deal with the struggle for kingship in heaven between older and younger gods.

The first myth centres on Kumarbi, the father of the gods, who may be equated with the Sumerian Enlil. However, Kumarbi was not the first god. Before him, Alalu was king in heaven and he was deposed by Anu. Then Kumarbi made war on Anu and bit off his penis. Anu's sperm impregnated Kumarbi and in due course there are produced three "terrible gods", apparently all aspects of the weather god. At this point, the tablet is mutilated, but the next episode is probably the victory of the weather god over Kumarbi. In the second myth, the Song of Ullikummi, Kumarbi seeks revenge on Teshub who has deposed him. With the help of the Sea, the personified chaos, Kumarbi fathers a son, Ullikummi, who is then placed on the shoulders of Upelluri, a giant who lives in the midst of the sea. Ullikummi grows to huge size, to the alarm of Teshub, who organizes the gods to attack him. But the enterprise fails, and Ullikummi forces Teshub to abdicate. Then Teshub resorts to the wise god Ea, who devises a means to detach Ullikummi from his source of strength in Upelluri. Ea summons the gods to renew the struggle. The end of the myth is missing, but almost certainly concerns the restoration of Teshub and the defeat of Kumarbi and his son.

Originally a Hurrian deity, Teshub is depicted as both a warrior and storm god, girded with a sword, holding an axe and a three-pronged lightning fork, and wearing a horned helmet.

PERSIAN MYTHS

Ahura Mazdah and the battle between good and evil

MITHRA
Perhaps the best-known Persian deity is Mithra, because of the widespread cult which developed around him in the West. Originally, he was the personification of *mitra* ("contract") and so the preserver of law and order. He was also a god of war, described as riding in his four-horsed golden chariot against the demons and their worshippers, and closely associated with the sun. He eventually became the object of a mystery cult under the Roman Empire. Virtually every shrine to Mithra had a central relief of Mithra slaying the bull, an ancient Persian rite instituted by Yima, the first man. In Mithraism, the rite represents an act of the renewal of creation: by slaying the bull Mithra was believed to bring again Yima's reign over a world without hunger or death, and to assure his worshippers of immortality.

The religion of the ancient Persians is known only from the later Zoroastrian scriptures, the *Avesta*, and in particular from the body of hymns known as the *Yashts*. Natural forces were worshipped, but also there were deified concepts and social phenomena. The Persians recognized one supreme god Ahura Mazdah ("Wise Lord"), the all-embracing sky. Against him stood Angra Mainyu or Ahriman, god of darkness and sterility. Life was thus essentially a battle between the forces of good and evil. Between these two deities existed Vayu, god of air and wind. Another important god was Tishtrya, the rain god, whose myth exemplifies the universal Middle Eastern conflict story. Tishtrya goes down to the cosmic ocean in the form of a white horse with golden ears and trappings, where he meets Apaosha, the demon of drought, as a black horse. They fight for three days and at first Apaosha is victorious and drought prevails on the earth. However, Tishtrya appeals to Ahura Mazdah, who feeds him with sacrifices and so makes him strong. He overcomes Apaosha and the rains flow again. Another figure of Persian myth is the fertility goddess Anahita, source of all waters on earth, of human reproduction, and of the cosmic sea. The familiar myth of the disappearing god occurs in the form of Rapithwin, lord of the noonday heat and the summer months: each year the demon of winter invades the land, and Rapithwin retreats beneath the earth to keep the subterranean waters warm.

Some time in the 6th or 7th century BC the prophet Zoroaster formalized the inherent dualism of Persian faith. Ahura Mazdah became alone worthy of absolute worship. The main Zoroastrian myths deal with creation. Ahura Mazdah creates the whole beneficent universe, including Gayomart, the archetypal man, but Angra Mainyu, leader of the demon hordes, creates his own evil offspring – vicious animals, whirlwinds, sandstorms and disease, which attack the cosmos and shatter its ideal state. This conflict is destined ultimately to end in the victory of good over evil.

Under the Achaemenids, Ahura Mazdah was adopted as the patron of the royal house, and was symbolically represented, following Babylonian and Egyptian models, as spreading his protective wings over the king.

INDIA

*The group of three gods in the classical Hindu pantheon –
(from left) Brahma, Shiva with his bull mount Nandin below,
and Vishnu – are seen dancing to the music of the divine
musicians, the Gandharvas, in this 12th-century stone sculpture.*

Throughout the history of Indian culture there has been a continuous interaction between the different religious, linguistic and social groups, and this has resulted in a richly textured mythology, rivalling the whole of the European corpus in quantity and diversity. An enormous bulk of narrative is preserved in the regional languages of India, but in the main the most popular myths have achieved wider currency by being adopted into the supra-regional language, Sanskrit, and collected together in the *Puranas*, which from the 4th century onward took over from the epics (the *Mahabharata* and the *Ramayana*) as the great storehouses of religious and mythic traditions.

Underlying this rich variety of myth is the central theme of the tension between creation and destruction. A characteristic feature of Indian thought is the process by which order is brought out of chaos and the universe dissolved back into chaos in an immense cyclic pattern. Another basic theme is that things are not what they seem, and thus all reality is in some sense delusory. Most notable of all is the way in which the storytellers are often consciously manipulating their materials, developing and modifying them in what amounts to a deliberate critique of other forms of the same myth.

The oldest grouping of gods in the Vedic pantheon (often said to total thirty-three) gave way, as the religion developed into Hinduism, to the concept of the *trimurti*, a formal grouping of Brahma with the two deities who later become dominant, Vishnu and Shiva: Brahma is held to be the originator, Vishnu the maintainer and Shiva the destroyer of the cosmos. More recently, a grouping of five gods (Vishnu, Shiva, Devi, Surya and Ganesha) has been preferred.

SACRED SITES

HIMALAYA ("abode of snow"). In the Himalaya are Shiva's favoured residence on Mount Kailasa, the mythical Mount Meru (the navel of the world and the site of Brahma's and Indra's heavens) and Mount Mandara, used as the paddle in the churning of the ocean (see p.71). Personified, the great range is father by his wife Mena of Shiva's consort, Parvati, "daughter of the mountain". There is also a myth that the mountains were once flying elephants until Indra punished them for their stubbornness by cutting off their wings.

GANGA (Ganges). The most holy of the three great river goddesses of Hinduism (the others are the Yamuna and Sarasvati, all three joining according to tradition at Prayaga, modern Allahabad). (Another formulation lists seven sacred rivers.) Brought down from heaven by Bhagiratha, Ganga's fall was cushioned by Shiva's matted locks as he meditated on Mount Kailasa. Because she penetrated also to the underworld, she is said to water the three worlds. Ganga also nourished the embryo born as the six-headed Skanda or Karttikeya.

MATHURA. The city ruled by Kamsa, the enemy of Krishna, and surrounded by Brindaban, the locale of Krishna's youthful exploits.

AYODHYA. Identified as the capital of the kingdom inherited by Rama from his father Dasharatha, and therefore the city in which his ideal rule was manifest.

VARANASI (Benares). Also called Kashi ("city of light"), this is Shiva's city, where he resides in person, and is sometimes believed to survive the periodic dissolution of the universe. Residence here is thought by devout Hindus to ensure that one gains release; it is also the best place to be cremated.

KEY TO MAP

- ● City or site of special religious or cultural significance
- ● Other city
- ▨ Mountainous region

Present-day country: **PAKISTAN**

RELIGIONS OF INDIA

HINDUISM denotes the group of religious traditions that developed by stages from the Vedic religion brought into India by the Aryans, or that claim such descent. An early emphasis on animal sacrifice tended to give way to vegetarian offerings, female deities became more important, and devotional religion proved popular. Vishnu or Shiva is often seen as the supreme deity. A distinctive Hindu concept is that of transmigration: continuing rebirth in a series of lives, until one can achieve final release by knowledge, by actions or by devotion.

BUDDHISM arose in the 6th-5th centuries BC in eastern North India at a time of growing discontent with the dominance of sacrificial orthodoxy. Siddhartha Gautama, the Buddha ("Enlightened"), propounded a pragmatic approach to the search for release from the cycle of rebirths. He believed that humanity's problems were brought about by cravings and the belief in an eternal soul. His message of the Eightfold Path which leads to Nirvana (the extinction of craving and the dissolution of the individual) spread along trade routes within India and beyond, travelling through Central Asia to China and Japan in its Mahayana form, while the Theravada form established itself in Sri Lanka and Burma.

JAINISM looks to Mahavira, the Jina ("Conqueror") and a contemporary of the Buddha, as its last great teacher. He preached an especially austere form of religious endeavour, emphasizing among other things the presence of living souls in a very wide range of creatures and the corresponding duty to avoid taking life (the concept of *ahimsa*).

ORIGINS OF THE WORLD

Sacrifice and conflict

In the developed cosmology of Hinduism, the world undergoes regular cycles of emanation and reabsorption. In this 17th-century painting, Vishnu rests between one period of emanation and the next on the snake Ananta, while Shri massages his feet. In the upper register (from the left) are shown Vishnu riding on Garuda (who has a snake in his mouth), Brahma and Shiva.

THE VEDIC PANTHEON
The earliest Indian texts are the Vedic hymns, orally composed and transmitted in four collections from around the beginning of the 1st millennium BC and long regarded as too sacred to be written down. These collections, containing poems of praise and invocation to numerous deities, but usually only alluding to the myths about them, are the earliest part of the *Vedas*, the Vedic literature, continued in the *Brahmanas* (devoted to the sacrificial ritual but a rich storehouse of myths), the *Aranyakas* and the *Upanishads* (speculative texts which nonetheless make use of myth to communicate their ideas).

The (predominantly male) Vedic deities, the Devas, display very human characteristics. There are often said to be thirty-three of them, later usually divided equally between the three regions of heaven, atmosphere and earth. Their chief attribute is their power, and hence their ability to help mankind.

In Indian thought the origin of the world is not an act of creation, but an act of arrangement, the making of order out of chaos – a point on which all the cosmogonic myths, as well as the formal theologies, agree. However, beyond this there is little consistency. The origin myths comprise a varied collection of vivid metaphors, drawn from all kinds of human activity. Especially in the later Vedic literature, the metaphor is that of animal sacrifice. In one hymn Vishvakarman, "the maker of all", is represented as celebrating the first sacrifice, that of creation. In another hymn Purusha, a cosmic person or primal being, is sacrificed, and from his dismembered body are produced all the entities of the universe, from the traditional Vedic gods, through the atmosphere, heaven and earth, to animals and man; however, only one quarter of him is manifest in this way, as the remaining three quarters constitute immortality in heaven. Reflecting these ideas of sacrifice are the sacrificial rituals, considered as a re-enactment of creation, and thus vital to the maintenance of the cosmos.

From the Vedic hymns onward, allusions are made to the Golden Germ or embryo, a world egg floating on the primeval waters of chaos, from which arises the first deity as the maker or orderer of the world. The analogy of pregnancy implied in this concept is made explicit in several myths, of which the best known is that of Prajapati ("the lord of progeny") who produces children by the power of his asceticism, among them a daughter, the Dawn. However, he becomes sexually aroused by his daughter and attempts to commit incest with her. In her shame and terror she becomes a deer, whereupon Prajapati takes the form of a stag and spills his seed, which gives rise to the first men. Alternatively, Prajapati actually mates with the Dawn in one animal form after another, and so he creates or procreates "all the pairs, even down to the ants".

Descriptions of Heaven and Earth as the divine parents also occur. In some hymns the goddess Aditi, "the limitless one", impregnated by Daksha, "ritual skill", bears the seven major gods (called therefore

Adityas), as well as the Sun, who is the eighth god, originally born dead. The gods then produce the cosmos out of chaos. However, just as Daksha is born from Aditi, so too Aditi is born from Daksha, because the two principles are interdependent.

One of the minor Vedic deities is Tvashtr, the divine carpenter or architect, whom some hymns declare to have fashioned Heaven and Earth or to have created all forms. Two hymns ask the question: "What was the wood, what was the tree out of which they shaped heaven and earth?"; and the second hymn (the one that speaks of Vishvakarman as celebrating the first sacrifice) adds the images of the potter and the smith, also found elsewhere. Alternatively, Tvashtr's cosmogonic role is secondary: he makes the thunderbolt for Indra to slay Vritra, so fixing the earth and releasing the waters. Indra's slaying of Vritra (see p.72) is an example of creation through opposition and strife, with the forces of chaos given a degree of personality. This is an aspect of the broader conflict between the Devas (the gods, who are friendly toward mankind) and the Asuras (the anti-gods). In the myth of the churning of the ocean (see panel, below) out-and-out conflict between these groups is turned into a formalized contest, a kind of tug of war.

SNAKES IN MYTH
Snakes – typically envisaged as cobras – play a major role in Indian mythology. Vasuki, who in the churning of the ocean is used as the rope, is one of several kings of the *naga*s or snakes. Elsewhere the world is said to rest on his multiple heads and when he moves there is an earthquake. He and another snake, Takshaka, and their descendants, are thought to contain a jewel within their hoods. Ananta ("infinite") or Shesha ("remainder") is the cosmic serpent on whose coils Vishnu rests in the cosmic waters during the intervals between the emanations of the cosmos. All three are said to be sons of Kadru, a daughter of Daksha and ancestress of all snakes, while her sister is mother of Garuda, the divine bird who is their great enemy.

The churning of the ocean

This myth, first found in the Brahmanas, *is popular in the* Puranas. *Here an intermediate form is condensed from the* Mahabharata *(one of the two great Sanskrit epics composed between the 4th century* BC *and the 4th century* AD*). It focuses on winning the* amrita *("immortal": that is, the elixir of immortality). With the ambiguity that is so characteristic of Indian myth, the cosmos is already in some sense in being before the production of this and other essentials.*

The gods, assembled on Mount Meru, began to ponder how to win the *amrita*. Vishnu suggested: "Let the Devas and the Asuras churn the pail of the ocean, and then the elixir will emerge as the ocean is churned, along with all herbs and jewels."

They went to Mount Mandara, uprooted it, and set it on the back of a tortoise as the paddle. Then they used the snake Vasuki as the rope and began to churn the ocean. The Asuras and Danavas took hold of one end of

Vasuki and the Devas of the other, twirling Mount Mandara about, so that its trees toppled and the friction set them alight. Indra put out the fire with water from his clouds, but the sap of all the plants flowed into the ocean, and the ocean turned to milk and then to butter.

With a final effort, they churned some more, and thus arose the Sun, the Moon, the goddess of fortune, other treasures and lastly the divine physician Dhanvantari bearing the elixir. Vishnu deluded the Asuras into surrendering the elixir and gave it to the Devas to drink. However, Rahu snatched a drop; but, before he could swallow it, Vishnu decapitated him. Ever since there has been a constant feud between Rahu and the Moon (with which *amrita* is identified): this explains the waxing and waning of the moon, disappearing and reappearing from down his severed throat. Enraged, the Asuras offered battle but were defeated. The victorious gods put Mount Mandara back in its proper place.

This 18th-century Kangra miniature depicts the churning of the ocean, with the anti-gods hauling at the heads of the snake Vasuki and the gods at his tail.

INDRA

Warrior and king of the gods

Indra, armed with swords and elephant goad, rides on his great white elephant Airavata, caparisoned like a South Indian temple elephant, in a detail from a 19th-century painting (right).

INDRA'S TITLES

As befits a god whose most prominent attribute is his strength, many of Indra's titles allude to this:

SHAKRA ("mighty"). This is such a frequent title that it becomes an alternative name for him.

SHACHIVAT ("possessing might").

SHACHIPATI ("lord of might"). This was later reinterpreted as "husband of Shachi", thus providing him with a consort.

SHATAKRATU ("having a hundred powers"). This title was also reinterpreted, as "celebrating a hundred sacrifices". Indra is also called the "thousand-eyed", originally in token of his omniscience. Some later narratives, as part of his general decline in esteem, suggest that Gautama's curse for Indra's adultery with Ahalya was not the loss of his testicles but the appearance of female genitals all over his body – a curse subsequently commuted into a thousand eyes.

Indra was the most popular deity among the poets of the first and best-known of the Vedic hymn collections, the *Rigveda*. Around a quarter of its hymns invoke him. He is the dominant god of the middle region of the atmosphere, and is described in more anthropomorphic terms than most other deities. His body is huge and mighty, his arms are powerful in order to wield his weapons, his hair is tawny, his belly is distended with intoxicating soma. Above all, he is the most outstanding warrior of the Vedic pantheon.

Chief of the gods, Indra is their leader against the Asuras and the main focus of the myths alluded to in the Vedic hymns. Born from Heaven and Earth (whom he separates for ever), he begins at once to display his characteristic energy. The stories about his birth and youthful exploits concern his rivalry with the more mysterious deity, Varuna, who seems once to have been the ruler of the gods but to have been gradually ousted by Indra. Whereas Varuna represents the static and juridical aspects of sovereignty (symbolized in his guardianship of *rta*, or cosmic order), Indra represents more immediately the power on which kingship relies. The principal myth about Indra tells of his battle with the serpent Vritra (see panel, below), but he also engages in conflict with many other hostile forces, as well as aiding the Aryans in their battles on earth. Sometimes he is described as destroying hostile powers in general, sweeping away the Asuras or consuming the Rakshasas (malevolent minor

The slaying of the serpent, Vritra

Indra's slaying of Vritra is commonly alluded to in the Vedic hymns. Here is a slightly abbreviated adaptation of one hymn from the Rigveda.

Indra's heroic deeds now let me proclaim, which he who wields the thunderbolt performed in the beginning. He slew the snake, cut a channel for the waters, and split the entrails of the mountains. Like lowing cows, the flowing waters made their way downwards straight to the sea. Exulting in his virility like a bull, he took the *soma* and drank the pressed juice from the three bowls. The generous one seized his thunderbolt as his weapon and killed the first-born of dragons. So, O Indra, in that instant you brought forth the sun, the sky and dawn. Since then you have found no enemy to match you. With his great weapon Indra slew the shoulderless Vritra. Like the trunk of a tree with its branches lopped, the dragon lay prostrate on the ground. Over him, as he lay like a broken reed, the rising waters flowed for mankind, the waters that Vritra had enclosed with his might. The waters flow over Vritra's hidden corpse, for he who found Indra too mighty a foe has sunk into long darkness. You, o brave god, won the cows, you won the *soma*, you released the seven streams so that they flow.

Indra's seduction of Ahalya

*I*n the Ramayana *(the other great Sanskrit epic composed over much the same period as the* Mahabharata*), Vishvamitra tells Rama the story about Indra seducing Ahalya, the wife of the great sage Gautama.*

In a hermitage Gautama, accompanied by Ahalya, performed austerities for many years. Indra, learning one day that the sage was absent, dressed himself as the ascetic and went to Ahalya to say that he wanted to have intercourse with her. The woman recognized the thousand-eyed Indra in his ascetic attire, but out of curiosity about the king of the gods agreed to his demands. As he left her he met Gautama returning from his bathing, and the sage angrily declared to him: "Since you have taken my form and done this evil, you fool, you shall lose your testicles." At once Indra's testicles fell to the ground. Then he cursed his wife, saying: "You shall live invisibly in this hermitage, subsisting just on air and lying on ashes, until Rama, son of Dasharatha, visits this forest. Only then, by giving him hospitality, will you joyfully regain your form in my presence."

Vishvamitra goes on to tell how the gods replace Indra's testicles with those of a ram, and then they enter the hermitage, where Ahalya eagerly greets Rama and is freed from the curse.

powers) with his thunderbolt. By his victory over Vritra, Indra gave form to the previously formless chaos, and activated the process of differentiation and evolution. By killing the serpent he separated land from water, upper regions from nether, and caused the sun to rise in an act of creation that is repeated every morning. This episode established him as the great champion against all forms of resistance and obstruction. However, in a priestly reworking of the Vritra myth, Indra overthrows Vala with a hymn or by other ritual means.

In his ready indulgence in the exhilarating drink *soma*, Indra has much in common with the swashbuckling, hard-drinking Aryan warrior whose hero he was. Pressed from a plant whose identity remains controversial, this juice was central to Vedic sacrificial rituals. After he has drunk it, Indra's belly is said to be like a lake, and he swells to a terrifying size, filling the two worlds, Heaven and Earth. The juice empowers him to make the sun rise, and perform his mighty deeds.

The *Vedas* imply approval when they mention Indra outsmarting Vritra and striking him in the back, but in later Hinduism the god's role as a paragon of the warrior ethic is diminished. Vritra is regarded as a brahman (whom it is a heinous offence to kill), and Indra must therefore expiate his sin. He slays Namuci only by getting round the terms of the non-aggression pact they have made with each other, disguising or more exactly transforming his thunderbolt (*vajra*) by wrapping it in foam. Another of his victims, Trishiras ("Three-headed"), is considered to be his half-brother. He seduces the sage Gautama's wife, Ahalya, and suffers the sage's curse. This kin-killing, contract-breaking and adultery become a standard theme of the *Puranas* – Indra as triple sinner – and in consequence he loses his lustre, his strength and his looks.

Indra by the classical period became the god of rain. In some versions of the churning of the ocean myth, among the treasures to emerge is Surabhi, the cow of plenty, who becomes the mother of all ordinary cattle. The *Mahabharata* records that one day she came to Indra in distress over the harsh treatment of a son of hers, a bull, at the hands of some peasants. He asked why she was concerned about just one son among thousands. When she persisted in her complaint, he responded by raining down on the spot so heavily that the ploughing had to stop – the warrior god harnessed to agriculture. Thus, Indra's thundering becomes superintendence of rain in another domestication of his once martial attributes.

In classical Indian mythology, Indra is often humiliated by younger deities. Krishna, having persuaded his people to cease worshipping Indra, lifted Mount Govardhana to protect them from Indra's rains. In the ensuing conflict Indra, armed with bow and arrow, is seen attacking Krishna, mounted on Garuda, in this Mughal illustration from a manuscript of c.1590.

BRAHMA
The creator god

Brahma, the creator and giver of boons, is a frequent figure in the later mythology, usually in a subordinate role to the other two great gods, Vishnu and Shiva. There does seem to have been a period during the early centuries AD when Brahma was the focus of a cult, presumably as the creator deity; however, this has long gone. There are several passages in the epics where Brahma, also called Pitamaha, the Grand Father, is credited with some of the cosmogonic myths associated in the later Vedic period with Prajapati. Among them is the story of how he produces a lovely young woman, as a daughter, from his own body. He is smitten with her beauty, and as she walks around him as a gesture of respect, his wish to stare at her beauty causes a succession of faces to appear. The union of father and daughter produces Manu, the first man.

As he meditates, Brahma emits from himself both the material elements of the universe and the concepts through which we understand them. The duration of the universe is counted in terms of Brahma's lifespan of a hundred years, each made up of 360 days, which are each equal to 1,000 years of the gods, each day of which makes a human year. In each day of Brahma the universe is created; in each night it is reabsorbed. Within each cycle, from emanation to dissolution, there are four successive ages, from the best, the Krita Yuga, to the worst, the Kali Yuga. Eventually, Brahma's creative activity is trivialized into a readiness to grant boons to anyone who performs penance or asceticism, regardless of the consequences.

BRAHMA AND BRAHMAN
The concept of Brahma as a male deity, a personalized form of the neuter abstraction Brahman, is found particularly in the two great Sanskrit epics. Essentially, he is a fusion of a creator deity with the impersonal Brahman propounded in the *Upanishads*, which see the goal of religious endeavour as some kind of union with this absolute, whereas the popular forms of religion attested in the epics prefer a more personal and devotional approach. Eventually Brahma suffered a decline in prestige compared with Vishnu and Shiva (perhaps because he is especially linked with the brahmans, the guardians of tradition and specialists in ritual, just as Indra was linked with the warriors, the *kshatriyas*).

Brahma as giver of boons

The following story from the Mahabharata *is one of many illustrating Brahma's role as boon-giver to the Asuras.*

Three Daitya brothers undertook strenuous austerities, and Brahma granted them boons. They asked for total invulnerability, but the Grand Father said that there was no such thing. They then asked: "Let us establish three cities on earth and ourselves wander in the world until, after a thousand years, we come together again, the three cities join into one, and the best of gods destroys the united cities with a single arrow." Brahma agreed and the cities were built by Maya, the great Asura: one of gold in heaven, one of silver in the air, one of iron on the earth. The three brothers overwhelmed the three worlds and ruled for many years. Millions of demon leaders flocked to the cities and Maya, by his magic, provided whatever they wished. The gods became angry at this moral laxity, and at the moment when they united, Shiva burned up the triple city and all the Asuras, and hurled them into the western ocean.

VISHNU

Protector of the world

In the *Rigveda* Vishnu, the "wide-strider", is repeatedly praised for having taken three strides that measured out and pervaded the cosmos, thus affirming the habitable universe for gods and humans alike. He is a friend and ally of Indra, helping him in his conflict with Vritra and in spreading out the spaces between heaven and earth. He is benevolent, never inimical to humanity, and willing and able to bestow favours on his worshippers.

Vishnu's pervasiveness is also apparent in his identification with the cosmic pillar, the centre of the universe which leads to and supports the heavens; in ritual, this is the stake to which the Vedic sacrificial victim was tied. In later Vedic literature, Vishnu's activities take on a more narrative form – for example, when he takes the form of a dwarf to regain the world from a demon (see p.76). His benevolence and his activities are beginning to be given expression in a form which in due course reaches its culmination in the avatar concept.

Vishnu's consort Shri, goddess of prosperity and good fortune, known also as Lakshmi, is often reckoned one of the good things that emerged from the churning of the ocean (see p.71): she is naturally attracted to Vishnu, who oversees the operation, and he in turn is entitled to the lovely goddess by virtue of his role. Shri was consistently linked with Vishnu by the late epic period, but several early myths relate how Indra loses, acquires or regains the boon of Shri's presence, which is associated with fertility. One myth tells how when she sat down next to Indra he began to pour down rain and the crops grew abundantly.

Vishnu with his consort Shri on a 7th-century stone relief. By the late epic period, Shri was linked with Vishnu, and as his consort she became symbolic of loyalty – a model Hindu wife, loyal and submissive to her husband. Other names for Shri denote the lotus.

Vishnu's three strides

*I*n the hymn of praise to Vishnu in the Rigveda, *quoted below, the poet concentrates on the three strides, which in their earliest form symbolize his might and omnipresence, traversing the earth and sky and the regions beyond mankind's knowledge, and growing to great dimensions.*

"Vishnu's heroic deeds now let me proclaim, who measured out the earthly realms, who supported the upper dwelling-place, striding widely as he took his three steps. For his heroic deeds they praise Vishnu, who haunts the mountains wandering freely like a wild animal, in

This detail from a 19th-century painting shows Vishnu riding with his consort Shri on the celestial bird Garuda.

whose three wide strides all beings dwell. Let my inspiring thought go forth to Vishnu, the mountain-dwelling, wide-ranging bull, who alone with just three steps measured out this long, extended dwelling-place, whose three steps, unfailingly full of honey, rejoice in his energy, and who alone has triply supported earth and heaven and all creatures. May I reach his dear path, where men devoted to the gods rejoice, for there in wide-striding Vishnu's highest footstep is closeness, a fountain of honey. We wish to go to your abodes, where there are many-horned, untiring cattle. There the highest footstep of the wide-ranging bull shines down greatly."

VISHNU'S INCARNATIONS

The avatars

Various animal and human figures were viewed as examples of Vishnu's benevolent activity on earth, and identified with him as his avatars or incarnations. These appear successively whenever the world is in danger from evil. The number became fixed at ten, although their precise identities were flexible. For example, a passage in the *Harivamsha* (a supplement to the *Mahabharata*) has the lotus (arising from Vishnu's navel) instead of the fish and tortoise; it also includes Dattatreya (who grants Arjuna Karttavirya his hundred arms), while omitting the Buddha. However, the usual list of Vishnu's avatars is that given here (left) and depicted in the 18th-century miniature below. The avatars illustrated, surrounding a central depiction of Vishnu and Shri, follow the sequence in the list (in rows from top left), except that the sixth is Rama and Sita (with Hanuman), the seventh Krishna playing his flute with Radha, and the eighth Parashurama.

THE TEN AVATARS

MATSYA, the fish, protects Manu, the first man, during the great deluge. Manu rescues a small fish from the jaws of larger ones, tends it as it grows to enormous size and returns it to the ocean. Later the fish warns him of the coming flood, advises him to build a boat and stock it with the seed of all things, and then tows the boat to safety.

KURMA, the tortoise, supports Mount Mandara on his back at the time of the churning of the ocean (see p.71).

VARAHA, the boar, is manifested when the earth is plunged into the ocean. With his tusk, he raises the earth, conceived as a beautiful woman, out of the water again.

NARASIMHA, the man-lion, is the form that Vishnu takes to kill the demon Hiranyakashipu, to whom Brahma has granted invulnerability: he cannot be killed by men or gods, by weapons or blunt objects, by day or by night, within or outside his house. When Hiranyakashipu terrorizes the universe, Vishnu becomes half man, half lion, and emerges to disembowel the demon at twilight on his own veranda.

VAMANA, the dwarf, is the form taken by Vishnu when he comes to save the world from Bali (another demon) and all his minions. In the guise of a dwarf, he begs from Bali as much land as he can cover in three strides. When the dwarf's wish is granted, Vishnu transforms himself into a giant and thus wins back the world.

PARASHURAMA is a brahman who kills the hundred-armed Arjuna with his axe, annihilates all the warrior class thrice seven times, and beheads his mother at his father's command.

RAMA AND KRISHNA, the seventh and eighth avatars, are major figures in Hindu myth in their own right (see pp.77-9).

THE BUDDHA is the ninth avatar. He misleads the sinful to ensure their punishment.

KALKIN, the tenth and future avatar, is a millennial figure, who will establish a new era. He will appear as a warrior on a white horse; indeed, in South Indian popular belief he actually is a horse.

RAMA

The righteous avatar

Rama is now one of the two most popular incarnations of Vishnu, although his cult was much later to appear than that of Krishna (see pp.78-9). He is the hero of the *Ramayana* (from which the account below is compressed), and in the core of that text his story shows some analogies with the Vedic myths of Indra: for example, he receives Indra's magic weapons and later also the aid of Indra's charioteer, and his killing of Valin is reminiscent of Indra's underhand assault on Namuci (see p.73). His wife, Sita, appeared in Vedic literature as the deified Furrow, the wife of Indra.

Dasharatha, the childless king of Ayodhya, performs a sacrifice in order to be granted sons. At the gods' request, Vishnu becomes incarnate as Dasharatha's four sons to destroy Ravana, evil king of Lanka. Of the four, Rama and Bharata play the chief roles, while the twins Lakshmana and Shatrughna each attach themselves to one of their half-brothers as loyal companions. The sage Vishvamitra comes to court to demand Rama's help on a mission against marauding Rakshasas, and once this is successfully accomplished takes Rama and Lakshmana to King Janaka's court. Here we learn of Sita's miraculous birth and adoption by Janaka, and of Shiva's bow, which no man has strength to string: Rama not merely bends but breaks the bow, and marries Sita.

Later, Dasharatha determines to install Rama as his heir, but his stepmother contrives to have him supplanted by her son, Bharata, and banished to the forest for fourteen years. Rama prepares for his departure with no protest whatsoever, and sets off accompanied by his wife Sita and his brother Lakshmana. Despite Rama's resolve to live like an ascetic, his role as warrior now comes to the fore in protecting the defenceless sages who have their hermitages in the forest. The hideous but amorous female Rakshasa, Shurpanakha, makes advances to the brothers. Infuriated by their disdain, she attacks Sita, whereupon Lakshmana mutilates her as a punishment. She then seeks vengeance from her brother Ravana, king of Lanka, whom she incites to abduct Sita. Ravana, disguised as a mendicant, carries Sita off to Lanka.

Rama and Lakshmana, meanwhile, in great distress, start searching for Sita, and during their search meet Hanuman, minister of Sugriva, the exiled monkey king. Sugriva enlists Rama's help in ousting his usurping brother Valin, and Rama kills Valin as the two brothers duel. After many adventures Hanuman discovers where Sita has been taken. (In the developed Rama cult, Hanuman becomes the pattern of devoted service to the deity: see margin, right.)

While Rama and Sugriva's monkey subjects march southward, the Rakshasas prepare for war. A long series of duels ensues, resulting in the deaths of all the most fearsome Rakshasa champions at the hands of Rama, Lakshmana and the monkey chiefs. Finally only Ravana is left. His duel with Rama is protracted but, after Rama receives divine help in the form of Indra's chariot and charioteer, Ravana too is killed and victory won. Because of qualms about Sita's virtue, Rama coldly spurns her and Sita undergoes an ordeal by fire. The gods appear to Rama and reveal that he is in fact an incarnation of Vishnu, and the god of fire hands Sita back to her delighted husband, unharmed and exonerated. Dasharatha too appears and blesses his sons, telling Rama to return to Ayodhya and resume his reign (the fourteen years of exile having at this point expired). Rama reigns righteously for a thousand years.

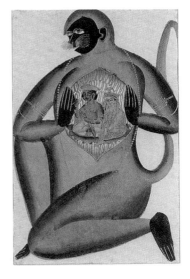

A 19th-century Kalighat drawing of Hanuman. In one story, Hanuman, given a pearl necklace by Rama, cracks open the pearls with his teeth. When Lakshmana protests, he declares that he is testing whether the pearls contain the name of Rama. Further challenged, he tears open his chest to reveal Rama and Sita enthroned in his heart.

HANUMAN, THE LOYAL HELPER

Hanuman shows outstanding devotion to Rama from the moment they meet. Rama entrusts his ring to Hanuman as a token for Sita, when parties of monkeys go off to search for her. When Hanuman's troop learn that Sita is on the island of Lanka, he resolves to make an extraordinary leap over the sea to find her. Once on Lanka, Hanuman reveals himself to Sita, producing Rama's ring. Instead of hurrying back in secret, Hanuman then embarks on a course of ostentatious destruction and allows himself to be captured by Ravana's son. The angry Ravana is dissuaded from killing Hanuman outright and merely sets fire to his tail, but Hanuman uses it as a brand to complete the destruction of Lanka. When Rama and Lakshmana are wounded in the battle, Hanuman hurries off to the Himalayas to fetch the mountain on which a healing herb grows.

KRISHNA, THE ADORABLE

The eighth avatar of Vishnu

KRISHNA, THE BUTTER THIEF
Krishna's childhood pranks centre on his frequent thefts of butter. He dug it out by the handful from the pot, smearing it all around and offering a ball of it to his companions or the marauding monkeys as he crawled about the floor. Slightly older, he raided neighbours' houses, clambering onto a friend's shoulders or using a stick to knock down pots placed out of reach. It was after one such escapade and the complaints it attracted from other *gopis* that his foster-mother Yashoda tied him to a mortar. Older still, he and some companions waylaid the *gopis* as they took their butter, curds and milk to market and demanded a "gift" of some of it as the price of letting them pass. The detail (above right) of Krishna stealing butter from Yashoda is based on a Jain painting.

Krishna figures in the *Mahabharata* as a companion to its heroes but is then himself the focus of its supplement, the *Harivamsha*. His story is most notably recounted in the *Vishnu Purana* (from which the following outline is condensed) and the *Bhagavata Purana*.

It is prophesied that Devaki's eighth child will kill King Kamsa, so the king imprisons her. However, her husband smuggles the child out and exchanges it with the new-born child of Nanda and Yashoda, who bring up their adopted one among the cowherd folk in Brindaban. Kamsa, realizing that he has been outwitted, vainly institutes a Herod-like slaughter of all male children. Right from birth Krishna demonstrates marvellous abilities: he sucks the life out of the demoness Putana, uproots a pair of trees with the mortar to which he has been tethered by Yashoda to restrain him, and kills the snake Kaliya, all with his half-brother Balarama. He urges his foster-father to cease worshipping Indra and, when Indra retaliates with a deluge, lifts up the local hill, Mount Govardhana, as an umbrella over the cowherds and their cattle; Indra thereupon recognizes Krishna as the lord of cattle. Krishna and Balarama sport with the young women of the tribe (the *gopis*), who proceed to fall in love with Krishna.

Krishna kills the bull-demon Arishta, the horse-demon Keshin and

Radha and Krishna

*A*s he grew up in Brindaban, the pranks which Krishna played on the gopis changed into dalliance with them.

On one occasion Krishna stole their clothes as they were bathing in the Yamuna river and refused to return them until they had emerged naked one by one with their hands raised in supplication. Before long, all the cowherd girls were in love with the enchanting Krishna and, whatever the obstacles in their way, responded to his summons. At the sound of his flute on autumn evenings, they left their homes and husbands to join him in the forest along the Yamuna and there to dance with him the *ras* dance: each girl thought she had Krishna as her exclusive partner and was in ecstasy.

Even as the *ras* dance was continuing, Krishna slipped away with one of them. The other *gopis* disconsolately tracked their footprints and eventually the dance was resumed. Radha was indeed Krishna's favourite: she stole his heart even as a child. Her passionate love for Krishna, whether as mistress or wife (the traditions vary), and the depths of her longing for him after they had become estranged, are central to the story. But the longing was mutual: Krishna pined for her and was ready to abase himself before her to make amends. His dark form (his name means "dark") and her golden beauty complemented each other.

Kamsa's champion wrestler, before killing the evil Kamsa himself. He repeatedly defeats the wicked king of Magadha, Kamsa's father-in-law, Jarasandha; he leads the Yadavas, his clansmen, from Mathura to the new city of Dvaraka. He carries off Rukmini as his bride, as well as marrying many other wives. Rukmini bears his son Pradyumna, who in turn has a son Aniruddha. The demon Bana captures Aniruddha, who loves his daughter, and Krishna comes to his grandson's rescue: the resulting fight is so terrible that the dissolution of the world seems imminent, but Bana's ally Shiva acknowledges Krishna as highest god and identical to himself, whereupon Krishna spares Bana and frees his grandson. Another grandson, Samba, similarly carries off Duryodhana's daughter, and is captured by Duryodhana, and freed by Balarama.

Some Yadava lads dress up Samba as a woman and ask some sages what sort of child she will bear. Offended by their behaviour, the sages curse "her" to bear a pestle that will annihilate the Yadavas. The pestle is ground to powder and thrown into the sea, but the powder turns to reeds and one lance-like piece is swallowed by a fish, which a huntsman catches. In due course the Yadavas, along with Krishna and Balarama, indulge in a drinking bout and, when they quarrel, pick up these reeds and kill each other. Balarama sits down beneath a tree to die and, as Krishna sits lost in thought, the hunter who had found the lance-like piece and tipped his arrow with it approaches and shoots Krishna in the sole of his foot (his one vulnerable spot), mistaking him for a deer. Krishna dies and resumes his divine nature.

Radha and Krishna seated in a grove by the Yamuna, shown in a Kangra painting of c.1785 (see panel, opposite). The flowering of nature and the pairs of birds symbolize their amorous sentiments, while the plantain leaves echo the shape of Radha's thighs in a regular Indian conceit. Krishna's affair with Radha is treated as an allegory for the intimacy of deity and devotee.

SHIVA

The erotic and ascetic combined

Shiva on his bull mount Nandin, as depicted in an early 19th-century painting commissioned by the East India Company (the British colonial authority) from a local artist. A sculpture of a recumbent Nandin is regularly sited facing the main sanctuary of Shiva temples.

THE LINGA

Shiva is worshipped in the form of a linga, or sacred phallus (below). According to one myth, Vishnu and Brahma were arguing about who was greatest, when Shiva appeared as a blazing pillar – the linga. Brahma, as a wild goose, flew up to look for the pillar's top, while Vishnu, as a boar, dived down to look for the bottom. Both failed, and they were thus compelled to admit to Shiva's authority.

The erotic and ascetic aspects of Shiva combine in the story of how, smeared with ashes and unrecognizable, he visits a pine forest where sages are practising asceticism. The sages suspect him of try-ing to seduce their wives and curse him to lose his phallus. The castration works, but only with Shiva's secret complicity. Then the world grows dark and cold, and the sages lose their virile powers. Normality returns only after they have propitiated Shiva by making a linga.

Shiva appears in the *trimurti*, the sacred grouping of three, as the destroyer. His origins are in the Vedic Rudra, the "howler" or "ruddy one", a malevolent storm god, later called *shiva* ("auspicious") in order to propitiate him. Among the complex of Indian deities, Shiva is a wrathful avenger, as well as a herdsman of souls. With similar ambivalence, he is not only linked with yoga and asceticism (he sits meditating on lofty Mount Kailasa), but also has a pronounced erotic aspect.

Shiva's wife appears variously as Sati and Uma or Parvati. He is also sometimes paired with the "inaccessible" Durga and the dark goddess Kali. In painting he is usually shown as pale or ashen-faced, with a blue neck, caused by swallowing the poison which was generated at the churning of the cosmic ocean and threatened to destroy mankind: this is an example of Shiva as protector (another is the myth of how he broke the fall of the river goddess Ganga when she crashed down from heaven to cleanse the world). Other attributes of Shiva include a necklace of skulls, a garland of snakes, the coiled locks of an ascetic, the crescent moon, and a third eye of illumination (and destruction).

The disruption of Daksha's sacrifice

The father-in-law of Shiva, lord of cattle, was Daksha, a Prajapati (lord of creatures), who had sprung from Brahma's right thumb. This story, based on an account in the Mahabharata, *concerns a horse sacrifice Daksha had arranged in accordance with Vedic rites. Shiva's wife Sati is Daksha's daughter.*

In one account, Shiva pulls a lock from his hair and from it creates a many-armed monster which is unleashed on Daksha's sacrifice.

All the gods, headed by Indra, decided to attend the ceremony. Sati, the wife of Shiva, saw the gods riding there in their chariots, which shone with blazing light. "Illustrious one, why don't you go too?" his wife asked, but Shiva told her that the gods had decided he was to have no share in any sacrifice. Then she said, "Lord, among all beings you are superior. Yet I am ashamed because you are denied a share of the sacrifice."

Stung by this speech, the lord of cattle summoned his powers of yoga, seized his powerful bow and attacked the sacrifice with his terrifying servants. Some of them roared, some let out horrible laughs, others sprinkled blood on the fire; some tore out the sacrificial stakes and others devoured the officiating priests. Then the sacrifice took the form of a deer and flew upward, but Shiva pursued it with bow and arrow.

In mid-air Shiva's anger was distilled into a drop of sweat on his forehead. Where this drop fell to earth, an enormous fire broke out, and from it appeared a squat hairy man with bright red eyes and monstrous teeth, who burned the sacrifice to ashes, and caused the gods to flee in fear. This was Disease, who brought grief and mourning wherever he went, until Brahma promised Shiva a share in future sacrifices, begging him to moderate his anger and bring the pestilence he had created under control. Responding to Brahma's entreaties and the prospect of a share in sacrifices, Shiva divided Disease into many forms. Thus it was that everything came to have its own ailment – headaches for elephants, sore hooves for bulls, salinity for the earth, blindness for cattle, coughing for horses, crest-splitting for peacocks, eye diseases for cuckoos, hiccups for parrots, exhaustion for tigers, and fever for mankind.

In an alternative account, the sacrifice ends in a celestial brawl, leaving deities with broken noses, smashed jaws and torn hair. Daksha's head is ripped off by Shiva and hurled into the sacrificial fire. After Shiva's anger has abated, he gives Daksha a goat's head in place of his own. Another variant has Brahma intervening after Shiva's blazing trident has pierced the chest of Vishnu, protector of this world. Brahma finally persuades Shiva to propitiate Vishnu, and it is their reconciliation that restores the harmony of the universe.

THE LORD OF THE DANCE
As Nataraja, Shiva is the lord of the dance, the source of all movement in the universe. The cosmic dancer is represented in sculpture (below, an 11th-century South Indian bronze) as a four-armed figure encircled by flames – the process of universal creation. His steps are intended to relieve by enlightenment the sufferings of his devotees: hence, he balances on the back of a dwarf who symbolizes ignorance. His gestures and the attributes he is holding symbolize aspects of his divinity: the drum (creation) in his back right hand, the tongue of flame (destruction) in his back left hand, the gesture of protection (front right hand), and the raised leg symbolizing release.

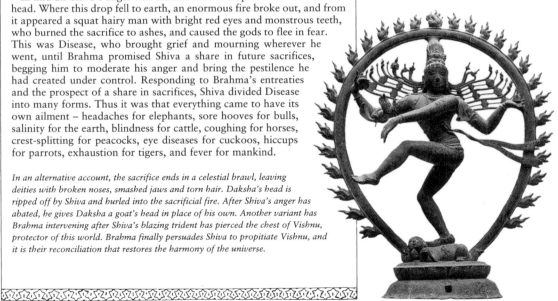

DEVI

The manifold goddess

A four-armed Devi as consort of Sadashiva, a form of Shiva, dances on a dwarfish figure in this 12th-century bronze.

Under the name Devi ("the goddess") or Mahadevi ("the great goddess") are often grouped the various individual goddesses of the classical Hindu pantheon. This composite goddess is often regarded as a major deity. She is either linked with Shiva (because of Parvati's role as Shiva's wife), and benign; or she is completely independent, in which case her fearsome aspects tend to predominate. Parvati or Uma, Shiva's wife, is a reincarnation of his first wife, Sati, following her self-immolation in the fire out of shame at Shiva's exclusion from her father Daksha's sacrifice (see p.81). As a young woman she undertakes the most extreme austerities in order to win Shiva again as her husband, and refuses to be put off by his uncouth attire and habits. Their life together is generally portrayed as idyllic: Parvati domesticates the unworldly and ascetic deity.

Durga ("hard to approach") is a warrior goddess, unapproachable by suitors and invincible in battle. Her main role is to combat demons who threaten the stability of the world. Sometimes she is said to arise from Vishnu as the power of sleep or as his creative power; sometimes she emerges from Parvati when Parvati becomes angry; and sometimes she is created by all the male gods pooling their attributes to form her as their champion against a demon. Even more terrifying is Kali, who springs from Durga's forehead when she gets angry (see panel, opposite).

Other fearful goddesses (Candi, Camunda, Bhairavi and the like) are

Durga and the buffalo

The main myth about Durga is her killing of Mahisha, the buffalo. The Devas, after being subdued by Mahisha, go to Shiva and Vishnu for help. As they listen, the gods' anger coalesces into a goddess.

The demons rushed toward the goddess, who killed them in hundreds, felling some with her club, catching others in her noose, slicing others with her sword, and piercing others with her trident. Meanwhile Mahisha himself, in buffalo form, terrorized her troops. Then he attacked her lion, and Durga became furious. She caught him in her noose, whereupon he quitted his buffalo shape and became a lion himself. She cut off its head and he emerged as a man, sword in hand. As she pierced the man, he became a great elephant, seizing her lion with his trunk, but she cut off his trunk with her sword and he resumed his buffalo form. Lightly tossing aside the mountains he hurled at her, she leaped on him, pinned his neck with one foot and pierced him with her trident. Then she cut off his head with her mighty sword.

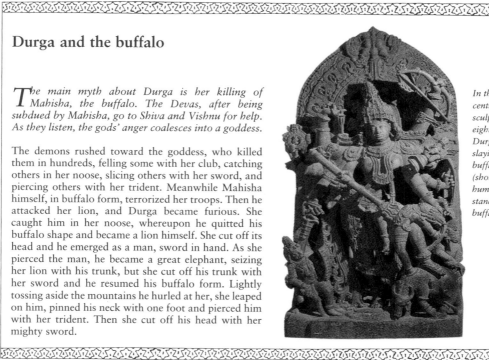

In this 13th-century sculpture, an eight-armed Durga is slaying the buffalo, Mahisa (shown as a human figure standing on the buffalo).

Kali

The role of Kali ("the dark one" or "time") is to destroy demons who threaten the cosmic order, but she herself is liable to become so drunk with blood on the battlefield that she begins to destroy the world. She is frequently portrayed as an emaciated hag, wearing a necklace of skulls or severed heads, frequenting battlefields or cremation grounds. In one myth Kali confronts the demon generals Chanda and Munda, and then kills the self-reproducing demon, Raktabija:

Kali was dark and gaunt, with protruding fangs, and wore a necklace of human heads and a tiger-skin. Roaring, she killed the demons. Next she was summoned by Durga to help against the demon Raktabija, who had the power to produce replicas of himself from every drop of blood that reached the ground. Durga and the Matrikas ("little mothers", usually seven) wounded him repeatedly, but only found they

A painting of Kali, holding a severed head in one of her hands, as sold to pilgrims to her shrine at Kalighat.

had even more to deal with. Then Kali gleefully appeared and defeated the demon, catching his blood before it fell, and sucking his body dry, while swallowing all the little Raktabijas with her gaping mouth.

The Thugs (who engaged in ritual murder by strangling) validated their practices by a variant of the Raktabija story. Tiring from her exertions, Kali made two men from the sweat on her arms and gave each a square of cloth, telling them to continue killing the demons without shedding any blood. Soon all the demons were strangled, and Kali told the men to keep the cloths and continue to offer victims as sacrifices to her.

Animal sacrifices are part of the worship of local goddesses throughout India, but the most spectacular manifestations relate to Kali. At her temple at Kalighata, goats are sacrificed daily, and there are traditions that human sacrifice was made to her here in the past.

sometimes regarded as separate individuals and sometimes totally identified with Kali. There are yet other goddesses concerned with more specific problems, including Sitala (the goddess of smallpox and, since its eradication, of various skin diseases), Manasa (the Bengali goddess of snakes), and Hariti and Shashti (goddesses of childbirth), as well as groupings of goddesses. In addition, there are the village goddesses, often worshipped with the sort of bloody animal sacrifice long abandoned in other forms of Hinduism. These deities are often seen as independent and uncontrolled: myths about Kanyakumari ("maiden princess") centre on her being prohibited from marrying Shiva, and on the power of her virginity. Alternatively, they are regarded as married to their village. To many of these goddesses a buffalo sacrifice is offered, echoing the myth of Durga's slaying of Mahisha, the buffalo demon. Sometimes they control or inflict disease.

Minakshi ("fish-eyed"), the goddess enshrined at Madurai, is said to have been born with three breasts and to have been brought up as a boy by her royal parents. She succeeds her father as ruler and subdues the entire world. One day she arrives at Mount Kailasa and challenges Shiva; but when they meet, she suddenly assumes a feminine modesty and shyness, and also loses her third breast: this image of the warrior queen pacified or domesticated by Shiva mirrors the myths about Parvati domesticating Shiva's wildness.

MARIYAMMAN
A common name for the village goddess is Mariyamman. She is said to have been a young brahman girl wooed and married by an untouchable disguised as a brahman; when she discovers the deception she kills herself and is transformed into a goddess, who punishes the untouchable by burning him to ashes.

SHIVA'S FAMILY CIRCLE

Shiva, Parvati, Skanda, Ganesha

Hindu art often portrays the members of the family sitting in a cosy circle, although this is hardly an ordinary family (see below). In this tableau, each of the family has a vahana *or mount, representing an aspect of the deity's nature. For example, Parvati has the lion (her killer instinct, as Durga), Ganesha his rat or mouse (ability to overcome obstacles).*

SKANDA AND GANESHA

Skanda's birth is usually linked with the first lovemaking of his parents. This is interrupted by the gods (who fear the offspring will possess excessive powers). Shiva spills his semen, and the fiery substance, too hot to handle, passes from one god to another until it reaches the Ganga, where it is incubated. Suckled by the six Krittikas (the personified Pleiades), Skanda defeats the demon Taraka and so rescues the world. He becomes the general of the gods and is accepted by Parvati as her own child; indeed, milk flows from her breasts in affection when she first sees him.

Parvati wants a child of her own who will protect her from intrusions. She makes Ganesha out of the rubbings from her body as she is bathing, and puts him on guard outside her rooms. When Shiva himself tries to enter, Ganesha refuses to admit him; and Shiva knocks off his head. Parvati demands he be brought back to life. Shiva casts about for the first head he can find as a replacement, and this is how Ganesha gets his elephant head (below).

Domesticating the ascetic Shiva, Parvati introduces him to family life. The texts often allude to domestic details, such as their son Skanda playing with Shiva's skull ornaments, or mistaking his crescent moon for a lotus bud. Several myths record bickering between Shiva and Parvati. One starts in playful mood: Parvati puts her fingers over Shiva's eyes from behind, but this plunges the world into darkness, whereupon Shiva angrily makes a third eye appear in his forehead. Sometimes they squabble over dice, or Shiva taunts Parvati with being dark-skinned, so she performs austerities to gain a golden complexion (in some versions her discarded dark complexion becomes Kali). Bengali myths often portray Shiva as a cannabis-smoking layabout, Parvati as a grumbling if long-suffering wife.

JAIN MYTH

A response to Hinduism

In both its cosmology and its "universal history" (an elaborate view of the history of the world), Jainism has inherited a great deal from Hinduism, while developing the material in quite specific ways, in particular by a rationalistic tendency. This is nonetheless combined with a delight in huge numbers and elaborate schemes, resulting in a plethora of names of deities, cosmographic details and fantastically long time periods.

The Jain universal history centres on the sixty-three prominent figures known as the Shalakapurushas – a series of spiritual and temporal leaders spaced out in each half of the cycles of ascent and descent through which the universe is perpetually passing.

Each series consists of twenty-four Tirthamkaras or Saviours, twelve universal Emperors, and nine triads of heroes, each comprising a Baladeva, a Vasudeva and a Prativasudeva. Although at least the names of some of the Shalakapurushas of the previous and next halves of the cycle are recorded, those whose myths are narrated belong to the current half, which is one of decline.

The pattern of triads of heroes is obviously modelled on the Hindu mythology of Krishna. The Baladeva is always the older half-brother of the Vasudeva, and the Prativasudeva is an evil opponent; even iconographic representations of the Baladevas and Vasudevas largely agree with the Hindu depictions of Balarama and Krishna. The Vasudeva, as the more powerful warrior, increasingly occupies the foreground, compared with the gentler Baladeva, but because of the sin he has incurred in fighting will go to hell; the Baladeva, however, renounces the world, takes ordination and reaches release.

The birth of Parshvanatha, the twenty-third Tirthamkara or Saviour, as depicted in a Jain manuscript of the 15th-16th centuries. Images of Parshva are often distinguished by a canopy of cobra's hoods. In a previous birth Parshva rescued a snake from being burnt in a brahman's sacrificial fire and, after his rebirth as the twenty-third Tirthamkara, was attacked by the brahman in demonic form and shielded by the snake, now a prince, Dharanendra.

Jain cosmology

*T*he Jain universe is a triple world system, which is commonly depicted in the form of a cosmic man.

The underworld comprises seven regions or levels, inhabited by different types of demons. The middle world has at its centre the circular continent of Jambudvipa (as in the usual Hindu cosmology of the *Puranas*), centred on Mount Mandara (or Meru) and ringed by the Salt Ocean. Outside this again are seven continents and seven oceans alternating in concentric circles. The upper world begins above the peak of Mount Mandara, is usually spindle-shaped and has eight levels, above which again come two further regions inhabited by the different classes of gods. Higher still, at the apex of the system, the crown of the cosmic man's head, comes the abode of released individuals. In contrast to the Hindu concept of four Yugas or periods of progressive decline, the Jain theory of cosmic periods envisages each "wheel of time" or cycle as comprising two halves, one of ascent and one of descent, each divided into six ages in which the conditions of life steadily improve or worsen.

JAIN VERSIONS OF HINDU MYTH
The obvious influence of the Krishna myth may be a consequence of Jainism's spread westward to the Mathura area, but once absorbed the myth was put to specifically Jain use – partly as a critique of Hindu myth generally. The Rama story (see p.77) was even more popular among Jains. Usually the Rakshasas and monkeys are turned into Vidyadharas, semi-divine masters of magic, while Lakshmana (not Rama) kills Ravana, who is depicted as a pious Jain, whose only weakness is his passion for Sita.

THE ENLIGHTENED ONE

Myths of Buddhism

Buddhism is a philosophy of salvation, so in theory it has no use for mythology. In practice Buddhists in all countries have turned to the local mythologies to fill out their world-view. In India, where Buddhism began, ideas about the Buddha were clothed in the garments of Hindu mythology. The Hindu gods become spectators of and minor actors in the drama of Gautama's quest for understanding which culminated in his becoming the Buddha, the Enlightened One. With the emergence of the Mahayana ("great vehicle") around the beginning of the Christian era, mythological elements became much more prominent. The cult of Bodhisattvas became the basis for a flourishing Buddhist mythology, although the old motifs and stories still appear. At first, these Bodhisattvas seem mainly to have personified different aspects of the Gautama's character, but soon developed a very real identity. Maitreya typifies *maitri* ("friendliness"): life under him is the Buddhist millennium, but meanwhile from the Tushita heaven he visits this world in various forms to save and teach.

The Buddha's life

According to many accounts, the Buddha's mother, Queen Mahamaya, had a dream that a Bodhisattva came down into her womb in the form of a white elephant holding a lotus in its trunk, while at the same time the whole of nature manifested its joy.

The brahmans interpreted this as foretelling the birth of a son who would be either a universal emperor or a Buddha. His birth was miraculous: standing grasping a tree, his mother bore her son from her side. Brahma and the other gods received the child, who took seven steps, and declared that this was his final birth.

Brought up in luxury, Gautama is supposed to have been shielded from all disturbing aspects of life, to have married and had a son, Rahula ("fetter"). One day a series of chariot drives around the town revealed to him the problems of old age, sickness and death, as well as the serenity of a wandering ascetic. Stealing

A statue of the Buddha, with the cranial protuberance, elongated earlobes and urna between the eyes – among his thirty-two major marks.

away by night from the ties of family and position, he began a search for enlightenment.

Seven years after leaving home, the Buddha determined to remain seated under a tree (later known as the Bodhi tree, at modern Bodh Gaya) until he had resolved the problem of suffering. In heaven the gods began to rejoice, while Mara, god of death and desire, assailed him with distractions. After forty-nine days Gautama attained enlightenment – he became a Buddha. For another seven weeks he sat meditating, while the snake king shaded him with his seven hoods. At first he despaired of finding anyone capable of grasping the truths he had mastered, but when Brahma urged him to preach, he yielded to the god's urgings. During his ministry he converted most of his family. To convert his mother he ascended to the Heaven of the Thirty-three Gods, whence Sakka (Indra) and the other gods escorted him back to earth.

The Buddha's previous lives

The perfection achieved by a Buddha can only be achieved over a long series of previous existences, during which the Bodhisattva prepares himself for his final life by cultivating the requisite moral qualities, foremost of which is giving. Many of the stories of the Buddha's lives are folktales adapted to this purpose. In one, the Buddha in a past life is a hare, which, realizing that it has no food to offer any guest, decides that it will offer its own flesh. Sakka (Indra), to test its resolve, comes to the hare as a beggar, and the hare invites him to make a fire and prepares to throw itself into it. Sakka intervenes to prevent him, and to commemorate the episode draws an image of the hare on the moon. In the following tale, the last and longest from the Jataka ("birth stories") book of the Theravada scriptures, Prince Vessantara is the Buddha's last human birth before that as Gautama (in between comes a birth as a god in the Tushita heaven).

Vessantara, son and heir of King Sanjaya, lived in the capital with his wife Maddi and their young son and daughter. His generosity was extraordinary. He had a magical white elephant which always ensured rain, but one day he gave it away to envoys from another kingdom. The citizens were enraged, and forced the king to banish him. Maddi opted to share his exile, and take their children along too. Vessantara gave away all his possessions. and travelled on a long journey with his family to a Himalayan valley, where they settled down. An old brahman called Jujaka, nagged by a young wife who demanded servants, arrived to ask him for his children, and Vessantara surrendered them all. Next morning Sakka, fearing that Vessantara might give away his wife too, disguised himself as a brahman, begged her from Vessantara, and returned her to him (as she was now a gift, Vessantara was no longer able to dispose of her). Meanwhile, Jujaka and the children arrived at Sanjaya's court, where Sanjaya ransomed his grandchildren and Jujaka gorged himself to death. Full of remorse, Sanjaya took his retinue to the mountain and invited Vessantara and Maddi to return. All were reunited and Vessantara became king.

The roundel on this railing around the great Buddhist stupa at Amaravati shows a scene from the Jataka stories.

This stone relief from East India (9th-10th century) shows Avalokiteshvara, the Bodhisattva who "looks down" in compassion, holding in his left hand the lotus, and giving the gesture of reassurance with his right hand. His elaborate sacred thread and jewelry emphasize his lay status. In China he came to be known as the goddess Guanyin (see p.96).

BODHISATTVAS

The concept of the Bodhisattva ("he whose essence is Bodhi, enlightenment", in effect a future Buddha) is common to the whole of Buddhism but becomes especially important in the Mahayana. Here the emphasis is on the Bodhisattva's willingness to share his merit with any who call on him in faith. Illustrated above is Avalokiteshvara, "the lord who looks down" (also called Padmapani), whose outstanding characteristic is compassion. Other important Bodhisattvas include: Maitreya ("friendliness"); Manjushri, ("affably majestic"), whose task is the removal of ignorance; and Vajrapani, "the one who has a thunderbolt in his hand", who is the destroyer of evil.

CHINA

The interior of the roof of the Qiniandian (Hall of Prayer for a
Good Harvest) at the north end of the Temple of Heaven complex
in Beijing. In this hall the emperor, in his capacity as heaven's
representative on earth, offered prayers for a good harvest.

Chinese mythology can be traced back nearly 4,000 years, although extensive remains in northern China attest to widespread human occupation from *c.*3000BC onward. The Xia, an evidently tribal people, dominated much of this region from *c.*2000BC or earlier to c.1500bc. Their totem was originally the snake, which occurs in some of China's oldest myths. Later, it developed into the dragon, a lasting symbol of Chinese mythology and culture (see p.92).

The Yin people challenged Xia rule and established the Yin or Shang dynasty *c.*1500BC. They mastered bronze-making and their emblem was the "red bird", symbol of the south. The Yin evidently sacrificed to many divinities, including the sun, moon, clouds, earth, mountains, rivers and the four cardinal directions. Their greatest deity was Shang Di, revered as ancestor of the dynasty. People sought to contact spirits by reading cracks on scorched "oracle bones" and through other shamanistic practices, such as chanting, dancing and ecstatic trances.

During the succeeding Zhou dynasty, families adopted hereditary surnames and ancestor worship became widespread. But the old deities never died out and the earth, rain and river gods remained popular. Zhou rulers preferred to worship Tian ("Heaven"; see p.100).

Toward the end of the Zhou dynasty, a number of new political philosophies emerged. The way of life founded by Confucius (a latinization of Kong Fuzi or "Master Kong"; 551-479BC) was based on ritual, filial piety and education, and dominated Chinese life until the advent of communism. A second great school, Taoism (see p.98), advocated a non-interventionist state and a return to rural simplicity. Above all, it believed that humanity should live in harmony with nature and not seek to dominate it. The Yin and Yang (that is, the female and male principles; see p.90) should be in equilibrium.

Confucians tended to be agnostic toward traditional gods and spirits. However, in response to the arrival of Buddhism (see p.96), Taoism developed a more religious character, as well as its own mythology. Taoism, Buddhism, Confucianism and older traditional beliefs lived together in a spirit of mutual respect and influence. This amicable coexistence accounts for the rich cultural heritage of Chinese myth.

THE FIVE ELEMENTS AND THE FIVE SACRED MOUNTAINS

It is not known why, but since ancient times the number five has held a special significance for the Chinese. For example, the material structure of the world is said to be made up of Five Elements (Wood, Fire, Soil, Metal and Water), dynamic interacting forces. Each element is associated with one of five seasons (including a mystical "centre"), one of the cardinal directions (again including the "centre": see also p.21), and a planet:

Wood	Spring	East	Jupiter
Fire	Summer	South	Mars
Soil	Summer	Centre	Saturn
Metal	Autumn	West	Venus
Water	Winter	North	Mercury

From ancient times mountains have been revered as active deities which respond to prayers and sacrifices. Five mountains were recognized by Chinese rulers as particularly sacred: Hengshan (Northern Peak and Southern Peak: the Pinyin spellings are identical); Huashan

(Western Peak); Songshan (Central Peak); and Taishan (Eastern Peak). The most prestigious was Taishan. It is near Qufu, the birthplace of Confucius, and over the centuries was granted various aristocratic ranks, from duke to emperor. No emperor would presume to sacrifice there unless his reign had been outstanding. Apart from these five, there are other mountains sacred to Buddhists and Taoists, while Kunlun, outside the old empire in the far west, was regarded as the abode of the gods, almost a colony of heaven.

KEY TO MAP

🔺 Sacred mountain

● City (traditional name in brackets)

ᴖᴖᴖ Ancient Chinese frontier (c.220AD)

····· Present-day frontier

Present-day country: VIETNAM

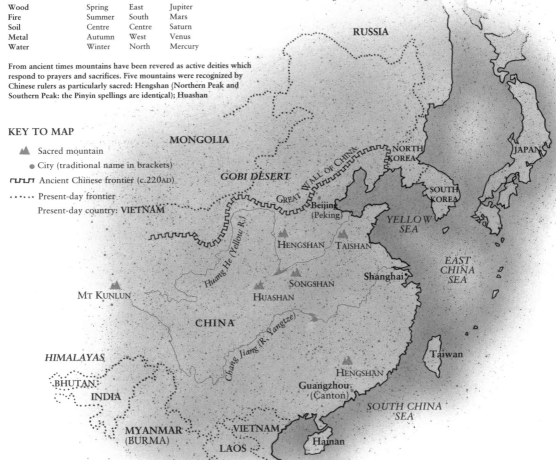

CHINESE DYNASTIES	
Xia	c.2000-c.1500 BC
Shang or Yin	c.1500-1050 BC
Zhou	1050-221 BC
Qin	221-206 BC
Han	202 BC-AD 220
Wei, Jin and Northern and Southern	220-581
Sui	581-618
Tang	618-907
Five Dynasties and Ten Kingdoms	907-960
Song	960-1279
Yuan	1276-1368
Ming	1368-1644
Qing	1644-1911

ORDER OUT OF CHAOS

Pan Gu and Hun Dun

YIN AND YANG
Yang, which originally meant sunshine or light, and Yin, which meant shadow or darkness, came to be regarded as the two cosmic forces which interacted to produce the phenomena of the universe. Yang represents masculinity, activity, heat, dryness, hardness, and so on, while Yin represents such qualities as femininity, passivity, cold, wetness and softness. Yin and Yang qualities often occur as contrasting pairs, such as life and death, female and male, even good and evil. On a more philosophical plane, Yin and Yang were seen as complementary and mutually dependent. The red lacquer panel (above) bears the symbols for Yin and Yang, surrounded by the Eight Symbols used in divination.

The most important Chinese account of creation describes how the world was formed by a primal deity called Pan Gu, whose cult survives among the minority peoples of South China, such as the Miao, Yao and Li. He is said to have been the offspring of the Yin and Yang, the two vital forces of the universe (see illustration, left; the creature at the bottom of the panel may represent Pan Gu). In the darkness of a huge primordial egg, Pan Gu came into being and grew for eighteen thousand years, until the egg split open. The light and clear parts of the egg floated up to form the heavens and the heavy and opaque parts sank to form the earth.

Pan Gu stood up. To prevent the fluid earth and sky from coming together again, he grew taller, forcing the ground and the heavens apart by ten feet a day. After another eighteen thousand years, the earth and sky solidified in their present positions, and Pan Gu wearily lay down to rest. He died, and his breath became wind and cloud, his voice thunder, his left eye the sun, his right eye the moon, and his hair and whiskers the stars in the sky. The other parts of his body became the elements that make up the earth, including mountains, rivers, roads, plants, trees, metals, gems and rocks. His sweat was transformed into rain and dew.

The Pan Gu myth reached this form in the 3rd century AD, although Pan Gu himself is referred to in earlier texts. In one of many later variations, the alternation of the night and day is explained by the opening and shutting of Pan Gu's eyes.

The death of Chaos

Among the best sources of ancient Chinese mythology are the allegorical stories which are to be found in the works of the classical philosophers. A good example of these is the brief but well-known creation story about the death of Chaos, which is to be found in the Zhuangzi, a work written by the early Taoist scholar of that name around the 4th century BC. This myth presents the two interacting principles of the primordial universe and the chaos which lay between them in anthropomorphized form as three emperors.

Shu, emperor of the Northern Sea, and Hu, emperor of the Southern Sea, often came together in the territory of Hun Dun ("Chaos"), emperor of the Centre, who was most hospitable to them. One day Shu and Hu discussed how they could repay Hun Dun's kindness. They observed how they each had seven bodily orifices, which enabled them to see, hear, eat and so on, while Hun Dun did not have a single one. The two emperors decided to show their gratitude to Hun Dun by boring holes in his body with chisels and drills, at the rate of one hole per day. After seven days they had completed their work, but unfortunately Hun Dun had been killed in the process. At the moment Chaos died, the ordered world came into being.

NŰ GUA AND FU XI

The creation of humanity; flood myths

Stories about the creator goddess Nü Gua and the creator god Fu Xi are among China's oldest myths. The provenance of these deities is obscure, but both names are derived from words meaning gourd or melon, fruit which also occur in the fecundity and origin myths of other cultures. In the Han dynasty they were often depicted as a married couple, with human heads and entwined serpents' tails, but it is possible that originally Nü Gua and Fu Xi were separate gods whose stories became linked, as, for example, those of Zeus and Hera may have been by the ancient Greeks (see p.132). Their serpentine tails indicate a possible connection with the snake totem of the early Xia people.

Nü Gua and Fu Xi are referred to in many books from the 4th century BC onward in connection with several different myths. These have three main themes: the creation of humanity, its early struggles against natural disasters (especially floods), and ancient warfare. Nü Gua was particularly revered as the creator of the first people (see panel, below) and as their protector.

One important myth relates how, while the goddess was living on earth, a quarrel arose between the Fire God and ruler of the universe, Zhu Rong, and the Water God, Gong Gong, sometimes said to be Zhu Rong's son. The Fire God governed the universe firmly but wisely, ensuring that the sun appeared regularly in the sky and that the people Nü Gua had created enjoyed favourable conditions to carry on their daily lives. Gong

FU XI, THE FIRST EMPEROR
During the Han dynasty (202BC–AD220), new dynasties were devised to account for obscure early periods of history. Many myths were rewritten as fact, and some key mythical figures became emperors. Fu Xi was declared to have been the first emperor of all, one of "Five Emperors of High Antiquity", and his reign was fixed at 2852BC to 2737BC. One myth gave him four faces (each overseeing one of the four directions), which the official historians turned into four government ministers. He was made into a culture hero, accredited with having taught people to fish with nets and to rear domestic animals. He was also reputed to have devised musical instruments and to have invented the first Chinese script, replacing knotted strings as a means of communication.

The race of mud

Nü Gua is said to have come to live on earth from heaven after the separation of the heavens and the earth and the creation of the hills, rivers, animals and plants. The following myth relates how she formed the human race from mud.

After some time on earth Nü Gua grew lonely, feeling that something was still missing from the world. One day she saw her reflection in a pool and had an idea. She scooped up a handful of mud and fashioned it into a tiny copy of herself: the first human. When the goddess put the creature down, it came to life at once and started to shout and dance with joy. Pleased with her handiwork, Nü Gua took more mud and made a host of people. They wandered off into the countryside, but she could always hear their voices and never felt lonely again.

The goddess soon realized that to populate the whole world she must produce people more rapidly and efficiently. She dipped a vine in watery mud, then flicked it so that the mud flew off in all directions. Each drop of mud turned into another human being. Nü Gua soon populated the world and could rest from her labours. Later, when some people had grown old and died, she taught humans how to reproduce and raise children.

An early 20th-century painting of Nü Gua, portrayed with a serpent's body.

Gong, an ugly creature with a snake's body and a human head covered with a shock of red hair, envied Zhu Rong and was determined to wrest control of the universe from him. The battle between the two gods raged fiercely, first in heaven and then on earth. Gong Gong mustered all the creatures of the sea and rivers to attack the forces of the Fire God, but in the end they could not withstand the burning heat of the sun, which boiled the water in their bodies and left them scorched and helpless.

Gong Gong's plans for domination came to nothing, and his disappointment soon turned to anger. In a rage he butted Imperfect Mountain with his head, causing it to collapse into a pile of rubble. This curiously named mountain was the main prop of heaven in the northwest of the world, and once it was removed a great hole appeared in the sky, which was matched by a depression which appeared in the land to the southeast. The world was thrown off balance and people suffered greatly in the disasters which followed: fires swept through the hills and forests and floods engulfed the plains. The water rushed toward the southeast, where the land was now lower; this is said to be the reason why China's big rivers flow roughly from west to east.

Nü Gua could not stand idly by and watch her children suffer. To repair the hole in the sky she went to a river bed and selected a large number of stones. Then she constructed a furnace and smelted the stones until they could be shaped into the forms she required. Flying up to heaven, the goddess pressed the molten stones into the gaps in the sky and moulded them until no cracks remained. To ensure that the sky did not break again, Nü Gua decided to kill a giant tortoise and use its four legs to support heaven in place of Imperfect Mountain. After she had done this she burned rushes and used the ashes to block the gaps in the river banks, thus controlling the floods.

A bronze tortoise in the Forbidden City (Imperial Palace) in Beijing. Tortoises were a symbol of strength and permanence, able to support heavy loads on their backs. According to myth, the goddess Nü Gua used the legs of a tortoise to hold up the heavens after the collapse of Imperfect Mountain (see right).

Yu the Great

*T*here are numerous Chinese myths about an ancient flood, besides those involving Nü Gua and Fu Xi. *The most popular concerns a heroic figure called Yu the Great. In its original version, Yu was a dragon, or else a creature half human and half dragon in form, whose father, Gun, had been sent down from heaven to control a flood. In the following, later, version of the myth, Yu is represented as entirely human.*

The mythical Emperor Shun appointed Yu to find a means of controlling the waters of a great flood.

Yu, mythical founder of the Xia dynasty, was originally said to be a dragon, and each emperor was seen as the incarnation of this creature. The dragon (above) is in the Forbidden City.

For thirteen years Yu laboured unceasingly, his hands growing worn with toil and his feet calloused: he was barely able to hobble. His skin was black through exposure to the sun and he was as thin as a rake.

At last his suffering was rewarded. By making artificial canals he drained the water off into the sea. In recognition of his services, Shun abdicated in his favour, and Yu became the first emperor of the Xia dynasty. He is said to have reigned from 2205 BC to 2197 BC, and his supposed tomb is still to be seen near present-day Shaoxing in Zhejiang Province.

The gourd children

Fu Xi and Nü Gua myths also occur in the oral traditions of the Miao and Yao peoples of South China, usually in a much livelier and more complete form than the written versions of the more populous Han Chinese. This is a shortened version of the Fu Xi and Nü Gua legend told by the Yao people of Guizhou Province.

One summer's day a long time ago a man was working in his fields when he heard a rumble of distant thunder. He sent his two children, a boy and a girl, indoors, and hung an iron cage under the eaves of the house. Soon it started to rain so heavily that the man took a sharp fork of the kind used for catching tigers, opened the cage door and stood guard in front of the house.

Suddenly there was a great flash of lightning and a crack of thunder, and down from the clouds flew the Thunder God, holding an enormous battleaxe. The man lunged at the god, impaled him on his fork, and in one movement pushed him into the cage and slammed the door shut. As soon as the Thunder God had been captured, the rain stopped and the wind died down. Next morning the man went to market to buy herbs and sauce in which to pickle the god after he had killed him. He told the children that while he was away they were not on any account to give the Thunder God any water to drink. As soon as the man had gone, the Thunder God pleaded so piteously for just one drop of water that the children granted him his request. At once the god revived and burst out of his cage. To

Wen Zhong, the Minister of Thunder. In ancient myths the Thunder God is described as a hideous beast, but later traditions ascribed all natural phenomena to a heavenly government which mirrored the earthly dynastic administration.

repay the children's kindness, he pulled out a tooth and told them to plant it in the ground and perish. Then he left. The children planted the tooth, and within minutes it had grown into a gourd plant which only a few hours later began to bear a gourd. The rain returned and water started to cover the earth. On returning home from market, the man told his children to climb inside the gourd. Meanwhile, he built a boat and floated to heaven to appeal to the Lord of Heaven to end the flood. The Lord of Heaven listened to his pleas and ordered the Water God to end the deluge. In his haste to obey, the Water God made the flood subside so rapidly that the man's boat crashed to earth and he was killed. However, the children bounced harmlessly in their gourd, the flood's only survivors.

It is not known what the children's original names were, but they are known from this point as Fu Xi ("bottle gourd"). They lived happily together, and when they grew up the young man suggested they get married. His sister was reluctant because they were siblings, but said she would consent if her brother caught her in a chase. He did so, they married, and the sister changed her name to Nü Gua, another word meaning gourd or melon.

Later, Nü Gua gave birth to a ball of flesh. They sliced it into many pieces, which they took with them up the ladder leading to heaven. A gust of wind blew the pieces of flesh all over the earth. Where they landed, they became people: thus humanity was re-established.

SUN, MOON AND STARS

Myths of the heavenly bodies

Part of the top section of a 2nd-century BC funerary banner depicting the passage of a soul to the realms of the Immortals. The large red disc represents the sun and the crow is its spirit. When Yi the divine archer shot the first sun, the solar crow inside it fell dead at his feet (see opposite).

The sun, moon and stars figured prominently among the animistic deities of ancient China, and the sun and the moon continued to be honoured in sacrificial ceremonies down to the early 20th century. Altars to the sun and moon are still to be found in the Chinese capital, Beijing, although they are no longer used. However, the sun was never singled out as supreme deity, and in the hierarchy of deities recognized by the imperial state both Sun and Moon ranked after Heaven, Earth, the Imperial Ancestors, the Gods of Grain and Soil and Confucius.

Most Chinese have a sentimental attachment to the moon, and particularly to the full moon, whose round shape symbolizes the reunion and completion of the family circle. The Mid-Autumn Festival, which is held on the 15th day of the eighth month in the lunar calendar, when the moon is full, is still very popular. On that evening families come together and, among other things, eat round "moon cakes".

Stellar gods, each associated with a particular star or group of stars, existed from ancient times and were especially numerous in the Taoist pantheon. They included gods of literature, longevity, happiness, and so on. Most stellar myths were a comparatively late development in Chinese religion and folklore, but one famous star myth, about Yi, a divine archer with magic powers, dates at least as far back as the 6th century BC. According to this myth, there were originally ten suns encircling the earth. They all lived in a giant tree called Fu Sang which grew in a hot spring beyond the eastern horizon, and were all sons of the Lord of Heaven, Di Jun, and of the goddess Xi He, who had decreed that only one sun should appear in the sky at a time. Xi He escorted each sun around the sky in her chariot and then brought him home to the Fu Sang tree at the end of the day. Next day it was the turn of the second sun, and so on until the turn of the first sun came round again.

The years rolled by, and this arrangement seemed as though it would continue for ever. But this was not to be, because the ten brothers began to find their duties irksome and resented the discipline imposed by their mother. They started gathering together on the branches of the Fu Sang tree and discussing how they could break free of the regime which had been imposed upon them. Together they hit on a plan. One day, without warning, all ten suns appeared in the sky all at once. They had burst out of the Fu Sang tree together and, as they thought, would now be able to stay in the sky as long as they pleased.

At first the people on earth were delighted by all the light and warmth which the ten suns provided. But when their crops withered and perished in the fierce heat, the people became desperate and sought a method of curbing the suns' power. The earthly ruler at that time was Yao, who was later canonized, together with Shun and Yu (see p.92), as one of the three sage rulers of antiquity. Yao was a humble man who lived frugally in a thatched cottage and ate coarse grains and soup made from wild plants. He suffered the same privations as his people and was deeply concerned for their welfare. He prayed to Heaven to intervene on behalf of humankind, imploring Di Jun to restore the old order whereby only one sun appeared at a time.

The Lord of Heaven, Di Jun, heard Yao's prayers and immediately ordered the nine extra suns to return to the Fu Sang tree. But the suns were enjoying their liberty so much that it would clearly take more than words to get them to fall into line. Di Jun decided to send one of his most powerful assistants, Yi, to earth to tackle his recalcitrant sons, and at the same time to solve a number of other problems Yao was facing.

Yi was known as an expert archer, so before he left for earth Di Jun gave him a red bow and a quiver full of white arrows. The Lord of Heaven did not intend Yi to harm the suns, but merely to frighten them into obeying Di Jun's orders. Together with his wife Chang E (see panel, below), Yi descended to earth, and when he saw the state to which the people had been reduced he became very angry. He at once took an arrow from his quiver and shot it into the sky. There was a thud followed by a cascade of sparks, which sprayed out in all directions from one of the suns. Then, amid a shower of golden feathers, a large three-legged crow fell from the sky at Yi's feet, its breast pierced by a white arrow. This was the spirit of the first of the ten suns. (It has been claimed that the crow in the sun is evidence of the ancient Chinese observation of sunspots.)

Killing one sun had little effect on the climate, so Yi took another arrow and carried on shooting the suns until only one was left in the sky and the climate returned to normal. As a consequence of this feat, Yi became a great hero among the people.

COWHERD AND WEAVING MAID

The star Vega in the constellation Lyra is known to the Chinese as Weaving Maid. She was the daughter of the Sun God, who, out of concern for her loneliness, married her to Cowherd. But the happy couple spent all their time making love, instead of attending to their respective duties. The Sun God was displeased and condemned them to be separated, one on either side of the Celestial River (Milky Way). Once a year, on the seventh day of the seventh month, magpies congregate at the Celestial River to form a bridge so that Weaving Maid may cross over to meet Cowherd. If it should rain that day, the magpies take shelter and the luckless couple must wait another year.

Chang E and the moon

*A*fter Yi had killed the nine suns, Di Jun was angry and condemned Yi and his wife, Chang E, to live on earth as mortals. Yi went in search of the elixir of eternal life possessed by the Queen Mother of the West, a tyrant goddess who lived on Mount Kunlun. She gave him enough elixir for two, but warned that if one person took it all he or she would leave the world for higher regions.

Yi took the elixir back home to his wife, Chang E, who was missing her former trouble-free life in heaven. Having learned from her husband about the goddess's warnings, she considered taking all the elixir and returning to heaven. But she was worried that she would be condemned by the other deities for deserting her husband, so she decided to consult an astrologer. He suggested that she should go to the moon, where she would be free from the travails of mortal life and the accusations of the gods and goddesses.

An early 20th-century depiction of Chang E ascending to the moon after taking the elixir of immortality. Her husband, Yi the divine archer, looks on in dismay as she floats away.

Moreover, he promised, when she arrived on the moon she would be wonderfully transformed.

Chang E agreed with this plan. One day, when Yi was out, she stole the elixir from where it was hidden in the rafters, swallowed the whole bottle and immediately floated to the moon. She tried to call out but could only croak, because she had turned into a toad. Her only companions on the moon were a hare, which continually pounded medicinal herbs with a mortar, and an old man vainly trying to chop down a cassia tree.

When Yi found his wife and the elixir missing, he knew at once what had happened. He realized that it had been a mistake to attempt to escape from the mortal existence which had been granted to him.

In a later version of the myth, Chang E is restored to human shape and lives in the Palace of the Moon, while Yi, his errors forgiven, returns to heaven.

CHINESE BUDDHISM

Amitabha and Guanyin

Buddhism first began to win Chinese converts in the 2nd century AD and soon became very popular, eventually coming to occupy a position alongside Taoism and Confucianism as one of the three great belief systems of China. Indeed, it has long been of far greater importance in China than in its native India. The original founder of Buddhism, Gautama Sakyamuni or the Buddha (born *c.*560BC and usually called Fo in Chinese), promised salvation only to those who obeyed Buddhist law and lived a life of asceticism, renouncing all worldly pleasures. Eventually, freed from all attachments to this world, such people would escape the cycle of birth and death and enter the blessed state known as Nirvana. This process was inevitably long and painful, and meant renouncing all emotional ties to family and friends and living a monastic life.

The Chinese, however, preferred to worship the manifestation of the Buddha called Amitabha (Emituofo in Chinese), who was said to reign in a Western Paradise. He vowed to give salvation to all those who repented their sins and called upon his name. The state of bliss could be achieved by faith rather than just asceticism, and was therefore open to more people. After Buddhism became established in China, countless images of Amitabha, enthroned upon a lotus flower, appeared in temples throughout the country.

Myths about the life of Buddha became well known in China, often embellished to make them more acceptable to the Chinese cast of mind. The role of storyteller was taken on by monks, some of whom recorded the myths in chapbooks. One story relates how a disciple of the Buddha called Maudgalyayana, rendered as Mulian in Chinese, descended into hell to rescue his mother (see opposite). This appealed to the Chinese, because it not only expressed the Buddhist idea of karma (the doctrine that good or bad acts have inevitable consequences in this and future lives) but also the traditional Chinese virtue of filial piety. In the Buddhist calendar the important Avalambana ("Hanging Down") Festival marks the time when monks emerge from their traditional retreat during the rainy season. The name of the festival derives from a Hindu myth about an Indian ascetic, who saw his ancestors hanging upside down as a result of his withdrawal from the world and consequent failure to marry and provide descendants to keep up sacrifices to the dead.

Amitabha was frequently attended by the Bodhisattva Guanyin, often called the Goddess of Mercy. Bodhisattvas were a feature of the Mahayana form of Buddhism which became popular in China and Japan. They are beings who hesitate to enter the state of Nirvana because they wish to save suffering humanity. Their compassion and promise of salvation introduced a new and human element into Chinese religious life. Originally, Guanyin was in fact the male Indian Bodhisattva Avalokiteshvara (see p.87), whose name was taken by the Chinese to mean "listening to the cries of the world". Soon after being introduced into China, Avalokiteshvara came to embody Chinese motherly virtues of compassion, and changed from a male Bodhisattva to a female one. Many stories were written about her. For example, she saved the holy books of an early Chinese Buddhist pilgrim returning to China from India, and was able, for those who invoked her, to break the chains of prisoners, remove venom from snakes, and deprive lightning of its power. Mothers prayed to her on behalf of their children. Sometimes she was depicted with many arms, indicating the extent of her powers of intercession.

A late 13th-century wooden figure of the Bodhisattva Guanyin. Derived from an Indian male original, in Chinese Buddhism she became the Goddess of Mercy.

Radish and Lady Leek Stem

Every year, during the Buddhist Avalambana Festival, plays about the character Radish used to be performed in villages and towns throughout China. They often lasted several days and contained so many embellishments that the details of the original story were all but lost and the drama was transformed into a purely Chinese entertainment. This is a brief outline of the story, as contained in a 9th-century source.

Buddha had a pious disciple called Radish, who had to go on a long journey. Before he went, Radish entrusted his mother, Lady Leek Stem, with a sum of money to give to Buddhist monks who came to her door to beg. But while Radish was away, his mother gave nothing to the monks and lied to her son when he returned, saying that she had carried out his wishes. In consequence, when Radish's mother died she went straight to hell and suffered terrible torments.

By this time, Radish himself had grown in wisdom and piety until he had attained the

Yanluo or Yama, the King of Hell, in his court. The king looks on as various devils chase the souls of the condemned to their appropriate punishment quarters.

enlightened status of *arhat*, or saint. He was renamed Mulian. Newly enlightened, he learned that his mother was in hell, and determined to rescue her. On the way, he met Yama (Yanluo), the King of Hell, who tried to discourage him with a stern pronouncement: "Sentences decreed at Taishan [one of the sacred mountains: see map on p.89] are not easily reversed. They were drafted in Heaven and endorsed by Hell. The retribution that sinners meet arises from their past deeds. Others have no power to save them."

Undeterred, Mulian called upon all the officials responsible for the sentencing, recording and despatching of sinners, and visited many departments of Hell. Eventually he learned that his mother was in one of the lower infernal reaches, the Avici Hell. On his way there, he encountered fifty bull-headed (or horse-headed) demons, each with fangs like a forest of swords, a mouth like a bowl of blood, a voice like thunder and eyes like lightning. He waved a magic wand, given to him by the Buddha himself, and the monsters vanished.

Once in Avici Hell, Mulian asked the jailer where his mother was. The jailer climbed a high tower, waved a black banner and beat an iron drum, crying: "Is there a Lady Leek Stem in the first compound?" There was no answer. He asked the same question of each jail compound and found her in the seventh, nailed to a bed by forty-nine long nails. But Mulian was unable to release her, a deed which, given her sins, only the Buddha could perform.

Mulian went to the Buddha and described his mother's pitiful condition. The Buddha was merciful, and after the Avalambana Festival, on the fifteenth day of the seventh month, freed Lady Leek Stem from Hell. To find her, Buddha told Mulian to wander through the streets of the city where he lived, begging at random until he came to the house of a wealthy man. When he got there, a black dog would run out and tug at his cassock. This dog would be his mother.

Mulian did as Buddha requested, and found the dog. However, his mother resumed her human form only after her son had recited the scriptures for seven days and seven nights in front of the Buddha's pagoda, confessing, praying and observing abstinence.

After the episode Mulian advised his mother that because reincarnation as a human being and conversion to good thoughts were hard to achieve, she should immediately endeavour to lay up a store of blessings by doing good works.

TAOIST MYTH

Gods and Immortals

This woodcut depicts the Immortals Cao Guojiu and (with his crutch) Li Xuan.

The Immortals Han Zhongli and the blue-robed minstrel, Lan Caihe.

Taoism, one of China's two great indigenous belief systems, takes its name from the word Tao ("way" or "path"), which in Pinyin (see p.89) is properly transliterated as Dao. To Taoists this did not mean a particular spiritual path to be followed, but a principle of existence which caused all things. For the Confucians every phenomenon or human institution had its own particular Dao. However, for Taoists there was only one Dao for everything. Wisdom and enlightenment came if an individual understood the Dao and lived in harmony with it.

Taoism was well established by 100BC. The founder of philosophical Taoism was a man (later deified) known as Laozi, which means "The Old Master". Although later tradition gave him a name and invented details of his career, nothing is known for certain about him, and it is possible that the book attributed to him (*Dao De Jing* or *The Classic of The Way and its Power*) was an anonymous compilation.

Faced with the arrival and growing popularity of Buddhism (see p.96), Taoism, originally a philosophical system, took on the character of a religion. It absorbed many of the popular mystical cults which abounded in China, taking as its founders the mythical "Yellow Emperor", supposed progenitor of the Chinese race, as well as Laozi. It adopted the trappings of religion – temples, monks, images, incense – from Buddhism, and evolved a pantheon of animistic deities, heroic figures from the past, and various other figures. Some Taoists indulged in alchemy, seeking to concoct an elixir of longevity or immortality. Taoist writers compiled a new mythology of spiritual beings who were not gods but human beings said to have achieved immortality through Taoist practices, and to be capable of magical deeds and supernatural methods of locomotion.

Taoist divinities consisted of humanized planets and stars, ancient heroes (including the presiding spirits of various occupations), all human activities (including scholarship, commerce, robbery, fornication and drunkenness), and animals such as dragons, tigers, snakes and grasshoppers. Taoist priests made their living mainly through driving away malignant spirits, on whom evils of all sorts were blamed. It was therefore necessary for a priest to know which spirit was responsible and to choose the appropriate remedy, whether it be charms, religious ceremonies, drugs or attention to the alignment of buildings.

Central to Taoist mythology are the Eight Immortals, who are often depicted in art. Their origin is comparatively recent, accounts of how they achieved immortality not appearing before the 15th century AD. However, some of their names are mentioned earlier.

The eight figures achieved immortality in different ways. The first to do so was Li Xuan, or Iron Crutch, who was taught the secret by Xi Wang Mu, Queen Mother of the West (see p.95). As he had a club foot, the Queen presented him with an iron crutch, and

A bronze figure of Laozi on a buffalo. After writing the Dao De Jing *he is said to have disappeared into the west riding a water buffalo.*

this is how he acquired his name. Li Xuan in turn taught the Way to Zhong-li Quan, who became Messenger of Heaven and is often depicted with a fan made of feathers.

Next came Lü Dongbin, perhaps the most famous of the Eight Immortals. While visiting an inn he met a man called Han Zhongli, who started to heat a pot of wine. Lü fell asleep and dreamed that he was promoted to high office and enjoyed good fortune for fifty years. But then his luck ran out, he was disgraced and his family ruined. When he woke up he realized that only a few minutes had passed: he was still at the inn and Han Zhongli had not finished heating the wine. As a result of this dream Lü Dongbin became convinced of the vanity of worldly ambition, and followed Han Zhongli into the mountains. to seek the Dao (whose essence is to be found in nature) and to achieve immortality. Lü Dongbin is sometimes depicted in art carrying a sword.

Han Xiang was said to be the great-nephew of Han Yü, a Tang dynasty essayist and philosopher. He became a disciple of Lü Dongbin, who, when he had almost reached immortality, took him to heaven to the tree which bore the heavenly peaches of eternal life. Han started to climb the tree but slipped and fell to earth, achieving immortality as he was about to hit the ground. He is shown carrying a bouquet of flowers.

Cao Guojiu was a brother of Empress Cao of the Song dynasty. Disillusioned by corruption at court he went into the mountains to seek the Dao. He came to a river and, having no money, tried to impress the boatman by showing him his golden tablet for admission to court. The boatman said: "You seek the Dao, yet you try to pull rank with me?" Cao was ashamed and threw the tablet into the river. The boatman happened to be Lü Dongbin in disguise. He took Cao as his disciple and taught him the Dao. Cao Guoju is shown carrying his golden tablet.

The sixth immortal was Zhang Guo, who lived at the time of Empress Wu of the Tang dynasty. He is often depicted riding on a white mule, facing either the animal's head or its tail. The mule was capable of travelling thousands of miles a day and when not required could be folded up and put into a bag. Old Man Zhang Guo, as he is often called, was most famous for his skill at necromancy. He could also grant offspring to childless or newlywed couples, and his picture was often hung in the bridal chamber. He may be represented holding peaches of immortality and the bag containing his folded mule.

Lan Caihe was either a girl, or a man "who didn't know how to be a man" as one writer put it enigmatically. Her family dealt in medicinal herbs. When she was collecting herbs in the mountains she came across a beggar dressed in filthy rags, his body covered in sores. Washing and dressing his wounds proved difficult, but she did not give up. The beggar was Iron Crutch Li in disguise, and her kindness to him was rewarded with eternal youth. Now an Immortal, Lan toured the country as a minstrel, clad in a tattered blue gown, urging people to seek the Dao. She (or he) is sometimes depicted holding a basket of fruit.

He Xiangu, the only Immortal who was definitely female, acquired her gift after a spirit told her to grind up and eat a "mother-of-pearl stone", which was to be found on the mountain where she lived. She is depicted as a maiden holding either a peach or a lotus blossom.

The most famous story in which the Immortals are all involved together concerns a voyage which they undertook to view the wonderful sights of the undersea world. Instead of travelling on clouds, which was their usual method of locomotion, they decided to demonstrate their magical powers by throwing the objects they were carrying into the sea and using them as boats or rafts. During their journey, the son of the Dragon King of the Eastern Sea stole Lan Caihe's musical instrument and took him prisoner. The others then declared war on the Dragon King and defeated him after a fierce battle, after which Lan Caihe was freed.

Lü Dongbin (left) and He Xiangu, the only Immortal who was definitely female.

The Immortals Zhang Guoli (Old Man Zhang Guo) and (right) Han Xiang.

The Jade Emperor and his court

In ancient times the supreme ruler of heaven was given various names, depending upon which dynasty was in control. Confucians, taking their cue from the founders of the Zhou dynasty, preferred the impersonal name Tian ("Heaven"), although in the popular mind he remained a person rather than an abstraction. Eventually, a deity called Yuhuang, or the Jade Emperor, emerged as the supreme ruler of heaven and his position was confirmed by one of the Song dynasty emperors, who claimed to receive direct instructions from him. His cult mingled both Taoist and Buddhist beliefs.

The Jade Emperor lived in a palace and was attended by a vast bureaucracy, just like his earthly counterpart. His chief assistant was Dongyue Dadi, or Great Ruler of the Eastern Mountains, who had no less than seventy-five departments in his office, each supervised by a minor deity. The emperor's wife was Wang Mu Niangniang, another name for Xi Wang Mu (Queen Mother of the West) who lived on Mount Kunlun (see also panel, p.95). The only human with whom the Jade Emperor dealt directly was the emperor of China; lesser mortals were the responsibility of his officials, who included gods and goddesses, Buddhas and Bodhisattvas, deceased emperors and empresses, celestial beings and immortals. A lively description of the heavenly regime occurs in the 14th-century novel *Journey to the West*, otherwise known as *Monkey*, in which Sun Wukong, the Monkey King, goes up to heaven, steals the peaches of immortality which grow there, and takes on the whole heavenly hierarchy in combat before being captured by Buddha. The benign Bodhisattva Guanyin (see p.96) intercedes for him, and he is allowed to accompany and protect Tang Seng, a Buddhist pilgrim, during his journey to India.

By the time that the Jade Emperor had become recognized as supreme ruler in heaven, beliefs of the main religions of China had already started to intermingle. For example, Taoists were quite ready to accept the Buddhist, and therefore ultimately Indian, theories of karma and reincarnation. Indeed, they were already widely accepted by the Chinese population in general, except for some believers of Islam and other religions. It therefore became important for the heavenly bureaucrats who served the Jade Emperor to keep a record of the successive incarnations of those living on earth, so that an individual's total balance of merit and demerit could be calculated. This balance would determine the nature of the individual's next reincarnation. Animals had to be included in the incarnation register, since particularly virtuous animals could be reincarnated as humans.

This plate is decorated with a scene from the novel Journey to the West *and shows Guanyin with the Monkey King, who has stolen the peaches of immortality.*

MYTHS OF THE FAMILY

Filial piety and household gods

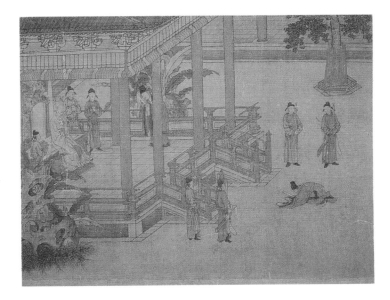

A son abases himself before his father in this illustration from an edition of the Chinese classic collection of moral tales, The Twenty-Four Examples of Filial Piety, compiled in the 14th century.

In Chinese families much emphasis was traditionally placed on respect for elders, particularly for parents and grandparents. This even extended to the long dead: a family treated its ancestors in many ways as though they were still alive, conducting ceremonies in their honour on their birthdays and on the anniversaries of their deaths. During these ceremonies, offerings of food were made to their spirits.

Reverence for the older generation was a recurrent theme in Chinese literature and drama, and myths extolling models of filial piety were required reading for the young. The best-known collection of such exemplary tales is *The Twenty-Four Examples of Filial Piety*, which was compiled by Gui Jujing in the 14th century. The stories were drawn from different periods of Chinese history, and although they were each assigned a time and a place to give them a ring of authenticity (a common practice in Chinese storytelling), they are distinctly far-fetched. For example, the reader is told how a certain Lao Laizi put on a jester's clothes and played like a child – at the age of seventy – to please his parents. In one tale, a son lay naked on the ice to melt it so that he could catch fish to feed his mother and father, while in another a son cut some flesh from his thigh to make soup for his parents when they were sick.

Like any other Chinese institution, the household had its own gods and spirits. Pictures of guardian door gods were pasted on either side of the front door, and there were gods of the bedchamber and even of the privy. The most important household deity was the kitchen god, whose duty it was to make an annual visit to heaven to report on the family's behaviour. On the twenty-third day of the twelfth month, the mouth of his image would be smeared with a sweet paste so that he would not be able to open it to make his report.

LADY SILKWORM

A girl's filial piety led to the arrival of silk in the world. In ancient times there was once a man who had to leave home on business for a long time. His young daughter missed him greatly. One day, as she was grooming her stallion, she declared: "I'd marry anyone who brought father home." Suddenly, the stallion bolted and disappeared into the distance.

The next day, in a distant town, the father was surprised when the stallion galloped up to him, neighing. Thinking that something must have happened to the family, he jumped on the horse's back and galloped home. When he arrived he was relieved to find nothing amiss, and asked his daughter what had made the horse come to fetch him. She said that the horse must have known that she missed her father. The man was grateful and for the next few days gave the horse extra helpings of the best fodder. But the horse did not seem happy and hardly touched its food, and every time the girl came near, it became very excited, neighing and rearing up. After several days the girl remembered her words while grooming the horse, and told her father. Furious that a horse should dare to think of marrying his daughter, he slaughtered the stallion and laid its skin out in the sun to dry.

Later, when the girl and her playmates were taunting the skin as though it were alive, it suddenly wrapped itself around her and flew off into the distance with her. Her father and his neighbours eventually spied the skin on the top of a tree. Inside it, the girl had become a caterpillar-like creature, Can Nü (Lady Silkworm). As she waved her horse-like head from side to side, a fine, glossy white thread emerged from her mouth. Everyone was amazed and said that it was the finest and strongest thread they had seen, and they realized that it could be spun and woven into beautiful garments.

TIBET AND MONGOLIA

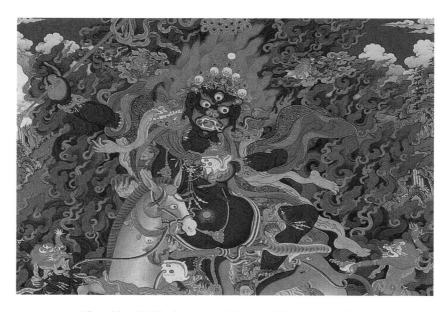

The goddess dPal-ldan lha-mo, wrathful slayer of the enemies of religion,
as depicted in a thangka (scroll painting on canvas) from the Potala Palace,
Lhasa. The ferocity of the imagery is typically Tibetan.

Centuries before Buddhism came to Tibet, a shamanistic culture held sway over both Tibet and Mongolia. The earliest myths tell how the world is created and sustained by many gods and demons who reside in countless special places on earth, in the heavens and in subterranean labyrinths. Such spirits were honoured with offerings on the mountain passes to ensure safe passage. Their assistance was called upon before the start of any undertaking, and they were exorcised by priestly rituals whenever they caused trouble, stagnation or sickness.

Only a shaman in trance had the ability to travel the three realms and understand the intricate workings of the universe. He could divine the causes of illness and misfortune, or retrieve lost souls abducted by spirits. It was he who recommended the appropriate sacrifice, typically the weaving of a "thread cross" (*mdos*) and the presentation of a ransom to the offended or malicious spirit.

In Tibet the ancient mythology of shamanism was overthrown when the 8th-century king, Khri Srong-lde'u-btsan, made up his mind that the most potent civilizing force was Buddhism. Full of admiration for the sophisticated cultures of his Buddhist neighbours, Khri Srong-lde'u-btsan sent messengers to India in search of the most learned men of his day. He was advised to send for a *tantrika* (practitioner of occult religion) known as Padmasambhava. Honoured by the king's gift of gold, Padmasambhava accepted the invitation to Tibet and with the help of local spirits established the "inconceivable" (bSam-yas) temple. Modelled on Buddhist concepts of cosmology, the three-storeyed central tower represented the world mountain Sumeru, while around it were shrines in the positions of the minor continents of the world, and the sun and moon. In the adjacent monastery Buddhist texts were translated from Sanskrit to Tibetan. Padmasambhava resided in a nearby cave with his closest disciples. When the time came for his departure from Tibet, he promised that he would return there every month, on the tenth day of the waxing moon, in order to bless anyone who called out his name.

TIME CHART

Throughout the prehistoric period, the wandering shamans of Tibet and Mongolia shared a similar mythological outlook, although the details of their storytelling varied widely from area to area. After the 13th century, their religions began to correspond more exactly, as Buddhism was transmitted from Tibet to Mongolia. In the 16th century, Mongolians coined the term "Dalai Lama" and applied it retrospectively to two generations of teachers. Ever since, the Dalai Lamas of Tibet have remained a key element in the unification of Tibeto-Mongolian religious culture.

c.120 BC	Gri-gum, last of the sky-descended kings, killed by Lo-ngam
AD 433	King Lha-tho-tho-ri receives Buddhist texts and sacred objects
670-692	Tibetan empire at height of military power
762	Invitation to Padmasambhava to visit Tibet
763	Founding of bSam-yas monastery
794	Indian Buddhism declared superior to Chinese
1252	Mongolian invasion of Tibet
1270	Mongolia converted to Sa-skya school of Tibetan Buddhism
1543	Bestowal of the title "Dalai Lama" by Altan Khan of Mongolia
1577	First anti-shamanist edict by Altan Khan
1642	Dalai Lama V takes power in Tibet

PRONUNCIATION GUIDE

The Tibetan language is written in syllables. At first sight, the complex spelling of many of the syllables makes them seem impossible to pronounce. However, most syllabic prefixes and suffixes are silent, so that the first step for the Western reader who encounters Tibetan names may be to look for the vowel in each syllable and vocalize that, together with the preceding consonant. If a consonant follows a vowel, this often has the effect of raising the vowel's tone. Difficulties may occur with the rule that transforms the pronunciation of bya to ja, pya to cha, and phya to chha. For example, the Tibetan name of the Buddhist god Avalokiteshvara (in the Sanksrit version) is written sPyan-ras-gzigs, pronounced chen-ray-zee. With the introduction of Buddhism from India, Sanskrit names and terms found their way into the country, and many of these are used in the text of this chapter.

KEY TO MAP

Old kingdom of Tibet
------ Southern edge of Mongol Empire, mid-13th century
Heartland of Buddhism, from 6th century BC
Migration of Buddhism, from India to Tibet
Yar-lung valley: tombs of the Tibetan kings.

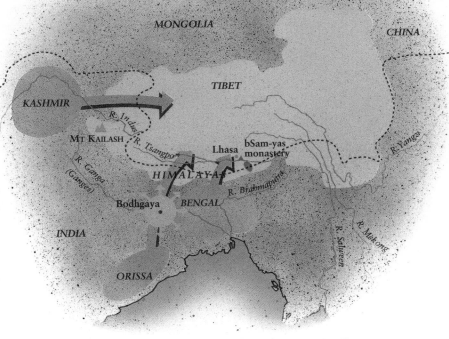

Padmasambhava, who brought Buddhism to Tibet, is still worshipped there. He is thought to dwell on a copper-coloured mountain, surrounded by devotees.

PADMASAMBHAVA AND THE INCONCEIVABLE TEMPLE

As Padmasambhava made his way over the Himalayan mountains and through the valleys, he supposedly employed his magic nail (*kila*) to pin down and bring under control all those malignant spirits of the land who wished to show hostility to the new religion. Arriving in Tibet he found the king's new temple in disrepair, because demons were tearing down at night all that the men could construct by day. So Padmasambhava set the local spirits to work and with their assistance the building was soon completed. Then, to ensure its longevity and auspiciousness, Padmasambhava consecrated the temple with rites of the magic nail.

THE KING'S GIFT

In honour of his *guru*, King Khri Srong-lde'u-btsan offered his youngest bride, the princess Ye-shes mTsho-rgyal, to act as divine consort in the esoteric rites. She remained with Padmasambhava throughout his stay in Tibet and was responsible for the transmission of many of his most important doctrines. It was she who oversaw the concealment of "the hidden treasures" (*gter-ma*) – religious instructions destined to be revealed at a future time when the world would be in need of fresh, uncorrupted revelation.

THE BUDDHIST TEACHINGS

Padmasambhava taught the Buddhist way of "blood sacrifice". Slaughter of innocent animals in religious ritual was prohibited. Yogins, instead, were to imagine their own blood as symbolic of sexual passion and surrender this to the deity. Their bones were thought of as the bones of anger and their flesh as a quivering mound of ignorance. Renouncing the world, Buddhist practitioners symbolically offered their own skulls as cups, filled with the "flowers" of their sense-organs so that all they experienced was in honour of the deity.

MYTHS OF ORIGIN

Radiant, Black Misery and the karmic wind

THE MONKEY AND THE OGRESS
Once a saintly monkey made his way to
the Himalayas to enjoy the ecstasy of
undisturbed, profound meditation. The
beauty of his personality captivated the
heart of a female rock-demoness, whose
attempts at seduction (illustrated right, in
the cave at the lower right corner) were
unable to weaken the monkey's vow of
chastity. So she suffered the pangs of
unrequited love. But a frustrated, angry
demoness is a great danger in this world,
and bearing this in mind, and full of
sympathy for her suffering, the monkey
finally succumbed to her entreaties. In due
course, six children were born of their
union and from these, it is said, the entire
population of Tibet eventually descended.

As pious Buddhists, Tibetans believe
that their original ancestors were the holy
Bodhisattva sPyan-ras-gzigs
(Avalokiteshvara) in the guise of a monkey
and the goddess sGrol-ma (Tara) in the
form of a rock ogress (*brag srin mo*).
These patron deities of Tibet have
watched over their descendents ever since
– especially Avalokiteshvara who has
repeatedly become manifest for his people
in the form of the Dalai Lama. Tibetans
account for the variety of personality types
by claiming that the first six monkey
children included one representative from
each of the six realms known to Buddhist
cosmology.

At one time, the old myths say, when nothing whatsoever existed, two
lights were born. One was black and called Black Misery (*myal ba nag po*),
the other was white and called Radiant (*'od zer ldan*). Then, out of chaos
arose multicoloured streams of light which separated like a rainbow, and
from their five colours arose hardness, fluidity, heat, motion and space.
These five elements came together and fused to form a huge egg. Then
Black Misery produced the darkness of non-being from that egg, and filled
the darkness with pestilence, disease, misfortune, drought, pain and all
kinds of demons. Radiance filled the world with the light of auspicious
becoming. He sent forth vitality, well-being, joy, prosperity, longevity and
a host of beneficent gods who poured their blessings onto creation. As the
gods and demons met together and mated, all kinds of creatures were born
from the resulting eggs. These children, in turn, "made magic" with one
another until the world was filled with their progeny. The stories of these
beings are often highly localized. The mountains, trees, rocks and lakes
that make up the sacred landscape are seen either as the abodes of these
gods and demons, or as the gods and demons themselves.

The mythology of Buddhism gradually replaced all these indigenous
ideas. The new concern was to account for periodic cycles of cosmological
time. To the Indian sage, local spirits and demons pertain to the realm of
maya, or illusion. According to Buddhist belief, the present universe is the
residual effect of karma – deeds done by the inhabitants of a universe now
ceased. It is the wind of karma that first stirs in the empty universe, not the
creative whim of a demiurge. Eventually this karmic wind becomes so
thick and dense that it can support the rainfall precipitating from above.
A cosmic ocean then arises, and at its centre towers the world mountain
Sumeru. When the outer container of the universe is complete, after millions of years of evolution, the sentient beings whose destiny it is to dwell
within the world begin to manifest. At first they have bodies made only of
mind and they dwell in the sky. Eventually they take on solid, fleshy form
and inhabit the material earth. After aeons of wrongdoing, they inhabit the
deepest pits of hell in the bowels of the earth and there they remain until
the universe itself begins to crumble at the end of time.

MYTHS OF THE ANCIENT KINGS

The sky-descended rulers

Before the dawn of history, Tibet is said to have been held together by a succession of non-human rulers, the first of whom were the black *gnod-sbyin* – demons armed with bows and arrows. Subsequent races of demons had different weapons, such as hammers and axes, slings and catapults, and tempered steel. The ruling spirits included the heroic *ma-sang* brothers, who gave Tibet the name Bod, by which it is still known today.

The first human ruler descended from the sky onto a mountain in Kong-po. At the end of his reign he ascended back to the heavens by means of a *dmu* cord, leaving no earthly remains. His six descendants did the same, but the seventh of his royal line cut the magic cord at the close of his life and was buried in the earth. Thus began the cult of the royal tombs, which until the 9th century AD were constructed in the Yar-lung valley and kept under constant supervision by guards.

After twenty-seven generations of human kings, Lha-tho tho-ri came to the throne and, in the water-bird year of 433AD, at the age of sixty, became the first king to learn of Buddhism. Legend has it that the sky one day filled with rainbows, and Buddhist texts and images fell onto the roof of his palace. He was unable to fathom the sacred writings, but it was prophesied that their meaning would be revealed to his family after five generations. Worshipping the miraculous objects as sacred, Lha-tho tho-ri lived to be one hundred and twenty, although his body appeared no older than sixteen.

Five generations later, in fulfilment of the prophecy, King Srong-btsan sgam-po commissioned an alphabet for the Tibetan language, thus introducing the art of writing. Among the king's five wives were two Buddhist princesses from China and Nepal, and as part of their dowries both queens brought with them precious statues of the Buddha and Buddhist saints. At their insistence, Srong-btsan sgam-po began to tame the wild terrain of Tibet, which was thought to be a malignant ogress, and prepare the country for the reception of their foreign religion. Demonstrating her skill in the Chinese art of geomancy, the Chinese queen, Kong-jo, pointed to places in the land where temples could be built to press down upon and subdue the demoness's body.

THE SEVERING OF THE CORD
The first Tibetan king not to return to heaven by a cord at the end of his reign was Gri-gum, and his was the first royal tomb in the land. Enraged by the prophecy of his shamanic soothsayer that he was to die by the sword, and determined to prove otherwise, Gri-gum challenged his ministers to a duel and the challenge was accepted by Lo-ngam, keeper of the king's horses. For superstitious reasons, the king went into battle surrounded by a herd of yaks with bags of soot upon their backs. Wearing a black turban fastened on his forehead with a shining mirror, he had the corpses of a fox and a dog draped upon his shoulders. As soon as combat began, the sharp horns of the yaks burst the bags of soot and the air was filled with a dense cloud of black dust. Wildly waving his sword above his head, Gri-gum severed the magic rope that connected him with heaven, and inflicted no injury upon his opponent. Deserted by his protector gods who felt aggrieved at the stinking corpses on his shoulders, Gri-gum was slain by Lo-ngam who carefully aimed an arrow at the only thing visible in all that cloud of gloom – the shining mirror on the king's forehead. The painting (above left), from the Buddhist period, depicts the fatal shot.

THE STATUE OF THE GREAT LORD
The large, jewel-encrusted golden image of the twelve-year-old Buddha that Queen Kong-jo brought with her from China is nowadays to be found in the Ra-sa 'phrul-snang temple, built upon a lake in Lhasa formed of the ogress's heart's blood. The statue, known as Jo-bo chen-po ("Great Lord"), is popularly believed to have been fashioned by a divine artist during the lifetime of the Buddha, and remains the most revered image in the whole of Tibet.

KING GESAR

The warrior-king

King Gesar in full armour. Telling of treachery, deceit, cowardice, greed, envy and other human shortcomings, the stories of Gesar's adventures twist and turn in an unpredictable manner.

The legends of King Gesar (Gesar Khan) are well-known throughout the Tibeto-Mongolian world. This is primarily an oral tradition: many episodes of the narrative are recited by wandering bards who enact the exploits and sing of the hero's valour, cunning and magical skills. Even today the massive cycle of legends surrounding this figure has not been set down fully in writing, but its extent is estimated to be more than five times that of the Bible.

Permeated in its present form with the ideology and mythologies of Buddhism, the Gesar cycle nevertheless retains memories of many older shamanic gods whose myths are included within it – powerful mountain deities as well as numerous lesser spirits of the places where the stories take place. It is these beings who appoint Gesar to undertake his earthly mission. Embittered by bad luck, and angry with the gods and all their worshippers, an old woman and her three sons die with curses against all religion upon their lips. Destined to become demonic monsters in their next lives, these four pose an unprecedented threat to order and harmony among mankind. The gods choose Gesar from among their own number to descend from heaven in order to do battle with these demons and their successors as they arise on earth. Unwilling at first to do what the others command, Gesar attempts to avoid fleshy incarnation by assenting to his mission only upon the fulfilment of certain "impossible" conditions. "I demand", he says, "that my father be a god and my mother a snake-demon (*klu*). I wish for an immortal horse that can fly through the sky and speak the languages of all men and animals. I insist upon a magnificent saddle encrusted with jewels and a helmet, armour and sword that are not of human manufacture. Likewise a bow and arrow of miraculous origin and strong, heroic companions. I also wish for a wife of such beauty that all who see her will willingly enlist to fight in her service, and an uncle whose clever stratagems will enable me to win every battle. Finally, I also insist that each one of you who is to remain here so comfortably while I am gone watch over and protect me at all times and come to my aid whenever I should call." These conditions are all satisfied, and Gesar has no alternative but to make his earthly journey.

Gesar's birth, from a white egg marked with three eye-shaped spots that issue from the crown of his mother's head, is reminiscent of shamanic myths of origin. Heralded by excellent omens, he arrives on earth with three eyes, but one is at once plucked out by his terrified mother. Although pledged to restore order and harmony in the world, Gesar often becomes forgetful of his mission in the aftermath of his victories and requires the prompting of his guardian angel (now identified as a Buddhist *dakini*) to set his feet back on the path. Though saturated with the magical and the divine, the cycle is firmly rooted in human experience, and indeed many Tibetans alive today claim themselves to be the descendents of the characters from the narratives – even of Gesar himself.

After a life of stirring adventures as a ruthless and powerful warrior king, crushing violent injustice wherever he encounters it, Gesar and his companions retire to meditate in caves on the slopes of the sacred mountain Margye Pongri. Three years or more later, having been purified by religious rites of all the negative effects of a lifetime of war and bloodshed, Gesar returns home to heaven in the knowledge that he will one day be obliged to visit earth again – because evil can never be permanently eradicated from this world.

THE TAMING OF THE GODS

The impact of Buddhism

Under the influence of Buddhism, the chaotic forces of nature, variously feared and honoured by the shamanic tradition, were made to fit harmoniously into the Indian cosmological model. Old shamanic rites were adopted by the Buddhist clergy and heavily overlaid with Buddhist liturgy and symbolism. Monks adorned their temples with such archaic paraphernalia as the shaman's divination arrow, his magic mirror and precious pieces of fine rock crystal. From the trimmings on the old shaman's tunic were derived theatrical costumes for the "Buddhist" dances of the eagle, stag, snow-lion and skeleton. The shaman's eagle, by which he once ascended to his nest in the world tree, became identified with the Indian Garuda; the stag was said to be the one who first heard the teachings of the Lord Buddha in the deer park at Varanasi; and the snow-lion became identified as the mount of such Buddhist deities as Vairocana or Manjusri. The dancing skeletons of the wounded shaman's own traumatic initiation by dismemberment became the guardians of the sacred Vajrayana charnel grounds. Buddhist priests often assumed the role of oracular mouthpiece for converted shamanic deities. They appropriated the shaman's bow and arrow or drum, and the broad, fur-trimmed hat and gown of the "black-hat sorcerer" (*zhva nag*) festooned with shamanic symbols of the cosmic tree (world mountain), sun and moon, snake-like ribbons and the divination mirror, with trimmings of bone, fur and feathers.

The apotheosis of Padmasambhava

Padmasambhava, the Indian mystic who brought Buddhism to Tibet (see pp.102-3), is worshipped there as "the second Buddha".

He is believed to have miraculouly emanated as an eight-year-old within the heart of a lotus blossom. Raised by the king of Oddiyana, he was banished after murdering a king's minister, and condemned to live as a penitent ascetic in the charnel grounds beyond the borders of human habitation. There he conversed with supernatural beings (*dakini*) and attained great spiritual power.
    Ordained by the Buddha's cousin, he lived for more than a thousand years as a follower of the Buddhist path.

Padmasambhava, "the guru with eight names", is depicted here in wrathful guise, on a tiger.

THE *KILA*
The cult of Vajrakıla, the deified wrathful spike or peg (*kıla* in Sanskrit; *phur-ba* in Tibetan), originated in India but seems to have been lost there, and is seen today as a characteristic of Tibetan Buddhism. The spike is the embodiment of a powerful god, and by merely hammering it into the ground all malign influences are subdued. If pegged into the corners or at the entrance of a sacred site, the spike creates a magic barrier which evil cannot cross. The illustration shows a *kila* with its tiny demon effigy, which is symbolically pierced in ritual; four miniature spikes supplement the main one.

MONGOLIAN SHAMANISM

Encounters with the spirit realm

THE EAGLE AND THE SNAKE
When the world was still young, the king of all flying creatures ordered the wasp and the swallow to go out and taste the flesh of all living creatures. The two subjects were to report back to him in the evening and declare which meat was sweetest, and most suitable for the diet of a king. As it was a beautiful day, the swallow lost himself in transports of joy – singing and soaring in the light blue sky. The wasp, on the other hand, did as he was told and spent the day biting whomsoever he met and tasting their hot blood. When the two met up at the end of the day, prior to reporting back to the king, the swallow asked the wasp for his verdict. "Without doubt," said the wasp, "the sweetest food to eat is humans." Fearing that this judgment could cause great trouble for the future, the swallow pulled out the wasp's tongue with his beak, so that when the king asked for his verdict that night, all the poor creature could do was buzz incoherently. "We have decided, your majesty," said the swallow, "that the meat most suitable for a king is the flesh of serpents." To this day the eagle and the hawk, both descendants of that ancestral ruler of all flying creatures, love to dine on snakes.

The cosmos of the Mongolian shaman is vertical in structure – blue eternal heaven above, mother earth below. The father of heaven rules ninety-nine realms (*tngri*), fifty-five of which are located towards the west and forty-four towards the east. The earth mother's domain is made up of seventy-seven *tngri*. All these realms are interconnected, and sustained by a web of life in which every living being, both above and below, has its part to play. The whole is shaped like a cosmic tree with spreading branches on every level, and there are holes between the layers through which the shaman can climb.

Among the first shamans in ancient times was a fifteen-year-old youth called Tarvaa who, having fallen ill and fainted, was mistaken for dead. In disgust at the haste with which his relatives removed his body from the house, Tarvaa's soul flew off to the spirit realm where he was accosted by the judge of the dead and asked why he had come so early. Pleased by the boy's courage in travelling to that realm which no living man had ever reached, the lord of the dead offered the boy any gift of his own choosing to take back with him to life. Shunning wealth, pleasure, fame and longevity, Tarvaa chose to return with a knowledge of all the wonders he had encountered in the spirit realm, and the gift of eloquence. By the time he returned to his body, crows had already pecked out the eyeballs. Although now blind, Tarvaa could foresee the future, and he lived long and well with his tales of magic and wisdom brought back from the far shore of death.

Shamans that have followed Tarvaa have, to this day, woven into their costumes knowledge of light and darkness, of the deities above and below, and of spirits both benevolent and malign. While resting in the world tree, fledgling shamans learn the way of sacrifice to ensure harmony and order within the web of life. They return to men with a knowledge of the five gods of wind, the five gods of lightning, the four gods of the corners, the five of the horizon, the five of entrance and the eight of borders. They know the seven gods of steam and the seven of thunder and the countless numbers of other gods. Such knowledge gives them great power to put at the disposal of their fellow men, and they are able to summon whomsoever they please with their drums. Early shamans were apparently so powerful that they could call back the souls of those long deceased, so that the lord of the dead feared that his realm would be emptied around him. In a fit of rage, he reduced the originally double-headed shamanic drum to its current single-headed style in order to protect his sovereignty.

Animals as familiars and helpers feature greatly in the cosmology of the shaman. The bat, for example, hangs upside-down in order to watch the sky and will warn us should it ever show signs of collapse. The marmot watches the sun, forever hopeful of catching it. Long ago, this creature was a man, and is said to have shot down six of the seven suns that dessicated and scorched the earth causing famine and misery to all beings; the seventh sun now keeps setting and rising in order to escape the final arrow.

Cats and dogs feature in shamanistic creation myths. There was a time long ago when the seas of the world were still mud and the rising mountains no more than hillocks. Then god created the first man and woman of clay and set a cat and a dog to watch over them while he went to fetch the waters of eternal life from the spring of immortality. However, while he was away, the devil distracted these animal guards by offering them milk and meat, and urinated on the newly created creatures. God was angry to find the fine fur of his handiwork so defiled and he ordered the cat to lick off the fur – all except the hair of the creature's heads which alone remained unpolluted. The cat's rough tongue took off all the dirty hair it could reach, leaving sparse stained hairs on the armpits and groin. What the cat licked off, God put on the dog. He then sprinkled his creations of clay with the sacred waters of the eternal spring, but because of the devil's defilement he was unable to grant us immortal life.

Buriat shamans traditionally begin their calling and dancing with the words, "If the swan ever sets off, listen to me, my soldiers of the birch grove, listen to me my Khudar with birch brims, listen to me my Oikhon with water edges." The banks of the river Khudar are covered with birch groves and, long ago, on the little island of Oikhon on Lake Baikal, Khori Tumed saw nine swans fly down from the northeast. Taking off their feathered dresses, they became nine beautiful girls who bathed naked in the lake. Khori Tumed silently stole one of the dresses so that only eight swans were able to fly off after bathing. He married the one who remained and she bore him eleven sons. They were very happy together, but Khori Tumed would never reveal to his wife where he had hidden her swan dress. One day she asked him again, "Oh please let me try on my old dress. If I try to walk with it out of the door, you may easily catch me, so there is no danger of my escape." This time he was persuaded, and let her try it on. Suddenly she flew up through the skylight of their *yurt* (tent of skins). Khori Tumed was just in time to catch her ankles and he pleaded with her to stay at least long enough to give names to their sons before departing. She agreed to this, and the eleven sons became men. Then Khori Tumed let his swan wife go and she flew around the tent bestowing blessings upon their clans before disappearing back to the northeast.

Since the introduction of Buddhism to Mongolia in the 13th century, such shamanic myths have become devalued and lost. The Mongolian Buddhist figure of the "white old man" represents all that remains of a once proud shamanic deity who ruled all heaven and earth. It is said that the old man was converted during a meeting with the Buddha, and that he now acts as an assistant to the clergy and as a supporter of the Buddhist path, his magic staff now a mere walking stick.

INITIATION

Shamans have spoken of their youthful initiation: the spirits of ancestors force themselves upon the young person and cause his personality to crumble. As the neophyte shaman experiences the dismemberment of his physical body, his spirit takes refuge in a nest upon one of the branches of the world tree. There it stays until it has been nurtured back to health and the spirits that attend it have taught it how to see the world from the high vantage point of the tree.

The burning of the yellow book

Sheep have special importance in Mongolian belief. At the end of every year the breast-bone of a sheep is offered to the fire god who maintains fertility among the herds. Shamans know that a sheep's shoulder-blade is capable of accurate prognostication, and that this power derives from the burning of the yellow book.

The yellow book of divination belonged to a king to whom its pages unfailingly revealed the culprit of any crime. The king had a beautiful daughter whom he kept hidden from the world, and his servants all knew that if they revealed her identity to any stranger they would be discovered by the yellow book and punished. To confuse the book, a certain Tevne dug a deep pit in the ground and into it enticed one of the princess's maidservants. Over the hole he built a fire, placing a kettle of water on top. He took a length of iron pipe, wrapped with cotton at one end, and passed it through the kettle in order to be able to speak to the old woman below. Speaking through the pipe, she told him how to identify the princess, and then he let her go. When, later, Tevne picked out the princess from a number of similar-looking girls, all dressed alike, the king was furious but was forced to bestow upon him the hand of his daughter. Consulting his magic book, the king learned that the informant was a man with earthern buttocks, a body of fire, lungs of water and an iron pipe for vocal cords. Unable to fathom the riddle, he lost faith in his yellow book and burned it. Sheep licked up the ashes, and became imbued with divinatory power.

JAPAN

Every Shinto shrine has a simple torii *(gateway) at the entrance to its precincts.*
This torii *rising from the sea is linked with the Miyajima shrine near Hiroshima,*
sacred to the three divine daughters of the storm god Susano.

Lying off the northeast coast of the Eurasian landmass, from which it is separated by the Tsushima Straits, Japan is at once *in* East Asia, but not really *of* East Asia. Its history, in the strict sense of a literate historical tradition, began late by Western standards: the conventional starting date is 552AD when the king of the Korean kingdom of Paekche (near modern Pusan) sent some Buddhist missionaries to the emperor of Japan as a gesture of good will. At that time, the principal Japanese institution was the *uji*, or clan. Each *uji* seems to have controlled its own territory and to have been composed of both commoners and aristocrats, and almost certainly had its own mythology, which centred on a divine ancestor.

By the beginning of the 6th century, one of these clans (sometimes referred to as the Yamato clan, from the region of central Honshu that still bears this name) had managed to gain effective hegemony over the others – and, by extension, so had its divine ancestors. The imperial family, which has continued in an unbroken line to the present, soon became the primary focus of Japanese myth.

The native religion of Japan, Shinto, is based on the worship of a multitude of gods, spirits and objects of reverence. Its mythology concentrates on tales of the sun goddess Amaterasu and the adventures by which her descendants unified the Japanese people. With the introduction of Buddhism came a period of cultural borrowing, initially from Korea, later from China, the "mother civilization" of East Asia. Buddhism mingled with Shinto in complex ways, but from the 17th century there was a strong Shinto revival, culminating in the adoption of Shinto as state religion under the Meiji government (1868-1912).

SOURCES OF JAPANESE MYTH

The primary source for Japanese mythology, the *Kojiki*, or Record of Ancient Matters, is the oldest surviving imperial genealogy. The final text was compiled by a courtier named Ono Yasumaro from several earlier texts (no longer extant) after receiving a commission from the Empress Gemmei in AD711. The work was formally presented at court four months later, in the first month of AD712. Written in a curious mixture of archaic Japanese and Chinese, the *Kojiki* begins with the creation of the world, the origin of the gods, the divine ancestry of the imperial family, and ends with the death of the Emperor Suiko in AD641.

The second major source is the *Nihonshoki*, or Chronicle of Japan, compiled by several scholars at around the same time as the *Kojiki*, and completed in AD720. Except for its poetry, the *Nihonshoki* is written in classical Chinese and is strongly influenced by Chinese (and Korean) historical and mythological traditions and dynastic chronicles. For this reason, the *Nihonshoki* is, on the whole, less reliable than the *Kojiki* as a source for indigenous myth.

Other sources include the *Kogoshui*, or Gleanings from Ancient Stories (AD807), various *norito* (ancient Shinto prayers), the *fudoki* (8th-century provincial "gazetteers"), and the first great anthology of Japanese poetry, the *Manyoshu* (c.AD760).

TIME CHART

660 BC	Traditional date for accession of first emperor, Jimmu-tenno
4th-5th centuries AD	Rise of Yamato court, traditionally after an invasion of Yamato from the southwest
AD 552	First Buddhist missionaries reach Japan from the Korean kingdom of Paekche
AD 710	Foundation of Nara, first permanent capital of Japan, modelled after the Tang capital Changan (modern Xian)
AD 712	*Kojiki* myth compilation presented to Empress Gemmei
AD 720	Completion of *Nihonshoki* myth compilation
794-1868	Heian (modern Kyoto) serves as imperial capital of Japan
1192	First military government (shogunate) established at Kamakura
1600	Japan unified after Battle of Sekigahara
1603-1868	Tokugawa shogunate: a time of national isolation
1868-1912	Meiji period: the restoration of imperial power
1872	Shinto adopted as state religion
1946	Emperor denies his own divinity

MYTHIC SITES AND SACRED PLACES

MOUNT TAKACHIO Mountain in Kyushu where Honinigi descended from heaven (see p.120).
ISE Site of the Grand Shrine of Amaterasu and the Rice God; the most sacred place in the Shinto religion (see p.115, margin).
THE HI RIVER Now in Shimane Prefecture. Susano is believed to have landed near its headwaters when he was banished from heaven (see p.117).
IZUMO-TAISHA Site of the Grand Shrine of Okuninushi (sometimes called Daikokusama), offspring of Susano and the protector of the imperial family (see pp.118-20).
KUMANO Site of Jimmu-tenno's encounter with the bear spirit (see p.122).
THE KANTO PLAIN Site of Yamato-takeru's battle with the Emishi (see p.122).
URAGA STRAITS Here Yamato-takeru's consort sacrificed herself to a water spirit on a rough sea crossing, to calm the waves (see p.122).

SHINTO

Shinto, "The Way of the Gods", centres on the worship of *kami*, divinities believed to inhabit every distinct phenomenon in nature, including human beings. From 1872 to 1945 Shinto was the state religion of Japan, but after the Second World War it reverted to being a "congregational" religion, in which each shrine, or *jinja*, is only loosely related to the others. The most important annual event at every *jinja* is the *matsuri*, or shrine festival. An image of the local *kami* is carried around the neighbourhood on the shoulders of young men and women – thereby sanctifying both the vicinity and the carriers.

HOKKAIDO
Sado
HONSHU
KANTO PLAIN
Edo (Tokyo)
Ugara Straits
SEA OF JAPAN
Oki
Biwa Lake
MT HIEI
Heian (Kyoto)
Nara
Ise
Izumo-taisha
R. Hi
YAMATO
Kumano
Wakayama
PACIFIC OCEAN
KOREAN KINGDOM OF PAEKCHE
Tsushima
SHIKOKU
Inland Sea
Tsushima Strait
MT TAKACHIO
KYUSHU

KEY TO MAP

→ Route of conquest of Yamato by Jimmu-tenno, legendary first emperor of Japan, c. AD300–400
Kanto Plain
◆ Site of mythical episode
▲ Mountain site of mythical episode
■ Sacred site

IZANAGI AND IZANAMI

The primal couple

In the beginning, when the earth was young and not yet fully formed (the *Kojiki* describes it as "resembling floating oil and drifting like a jellyfish"), three invisible gods came into existence in what the Japanese call Takamagahara, or the "High Plains of Heaven". The oldest was called Amanominakanushi-no-kami, or "Lord of the Centre of Heaven". He was soon followed by Takamimusubi and Kamimusubi, both of whom were powerful *kami* in their own right. These three, together with two lesser divinities (Umashiashikabihikoji-no-kami and Amanotokotachi-no-kami), formed the five primordial "Separate Heavenly Deities". Then came seven more generations of "heavenly" gods and goddesses, culminating with the Japanese primal couple: Izanagi and his sister and wife, Izanami, in full Izanagi-no-Mikoto ("The August Male") and Izanami-no-Mikoto ("The August Female").

Commanded by the deities to "complete and solidify this drifting land", Izanagi and Izanami stood on the Floating Bridge of Heaven (perhaps a rainbow) and stirred the brine below with a jewelled spear. When they lifted up the spear, the drops formed an island called Onogoro, the first solid land. Shortly afterwards, they descended to the new island, erected a

This 19th-century print shows Izanagi and Izanami with the jewelled spear on the Floating Bridge of Heaven. They were the eighth pair of divinities to appear after the creation of heaven and earth out of the primordial chaos.

"heavenly" pillar and built a palace. Then they decided to procreate. Izanagi asked his sister how her body was formed. She replied that in one place it was formed insufficiently. Izanagi said that one place in his own body was formed to excess, and suggested that they unite these two parts. The divine couple invented a marriage ritual which consisted of them both walking around the heavenly pillar, Izanagi from the left and his sister from the right. When they met, the two exchanged compliments and then had sexual intercourse.

In due course Izanami gave birth, but their first-born turned out to be the deformed Hiruko ("Leech-Child": see right), which the unhappy couple placed in a reed boat and consigned to the sea. During a "grand divination", the gods concluded that the birth of the leech-child was the fault of Izanami, because she had spoken first during the courtship ritual. Armed with this information (which serves to this day to legitimize sexual inequalities in Japan), the couple returned to Onogoro and performed the ritual again. This time Izanagi spoke first when they met at the column, and Izanami duly gave birth in abundance. First, she produced a series of islands (that is, the Japanese archipelago), then a series of gods and goddesses, including the gods of wind, of mountains and of trees. But during the birth of Kagutsuchi (or Homusubi), the Fire God, her genitals were so badly burned that she fell sick and died. However, even in her death throes Izanami continued to engender deities – in her faeces, urine and vomit. Izanagi was inconsolable at her loss, and as he wept, his tears gave rise to yet more deities. Later, his sadness gave way to a terrible rage, and he decapitated the Fire God for causing the death of his beloved wife. From the dead Fire God's remains emerged yet another set of divinities.

Izanagi decided to visit Yomi, the underworld land of the dead (see panel, below), in an attempt to bring Izanami back to life. When Izanami appeared at the entrance to Yomi shrouded in shadows, Izanagi greeted his wife warmly and begged her to return with him. She agreed to discuss his request with the gods in the underworld, and before withdrawing into the darkness she warned her husband not to look at her. But Izanagi was consumed with such a strong desire to see his beloved that he broke off a tooth from the comb which he wore in his left hair-bunch and lit it to make a torch. He entered the land of the dead and saw at once that

THE LEECH-CHILD
The idea that a deformed first child (or set of twins) may be unworthy, and for this reason should be abandoned to die, has many resonances in world mythology. Similar circumstances occur in many stories, including those of Moses, Perseus (see p.156) and Romulus and Remus (see p.174). It is possible that the story of the leech-child born to Izanagi and Izanami reflects an ancient Japanese ritual in which the birth of a first child was marked by putting a clay figurine in a reed boat and floating it away as a scapegoat.

The Land of Darkness: the Japanese underworld

The subterranean world of the dead is known also as the Land of Darkness (Yomi-tsu-kuni), the Land of Roots and the Deep Land.

The description of Yomi given in the Kojiki may reflect the late prehistoric Japanese practice of burying the dead in stone-lined chambers deep within large tumuli (or kofun). Izanagi's expedient of rolling a large boulder across the entrance to Yomi perhaps echoes the final sealing of such a tomb. The boulder may also be a metaphor for the insurmountable barrier between life and death.

There are striking similarities between this story and two well-known Greek myths: the story of Persephone (see p.142), whose ingestion of pomegranate seeds in Hades ties her to the land of the dead in winter, and the story of Orpheus' attempt to rescue his beloved Eurydice from the same realm (p.165).

Whether elements of these Greek myths somehow diffused to ancient Japan, or whether the parallels reflect a universal tendency in human myth-making, is disputed by scholars. In many cultures eating the food of the dead is said to create a bond with them. When Izanami meets her husband at the entrance to the land of the dead, she wishes that he had come sooner because she has already "eaten at the hearth" there. This act may explain her dramatic transformation from loving wife into raging demon.

Izanami was a rotting, maggot-riddled corpse. Terrified at the sight of her, Izanagi turned and fled. Izanami, outraged by Izanagi's betrayal of her wishes, sent the evil "hags of Yomi" to pursue him, followed by the eight thunder deities and a horde of warriors. When he reached the pass of Yomi, which led back to the land of the living, Izanagi found three peaches with which he pelted his pursuers, forcing them to retreat. Finally, Izanami, now a fully-fledged demon, joined the pursuit herself, but before she could reach him, Izanagi closed the pass with a huge boulder. The two faced each other on either side of the boulder and "broke their troth".

Feeling polluted by his experience in Yomi, Izanagi decided to purify himself in the time-honoured Japanese way: by taking a bath. Arriving at the mouth of a small stream in Hyuga (northeast Kyushu), he disrobed. A variety of gods and goddesses were born from his discarded clothing, and others emerged as he bathed. Finally, Izanagi gave birth to three of the most important divinities in the Shinto pantheon: the Sun Goddess, Amaterasu-no-mikoto (literally, "August Person who Makes the Heavens Shine") appeared when he washed his left eye; Tsuki-yomi-no-mikoto ("The August Moon") came out of his right eye; and Susano-no-mikoto ("The August Raging Male") emerged from his nose. Surveying his three noble children, Izanagi decided to divide his kingdom among them. He gave his sacred bead necklace, a symbol of sovereignty, to Amaterasu, with the injunction that she should rule the High Plains of Heaven. To one son, the Moon God Tsuki-yomi (in Japanese mythology the moon is seen, unusually, as male), Izanagi entrusted the realms of the night. To the other son, Susano, he assigned the rule of the ocean.

Amaterasu and Tsuki-yomi obediently accepted their assignments. Susano, however, wept and howled. When Izanagi asked him the cause of his distress, Susano replied that he did not want to rule the waters but wished instead to go to the land of his mother Izanami. Angered by Susano's defiance, Izanagi banished him and then withdrew, his divine mission completed. According to one version of the myth, he ascended to heaven, where he lives to this day in the "Younger Palace of the Sun". He is also said to be enshrined at Taga (in Shiga Prefecture, Honshu).

The offspring of Izanagi

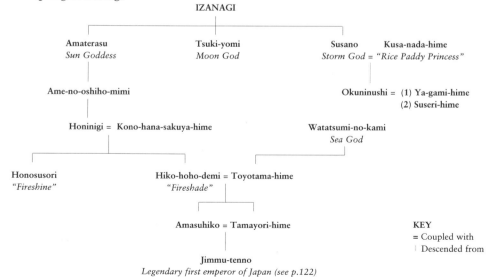

IZANAGI

Amaterasu
Sun Goddess

Tsuki-yomi
Moon God

Susano   Kusa-nada-hime
Storm God = *"Rice Paddy Princess"*

Ame-no-oshiho-mimi

Okuninushi = (1) Ya-gami-hime
                (2) Suseri-hime

Honinigi = Kono-hana-sakuya-hime

Watatsumi-no-kami
Sea God

Honosusori
"Fireshine"

Hiko-hoho-demi = Toyotama-hime
"Fireshade"

Amasuhiko = Tamayori-hime

Jimmu-tenno
Legendary first emperor of Japan (see p.122)

KEY
= Coupled with
Descended from

AMATERASU AND SUSANO

The contest of the sibling deities

When the Storm God Susano was banished by his father, Izanagi, he announced his intention to take leave of his sister, the Sun Goddess, Amaterasu. The goddess suspected her brother of wanting to usurp her lands and prepared herself for battle, arranging her long hair in bunches and arming herself with a bow and two quivers of arrows. She shook her bow furiously and stamped and kicked the earth beneath her feet while she waited for him. Susano assured her he had no evil intentions. He suggested that they could prove which of them was mightier by having a contest of reproduction: whichever of them bore male deities would be vindicated.

The contest began with the Sun Goddess asking for her brother's sword. She broke this into three pieces which she chewed up and then spat out as three graceful goddesses. Next, Susano took the long strings of *magatama*, or fertility beads, which Amaterasu wore around her hair-bunches, hairband and arms. From these he produced five male gods and proclaimed himself the victor. Amaterasu pointed out that her brother's male offspring had come from her possessions and that in fact *she* had won the contest. Susano refused to concede and celebrated his victory by breaking down the ridges of the divine rice paddies and covering up the irrigation ditches. Then he defecated and strewed his excrement in the hall where it was customary to taste the first fruits of the harvest. Finally, Susano skinned a "heavenly" dappled pony (probably a reference to the stars) and hurled it down through the thatched roof of the sacred weaving hall (see panel, below), where Amaterasu and her maidens were weaving. One of the maidens was so alarmed by this that she banged her genitals against the shuttle of the loom and died. Amaterasu fled in terror. The *Nihonshoki* includes a version of this story in which Amaterasu herself was the victim of her brother's violent prank, although she was merely injured, not killed.

THE SUN GODDESS
The Sun Goddess Amaterasu, the elder daughter of Izanagi, is one of the greatest deities in Japanese myth. She was born out of her father's left eye as he washed after returning from Yomi, the underworld. Amaterasu is worshipped both as a spiritual divinity and as a sacred ancestor of the imperial family. She was once worshipped in the imperial palace itself, until it became politically expedient to put the authority of the emperor beyond the power of the priestesses and erect a shrine to her elsewhere. The main shrine to Amaterasu is at Ise, in Mie Prefecture. This is the most important Shinto shrine in Japan. The main building is a thatched, unpainted hut of cypress, constructed in ancient Japanese style. It is regularly rebuilt in wood in exactly the same form: from the 7th century to the 17th century it was rebuilt every twenty years; since the 17th century it has been rebuilt every twenty-one years.

The sacred weaving hall

Neither the Kojiki nor the Nihonshoki *is precise as to the purpose of the sacred weaving hall, or what indeed Amaterasu and her maidens were weaving. However, several possibilities have been suggested.*

Amaterasu was a priestess-queen, responsible for weaving the clothes of the gods, and the weaving hall may have been her workroom. Some authorities suggest that she and her female attendants were making garments to be worn by priestesses officiating at ceremonies connected with the sun cult. A more profound possibility is the notion that they were weaving the fabric of the still incomplete universe. Susano's actions can perhaps be seen as a chaotic assault upon the cosmos or universal order. The sacred weaving hall, as a scene of creation, would be a fitting arena for the confrontation between the divine embodiments of cosmos (Amaterasu) and chaos (Susano).

A 19th-century print of Amaterasu and some of her handmaidens in divine splendour.

THE DIVINE CRISIS

Amaterasu's removal of the sun

THE DAWN GODDESS
In her capacity as a prototype of the female shaman, or *miko*, who regularly engaged in ecstatic dancing, Ama-no-uzume, the dawn goddess, appears again later in the story as told by the *Nihonshoki*. On this occasion she displays her charms in order to distract a local solar deity called Sarutahiko, or the "Monkey Prince", who had attempted to block the descent from heaven of Amaterasu's grandson, Honinigi. She and Sarutahiko eventually married, and from their union is said to have sprung an historically attested clan of female Heian court dancers called the Sarume.

Amaterasu emerging from her cave, thereby restoring sunlight to the world, as depicted in a 19th-century print triptych. Some scholars have interpreted this event as the return of spring after the darkness of winter. This would make the erotic dance in front of the cave, which leads to Amaterasu's emergence from hiding, a kind of fertility ritual. However, others think the episode is derived from observation of a solar eclipse.

The Sun Goddess Amaterasu was badly frightened when her brother Susano hurled a skinned horse through the roof of the sacred weaving hall (see p.115). Her decision to withdraw into what the *Kojiki* calls the "Heavenly Rock Cave" (or Ama-no-iwato) produced a divine crisis analogous to the crises found in almost every ancient mythology, such as the Egyptian account of the temporary triumph of the evil god Seth (see p.44) and the Greek myth of the abduction of Persephone (see p.142), both of which caused all manner of disasters to befall the world. Some scholars interpret her withdrawal as a symbolic death and entombment; however, it may equally be a metaphor for a total eclipse of the sun, precipitated by the event that the Sun Goddess had just witnessed.

Amaterasu's self-imposed retirement plunged both the High Plains of Heaven and the Central Land of the Reed Plain (that is, the mortal realm) into total darkness. As a result, the rice paddies lay fallow, and various calamities ensued. In desperation, the "eight-hundred myriad" gods came together in solemn assembly by the heavenly river to discuss ways of coaxing Amaterasu from her hiding place. (In this context, the Japanese number eight, or *ya*, is a sacred number, implying many or an entire contingent rather than a specific total.)

Omori-kane-no-kami, the wise son of Takamimusubi, was directed to come up with a solution. After the sounds of certain "long-crying" birds (probably roosters) failed to produce the desired result, Omori-kane and his fellow divinities conceived an elaborate stratagem. First, they constructed a magical mirror which they suspended from the branches of a sacred sakaki tree uprooted from a mountain forest. Then, while several divinities held magical objects and performed a solemn liturgy, a beautiful young goddess called Ama-no-uzume (in this context seemingly a dawn goddess, like the Roman Aurora, the Greek Eos or the Vedic Indian Ushas, although none of the ancient sources actually characterize her in this way) climbed on top of an overturned tub and performed an erotic dance.

Ama-no-uzume's aim was to trick the sun into re-emerging, by employing methods consistent with those of the ancient *miko*, or female shaman. When she exposed her breasts and pushed her skirt down to her genitals, the assembled gods laughed so uproariously that the High Plains of Heaven shook as if struck by an earthquake. The sound even penetrated to where Amaterasu was hiding. Her curiosity aroused by the commotion, she opened the door of the rock-cave by just a crack and called out: "Why is Ama-no-uzume singing and dancing, and all the eight-hundred myriad deities laughing?" The young goddess replied for them all: "We are rejoicing because here is a deity superior to you." While she was speaking, two gods aimed the mirror in the direction of the partially open door and another god, whose name includes the word for strength (*chikana*), concealed himself nearby.

Catching sight of her reflection, Amaterasu slowly came out of her refuge and approached the mirror. As she gazed intently at herself, the god who was in hiding nearby suddenly grabbed her by the hand and pulled her all the way out. Another divinity stretched a magic rope (*shiru-kume*) across the doorway, saying: "This is as far as you may go!" Things rapidly returned to normal after this, and the sunlight returned to both heaven and earth. The divine crisis had been resolved.

The eight-hundred myriad deities then reassembled to deliberate over the fate of the one who had caused the crisis, the wilful and destructive Susano. The punishment imposed on him was severe: the gods fined him "a thousand tables of restitutive gifts", cut off his beard and the nails of his hands and feet, and finally expelled him from heaven, forcing him to descend once more to the Land of the Reed Plain.

Susano and the Food Goddess

Susano, the God of Storms, was consistently a source of mayhem. Before his banishment to the Central Land of the Reed Plain, Susano's troublesome disposition brought him into conflict with almost everyone who crossed his path. According to some sources, one such unfortunate was the Food Goddess, Ogetsu-no-hime.

In an incident unrelated to the main narrative, Susano is said to have ordered Ogetsu to give him something to eat. She responded to this demand in an unusual manner not at all to his liking – that is, by withdrawing the food from her nose, mouth and rectum. In retaliation for this perceived insult, he slew her.

However, the death of Ogetsu serves a positive purpose in Japanese myth. Her body parts yielded the basic food crops on which the Japanese still subsist: in her eyes grew rice seeds; in her ears, millet; in her genitals, wheat; in her nose, red beans; and, in her rectum, soy beans.

This story recalls the ancient Chinese myth of Pan Gu (see p.90), a primordial giant whose remains became the raw material of creation, including foodstuffs: his skin and hair became plants and trees. However, most scholars believe that the Ogetsu story pre-dates the beginning of intense Chinese influence on Japan in the 6th century AD. In fact, the Japanese account of the Food Goddess's fate is curiously similar to an Indonesian myth in which a goddess called Hainuwele was wrongfully slain and dismembered; her body parts were subsequently buried, and from them, it is said, emerged the staple food plants (for example, yams) which are cultivated in that part of the world. There may be a very ancient link between Ogetsu and Hainuwele, both tales deriving ultimately from a common Southeast Asian prototype.

In the *Nihonshoki*, the slayer of the Food Goddess is given as Tsuki-yomi, the Moon God, rather than Susano. When Tsuki-yomi reported what he had done to the Sun Goddess, Amaterasu, she rebuked him, vowing never to set eyes on him again. That is why the sun and the moon dwell apart from each other. Several authorities suggest that this version of the story is the more ancient one, and that the compiler of the *Kojiki* substituted Susano for Tsuki-yomi in order to underscore the god's violent nature.

THE IZUMO CYCLE

Susano's descent to earth; Okuninushi and the White Rabbit

The Storm God Susano with his wife, Kusa-nada-hime, whom the god turned into a comb to save her from an eight-headed dragon.

After his banishment from heaven, Susano went down to earth to the land of Izumo (see map, p.111). His first adventure there forms a bridge passage to a distinct group of myths set in this region and known as the Izumo Cycle. The character central to the cycle is the region's principal divinity, Okuninushi (or Daikokusama), the "Great Lord of the Country", who was the descendant of Susano and Kusa-nada-hime, possibly their son (see family tree, p.114).

The exiled Susano found himself near the headwaters of the Hi River. Noticing a pair of wooden chop-sticks floating in a stream, he reasoned that there must be people living up-river, and so he set out to find them. He soon encountered an elderly couple and a beautiful young woman, all weeping bitterly. The couple told the god that an eight-tailed, eight-headed creature called Yamato-no-orochi had devoured seven of their eight daughters, and that the monster was about to take their youngest offspring, Kusa-nada-hime ("Rice Paddy Princess") as well. The god revealed his identity and offered to slay the dragon in return for Kusa-nada-hime's hand in marriage. When the couple readily agreed, he turned the princess into a comb, which he inserted into one of his hair-bunches. Then he instructed them to fill eight large tubs with *sake* (rice wine) and to place these on eight platforms surrounded by a fence with eight openings.

Yamato-no-orochi eventually arrived, stuck his eight heads through the openings and began to lap up the *sake*. Susano waited until the creature was dead drunk before coming out of hiding and hacking it to pieces with his sword. In the course of chopping up the middle tail, he discovered inside it the famous sword that would later be named Kusanagi, or "Grass Mower" (see p.122). Then he changed Kusa-nada-hime back to her human form, married her, and built a large palace at Suga in Izumo.

The most famous story in the Izumo Cycle is that of Okuninushi and the White Rabbit. Okuninushi had eighty brothers, all of whom wished to marry the beautiful princess Ya-gami-hime of Inaba. One day the brothers set out for Inaba to woo the princess, with Okuninushi bringing up the rear as their attendant. On the journey they came upon a rabbit without fur lying by the side of the road, obviously in great pain. The brothers told the suffering creature that he might get his fur back if he bathed in salt water, but this remedy only made his condition worse.

Okuninushi eventually arrived on the scene and asked the rabbit why he was crying. The rabbit replied that he had been on the island of Oki and had wanted to cross over to Izumo, but there was no bridge. He had persuaded a family of crocodiles to form a living bridge across the water. In return for this favour he had promised to count the number of crocodiles lying end-to-end as he ran over them and thereby determine whether they or the creatures of the sea were more numerous. But a few bounds short of the end of the living bridge the rabbit had revealed that his promise was a ruse, intended solely to get him across the water. Enraged, the crocodile lying at the end of the chain had seized the foolish rabbit and skinned him alive.

Okuninushi told the rabbit to go to the river-mouth and wash himself in the pure water. Then he was to roll on ground sprinkled with the pollen of kama grass. The rabbit, who was actually a deity, did as he was instructed, and his snow-white fur soon returned. Okuninushi was rewarded for his help by the grateful rabbit, who assured him that he and not any of his brothers would gain the hand of Ya-gami-hime. The eighty

The ordeals of Okuninushi

Okuninushi's union with Ya-gami-hime provoked several murderous attacks on the young god by his eighty jealous brothers. His attempt to resolve the dispute involved him in an even more deadly conflict with the mighty Storm God, Susano.

On two separate occasions the vengeful brothers succeeded in killing their sibling, only to find him restored on both occasions by his mother who interceded with the gods on his behalf. The brothers first heated a large rock to white-hot intensity and rolled it down a mountain toward him. Thinking that it was a boar which his brothers wanted him to stop, Okuninushi caught the rock and was burned to death. The second attempt involved the brothers crushing Okuninushi to death in the fork of a large tree. After this experience Okuninushi, urged on by his worried mother, decided to put an end to the rivalry by seeking the counsel of Susano, the Storm God, who now lived in the underworld.

Upon his arrival at Susano's palace, Okuninushi noticed the beautiful Suseri-hime, Susano's daughter. She and Okuninushi fell deeply in love and were soon married. However, this impetuous act angered Susano, and he too decided to do away with Okuninushi. Feigning acceptance of his new son-in-law, he bade him sleep in a room that turned out to be full of snakes. Fortunately, Okuninushi's bride gave him a magic scarf that drove off the snakes when it was waved at them three times. The next night, when Susano told Okuninushi to sleep in a room full of centipedes and bees, the scarf saved him again.

Finally, his angry father-in-law shot an arrow into a large plain and instructed Okuninushi to fetch it. The young god did as he was told, but no sooner had he begun his search than Susano set fire to the grass growing in the plain. Okuninushi looked in vain for a way out of the inferno until a mouse came to his rescue. The mouse told the anxious god to stamp his feet, because the ground was hollow. Okuninushi took the advice of the mouse, stamped his feet and a hole opened up. He took refuge in the hole while the fire passed over him harmlessly. Meanwhile, the mouse had searched for and found the arrow, which he gave to Okuninushi.

Okuninushi returned the arrow to Susano, who now began to feel a little more kindly disposed toward his son-in-law. All the same, Okuninushi made plans to escape from the older god's sphere of influence. One day, after Okuninushi had washed Susano's hair, the Storm God fell asleep. Seizing his opportunity, Okuninushi tied the slumbering Susano's hair to the rafters of the palace. Then, armed with his father-in-law's mighty bow and sword, and carrying Suseri-hime on his back, Okuninushi left Susano's underworld palace and set out for his own country, the Land of the Reed Plain.

It was only when Okuninushi had gone some distance that Susano started off in pursuit of his daughter's abductor. When he came within shouting distance of the fleeing couple, at the border of the underworld and the land of the living, Susano decided not to follow the happy pair. Instead, he shouted to Okuninushi the advice he had sought in the first place: how to end the quarrel with his brothers. The Storm God told him that he would defeat his brothers if he fought them with the bow and sword which he had taken from his palace.

brothers were furious at Okuninushi's success, and the struggles between Okuninushi and his jealous brothers are the basis for a number of other stories (see panel, p.119). These conflicts, in which Okuninushi was victorious, reduced Izumo to anarchy, which the shrewd Amaterasu turned to her advantage. She wanted to extend her rule to the region, and she dispatched one of the sons borne to her in the contest with Susano to assess the situation. After learning of the upheavals there, the Sun Goddess dispatched another son to subdue the region. When this son failed to return after three years, she consulted with her fellow divinities and decided to send a god called Ame-no-waka-hiko to find out what had happened to him. However, Ame-no-waka-hiko turned traitor and, after marrying Okuninushi's daughter, schemed to take control of the land. After eight years Amaterasu sent a divine pheasant to him to ask the reason for his long absence from heaven. Ame-no-waka-hiko shot the bird with an arrow, which passed through it and reached the god Takamimusubi, who sent it straight back: it killed the traitor as he lay in bed.

Exasperated by these failures, Amaterasu sent two of her most trusted divine colleagues, Takamimusubi and Kamimusubi, to inform Okuninushi that he must surrender the land to the Sun Goddess. Seated on the tips of their upturned swords, which had embedded themselves in the crest of a wave just off the beach at Inasa in Izumo, they delivered the Sun Goddess's ultimatum. Okuninushi, much impressed by this display, asked one of his sons for an opinion. The young god advised capitulation, an assessment with which Okuninushi eventually concurred, with the proviso that a place should be reserved for him among the major deities worshipped at Izumo. Amaterasu agreed to this. After Ise (see p.115, margin), Izumo is the most important Shinto shrine.

After Okuninushi's surrender, Amaterasu sent her grandson Honinigi to earth bearing three sacred talismans of sovereignty: the Divine Mirror which had helped to trick Amaterasu into leaving the cave of darkness (see pp.116-7), the Kusanagi sword found by Susano in the tail of the dragon (see p.118), and the *magatama* beads which had produced many offspring (see p.115). Replicas of these talismans are still presented to each new emperor at his enthronement.

FIRESHINE AND FIRESHADE

Honinigi, the grandson of Amaterasu, had two sons, Honosusori ("Fireshine") and Hiko-hoho-demi ("Fireshade"). Fireshine, the eldest, supported himself by catching sea creatures with his fishhook, while his younger brother, Fireshade, was a landsman who hunted animals. Dissatisfied with his lot, Fireshade proposed that they exchange occupations. They did so, but Fireshade was no more successful in the new role than in the old. To make matters worse, he lost the fishhook and was unable to return it when his brother demanded it back. The hapless former landsman offered several substitute hooks, but only the original would satisfy Fireshine. Deeply embarrassed, Fireshade drifted far out to sea and finally reached the palace of the Sea God, Watatsumi-no-kami. Not only did the god find the missing fishhook, in the mouth of a redfish, but he also gave the newcomer his daughter's hand in marriage.

After several years of living comfortably in his father-in-law's palace, Fireshade began to long for his homeland. As a parting gift, the god gave him two magic jewels: one to make the sea rise and another to make it fall. He also arranged for his son-in-law to ride home on the back of a friendly crocodile.

Fireshade returned the fishhook to Fireshine, but the latter continued to make trouble, and so Fireshade threw the jewel that makes the sea rise into the water, causing his elder brother to panic and beg forgiveness. Thereupon, Fireshade threw the other jewel into the sea. When the water receded, a grateful Fireshine vowed to serve his younger brother forever. Fireshade's grandson was the first Emperor, Jimmu-tenno (see p.122).

This 19th-century print (right) depicts Fireshade riding home on the crocodile.

GODS, HEROES AND DEMONS

Inari, Hachiman and the Oni

The Shinto pantheon includes a number of major divinities not mentioned in the myths summarized so far. One is Inari, the Rice God. Closely related to Ogetsu-no-hime, the Food Goddess (see p.117), Inari is widely venerated not only as the deity who ensures an abundant rice harvest, but also as the patron of general prosperity. As such, he is especially worshipped by merchants. Inari's messenger is the fox, and a pair of these creatures invariably flanks his image at every Inari shrine.

In ancient times, Inari was considered the patron of swordsmiths as well as of merchants and rice farmers. Other popular divinities of this sort include Kamado-no-kami, god of kitchen ranges, and Ebisu, the *kami* who oversees work. Finally, the Shinto pantheon includes a great many deified historical (or quasi-historical) figures. One of the most important is the Emperor Ojin (died c.394ad), who was famed for his military exploits and later deified as Hachiman, God of War. It is still customary in many regions for young men to celebrate their coming-of-age ritual (at the age of twenty) at one of the numerous Hachiman shrines.

Demons

Shinto, like other traditional belief systems, has its dark side. Those who have sinned are condemned to the Japanese equivalent of hell: a subterranean realm called Jigoku, consisting of eight regions of fire and eight of ice.

The ruler of Jigoku is called Emma-ho, who judges the souls of male sinners and assigns them to one of the sixteen regions of punishment according to the nature of their misdemeanour. Emma-ho's sister judges female transgressors. As part of the judgment process, the sinner's past sins are reflected back at him in a vast mirror. The souls of the dead can be saved by the intercession of *bosatsu* or Bodhisattvas (see p.123). Another class of demon, found both in Jigoku and on earth, is made up of beings called Oni.

These malevolent forces are responsible for all sorts of misery, including disease and famine, and are also capable of stealing souls and possessing innocent people. Although some Oni are believed to be endowed with the facility for assuming human or animal forms, or both, most are invisible. Diviners (for example, *miko*: see p.117) and especially virtuous people can sometimes detect these demons.

Generally, the Oni are thought to be of foreign origin, having possibly been introduced into Japan from China, along with Buddhism – a way of life to which they are sometimes converted.

This ivory and root wood sculpture of the 19th century shows numerous Oni with two warriors who have subdued them, including a figure called Shoki the demon-queller, who stands with his foot on one of the defeated demons.

THE REALM OF SAGA

The exploits of Jimmu-tenno and Yamato-takeru

THE NAMING OF YAMATO-TAKERU
Yamato-takeru, the famous name by which O-usu-no-mikoto was known, means "Brave One of the Yamato". He acquired this name as a young man.

O-usu-no-mikoto's first exploit was to kill his elder brother for not showing proper respect to their imperial father. Impressed by his son's ferocity, the emperor decided to send him off on a dangerous mission to kill two mighty warrior brothers named Kumaso. Disguised as a woman, O-usu managed to insinuate himself into the brothers' palace and was invited to attend a feast. When the festivities were at their height, O-usu suddenly withdrew the sword he had concealed beneath his female garments and stabbed the elder Kumaso through the chest, killing him instantly. The younger Kumaso brother fled in terror, but O-usu managed to catch him and stab him in the buttocks. As the injured man lay dying, he bestowed upon his killer the name by which he would henceforth be known.

Jimmu-tenno sets out on his journey east, to find new lands to rule. The bird-like creature may be a winged being called Sawo-ne-tsu-hiko which guided Jimmu and his brother across the strait which separates Kyushu from Honshu.

One section of the *Kojiki* focusses on the "Age of Men", dominated by heroic quasi-historical figures rather than by gods. The first such figure in the Japanese tradition is Jimmu-tenno (or Kamu-yamato-iware-biko as he was also called), grandson of Fireshade (see p.120) and founder of the imperial family. There is some evidence that he was not in fact the first of the line but had an elder brother, Itsu-se, who was killed in battle during the brothers' move east, to find the best place from which to rule their kingdom, and also to look for new territories. After burying his fallen brother, Jimmu continued eastward into the Kumano region (modern Wakayama Prefecture). Here, a local deity, taking the form of a bear, cast a spell over the invaders which put them into a deep sleep.

Then one of Jimmu's retainers learned in a dream of a magic sword, sent by Amaterasu and her fellow divinities to help Jimmu pacify the central Land of the Reed Plain (that is, Yamato). Awaking, the retainer located the sword and presented it to Jimmu. The army then continued its eastward march, guided by a giant crow sent down by heaven. As the soldiers moved deeper into Honshu, the local rulers paid homage to Jimmu. Finally reaching Yamato, Jimmu built a palace there, married a local princess of divine ancestry (Isuke-yori-hime), and settled down to rule his new realm.

The greatest of all Japanese legendary heroes is Yamato-takeru, originally called O-usu-no-mikoto. After several exploits in his youth, Yamato-takeru was sent by his father, Keiko, to subdue the land of Izumo by killing its chief, Izumo-takeru. This mighty warrior agreed to a duel with Yamato-takeru, and to exchange swords for the fight. When the contest began, Izumo-takeru was unable to draw Yamato's sword (it was not a real sword but an imitation), and so was easily killed.

The next mission assigned to Yamato-takeru by his father was the pacification of the Eastern Barbarians, or Emishi. He set off with the magic Kusanagi sword found by Susano (see p.118) and a magic bag, both given to him by his aunt, Yamato-hime, at the Ise shrine. En route he met a princess, Miyazu-hime, and fell in love with her, promising to marry her on his return. When he arrived in Sagamu (modern Kanagawa province) he was implored by a local chieftain to dispatch an unruly deity who lived in a great pond in the middle of a grassy plain. This was a trick: as soon as he entered the plain the chieftain set fire to the grass. However, the Kusanagi sword then started wielding itself to mow down the blazing grass (hence the name by which this sword was later known: the Grass-Mower). Opening the magic bag, Yamato-takeru found fire-starting equipment, with which he set a counter-fire and escaped from the trap.

It was during the long journey back to his homeland that Yamato-takeru brought about his own downfall. Before setting off he married Miyazu-hime and left the Kusanagi sword in her care. In the pass of Ashigara he killed a mountain deity in the form of a white deer. Later, on Mount Ibuki, he encountered another deity, embodied as a white boar, and violated a taboo by proclaiming that he would kill the creature. Because of these transgressions, he was soon afflicted by a mortal illness. Dying, the hero made his way to the coast at Otsu, near Ise, to collect another sword he had left there. Then, singing a song about the beautiful homeland he would never see again, he proceeded to the plain of Nobo, where he finally died. Before his body could be buried in the tomb erected by the emperor, it transformed itself into a giant white bird which soared off in the direction of Yamato.

BUDDHIST MYTHS

Three figures of mercy

The death of the Buddha, as depicted in a Japanese handscroll of the 17th century. Buddhism developed rapidly in Japan in the 7th and 8th centuries.

The Shinto religion has co-existed with Buddhism for more than 1,500 years in Japan. As a result, there has been a great deal of cross-fertilization between the two faiths, and many Shinto *kami* have long since taken on a Buddhist cast. For example, the god of war, Hachiman, is also referred to as a *bosatsu* – that is, an incarnation of the Buddha (from the Sanskrit *bodhisattva*). The merging of Buddhist and Shinto teachings is often referred to as Ryobu-Shinto, or "Double-Shinto". However, there are also a great many *bosatsu* who have little, if anything, to do with Shinto, and whose roots go back to China and, ultimately, to Buddhism's birthplace in northern India.

Of all the major Buddhist deities, three figures loom especially large in the popular tradition: Amida, Kannon and Jizo. Amida-butsu ("Buddha"), who derives from the Sanskrit figure Amitabha, is a Bodhisattva who voluntarily postponed his own salvation (that is, his entry into Nirvana) until all human beings had been saved. He is the central figure in the "Pure Land" sects (Jodo-shu and Jodo-shinshu), which are grounded on the belief that the faithful, by invoking Amida at the hour of death, are able to be reborn into the beautiful "Pure Land" where they will be free from pain and want until ready for the final Enlightenment.

Kannon, the equivalent of the Chinese Guanyin (see p.96) and the Indian Avalokiteshvara (see p.87), is widely worshipped under several names. He is the *bosatsu* to whom believers turn for mercy and wise counsel. He is at once the protector of children, of women in childbirth and of dead souls. One of his most popular manifestations is Senju Kannon, or the "Kannon of a Thousand Arms" – all of which are stretched out compassionately toward the worshipper. In Japanese iconography he is typically shown with a miniature Amida on his head, as he was seen as the companion of this Buddha.

Jizo is also concerned with children, especially the souls of those who have died. Small Jizo-yas, or temples to Jizo, are ubiquitous in Japan. But he is also the protector of all who suffer pain, and is believed able to redeem souls from hell and bring them back to the Western Paradise.

Kannon, shown here (on a late 19th-century sword-guard) standing on the back of a carp, is sometimes illustrated as a thousand-armed figure, sometimes in other forms (for example, as a seated two-armed figure holding a lotus, or as a horse-headed figure with a third eye). The cult of Kannon was introduced into Japan from Korea shortly after the arrival of Buddhism in the islands.

GREECE

*The most famous of all Greek temples, the Parthenon
at Athens (seen from the east, above), was built
between 447BC and 438BC by the architects Callicrates
and Ictinus under the supervision of the great sculptor
Pheidias (c.490-430BC). It was dedicated to the city's
patron goddess, Athene Parthenos (Athene the Virgin).*

The rich legacy of stories, decorative images and temple architecture inspired by the gods and heroes of ancient Greece has exercised a powerful influence on Western culture. Except during the so-called Dark Ages and the early Middle Ages, successive generations, from Roman times through the great revival of ancient culture in the Renaissance right up to the present day, have admired, adopted and adapted the Greek mythological heritage.

Every city of the ancient Greek world – which stretched from southern Italy to the coast of Asia Minor and included all the islands of the Adriatic and the Aegean – had its own myths, heroes and religious festivals. This complicates our understanding of Greek mythology, because even for the most important events in the biographies of the major divinities, innumerable, often incompatible, accounts circulated. At the same time, there were rites and festivals, such as the Olympic games, in which all Greeks participated, and certain heroes, such as Herakles (see p.148), to whom shrines were dedicated throughout the Greek world. The epics of Homer were among the considerable number of stories and works of literature which were known to Greeks throughout the Hellenic world. The development of a standard core of universally familiar stories helped create a sense of Greek nationhood, linking the city-states in opposition to the "barbarians" by whom they felt they were surrounded. Many of the Greek myths that are best known today are the product of this tendency toward the evolution of a canonical mythology.

MOUNT OLYMPUS
Greece's highest mountain, revered as the home of the chief deities (the Olympians), headed by Zeus. The others were: Aphrodite, Apollo, Ares, Artemis, Athene, Demeter, Dionysos, Hephaistos, Hera, Hermes, Hestia and Poseidon.

DELPHI
Regarded as literally the centre of the world, Delphi was dedicated to Apollo. Its famous oracle, consulted by all the major cities, features frequently in Greek mythology and history (see p.138).

ATHENS
The biggest and one of the most powerful cities in the classical Mediterranean, Athens was the cultural capital of the Greek world. Athenian literature and art are a primary source for Greek mythology and Athens is the home of the most famous Greek temple, the Parthenon (see opposite). Built in the 5th century BC, its centrepiece was a magnificent, 40-foot (12-metre) high ivory and gold statue of Athene by Pheidias, who also built the statue of Zeus at Olympia (see below, left).

Map labels:
THRACE
BLACK SEA
MACEDONIA
Hellespont
Troy
Mt Olympus
ASIA MINOR
Corfu
THESSALY
AEGEAN SEA
Delphi
Aulis
Ithaca
Thebes
ATTICA
Corinth
Eleusis
Olympia
Mycenae
Athens
Argos
PELOPONNESE
Delos
Sparta
Naxos
Cos
Cythera
MEDITERRANEAN SEA
CRETE
Knossos

Inset map labels:
GAUL
BLACK SEA
SPAIN
ITALY
GREECE
Pillars of Herakles
Athens
Crete
MEDITERRANEAN SEA
EGYPT

KEY TO MAP
Area of Greek settlement, c.550BC
● Important city
■ Important religious site
Region: *GAUL*

OLYMPIA
The site of the Olympic games, a four-yearly festival in honour of Zeus (see below), at which athletes from all over the Greek world competed in emulation of the heroes of myth. The games were abolished only in AD393 by the Christian Roman emperor Theodosius I, probably because of their pagan associations.

THEBES
Reputedly founded by Cadmus (see p.130), Thebes provides the backdrop for tragic dramas such as Sophocles' *Oedipus the King* and Aeschylus' *Seven Against Thebes*. In the mid-4th century BC it was briefly the leading Greek power.

SPARTA
The centre of a powerful, austere and militaristic state, Sparta left little architecture or literature. It features in myth as the city of Menelaus (see p.157).

ARGOS
Argos and its citizens, the Argives, play a central role in Greek epic and tragedy, but the city itself was of little importance after c.500BC.

TROY
The city of the legendary King Priam, Queen Hecuba and their sons, including the heroes Hector and Paris. They and the city were immortalized by Homer in his great epic, the *Iliad*, the story of the Trojan war (see p.157).

A reconstruction of the 42-feet (13-metre) high statue of Zeus, which stood in his temple at Olympia. Completed c.430BC and made of ivory and gold, it was the masterpiece of Pheidias.

TIME CHART *(most dates are approximate)*

1600-1100 BC The Mycenaean Age, or late Greek Bronze Age
1400-1100 BC The Minoan Age, named after Minos, legendary king of the island of Crete (see p.150), where a distinctive culture develops
1100 BC Probable time of the Trojan war
1100-800 BC The Greek Dark Ages, about which little is known
800-700 BC The Age of Homer: the city-state and alphabet develop
750-550 BC The Age of Expansion. Many cities establish colonies abroad
700-600 BC The Age of Tyrants. A time of much social disruption
600-400 BC The Age of Democracy. Athens, the first democratic state, reaches the zenith of its power under Pericles (c.495-429BC)
490 BC Athens and its allies defeat Persia
431-404 BC Peloponnesian war, ending in the defeat of Athens by Sparta
400-300 BC The Age of Alexander the Great (365-323BC), whose conquests take Greek culture to the frontiers of India
338 BC King Philip of Macedonia wins supremacy over all Greece
336 BC Philip's son Alexander succeeds as ruler of Greece
330 BC Alexander conquers Persia
300-1 BC The Age of Kingdoms. After Alexander's death in 323BC, his empire splits into several large dominions which, like Greece itself, are eventually conquered by the Romans

MYTH AND SOCIETY

Public and private observances

THE PANATHENAIA

This sculpture (right), from the frieze on the Parthenon, shows Athenians leading a sacrificial bull during the annual Great Panathenaia, an ancient festival in honour of their patron goddess, Athene. During the festival, which was the most important and splendid religious event in the Athenian calendar, leading citizens and representatives from all the city's territories brought animals to be sacrificed to the goddess. The sacrifices took place at the high point of the celebrations, when a great procession ended in the presentation of a new embroidered robe (*peplos*) to Athene's statue in the Parthenon, her chief temple.

A red-figure oinochoe (wine cup) of c.450-400BC, decorated with a scene from a sacrificial ritual. Sacrifice to the gods, as an act of thanksgiving, supplication or propitiation, was integral to Greek religious practice. At official rites such as the Panathenaia (see above), animal sacrifice was usual, but in their private devotions people would often make offerings of vegetables, honey or cheese.

Although the origins of ancient Greek religious beliefs remain shrouded in obscurity, the Greek pantheon was clearly well established by *c*.750BC. Its major figures feature prominently in the great epics of Homer, the *Iliad* and the *Odyssey* (see p.157), which were probably composed around that time and show signs of a very long poetic tradition.

The Greeks believed that their lives and destinies were governed by a great number of divinities, the most important of which were the Olympians, the gods and goddesses who lived on Mount Olympus (see p.125). A statue of the god Hermes might mark the doorway of a Greek home, while the hearth was sacred to Hestia (see p.144). Heroes, who were usually the offspring of a god and a woman, were worshipped as eternal spirits who could intercede on behalf of mortals. Their valour and nobility were regarded as exemplary, and their conflicts against monsters (see p.147) were popular subjects of art and literature. Many states claimed a deity or hero as founder or protector, supporting the claim with myths such as that of the contest between Athene and Poseidon (see p.136). Noble families often claimed descent from a hero, such as one of the Argonauts (see p.154).

A host of positive abstract qualities, such as "Justice" and "Youth", were also worshipped as divinities. On the darker side, Greeks feared becoming the victims of the forces of darkness, such as the Furies or the sorceress Hekate (see p.146).

The Olympians (see p.125) were the objects of the most popular and widespread cults. Most religious rites in their honour took place in sanctuaries dedicated to the relevant god or goddess, whose statue stood in a temple which was the focal point of the sanctuary. In front of the temple, in the open air, priests performed sacrifices at an altar as worshippers watched, sometimes from a *stoa* (covered colonnade), and then ate the roasted meat of the sacrifice. Votive offerings, placed around the temple and on its steps, included statues made of bronze, marble and, for the less affluent, terracotta. Outside the sanctuaries of the Olympians, offerings to other divine or semi-divine figures, such as heroes, were made at many individual shrines and altars.

Temples were important public centres for the expression of state culture. Their friezes and pediments often depicted mythological battles between the forces of civilization, represented by the city-state and the Olympians, and the forces of transgression and barbarity, represented by giants and monsters. Athenians in the 5th century bc possessed two institutions for the telling of myth on the grandest scale: the theatre and the poetry recital. Athens invented the theatre as a great public spectacle where some 16,000 citizens could see tragedies which were almost always based on myths and legends. Poetry, in particular that of Homer and Hesiod, was publicly recited by professional performers called rhapsodes. The entire *Iliad* and *Odyssey* were recited at the Great Panathenaia (see margin, opposite). Poems incorporating myths were commissioned and publicly recited to celebrate events such as a citizen's victory at the Olympic games.

Education and intellectual life were underpinned by mythology. The myths told by Homer and Hesiod were central to the teaching of literacy, and myths were a topic for discussion among philosophers, scientists and historians from the 5th century BC onwards.

The gods and goddesses often adorned Greek personal jewelry. These 7th-century BC bronze pectoral plaques from Camirus, Rhodes, bear the image of the goddess Artemis.

The symposium

Many household objects were decorated with mythical scenes, especially the cups, jugs and mixing bowls used for the symposium, in Greek symposion ("drinking together").

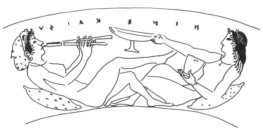

The symposium was an important social event for Greek men. They gathered to lie on couches and drink (wine-drinking was heavily ritualized), converse, generally enjoy themselves, and cement political and social ties. Men regularly recited poems with mythological themes and sang songs by famous poets. The only women present would be hired to provide music, dancing and sex. The illustration (above), taken from a pot, depicts two naked women who may be entertainers at a symposium.

The standard Greek alphabet (only capitals, used for most inscriptions, are given), with their usual English transliterations below:

Α β Γ Δ Ε Ζ Η Θ Ι Κ Λ Μ Ν Ξ Ο Π Ρ Σ Τ Υ Φ Ψ Χ Ω
A B G D E z E th I K L M N X O P R S T Y/U PH PS CH O

THE GREEK LANGUAGE
Our knowledge of the mythology of the Greeks is aided by the fact that countless inscriptions and documents have been found all over what was the ancient Hellenic world. Greek, like Latin and English, belongs to the Indo-European family of languages. It has been a written language for about 3,000 years, and although modern Greek differs considerably from the ancient language, it uses an alphabet (see bottom of page) largely unchanged for about 2,500 years. The alphabet developed from a Semitic one (probably Phoenician) in *c.*950BC, and a number of local variants existed for many centuries. In 403BC the eastern variant called Ionic effectively became the standard Greek script when it was accepted as the official alphabet of Athens, the centre of Greek intellectual life. The humorous inscription on the pot illustrated (panel, left) is written back to front, as was common practice. It reads: ΠΙΝΕ ΚΑΙ ΣΥ (PINE KAI SU), which means "You have a drink too!".

THE BIRTH OF THE GODS

The rise of the Olympians

A monumental stone head, believed to represent Gaia, the primal earth goddess of the Greeks.

Many myths circulated about the beginning of all things and no one version became universally accepted. The most comprehensive account, however, and the one which gained the widest currency, was related by the poet Hesiod in his *Theogony* in the 8th century BC (see panel, opposite). This was the first important attempt to produce a genealogy of the Greek pantheon from the many prevailing popular beliefs. As much a cosmogony as a theogony, it traced the detailed ancestry of the Olympian gods back to the creation of the world out of Chaos. An alternative account of the origin of the world was told by the Orphics, the followers of the mystic cult called Orphism. Their account was more abstract and philosophical in tone than Hesiod's and consequently had a much narrower popular appeal. It begins with Chronos ("time", an Orphic reinterpretation of the name Kronos) accompanied by Adrasteia ("necessity"). From Chronos come Aither, Erebos and Chaos ("upper air", "darkness" and "the yawning void"). In Aither, Chronos fashions an egg, from which is born Phanes, the creator of everything, a bisexual deity with gold wings and four eyes. Phanes is called by many names, including Eros, and has a daughter, Night, who becomes his consort. Night gives birth to Gaia and Uranos. When Zeus takes control he recreates everything anew, swallows Phanes and couples with Kore (Persephone) to produce Zagreus-Dionysos.

THE GENEALOGY OF THE GODS
The table (left) is a simplified representation of the genealogy of the universe and of the gods, according to Hesiod. The twelve Titans and their most important offspring are in italic type, the first Olympians in SMALL CAPITALS. The figures are Eros (top), Okeanos (bottom left) and Helios (bottom).

KEY
Okeanos Titans and their offspring
POSEIDON First generation of Olympians
= Coupled with
   Gave rise to the birth of

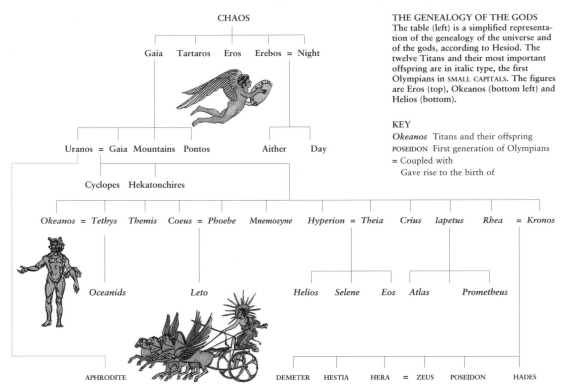

CHAOS

Gaia   Tartaros   Eros   Erebos = Night

Uranos = Gaia   Mountains   Pontos   Aither   Day

Cyclopes   Hekatonchires

Okeanos = *Tethys*   *Themis*   *Coeus* = *Phoebe*   *Mnemosyne*   *Hyperion* = *Theia*   *Crius*   *Iapetus*   *Rhea* = *Kronos*

Oceanids   *Leto*   *Helios*   *Selene*   *Eos*   *Atlas*   *Prometheus*

APHRODITE   DEMETER   HESTIA   HERA = ZEUS   POSEIDON   HADES

The ancestry of the gods

*H*esiod's Theogony *opens with the simple statement, "First of all Chaos came into being", but it is unclear whether Chaos (the yawning void) is conceived of as a divinity. After Chaos (perhaps as progeny, but again this is ambiguous) came Gaia or Ge (the earth), Tartaros (the underworld), Eros (desire), Erebos (the gloom of the underworld) and Night (the gloom of the earth). Then Night coupled with Erebos to produce Aither (the ether, or bright upper air) and Day (the brightness of the world).*

By herself Gaia gave birth to Uranos (the sky), "so that he might surround her and cover her completely and be a secure home for the blessed gods forever", and then to the Mountains and Pontos (the sea). She coupled with Uranos to produce the first divinities: twelve mighty Titans (six male and six female); three Cyclopes, called Brontes ("Thunder"), Steropes ("Lightning") and Arges ("Bright"); and three monsters with a hundred hands each, the Hekatonchires, called Cottus, Briareus and Gyes. Uranos was appalled by his children and locked them in the bowels of the world, but in revenge Gaia persuaded the youngest Titan, Kronos, to castrate his father and seize power. The blood from Uranos' wound spawned giants, nymphs and the Furies, while his severed genitals fell into the sea and turned to white foam, from which was born Aphrodite, the goddess of desire and sexuality.

The Titans populated the world with demi-gods by coupling with nymphs or each other: the offspring of Hyperion and his sister Theia, for example, were Helios (the sun), Selene (the moon) and Eos (the dawn). Another Titan, Iapetus, married the Oceanid Clymene, who produced four children, of whom the most famous were Prometheus ("Forethought"; see pp.130-31), and Atlas, who, after the defeat of the Titans, was condemned by Zeus to hold up the heavens at the western extremity of the world (see p.149): the Atlantic is named after him. Their brothers were Menoetius and Epimetheus ("Afterthought"), husband of Pandora (see p.131). Naïve and rash, Epimetheus was the antithesis of Prometheus. Kronos had several children by Rhea, but he was afraid of being overthrown by them, and swallowed each baby as it was born. However, when Rhea gave birth to Zeus, she deceived her husband by clothing a stone like a baby, which he swallowed instead of the real child. Hidden from his father, Zeus grew up and planned his revenge. He was victorious in a great battle against the Titans, the Titanomachy, after strengthening his position by a trick. Metis, the daughter of the Titan Okeanos (Ocean), served Kronos a drink which made him regurgitate Zeus's brothers and sisters (Poseidon, Hades, Hera, Demeter and Hestia), who joined forces with Zeus. He was supported by the Cyclopes and the Hekatonchires, whom Kronos had kept imprisoned, but Zeus had freed.

After the fall of the Titans, Zeus was challenged by monstrous giants who had sprung from the blood of Uranos. In the ensuing Battle of the Giants, the Gigantomachy, Zeus led the gods to victory and was established as supreme controller of the heavens and earth. He declared that Olympus, the highest mountain in the world, would be a home for the victorious gods and goddesses.

HESIOD, PEASANT AND POET
Hesiod was a farmer, rhapsode (professional reciter of poetry) and authoritative writer on ethics and theology who lived at Ascra in Boeotia *c.*700BC. Two of his major poetic works, the *Theogony* and *Works and Days*, have survived in full, and several are known from fragments or titles alone. The *Theogony* is, in effect, a summary and skilful retelling of prevailing myths about the origins of the world and the gods who ruled it. The *Works and Days*, on the other hand, is more practical in content and is largely taken up with an account of the agricultural year. In the first part, however, Hesiod advises his brother Perses to live his life by the rules of justice, telling him many myths by way of illustration.

THE ORIGINS OF HUMANITY

Prometheus, Pandora, Deucalion, Pyrrha

A black-figure bowl from Laconia in the Peloponnese, showing the torment imposed by Zeus on Prometheus, bound to a tree (more often, a rock) as an eagle plucks at his liver (see panel, opposite). His brother, the Titan Atlas, looks on.

BORN FROM THE EARTH

The Athenians had their own myth of a man born from the soil. The god Hephaistos tried to rape Athene, and when she fended him off, he ejaculated on her thigh. She wiped off his semen with a piece of wool and threw it to the ground in disgust. From this piece of wool was born Erichthonius, a future king of Athens, who was often depicted as part serpent, owing to his connection with the earth.

The Thebans told how Cadmus, the founder of Thebes, killed a great serpent at the site of the future city. He took the serpent's teeth and sowed them in the ground, and from them sprang armed men who fought and killed each other until only five were left. They were called the Spartoi ("sown men"), from whom were descended the noble families of Thebes.

Greek mythology offers no single account of the origins of the human race, attributing the creation of the first people to the earth (Gaia), the Titans, or the Olympians. The idea of birth from the earth itself – "autochthony" – is often encountered. According to one myth, the first man was Pelasgus, who sprang from the soil of Arcadia in the Peloponnese and founded the race of Pelasgians, an ancient non-Greek people whose descendants were still to be found in some villages as late as the 5th century BC.

Another myth tells how Zeus sent a great flood to destroy humanity as a punishment for the misdeeds of the Titan Prometheus (see panel, opposite). Deucalion, son of Prometheus, and his wife Pyrrha, daughter of Epimetheus and Pandora, were warned by the Titan and built an ark in which they survived the deluge. When the waters subsided, Deucalion and Pyrrha went to Delphi to pray to the Titan Themis, who in some accounts is said to be the mother of Prometheus. She told them to throw over their shoulders the bones of the being from whom they were both descended.

Bewildered at first, the couple soon realized that Themis must be referring to Gaia, the earth, whose bones were the stones in the ground. As each stone they hurled behind them landed, it turned into a human being: those thrown by Deucalion became men and those thrown by Pyrrha turned into women. The human race was thus re-created from the soil. At Athens Deucalion is said to have founded a temple in honour of Zeus, whose wrath had now finally abated. In one, simpler, variant of this myth, after the flood the pair made a sacrifice to Zeus, who was placated and promised to grant Deucalion one wish. He asked for the re-creation of humanity.

Greeks looked upon Deucalion as the ancestor of their nation, the first king and the founder of numerous towns and temples. The subsequent development of humanity was explained in the myth of the ages, or races, of man, the best-known version of which was told by Hesiod in the *Works and Days*. In the time of Kronos, Hesiod wrote, the gods made the first men, the Golden Race, who did not suffer old age, sickness or toil, because the earth gave them fruit without labour. They all died – it is not clear why – as if falling asleep, but existed still as holy spirits who protected humans. Zeus and the Olympians then created a Silver Race, who took a century to mature, were arrogant and violent, and did not worship the gods. Zeus hid them underground, where they too continued to exist as spirits.

Zeus also created the last three races. The third race, the Race of Bronze, discovered metals and took steps toward building a civilization, but ended up slaughtering each other and passed ignominiously into the Underworld. Next came the Race of Heroes (according to Hesiod: not all accounts include them), born of human mothers and divine fathers. They were valiant mortals of superhuman strength, and after death they went to the Islands of the Blessed. The fifth race was the Race of Iron, modern humanity, for whom good was always mixed with evil, and toil was necessary. This race would pass away, said Hesiod, when children were born grey and men dishonoured their parents, destroyed cities and praised the wicked.

Prometheus and Pandora

The myths of Prometheus and Pandora helped to explain the hardships which beset humanity. The story of Pandora, created after man and the source of many human woes, served to justify to Greeks the inferior position of women in society.

Although Prometheus had not joined the Titans in opposing Zeus (see p.129), he still resented the defeat of his race and sought to get his own back by fostering men, who had been treated as equals in the days of Kronos but were now regarded as beneath the gods. (In one account, Prometheus himself created the first man, Phaenon, from clay and water.)

Zeus became furious at the way Prometheus protected the new race, and in revenge withheld fire from humans, who were forced to live without heat and light. But Prometheus came to their aid and stole a flame from the forge

The creation of Pandora is depicted on this early 5th-century Attic red-figure vase. It shows (left to right): Zeus, Hermes, Hephaistos and Pandora.

of the god Hephaistos, hidden in a stalk of fennel.

Zeus then asked the god Hephaistos to fashion the first woman, Pandora, from earth. After Athene and the other goddesses had adorned her with beauty, finery and allure, and Hermes had taught her how to deceive, she was sent with a jar ("Pandora's box") as a gift for Prometheus' brother Epimetheus. He took her into society, whereupon she opened the jar and released its contents: evil and sickness. Only hope remained inside.

Having thus punished humans, Zeus turned on Prometheus, binding him to a rock and sending an eagle to peck at his liver. Every time the bird tore out the organ it grew back and the Titan torture recommenced (see illustration, opposite). Prometheus' agony lasted for thousands of years, until he was freed by Herakles.

ZEUS

King of the gods

A greater than life-size bronze statue, almost certainly of Zeus, dating from c.450BC. The god would originally have wielded a thunderbolt.

(see p.129)

Zeus came to power by a combination of violence and trickery and, once established, his rule was permanent and unchallengeable. He took the heavens as his particular domain (his name appears to be derived from an ancient root meaning sky, suggesting that he was originally a sky god), while his brothers Poseidon and Hades became lords of the sea and the underworld respectively. In one account this division of realms was made by drawing lots, but the supremacy of Zeus was never doubted. He married and then swallowed Metis ("cunning intelligence"), who had helped him to defeat Kronos, and with Metis inside him he could not be tricked or manipulated as he himself had tricked and manipulated his way to power.

Next, Zeus married Themis ("right"), the goddess of fixed order, and with her produced the Fates, the seasons, good order, justice and peace. Finally he married Hera, his sister, and their progeny consisted of Ares (the god of war), Hebe ("youth"), Eileithyia (the goddess of childbirth) and, in some accounts, Hephaistos (the craftsman-god). Zeus sired the remaining divinities of the Olympian order, with the exception of Aphrodite, through various other liaisons. There are many myths about Zeus's relationships with human and divine females (and males), many of which are set against the background of his tempestuous relationship with Hera (see margin, below, left, and opposite page). In fact, very few stories about Zeus and Hera are not directly related to their stormy marriage, which is one of the chief sources of conflict in Greek mythology. Typically, the goddess is depicted as a bitter figure, constantly persecuting the objects and offspring of Zeus's adulterous liaisons, almost without exception. However, the persecution is not always one way. In one myth, Zeus becomes so angry with Hera that he attaches an anvil to each of her ankles and hangs the goddess from Mount Olympus. Homer frequently depicts Hera's conflict with Zeus, often with wry amusement. Despite Zeus's extramarital affairs and Hera's inevitable jealous anger, their so-called Sacred Marriage symbolized the importance of wedlock in Greek culture.

Zeus was the supreme power on Olympus. He chaired the council of the gods, and his authority and plan established the course of all things. One of the Seven Wonders of the ancient world was the magnificent gold, ivory and marble sculpture of Zeus at Olympia (see p.125). Standing around forty feet (twelve metres) high, the statue was an embodiment of the god's awesome power. In the human world, Zeus was believed to guarantee the power of kings and the authority of a city's laws. He was also the guardian of social order, and his many manifestations included Zeus Xenios (upholder of "guest-friendship", the courteous social relations between families and cities), Zeus Hikesios (protector of those seeking sanctuary) and Zeus Horkios (protector of the sanctity of oaths). The symbols of Zeus's power were thunder and lightning, as befitted the god of the heavens, and the eagle, the king of the birds. He was often depicted holding a sceptre, the sign of royal power, or a thunderbolt.

Cleanthes (*c*.330BC-*c*.232BC), who from 363BC headed the Stoic school of philosophy, looked upon Zeus in a more abstract way, regarding him as the essential ether of the living universe. In his most notable work, the *Hymn to Zeus*, Cleanthes hails the god as "master of the universe". The philosopher continues: "Nothing on earth, nor in the heavens, nor in the sea, is produced without you."

HERA

Hera, the sister and wife of Zeus, was a major figure in the Greek pantheon in her own right, although there are few stories of her exploits that are not connected with her turbulent marriage to Zeus. There were several important temples to Hera, who was particularly associated with fertility and the sanctity of marriage. The most famous was the Heraion at Argos in the Peloponnese.

THE COUPLINGS OF ZEUS

Human and divine consorts

Greek myth credited Zeus with a string of affairs with both divine and human consorts. Sometimes, for practical reasons or to prevent the interference of his jealous wife Hera, he was obliged to adopt a different form, such as that of a beast, to approach the object of his desire. In any case, he could not appear before mortals in his full divine splendour because the sight was so overwhelming that it meant instant death – the fate which befell Semele. The most famous liaisons of Zeus are given below and continued on p.135: the first three consorts were divine, the others human (see also table on p.134).

Metis
Zeus married the Titan Metis immediately after his accession to power and impregnated her. Gaia and Uranos had prophesied that Metis was destined to bear remarkable offspring: a goddess, Athene, who would equal Zeus in wisdom, and a son, who would become king of gods and men. To prevent the births, Zeus swallowed Metis. Although the son was never conceived, Athene was born, fully armed, from her father's head.

Leto
The daughter of the Titans Coeus and Phoebe, Leto mated with Zeus and conceived divine twins, Artemis and Apollo. Artemis was born on Ortygia, but Leto was forced to travel the world, racked with pain, looking for a place to give birth to Apollo. The jealous Hera prevented her daughter Eileithyia, the goddess of childbirth, from hearing Leto's anguish. Eileithyia was only allowed to attend to the birth when the people of Delos, an island in the Aegean, agreed to permit the birth of Apollo on its

GANYMEDE
Zeus's consorts were not all female. They included Ganymede, the son of King Tros of Troy and famous for his beauty. Zeus became besotted with the youth and decided to kidnap him, so he sent an eagle to pluck Ganymede from the Trojan plain and bring him to Mount Olympus, where he became the cup-bearer to the gods. In another version of the myth, Zeus changes into an eagle and seizes Ganymede himself. The above terracotta figurine of *c.*450BC, a roof sculpture from Olympia, shows Zeus carrying the youth.

The goddess Athene springs, fully armed, from the head of Zeus. In some accounts, the smith-god Hephaistos aided the birth by splitting the god's head open with his axe. A panel from an Attic black-figure amphora, c.540BC.

The consorts and offspring of Zeus

In this table, Zeus's consorts are in **bold**, his offspring in *italics*.

DIVINE CONSORTS

Hera, wife and sister of Zeus.
Ares, god of war, who coupled with Aphrodite and backed Troy against the Greeks (see p.158).
Hebe, goddess of youth, cupbearer to the gods and celestial wife of Herakles.
Eileithyia, goddess of childbirth; Hera commanded her to try to prevent the births of children whom Zeus fathered by other consorts.

Metis, daughter of Okeanos and Thetys (see p.133).
Athene, goddess of wisdom and heroes, born fully grown and fully armed from Zeus's head.

Themis, earth goddess and Titan, daughter of Uranos and Gaia.
The Horai (Seasons), *Moirai* (Fates), *Eunomia* ("order"), *Dike* ("justice") and *Eirene* ("peace"): female deities governing human and divine destinies. The Fates were depicted as three women: *Clotho,* who span the thread of life; *Lachesis,* who measured it out; and *Atropos* who cut it. They were also sometimes said to be the offspring of Night.

Eurynome, a sea nymph, depicted as a woman with the tail of a fish.
Three Graces, divine attendants of Aphrodite: *Aglaia* ("splendour"), *Thalia* ("good cheer") and *Euphrosyne* ("merriment").

Demeter, goddess of crops and the land and a sister of Zeus. A pre-Greek deity in origin (see p.142).
Persephone, carried off by Hades to be queen of the Underworld.

Hera, fully armed. This image of the goddess is taken from an amphora.

Mnemosyne ("memory"), a Titan, the daughter of Uranos and Gaia.
The Muses, nine divinities of the arts, history and astronomy.

Leto, a Titan (see p.133).
Apollo, great god of prophecy, music, archery and medicine.
Artemis, goddess of the hunt, the forest and wild animals; also of virginity, childbirth and female diseases.

Maia (see opposite), daughter of the Titan Atlas.
Hermes, messenger of the gods.

Thetis, a sea nymph. It was prophesied that she would bear a son greater than his father, so Zeus passed her on to Peleus, king of Thessaly, by whom she bore the great hero Achilles (see p.158).

HUMAN CONSORTS

Io, daughter of Inachus, first king of Argos (see p.165).

Epaphos, ruler of Egypt and Africa.

Europa, a Phoenician princess (see margin, opposite).
Minos, the owner of the monstrous Minotaur and of the Labyrinth (see pp.150-51).
Rhadamanthus, who, like Minos, became a judge of the dead in the underworld.

Semele, daughter of Cadmus, the founder of Thebes (see p.135).
Dionysos, Olympian (see p.140).

Danaë, princess of Argos (see p.135).
Perseus, the hero who slew the Gorgon Medusa and saved Andromeda from being eaten by a sea monster (see p.156).

Leda, princess of Sparta (see opposite).
Castor and *Polydeuces,* twins who became semi-divine. They were known as the Dioscuri, in Greek *Dios kouroi* ("sons of Zeus").
Helen, whose elopement with Paris caused the Trojan war.
Clytemnestra, wife and murderer of Agamemnon, king of Argos, who led the Greeks against Troy.

Antiope, Theban princess whom Zeus approached after taking on the form of a satyr.
Zetheus and *Amphion,* joint rulers of Thebes who built its walls.

Alkmene, queen of Tiryns (see p.135).
Herakles ("Glory of Hera"), the greatest Greek hero (see p.148), persecuted by Hera throughout his career.

Ganymede, a beautiful Trojan youth (see p.133).

soil: thereafter Delos became one of the main centres of the worship of Apollo (see p.138).

Maia

Maia was the daughter of the Titan Atlas (see p.129). She was also one of the Pleiades – seven nymphs whom Zeus later changed into stars – and lived in a concealed cave, which allowed Zeus to consummate his desire without attracting the attention of Hera. Nothing else is known of Maia, except that she gave birth to the god Hermes.

Alkmene

Alkmene (see illustration, below right) was married to Amphitryon, king of Tiryns, who like her was a descendant of the hero Perseus. When Amphitryon went away to war, Zeus visited Alkmene in the form of her husband on the day before he was due to return. The god lengthened the night to three times its normal length to extend his pleasure, and when Amphitryon returned he was taken aback by his wife's lack of sexual ardour, while she in turn was surprised that her husband had apparently forgotten the previous night's pleasures. The couple eventually learned the truth from the blind, androgynous prophet Teiresias.

Alkmene bore twin sons. The elder, by Zeus, was Herakles, greatest of all heroes. The younger, by Amphitryon, was Iphikles, whose son Iolaus helped Herakles to kill the Lernean Hydra (see p.149).

Danaë

Acrisius, the king of Argos, was told by an oracle that a son born of his daughter Danaë would kill him, so he locked her in a bronze tower or chamber in his house. Zeus entered the room in the form of a shower of gold and coupled with her, as a result of which she conceived and bore Perseus, whom she kept hidden from Acrisius in the chamber. After four years the king discovered the truth and locked his daughter and grandson in a chest, which he threw into the sea. But Danaë and Perseus were washed ashore and, after many adventures (see p.156), returned to Argos. One day, while taking part in games, Perseus threw a discus which struck and killed Acrisius, thus fulfilling the oracle's prediction.

Leda

Leda was married to Tyndareus, king of Sparta. Zeus came to her in the form of a swan, and she produced four children from two eggs. From one sprang Polydeuces (better known by the Latin version of his name, Pollux) and Helen, and from the other Castor and Clytemnestra. Castor and Polydeuces, who are rarely separated in the myths involving them, journeyed with Jason as part of the crew of the *Argo* on the quest for the Golden Fleece (see p.154). Clytemnestra married King Agamemnon of Argos, and Helen married Agamemnon's brother, King Menelaus of Sparta. The sisters play an important role in the story of the Trojan war and its aftermath: Helen's elopement with the Trojan prince Paris precipitated the war (see p.157), and Clytemnestra was responsible for the murder of her husband on his triumphant return from the conflict (see p.161).

Semele

Zeus, disguised as a mortal, had an affair with Semele, the daughter of Cadmus, founder of Thebes. Hera, out of jealousy, disguised herself as an old woman and persuaded Semele to ask her lover to show himself to her in his full glory. Zeus agreed reluctantly to Semele's request, aware that his appearance in full magnificence, riding in his celestial chariot amid great thunderbolts and lightning, would be too much for any mortal to endure. The unfortunate Semele was burnt to a cinder. However, Zeus saved their unborn child, Dionysos, from her ashes (see p.140).

EUROPA AND THE BULL

The myth of Zeus's liaison with Europa, the beautiful daughter of King Agenor or, in some versions, of King Phoenix of Phoenicia, was almost certainly Cretan in origin, as its location (Crete) and connection with the story of King Minos suggest.

One day, Zeus took on the form of a white bull to approach Europa while she was picking flowers with her friends in a meadow near the sea. The beast's gentleness and beauty overcame her fear, and she was tempted to sit on its back. It wandered down to the seashore and suddenly plunged into the water and swam away, carrying the helpless Europa with it. They came ashore near Gortyn on Crete, where Zeus turned into an eagle and coupled with the kidnapped girl. She later married the Cretan king, Asterius, who adopted the offspring of her union with Zeus: Minos, Rhadamanthus and, in some versions, Sarpedon.

Meanwhile, Europa's brothers had been sent on an unsuccessful search for her. One of them, Cadmus, ended up in Boeotia on mainland Greece, and became the first king of Thebes (see p.130).

The vase below, painted by Python in c.330BC, shows Zeus's unwitting lover Alkmene about to be sacrificed on a pyre by the jealous Amphitryon, in a version of the myth by the dramatist Euripides. The fire is doused at the last minute by the intervention of the Olympian goddesses.

ATHENE

The virgin goddess

A marble statue of c.350BC portraying Athene as the bringer of peace. The goddess sports her helmet and aegis or breastplate (the head of the Gorgon Medusa), but is otherwise unarmed.

One of the most powerful goddesses in the Greek pantheon was Athene, whose birth, fully armed from the head of Zeus, inspired the common representation of her in armour with helmet, spear and shield. She was also usually depicted wearing her aegis, a sort of breastplate or protective robe which she adorned with the head of the Gorgon Medusa, given to her by the hero Perseus (see p.156). As a military figure and great counsellor, Athene was revered by kings and was often associated with the founding of a city's acropolis or citadel, where the royal palace was usually situated. She was also the protector of heroes. In myth, Odysseus was her particular favourite, since his skills of guile, wise counsel and cunning were close to her own qualities. With her aid he devised the wooden horse by means of which Troy was captured. She also assisted Herakles and Perseus in their adventures.

Athene was revered as the defender of cities, especially Athens, of which she was patron and which was the centre of her cult. According to myth, she and Poseidon quarrelled over the patronage of the city and of Attica, the surrounding region. The Athenians suggested that the two Olympians each invent a practical gift for Athens: the best invention would be rewarded with the protectorship of the city. Poseidon hit the Acropolis with his trident and a saltwater spring immediately gushed from the spot where it had struck (in another account his blow produced the first horse). Athene then touched the Acropolis with her spear and produced the olive tree, a source of oil for lighting, cooking and perfume. Delighted at Athene's invention, the Athenians (or in some versions their first king, Cecrops) chose her as their patron. To placate Poseidon, who had flooded the plain around the city in his anger at losing the contest, they agreed that he would also be worshipped at Athens. In classical times the sacred olive tree and the supposed mark of Poseidon's trident were still shown to visitors to the Acropolis.

As her unusual birth might suggest, Athene was particularly associated with activities of the head: she rivalled her father Zeus in wisdom and took after her mother, Metis, in possessing "cunning intelligence". One of her symbols was the owl, the wisest of birds. Like Hephaistos she was a patron of skilled crafts, for example ship and chariot building, and also of such traditionally female domestic activities as spinning and weaving. (Despite her association with these wifely skills, however, Athene was an unmarried virgin goddess.) The goddess was also credited with the invention of the potter's wheel, the first vases and the flute. She loved the sound of the instrument, which was said to have been inspired by the lamenting voices of the other Gorgons after the death of Medusa, although another account claimed that the flute imitated the eerie whistling noise made by Medusa as her throat was slit. But one day Athene caught sight of her reflection as she played the instrument and threw it away in disgust at her distorted features. She put a curse on anyone who might pick up the flute; this curse fell on Marsyas the satyr (see p.138).

A silver four-drachma coin from Athens, bearing an owl, symbol of Athene's wisdom, and the letters "AΘE" (ATHE), an abbreviation of Athene and Athenai (Athens).

Athene was regularly referred to by the cult titles of Pallas (a word which probably means "girl", a reference to her virginity) and Tritogeneia ("born of Triton", a stream in Crete near her supposed birthplace), and was known as *glaukopis* ("grey-eyed"). Of the many cults of Athene, the festival of the Great Panathenaia at Athens was the most celebrated (see p.126). During this event the Athenians presented a sacred robe (*peplos*) to her statue in the Parthenon.

POSEIDON

God of the sea

Poseidon, the brother of Zeus, is an awesome and violent god who is associated with many of the elemental forces of nature. He rules over the sea, particularly its storms and violent weather. He usually carries a three-pronged fork, the trident, which resembles a fisherman's spear. Poseidon is also the presiding deity of earthquakes and is often referred to by the cult title Enosichthon ("Earth-shaker"). He could split the earth and mountains with a blow of his trident, as he did when the Olympians fought the Giants (see p.129). In art, he closely resembles Zeus in appearance and posture, except that he wields his trident rather than a thunderbolt.

The contest for Athens (see opposite) was one of a number of myths to depict Poseidon in opposition to Athene. In the story of Odysseus, Athene supported the warrior hero but the god compelled him to wander the seas. Another myth tells how Poseidon took the form of a horse (in some accounts it was a bird) to couple with the Gorgon Medusa in a temple dedicated to Athene. The goddess was said to be so furious at this act of sacrilege that she turned Medusa's hair into snakes. When the hero Perseus cut off Medusa's head (see p.156), the offspring of her union with Poseidon – the winged horse Pegasus and a son called Chrysaor – sprang from her blood. Through Chrysaor, Poseidon was the ancestor of some of the most famous monsters of Greek myth: the Echidna and her offspring Cerberus, the Chimaera, the Hydra and the Sphinx (see p.147); and the Nemean lion (see p.149).

Poseidon's turbulent love life produced a string of other monsters, sea creatures and marine divinities. He was married to the sea nymph Amphitrite – she was either an Oceanid or a Nereid – and they had a son, Triton, who was human above the waist and fish below. (Triton was represented by a conch shell.) However, like Zeus, Poseidon fathered most of his offspring through acts of infidelity. With Gaia he fathered Antaeus, a giant whom Herakles fought and killed, and Charybdis, a sea monster that spewed out water three times a day and was a danger to ships. When Poseidon made advances to Scylla, a beautiful nymph, the jealous Amphitrite dropped magic plants into the water where she bathed and Scylla was transformed into a dog-headed monster which, like Charybdis, became a hazard for passing sailors.

Poseidon's symbols include the trident, the bull (possibly representing his aggressiveness), and the horse (he is said to have created the first horse for the Athenians and was known by the cult title of Horse-tamer). The god was worshipped at many temples, the best preserved of which occupies a beautiful clifftop site overlooking the sea at Sounion in southern Attica.

There were many water deities besides Poseidon. Pontos (the Sea) was produced by Gaia at the earliest stage of creation. Two Titans, Okeanos (the Ocean, a great river which, the Greeks believed, surrounded the world) and Tethys, produced the Oceanids, or sea nymphs. Pontos and Gaia produced Nereus, the "old man of the sea" who had the gift of prophecy. Nereus coupled with Doris to father the Nereids, fifty sea nymphs who included Thetis, the mother of Achilles, and Galateia, who was loved by the Cyclops Polyphemus.

Poseidon, with his trident and a fish, painted by the late 6th-century BC artist Oltos on a red-figure wine cup.

Poseidon (right) and Amphitrite, from a vase fragment. The dolphin represents Delphinos, one of Poseidon's followers.

APOLLO

The brilliant god

Apollo, the patron of music, playing the cithara, a type of lyre, depicted on a red-figure stamnos (wine jar), c.5th century BC.

According to myth, Apollo was the son of Leto and Zeus and the twin brother of the goddess Artemis. He was born on Delos, the site of his most important cult festival and because of this he is often called Delian Apollo. The other principal site of Apollonian worship was Delphi (see panel, below). His grandmother was the Titan Phoebe and he was often referred to by the masculine form of this word, Phoebus ("Brilliant"). Later he came to be associated with light and the sun.

Apollo had one of the widest ranges of divine attributes. He was mainly represented as a beautiful young male. The patron of archery and bows, his arrows brought plague and sickness to humans, but paradoxically Apollo was also the patron of medicine; he was the father of Asklepios, the greatest of mythical doctors. The patron of music and the arts, he was often depicted with a lyre (see illustration, left). One myth tells how the satyr Marsyas picked up the flute which Athene had cursed (see p.136) and dared to challenge Apollo to a music competition. Like most Olympians, the god hated to see his prowess challenged, and when Marsyas lost the competition Apollo had him flayed alive for his insolence.

Apollo had many loves, most which ended in tragedy. Cassandra, the daughter of King Priam of Troy, agreed to give herself to Apollo, who in return promised her the gift of prophecy. When she reneged, Apollo added a twist to his gift, by ensuring that she was never believed.

Delphi, the centre of the world

According to one myth, Zeus released two eagles from opposite ends of the earth to discover the exact centre of the world. They met at Delphi, which became one of the Greeks' most important religious sites and the focus for the worship of Apollo.

Zeus marked the spot at Delphi where the eagles met with a large stone called the *omphalos* ("navel"), which was guarded by a monstrous serpent, Pytho. Apollo established his sanctuary there and slew Pytho, an act for which he did penance in Thessaly for nine years before returning to Delphi. The oracle he founded at Delphi was consulted by cities and individuals, and its prophecies feature in both myth and history. At the temple of the oracle was a priestess, called the Pythia

A consultation of the Delphic oracle. Themis ("fixed law") sits on the tripod (left). From a red-figure bowl of c.440BC.

(from Pytho, whence also Apollo's commonly encountered epithet "Pythian"), who sat on a tripod to deliver prophecies in response to a visitor's questions. Her answers were delivered in a frenzy of inspired ravings which were transcribed by priests into verse or prose. These predictions, the Greeks believed, always came true, although they were often misunderstood at first.

Delphi was the home of the Pythian games, a great athletic festival believed to have been founded by Apollo which was held in the god's honour every four years. The games took place in the third year of the Olympiad, the four-year interval between the more famous sporting festivals which took place in honour of Zeus at Olympia. The period between Pythian games was called a Pythiad.

ARTEMIS

Chaste goddess of the hunt

Artemis has a wide range of functions in Greek mythology, like her twin brother Apollo. A virgin goddess, she was fiercely protective of her own chastity and that of her companions (see panel, below). She was goddess of the hunt and often ran in the wild with her female attendants. Although she killed animals, she was also the divine protector of young creatures. With similar contradiction, as the goddess of childbirth she protected women in labour, but she also brought death and sickness to women.

Like Apollo, Artemis was represented with a bow. She was usually depicted as a young woman in hunting garb, sometimes with young animals, and often sporting horns in the shape of crescent moons: she was frequently associated with the moon, in the same way that Apollo was associated with the sun. Many of her numerous cults were connected with female times of transition such as birth, puberty and death. On reaching puberty, noble Athenian girls went through Artemisian initiation rites at Brauron, a few miles from Athens, where they were called "bears" – the she-bear was a symbol of the goddess.

IPHIGENEIA

Artemis is associated with the sacrifice of Iphigeneia at Aulis, where the Greek expedition against Troy was gathering (see p.157). Agamemnon, the Greek leader, provoked the wrath of Artemis – either by killing a stag in a sacred grove of the goddess, or by boasting that he was a better hunter than Artemis. The goddess angrily stopped the winds and demanded the sacrifice of Iphigeneia, his virgin daughter, before the fleet could sail. Agamemnon agreed, but (in one version) a stag replaced Iphigeneia at the last moment. She was spirited to Tauris to become a priestess of Artemis.

The wrath of Artemis

*A*rtemis, *like Athene, was a virgin, and if seen by mortals or crossed in her pursuit of chastity she exacted a fierce revenge. Several myths illustrate her wrath, of which these are some of the most famous.*

Actaeon, a hunter, lost his way in the woods and inadvertently came across Artemis bathing in a pool. Artemis was outraged to have been seen naked and turned Actaeon into a stag. He was pursued and torn to pieces by his own hounds.

Callisto was one of the nymphs who attended Artemis. As she slept alone, exhausted after the hunt, Zeus saw her and raped her. Callisto tried to conceal her loss of chastity from Artemis, but after some months the goddess spotted her pregnancy as they bathed. In a rage, Artemis exiled Callisto, exposing her to the jealousy of Hera. When Callisto bore a son, Arcas, Hera discovered

Artemis and her brother Apollo slaughter the Niobids. Their grieving mother, Niobe, asked Zeus to turn her into a marble statue, which continued to shed tears.

her husband Zeus's transgression, and in anger turned Callisto into a bear. She was then shot by Arcas and turned into the constellation Ursa Major (the Great Bear).

Niobe, wife of Amphion, king of Thebes, was the daughter of Tantalus (see p.146) and grand-daughter of the Titan Atlas. She had seven sons and seven daughters (the Niobids) and rashly boasted that she was much more fortunate than Leto, the mother of Artemis and Apollo, who had only two children. Leto was enraged and summoned her children to punish Niobe. Artemis shot the seven girls and Apollo the seven boys.

Orion, a great hunter, tried to ravish Artemis. She produced a scorpion from the earth which killed both Orion and his dog. Afterwards, Orion became a constellation and his dog became Sirius, the Dog Star.

DIONYSOS

God of wine and altered states

PENTHEUS
The most famous tale of tragic opposition to Dionysos is that of Pentheus, memorably told in Euripides' *Bacchae* ("Bacchants"). Pentheus, the grandson of King Cadmus of Thebes, discovers that all the women have left their homes to roam ecstatically in the hills. They are following an "Eastern Stranger", who is claiming to bring the new cult of Dionysos. Pentheus has the stranger (who is really Dionysos in disguise) captured, but he easily escapes. Pentheus is possessed by Dionysos and, dressed as a woman, goes into the hills to spy on the orgiastic revelries of the Bacchants. However, they catch him and, led by his own mother Agave, tear him to pieces in a frenzy. The above detail, from a red-figure drinking vessel of *c.*490BC, depicts the death of Pentheus.

When people were drunk, acting, or in a state of religious ecstasy, they were believed to be in the realm of the god Dionysos, who presided over illusion and altered states. He often appeared in disguise, for example as an animal (usually a bull or lion) or a human (male or female), and is therefore sometimes hard to recognize and define. Although he fought in the battle against the Titans (see p.129), Dionysos is often depicted as effeminate and ridiculous. The playwright Euripides famously called him "most gentle and most terrible".

Also known as Bacchus, Dionysos was the god of wine in all its aspects. Wine was always a sacred drink in Greece and its consumption was ritualized: it played a part in most religious festivals and there were celebrations to mark both the grape harvest and the opening of new casks, over which Dionysos presided. He was the object of a mystic cult whose initiates were promised an afterlife of continual drinking and revelling. In one important story, the god himself underwent a resurrection, which explains one of his cult epithets, "twice-born". Zeus and Persephone had a child called Zagreus (another name for Dionysos). The jealous Hera prompted the Titans to devour the baby, but its heart was saved by Athene and returned to Zeus. Dionysos was then carried by his lover Semele, the daughter of Cadmus, king of Thebes. On her demise (see p.135), Zeus saved the unborn child and stitched him into his own thigh, from where he was born. Thus, Dionysos, alone of the gods on Olympus, had partly mortal parentage. His precise birthplace was debated even in Homer's time, when different traditions located the site in Draconium on the island

Dionysos and the pirates (see opposite page), painted on the bottom of a bowl. The god, who has caused vines to grow from the mast, has turned the pirates into dolphins.

of Cos, on the island of Icarus, near the river Alpheus in Elis, and at Thebes. Zeus entrusted Dionysos after his birth to the care of nymphs on Nysa, a mountain of unknown location but sometimes placed in Egypt.

Although an ancient god, Dionysos was often depicted as a newcomer who travelled among humans bringing gifts, demanding recognition and punishing those who did not accept him. He faced much opposition on these journeys, which are often said to start "from the east". Fleeing from the king of Thrace, Lycurgus, the god jumped into the sea to seek refuge with Thetis, a former consort of Zeus. Lycurgus was struck blind and pulled apart by Dionysos' supporters. In Argos, the daughters of Proteus refused to accept the god, so he drove them mad in punishment. In Orchomenos, the daughters of Minyas refused to worship the new deity and stayed at home weaving. Dionysos took the shape of a girl to warn them to change their minds, but to no avail: they too were driven mad. In Athens, in the age of King Pandion, Dionysos was received by Icarius and gave the city wine in gratitude. When the people felt the effects of the gift, they thought they had been poisoned and turned on Icarius and killed him. When the king's daughter, Erigone, found his corpse and hanged herself in grief, a plague struck Athens and ceased only when a festival was established to honour both her and Icarius.

One of the most vivid stories tells how the god was captured by pirates. They tried to tie him up, but the knots kept untying of their own accord. The pirates still refused to release him, so he amazed them with a series of wonders. He made delicious wine flow around the ship and caused vines and ivy to grow over the vessel; finally he turned himself into a fierce lion, at which the sailors leapt into the sea in terror and were turned into dolphins (see illustration, opposite).

Dionysos was portrayed in art both as a youth and as a bearded adult, often with satyrs and maenads, his female followers (see panel, below), and clutching a drinking vessel amid some celebration.

Satyrs and maenads (see panel, below), followers of Dionysos, engage in a Dionysiac rite under the god's influence. This scene, appropriately, decorates a drinking vessel.

Satyrs, maenads and the theatre

A red-figure drinking cup of c.490BC showing actors preparing to take part in the satyr play.

The mythical male followers of Dionysos were the satyrs, creatures who were part man and part goat with horses' tails. His female followers, both in myth and reality, were called Bacchants ("women of Bacchus") or maenads ("mad women").

Satyrs were addicted to wine, revelry and lust and were usually depicted naked, in a permanent state of sexual arousal. They often pursued maenads, but were happy to consummate their desire with any creature or even with inanimate objects. The Athenian satyr play was a bawdy comedy, usually performed after a tragedy, with a chorus of men in satyr costumes. In Athens, drama took place at two festivals of Dionysos, the Great Dionysia and the Lenaia. His cult involved, in particular, an ecstatic release brought on by dance, music and wine, hence one of Dionysos' cult names, Lusios ("releaser").

Maenads dressed in faun skins and wore garlands of ivy. Each carried a *thyrsus*, a staff with a pine cone-like decoration on the end, and gathered in a ritual group to go to the mountains, where they would sing and dance to exhaustion in celebration of the god. It was said that maenads would rip apart a sacrificial animal with their bare hands and eat it.

GODDESSES OF THE SOIL

Demeter and Persephone

The remains of a painted marble statue of Kore (Persephone) from Athens (c.510BC). She is holding an apple or pomegranate.

THE ELEUSINIAN MYSTERIES
The mysteries at Eleusis in Attica were the most famous and widely celebrated mystery cult in the ancient Greek world. Its initiates were promised a special life in the underworld after death, and its rites were kept secret so successfully over hundreds of years that even today we cannot fully know what happened. Anyone, even women and slaves, could be initiated. The mystic initiation festival was an international occasion, and each year, in September and October, a truce in any current wars was declared for 55 days to allow its celebration. Great processions went from Athens to Eleusis with songs and other ritual celebrations. The initiation festival, over a two-day period, involved a dramatic enactment of a myth of Demeter and Persephone, a revelation of sacred objects and the uttering of certain prayers. The initiates fasted. Central to the cult were the agricultural motifs of the story of Demeter.

The goddess Demeter ("Grain Mother" or "Mother Earth"), daughter of Kronos and Rhea and sister of Zeus and Hades, was believed to protect crops and the bounty of the soil. Her cults also concern female fruitfulness, and she is probably related to the ancient Great Mother. Her daughter Persephone, who is often simply called Kore ("maiden"), was said to be a queen of the underworld. Mother and daughter are usually represented together.

The two figures are linked in a myth which was important for the mysteries at Eleusis, the central cult of mystic initiation in Greek society. One day, Persephone was picking flowers in a meadow with the Oceanids, the daughters of Okeanos and Tethys, when Hades kidnapped her in his chariot and took her to the underworld. She called on Zeus for help, but he failed to hear her in his distant temple, and only Hekate, a goddess of sorcery, and Helios, the sun, heard her cries. Catching the echo of her daughter's voice on the sea, Demeter tore off her headdress and, carrying torches, wandered the earth for nine days without food or sleep. On the tenth day she met Hecate, who sent her to Helios. He told her what had happened and blamed Zeus, who had given Hades permission to take Persephone as his wife. Grief-stricken and furious, Demeter refused to stay on Olympus and wandered out into the world of humans disguised as an old Cretan woman called Doso.

Eventually she came to Eleusis, where, at the instigation of his daughters, the kindly King Celeus hired her as an attendant for his wife Metaneira, who at once recognized Demeter's nobility and offered her a seat and a drink. The disguised goddess refused, preferring to stand in silence until a slave called Iambe, the daughter of Pan and Echo, made her laugh with her jokes and eased her grief. (This is the origin of "iambic" poetry, which is characterized by lampoons and satire.) Metaneira asked Demeter to nurse her child, Demophöon. The goddess surreptitiously fed him on ambrosia, the food of the gods, and each night laid him in the fire to make him immortal. One night she was disturbed by Metaneira, who screamed in horror at the sight of her nurse putting the child in flames. Demeter hastily withdrew him and revealed herself as a goddess, angrily telling Metaneira that Demophöon would now die like any other mortal. She ordered the establishment of the Eleusinian mysteries in her own honour, and then left her hosts.

When Demeter's grief for Persephone returned, she decided to withhold the grain from the earth. Zeus and the other gods pleaded with her to let the crops grow, but she refused, threatening to starve humanity unless she saw her daughter again. Zeus relented and sent Hermes to bring back Persephone from the underworld. Hades agreed to let Persephone return to her mother, but persuaded her to eat some pomegranate seeds, which were a symbol of unbreakable wedlock. Demeter was delighted to receive her daughter and asked if she had eaten anything in the underworld; if so, she would have to return to Hades forever. As she had eaten the pomegranate seeds, it looked as though Persephone would be lost, until Zeus intervened. Persephone, he declared, would spend two-thirds of each year on Olympus and return to Hades for the winter.

Mother and daughter celebrated together and fruitfulness returned to the land. At Demeter's instigation the son of Celeus, Triptolemus (who is sometimes associated with Demophöon), took the arts of agriculture to all peoples of the world.

ARES AND APHRODITE

War, love and sex

Although Ares, the god of war, was worshipped across the Greek world, there are very few myths about him. A son of Zeus and Hera, he is generally depicted as a strong, even brutal warrior, but apart from his appearances on the battlefield, it is primarily as the lover of Aphrodite, the great goddess of love and desire, that he figures in Greek myth. Aphrodite's name means "born of foam": she was believed to have sprung from the foam of the sea at the point where Uranos' severed genitals fell (see p.129). She was brought to Cythera in Cyprus, where she was decorated and anointed by her attendants, the Graces and the Seasons. She was commonly called "lover of laughter", and was associated with all aspects of sexuality, marriage and physical attraction. Often the goddess was depicted naked and accompanied by Eros, the winged god of desire.

Aphrodite was married to the craftsman-god Hephaistos (see p.145) but also took several lovers. The story of her affair with Ares is recounted in Homer's *Odyssey*. Helios, the Sun, spotted Aphrodite and Ares together, and told Hephaistos. The craftsman produced a wonderful net, as fine as gossamer and as strong as adamantine, which fell over the couple as they lay together in bed, capturing them in the act of adultery. Hephaistos triumphantly summoned the gods to witness the outrage, but they only laughed, Hermes and Apollo joking that it was worth the shame of being caught just to sleep with Aphrodite. Ares was freed when he agreed to pay Hephaistos in recompense. The lovers fled the scene in embarrassment.

Another of Aphrodite's loves was Adonis, a beautiful youth and hunter. The goddess warned him of the dangers of hunting, but he continued to frequent the woods and was killed by a wild boar which gored him in the groin. Ritual songs of lament for Adonis were sung each year at the Athenian festival of the Thesmophoria.

THE CHILDREN OF APHRODITE

Aphrodite bore several offspring as a consequence of her numerous liaisons. These are among the most notable:

AENEAS, son of Aphrodite and a Trojan prince, Anchises, whom she had seduced (and terrified) while he was a shepherd in the hills. Aphrodite protected Aeneas in battle at Troy; after Troy's defeat he escaped to found Rome (see pp.172-3).

EROS ("desire"), the winged god who often accompanies images of Aphrodite. He is often called her child, but for the Greeks his parentage was a famous problem. Ares is sometimes said to be his father. Eros is usually depicted with bow and arrows.

HERMAPHRODITE, the child of Hermes and Aphrodite. He was loved by Salmacis, a water nymph. He tried to avoid her, but when he dived into the spring in which she lived, she embraced him until they became fused. He prayed as he died that all who entered the spring should also acquire both male and female attributes: hence the English word "hermaphrodite".

PRIAPUS, a rustic god of fertility who protected gardens and orchards. He was represented as an ugly old man with a large erect phallus. There are many comic and obscene stories about Priapus, whose paternity was variously attributed to Hermes, Dionysos, Pan and Zeus.

A terracotta figure representing the birth of Aphrodite, who is depicted rising from the waves, flanked by cockleshells. It was made in the late 1st century BC in Magna Graecia ("Great Greece"), the Greek areas of southern Italy.

HOME, HEARTH AND FIRE

Hermes, Hestia and Hephaistos

Hermes, in winged hat and sandals, is depicted as the transporter of souls to the underworld on this terracotta plaque from southern Italy. He is stepping into a chariot where Aphrodite, who bore their child Hermaphrodite (see p.143), awaits. The vehicle is drawn by Eros and Psyche.

HERMES THE THIEF

The Homeric *Hymn to Hermes* gives a witty account of the god's birth. The son of Zeus and Maia, a daughter of the Titan Atlas, he was born at dawn. By midday he had invented the lyre and learned how to play it. As god of windfalls, he had found a tortoise by the mouth of the cave where he was born. He had stretched a hide across the shell, fashioned strings and a bridge, and immediately struck up a playful and erotic hymn to his parents. In the evening of that same first day, Hermes stole Apollo's cattle, driving them backwards to confuse their owner. (He had even made himself special shoes to aid the trick.)

Apollo caught up with him and took him to Zeus for punishment. Hermes first lied and tried to use his age as a defence; then he played his lyre so beautifully that Apollo agreed to accept it as a gift, in return for dropping all charges. Apollo and Hermes are often associated as companions in later myth.

The god Hermes and the goddess Hestia were often linked as co-protectors of the home. A statue of Hermes stood by the door of the house, its boundary, and was thought to bring luck (he also presided over windfalls and lucky finds). As this position might suggest, Hermes was not a figure of stability and permanence, like Hestia, so much as one of motion, transition and exchange. This can be seen in the many different spheres in which Hermes operated. The counterpart of the Roman god Mercury, he was the messenger of the gods, and was commonly depicted wearing winged sandals and a *petasos* or traveller's hat (with or without wings), and carrying a herald's staff, which could double as a magic wand. Hermes was the god of travellers and roads, and in Attica his statue marked crossroads. He was also known as Psychopompos ("transporter of souls"), because he was said to escort the souls of the dead to the underworld: it was doubtless for this reason that Zeus chose Hermes to bring Persephone from Hades (see p.142). The god's staff was often adorned with two intertwined snakes, which were symbols of the soil and the underworld.

Hermes represented transaction and exchange. He was the god of the marketplace and the patron of merchants – and of thieves. This dual role of proper and improper exchange applied in the realm of language: he was the carrier of the divine word to mortals, but he also purveyed devious and corrupt communication – lies, false oaths and deceptions. When a sudden silence fell in a conversation (in other words, when communication was broken), the Greeks used to say: "Hermes is passing." His communicative gifts were put to good effect in his most famous exploit, the killing of the hundred-eyed monster Argos. He lulled Argos to sleep with stories before despatching him and earning his most common title, Argeiophontes, "slayer of Argos".

Hestia, the virgin goddess of the hearth, was associated with stability, permanence and prosperity, and was usually represented as an austere woman, seated and shrouded in robes. There were few stories about her in the mythic tradition, but she was clearly of great symbolic and ritual importance. She was said to attend the naming and legitimation of children, which involved carrying them around the hearth in a ritual called the Amphidromion. Every house had its hearth, and thus its focus for the worship of Hestia.

Hephaistos, the equivalent of the Roman god Vulcan, was the god of fire and volcanoes, and a divine inventor and builder of magical things. His name was often used in Greek poetry simply to mean "fire", but he was usually represented as a lame smith who forged remarkable objects. He is portrayed as more benign and less wrathful than most of the Olympians, although not necessarily less passionate, as his attempted rape of Athene demonstrates (see p.130).

The god's cult originated in Asia Minor and nearby islands, especially Lemnos, and one of his chief cult sites was on Mount Olympus in Lycia (in what is now southeast Turkey), called Lycian Olympus to distinguish it from its more famous namesake. In myth, Hephaistos was sometimes described as the child of Zeus and Hera, but more commonly he was said to be the child of Hera alone, who bore him without a father in order to avenge the motherless birth of Athene from the head of Zeus. In some accounts, Hephaistos was born first and subsequently assisted at the birth of Athene (see margin, right). The two deities were often associated as the source of the arts and technical skills.

Hephaistos was lame, and on account of this was often the target of jokes among the other gods of Olympus. He was married to Aphrodite, the goddess of sexuality, but there was a price for being the consort of such a desirable goddess: he was frequently cuckolded, most famously by Ares (see p.143). When Hephaistos was born, Hera was so ashamed of her child's disability that she threw him from heaven into the Ocean, the great river which surrounded the world. He took his revenge by sending Hera a beautiful golden throne he had made, which gripped her tight with invisible straps when she sat on it. Only Hephaistos could free her, but he refused even to leave the Ocean unless he could marry Aphrodite. Attempts to bring Hephaistos back to Olympus failed until Dionysos got him drunk, sat him on a mule and led him back to the other gods, who howled with laughter at the sight of him. A spirit of reconciliation prevailed: Hephaistos released his mother and was given the hand of Aphrodite. The story of the return of Hephaistos to Olympus is one of the most frequently encountered myths about the god, and was often depicted on Greek vases.

The technical skills of Hephaistos were a compensation for his physical handicap. As well as making the golden throne for his mother Hera, the god also made golden female attendants to help him at his work, golden guard dogs which never slept for the palace of Alcinous (as reported in the *Odyssey*), and many other magical creations. After he had been thrown into the Ocean he was comforted by Thetis, at whose request he made a shield for her son, the hero Achilles, which is described at length in Homer's *Iliad*. In many stories, Hephaistos' forge was placed on or near Mount Olympus in Greece and sometimes under the ground, particularly in areas of volcanic activity. The Cyclopes, who forged Zeus's thunderbolt, were said to be his assistants.

Hephaistos is commonly portrayed wearing the short tunic worn by smiths and other craftsmen, as on the above Greek red-figure container of the 5th century BC, which was found in an Etruscan tomb at Vulci in Italy. The god (centre) is holding the axe with which he has just split open the head of Zeus (right) to release Athene (see also p.136). Poseidon stands on the left.

THE UNDERWORLD

The kingdom of Hades

The underworld is frequently encountered in Greek myth. It was ruled by the god Hades (a name also used to mean the underworld itself). Hades was a brother of Zeus and Poseidon but he was usually excluded from the list of Olympians, because his realm was opposed to the celestial Olympus. The underworld was where the souls of dead mortals were judged and, if necessary, punished in the dark infernal regions of Erebos or Tartaros. However, it also encompassed the lands of the divine dead, the Elysian Fields or Islands of the Blessed. One tradition, followed by Homer, placed Hades in the sunless region beyond the great river Ocean which surrounded the earth, but as the Greeks discovered more of the world a new tradition located it in the centre of the earth, connected to the land of the living via unfathomed caves and by rivers which flowed partly underground, such as the Acheron in northern Greece. The Acheron (river of woe) was one of five infernal rivers. The others were: the Styx (river of hate), which surrounded the underworld, Lethe (river of forgetfulness), Cocytus (river of wailing) and Phlegethon or Puriphlegethon (river of fire). Charon, the boatman of the underworld, ferried the souls of the dead across the Styx and, in some accounts, the other rivers.

This red-figure vase shows most of the important characters associated with the Greek underworld. In the centre the god Hades, ruler of the underworld, is enthroned in his palace; standing next to him is his consort Persephone. The other figures shown are (anticlockwise from top left): Megara, the wife of Herakles, and two of her children (see p.148); Orpheus with his lyre, leading some of his cult followers, the Orphics (see p.165); Sisyphus, a king of Corinth, who tried to cheat death and was condemned by the gods forever to push a rock to the top of a mountain: every time he almost reached the top, it rolled back down again. He is whipped by one of the Furies (Erinnyes), fierce goddesses who sought out the guilty on earth and meted out punishment to the dead; the god Hermes (see p.144), here in his role of Psychopompos, "Transporter of the Souls"; Herakles and Cerberus, the three-headed dog that guarded the gates of the underworld (see p.149); another Fury; Tantalus, a king of Asia Minor, who in one account stole ambrosia and nectar from the gods; his infernal punishment was to suffer eternal thirst and hunger, with food and drink always just beyond his reach – hence the word "tantalize"; Minos (see pp.150 and 162), Rhadamanthys and Aeacus, the three judges of the dead, who assessed the past life of anyone who entered the underworld, in order to determine how they would be treated; and two penitents before a seated fury.

HEROES AND MONSTERS

The world's prodigies

A bowl decorated with a painting of a Gorgon and the bodies of two of her victims.

In Greek myth the exploits of mighty and fearless individuals are second in importance only to those of the gods, and people revered these heroes in much the same way as they paid tribute to their ancestors. Indeed, the great heroes were often looked on as national ancestors, founders of the great families and cities of Greece.

The word "hero" was used as a term of address by the princes who inhabit the world of Homer's great epics, the *Iliad* and the *Odyssey*. In these earliest Greek texts the word seems to mean a great personage, a prince or a king, often with a large retinue and a special relationship with the Olympian gods and other deities. Achilles, for example, was said to be the son of Thetis, Sarpedon the son of Zeus, and Odysseus the favourite of Athene.

Heroes were figures of the past for Homer (*c.*750BC or earlier), but not figures of religious worship, nor did they have special status after death. However, for Hesiod (*c.*700BC) they were one of the five races of men who had so far existed (see p.131), a special group who in his time lived under the earth and received special honour and offerings from the living. By the 5th century BC the hero cult had become a popular form of religious worship; to have a hero on your side was believed to be a great advantage, and people made offerings to heroes at shrines which were usually built on the supposed site of their death or burial. There were many local heroes, and many great figures of myth were honoured as heroes in particular places, for example Oedipus at Colonus, Ajax at Salamis and Theseus at Athens (see p.150).

It was believed that honouring a hero with cult offerings helped to secure his aid in times of crisis, while insulting him risked incurring his wrath. Heroes could demonstrate both good and evil power. For example, Herakles, the great civilizer who rid the world of monsters, was driven mad for a time by the goddess Hera and massacred his own wife Megara and their children (see p.149 and illustration opposite). Another example is Oedipus, the wise and benevolent king of Thebes, who unwittingly committed the deadly crimes of parricide and incest (see p.163).

MONSTERS

The heroes of Greek myth were often confronted by monstrous creatures. These are some of the most notable:

ECHIDNA, a creature with the upper body of a nymph and the lower body of a repulsive serpent, was the mother of several other monsters: Cerberus, the Hydra, the Chimaera, the Sphinx and the Nemean Lion.

GORGONS, three snake-haired women, Stheno, Euryale and Medusa, whose look could turn people to stone (see p.156).

SIRENS (right), female creatures, often depicted with wings, who lured sailors to their deaths with their bewitching song (see p.161).

THE SPHINX (right), literally "strangler", a being with the face of a woman, the body of a lion and the wings of a bird. It asked riddles and destroyed those who could not answer (see p.163).

GRAEAE, "aged ones", three old sisters of the Gorgons, who had to share one eye and one tooth (see p.156).

THE HYDRA (right), "water-snake", a huge serpent (see p.149) with nine or more heads.

CERBERUS, a monstrous three-headed dog which guarded the gates of the underworld (see p.149 and illustration opposite).

THE CHIMAERA, a lion-like, fire-breathing creature with a goat's head on its back and a serpent for a tail.

HERAKLES

The archetypal hero

Herakles, who was called Hercules by the Romans, was the only hero honoured throughout the Greek world and the only human to be granted immortality among the gods. He sums up much of the paradox of heroism as portrayed in Greek myth. He vanquished monsters and struggled with Death to save a friend, yet he was also the victim of his lust and greed: he raped women, destroyed cities and in his madness killed his own children. In later Greek writing, Herakles became a philosophical hero who chose the path of virtue and underwent suffering to pursue it. In this guise he entered Christian traditions.

According to myth, Herakles was the son of the illicit liaison of Zeus and Alkmene, who was descended from the hero Perseus. Alkmene was an unwitting party to the adultery (see p.135), which may explain why Zeus's wife Hera chose to take her jealousy out on Herakles rather than his mother. Hera persecuted the hero throughout his life, occasioning many of his heroic exploits, including the celebrated Twelve Labours. Hence, the common explanation of the name Herakles: "glory of Hera". His mettle was tested within a few days of his birth, when he was laid in a crib (a shield in some accounts) with his half-brother Iphikles. Hera sent monstrous snakes to destroy the infants, but Herakles strangled them.

The hero was often engaged in combat. He killed Cycnus, the robber son of Ares, who lived in Thrace, and King Syleus of Aulis, who compelled strangers to work in his vineyard and then slit their throats. He fought against the Lapiths, a fabulous race from Thessaly, and against the Egyptians. In these and many other myths Herakles is portrayed as the greatest of fighters, whose exploits took him all over the world. He went on the expedition of Jason and the Argonauts (see p.154), taking Hylas, his young male lover, with him. But when Hylas went to fetch water and was snatched by water nymphs, Herakles spent so long looking for him that the *Argo* sailed on without the hero.

An Attic red-figure vase (c.5th-century BC) depicting the apotheosis of Herakles, who is carried off to Olympus in a chariot accompanied by gods. His funeral pyre and attendants are shown at the bottom of the scene.

Herakles was often characterized as a slave to his passions. In Greek comedy he was depicted as a drunkard, a glutton and a lecher, and in myth he was said to have slept with the fifty daughters of one King Thespios in a single night. Indeed, it was his lust that led to his death. Herakles married Deianeira, daughter of King Oenus of Aetolia, after defeating the river god Achelous to win her hand. Some time later he killed a Centaur, Nessus, who tried to rape his new wife; as the Centaur was dying, the creature gave Deianeira a potion which, he claimed, would keep her husband's love forever. She decided to put it to the test when Herakles fell for Iole, daughter of King Eurytus of Oechalia, and went as far as slaying her father and brothers and sacking their city to win her. Deianeira, in an attempt to regain his affections, smeared a shirt with the Centaur's potion and sent the garment to her husband. But Nessus had lied: the potion was really a terrible poison, which destroyed Herakles' body. Deianeira killed herself in grief, but the dying Herakles was carried by their son, Hyllus, to Mount Oeta, where the hero ordered a funeral pyre to be built.

Herakles lay on the pyre, which then was lit by Philoctetes, the only one of his followers prepared to carry out this grim task (for which he received the grateful hero's bow and arrows). As the flames took hold, a cloud appeared and took Herakles up to heaven amid a glorious display of thunder and lightning. He entered Olympus, the realm of his father Zeus, where he was granted immortality, reconciled with Hera, and given Hebe, the goddess of youth, as a new wife.

The Labours of Herakles

The most famous exploits of Herakles were eventually systematized in the story of the Twelve Labours. The most common version of the myth recounts how Hera sent Herakles into a fit of madness, during which he killed his wife and children. The oracle at Delphi told him that in penance he must serve Eurystheus, king of Tiryns, for twelve years. Eurystheus imposed twelve gruelling tasks on his servant, as related below. The first six labours took place in the Peloponnese.

Herakles wrestles the Nemean Lion, as Athene (right) looks on. A black-figure vase of c.550BC.

1. **The Nemean Lion.** Herakles was sent to the land of Nemea to kill a monstrous lion, whose hide was impervious to any normal weapon. The hero fashioned a huge club with which he battered the lion before strangling it and cutting through its skin with its own claws. He donned the lionskin, which rendered him invulnerable.

2. **The Lernaean Hydra.** The hero had to slay this nine-headed water-snake, which lived in a swamp near Lerna; but whenever Herakles cut off one head, two more grew in its place. Herakles was aided by Iolaus (the son of his half-brother Iphikles) who cauterized each decapitated neck with a burning torch, preventing the growth of new heads.

3. **The Cerynean Hind.** This bronze-hooved and golden-horned beast lived on Mount Cerynea and was sacred to Artemis: Herakles had to capture it unharmed or incur her anger. After a year's pursuit he wounded the beast and carried it back to Eurystheus, whom he blamed for the hind's injury, thereby avoiding the wrath of Artemis.

4. **The Erymanthian Boar.** A monstrous boar was ravaging the area around Mount Erymanthus and Herakles was ordered to bring it back alive. On the way, he defeated the Centaurs in battle. He eventually returned to Eurystheus with the boar, which terrified the king so much that he hid in a bronze urn.

5. **The Augean Stables.** Augeas, son of Helios, owned great herds of cattle. They were kept in stables that had never been cleaned out and were piled high with the enormous quantities of dung that had built up over many years. Herakles was given the noisome task of cleaning out the filth in just one day, which he achieved by diverting the rivers Alpheus and Peneus through the stables.

6. **The Stymphalian Birds.** Lake Stymphalos in Arcadia was home to a flock of monstrous birds that ate humans and had beaks, claws and wings of iron. Herakles was commanded to get rid of them. He frightened them out of their trees by clashing bronze castanets, and then shot them one by one with his bow.

7. **The Cretan Bull.** A giant bull was running wild on the island of Crete and terrifying the population. On the orders of Eurystheus, Herakles captured it and brought it back alive to Tiryns.

8. **The Mares of Diomedes.** Herakles was commanded to bring back a herd of mares belonging to the Thracian Diomedes, who fed the beasts on human flesh. Herakles killed him and fed him to his own mares, which he tamed and took back to Eurystheus.

9. **The Girdle of Hippolyte.** Hippolyte, the queen of the warlike Amazon women of Asia Minor, possessed a beautiful girdle which was coveted by the daughter of Eurystheus. Herakles fought and defeated the Amazons and killed Hippolyte, taking the girdle from her corpse.

10. **The Cattle of Geryon.** Geryon, a three-bodied monster, lived in the far west and kept red cattle, helped by a giant herdsman and his hound. Herakles borrowed the Cup of the Sun to sail on Okeanos, the Ocean (see p.137), to Geryon's land. He killed Geryon, the herdsman and the hound, and returned to Eurystheus with the cattle. The Pillars of Herakles (Straits of Gibraltar) mark this most westerly point of Herakles' adventures.

11. **The Apples of the Hesperides.** The Hesperides were nymphs of the far west, daughters of the Titan Atlas. They tended a tree bearing golden apples which Herakles was ordered to bring back. Herakles slew Ladon, a dragon guarding the tree, and stole the apples.

12. **Cerberus.** Herakles' final task was to bring up the fierce three-headed dog, Cerberus, which guarded the gates of the underworld. The hero entered the underworld, wrestled with Cerberus, and dragged him off to show Eurystheus (see illustration on p.146). Herakles then sent him back to the underworld.

THESEUS

Athenian hero and statesman

A vase of c.480BC (reconstructed below) shows Theseus fighting Sciron (left) and Procrustes (right) on the way to Athens. The vase, from an Etruscan site at Cerveteri in Italy, was made by the painter and potter Eurphonios and probably painted by Onesimos. They were among the finest Greek artists of their time.

ARIADNE

After Theseus left the Labyrinth on Crete, he took Ariadne and his young companions and sailed for Athens. When they reached the island of Naxos, he deserted Ariadne, leaving her asleep on the shore, either because he had forgotten her, or, as it is more frequently recounted, as an act of deliberate male treachery.

However, the story of Ariadne has a happy ending. The god Dionysos, accompanied by his full retinue, discovered the girl weeping on the beach and married her amid great celebrations which were attended by the gods. He later turned her into the Corona, a constellation for sailors to steer by. The Athenian red-figure cup below (c.390-380BC) shows Dionysos and Ariadne accompanied by Eros, the winged god of love.

Theseus was a distinctively Athenian hero, but his early life followed a common pattern: an unusual birth, the return to a home from which he had been separated at an early age, exploits against monsters to prove his manhood, and subsequent kingship. Theseus' father was Aegeus, king of Athens, although in many accounts his paternity is attributed to Poseidon. Aegeus was childless and went on a journey to Delphi to consult the oracle, which warned him not to "undo the wineskin's mouth" until he got home, or one day he would die of grief. But on the way back to Athens he visited King Pittheus of Troezen, who got Aegeus drunk and gave him his daughter Aethra to sleep with. She became pregnant, and when Aegeus left Troezen, he told Aethra that if the child was a boy he was to come to Athens as soon as he could lift a particular rock, under which Aegeus had left a sword and a pair of sandals as tokens of recognition. The child was Theseus, who as a young man was told of his true origins by Aethra. He retrieved the sword and sandals and set out for Athens.

On the way he tested his mettle by defeating a string of monsters and brigands. Near Corinth, for example, he slew Sinis, known as Pityocamptes ("pine-bender"), who would strap travellers between two bent-over pine trees and then let them go, tearing the unfortunate victims in two. At Megaris he met Sciron, who made travellers wash his feet and while they knelt would kick them into the sea to be eaten by a huge turtle. Theseus hurled him over a cliff. At Eleusis he defeated Cercyon, who forced travellers to wrestle with him to the death. Between Eleusis and Athens the hero killed Procrustes, who fitted all travellers to the same bed: those who were too long he chopped down to size, while those who were too short he would stretch to the right length. Finally, Theseus arrived at his father's city, where the sorceress Medea tried to poison him (see p.153). The attempt was thwarted when Aegeus recognized the sword and sandals and greeted his heir. Theseus' first exploit in his father's service was to capture a bull (the same one that Herakles had brought back from Crete: see p.149) which was terrorizing the area around Marathon in Attica.

Athens was forced to pay a tribute of seven boys and seven girls to Minos, king of Crete, and Theseus volunteered to accompany the victims.

Phaedra, the tragic queen

One of the most famous episodes in the mythology of Theseus is the tragedy of Phaedra, his second wife. Her story was told by the dramatist Euripides in his celebrated play, Hippolytus.

After the death of his Amazon wife Antiope (see below), Theseus married Phaedra, a Cretan princess who was often said to be the sister of Ariadne. His son from his first marriage, Hippolytus, was by now grown up, but refused any contact with Aphrodite, the goddess of sexuality, preferring to spend his time hunting in the hills in devotion to Artemis. Aphrodite grew angry at this snub to her authority and plotted his downfall by making Phaedra fall madly in love with her stepson. Phaedra tried to conceal her desperate passion, but her nurse revealed it

to Hippolytus, who fled in disgust. Phaedra killed herself, but left an incriminating letter in which she accused Hippolytus of rape. Theseus found the letter and, with the permission of his divine father Poseidon, put a curse on his son. When Hippolytus was out in his chariot, a monster rose from the sea and terrified his horses, so that he was dragged to his death.

Hippolytus' corpse was carried back to his father, who learned the truth of his son's innocence from Artemis. With Theseus' blessing, the goddess established a cult in honour of the dead Hippolytus.

A krater (large pot for mixing water with wine) depicting Hippolytus, dragged to his death by his own horses through the deviousness of his stepmother, Phaedra.

The children were to be fed to the Minotaur, a monstrous hybrid of man and bull which Minos kept in the Labyrinth, an underground maze built by Daedalus (see p.162). But Ariadne, the daughter of Minos, fell in love with Theseus and gave him a ball of twine, by means of which he could enter the Labyrinth and retrace his footsteps out again. Guided by the monster's distant bellowing, Theseus followed the children into the dark maze, reaching them just as the terrifying creature was about to slaughter them. He grappled with the beast and beat it to death before leading the children out of the Labyrinth to where Ariadne was waiting. They all set sail for Greece, but on the way Theseus abandoned Ariadne (see margin, opposite). He returned to Athens in triumph, but forgot the instructions of his father, who had told him to set a white sail if all was well or a black sail if disaster had befallen his mission. Theseus sailed into Athens with the black sail still flying. When Aegeus saw it, he assumed his son was dead. Stricken with grief, he threw himself into the sea, which from that time was known as the Aegean. Thus, the prophecy delivered to Aegeus at Delphi (that he would die of grief) was fulfilled. Theseus succeeded him as king.

After his return from Crete, Theseus fought with Herakles against the Amazons (see p.148). As his share of the spoils he received an Amazon warrior, Antiope, by whom he fathered Hippolytus (see panel, above). The Amazons later invaded Attica, but Theseus defeated them again (Antiope died in the battle). This victory was depicted in much Athenian art of the 5th century bc, most notably on the Parthenon. Theseus' next campaign began when he attended the wedding Perithous, king of the Lapiths in Thrace. Centaurs attacked the nuptial feast, and Theseus helped fight them off in a battle also depicted on the Parthenon.

THESEUS THE STATESMAN
The city of Athens and the Acropolis were believed to have existed long before Theseus, and the Athenians told of earlier notable kings such as Cecrops (the city's mythical founder), Erechtheus and Theseus' own father Aegeus. But Theseus was particularly revered for bringing all the different towns and villages of Attica, the region of which Athens was the chief city, under a single ruler as a unified state. Every assembly and law court of Athens was believed to be part of the heritage of Theseus. The legends about him articulated the ideals of the democratic state, and he appeared in Athenian myth as a good king, praised for his justice.

Evidence of the real Theseus – if he existed at all – is lacking. Cimon, a politician of the 5th century BC, discovered huge bones on the island of Scyros, to which the Athenian king was believed to have retired. The bones were claimed as those of Theseus and were reburied at Athens with all the honour due to a sacred hero of the state.

JASON

The great adventurer

The adventures of Jason, a prince of Iolcus in Thessaly, were as popular as those of Odysseus. Jason's early life, like that of Theseus, was marked by his early isolation from court and eventual return as a young man to claim his royal birthright. When Pelias, the brother of Jason's father King Aeson of Iolcus, seized the throne, Jason was sent away by his mother to Mount Pelion to be educated by Chiron, a wise Centaur, who taught him the arts of music, medicine, hunting and warfare. When he was twenty, he returned to Iolcus and on his way came upon a river, where he met an old woman – really the goddess Hera in disguise – who asked him to carry her across. He was glad to assist, and thereby won the protection of the goddess on his subsequent adventures.

In helping Hera across the river Jason lost a sandal and arrived at Iolcus with one bare foot. Pelias had been warned by an oracle to beware the arrival of a stranger with only one shoe and was terrified by Jason's approach. He craftily agreed to yield his throne to his nephew if the young man would complete one seemingly impossible task, namely to bring him the famous Golden Fleece from Colchis at the furthest end of the Black Sea. Jason accepted the challenge and won the fleece after many adventures in his ship, the *Argo* (see pp.154-5).

The hero returned home with Medea, the daughter of Aeëtes, to find that Pelias had put Aeson to death. Medea helped Jason to avenge his father's death by arranging the gruesome murder of Pelias. Many years after the tragic end of Jason's marriage to Medea (see opposite), the hero is said to have died when a piece of the *Argo*, which had been dedicated in a temple, fell on his head.

Jason is rescued by Athene (right, holding an owl, one of her emblems) from the mouth of the dragon guarding the Golden Fleece (see pp.154-5). The fleece hangs from a tree in the background of this scene, taken from a red-figure vase.

Medea, the sorceress queen

*A*fter his voyage with the Argonauts (see pp.154-5), Jason returned to Iolcus with the sorceress Medea, who is the focus of the tragic epilogue to his adventures. The Corinthian episode of her career forms the basis of the tragedy Medea by the great dramatist Euripides.

On their arrival in Iolcus, Jason and Medea plotted to avenge the death of Jason's father Aeson, the rightful king, who had been executed by Pelias. Medea persuaded the daughters of Pelias that she would change their father into a young man again by a spell, but to prepare him for his rejuvenation they must first chop him up and cook him. The daughters consented to this plan, killed Pelias and cooked the pieces of his body – only for Medea to reveal that she had tricked them.

In spite of the usurper's demise, Jason had no opportunity to occupy his father's throne, because the manner of Pelias's death caused such widespread outrage that he and Medea were forced to flee from Iolcus. The couple went to the Peloponese and settled in Corinth, where they had several children.

Many years later, King Creon of Corinth offered Jason an attractive political marriage with his daughter. Jason proposed to Medea that he should divorce her and that she should then go voluntarily into exile. Medea was furious at this betrayal and sent poisoned robes to Creon and his daughter, Jason's intended new bride, as a result of which both died in horrific agony.

Next, according to Euripides, she cut the throats of her own children to hurt their errant father. After the murders she escaped in triumph to Athens in the chariot of Helios, the sun, pulled by dragons. This is the

An Attic krater (see p.151) showing the death of the bronze giant Talos, who tried to stop the Argonauts from landing on Crete. Medea (left) gave him a sleeping draught. While he slept she unstopped the single vein in his body and he bled to death.

point at which Euripides' tragedy ends, with Jason left in misery in Corinth.

At Athens Medea married King Aegeus, father of the hero Theseus, and bore him a son, Medus, whom she wanted to succeed his father as king. When Theseus, Aegeus' rightful heir, arrived at Athens from Troezen (see p.150), Medea divined at once who he was. She attempted to get rid of him before he could produce the tokens of recognition by which he would reveal his identity to his father.

Medea convinced the king that the newcomer, whose heroic exploits on the way to Athens (see p.150) had already made him famous, wanted to depose him. Together they plotted to kill Theseus at a banquet held to celebrate his successful capture of the wild bull of Marathon.

Medea put poison in Theseus' wine, but as the hero was about to drink it Aegeus recognized him and knocked the wine cup from his hand. Realizing his wife's motives, Aegeus banished Medea and her children from his kingdom forever.

According to some sources, after her death the sorceress went to the Islands of the Blessed, where she married Achilles, the great Greek hero who had been killed during the Trojan war (see pp.157-9).

THE ARGONAUTS

Jason's quest for the Golden Fleece

This terracotta relief shows Athene (left) assisting a shipwright, possibly Argus himself, with the sail of the Argo.

THE ARGONAUTS

There is no definitive list of the members of Jason's crew, because prominent Greek families commonly claimed an Argonaut among their ancestors. However, there is little dispute over the number of Argonauts – fifty – or over some of the more famous figures, including the following:

ARGUS, shipwright, who built the *Argo*.

ATALANTA, huntress, the only woman Argonaut.

CASTOR and POLYDEUCES, the Dioscuri (see p.134).

HERAKLES (see pp.148-9), left behind when he went to look for his lover, Hylas.

IDMON and MOPSUS, legendary seers.

LYNCEUS, so sharp-sighted that he could see beneath the earth.

MELEAGER, brother of Deianeira, the wife of Herakles (see p.148).

NAUPLIUS, father of Palamedes, a noted trickster in Homer's *Iliad*.

OILEUS, father of Ajax (not to be confused with his greater namesake), a hero in the *Iliad* (see p.158).

ORPHEUS, great singer (see p.165) who played his lyre for the Argonauts.

PELEUS, father of Achilles, leading hero of the *Iliad*, and husband of Thetis, a sea-nymph.

PERICLYMENUS, son of Poseidon. He could take any form in battle, a gift of his father.

TELAMON, father of the greater Ajax, one of the most famous heroes of the *Iliad*.

TIPHYS, helmsman of the *Argo*.

ZETES and CALAIS, winged sons of Boreas, the north wind. They fought the Harpies who tormented Phineus (see opposite).

Jason's greatest exploits took place during his journey to obtain the Golden Fleece of Colchis at the behest of his uncle, the usurper Pelias. The fleece came from a magic flying ram which Hermes had sent to help Phrixus and Helle, the children of another of Jason's uncles, King Athamas of Boeotia, when their lives had been threatened by their stepmother Ino. They escaped on the ram, but Helle fell off and drowned in what was thereafter called the Hellespont ("Helle's sea"). Phrixus, however, reached Colchis, at the easternmost end of the Black Sea, where he sacrificed the ram to Zeus and gave its golden fleece to the local king, Aeëtes, who had received him hospitably. Since then Aeëtes had kept the fleece under the watchful eye of an unsleeping dragon.

For the voyage Jason ordered the construction of a ship, the *Argo*, which some sources call the first ship ever built. It was constructed by the shipwright Argus (see illustration, left) with the help of either the goddess Athene or Hera, and incorporated a bough taken from Zeus's prophetic oak tree at Dodona. The *Argo* was fitted with fifty oars, one for each member of the crew, the Argonauts, which Jason then assembled. Among the Argonauts (see left) were many of the most famous heroes of Greek mythology, including Herakles. When all was prepared, Jason and his fellow adventurers set sail for the land of the Golden Fleece.

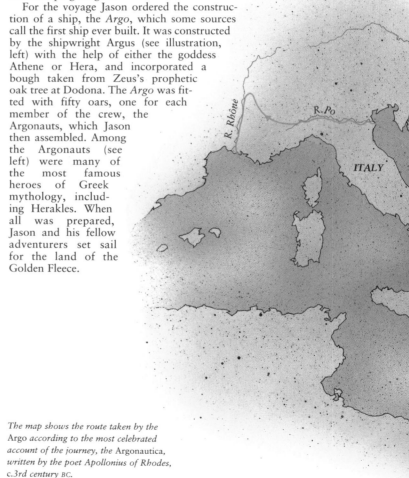

The map shows the route taken by the Argo *according to the most celebrated account of the journey, the* Argonautica, *written by the poet Apollonius of Rhodes, c.3rd century* BC.

THE ADVENTURES OF THE *ARGO*

(*Placenames in* SMALL CAPITALS *are marked on the map, below.*)

When the *Argo* reached LEMNOS, its first port of call, Jason found that there were no men on the island. In fact, the Lemnian women had killed them all after they had taken concubines because, the men had claimed, their womenfolk stank. The Argonauts, who were told merely that the men had been forced to flee, were invited to stay for several months to repopulate the island. Jason was taken by the island's queen, Hypsipyle, who bore him twins.

The Argonauts went on to CYZICUS, where they were well received by the local king and Herakles cleared the land of giants, but the visit ended in an unfortunate incident. When the *Argo* set sail it was driven back to shore at night by a storm. The Cyzicans, believing they were under attack from pirates, assailed the ship and were massacred by the Argonauts, equally ignorant of whom they were fighting. When the truth was discovered, Jason ordered funeral games for his former hosts.

The BEBRYCES, next on the *Argo*'s route, was a region ruled by Amycus, a son of Poseidon, who challenged strangers to box to the death. The strongest man on earth, Herakles (see p.148), had been left behind on the way from Cyzicus, but Amycus met his match in Polydeuces, who accepted his challenge and killed him.

The Argonauts sailed on, and near the mouth of the BLACK SEA encountered Phineus, a blind old man eternally plagued by Harpies, monsters with the faces of hags and the bodies and claws of birds, which snatched or defecated on his food. Zetes and Calais saw them off and the grateful Phineus gave Jason valuable guidance for the onward journey.

At this point the route to Colchis was barred by the SYMPLEGADES, two huge moving rocks near the mouth of the BLACK SEA which crashed together like cymbals, allowing no vessel to pass safely. Phineus advised the Argonauts to send a dove on ahead; if it succeeded in passing through the rocks, so would they. The dove negotiated the rocks with the loss of a tail feather, so the *Argo* – with the help of Athene and Hera – sailed through, but lost its helmsman, Tiphys. After this the rocks became fixed in position forever.

The Argonauts sailed up the River Phasis and finally reached COLCHIS, the land of the Golden Fleece. King Aeëtes said he would hand the fleece over only if Jason would fulfil certain tasks: yoke the king's bronze-footed, fire-breathing bulls; plough a field; sow dragon's teeth; and kill the giants who would spring from the planted teeth. The gods caused Medea, the

KEY TO MAP

Outward journey of the *Argo*

Homeward journey of the *Argo*

City or island: **Cyzicus**

Region: *GREECE*

R. Danube

BLACK SEA

COLCHIS

Sinope   Isle of Ares

Themiskyra

Symplegades

Heraklea

Samothrace

BEBRYCES

Cyzicus

Hellespont

GREECE

Iolcus

Lemnos

ASIA MINOR

Corfu

AEGEAN SEA

Corinth   Aegina

Anaphis

Karpathos

Crete

MEDITERRANEAN SEA

SYRTES

LIBYA

sorceress daughter of Aeëtes, to fall in love with Jason. She gave him magic potions, by means of which he succeeded in the tasks he had been set. He seized the fleece after Medea had bewitched the dragon guarding it. As the Argonauts fled from Colchis, Medea delayed the pursuing Aeëtes and his entourage by murdering her own brother, Apsyrtus, then dismembering him and hurling the pieces of his corpse out of the *Argo*.

There are many accounts of the long return journey of the *Argo* to IOLCUS. The adventures include Medea charming and destroying a bronze giant called Talos, whose only flaw was in his ankle, where the plug for the only vein in his body was located (see p.153). The *Argo* was also said to have sailed up the DANUBE and to have become stranded on the sandbanks of LIBYA at SYRTES. The heroes were forced to carry the ship overland on their backs for twelve days. Jason and Medea visited Circe, the witch of the *Odyssey* and Medea's aunt, who ritually purified them for the murder of Apsyrtus. Other monsters from the *Odyssey* were also encountered or passed before the ship at last returned to Iolcus.

PERSEUS

Slayer of Medusa

Perseus weaing his winged sandals and cap of darkness, carries off the head of Medusa, from a red-figure water jug of c.350-330BC.

One of the most commonly depicted figures in myth and art is Perseus, the son of Zeus and his human lover Danaë. He grew to manhood on Seriphos, an island in the Aegean, under the rule of Polydectes, whose brother Dictys, a fisherman, had saved Perseus and Danaë (see p.135). Polydectes fell in love with Danaë, but she refused his advances. He then invited all the nobles of Seriphos to a feast and demanded from each the gift of a horse. The poor Perseus joked that he could just as easily get the head one of the three Gorgons – fierce snake-haired monsters – as afford a horse. Polydectes took him at his word and gladly sent Danaë's protector on such an apparently impossible mission.

However, the gods Hermes and Athene came to the aid of Perseus. The hero was sent first to the Graeae, three old women with one eye and one tooth between them, who alone could direct him to the Gorgons. He stole their eye and tooth, and would not give them back until they had given him the information he needed. They told him to go to certain nymphs, who could give him a cap of darkness to make him invisible, winged sandals so that he could fly, and a leather bag. Hermes gave him a curved sword. Perseus flew to the Gorgons. Only one of them, Medusa, was mortal, but those who saw her face directly were turned at once to stone. Perseus looked at her in the reflection of a shield (in another version, his hand was guided by Athene) and decapitated her, putting the head in his bag. He flew back to Seriphos, rescuing Andromeda on the way (see below), and revealed the Gorgon's head, which turned Polydectes and his supporters to stone. The hero, who lived the rest of his life in peace and prosperity, gave Medusa's head to Athene, who wore it to petrify – literally – her enemies.

Perseus and Andromeda

One of the most famous episodes in the career of Perseus was his rescue of the beautiful Andromeda. It is a favourite subject of ancient Greek and Roman art.

Cassiopeia, wife of King Cepheus of Ethiopia, boasted that she was more lovely than the Nereids, fifty beautiful sea nymphs who were daughters of the Old Man of the Sea, Nereus, a divinity who lived in the ocean and helped sailors in distress. Poseidon, angered by the boast, flooded his kingdom,

This Greek vase (c.250BC) from southern Italy shows Perseus fighting the monster to save Andromeda.

and sent a sea-monster to ravage the land. Cepheus consulted an oracle and was told to sacrifice his daughter Andromeda to the monster by chaining her to a rock. As she lay on the rock, Perseus flew by and immediately fell in love with her. He offered to kill the monster, if he could marry Andromeda. Cepheus accepted the hero's offer, so Perseus took his cap of invisibility, winged sandals and curved sword and destroyed the monster. He released Andromeda and took her for his wife. She bore him a son, Perses, who became the heir of Cepheus.

THE TROJAN WAR

Homer's warrior epic

Menelaus (left), one of the Greek leaders, confronts the Trojan warrior Hector during the battle for Troy. From a vase c.610BC.

THE EPICS OF HOMER

The stories of the Trojan war and its aftermath were told first in a series of epic poems, of which the two most celebrated and influential were the *Iliad* and the *Odyssey*. They were both very widely performed and learned in ancient Greece and are traditionally said to be the work of a bard called Homer (below), about whose life almost nothing is known, except that he is supposed to have been blind and a native of Chios. Even in ancient times, scholars doubted that the *Iliad* and the *Odyssey* were written by the same person, or that each work was the product of one composer. Although both epics are believed today to be the end-products of a long oral tradition, they remain the glorious fountainhead of Western literature.

The bulk of the *Iliad* concentrates on only a few days of the Trojan War: the quarrel between Achilles, the greatest Greek warrior, and Agamemnon, the Greek leaders. The *Odyssey* tells of the return from Troy to his home on Ithaca of the Greek hero Odysseus (see p.160).

The *Iliad*, Homer's great poetic account of the war between the Greeks and the city of Troy in northwestern Asia Minor, was essential reading in ancient Greece, where its literary importance was fully recognized, and it served as a basic text in the Hellenic education system. For the Greeks, the epic told the history of their ancestors. Archaeological evidence shows that Troy, which from its size and situation near the coast was clearly of importance, was indeed destroyed by fire and abandoned c.1100. This was at the end of the Bronze Age, and the warriors in Homer are described as using bronze as well as iron. In ancient times Troy was also known as Ilion or Ilium, hence the title of the epic.

The story begins with Priam and Hecuba, the king and queen of Troy. When Paris, one of their fifty sons, is born, Hecuba dreams that she has given birth to a firebrand which destroys the city. The infant is abandoned, but he miraculously survives to become a shepherd. Later, as a young man, he defeats his brothers in a boxing match and is recognized as a son of Priam and welcomed back into the royal household.

Meanwhile, the wedding takes place of Peleus, a mortal, and the sea-nymph Thetis. An oracle has foretold that Thetis will bear a son greater than his father. This will be Achilles, the best of the Greek warriors (see p.158). The goddess Eris ("strife"), insulted because she was not invited to the wedding, sends a golden apple to the nuptial feast, inscribed "For the Fairest". Athene, Hera and Aphrodite each claim the prize, and Zeus appoints Paris to judge which of these goddesses is the fairest. If she wins, Athene promises to give Paris wisdom and victory in war. For her part, Hera promises him royal power, while Aphrodite promises the most beautiful woman in the world. The sensual Paris chooses Aphrodite as the winner and thereby earns Troy the everlasting enmity of Hera and Athene.

THE HEROES OF THE TROJAN WAR

According to Homer, many great warriors fought at Troy. These are the most famous:

GREEKS:

AGAMEMNON, leader of the expedition and described as the "most kingly".

AJAX, son of Oileus, known as the lesser Ajax. He raped Priam's daughter Cassandra in the sack of Troy and desecrated the altars of the gods, for which the Greek fleet was shipwrecked by the gods on the way home.

AJAX, son of Telamon, greatest warrior after Achilles. Stubborn and taciturn, he went mad when the dead Achilles' armour was awarded to Odysseus. He tried to kill the Greek commanders, but massacred sheep instead, and finally killed himself out of shame.

CALCHAS, seer of the Greeks, who interpreted the gods' omens.

DIOMEDES, an outstanding warrior, though often rash in council. He wounded first Ares and then Aphrodite on the battlefield.

MENELAUS, brother of Agamemnon and often depicted as ineffectual.

NESTOR, oldest of the Greeks, who gave advice at great length.

ODYSSEUS, craftiest and wisest of the Greeks, a supporter of Agamemnon. He conceived the idea of the Trojan horse.

TROJANS:

AENEAS, son of Aphrodite; he escaped the sack of Troy and, in Roman myth, went on to found Rome (see p.172).

GLAUKUS, Lycian ally of Troy, who exchanged armour on the battlefield with the Greek Diomedes as a sign of their long-established ties of guest-friendship.

HECTOR, son of Priam and leading Trojan warrior. His death forms the climax of the *Iliad*. Unlike any Greek warrior, Hector is depicted movingly with his family.

PARIS, son of Priam, a seducer and depicted as sensual and effeminate. He and Helen, whose abduction caused the war, lived apart from the palace. He fought with little success and usually with a bow, a coward's weapon.

PRIAM, king of Troy. He ransomed the body of his son Hector from Achilles, and perished when the city fell.

SARPEDON, son of Zeus, killed by Patroclus. Zeus was tempted to save his son but Hera reminded him of the mortality even of heroes.

Paris's prize is Helen, the daughter of Leda and Zeus (see p.135) and the wife of Menelaus, king of Sparta. Paris visits Sparta as an honoured guest, but then, with the help of Aphrodite, he elopes with Helen back to Troy.

All the Greek princes who had been suitors of Helen promise to protect her from any future outrage. Menelaus and his brother Agamemnon, king of Argos, summon these princes and muster a great expedition at Aulis to sail for Troy and avenge the abduction. Two warriors, Achilles and Odysseus, are at first reluctant to join the campaign. Achilles disguises himself as a woman on the island of Scyros, but is discovered when a war trumpet sounds and he alone reaches for a weapon. Odysseus pretends to be mad and ploughs the seashore, but his ploy is revealed when his own baby is placed before the plough. Once exposed, both men agree to join the expedition. The Greeks assemble at Aulis, but their fleet is held up by Artemis, who takes the Trojan side in the war. Agamemnon is forced to sacrifice his daughter Iphigeneia in order to secure good winds. The expedition finally sets sail for Asia Minor and establishes camp outside Troy, to which the Greeks lay siege for ten years.

During the siege, Agamemnon wins Chryseis, daughter of Chryses, priest of Apollo, as war booty. It is at this point in the saga that Homer begins his *Iliad*. The priest asks for his daughter back, and when refused prays to Apollo and implores him to destroy the Greeks. A terrible plague attacks the camp; after some days the reason for the plague is revealed and Agamemnon is forced to return Chryseis to her father. In his anger at this loss, Agamemnon claims for himself another woman, Briseis, who is a prize of the Greek warrior Achilles.

The warrior is outraged, refuses to fight any longer, and prays for the destruction of the Greeks so that they will regret his

Achilles

*A*chilles, as described in Homer's Iliad, was a typical Greek hero: strong, proud, fearless, passionate and wrathful. He was the best but also the most destructive of warriors, and as such embodied the paradox of Greek heroism also seen in Herakles.

The child of Peleus and the sea-nymph Thetis, Achilles was educated by Chiron, a wise Centaur. His mother dipped him in the River Styx as a baby to render his body immortal and invulnerable, except for the heel by which she had held him – hence the English phrase "Achilles' heel" to describe a crucial weakness. Achilles was offered a choice by the Fates: a long life of ease and obscurity, or a young death and immortal glory. He chose the latter.

Achilles became for the Greeks the model of the direct, noble man who could not bear dishonourable conduct such as Agamemnon's when he took his war-prize, the Trojan woman Briseis. At Troy he fought and killed Penthesileia, the Amazon queen, falling in love with her as she died.

Achilles (left) kills Penthesilea, the Amazon queen. An amphora (storage jar) of c.540BC made and decorated by Exekias, one of the greatest of all Greek potters and painters.

absence. Hector, Priam's eldest son and the chief Trojan warrior, now leads an advance from Troy and reaches as far as the ships of the Greeks, wounding and killing many heroes. Patroclus, Achilles' dearest friend, begs the idle warrior for a loan of his armour, so that the Trojans will think Achilles is fighting and retreat. Achilles is reluctant but eventually relents, warning Patroclus to be careful. But Patroclus fails to heed the warnings and, despite pushing back the Trojans, is killed by Hector.

Achilles' grief knows no bounds, and he returns to the battle to seek revenge. In a famous scene, he pursues Hector three times around the walls of Troy and finally kills him in single combat. A magnificent funeral is held for Patroclus, complete with funeral games, but the Trojans cannot do the same for Hector because Achilles has kept and desecrated his corpse. The angry gods force Achilles to accept the offer of a ransom and return Hector's body to Priam (the *Iliad* ends with Hector's funeral). Achilles dies when he is shot by Paris in the ankle, his only vulnerable spot, and his armour is awarded to Odysseus as the next best warrior. Shortly afterwards, Paris himself is shot and killed by the archer Philoctetes.

Since the death of its chief warrior, Hector, Troy has been doomed to fall. Odysseus has the idea of building a huge hollow wooden horse, in which the pick of the Greek warriors hide while their fleet sails away as if in defeat. The Trojans believe that the horse is an offering to the gods and bring it inside the walls. At night, the warriors slip out of the horse and open the city gates to the rest of the army, which has come ashore once more. Troy is sacked and razed by fire, Priam and his remaining sons are slaughtered, and Hecuba and the Trojan women are taken into slavery.

The Greek heroes Achilles and Ajax play checkers between battles. A detail of a 6th-century BC black-figure amphora by Exekias.

AFTER TROY

Odysseus and Agamemnon

Odysseus and his companion blind the Cyclops Polyphemus, from an amphora of c.510-530BC.

ODYSSEUS

Odysseus, a significant figure in the *Iliad* and the leading character in the *Odyssey*, was a common figure in Greek tragedy, well known for his guile and political pragmatism. For philosphers, Odysseus was the archetypal figure of the complex and calculating character, as opposed to the direct and noble Achilles. In some of the many accounts of his life he was said to be not the legitimate child of the hero Laertes, as Homer says, but the bastard son of Sisyphus, whose habitual trickery earned him the eternal punishment in the underworld of rolling a rock up a hill, only for the rock to roll down again as soon as the summit was reached (see p.146).

The prophet Teiresias foretells that Odysseus' death would come from the sea. In some accounts Telegonus, the child of Odysseus and Circe, sails to Ithaca and accidently kills his father.

The sack of Troy was not the end of the adventures of the Greek heroes. The Greeks told many myths of their separate homecomings, the most famous of which is Homer's great epic, the *Odyssey*, which is named after its hero, Odysseus (whom the Romans called Ulysses). It was said that the Greeks desecrated the altars of Troy when they sacked the city, as a result of which the gods became angry and caused storms to scatter the Greek fleet as it sailed for home. Many heroes subsequently ended up in Italy or Africa before reaching Greece.

After the ships of Odysseus and his followers become separated from the fleet they reach the city of the Cicones, which they sack. A further storm drives the ships off course and into a world of monsters and witches. Odysseus comes first to the land of the Lotus-Eaters, who give some of his men lotus blossoms to eat, wiping out their memories and inducing such lethargy that those who have eaten the flowers have to be carried back to the ships. The next adventure takes place on the island inhabited by Cyclopes, one-eyed monsters who live in caves and have no laws or social system. Odysseus takes some wine and some of his crew to explore the island, and in a cave finds signs of sheep farming. Against the advice of his crew, he insists on staying to see the shepherd. This is the Cyclops Polyphemus, who returns with his flock and, once inside the cave, blocks the mouth with a huge rock. He discovers the Greeks and eats two of them raw for dinner and two more for breakfast. The Greeks cannot escape, because only the Cyclops can move the rock to allow them out of the cave. However, Odysseus has a plan. He uses the wine to get the Cyclops drunk, and when asked his name, replies "Nobody". As the Cyclops lies in a stupor, Odysseus blinds him with a hot wooden stake. Polyphemus screams for help and some other Cyclopes come to ask what is causing him pain, to which he replies: " 'Nobody' is hurting me!" The other Cyclopes assume all is well and leave, whereupon Odysseus ties each of his men under a sheep, himself clinging to the belly of a ram. When the blind Cyclops lets his sheep out in the morning, the Greeks escape. From his ship Odysseus taunts the Cyclops, who curses him. The sea god Poseidon, Polyphemus' father, makes Odysseus wander the sea for ten years.

The sailors next come to Aeolus, king of the winds. Odysseus is given a sack of winds which allows the ships to sail within sight of Ithaca. But the hero falls asleep and his men open the sack, thinking that there is treasure in it. The winds escape and cause a storm which blows the voyagers back to Aeolus, and from there to the land of the Laestrygonians, cannibal giants who destroy all but one of Odysseus' ships and eat their crews.

The next episode takes place on the island of the goddess Circe, an enchantress. Half of Odysseus' crew approach Circe's palace in the woods, around which wolves, bears and lions play like tame animals. Circe invites them in and gives them a drugged drink, then turns them into pigs and locks them in a sty. The one man who has stayed outside returns and tells Odysseus of this latest disaster. With the help of Hermes and a magic plant, Odysseus is rendered immune to Circe's spells and forces her to free his men. The crew stay on the island for a year of feasting and Circe advises Odysseus on the remainder of his route. First, he must go to the underworld to consult the prophet Teiresias about how to get home. Teiresias tells Odysseus to go to a land which does not know the sea and make a sacrifice to Poseidon. This is the underworld, and while there, Odysseus sees the great heroes and heroines of the past and the great sinners being punished. Among those he meets are his fellow heroes from the Trojan War, Achilles and Ajax.

From the underworld, Odysseus travels past the island of the Sirens, monsters with the bodies of birds and the heads of women, whose irresistible singing lures sailors to a certain death at their hands. Odysseus escapes their enchantment by having himself strapped to the mast, as Circe has suggested, while his sailors row on, their ears stopped with wax.

The hero and his crew steer past the two sea monsters Scylla and Charybdis and eventually reach Thrinakia, the island of the Sun. Circe has warned them not to eat the Cattle of the Sun, but the ship is becalmed and the crew cannot resist killing the cattle in their hunger. The roasting flesh continues to low even on the spit and the cows' hides crawl about as if alive. The Sun, enraged, destroys the ship and all its crew except Odysseus, who survives the shipwreck to land on the island of Calypso, a goddess who keeps him in a cave for eight years as her unwilling consort. Odysseus is at last freed by the intervention of the goddess Athene. He makes a raft and on it comes to the land of the Phaeacians, a glorious and magically fertile place whose people entertain him in great luxury. Their king, Alcinous, sends Odysseus home in a magic ship laden with gifts.

Finally back in Ithaca, Odysseus finds his wife Penelope besieged by suitors and his son Telemachus threatened by rivals. Penelope has always refused to believe that Odysseus is dead, but can keep the suitors at bay with her tricks no longer. In disguise, Odysseus first tests the loyalty of his family and of the Ithacans. Then, with the help of Telemachus and his faithful retainers, the suitors are killed and Odysseus is reunited with Penelope after twenty years. The *Odyssey* ends with a celebration of the achievements of the wandering hero, and of the family and its values. For the Greeks, this latter message lent the work great moral significance.

Agamemnon, king of Argos

The story of the fate of King Agamemnon, the victorious Greek leader of the expedition to Troy, was repeatedly told by Greek writers, for example the playwright Aeschylus in his trilogy the Oresteia.

After the war Agamemnon returns in triumph to his palace at Argos with his prize and concubine, Cassandra, prophetess daughter of King Priam. But his wife, Clytemnestra, and her lover, Aegisthus, have prepared a trap. Clytemnestra greets her husband and leads him to his bath. After he has bathed, she makes as if to offer him a towel, then suddenly throws a net over his head, and the king is mur-

Agamemnon struggles under the net thrown by Clytemnestra (right) as Aegisthus (left) stabs him. An Attic krater of c.470BC.

dered. Cassandra is also killed by the queen.

Orestes, son of Agamemnon, away from home at this time, grows to maturity and returns to take his revenge. He enters the palace in disguise and kills both the usurper Aegisthus and Clytemnestra. (This was often said to be achieved with the help of Orestes' sister, Electra.)

As a matricide, Orestes is pursued by the Furies and flees to Delphi to be purified of his deed. He goes on to Athens, where he is tried and finally acquitted of his transgression thanks to the deciding vote of the goddess Athene. He returns to rule in Argos.

TRANSGRESSORS

Breakers of the natural order

DAEDALUS AND ICARUS
Daedalus is perhaps best known from the tragic story of his son, Icarus. King Minos of Crete was so enraged with Daedalus for his role in helping Theseus against the Minotaur (see right) that he imprisoned him and Icarus. In order to escape from the island, the craftsman made wings for himself and his son from wax and feathers. Daedalus warned Icarus not to fly too close to the sun, but when they took to the air his son forgot the warning. The wax in his wings melted and Icarus plummeted to his death into the sea below, which was called the Sea of Icarus after him. Daedalus reached Sicily (or mainland Italy in some accounts), where he lived for the rest of his days.

The above illustration is based on a bronze figurine of Icarus with his wings strapped on, prepared to fly.

Many Greek myths tell of transgressors and their punishment. These stories may have been told to help maintain the proper order of things, especially within the family, as many of the myths involve overstepping the bounds of sexual propriety. Almost all involve human protagonists, because the gods and goddesses could generally misbehave with impunity, while the misdemeanours of mortals were usually severely punished – a paradox of which the ancient Greeks themselves were well aware. These are some of the more notable transgressors:

Atreus and Thyestes, sons of Pelops, who was the son of Tantalus (see p.146). When Atreus thwarted his brother to take the throne of Argos, Thyestes seduced Atreus' wife Aërope. In revenge, Atreus invited Thyestes to a feast and served him up his own children. The children of Atreus were Agamemnon and Menelaus, who married Clytemnestra and Helen, perhaps the most famous of adulterous wives. A surviving son of Thyestes, Aegisthus, became the lover of Clytemnestra and abetted her murder of her husband, his cousin Agamemnon (see p.161).

Daedalus, revered by the Greeks as the greatest of mortal craftsmen and inventors, was also a transgressor. He was a member of the Athenian royal household but was forced to leave Athens after he had killed his nephew Perdix, a rival craftsman who had invented the saw, taking the idea from the spine of a fish. When Daedalus hurled the youth over a cliff he turned into a partridge (*perdix* in Greek). Daedalus fled and headed for Crete, where he entered the service of King Minos. Minos had prayed to Poseidon for a bull to offer the god in sacrifice, but it was such a splendid beast that the king had kept it for himself. This angered Poseidon, who made Minos's wife Pasiphaë fall in love with the bull. Daedalus built a life-size, hollow model of a heifer, in which Pasiphaë could hide in order to consummate her unnatural passion, as a result of which she bore the Minotaur, a savage beast which was half man and half bull. Angry at his craftsman, Minos ordered Daedalus to construct the Labyrinth as a prison for the monstrous hybrid. Later, Daedalus gave Ariadne the twine by means of which Theseus negotiated the Labyrinth to slay the Minotaur (see p.150).

Danaïds, the fifty daughters of Danaus, descendant of Zeus and Io (see p.134). They were forced against their will to marry the fifty sons of their uncle Aegyptus and, on the wedding night, forty-nine of the Danaïds killed their husbands. (The fiftieth, Hypermnestra, loved her husband Lynceus and from their union were descended Perseus and Danaë.) The forty-nine murderesses were punished in the underworld by eternally having to fill a water jar with a sieve.

Tereus, king of Thrace. He helped King Pandion of Athens, received Pandion's daughter Procne as his bride, and had a son by her, Itys. When Philomela, Pandion's other daughter, was visiting her sister, Tereus raped her and cut out her tongue so that she could tell no one. But Philomela wove a tapestry depicting her suffering and showed it to Procne. In revenge the sisters killed Itys, cooked him and fed him to his unwitting father, who discovered the outrage and pursued the sisters. Because they had all committed murder, they were turned into birds: for example, Procne became a swallow and Philomela a nightingale.

Oedipus

Oedipus was the most celebrated sexual transgressor in Greek myth. The most famous version of his story is that told by Sophocles in his play Oedipus the King. *Oedipus is the prime example of the Greek hero who possesses all the noble heroic qualities but is nonetheless condemned by fate to commit grave crimes against the natural order. Thebes, the setting of the story, was frequently the backdrop for Greek tragic drama.*

King Laius and Queen Jocasta of Thebes were told by the oracle at Delphi that their future child would kill his father and sleep with his mother, so when Jocasta bore a son, Laius pierced its feet and tied them together, and abandoned the child on a mountainside. However, a shepherd saved the baby and took it to Corinth, where he was adopted by the king and queen, Polybus and Merope. He was named Oedipus ("swollen foot").

Years later, Oedipus was taunted by a stranger at a feast that he was not the son of Polybus. The insult rankled and he consulted the oracle at Delphi, which told him that he would murder his father and marry his mother. Assuming Polybus and Merope to be his real parents, Oedipus decided to flee Corinth. On the road to Thebes he slew a stranger who had insulted him; this man was Laius, his father. At this period Thebes was plagued by the Sphinx, a creature which killed anyone who could not answer her riddle: "What has four legs in the morning, two legs at midday, three legs in the evening?" Oedipus challenged the monster and gave the correct answer, "man" (who crawls on all fours as a baby, walks upright in maturity and uses a stick in old age). The Sphinx hurled herself into the ocean and Oedipus was hailed as the city's saviour. He was asked to rule Thebes and marry its recently widowed queen – his own mother, Jocasta. By her he had four children, two sons, Polyneices and Eteocles, and two daughters, Antigone and Ismene. Thebes prospered under his rule.

Many years later, the city was plagued by drought, famine and disease. The oracle at Delphi told the Thebans that the trouble would end only when the killer of Laius was driven out. Oedipus undertook the search himself and eventually found out the truth from Teiresias (see p.165) and the shepherd who had saved him as a child. Oedipus blinded himself and went into exile. Jocasta hanged herself.

A painting from a kylix (shallow drinking cup) of c.470BC, showing Oedipus, with traveller's hat and staff, and the Sphinx, on the road to Thebes.

IXION

One notorious sexual transgressor was Ixion, king of the Lapiths, a fabulous race of Thessaly. He attempted to rape the goddess Hera, but she deceived him by putting in her bed a cloud in her shape, with which Ixion mated when he was drunk. Zeus punished Ixion for attempting to seduce his wife by condemning him to be tied to a burning wheel which would turn forever in the underworld. The offspring of Ixion and the cloud was Centauros, who later became a sexual transgressor himself by coupling with a mare to produce the first Centaur (see p.164). The above painting from a bowl depicts Ixion's punishment.

CENTAURS AND AMAZONS
Races of fabulous beings

Centaurs in battle with the Lapiths, as depicted on a temple frieze from Bassae in Arcadia, in the Peloponnese.

Amazons fighting against the Athenians, as shown in a frieze from the Parthenon, Athens, sculpted 447-432BC.

The Centaurs and the Amazons were fabulous creatures which were thought of as subverting the norms of civilized behaviour. They were often in battle against heroes, and both the Centauromachy (battle of the Centaurs) and the Amazonomachy (battle of the Amazons) were regular subjects of art and myth.

The Centaurs, descendants of Ixion (see p.163), had the torsos of men and the bodies of horses. They were often associated with sexual licence and violence. At the wedding of King Perithous of the Lapiths, the Centaurs attempted to carry off his bride, causing a battle in which Theseus aided the Lapiths. However, some Centaurs were wise and kindly, such as Chiron, who educated several heroes including Jason and Achilles, and Pholus, who played host to Herakles. (Unfortunately, Herakles' visit ended on a sour note when other Centaurs demanded to share the wine Pholus had offered him. They were beaten in battle by the angry hero. Another Centaur, Nessus, ultimately caused Herakles' death: see p.148.)

The Amazons were warlike women from the east who often dressed as Persians (and were therefore "barbarians"); they rode, shot and pillaged, and did not grow crops. Their weapon was usually the bow and, in some accounts, they cut off one breast to facilitate the drawing of a bowstring. (Some sources claim that Amazon means "without a breast", although Amazons are always depicted with two.) They were said to have men at home as slaves, to whom they returned for one month a year to procreate. Male children were abandoned to die, while females were brought up to be like their mothers. In the *Iliad*, Achilles kills the Amazon queen, Penthesileia (see p.158), and visitors to Athens were shown the supposed tombs of Amazons who had fallen in battle against Theseus.

TRANSFORMATIONS

Myths of metamorphosis; Orpheus

In Greek myths a crucial point in the narrative is often reached when a character changes shape, typically taking on the form of a plant, animal or some other natural feature. Among the best-known transformation myths is the story of Halcyone (or Alcyone) and her husband Ceyx, who presumptuously decided to call themselves Hera and Zeus. For this the gods turned them both into sea-birds. For seven days each winter, Aeolus, the king of the winds, kept the waves calm so that Halcyone, who had become the kingfisher or halcyon, could sit on her eggs undisturbed – hence the expression "halcyon days" to describe a time of peace and contentment.

Two transformation stories involved the nymph Echo. In the more famous of them, her garrulous stream of talk distracts Hera for long enough to allow Zeus to leave the scene of one of his affairs undetected by his wife. In punishment, Hera takes from Echo all but the briefest of voices. Echo falls deeply in love with Narcissus, the beautiful son of Cephisus, a river god, but when she tries to seduce him, all she can do is repeat his last words. Echo pines away until all that is left of her is her echoing voice. She curses Narcissus, who later comes to a pool and, seeing a reflection of himself, falls in love with the beautiful image, which he cannot possess. He too pines away, and as he dies he is transformed into the narcissus flower.

In the second myth, Echo is pursued by Pan, the god of woods and pastures, who was often portrayed with the legs and horns of a goat. She rejects his advances and flees, but Pan, in his anger at this rebuff, drives a group of shepherds mad, so that they pull the nymph apart. All that remains is her wailing voice, which reverberates around the mountains.

Hera also features in the myth of Io, a lover of her husband Zeus. Io, priestess of Hera, is the daughter of another river god, Inachus. Zeus desires her and takes the form of a cloud to couple with her, but when Hera grows suspicious he tries to deceive his wife by turning Io into a beautiful white heifer. Pretending to be fooled, Hera asks Zeus for the heifer as a gift, and once Io is in her possession she sets Argos, a hundred-eyed monster, to keep a constant watch over her. To free his mistress Zeus enlists the help of the wily Hermes, who lulls Argos to sleep with stories (see illustration, above right) and then cuts off his head. Not to be outdone, Hera sends a gadfly to torment Io. Maddened by the insect, she wanders the world miserably until she reaches Egypt. There, Zeus restores her to human form with a gentle touch (*epaphein*) which at the same moment impregnates her with a son, Epaphos, the founder of the royal families of Egypt and Argos and ancestor of the Danaïds (see p.162).

Teiresias or Tiresias, the most famous seer in the Theban legends, was said to have lived for seven generations. In one account, he sees two snakes copulating and strikes them with his stick, whereupon he is changed into a woman. Eight years later he comes across the same snakes copulating, strikes them again and is turned back into a man.

Later, Zeus and Hera are arguing about who has more pleasure in sex: Hera contends that women have far less than men. Teiresias, as the only person to know both sides of the story, is consulted. His answer, that women have nine times more pleasure than men, angers Hera so much that she strikes Teiresias blind. However, his blindness is compensated for by the gift of prophetic insight. It is Teiresias who reveals that Oedipus has killed his father and married his mother (see p.163).

Hermes prepares to cut off the head of Io's guardian Argos, whom the god has lulled to sleep with his stories. A vase painting of c.470BC.

ORPHEUS AND THE ORPHICS
One of the most widely known myths of transformation was the story of Orpheus and Eurydice, in which the great singer succeeded in bringing his beloved back from death in the underworld, only to lose her again. Orpheus himself was transformed from death to everlasting life, albeit in dismembered form.

Orpheus, a Thracian, was the son of Calliope, the Muse of epic poetry and eloquence, and was renowned as the greatest of all singers. He was married to Eurydice and when she died he was so broken by grief that he took his lyre and entered the underworld itself. As he played and sang, his music persuaded the gods of death to allow Eurydice to return to earth, on one condition: Orpheus must not look round as he led her back to the light. However, as he reached the exit of the underworld, Orpheus was overcome with fear and love and turned to look at Eurydice. She slipped back into the underworld forever.In his grief, Orpheus rejected all advances from women. A group of Thracian women became so incensed at this that they dismembered him, but to no avail: his disembodied head and lyre continued to sing. A temple was built over his head, from which prophecies were delivered.

Orpheus was believed to be the founder of a mystery religion, Orphism (see p.128).

ROME

*The Roman Forum was the religious, civic and commercial centre
of the city. It contained temples to Janus and Saturn, and also
a Temple of Vesta, where the flame of the city was kept
permanently alight.*

The Roman empire dominated most of the area of modern Europe and beyond for the first four centuries AD. Rome itself had a population of a million, while the empire accommodated fifty million or more, speaking well over a hundred languages, in addition to Latin, the language of the central administration.

The extent of Rome's sway is crucial to understanding its mythology. Over such a vast empire a single set of mythological and religious traditions could not have been sustained. The Egyptian myths of Isis and Osiris, the Greek myths of Oedipus and Agamemnon, the Celtic myths told in Britain and Gaul (modern France), were all in some sense *Roman* myths: the inhabitants of the empire, or parts of the empire, could think of them as their own.

The Romans absorbed the myths of their conquered subjects. For the modern observer, the result is an array of apparently contradictory images – temples of native Italian deities side by side with those of Greek or Eastern gods; high-ranking "Roman" priests standing shoulder to shoulder with the foreign, flamboyant, self-castrated priests of the Great Mother. No wonder some Romans debated what "real" Roman myth or religion might be.

Nevertheless, within this eclectic culture, a number of myths were seen as distinctively Roman. The best-known of these concern the foundation of the city (the myths of Aeneas and Romulus) and the legendary heroes of its early history. For the Romans the story of their city was the most important myth of all.

THE CITY OF ROME

Rome, to the inhabitants of the empire, was a sacred city, defined by a sacred boundary, the *pomerium*. It was within this religious space that many of the events of Rome's past were said to have taken place – their exact location still "known" and commemorated, even as late as the first centuries AD. Many of these episodes were part of the myth of Rome's founder, Romulus. The Lupercal (the cave in which he and his brother Remus were suckled by the wolf: see p.174) was identified with a cave on the slopes of the Palatine hill, which was embellished with ritual offerings. A primitive

wooden hut on the same hill, supposedly the dwelling-place of Romulus himself, was preserved right through the city's history. And the *pomerium* was traced back, despite various enlargements, to the plough furrow that Romulus marked out around his new city. A small pool in the Forum – the Curtian Lake – was said to mark the spot where a young Sabine warrior, Curtius, during the wars between Romulus and the Sabine people, had fallen from his horse and nearly drowned in a marsh. In these and other examples, the city of Rome acted as a constant reminder of the mythic tradition.

KEY TO INSET MAP

— Approximate line of *pomerium*, 1st century BC
● Altar of Peace
▲ Temple of the Great Mother
■ Site of the Lupercal
◆ Temple of Aesculapius

THE CITY OF ROME

Capitol · Forum · PALATINE HILL · AVENTINE HILL

KEY TO MAIN MAP

The city of Rome

The Roman Empire at its height, 2nd century AD

Limit of Roman control, 241BC

GODS AND THE EMPIRE

The Romans believed that their empire was acquired with the help of the gods, who rewarded Roman piety with military victories. Imperial conquests led to the absorption of new gods – those of the conquered peoples – and at the beginning of Roman expansion these were often similar in character to the existing deities of the city. As the empire stretched further afield the Romans encountered more obviously "foreign" deities, such as the Great Mother (see p. 171), who were harder to incorporate within Roman traditions.

TIME CHART	
753-510 BC	**Period of Monarchy**
753 BC	Legendary foundation of the city
509-31 BC	**Republican Period (Rome governed by elected magistrates)**
By 241 BC	Rome dominates most of Italy, including Sicily
218-201 BC	Rome's war against Hannibal
By 206 BC	Spain under Roman control
By 146 BC	Greece and the North African coast under Roman control
44-31 BC	Civil Wars, ending in the victory of the future emperor Augustus
From 31 BC	**Imperial Period**
31 BC-AD 14	Reign of Augustus, founder of imperial system. Augustus adds Egypt and parts of Germany to the empire; some later emperors add further territory
Mid-3rd century AD	Major series of barbarian invasions; empire in crisis
AD 284-305	Emperor Diocletian restores unity to empire
AD 307-337	Reign of Constantine; first emperor to be baptized a Christian
AD 364	Roman empire divided into Eastern and Western halves under different emperors
AD 476	Romulus Augustulus, last Roman emperor in the West, deposed

GODS AND GODDESSES

The borrowed pantheon; household gods and civic virtues

Venus (associated with the Greek Aphrodite) was thought to be the daughter of Jupiter, the wife of Vulcan and the mother of Cupid. She was supposedly the mother also of Aeneas. This wall painting from Pompeii shows the birth of Venus.

JANUS

The powers of Janus (god of doors and arches) were established by an early period in Roman religion. He had no Greek equivalent. Janus is depicted on coins as facing two ways, because of his link with entrances and exits (below).

It is no coincidence that the major gods and goddesses of the Roman pantheon were similar in character to Greek deities. Some of them were imported directly from the Greek world (for example, Aesculapius, god of medicine, derived from the Greek Asklepios who was introduced to Rome in 293BC on the instructions of an oracle following a devastating plague).

Other native deities were gradually reinterpreted, as Rome's contacts with Greece grew, to become the equivalents of particular Greek deities (for example, Jupiter as the equivalent of Zeus, Venus of Aphrodite). The Greek goddess Pallas Athene became Minerva, patron of crafts, to the Etruscans (whose pre-Roman civilization north of the Tiber flourished in the 6th century BC); and the Romans took over this goddess from their Etruscan predecessors. Diana, a goddess of the Italian woodlands, in due course became identified with the Greek Artemis. Apollo, the Greek god of light and intellect, also came to the Romans via the Etruscans, but did not attain prominence until the reign of the emperor Augustus (early in the 1st century AD).

There were no native myths in which these derivative deities played a part. Occasionally they appeared to men in visions, or came to fight alongside the Romans in battle (Castor and Pollux were said to have intervened in the battle of Lake Regillus in 496BC). But otherwise most of the narratives the Romans came to weave around their gods were borrowed from Greece, or were self-consciously invented following the Greek pattern. Ovid's poetic tales of transformation, the *Metamorphoses* (43BC-AD17), vividly render Greek myths in Roman guise. Especially noteworthy are the accounts of Jupiter deceiving his wife Juno (the Greek Hera) by giving his mistress Io the form of a cow; the nymph Daphne turning into a laurel tree to evade the appetites of Apollo; and the story of the hunter Actaeon, who observes the goddess Diana naked, and as punishment

Greek and Roman parallels

Deity	Greek "equivalent"	Major functions
Jupiter	Zeus	God of the sky; supreme god
Juno	Hera	Consort of Jupiter
Minerva	Athene	Goddess of wisdom
Apollo	Apollo	God of healing, poetry and music
Diana	Artemis	Goddess of hunting
Ceres	Demeter	Goddess of crops
Bacchus	Dionysos	God of wine
Mars	Ares	God of war
Venus	Aphrodite	Goddess of love
Neptune	Poseidon	God of the sea
Mercury	Hermes	God of commerce; divine messenger
Vesta	Hestia	Goddess of the hearth
Liber	Dionysos	God of ecstasy and wine
Saturn	Kronos	God of sowing and seed
Dis Pater	Hades	God of the underworld
Faunus	Pan	A god of the woodland
Cupid	Eros	God of love; son of Venus
Vulcan	Hephaistos	God of fire and forge
Aesculapius	Asklepios	God of medicine
Castor and Pollux	Castor and Polydeuces	Divine sons of Jupiter

Faunus, shown here in a wall painting, was an ancient Italian deity, whose attributes in Roman times assimilated those of the Greek god Pan.

The Lares were household gods worshipped in association with the Penates (gods of the storeroom, and hence the family's wealth). Household shrines often contained small statues of Lares, depicted as wearing a short tunic and holding a drinking horn and bowl (above).

GREEK AND ROMAN GODS COMPARED

Ancient authors themselves recognized a difference between Greek and Roman deities. Varro (a Roman writer of the 1st century BC) pointed out that in the earliest days of the city, Roman gods and goddesses, unlike their Greek counterparts, had never been represented in human form. A Greek historian, Dionysius, writing at about the same time, stressed the moral superiority of Roman over Greek deities: Romulus, he wrote, had raised the moral profile of the gods because, in founding the city, he had rejected all the old myths about the gods' dishonourable exploits.

MEN INTO GODS

Among the Roman gods were some who had started life as mortals. Rome's founder, Romulus, was supposedly deified at his death, becoming the god Quirinus. He was said to have mysteriously vanished, and then to have appeared in a dream to one of his citizens, explaining that he had been abducted to join the gods.

Later in the city's history the Roman Senate formally declared many of the emperors to be gods, after their death – and sometimes their wives and children too. One emperor, Vespasian, joked on his deathbed: "Oh dear, I think I'm becoming a god." Like all the immortals, these divine emperors were worshipped and had temples and cults dedicated to them.

The carved panel, above, found in Rome, shows the deification of the emperor Antoninus and his empress Faustina.

is transformed into a stag and harried to death by his own hounds.

The gods of Rome are conspicuously lacking in personality. Jupiter, as he appears in Virgil's *Aeneid*, lacks the tyrannical character and libidinous instincts of Zeus, while Venus has nothing of the sensuality or callousness of Aphrodite. Mars, unlike his Greek parallel the war god Ares, was associated with agriculture, reflecting the Roman concern with civic virtues and communal responsibilities: he also has a patriotic aspect as father of Romulus, first king of Rome. Especially shadowy were the ancient gods of the household, the Lares. Shrines to the Lares, a common feature of many houses, were often decorated with statues or paintings showing diminutive figures dressed in a short, flared, dog-skin tunic, carrying a drinking horn and an offering bowl (see p.169). But these deities played no part in any mythic tales: they had no individual names, and existed only as an undifferentiated group. Likewise, no stories ever became attached to the deities who personified human qualities – Fides ("faith"), Honos ("honour"), Spes ("hope"), and the like. They were merely emblematic, "standing for" the qualities to which they owed their names.

In addition to the household gods there were minor deities associated with various human activities. St Augustine, in his attack on paganism, found these an especially good subject for ridicule. In his broadside he listed the huge number of trivial deities who were said to supervise the wedding night of a Roman bride – Domiducus (the "leading-home" god), Subigus (the "subjecting" god), Prema (the "holding-down" goddess), and so on. Such deities were never represented in human form, and were never the stuff of mythical narrative.

The Great Mother

*O*ne of the most exotic deities introduced into Rome was the Great Mother (Magna Mater), borrowed from Asia Minor (modern Turkey) in 204BC. Many Roman writers described her arrival in Rome and the fantastic events that surrounded it. The following account is drawn largely from the poet Ovid, writing in the 1st century BC.

Hoping for victory in their war against the Carthaginians under Hannibal, the Romans consulted a local oracle, which gave a strange response: "The mother is absent: seek the mother. When she comes, she must be received by chaste hands." Puzzled, they applied to the Greek oracle at Delphi for a second opinion, and the oracle advised that they should "fetch the Mother of the Gods, who is to be found on Mount Ida". So they sent an embassy to King Attalus, in whose territory Mount Ida stood, and asked if they might remove the cult image of the Great Mother to Rome.

Attalus refused permission, but then the goddess herself miraculously spoke, saying that it was her own wish to go. Awed by these words, the king gave his consent and a boat was then built to carry the precious cargo.

The long voyage across the Mediterranean ended at Ostia, Rome's port at the mouth of the Tiber, where all the citizens came to meet the goddess. Men tried to pull the boat to shore, but it was grounded on a mudbank and could not be shifted. The Romans were afraid they would not be able to fulfil the terms of the oracle. But then Claudia Quinta came forward – a noblewoman who was wrongly accused of being unchaste, on the grounds that she dressed too elegantly and had too ready a tongue in arguments with men. Knowing herself to be innocent she stepped into the river mouth and held up her hands in prayer to the Great Mother. "If I am innocent of all charges," she exclaimed, "yield, goddess, to my chaste hands." She then drew in the boat effortlessly, and the cult image was escorted to its new temple.

The Romans always had mixed feelings about the Great Mother. On the one hand, her ecstatic cult, with its self-castrated priests, wild music and dancing, seemed foreign in character. On the other hand, because her homeland near Troy was the ultimate origin of the Roman race (according to the Aeneas legend), she was seen as a "native" deity.

A stone head (above) of the Great Mother (also known as Cybele).

A silver plate depicting Cybele in a chariot pulled by lions, sitting next to her "consort", the shepherd boy Attis.

THE FOUNDATION OF ROME

The destiny of Aeneas the Trojan

Aeneas is depicted in this Pompeii wall painting receiving treatment for his wounded leg. He has his arm around his son, and Venus, his mother, looks on.

Aeneas, in Greek mythology, was a minor Trojan hero in the conflict between the Greeks and Trojans. He was the son of Anchises and the goddess Aphrodite, who had prophesied before his birth that the child would one day rule over the Trojans and be the ancestor of an everlasting dynasty. From at least as early as the 3rd century BC, Aeneas was celebrated in Rome as the mythical founder of the Roman race; and the story of that foundation was told in the greatest of all Latin epic poems, Virgil's *Aeneid*, written in the 1st century BC.

When the Greeks destroyed the city of Troy, Aeneas escaped alive, carrying his father on his back, and in his arms his son (Ascanius) and the images of his ancestral gods. He embarked on a long and dangerous voyage around the Mediterranean (the aged Anchises died en route), eventually reaching Cumae on the shores of Italy. There he first of all consulted the Sibyl, a priestess of Apollo, who acted as his guide on a visit to the underworld. According to Virgil, he was here reunited with his father, who told him of the future greatness of the race he was destined to found, and showed him the souls of famous Romans of the future, waiting to be born.

From Cumae Aeneas set sail again, and landed in the Italian kingdom of Latium, where the king, Latinus, promised him the hand of his daughter Lavinia. An oracle had declared that she would marry a foreign prince. However, Lavinia had earlier been betrothed to Turnus, leader of another Italian tribe, the Rutilians. Partly as a result of this insult to Turnus, war broke out, in the course of which Aeneas and Latinus made an alliance with Evander, king of Pallanteum, the site of the future city of Rome. Eventually Aeneas killed Turnus in single combat.

Virgil's poem ends with the defeat of Turnus, but there were various traditions that told the rest of the story of the creation of Aeneas' dynasty. A few of these made Aeneas the founder of Rome itself. But more commonly it was said that Aeneas established the town of Lavinium (named after his bride); and that his son Ascanius founded a second town, Alba Longa.

The purpose of these versions, whereby Aeneas and Ascanius became the founders of the first "pre-Roman" Trojan settlements in Italy, was no doubt to make the story of Aeneas compatible with the other account of Rome's foundation, by Romulus, who was descended from the royal line of Alba Longa (see p.174).

Aeneas became an important symbol of Roman moral values – notably the piety shown by the heroic rescue of his father, and the perseverance and sense of duty that marked his early struggles to found the Roman race. This symbolism was particularly stressed in the reign of the emperor Augustus (31BC-AD14), whose family (the Julii) claimed direct descent from Aeneas. In one of his most magnificent building schemes, the "Forum of Augustus", the emperor displayed statues not only of Aeneas but also of Ascanius, the subsequent kings of Alba Longa, and the other ancestors who represented his direct link with Rome's founder.

Virgil's story of Aeneas includes an account of his love affair with the Carthaginian queen, Dido (see opposite). In earlier versions of Dido's story, Aeneas probably played no part; by bringing the two characters together, Virgil created one of the most renowned Roman legends of all.

Aeneas and Dido

In the course of Aeneas' wanderings around the Mediterranean, before he arrived in Italy, he landed at Carthage on the shores of North Africa. There, according to Virgil's Aeneid, *he fell in love with the Carthaginian queen, Dido.*

Dido was by birth a Phoenician from the city of Tyre. Forced to flee her homeland after the murder of her husband, she was completing the building of a new city at Carthage when Aeneas and his men were washed ashore nearby. She received them lavishly, and almost at once fell deeply in love with Aeneas. Encouraged by her sister, Anna, she began to accept her desire for the stranger and to hope for marriage.

One day, when she and Aeneas were on a hunting trip together, a storm blew up, and Aeneas and Dido found themselves sheltering alone in a cave. While the storm raged, they made love. From then on, they lived together as man and wife, and Aeneas behaved almost as if he were king of Carthage.

When the messenger of the gods came to remind Aeneas of his duty to found a new Troy in Italy, the Trojan decided that he must leave his beloved and con-

Aeneas and Dido embracing (above): a detail from a mosaic floor. The scene below, from the same site, shows the onset of attraction during hunting.

tinue on his journey. Dido soon discovered what his intentions were, and confronted him with his treachery. Though himself deeply upset, Aeneas could only plead that the gods had compelled him, and begged her not to make their parting doubly difficult.

In despair, Dido resolved on death. She built a vast funeral pyre for herself, pretending it was for a magical rite to bring Aeneas back, or at least to cure her love. After a sleepless night she rose to see Aeneas' ship already at sea. Cursing him and praying for everlasting enmity between Carthage and Aeneas' descendants, she climbed the pyre and, taking her lover's sword, mortally stabbed herself.

Aeneas did not escape Dido entirely. On a visit to the underworld, he met her ghost and attempted once more to justify his conduct. But Dido would not speak with him, and slunk away to be with the ghost of her husband.

The legend of Dido and Aeneas had close links with Rome's political and military history. Dido's prayer for enmity between Carthage and Rome provided a mythological justification for Rome's war against the Carthaginian Hannibal (218-201 BC).

ROMULUS AND THE KINGS OF ROME

The she-wolf and the myths of the past

THE WOLF AND THE TWINS
The image of Romulus and Remus, suckled by the wolf, was in due course used by Rome as a symbol of her growing power. In the early 2nd century BC, as Rome's military influence spread eastward, a monument depicting Romulus and Remus was erected even as far afield as the Greek island of Chios. In Rome itself the emperor Augustus often displayed the image of the wolf and twins next to that of Aeneas. Some Romans suggested that Augustus should take the name Romulus as his official title – but by a quirk of fate it was only the very last emperor, Romulus Augustulus, who did this. The mosaic above, from Roman Britain, illustrates the widespread symbolic power of the she-wolf idea.

The rape of the Sabine women, shown in a sculpted frieze on the Basilica Aemilia from the Forum at Rome. Another section of this frieze (late 1st century BC) shows the punishment of Tarpeia (see opposite).

The name of the city, Roma in Latin, comes from Romulus, its legendary founder. He and his twin brother Remus were offspring of Rhea Silvia, a woman of the royal line of Alba Longa, and the god Mars, who had seduced her in a sacred grove, where she was searching for water. When her uncle Amulius, the king, noticed her mysterious pregnancy, he imprisoned her; and as soon as the children were born, he had them abandoned on the banks of the Tiber to die.

The twins were found by a she-wolf, who suckled them until they were discovered by a shepherd (Faustulus) who brought them up as his own. When they were older, Romulus and Remus took to robbery, and on one occasion attacked some of Amulius' shepherds, who were guarding sheep on the Aventine hill (part of the future site of Rome). Remus was captured and brought before Amulius; and Faustulus chose this moment to explain to Romulus the facts of his birth (in one version he had observed the abandonment). After hearing the story, Romulus went straightaway to rescue Remus, murdered Amulius, and awarded the now vacant throne of Alba Longa to his grandfather, Numitor.

Romulus and Remus resolved to found their own city where the wolf had rescued them. However, a dispute arose between the twins about the exact location. Romulus, having received a sign from the gods, started to mark out a boundary around his chosen site on the Palatine hill; but Remus jumped over the boundary ditch (the original *pomerium*), as if to show how feeble a line of defence it was. Romulus saw this as sacrilege, killed Remus, and became sole king of the new city.

Romulus' immediate problem was manpower: he needed to populate Rome. So he established there a place of refuge where criminals and runaways from all over Italy could take up residence in safety as the first citizens. In order to find sufficient women, he resorted to a trick. He invited people from the surrounding areas – the Sabine tribes – to celebrate a joint religious festival, and in the midst of it gave a signal to his men to abduct the marriageable women.

In retaliation, the Sabine king, Titus Tatius, gathered his army and invaded Roman territory. After some fighting between the two sides, in which the Sabines penetrated Roman defences on the Capitoline hill, the Sabine women, now Roman wives, intervened, begging their fathers and husbands to cease hostilities. Peace was made, and the two peoples united. Until his death shortly after the war, Titus Tatius ruled jointly with Romulus. Then Romulus took charge of the whole community, ruling for a further thirty-three years – the first king of Rome.

Myths of Rome's history

*T*he boundary between Rome's early history and
Roman myth is hard to define precisely. As with
British accounts of King Arthur or King Alfred, factual
and legendary ingredients are mingled. Many of the
stories that Roman writers treated as "history" would
be seen, in modern terms, as "myth"; and they contain
many of the themes commonly found in mythology
throughout the world. In these stories the role of
women (their treachery or their chastity) is an especially
prominent topic.

During the conflict between Romans and Sabines that
followed the abduction of the Sabine women (see
opposite), a Roman woman named Tarpeia, the
daughter of the Roman commander in charge of the
Capitol, tried to betray the city to the enemy. She had
caught sight of Titus Tatius in his camp, and had fallen
in love with him. She agreed to let him into the city if
he promised to marry her. In another version of the
story her motive was greed: she coveted the Sabines'
gold bracelets, and asked for "what the Sabines were
wearing on their left arms". Titus Tatius penetrated
Rome's defences with her help, but he refused to
reward her treachery. She was crushed to death by the
Sabines, who indeed threw on top of her "what they
wore on their left arms" – not their bracelets but their
shields. A famous rock on the Capitoline Hill, the
"Tarpeian rock", from which traitors and murderers
were thrown to their deaths, was named after her.

The last king of Rome, Tarquin the Proud, was
brought down by the virtue of a Roman woman,
Lucretia. The king's son wanted to sleep with her, even
though she was married and renowned for her faithful
conduct. He came to her house while her husband was
away at war, and was hospitably entertained; and then
he held her down, sword in hand, and begged her to
make love to him. When she refused him, the young
Tarquin devised an irresistible form of blackmail: he
threatened to kill not only her but also one of his own
slaves, saying that he would leave their bodies side by
side, to make it look as if she, a noblewoman, had been
caught in adultery with a slave. Lucretia surrendered in
the face of the threatened shame, but after her attacker
had left her she summoned her father and husband,
and told them what had happened. Despite their pleas
and their assurances that she was guiltless, she killed
herself.

In revenge for her death, her relatives rose up against
the king, who fled to the nearby city of Caere. The
monarchy was overthrown, and Lucretia's husband
became one of the first magistrates (the consuls) of the
"free Republican" government that was established in
its place. The rape of Lucretia was the new Republic's
founding myth – and the title of "king" was from that
time on regarded with hostility in Rome.

*Later, the king of Clusium, attempting to restore
Tarquin to power, laid siege to the city of Rome.
However, according to legend he was defeated by the
heroic actions of Horatius Cocles, who with two other
defendants held off the enemy on their approach to the
Tiber bridge, and then swam to safety in their armour.*

The legendary seven kings of Rome

Name	Legendary dates of reign	Achievements	
Romulus	753-715 BC	Founder of Rome	*This Roman coin*
Numa	715-673 BC	Established major religious institutions	*shows Numa (on the left) making an animal sacrifice.*
Tullus Hostilius	673-642 BC	Renowned warrior	*He is carrying his*
Ancus Marcius	642-616 BC	Enlarged Rome	*priestly staff.*
Tarquin the Elder	616-579 BC	Founded Temple of Jupiter and Minerva on Capitol; other building activities	
Servius Tullius	579-534 BC	Constitutional reforms	
Tarquin the Proud	534-510 BC	Extended Roman territory; despotic ruler	

THE CELTIC WORLD

*This aerial view shows the fort of Dun Aonghusa, on Inishmore in
the Aran Islands, Ireland. Its triple drystone walls were said to
have been built by the mythical race, the Fir Bholg, who fled here
after being defeated in the first battle of Magh Tuiredh (see p.180).*

"Celtic" is essentially a linguistic term. The Celtic regions are those areas of Europe and Asia Minor in which related Celtic languages have been spoken at various times, ranging from Ireland in the west to Turkey in the east.

Unfortunately no single coherent system of pan-Celtic mythology is apparent. There are certain similarities between the Gaulish deities described by the Romans and the gods of the "insular" literatures (that is, those of the British Isles and Ireland). However, these correspondences are seldom simple or free from ambiguity.

The Roman interpretation of Celtic cults and deities is actually a source of obscurity. When Julius Caesar presents a Gaulish pantheon with what appears to be classical precision and clarity, he is actually reducing a multiplicity of deities to a uniformity derived from Roman preconceptions. Moreover, he gives his Gaulish gods Roman names.

It may be that the Continental Celts worshipped local, tribal deities. Where a Gaulish inscription uses a Roman god's name, sometimes the reference may be to a local deity equated with a Roman god; sometimes to a pan-Celtic deity given a Roman name.

According to Caesar, the greatest of the Celtic gods is the one he calls Mercury, almost certainly Lugus, the Irish Lugh. "Lugus", most scholars believe, means "The Shining One". The sun was venerated as life-giver and promoter of fertility and healing, with the wheel as its symbol.

Because no Continental Celtic myths have survived as narrative, the insular narratives are especially important as a source of mythological tradition. However, there are doubts about their accuracy. In Welsh, certain of the stories in the medieval Welsh collection the *Mabinogion* have been shown to be modelled on well-known international folktales, and accordingly cannot be taken with certainty as myths. Early Irish sagas no doubt draw upon archaic elements, but are now seen to be literary fictions typical of early European Christian civilization.

TIME CHART

9th century BC	Celts established north of the Alps and down to Mediterranean
6th century BC	Celts spread across modern France and former Czechoslovakia
c.400 BC	Celts invade northern Italy
387 BC	Celts sack Rome
280 BC	Galatae confederation enters Asia Minor
279 BC	Celts invade Greece and plunder shrine at Delphi
2nd century BC	Romans occupy Gaul
1st century AD	Romans occupy Britain
5th century AD	Anglo-Saxons invade England
5th-6th centuries	British Celts settle in Brittany

THE GOD LUGH IN PLACENAMES

The god Lugh provides a good example of the way in which placenames reflect the importance of certain deities. He is arguably the same as the Celtic god whom Caesar identified as Mercury and put at the top of the Gaulish hierarchy: Caesar's "Mercury" is "the inventor of all the arts", while in Irish Lugh is designated as "possessing, being skilled in, many arts". The Welsh cognate of Lugh is Lleu, and the older form of these names is Lugus, contained in the compound placename Lugdunon (in Latin form, Lugdunum). This is the linguistic source of the towns Laon and Lyon (the latter chosen by Augustus Caesar as the capital of Gaul and the site of his annual festival) in France, Leiden in the Netherlands and Leignitz in Silesia. Luguvalium, or Luguvallum, the Romano-British name of modern Carlisle, in northern England, is derived from *Luguvalos*, meaning "strong like Lugus" or "strong in Lugus".

KEY TO MAP

Areas of Celtic settlement, 4th–3rd centuries BC

Directions of temporary expansion by the Celts:

6th century BC

4th century BC

3rd century BC

THE CELTIC LANGUAGES

The whole of the British Isles was Celtic-speaking before and during the Roman occupation until the arrival of the Anglo-Saxons in England in the 5th century AD. There were two main linguistic branches of "insular" Celtic: Goidelic and Brythonic. Goidelic includes Irish and Scottish Gaelic, which still survive, and Manx, which died out in recent centuries. These last two languages arose from Irish colonization. Brythonic includes Welsh, Cornish (which died out in the 18th century) and Breton, the language of Brittany.

The Celtic languages of Continental Europe are known only from fragmentary evidence such as inscriptions and placenames.

PRONUNCIATION GUIDE

An accent signifies that a vowel is long. The stress in Irish is normally on the first syllable, in Welsh on the last but one.

In Irish, pronounce

c as English k	bh and mh as v
dh as th in then	th as th as in thin
gh plus a, o or u, as in got, only weaker	
gh plus i or e, as initial y in yet	
ch after a, o or u, as ch in Scottish loch	
s plus i or e like English sh	

In Welsh, pronounce

ll as English tl, articulated with force	
dd as th, as in then	f as v
w (as a vowel) as in oo in food	

ORIGINS AND EXPANSION OF THE CELTS

The Celtic regions extended from France (Gaul; Gallia), Iberia and Galicia in the west to Turkey (Galatia) in the east. The Celts first come into historical view in Greek writings of the 5th and 6th centuries BC. The historian Herodotus, in the 5th century BC, is the first to mention the Keltoi. About 400BC Celtic tribes invaded northern Italy; in 279BC other Celtic tribes plundered the shrine of Delphi in Greece; and in 280BC a confederation of Celts known collectively as Galatae crossed into Asia Minor. This was the age of expansion: the original home of the Celts was probably east of the Rhine, in what later became Bavaria and Bohemia, and westward to the Rhine itself.

THE CELTIC PANTHEON

A miscellany of gods

The wheel god depicted in this scene from the Gundestrup cauldron (see p.181) cannot be precisely identified, but the wheel symbol probably represents the sun and the turning cycle of the seasons.

THE DAGHDHA

The Daghdha, "The Good God", is also "The Mighty One of Great Knowledge". By mating with the goddess of war (who is in addition an earth goddess), encountered in one of her familiar roles, at a river, washing the heads and limbs of those who will die in battle, he secures victory for his people. He controls weather and crops, a function which invites comparison with the Roman Silvanus, a deity of woodlands, growth and tillage.

The Daghdha has two special attributes: a club, one end of which kills, while the other brings the dead to life; and a cauldron, from which, as Lord of the Otherworld, he dispenses never-ending hospitality.

Celtic goddesses (and to a lesser extent gods) are frequently represented in triple form. Irish myth has a triad of war-goddesses, sometimes treated as one deity, sometimes as three. Similarly, there are three goddesses called Macha, with the aspects of prophetess, warrior and matriarch. On the European Continent, female deities (Deae matres or Matronae) are depicted in threes. Similar groups, like the mother goddesses illustrated below, are found in Romano-Celtic Britain.

The druids, the priestly caste of the Celts, taught that everyone was descended from the god of the dead – in Irish, Donn, the "Dark One". But the title "Great Father" is reserved in Irish for the Daghdha, "The Good God", responsible for abundance and fertility. Sucellos, the "Good Striker", has Nantosvelta, a river goddess, as his consort.

Caesar names "Minerva" as Gaulish patron of arts and crafts, and the obvious Irish counterpart is Brighid, daughter of the Daghdha. Oenghus, son of the Daghdha, is sometimes identified by modern writers as the god of love, partly owing to the role he plays in helping the lovers Diarmaid and Gráinne (see p.184).

Nuadhu Airgedlámh in Irish (the Welsh equivalent is Nudd Llaw Eireint) is one of the leading figures in the so-called Mythological Cycle (see pp.180-81). An ancestor-god, king of his people, he loses an arm in battle against invaders and has it replaced with one of silver: his epithet means "of the Silver Arm (or Hand)".

The Gaulish Taranis is the "Thunderer", equated with Jupiter by the Romans. He is widely distributed, but is not found in Ireland.

Ogmios, who in Gaul was linked with eloquence, may be connected with the Irish god Oghma, the supposed inventor of the Ogham alphabet, which consists of strokes and notches cut in wood or stone.

There are a few deities known from Irish narrative tradition whose functions are clearly defined. Dian Cécht is the Divine Physician, who sang his incantations over a well into which the mortally wounded were cast and from which they rose again healed. Goibhniu is the prime figure in a triad of craftsman-gods, the others being Luchta and Creidhne; he is also host at the Otherworld Feast, where an intoxicating drink made all those who drank it immortal. Manannán is associated with the ocean and with the sea journey to the joyous Otherworld. Maponus, venerated in Gaul and Britain, and equated with Apollo, is the Divine Youth – the equivalent of the Irish Oenghus.

A typically Celtic coin, made in Gaul, 1st century BC, perhaps showing a deity.

Cernunnos, the antlered god

ernunnos, the "Horned One", is the name applied to various images of a male deity with antlers. He is Lord of Animals (domestic and wild), dispenser of fruit, grain or money, a god of fertility and abundance. He has been equated with Dis Pater, god of the dead. He almost certainly pre-dates his Celtic representations.

In general, horns symbolize aggressiveness and virility. In one Gaelic folktale, travellers to a mysterious island eat apples they find there, and immediately grow antlers. In one Scottish historical legend, warriors preparing for combat are seen suddenly to sprout antlers.

The earliest recorded depiction of Cernunnos is a rock carving of the 4th century BC in northern Italy, showing an antlered god who wears on each arm a twisted band of precious metal known as a torc (a common attribute of divine figures, usually worn as a neck-ring). He is accompanied by a ram-headed serpent and a small figure with an erect penis.

The name Cernunnos has been found only once, on a relief dedicated by sailors early in the 1st century ad. The god has the ears of a stag, and a torc hangs from each of his antlers.

He is often depicted with animals, sometimes with a bull. On a relief at Rheims, he appears seated like a Buddha, flanked by Mercury and Apollo, with a stag and a bull at his feet. The animals here are being fed from a large bag from whose mouth pours what appears to be grain. Other Gaulish images show the antlered god sitting entwined with two ram-headed serpents who eat from a heap of fruit on his lap.

Two British representations are noteworthy. A stone relief from southwest England shows the god with two large ram-headed serpents forming his legs; these rear up next to open purses of money on either side of him. A silver coin, *c.* AD20, from southern England shows the deity with a wheel between his horns. As the wheel is a solar symbol, this image perhaps represents fertility and the rebirth of the earth in the spring.

The serpent association is suggestive, as the serpent is a widespread symbol of fertility and regrowth, connected with the Underworld. In Gaelic tradition it re-emerges on St Bride's day, marking the return of spring. The ram-headed serpent connected with Cernunnos thus doubly symbolizes virility and renewal.

Cernunnos: a striking and well-known detail from the Gundestrup Cauldron (illustrated in its entirety on p.181). The antlered figure is seated cross-legged, wearing one torc and carrying a second, and is accompanied by a ram-headed or ram-horned serpent. The "Buddha posture" may be of Eastern origin.

MYTHS AND GODS OF IRELAND

The Mythological Cycle

THE VICTORY OF LUGH AT MAGH TUIREDH

Before the Second Battle of Magh Tuiredh, the Tuatha Dé gather at Tara for a royal feast, to which entry is restricted to practitioners of the arts. A handsome young warrior, Lugh, dressed like a king, approaches. He claims the right to enter, as he is "skilled in all the arts": he claims to be a wright, harpist, warrior, poet, sorcerer, physician, cupbearer, and to have many other skills besides. Nuadhu gives him the king's seat, and he takes over the preparations for the battle.

Lugh's grandfather is Balar of the Evil Eye, one of the Fomorian leaders. It was prophesied that Balar will be killed by his own grandson; and so Balar had his only daughter imprisoned in a cave where she was seduced and gave birth to triplets. Balar cast these children into the sea. But one was saved and reared by a smith: this survivor was Lugh.

Balar has an eye with a venomous gaze which when opened can disable an army of many thousands. As soon as Lugh sees the eyelid raised in battle, he casts a sling stone at it, which carries the eye through Balar's head. As a result it is Balar's own troops who are slaughtered by the eye's fatal glance.

THE TWO BATTLES

Irish myth tells of the First and Second Battles of Magh Tuiredh in two distinct accounts. The major account is that of the Second Battle. The story of the First Battle is textually later, and is in some respects derivative.

The stories are placed in context by *The Book of the Conquest of Ireland*, commonly known as *The Book of Invasions*, a monastic construction which purports to enumerate the successive invasions of Ireland since the Deluge.

The central story of the body of Irish myth which scholars call the Mythological Cycle tells of the First and Second Battles of Magh Tuiredh (Moytirra). The myth is concerned with a conflict between two armies of supernatural beings and the establishment of cosmic and social order.

The background is supplied by an account of five peoples who successively invade the country. First comes Cessair, daughter of Bith, son of Noah, forty days before the Flood. All her company perish except one Fintan mac Bóchra, who lives for another 5,500 years in the form of a salmon, an eagle, and a hawk, acting as witness to the subsequent events.

The second invasion, 300 years after the Deluge, is that of Parthalón, a descendant of Japheth, son of Noah. His people establish a settled way of life: four plains are cleared and made habitable, cattle are introduced and houses built, and ale is brewed. The enemies of the race are the Fomorians, descended from Noah's son Ham, whom Noah had cursed; on account of that curse they are monstrous beings, one-armed and one-legged. Parthalón and his people are finally destroyed not by their enemies but by plague. There is only one survivor, Tuan mac Sdairn.

Thirty years after Parthalón's invasion comes Nemhedh, whose descendants in due course attack the Fomorians in their island stronghold. Most are killed in the attempt, but those who survive the battle (one boat's complement of thirty men) scatter from Ireland in various directions – Britain, the "northern islands of the world," and Greece.

The next two invasions are both led by descendants of Nemhedh. From those who have been driven into servitude in Greece come the Fir Bholg, the "Men of Bags or Sacks", a name given to them because during their Greek exile they were forced to make arable land by covering rocks with earth which they carried in bags. They have five leaders and divide the land between them into five provinces – hence the division of Ireland into Ulster, Leinster, Connacht, Munster, with Meath as the centre. They hold the country for thirty-seven years and institute kingship. The last of their kings, Eochaidh mac Eirc, is the prototype of the good ruler, beginning a long tradition linking fertility with justice. In his reign no rain falls, only dew, and there is no year without harvest; and falsehood is banished from Ireland.

The fifth invasion is that of the Tuatha Dé Danann, descendants of the people who have exiled themselves to "the northern islands of the world". Their arrival leads to the First Battle of Magh Tuiredh, fought against the Fir Bholg, in which the latter are defeated. While in the "northern islands", the Tuatha Dé have become skilled in druidry, heathen lore and devilish knowledge. They bring to Ireland four talismans: the Stone of Fál which shrieks when a lawful king sits on it; the spear of Lugh which ensures victory to anyone who holds it; the sword of Nuadhu from which no one can escape when it is drawn from its scabbard; and the Cauldron of the Daghdha (see panel, opposite).

At the First Battle, the leader of the Tuatha Dé Danann, Nuadhu, has his right arm severed at the shoulder by a blow from Sreng, a Fir Bholg warrior. Sreng becomes leader and makes peace with the Tuatha Dé, leaving all of Ireland to them except Connacht, which he chooses for his own people. But Nuadhu loses the kingship, because a man with a physical blemish cannot be ruler, and Bres becomes king in his stead.

Soon Bres's rule becomes mean and oppressive. Even the Daghdha is reduced to digging and building a fort for the king. After he is satirized by a poet, Coirbre, he is forced to renounce the kingship and sets out to gather an army of the Fomorians against the Tuatha Dé. Meanwhile the physician Dian Cécht fashions a silver arm for Nuadhu. He is reinstated as king, but abdicates in favour of Lugh, a stranger who impresses the court at Tara with his skills in all the arts. In the ensuing Second Battle, Lugh is victorious and the Fomorians are driven back to the sea. Bres, whose actions brought about the battle, is spared by Lugh in return for revealing the secrets of agricultural prosperity. Two prophecies from the war goddess Morríghan after the battle, one of cosmic order and prosperity, the other of chaos and the end of the world, round off the great myth.

In the chronology of *The Conquest of Ireland*, all these invasions precede the coming of the Gaels, the Sons of Míl. The name in full, Míl Espaine, is simply a borrowing from the Latin *miles Hispaniae*, "soldier of Spain" (the Latin for Ireland, *Hibernia*, was believed to be derived from *Iberia*, "Spain"). The Sons of Míl land in the south-west of Ireland on the feast of Beltane (May 1st) and overcome the Tuatha Dé Danann in battle. Then they set off towards Tara and inflict a final defeat. Then the poet Amhairghin divides Ireland in two, giving the half of the country that is underground to the Tuatha Dé Danann, who are exiled to the hills and fairy regions.

The Daghdha's cauldron

The cooking pot of the Great Father has a central role in the Otherworld Feast. The literature also describes various parallel treatments of the same idea. At the Feast of Goibhniu the god of the Underworld is the Divine Smith: those who eat and drink at his table neither age nor die. There is also the Cauldron of Da Derga, which cooks continually for the men of Ireland. The Daghdha's Cauldron, being that of the Great Father, can simply be taken as the type of them all.

The cauldron of the Daghdha is a source of plenty: "no company ever went away unsatisfied". The Second Battle of Magh Tuiredh contains a story of the Daghdha's humiliation. During a truce before battle with the Daghdha, the Fomorians prepare a vast meal of porridge for him, knowing it to be a favourite food of his. The idea was to mock him. They filled the cauldron with 80 measures of new milk and the same quantity of meal and fat,

The Gundestrup Cauldron, a 14-inch (36-cm) high silver vessel for ritual feasts, found in five pieces in a Jutland peat bog.

along with goats, sheep and swine. Then they boiled the mixture and poured it into a hole in the ground. The Daghdha was then ordered to consume the entire meal or be slain. The god ate the meal and scraped out the remains with his finger. Afterwards he fell asleep. When he woke up he saw a beautiful girl but was unable to make love to her because his belly was so enormously distended with the "porridge".

There is also a Cauldron of Rebirth in Welsh literature, notably in the story of Branwen, daughter of Llyr. The corpses of dead warriors are put into the vessel, a fire is kindled beneath it, and next morning the warriors spring forth as fierce as ever, except that they cannot speak.

The cauldron in the story is of Irish origin. The Cauldron of Rebirth is not an Irish idea, but there are parallels in the Irish notion of bringing the slain back to life by bathing them in a milk-filled trench or casting them into a well over which spells had been chanted.

THE HERO OF ULSTER

Tales of Cú Chulainn

THE BACKGROUND
The epic narrative of *Táin Bó Cuailnge* (The Cattle Raid of Cooley) brings together the deeds of the Irish heroes, pitching the "Men of Ireland" (Connacht) against the "Men of Ulster". An assemblage of tales (probably written *c.*AD700), the Táin includes various prefatory stories which give an added dimension to the narrative, among them the story of Deirdre, which explains how the Ulster hero Ferghus came to be on the Connacht side. A later, harmonized version of the epic sets the scene of the conflict as follows. Ailill, King of Connacht, and his wife Medhbh, talking in bed, argue over a great bull – the White-horned – which had originally been hers but had joined the King's herd, unwilling to be the property of a woman. She swears she will find another as good, but the only suitable animal is the Brown Bull of Cooley. Messengers are sent to the owner and offer generous terms, but they are heard boasting that if the bull is not given freely they will take it by force. War inevitably follows.

Cú Chulainn's association with hounds derives from the occasion in his youth when he killed the watchdog belonging to Culann the Smith (see margin, opposite). This hound sculpture, despite its modern appearance, is from the Romano-Celtic shrine at Lydney in Gloucestershire, southwest England.

In the war between the Men of Ireland and the Men of Ulster (see margin, left), Ferghus is appointed to guide the Connacht army, but his feelings for his own people cause him to lead the army astray and send warnings to Ulster. As a result of an old curse (laid on them for their brutality toward a supernatural woman, Macha), the Ulstermen are stricken with a debilitating illness, which comes upon their warriors in times of danger. Only Cú Chulainn and his human father Sualtamh (his divine father is the god Lugh) are exempt from the curse, and set out to meet the enemy.

Cú Chulainn kills a hundred warriors, and then, with Medhbh's agreement, engages in a long series of single combats at a ford, fighting a different warrior every day. He defeats them all. Then he turns back to defend his own territory and finds the Brown Bull being driven away. He kills the warrior who is leading the raid, but loses the bull nevertheless – a cause of the utmost dismay to the hero.

Lugh comes to Cú Chulainn's aid, curing his wounds as he lies asleep for three days and nights. Meanwhile the boys of Ulster fight three battles against Medhbh's warriors. They kill three times their own number, but a hundred and fifty of them are lost in the process. Cú Chulainn awakes and hears of this disaster, and slaughters a hundred and thirty kings, women, children and churls in a fury of revenge.

At last Medhbh calls upon Fer Diadh, Cú Cuchlainn's foster-brother, to fight him. For three days they fight without advantage on either side. Each night Cú Chulainn sends herbs to heal Fer Diadh's wounds, and Fer Diadh sends food to Cú Chulainn. On the fourth day Cú Chulainn choses to fight at the ford where his record in combat is unblemished. For a long time they battle, until Cú Chulainn calls for the *gae bolga*, the terrible weapon which he alone has been taught to use by Scáthach, a woman warrior who once instructed both the foster-brothers. The weapon enters the body as a single barb but increases to twenty-four barbs in the wound. Fer Diadh is killed by this brutal device, and Cú Chulainn sings a lament over him.

Cú Chulainn's father Sualtamh comes to the site of the battle, and Cú Chulainn, prostrate from his wounds, sends him to rouse the Men of Ulster. Conchobhar, the Ulster king, summons his warriors, and he and Ferghus fight shield to shield. Ferghus strikes three mighty blows so that Conchobhar's magic shield screams aloud. Cú Chulainn hears the scream and rises in a warlike fury. Ferghus, who has promised that he would never face Cú Chulainn in battle, retreats with the men of Leinster and Munster. Cú Chulainn plunges into battle, defeats the last of the bands and overtakes Medhbh. He spares her life because she is a woman, and allows her army to pass across the Shannon into Connacht.

Medhbh has sent the Brown Bull to Connacht for safety. Arriving there, he utters three mighty bellows. The White-horned Bull hears them and comes to fight him. All the surviving warriors assemble to watch. The great bull-fight continues into the night and is conducted all over Ireland. In the morning the Brown Bull is seen carrying his defeated rival on his horns. He gallops back to Ulster, scattering fragments of the dead White-horned's flesh. When he comes to the border of Cooley, his heart breaks and he dies. Ailill and Medhbh make peace with Cú Chulainn and the Men of Ulster. For seven years there is no war between them, and nobody is killed.

The death of Cú Chulainn

In the war against Medhbh, Queen of Connacht, Cú Chulainn slays a warrior, Cailidín, whose wife subsequently gives birth to three sons and three daughters. Medhbh sends these children abroad to study sorcery and on their return has them despatched against Cú Chulainn.

Conchobhar, hearing that treachery is planned, ordered Cú Chulainn to remain in Emhain Mhacha until the fighting was over. The hero was guarded there by women, the daughters of kings and nobles, among them Niamh, his mistress, and by the druids of Ulster. His guardians took him to a certain valley for his safety, but when Cú Chulainn saw the place he recognized it as the Valley of the Deaf and refused to enter.

At the same time, the children of Cailidín conjured up phantom battalions around the valley, making Cú Chulainn believe that the land was overrun with raiding warriors and that the sounds he heard were those of battle. Disconcerted by this clamour, and feeling himself insufficiently prepared for battle, he ordered his horses to be harnessed to his chariot, but Niamh embraced him and persuaded him to stay with her. Then Conchobhar ordered his attendants to take Cú Chulainn into the Valley of the Deaf immediately, because he would not hear the battle cries there. Reluctantly, the hero went with them, after a visitation by women, poets and harpists.

The children of Cailidín looked for him in vain. Thinking that Cathbhadh the druid must have concealed him, by magic arts they flew like birds, searching the entire province until they came to the Valley of the Deaf. Here they saw the Liath Macha (The Grey) and the Dubh Saingleann (The Black), Cú Chulainn's horses, with Laegh the charioteer in charge of them. They understood then that Cú Chulainn was there too, hearing the noise and the music around him.

Then the children of Cailidín gathered sharp downy thistles and puff-balls and fluttering withered leaves of the woods, and made armed warriors of these things, so that there was not a peak or a hill around the valley which was not filled with troops. The whole land was full of wild battle cries audible even in the clouds of heaven, and with the noise of horns and trumpets.

Cú Chulainn believed that the Men of Ireland were plundering the entire province. But Cathbhadh the druid persuaded him it was only the spectral hosts conjured up against him by the children of Cailidín. Then Badhbh, daughter of Cailidín, took the form of Niamh and asked Cú Chulainn to fight the Men of Ireland. Cathbhadh and the women all tried to stop him but could do nothing. Cú Chulainn heard the great cries as loudly and terribly as before, and saw many strange and horrible phantasms. The real Niamh told him it was not she but Badhbh who had come to him in her form. But he did not believe her, and went to do battle.

The sons of Cailidín had prepared three magic javelins. The first of these killed Cú Chulainn's charioteer, the second wounded the Liath Macha, and the third stuck Cú Chulainn himself. Realizing that death was near, he tied himself to a pillar-stone so that he could face his enemies standing upright. For three days no one dared approach him, until one of the daughters of Cailidín came in the form of a crow and landed on the stone. Then everyone knew that Cú Chulainn was dead.

HOW CU CHULAINN GOT HIS NAME

King Conchobhar invited his foster-son Sédanta (later to be called Cú Chulainn) to a feast given by Culann the Smith, but the boy was busy playing and promised to come later. The king forgot about the boy, so that when Sédanta eventually arrived, he was attacked by Culann's hound. The boy then killed the beast with his bare hands. Everyone else was upset that the king's foster-child had been threatened, but Culann lamented that he was now unguarded. The boy offered to act as a watchdog himself until he could rear a whelp of the same strain. Cathbhadh the druid told him that henceforth his name would be Cú Chulainn, which means "the hound of Culann".

DEIRDRE

Following a prophecy that she will be very beautiful but will bring death and ruin to the men of Ulster, King Conchobhar has the baby Deirdre fostered in secret in order to marry her himself when she is of age. One day, as a young woman, she sees her foster-father flaying a calf outside in the winter snow and a raven drinking the calf's blood, and says to her nurse Lebhorcham: "Dearly would I love any man with those three colours – his hair like the raven, his cheek like blood and his body like snow." Lebhorcham tells her that such a man lives nearby: Naoise, son of Uisneach. They meet and flee together to the wilds of Scotland. Conchobhar invites them back and sends the great warrior Ferghus to escort them. But when they arrive at Emhain, Conchobhar has Naoise put to death (at the hands of Eoghan) and Deirdre brought to him with her hands bound behind her back. Enraged at this treachery, Ferghus and his men ravage Ulster and transfer their allegiance to the hostile court of Medhbh, queen of Connacht.

Deirdre is forced to live with Conchobhar. When he asks her after a year (during which time she has not once smiled or raised her head from her knee) what she hates most, she replies: "You and Eoghan." The king tells her she must live with Eoghan, and next day the two men take her off in a chariot – "a sheep between two rams", as Conchobhar says. As the chariot moves on, it comes near to a rock, and Deirdre dashes her head against the rock and dies, ending her misery.

FINN AND HIS WARRIORS

The Fenian myths

THE HUNTING OF THE BOAR

The boar was a leading symbol for the Celts. There is evidence for boar sacrifice, and the Gaulish deity Mercury Moccus (*moccus* is a Latinized form of the Gaulish word for "pig" or "swine") may have been a protector of boar hunters. The animal has a prominent role in the popular folktale of Diarmaid and Gráinne.

Gráinne is betrothed, unwillingly, to Finn, who is at this time an aging widower. On the night of the wedding feast Gráinne elopes with Diarmaid, whom she has put under a spell. When Finn and his men pursue the fugitives, Oenghus, god of love and Diarmaid's foster-father, spirits them away to safety. The couple wander through Connacht and Munster, and in due course become lovers. They live happily until the day of the great hunt of the magic boar of Beann Ghulban (Ben Bulben) in Sligo. The boar had once been Diarmaid's foster-brother who, it has been foretold, would bring about Diarmaid's death. Diarmaid is wounded by the boar and his only chance of life is a draught of water from the healing hands of Finn. Twice Finn comes with the water, but when he remembers Gráinne he lets it trickle through his fingers. Diarmaid dies, and Oenghus bears away his body to Brugh na Bóinne, the ancient burial ground of Newgrange, in County Meath.

The illustration, above right, shows a bronze cult wagon of the 6th or 7th century BC.

Many Celtic boar images show the creature with raised dorsal spines. In one version of the story of Diarmaid and the hunting of the boar, the boar has a poisonous dorsal spine which gives Diarmaid his death wound.

The great literary corpus which scholars call the Fenian Cycle takes its name from Finn (modern Gaelic: Fionn) and his followers, the Fian, a band of warrior-hunters once thought to have been active in the 3rd century AD, but now attributed to myth. Finn and his heroes were conspicuous in the later Middle Ages, but it is clear that this represents a surfacing, and to some extent a re-making, of a narrative tradition already known in much earlier times. References to Finn from the 8th, 9th and 10th centuries connect him with fighting, wooing and hunting, and bring him into conflict with supernatural beings in encounters localized throughout Ireland. Later he is represented as a warrior-seer. He is possibly identifiable with the god Lugh: both names mean "Fair One" or "Bright One", and Lugh fights with the one-eyed Balar, just as Finn fights with "One-eyed" Goll, his chief Otherworld adversary (otherwise called Aodh, or "Fire"). By the end of the 12th century, the Fian (often depicted as giants) occupied a pre-eminent position in Gaelic tradition, evident in folktales and ballads of Scotland as well as Ireland.

The great 12th-century literary compilation *The Colloquy of the Old Men* identifies Finn as the son of Cumhall, head of the House of Baoisgne, at enmity with Goll, head of the House of Morna. Finn is both hunter and poet, and functions outside the bounds of settled society. According to some stories, he acquired his gift of prophecy and supernatural knowledge by imbibing the drink of the Otherworld; another tradition, which persists in folklore to the present day, claims that he once touched the Salmon of Knowledge with his finger (see panel, opposite).

Finn has a son, Oisín, whose mother is an Otherworld deer-woman who rears Oisín in the wilderness. Traditionally Oisín is the poet of the Fian. One of the major themes of the Fenian ballads which he supposedly composed is the threat posed by the Vikings. In Gaelic belief the fabulous land of Lothlind (later Lochlann, "Norway") is the home of the Vikings, who are themselves represented as beings of an otherworld.

The Fian, being hunters in the wilderness, have a natural affinity with animals. Finn's favourite hounds, Bran and Sceolang, are his own metamorphosed nephews (or nephew and niece). One of the most conspicuous of the Fenian heroes is Conán, the troublemaker, whose name means "Little Hound". In Scottish tradition Finn's foster-mother, Luas Lurgann ("Speed of Shank"), possesses the swiftness of deer.

The Colloquy of the Old Men tells of a division of Ireland: the nobility express their preference for towns, fortresses and treasures, while the Fian choose Ireland's cliffs and estuaries, forests and wildernesses, her beautiful speckled salmon and her game. Oisín and Caílte (modern Caoilte) are both pictured as having survived the other members of their band long enough to meet St Patrick. Accompanying the saint on a journey through Ireland, they (in later versions) argue about paganism and Christianity.

Diarmaid, whose fame centres on his role in the elopement of Diarmaid and Gráinne, is the handsome young hero of the Fian. In folktales he has a "love-spot": any woman who saw it would fall helplessly in love with him. He is sometimes known as Diarmaid Donn, suggesting a link with Donn, the god of the dead.

Conán the Bald is a brother of the great warrior Goll, son of Morna, who is both Finn's follower and his rival. In 12th-century literature Conán is portrayed as impulsive and malicious, whereas in post-medieval narratives he is a comic figure. One story tells how the Fian find themselves stuck to the floor by the hostile magic of their adversaries in an Otherworld dwelling, the Rowan-tree Hostel. Eventually all are released except Conán, who has to be torn from his seat, leaving the skin of his buttocks on the floor.

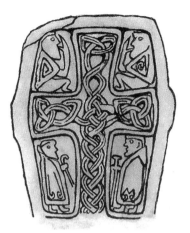

The thumb-sucking figure on this Celtic cross is probably Finn. Whenever he required to draw upon his magical wisdom, he had only to put his finger on his "tooth of knowledge" (see panel, below).

Finn and the Salmon of Knowledge

*T*he eo fis, *the Salmon of Knowledge, acquired its supernatural wisdom through eating the nuts of nine hazel trees which fell into the Well of Seghais, the spring of the Otherworld in which it lived, and made bubbles of mystic inspiration. This well is taken to be the source of the two great rivers of Ireland, the Boyne and the Shannon. Linn Feic, a pool on the Boyne, is represented as one of the homes of the salmon.*

When Finn was a lad (and his name was not Finn but Demhne), he went to seek instruction from one Finn the Poet, who has been described as an emanation of the timeless wisdom of the River Boyne. Finn the Poet had been waiting seven years for the Salmon of Linn Feic, because it had been prophesied that eating the salmon would bring him boundless knowledge. The salmon was caught and entrusted to Demhne to cook; but the poet told him not to eat any of it. When the lad brought him the cooked salmon, he told the poet that he had not eaten any of it but described how he had

burned his thumb on the salmon and then put his thumb in his mouth. The poet said that the boy's name from then on would be Finn, and that he was the one to whom it had been given to eat the salmon. So the lad then ate the flesh of the fish. He learned the three qualifications of a poet – that is, "knowledge that enlightens", "chewing the pith" and "incantation from tips" (possibly the fingertips). Whenever, in the future, the hero put his thumb in his mouth and sang "Chewing of the pith" (perhaps raw or taboo flesh), whatever he did not know would be revealed to him.

Another version, which is followed by modern folktales, of how Finn received his gift of prophecy gives a similar account. The young boy is entrusted with the cooking of the salmon, which must be prepared with the skin unblemished. A blister rises on the skin and Finn presses it down, burning his finger in the process. He puts his finger in his mouth to ease the pain and discovers the prophetic gift.

GODDESSES

Motherhood, war and sovereignty

THE HORSE GODDESS
The horse goddess Epona, the Divine
Horse, was venerated throughout the
Celtic world, from Britain to the Danube.
She had the unique honour among Gaulish
divinities of being given a festival by the
Romans; in particular, the Gaulish cavalry
in the Roman army were her devotees.
Epona has associations with water,
fertility and death – aspects which seem to
connect her with the Mother Goddess.

The cult of the mother goddess has left clear traces in Celtic mythology.
The Irish Tuatha Dé Danann are the family of the goddess Danu; while in
Wales the gods are descended from Dôn. Anu, an earth goddess linked
with Danu, is described as the mother of the gods of Ireland.

War goddesses appear under a variety of names: the Morríghan,
Bodhbh (or Badhbh), Nemhain, and Macha. Other goddesses instruct or
give birth to heroes. Scáthach, "The Shadowy One", taught Cú Chulainn.
Medhbh of Connacht, who leads the armies of the Men of Ireland, is
identifiable with sexual power: no king may rule in Tara without having
first mated with her. Sex and war also occur together in Flidhais, the only
partner who could satisfy Ferghus: a Celtic equivalent of the Roman
Diana, she is goddess of the moon and hunting. Diana is conflated too
with Continental Celtic goddesses of the hunt, such as Abnoba of the
Black Forest, and Arduinna, patronesses of wild boars, from the Ardennes.
Bodhbh and Nemhain are to some extent interchangeable with the
Morríghan. Their cries struck such terror that warriors died on hearing
them. Boann, the divine spirit of the River Boyne, was the wife of Nechtan,
a water god. She mates with the Daghdha (as does the Morríghan) to
produce Oenghus, god of love. When she broke a prohibition against
visiting Nechtan's well, the waters rose and engulfed her, becoming the
Boyne, the great river of Irish myth.

All these attributes come together in the concept of Sovereignty. The
king in myth is "married" to his kingdom in a ceremony, at which a
libation is offered him by his bride, Sovereignty. The Sovereignty of
Ireland may appear as an ugly hag, symbol of the desolate and bloody
kingdom. However, when kissed by the rightful claimant to kingship, she
becomes a beautiful girl who reveals herself as a goddess.

Brighid and St Bride

*T*he pagan goddess Brighid was so popular that
she has been taken over as a Christian saint
(St Bride of Kildare), with the same attributes
of fertility and the ability to strike terror in a
hostile army.

The name Brighid derives from the Celtic root
brig ("exalted"), which is often found in place
and tribe names, and suggests that she was a
goddess of sovereignty. The daughter of the
Daghdha, she was expert in poetry and arcane
learning. Her two sisters, also
called Brighid, were associated
with the arts of healing and with
craftsmanship. The three were

*The Romano-Celtic goddess Minerva
(above) is identified with Brighid. Both
were commemorated by an eternal flame.*

often treated as a single deity.

The cult of St Bride, which had a
conspicuous fertility aspect, perpetuated the
name of the goddess. The saint took over many
divine functions: her cows yielded a lake of
milk; her food supply was inexhaustible; one
measure of her malt made ale for all her
churches. Her festival is February 1st, the pre-
Christian feast of Imbolg, associated with the
lactation of ewes, and one of the four great Celtic
seasonal festivals. In popular belief St Bride
protects flocks, is guardian of the
family hearth, and presides over
childbirth. She is the foster-mother
of Christ.

OTHERWORLDLY VOYAGES

Conla, Mael Dúin and Bran

The Irish Adventures and Voyages tell of journeys to the Otherworld, a mysterious, ambiguous place. Although its powers can be hostile, it is essentially a place of timeless content, feasting and enchanted music, where old age and death are unknown. It may be entered through caves or lakes, or through chance encounters with its representatives, who invite or entice mortals to one of its dwellings. Its many names include the Plain of Two Mists, the Land of the Young and the Land of the Living. In the Voyages it is often the Promised Land of the west, located in the ocean or beyond the seas.

In the Adventure of Conla, a woman seen only by Conla calls him to the Plain of Delight. Conla's father, Conn of the Hundred Battles, orders his druid to prevent the invisible woman, whose voice they could all hear, from luring away his son. The druid's chanting drives her off, but as she disappears she throws Conla an apple. For a whole month this apple sustains him: he refuses all other food or drink, and the apple does not decrease. A great longing comes upon him to see the woman again. When she appears a second time and tells Conla that they can go together in her ship of glass, he follows her. They sail away in a crystal coracle, never to be seen again.

The Voyage of Mael Dúin's Ship tells how Mael Dúin sets out to avenge his father's death. This entails a sea journey, and a druid's instructions as to the building of the ship and the exact number of the crew. This last injunction is violated by Mael Dúin's foster-brothers, who swim out and join the vessel. When the ship reaches the island where the slayer of Mael Dúin's father lives, a great storm arises and drives them out to sea. Then Mael Dúin and his men let their craft sail wherever God pleases. Their voyage brings them to thirty-one islands, each with its own terrors and wonders. There are swarms of ants, each as big as a foal. There is a beast that has feet like a hound's and prances before the voyagers, overjoyed to see them because it longs to eat both them and their boat. And on another island, demons are having a horse-race.

After many adventures the voyagers come upon a silver pillar, with a silver net reaching far out from its top. The ship sails through the mesh and one of the company cuts a piece of it to lay on the altar at Armagh, should they ever reach home again. At length they come to the Land of Women. After feasting, each man sleeps with a woman, and Mael Dúin sleeps with the queen, who invites the visitors to stay with her and live there forever, enjoying the pleasures they have already tasted. After some time Mael Dúin's companions prevail upon him to leave. The queen throws a ball of thread to him as their boat sets sail; he catches it and by pulling on the end she still holds she draws the ship back to land. This happens three times. Then Mael Dúin lets another man catch the ball of thread; it clings to his hand, but one of the crew cuts off his arm and they all sail away. After other marvellous encounters they see a falcon flying southeast and, following it, in due course come home to Ireland. They lay the piece of silver mesh on the altar of Armagh and recount all that has happened to them.

Some experts hold that both the Adventures and the Voyages are pagan myths with Christian colouring or interpolations. Others maintain that the Voyages are Christian compositions, and the Adventures pagan. However, an increasingly influential body of scholarship regards them both as Christian allegories.

A gold model boat, with mast and oars, dating from the 1st century BC, from Broighter, County Derry, Northern Ireland.

THE VOYAGE OF BRAN

The *Voyage of Bran*, a prose tale interspersed with poetry, is now generally agreed to be an allegory of the progress of the soul. A woman comes to Bran, bearing the branch of a tree, which she has brought from the Underworld. She urges him to set out for that magical place. She prophesies the birth of Christ: a lord without beginning or end, born of a virgin. Bran and twenty-six companions cross the Delightful Plain, a paradise where there is no sin, and come to the Island of Merriment, where the inhabitants do nothing but laugh and shout. Next they reach the Island of Women, a place of libertine delights. One of the voyagers, Nechtán, pines for home, so the queen of the island allows them to leave, but warns them not to set foot on land. When they reach Ireland, Nechtán does precisely that, and at once turns to ashes. When Bran announces his own name, those assembled on the shore say: "We do not know him, but the Voyage of Bran is one of our ancient stories." Bran, from the ship, gives an account of his adventures, and then sails away, never to be heard of again.

STORIES OF WALES

The *Mabinogion*

THE WONDROUS HEAD
The Second Branch of the *Mabinogion* introduces the three members of the family of Llyr: Branwen, Manawydan and Brân the Blessed. Manawydan and Brân were evidently linked in ancient tradition as sons of the sisters of Beli the Great, an ancestor-deity of several of the royal lines of Wales.

The gigantic Brân leads the Britons to war against the Irish, over whom victory is won only when the magic cauldron of rebirth, which the Irish possess, has been destroyed. Brân, wounded in the foot (like Bron the Fisher King in Arthurian romance), commands his head to be cut off by the seven survivors of the battle. They bury the head at the White Mount in London in order to protect the kingdom, and while they spend seven years feasting at Harlech, and eighty years at Gwales in Penvro, the severed head remains undecayed, "as good a companion as it ever was".

Although mythic elements have been uncovered in medieval Welsh tales, the rich literature of Wales is not, in the eyes of many scholars, so obviously a repository of myth as the early literature of Ireland. There is only one significant Welsh collection: the *Mabinogion*. Its tales were primarily compiled for entertainment by literary and antiquarian-minded entertainers at the court of the Welsh nobility, but larger social and political concerns must have exercised their own conscious and unconscious influences over the retelling of the old stories.

The main narrative of the *Mabinogion* is divided into the Four Branches of the Mabinogi – the stories of Pwyll, Branwen, Manawydan and Math. (*Mabinogion* is a 19th-century title.) The First and Third Branches concern the family of Pwyll, the Second Branch the family of Llyr, and the Fourth Branch the family of Dôn. Pryderi, son of Pwyll, features in all four branches.

Of the other tales, outside the Four Branches, the story of Culhwch and Olwen is generally regarded as the oldest in the compilation. Culhwch wins the hand of Olwen, daughter of Chief Giant Ysbaddaden, who sets a number of impossible tasks as a condition of his consent. Culhwch recruits some extraordinary men, each of whom has a magic skill, and with their assistance he performs the tasks and wins the girl. In the course of the story Arthur makes what is probably his earliest appearance in Welsh prose, helping Mabon (son of Modron) and Culhwch hunt (over Ireland, South Wales and Cornwall) the magic boar Twrch Trwyth, between whose ears lie a wonderful comb and shears.

The stories of Pwyll contain a number of international folk themes, which cannot be taken as ancient Celtic myth. But his name means "sense" or "wisdom", and is thus reminiscent of the Irish Daghdha's epithet, "of great knowledge"; and the name of his bride, Rhiannon, comes from Rigantona, "Great, or Divine, Queen". Rhiannon and their son Pryderi have been linked with Modron and Mabon ("Great Mother" and "Great Son"), and some scholars have seen a connection between Rhiannon and the horse goddess Epona (see p.186).

Dôn, whose family dominates the Fourth Branch, may be the equivalent of the Irish Donu (Danu), "Mother of the Gods". Math, lord of Gwynedd, can only live if his feet are in the folds of a virgin's lap – that is, except when war makes this impossible. His nephew Gilfaethwy seduces the virgin Goewin with the help of his (Gilfaethwy's) brother Gwydion during Math's absence on a campaign. On his return Math takes revenge by turning the two brothers into animals. The next foot-holder is to be Arianrhod, daughter of Dôn. She fails a virginity test and gives birth to two boys, the second of whom Gwydion, now a human again, conceals. Arianrhod swears that this son of hers will not have a name until she gives him one herself; but is tricked by Gwydion into naming him Lleu Llaw Gyffes, "The Bright One of the Skilful Hand". She swears that Lleu will never have a human wife. Then Math and Gwydion conjure up a wife made of flowers, named Blodeuwedd: "Flower-Aspect". With her lover Gronw Pebyr, the treacherous Blodeuwedd plots to kill Lleu, who is wounded, and flies away in the form of an eagle. Gwydion seeks him out and restores him to human form. Gwydion tells Blodeuwedd that he will not kill her but instead, because of the shame she has brought on Lleu, he will turn her into a bird to which all other birds will be hostile – that is, an owl (Blodeuwedd means owl in modern Welsh).

THE ARTHURIAN LEGEND

Arthur and his knights

The Arthurian legend is rooted in Celtic tradition but only achieved its prodigious popularity when it became a dominant theme of medieval literature in Continental Europe, first and foremost in France. English and Welsh versions are all derived from or influenced by the French.

The essential link between Celtic verse and story and the Arthurian legend in European literature is *The History of the Kings of Britain*, composed in the mid-12th century by Geoffrey of Monmouth. Whatever genuine Welsh traditions Geoffrey may have drawn upon, Biblical and classical materials form a significant part of his legendary history.

However, Arthur was a known figure in Welsh tradition at least as early as the 8th century. In one of the earliest references, that of Nennius in his history of the Britons, Arthur is a war leader who defends his country against Saxon invaders. His name is unquestionably derived from Artorius, a well-known Latin name: it was the title of a Roman clan, the *gens Artoria*, and a 2nd-century Roman named Artorius is on record as living in Britain. The name of Arthur would, therefore, like other Latin names, have passed into the Celtic languages of Britain during the Roman occupation.

Nonetheless, most Arthurian tales place Arthur in a context of folklore and myth. In the Old Welsh poem *The Spoils of Annwfn*, Arthur visits the Otherworld, apparently to carry off the magic cauldron of the realm of the dead, which is also the City of Carousal, whose drink is sparkling wine. Arthur in general fights monstrous adversaries, giants or magic animals. In some 12th-century texts he is the ruler of a subterranean kingdom. In the topographical lore of the modern period, he is envisaged as a gigantic figure himself.

There are numerous parallels in all these stories with the tales of Finn (also envisaged, especially in folk tradition, as a giant) and his followers (see pp.184-5). Indeed, these two great cycles of narrative may draw upon a common fund of Celtic mythological tradition.

When Sir Bedivere throws Arthur's magic sword Excalibur into the lake, following the king's dying request, it is seized by the Lady of the Lake before hitting the water. The scene is shown here in a medieval illustration.

Merlin the magician

The Latin writings of Geoffrey of Monmouth provide the links between the legend of Merlin in Celtic sources and its subsequent development in Continental literature. Geoffrey's name Merlinus comes from the Welsh Myrddin (Merddin).

Originally Myrddin is a seer or prophetic madman who lives in what was British-speaking southern Scotland. The Irish story of the Frenzy of Suibhne (Sweeney) and the Scottish story of Lailoken (Llallogan) are versions of the Myrddin legend, which focusses on the Wild Man of the Woods. The protagonist of all three stories has lost his reason owing to the terror of battle, and is stricken with guilt at the deaths he has caused. The first two men, and in some versions Myrddin, subsequently see a dreadful vision in the heavens. This northern tale was brought to Wales some time after people from southern Scotland moved there in the 5th century (and was developed in the 9th and 10th centuries). Geoffrey links this story with the wonder-child Ambrosius, hero of a totally unconnected legend recorded in Nennius's history of the Britons (*c.*800). Geoffrey credits the child, whom he calls Merlinus Ambrosius, with the defeat of the magicians of King Vortigern.

NORTHERN EUROPE

*A detail from an elaborately carved wooden wagon from the late
9th-century ship burial at Oseberg, in southern Norway, with
snakes and monsters depicted in stylized form.*

The German-speaking peoples originally occupied the region of Europe enclosed by the Rhine, the Danube and the Vistula, living in separate tribes under kings and warrior leaders. As the power of Rome declined, they spread out in many directions, settling in southern Norway and Sweden, and in southern and eastern England. Other tribes moved eastward as far as southern Russia, and southward into Italy and Spain and even North Africa, but these invasions led to no lasting settlements. Conversion to Christianity came relatively early to Anglo-Saxon England and mainland Europe, but Denmark, Sweden and Norway retained the old religion, which was taken to Iceland when the Scandinavians set up a "free state" there. Not until the 11th century was Christianity established in the North, and we have plentiful records of earlier times from Iceland, where scholarship flourished after conversion and great interest was taken in the Scandinavian past. Our knowledge of myths comes mainly from the medieval literature of the Scandinavian northlands, particularly from Iceland in the late Viking age.

Germanic myths tell of the conflict between gods and monsters. The gods established order, law, riches, art and wisdom in both the divine and the human realms, while monsters and frost giants posed a constant threat to the state of things, seeking to bring back chaos. Such tales are those of a vigorous, restless people, accustomed to warfare, insecurity and hard weather – warriors who raided widely and fought one another, seeking new lands to settle. Scandinavians of the Viking age carried on this tradition, travelling far by sea in search of wealth and renown. The people turned to the Aesir and the Vanir, deities of sky and earth, to support law and order and to bring fertility. The gods also granted knowledge of past and future, inspiration in poetry and oratory, support for kings and victory in battle – and, after death, a welcome into the realm of ancestors.

TIME CHART

1st century BC	Germanic peoples living east of the Rhine
3rd-6th centuries AD	Period of Germanic expansion (Migration Period)
5th century	Settlement of Angles and Saxons in England
AD 597	Christianity brought to Kent, England
8th-11th centuries	Expansion of Scandinavians (Viking Age)
955 onward	Christianity encouraged in Denmark
AD 995	Conversion of Norway begun by Olaf Tryggvason
AD 1000	Christianity accepted in Iceland

SCANDINAVIAN DEITIES OF THE VIKING AGE

BALDER, son of Odin, doomed to die.
FREYJA, goddess of fertility, sister of Freyr.
FREYR, god of fertility and royal ancestors.
FRIGG, queen of heaven and wife of Odin.
HEIMDALL, watcher over Asgard, and known as father of mankind.
HOENIR, a silent god, companion of Odin.
LOKI, a trickster companion of the gods.
NJORD, god of sea and ships, father of Freyr and Freyja.
ODIN, god of magic, inspiration, battle and the dead, and ruler of the gods.
THOR, god of sky and thunder, protector of law and the community.
TYR, remembered as the binder of the wolf.
ULL, god with skis and bow, worshipped in Scandinavia.

KEY TO MAP

- Areas of Scandinavian settlement
- Direction of Viking expansion
- Viking trade route
- Viking exploration route
- – – – Early German peoples, c.100BC
- ▲ Burial mounds
- ⚓ Ship burial
- ◆ Viking town

EVIDENCE FOR THE MYTHS

The evidence for Germanic and Scandinavian mythology is rich, but fragmentary and scattered.

Most of the literature was produced in Christian monasteries. The prose tales known as the Icelandic sagas were composed long after conversion to Christianity but contain some memories of old beliefs and customs. Some pre-Christian poems about gods survive, and in the 13th century, Snorri Sturluson wrote a book in Icelandic, the *Prose Edda*, in which he recorded all he could learn of the old myths for the benefit of young poets.

Other historians writing in Latin, such as the Anglo-Saxon Bede (8th century) and the Dane Saxo Grammaticus (late 12th century), also provide valuable evidence about the myths.

The literary evidence is paralleled by the evidence from ancient artefacts. Pre-Christian burial sites include the famous ship burials at Sutton Hoo and Oseberg (see illustration, opposite page): men and women were buried or cremated in ships, and among the treasures found at burial sites are amulets and ritual objects in metalwork, as well as figurines, helmet plates and sword hilts.

Votive stones and altars from areas occupied by the Romans sometimes show native deities as well as Roman ones, and scenes from myth are found on memorial stones of the Viking age, especially those on the island of Gotland in the Baltic, and on the Isle of Man.

EARLY GERMANIC DEITIES

DONAR, god of sky and thunder (Anglo-Saxon name: Thunor).
FREA, chief goddess, wife of Wodan (Anglo-Saxon: Frig).
ING, fertility god with wagon, known to the Anglo-Saxons.
NEHALENNIA, goddess of fertility and the sea, worshipped on the coast of Holland.
NERTHUS, earth goddess, worshipped in Denmark.
TIWAZ, god of sky, law and battle (Anglo-Saxon: Tiw or Tig).
WODAN, god of the underworld, magic, inspiration, poetry and battle (Anglo-Saxon: Woden).

EARLY AND LOST GODS

Fragments of Northern myth

An eagle from a shield forming part of the treasure buried in a ship at Sutton Hoo in eastern England, 7th century AD. The eagle was used as a symbol of the god Wodan.

THE NAMING OF THE LANGOBARDS
A myth about Wodan and his wife Frea was related by Paul the Deacon in his Latin history of the Langobards, written as early as the 8th century. It tells how the goddess Frea was determined that Wodan should bring favour to the tribe of the Winniles, rather than the Vandals whom he had previously supported. She told the tribe to come out at sunrise with their women, who were to pull their long hair over their faces, so as to look like bearded men. Then she turned Wodan's bed toward the east, so that when he awoke he was facing the Winniles instead of the Vandals. "Who are these long-beards?" he exclaimed, and she told him that now he had given them a name, he must grant them victory. Thus, they acquired the name Langobards, a pledge of the god's favour. In this tale Wodan appears as a god of the sky rather than of the underworld.

This Swedish rock engraving from the Bronze Age shows a male figure with a spear – probably a sky god. There is also evidence for an earth goddess.

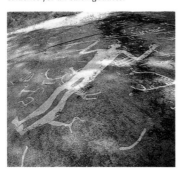

Early evidence for myth in Northern Europe includes a Bronze Age rock engraving of a figure with a spear (below left), who may have developed into Tiwaz, the Germanic god identified with the Roman war god Mars, but linked also with lawgiving. He may also be the deity whom Tacitus calls "god and ruler of all", worshipped in a sacred wood. Those entering the wood had to be bound – an idea linked with the Scandinavian Tyr, a later form of Tiwaz, remembered for his binding of the wolf (see p.195). The thunder god Donar, associated with the great oak forests of northern Europe, was identified with the Roman Jupiter and with Hercules. His symbol was the axe, standing for the power of lightning.

Anglo-Saxon literature contains traces of myths concerning a young god coming over the sea to bring blessings. The sea, like the earth, was associated with fertility, and a ship was one of the chief symbols of the fertility deities. In Denmark there was a powerful goddess remembered as Nerthus, and in the Netherlands a goddess of the North Sea coast called Nehalennia. There was also a queen of heaven and consort of the sky goddess Frea. Companies of female deities known as the Mothers (often depicted in threes) are shown on many stones of the Roman period in both Germanic and Celtic areas. Many of these are shown with infants: it is likely that women turned to them in childbirth and for help in rearing children. Another symbol of the fertility deities was the boar, also used as a protective charm in battle.

An important deity from early times was Wodan, identified with the Roman Mercury. Wodan brought good fortune in battle and was sometimes symbolized as a warrior on horseback, but he was a sinister figure, finally condemning his followers to defeat and death. Men were sacrificed to him by hanging. Though a guide to the underworld (like Mercury), he came also to be associated with the sky, and was symbolized by the eagle. Other symbols for him were the wolf and raven, creatures of the battlefield. He was linked with divination, the runic symbols, and the gift of ecstasy: he inspired both warriors and poets. The ancestor of kings, he granted them favours, upon which their success depended. Like Tiwaz he possessed a spear, and the power to bind and loose through his knowledge of battle-spells.

COSMOLOGY IN THE VIKING AGE

The World Tree and its realms

A detail of a hogback tombstone of the Viking age, from northern England. The relief depicts four such figures holding an arch – suggesting the dwarves who hold up the sky at creation.

This memorial stone of c.AD500, from Sanda, Gotland (below), appears to be an early diagram of the cosmos: the whirling disc of the heavens, the sun and moon below, and the World Tree in the centre. The ship at the bottom, found on many memorial stones, probably shows the departure of the dead from this world.

Icelandic mythological poems reflect a strong interest in the creation of the world and its ultimate destruction and re-creation. The earth is represented as a circle of land surrounded by ocean. In the ocean depths lies the World Serpent, while in the centre of the land is a mighty tree, the World Ash, Yggdrasil. The tree's roots go down into the underworld, and beneath them bubbles a spring, source of hidden wisdom. A nimble squirrel runs up and down the trunk, carrying messages between the eagle at the top and the serpent gnawing its roots. A hart feeds on the branches, and from its horns flow mighty rivers; here also there grazes a goat, which yields not milk but mead, for the warriors in Odin's hall. Yggdrasil probably means Horse of Ygg, one of Odin's names. He was said to have hung in agony from the tree, in voluntary sacrifice, to gain power over the runes which brought knowledge to those who could interpret them. Dew drops from Yggdrasil to earth, and the fruits of the tree give help in childbirth. This is the guardian tree of the gods, who hold their councils beneath its canopy. It is a symbol of universality, linking the different races of beings, and forming the centre of nine worlds. An earlier world-view may have been based on nine worlds set one above another in the Tree.

It is hardly possible to produce a consistent cosmological diagram or map from what the sources tell us, and no doubt there were varying traditions. Two races of gods, the Aesir (sky gods) and the Vanir (earth gods), are said to dwell in Asgard, apparently in the heavens; but the Vanir also have their realm of Vanaheim beneath the Earth. Among the Tree's roots lies Jotunheim, land of the giants, and also a realm of the dead, ruled by Hel, daughter of Loki the trickster (see p.195). Other worlds mentioned in the poems are those of the elves and dwarves, the heroes in Odin's hall, and the mysterious Mighty Powers (perhaps the fates). Jotunheim is beneath Asgard, yet can be reached by a long and dangerous journey overland; another such route links Asgard with the realm of the dead. A bridge,

THE WINNING OF THE MAGIC MEAD

Odin was responsible for bringing the mead of inspiration into the possession of the gods. When the Aesir and the Vanir, the two races of gods, made peace with each other, they all spat into a vessel, and so created a wise giant, Kvasir. Later he was killed by two dwarves, who mixed his blood with honey and so made the magic mead of inspiration, which filled three huge vessels. However, a giant, Suttung, whose parents had been killed by the dwarves, came seeking vengeance and took away the mead, which he hid inside a mountain. Odin set out to recover it for the gods. First, he caused nine men labouring for Suttung's brother Baugi to quarrel and kill one another, and then took their place, asking for nothing but a drink of mead as his wages. This Suttung refused, but Baugi helped Odin to creep into the mountain in serpent form, and there he slept for three nights with the giant's daughter, and persuaded her to give him three drinks of the mead. He swallowed the contents of all three vessels, flew back to Asgard in the form of an eagle, and spat out the mead again into vessels made ready by the gods: this scene is possibly depicted in the Gofland stone below. Thus the mead of inspiration came into their possession.

This panel from a stone in Gotland – an eagle with two figures – appears to show Odin returning to Asgard with the magic mead. The mead is shown pouring from the eagle's beak while two figures hold out cups to receive it.

Bifrost, giving access to Asgard, is guarded against the giants: this is said to be the rainbow linking heaven and earth, but may originally have been the Milky Way. The myths create a vivid picture of constant traffic between the realms, involving perilous journeys across vast expanses.

In the beginning was a great abyss, Ginnungagap, the Yawning (or perhaps Deceiving) Gap, full of latent energy. Layers of ice and sparks of fire came together to create the primeval androgynous giant Ymir, from whose body the giants and the first man and woman were engendered. The giant was fed by a primeval cow which licked the salty ice-blocks until the Sons of Bor emerged – three creator gods who slew Ymir and formed the earth from his body, the sea from his blood, and the sky from his skull. The sky was held aloft by four dwarves, creatures who bred like maggots in the earth. Another tradition is that a man and a woman were created when the three gods endowed two trees on the seashore with human form, breath and understanding.

The gods then established order, setting sun and moon on their appointed paths, framing laws, building fine halls in Asgard, and fashioning treasures in gold. At first there was war between two companies of the gods, the Aesir and the Vanir, but a truce was established, resulting in the brewing of the mead of inspiration (see margin, left), one of the treasures of the gods. Another treasure, which preserved their youth, was their stock of golden apples, guarded by the goddess Idun (see p.202). Other divine treasures were forged by dwarves. Odin had a gold ring, Draupnir, from which eight further rings dropped every nine nights; and a spear, Gungnir, governing the fortunes of war. Thor had his mighty axe-hammer Mjollnir, which caused lightning, and Freyr and Freyja of the Vanir possessed a golden boar which raced through the sky and the underworld, and a magical ship which was always favoured with a fair wind.

The fortification of Asgard

When the gods established their realm of Asgard, they needed a strong wall around it.

A skilled craftsman offered to build this for them, but demanded as payment the sun and moon, as well as the goddess Freyja as his wife. The gods agreed to this on condition that the work was finished in one winter, and that no man helped him: they felt sure that this was beyond the craftsman's powers, and that the payment would not be exacted. However, the builder was helped by his horse, a stallion of great strength and intelligence, which worked at night hauling rocks, and did twice as much as his master. Three days before the coming of spring, the wall was almost finished, and the gods were aghast. They blamed Loki, who had persuaded them to make the agreement, and accordingly it was he who decided to take action. He changed himself into a mare, and lured away the great horse, so that the wall was never completed. The builder fell into a tremendous rage, and when it became clear that he was a giant enemy from Jotunheim, the Aesir (gods of the sky) called on Thor, who slew him with his hammer. The outcome of Loki's encounter with the stallion was that he gave birth to a grey foal with eight legs: this was Sleipnir, the famous steed of Odin, on which he rode between the worlds (see p.196).

LOKI AND RAGNAROK

The trickster, the wolf and the last great battle

A furnace stone from Shaptun, Denmark, thought to show Loki with his lips sewn up by the dwarves to punish him for trying to cheat them when they forged the treasures of the gods (see p.194).

Loki, who plays an important part in the Northern myths, is a trickster figure, a thief and a slanderer, abusing the gods and putting them into jeopardy by his mischief, but also saving them through his cunning. He is a close companion of Odin and Thor, yet he gives birth to the monsters which will destroy them, and brings about Balder's death through his malice (see p.197). It is never clear whether Loki is god or giant. Certainly to some extent he is a creator figure, who caused the dwarves to produce some of the treasures of the gods and he himself gave birth to Odin's horse (see p.194), as well as monsters such as the World Serpent and Hel, ruler of the dead.

One of the monstrous children fathered by Loki was the wolf Fenrir. He grew up among the gods, and none but Tyr, who seems to be a later form of Tiwaz and a god of battle, dared to feed him. The wolf broke free from every chain, until Odin had the dwarves make a magical band, soft as silk yet invincibly strong, from such impalpable things as the root of a mountain and the noise of a moving cat. The wolf was suspicious, and would not let the band be put around his neck, unless one of the gods laid his hand between his jaws as a pledge of good faith. Tyr was the only one willing to do this. As the band tightened and held the wolf fast, the gods laughed – all except Tyr, who lost his right hand. The wolf was gagged with a sword between his jaws and fastened to a huge rock, where he remained bound until Ragnarok.

As a punishment for causing Balder's death, Loki was finally bound across three rocks, unable to break loose until the last great battle, when he joined the giants in the attack on Asgard at Ragnarok (see margin, right). In the course of the battle Loki and his chief enemy Heimdall, sentry of the gods, fought and slew one another.

RAGNAROK

Loki, having broken free from his bounds, led the giants against the gods in the last great battle, known as Ragnarok. The world was under constant threat from the giants, who coveted the gods' treasures and the goddess Freyja, and threatened a return to chaos and sterility. Odin collected the greatest heroes who had fallen in battle in Valhalla, so that they would support the gods. Thor wielded his hammer against the giants and kept them out of Asgard until Ragnarok.

A poem of *c.*AD1000, *Voluspa* (Prophecy of the Seeress), describes the creation and destruction of the world, as if in a vision. At Ragnarok the sons of Muspell from the region of fire shatter the bridge Bifrost, while the giants arrive by sea, with Loki as steersman. The monsters break loose and the wolf Fenrir devours Odin. Thor slays the World Serpent but is destroyed by its poison. The fire-giant Surt sets the earth ablaze, the sky falls, and the world is engulfed in the rising sea. But this is not the end, because the earth re-emerges, green and fair; the sons of the gods, together with a human pair who had sheltered in the World Tree, re-people heaven and earth; and a new and fairer sun journeys across the sky. This picture of destruction may be partly based on the terrifying eruptions of the Icelandic volcano Hekla in the early Middle Ages. But whatever the origin of the concept, the evidence of art and literature indicates that Ragnarok had a powerful hold over the imagination in the Viking age.

ODIN

Ruler of Asgard

ODIN AND VALHALLA
Odin was said to summon kings and
heroes who had died in battle to his Hall
of the Slain, Valhalla, where they spent
their time feasting and fighting, ready to
defend Asgard in the event of attack.
Valhalla may originally have been based
on the grave where the dead feasted with
their ancestors. But in the literature of the
Vikings the realm of the distinguished
dead was grander, and entered with
ceremony: the dead heroes were escorted
through the air to Odin's hall in Asgard
by warrior goddesses, the Valkyries.
Shown here (right) is a memorial stone
from Alskog, Gotland, depicting Odin's
eight-legged horse Sleipnir with a rider
(either the god or a dead hero) being
welcomed into the hall by a Valkyrie
with a horn of mead.

In Viking belief Odin, the All-Father, was ruler of Asgard, inheriting the
spear of Tiwaz which gave him control of battles. His predecessor Wodan
was the supreme god of the Langobards and other Germanic tribes (see
p.192). Odin, like Wodan, has close links with the underworld and the
dead. He was the god of kings, supporting promising young princes and
giving them magic swords and other gifts as pledges of his favour, but
ruthlessly destroying them when the time came. Cremation, often
necessary to dispose of the dead after battle, was linked with Odin's cult.

There are many tales of Odin's dedicated followers, the Berserks,
wearing bear or wolf skins in battle and seized with ecstasy, making
them impervious to pain. Odin's gift of ecstasy was also available to poets
and orators, and there are many references in Icelandic poetry to his
winning of the magic mead which gave inspiration (see p.194). He also
brought wealth to his followers, symbolized by his ring Draupnir, which
multiplied itself to ensure a supply of gold.

In addition, Odin was a god of magic and divination, especially in a
military context. Sacrifices were made to him of captives taken in war,
despatched by stabbing and hanging. Such sacrifices could be a form of
divination, as the last movments of the victim were held to foretell victory
or defeat. Odin himself hung as a sacrifice on the World Tree in order to
gain knowledge of the runic symbols used in divination. He also gave one
of his eyes for the sake of knowledge, and appeared on earth as an old
one-eyed man, in a cloak and broad-brimmed hat or a hood. His
constant companions were creatures of the battlefield, wolves and ravens;
and two ravens brought him news of battles from all over the world. Odin
was an accomplished shape-changer, sending out his spirit in bird or
animal form, and this, together with his ability to journey to the realm of
the dead, gives him something in common with the shamans of the
northern Eurasian peoples.

Balder, son of Odin

*M*any of Odin's journeys were motivated by his wish to obtain knowledge of the future. He consulted runes, and also the head of the wise giant Mimir, killed by the Aesir. He made dangerous trips to see other giants famed for their wisdom, and even called up the dead to question them. From them, he knew that he was doomed to be devoured by the wolf Fenrir, and that Loki was constantly plotting against the gods (see p.195).

The first serious threat to Odin came through the loss of his son Balder, described as the fairest of the gods and the one most loved by Odin and his wife Frigg, although in Danish tradition he was remembered not as a god but as a warrior son of Odin fighting on earth. Balder became plagued by evil dreams, and Frigg tried to protect him by asking all created beings, together with trees and plants and all objects of metal, wood and stone, to swear never to cause him harm. After this the gods were able to amuse themselves hurling weapons at Balder in sport, knowing he would remain unhurt. But Loki the trickster discovered that one little plant, the mistletoe, had given no oath to Frigg, since she had thought it too young to do harm. Loki made it into a dart, and gave it to the blind god Hother to throw at Balder, guiding his hand to be sure of a hit. When the dart pierced Balder, he fell down dead. Odin and the other deities were plunged into mourning. The gods took up his body and laid it on a funeral pyre built on his own ship, alongside the body of his wife Nanna, who had died of grief, and his horse.

When, after Balder's death, Frigg begged that someone should ride to Hel, the realm of the dead, and seek to bring back her son, it was Hermod the Bold, Balder's brother, who volunteered. He rode away on Odin's horse Sleipnir, journeying for nine days and nights through deep, dark valleys until he came to a golden bridge over the Echoing River. The maiden on guard there told him that he could not be one of

A bound giant: perhaps an allusion to the binding of Loki as punishment for his part in Balder's death. From a stone cross in Cumbria, England.

A silver pendant of the Viking era showing a messenger on horseback, evocative of Hermod on his journey to the underworld.

the dead, because the bridge resounded under his horse, as it had not done when five hosts of the dead had passed over it not long before. When Hermod told her that he was looking for Balder, she directed him down the northern road to Hel's gate, which Sleipnir cleared with an easy leap. Hermod entered the hall where Balder was sitting and stayed there three nights. He begged Hel, the ruler of the realm which bore her name, to let Balder return with him, but she replied that only the weeping of all people and all things in the world could bring this about.

Hermod returned to Asgard with the ring, Draupnir, which had been burnt on Balder's funeral pyre, as proof that he had fulfilled his mission. Then messengers went all over the world asking everyone to show their love for Balder by weeping him out of Hel. Not only men and women wept, but also stones, trees and metals, as such things weep when a thaw comes after frost. But at last they came across a giantess in a cave who refused to weep, declaring that Balder had been no use to her. It was believed this giantess was Loki disguised, maliciously preventing Balder's return.

So Balder remained in Hel, and when Loki's part in this became known he fled from the wrath of the gods and hid in the river as a salmon. He was caught in a magic net of his own devising, and the gods bound him across three stones, with snakes dropping poison on his face. His faithful wife Sigyn sat with a bowl and tried to catch the poison drops, while Loki's writhings caused earthquakes in the world. He remained bound until he was able to break loose at Ragnarok, the doom of the gods, and lead the giants against Asgard.

Balder's death led on inevitably to Ragnarok, when Odin was devoured by the wolf, and then avenged by his young son Vidar, who tore the monster apart. Vidar was one of the sons of the gods who replaced their fathers after Ragnarok.

THOR

The thunder god

In this Viking Age brooch from Birka, Sweden, two goats flank a "thunder-stone", actually a fossilized sea urchin – an object thought to have been dropped in thunderstorms.

RITUAL AND THE CULT OF THOR

Thor was especially popular in western Norway and Iceland: the robust comedy in many myths about him may be viewed as a sign of affection. When Christianity came to Iceland, Thor was the god whose cult was most difficult to eradicate. There were various rituals associated with him. A hammer was laid in the bride's lap at weddings, raised over a newborn child, and depicted on boundary stones.

Scandinavians wore silver hammer amulets: the ornate Swedish one below shows the god with eagle face, stylized beard, and a serpent symbol below. Thor's hammer was also carved on gravestones.

Deity of the community, guardian of those who farmed the land and met in local assemblies, Thor was also the sky god, akin to Jupiter and Zeus, his axe hammer a symbol of thunder and lightning. Thunder and lightning marked his path across the heavens, and rocks and mountains shattered before him. There are many tales, both savage and humorous, of his expeditions into Jotunheim, where he slew the giants, the enemies of the gods. He was a popular deity, pictured as a massive but somewhat homely figure, who had no horse but strode vigorously through rivers, or drove a wagon drawn by goats. Notorious for his huge appetite, he would even devour his own goats for supper, collecting their bones afterwards and restoring them to life by the power of his hammer. His red beard seems to have represented lightning (perhaps because of the mass of red fibres formed when lightning strikes a tree). We also hear of his fiery eyes, his tremendous strength and his fearsome anger. Memorial stones show his hammer as a weapon on a cord, sometimes thrown at enemies as well as being brought down on their skulls.

One early poem tells of a visit to the realm of the giant Geirrod, which Loki with malicious intent persuaded him to make. Thor had to summon all his divine strength to cross a raging river and avoid being crushed to death by the giant's two daughters, whom he slew together with their father. Another myth relates a famous duel with the giant Hrungnir who had managed to enter Asgard. The giant hurled a whetstone at Thor, and a fragment of it lodged in his head, but Thor demolished his foe with his hammer. His mostly deadly enemy was the World Serpent, which he once pulled up from the sea-bed. An earlier form of this myth may have been the familiar notion of the sky god overcoming the monster of chaos at the time of creation; however, in the Viking age it was at Ragnarok that Thor was said to vanquish the serpent, only to be laid low himself by poison.

Only when deceiving magic was used against him did Thor's strength appear inadequate. On a journey to the mysterious realm of Utgard, he met a giant so huge that Thor was able to walk into his glove as into a hall. The giant gave him a horn of ale to empty, which continually filled up from the sea; set him to wrestle with Age, which can defeat the strongest; and challenged him to lift a grey cat from the floor, which was actually the

World Serpent. All these were impossible tasks, yet Thor displayed such strength that the cunning giant was terrified: the level of the sea fell during the drinking test, and the world was almost destroyed when he heaved one paw of the cat off the ground (this could be another version of the myth of Thor pulling up the Serpent from the ocean depths).

Thor's mother was said to be Fjorgyn, a name used by poets for the earth. His wife was Sif, about whom little is known except that she was famed for her golden hair, which was once cut off by the mischievous Loki; but the trickster was so aghast at Thor's wrath that he had new hair of pure gold made for her by dwarves. This had an important result for the gods, as it led to the making of some of their most valuable treasures, including Thor's hammer (see p.194).

Thor fishes for the World Serpent

*O*ne of the most *popular myths of the Viking period was that of Thor's visit to the sea-giant Hymir. This encounter is described in some of the earliest surviving poems, and is depicted on three carved stones of the Viking age. There is an 8th-century stone from Gotland which appears to show Thor with the ox-head, rowing in a giant's boat.*

A detail from a stone from Cumbria, northern England, showing Thor fishing for the World Serpent.

According to one account, Thor went to the sea disguised as a youth, and asked if he might go fishing with the giant. Hymir was at first unwilling to take him, and told him to find his own bait; whereupon Thor went to the giant's herd of oxen, slew the largest and brought back its head.

They set out in the boat, and Thor rowed with tremendous power, until they were well beyond the giant's usual fishing grounds. Thor baited his hook with the ox-head and threw it overboard. The World Serpent in the ocean depths seized hold of it, and Thor hauled the creature up until its terrible head appeared above the waves.

Thor's prodigious strength increased as he hauled away, pushing his feet through the boat and bracing himself against the ocean floor. As the Serpent spat poison, Thor stared at it and raised his hammer, but the panic-stricken giant cut the line.

According to Snorri (in his Icelandic *Prose Edda*), the story-tellers disagreed as to whether Thor struck the Serpent, but it was thought that it escaped and fell back into the sea, while Thor threw the giant overboard and waded ashore.

THE THEFT OF THE HAMMER
One day Thor mislaid his hammer, the only effective weapon against the giants. Loki borrowed Freyja's falcon shape and flew far and wide in search of it, and at last he came back with the news that it was in the possession of the giant Thrym, and buried deep below the earth. The giant refused to give it back unless the goddess Freyja became his bride. Freyja was so enraged to hear this that, panting with fury, she shattered her famous necklace. The wise Heimdall counselled that Thor should disguise himself as Freyja in a bridal veil, and should journey with Loki to Jotunheim, the realm of the giants. Reluctantly Thor consented, and off he drove with Loki in his wagon, to the accompaniment of thunder and lightning. The giants greeted the bride with delight, but were somewhat surprised at her enormous appetite at the wedding feast, and alarmed by her fiery eyes glowing through the veil. The quick-witted Loki, disguised as the bride's attendant, soothed them with the assurance that Freyja's unusual demeanour was explained by the fact that she had neither eaten nor slept for eight nights, such was her longing for the wedding. At last the hammer was brought in and laid in the lap of the bride to bless her, and this was Thor's opportunity: he seized the hammer, demolished the bridegroom and wedding guests, and returned with Loki in triumph to Asgard.

FREYR AND THE VANIR

Gods of sky, land and water

This small phallic figure (about 3in/7.6cm high), from Railinge, Sweden, is thought to represent Freyr.

The main Scandinavian god of fertility and plenty was Freyr, whose name means "lord", possibly used as a title. He was one of the Vanir, a group of deities, male and female, mainly associated with the depths of earth and water, as opposed to the Aesir, the gods of the sky. The Vanir brought peace and prosperity to the land and support to the land's rulers, so long as the rulers caused no offence. The cult of Freyr was popular in Sweden in the Viking age, and gradually spread to Norway and Iceland. The Icelandic sagas tell of families who worshipped the god, and particular places dedicated to him. Like Odin and Thor, Freyr gave help and counsel, and divination was an important part of his cult. The Yngling kings of Uppsala in Sweden appear to have been identified with him after their deaths, and were thought to have brought prosperity to the land. Gifts of gold and silver were placed in Freyr's burial mound, and the image of the god was taken around Sweden in a wagon to bless the farms, just as the earth goddess Nerthus had journeyed around Denmark centuries earlier according to the Roman writer Tacitus.

One Vanir symbol was the golden boar, which travelled across the sky and underneath the earth like the sun. Although not a sky god, Freyr dwelt with the Aesir, and the sun played an important part in his cult. He was a god of peace, but his boar symbol appeared on warriors' helmet plates or as crests, affording protection in battle. The boar helmets of the Swedish kings of Uppsala (the Ynglings) were national treasures. Horses also were dedicated to Freyr, and it was said that he kept some in his temple. Another Vanir symbol was the ship, and Freyr had a special one of his own, in which he could travel wherever he wished: it could accommodate all the gods, but would fold up into a pouch when not in use. Ship-funeral was practised by royal families, as well as lesser folk, from the 7th century

The wooing of Gerd

*F*reyr *ventured to sit in Odin's seat, from which he could see into the worlds below. In the underworld he saw the beautiful Gerd, and was overcome with desire.*

Freyr felt it would be impossible to win Gerd in the realm of hostile giants. His mother Skadi begged Skirnir (unknown outside this tale) to help her son, and Freyr gave him a magic horse and sword, as the journey was long and perilous. When he reached the hall of Gymir, Gerd's father, his horse leapt through the flames surrounding the building. He offered golden apples to Gerd, and Odin's wealth-giving ring, but she refused to become Freyr's bride, even when threatened with the sword. Finally, when Skirnir persuaded her that refusal would unleash the gods' wrath, Gerd agreed to the marriage.

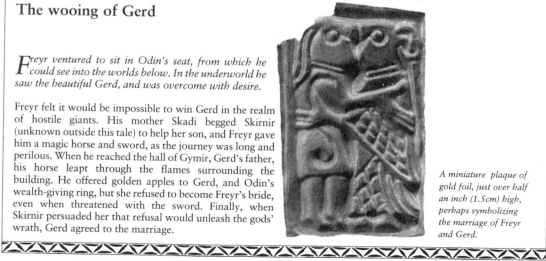

A miniature plaque of gold foil, just over half an inch (1.5cm) high, perhaps symbolizing the marriage of Freyr and Gerd.

The land-spirits

The land-spirits were said to dwell in hills, waterfalls, lakes and forests, or in great rocks.

Many tales tell of settlers coming to Iceland in the 9th century who made contact with the spirits of the new land, and received help from them in exchange for offerings of food. Such spirits assisted people in hunting, fishing and the rearing of farm animals, and gave good counsel about the future in dreams. One farmer who had lost much of

Dragon figureheads, and carved posts like this one from the Oseberg ship burial, were thought to protect against hostile forces. The land-spirits were said to object to ships with such figureheads entering Icelandic harbours.

his livestock went into partnership with a land-spirit, whereupon a strange he-goat joined his herd, and his goats thereafter flourished.

The land-spirits also included benevolent mountain giants, who protected men and women from hostile beings and helped in severe weather. Belief in such supernatural benefactors is found in the folklore of Scandinavia and other European countries, and survived long after the coming of Christianity. The land-spirits were prepared to defend the land against enemy attack, and showed anger toward people who broke the law. It is difficult to distinguish such beings clearly from the Vanir, although the land-spirits seem to have been worshipped individually by local people rather than by the community.

onward: both men and women were buried in ships or boats, or burned in them at cremation funerals, and a connection with the Vanir cult seems probable. Freyr's father was Njord, a god of some importance in the Viking age, associated with ships and the sea. His mother was Skadi, a mysterious goddess who travelled on skis and hunted in the northern forests. A tantalizing fragment of verse tells how the marriage of Njord and Skadi broke up because Njord could not bear to be far from the sea, while Skadi was only happy in the mountains.

Freyr wooed and won Gerd, a beautiful girl in the underworld, daughter of a giant. This union may have symbolized the sun's warmth penetrating the earth and producing corn. Tiny pieces of gold foil with the figures of a man and woman either embracing (see panel, opposite) or with a leafy branch between them, discovered in the foundations of houses and also at sacred sites, may represent this marriage of the god and goddess of the Vanir.

Other gods who may have belonged to the Vanir, apart from Freyr and Njord, are Balder (see p.197) and Heimdall, called the White God. Heimdall had links with the sea, and nine giant maidens, apparently waves, were said to have given birth to him. In an early poem he was represented as a begetter of children in the human world. Linked with Freyr is the Germanic Ing, hailed as the founder of the Yngling dynasty.

The goddesses also form an important part of the company of the Vanir, and are usually represented as the daughters of giants in the underworld. In addition there were the Elves, often mentioned in the poems along with the Aesir, and the land-spirits – supernatural beings attached to definite localities who could give help to farmers and fishermen. There were also certain wise giants (distinct from the frost giants) who could remember the earliest times before the coming of the sky gods.

No ruler could afford to ignore the Vanir, because good harvests and a prosperous reign were believed to depend upon their approval: there are tales of early kings being deposed or even killed by the people when good harvests were denied them.

Men in boar helmets, depicted on a bronze die for a helmet plate. Such devices invoked Freyr's protection over warriors in battle.

GODDESSES AND FEMALE SPIRITS

Freyja, Golden Apples, Valkyries and Norns

This Swedish pendant from the Viking period may show Freyja wearing the wonderful gold necklace, Brisingamen, reputedly made by dwarves.

The chief goddess of the Vanir, Freyr's sister Freyja, whose name means "lady", tends to be underestimated, because the emphasis in literature falls on the male gods. But she was a figure of power, worshipped not only by women (who left few records) but also by kings and heroes. She shared the Vanir symbols of boar and ship, and was linked with the horse cult, although her chariot was drawn by cats. One tradition maintains that she and her brother were married, and that this was the custom of the Vanir. She was reputed to have granted her sexual favours freely to all the gods, as well as accepting earthly rulers as her lovers, supporting them through their reigns and welcoming them after death. Jarl Hakon, the last pagan to rule in Norway, was said to be devoted to the goddess Thorgerd, who may be Freyr's bride Gerd; and both could be identifiable with Freyja. Like Freyr, Freyja was associated with riches: she wept tears of gold, and had a wonderful necklace (see illustration, left), a symbol of the Great Goddess from very early times.

Another figure who may represent Freyja is the goddess Gefion, who turned her four sons into oxen and broke up land in Sweden to form the Danish island of Zealand. The names Gefion and Freyja's alternative name Gefn are derived from the word for giving, and Freyja was a giving goddess, bringing fertility to land and sea and helping with marriage and childbearing. One side of her cult connects her to the preservation of the family, another to sexual abandon and sinister magic. The Icelandic sagas remember a ritual known as seid, in which a woman journeys through the land

The theft of the golden apples

Freyja plays a small but significant part in recovering the golden apples of immortality when they are stolen by a giant from their guardian, the goddess Idun, who watches over them in Asgard.

One day when Odin, Loki and Hoenir were journeying together, they tried to roast an ox for supper, but the meat would not cook properly. A great eagle (actually the giant Thiazi) perched on an oak above them offered to help in return for a share of the meal. When the ox was finally roasted, the bird carried off the greater part of the meat. Loki in fury struck at him with a pole, but the eagle flew off with the pole fixed to his body and Loki still attached to the other end. Loki was dragged across the ground, and Thiazi would not free him until he swore that he would bring him the goddess Idun and the golden apples of immortality.

When Loki reached Asgard, he lured the goddess with her golden apples out into the forest, on the pretext that he could show her apples even more beautiful than hers. Then the giant Thiazi in his eagle form swooped down and bore her off to Jotunheim, land of the giants.

Deprived of the apples, the gods began to grow old and wrinkled, and when they discovered Loki's part in the theft they threatened to kill him unless he brought Idun back. So Loki borrowed Freyja's falcon form and flew to Thiazi's hall, changed Idun into a nut, and flew off with her in his claws. Before long the giant pursued him in his eagle shape again, but as Loki flew into Asgard the gods set light to a pile of wood shavings, and Thiazi's wings were singed as he crossed the threshold in pursuit. He fell to the ground, and the gods slew him, and thus the precious apples remained in Asgard, continuing to ensure eternal youth for the gods.

and from a high platform answers questions put to her about the future: this is said to have been taught by Freyja to the gods. There is evidence that the goddess was served by priestesses, one of whom may have been the woman of high rank buried in the Oseberg ship (in southern Norway) in the 9th century, with fertility symbols such as apples and nuts and a splendid processional wagon (see p.190). Odin's wife Frigg has much in common with Freyja, and both may have developed from the earlier Germanic goddess Frea. They could both travel in bird shape, and are described as weeping goddesses (perhaps lamenting the fate of sons and lovers).

A late myth about Freyja (possibly the work of a Christian storyteller) tells how she obtained her famous necklace. It is said to have been the work of four dwarf craftsmen, and to have been greatly coveted by Freyja, who tried to buy it from them. However, the price set by the dwarves was that she should spend a night with each of them in turn, and Freyja consented so that the necklace might become hers. Loki told Odin of this, and was commanded to steal the necklace. He entered Freyja's bower in the form of a fly while she was asleep, and then became a flea and bit her on the cheek, causing her to turn over in bed so that he could undo the clasp and take the necklace away. When Freyja found it gone, she guessed that this was Odin's work, and demanded that he give it back. Odin consented, on condition that she brought about a war between two powerful kings, something which he desired for his own purposes. The tale then leads on to one of the great heroic legends of the Viking age.

The concept of mother goddesses and of female deities associated with special springs and lakes in the early period in Northern Europe continued into the Viking age. Some of these became transformed into local spirits; some, in the Christian period, were replaced by the Virgin Mary. Female beings also helped with women's crafts such as spinning, dairywork and healing.

Various companies of female spirits belonging to the Vanir were linked with the battlefield. Prime among these battle-spirits were the Valkyries, the choosers of the slain, sent out by Odin to decide the course of battle and conduct the noble dead to Valhalla. In the literature of the Viking age they are noble women on horseback, bearing spears, but there is also a tradition of fearsome giantesses who appear in dreams as omens of approaching slaughter, pouring blood over the land, devouring men in battle, or riding on wolves accompanied by birds of prey. They are often represented as companions of ravens – birds which flock to the battlefield to feast on corpses. A different aspect of the Valkyries is their role as family guardian spirits; such beings befriend young princes, give them a name and a sword, become their supernatural brides, teach them warrior lore, protect them in battle, and welcome them into the burial mound at death. There are many Valkyrie names, the simplest being words meaning battle, such as Hild. Many of these names are poetic inventions, with no basis in myth.

There are also individual goddesses of whom little is known, such as Skadi, Njord's wife, supposedly equipped with bow and skis (see p.201). Nanna (married to Balder), Sif (married to Thor), and Sigyn (married to Loki) are little more than names. Ran, wife of the sea-god Aesir, said to welcome drowned sailors to her hall, seems like her husband to be a personification of the sea.

Of greater interest are the Norns: that is, goddesses or giantesses said to decide the fates of mankind and the gods. They visited royal courts to plan the destiny of new-born princes, and were associated with the Well of Fate – the spring under the World Tree, a source of secret knowledge. There are references to three Norns, but sometimes a larger company is mentioned. There was also a cult of the Disir: goddesses for whom sacrifices, including human ones, were said to be made at Uppsala. Their main festival appears to have been in the autumn, the start of the new year, and the time of a major feast held for the gods.

Valkyries appear on many memorial stones of the Viking age on the island of Gotland, welcoming heroes with horns of mead.

THE DRAGON-SLAYERS

Beowulf and Sigurd

Panels from the door of a 12th-century church in Setesdale, Norway, show the reforging of Sigurd's sword, the testing of the sword on the anvil (above right), the dragon-slaying (above), the roasting of the heart, and the killing of Regin.

The myth of a hero who slew a great dragon was part of northern tradition. The outstanding version is the tale of the dragon Fafnir, slain by the young hero Sigurd the Volsung, which was popular from the 10th century onward.

Sigurd's father Sigmund was one of the greatest of Odin's heroes (indeed, he may have been the original dragon-slayer, as Sigurd is not mentioned in the early sources). When Sigmund fell in battle, Odin himself shattered the wonderful sword he had once given him. His widow Hjordis kept the fragments for her son, Sigurd, brought up at the court of her second husband Hjalprek. Sigurd was fostered by a cunning but evil smith Regin, who taught him many skills. One day when choosing a horse, he was helped by Odin, disguised as an old man, and so obtained the wonderful steed Grani, descended from Odin's horse Sleipnir. Regin told Sigurd of a great treasure guarded by the dragon Fafnir, his brother.

The story behind this treasure was complicated. There was a third brother, Otter, who had been eating a fish on the river bank in his animal shape when Loki threw a stone and killed him, taking his otter skin. When the three gods, Odin, Loki and Hoenir, happened to lodge with Hreidmar, father of the brothers, he imprisoned them and demanded as ransom for his son Otter that they cover the otter skin with gold. Loki was sent to capture a dwarf, Andvari, and take away all his gold, including a ring which could multiply wealth; but the dwarf put a curse on the ring so that it would bring destruction to anyone who possessed it. The whole treasure, including the ring, was needed before the skin was covered and the gods were free to depart. Fafnir then slew his father Hreidmar to obtain the gold, and turned himself into a dragon to guard his wealth.

Regin urged Sigurd to vanquish Fafnir and win the hoard. The smith forged two swords for him, but each one broke when tested, so Sigurd obtained the fragments of the sword Gram from his mother, and these Regin forged into a new weapon of tremendous cutting power. He advised Sigurd to dig a pit to sit in, and then stab the dragon from below when the creature crawled over it on his way to drink. But Odin in the guise of an old man appeared again, warning Sigurd that he would drown in the blood unless he dug a number of pits – advice that saved the hero's life. Sigurd stabbed Fafnir fatally under the shoulder. Regin then asked Sigurd to roast the dragon's heart for him to eat. In doing this Sigurd burned his finger and put it into his mouth, and as the blood touched his tongue, he was able to understand the speech of birds, and overheard them declaring that Regin intended to kill him. So Sigurd cut off Regin's head with his sword, loaded the treasure onto Grani's back and rode away. Possession of the fatal ring later brought about Sigurd's death, through the machinations of Brynhild, who was jealous of Sigurd's wife Gudrun.

The same tale is remembered in later medieval German tradition as that of Siegfried and the Hoard of the Nibelungs, but here there is little interest in the dragon-slaying.

A combat between a lion and serpent on a stone from St Paul's churchyard, London. A memorial for a Scandinavian who died in the mid-11th century, it shows the influence of the traditional dragon image.

Beowulf

A vivid word-picture of a fiery dragon appears in the Anglo-Saxon heroic poem Beowulf, *usually thought to date from the 8th century. Despite the poem's Christian background, the portrayal of monsters slain by the hero Beowulf has the flavour of pre-Christian legend.*

As a youth, Beowulf came from the land of the Geats to help the aged Danish king Hrothgar, and in a wrestling match killed the man-eating monster Grendel, who was breaking into the royal hall at night. When Grendel's mother came to avenge her offspring, Beowulf tracked the creature back to her lair beneath a lake and put her to death.

Beowulf went on to reign over the Geats for fifty years, until in his old age his kingdom was threatened by a dragon which for centuries had guarded a great treasure in a burial mound. Its wrath was aroused when a fugitive stole a rich drinking-cup from its

hoard, and that night it flew out to devastate the kingdom. Beowulf went to confront the beast, with a great iron shield to resist its fire, and a band of chosen warriors. His sword-blade could not pierce the horny skin, and as the dragon advanced his companions all fled in terror, except for one loyal young chieftain, Wiglaf. When the dragon seized Beowulf's neck in its jaws, Wiglaf pierced its underbelly with his sword. Beowulf drew his knife, and together they attacked the dragon until it fell. But Beowulf was weakened by the monster's poisonous breath. Dying, he bequeathed the hoard, with his neck-ring and armour, to Wiglaf.

The fire-breathing dragon in serpent form, winged so that it could fly through the night, may owe something to serpent monsters in early myth and legend. Beowulf's death has echoes of Thor's last battle at Ragnarok, when he slew the World Serpent but was afterwards overcome by its poison.

CENTRAL AND EASTERN EUROPE

*The central motif in this traditional Slav embroidery design from
North Russia is thought to represent the East Slav goddess
Makosh, who was the focus of a widespread fertility cult.*

Not one people but many, the Slavs range from Kashubians in the north to Macedonians in the south, each group with its own language reflecting a sense of separate identity. However, because of their relative youth among European peoples, the Slavs participate to a great extent in a shared mythic tradition. This tradition has eluded the preservative influence of written language, as the first writing came only in the 9th and 10th centuries with the conversion to Christianity, which ignored, misrepresented or condemned pagan practices. Details of early belief have to be pieced together by detective work. But economic backwardness and isolation (especially in Russia) have permitted the survival, albeit in distorted form, of a wide range of myths of ancient provenance.

The Slavs' mythology relates to supernatural beings, whom mortals encounter, usually at their peril. Names of pagan gods have been preserved, but little survives about their cults, except in exceptional cases such as that of the East Slav fertility goddess Makosh (illustrated above). Ancient beliefs relating to rites of passage or to shamanism are reflected in the folk tales. The Other World to which the shamans had access is inhabited or guarded by monsters, although the epic songs tell of how these malevolent beings, while still deriving their power from the Other World, have left it to threaten mankind in this world.

Also evident is the cult of dead ancestors, perhaps originally totemistic animals, vital today in folktales and popular beliefs about house spirits.

THE SLAV PEOPLES

The Slavs emerged with a distinct ethnic identity in about the 5th century AD. In the course of the next two centuries they split into three groups, pushing eastwards from a homeland probably in eastern Slovakia to occupy Bohemia, Poland and parts of Germany. Others pushed south through the Balkans, while others still went east and north to settle parts of present-day Ukraine and north-east Russia. The next millennium was a period of further expansion eastwards through European Russia to Siberia and into central Asia.

PRE-CHRISTIAN BELIEFS OF THE SLAVS

In the evolution of Slav mythological beliefs, three overlapping stages can be discerned:

LIGHT AGAINST DARK

A dualistic belief in a world governed by the creative force of light and the destructive power of darkness obliged mankind to enlist the aid of the good in placating or struggling against evil. With conversion to Christianity, the good forces became identified with the Church, but evil forces in the form of the revenant dead (such as vampires, or spirits dwelling in forests or streams) maintained their hold over the popular imagination.

THE CULT OF DEAD ANCESTORS

Each household was protected by dead ancestors, who determined its health and fertility. Beyond this purely local level, there was a general cult of a male fertility god, Rod, accompanied by mother and daughter deities, the Rozhanitsy. Elaborate rituals, linked with the calendar cycle of death and rebirth, probably included shamanistic practices of contacting the souls of dead ancestors in the Other World.

ELEMENTAL GODS

The final stage was the emergence of anthropomorphic elemental gods. Gods of the sun and fire express Slav reverence for the powers of light and, more particularly, respect for fire. In a developing culture the god of thunder not surprisingly became god of war, and a patron of trade emerged. Most pervasive of all are gods and goddesses of fertility.

KEY TO MAP

- Areas of Slav settlement, 6th century AD
- Expansion of Western Slavs, 5th–7th centuries AD
- Expansion of Eastern Slavs, 6–8th centuries AD
- Expansions of Southern Slavs, 7th century AD
- Areas of East Slav settlement, 10th century AD
- People: RUSSIANS

LINGUISTIC GROUPS OF THE SLAVS

The linguistic groupings of Slavs reflect the three directions of migration – west, south and east. By the time of the first written texts (9th-10th centuries), many of the modern Slav ethnic groups were already distinct. In the eastern area, Ukrainian and Belorussian emerged as distinct languages only after the 13th century.

WEST SLAVS	SOUTH SLAVS	EAST SLAVS
Polabians	Slovenes	Belorussians
Poles	Croats	Ukrainians
Kashubians	Serbs	Russians
Lusatians	Bulgarians	
Czechs	Macedonians	
Slovaks		

THE ANCIENT SLAV GODS

On the evidence of terminology, early Slav religion bore some relationship to Iranian belief, although some gods were of local provenance.

SVAROG, related to the Sanskrit *svarga* (sky). The most senior elemental god. He had two sons, DAZHBOG, god of the sun, and SVAROZHICH, personification of fire.
SVANTOVIT, a god connected with an ancestor cult. He had four heads which symbolized his great power and held a horn filled with wine, from the level of which he predicted the harvest. With the help of a sacred white horse Svantovit predicted the outcome of war. In East Slav areas Svantovit was represented by the ancestor cult of ROD, a deity of fertility,

light and creation.
PERUN was a god of thunder, lightning and war who in the late 10th century replaced Rod in aristocratic circles.
VELES, or Volos, was a deity of the dead and protector of flocks and trade.
MAKOSH, or Mokosh, great goddess of fertility, bounty and moisture, seems to have been unique to the East Slavs. (See illustration on opposite page.)
STRIBOG, god of winds to the East Slavs, is reflected in later Russian beliefs about stormy winds as vehicles for demons.
THE ROZHANITSY were mother-daughter goddesses of fertility, whose feast day marked the completion of the harvest. They were closely connected with Rod.

THE OTHER WORLD

The thrice tenth kingdom

NIGHTINGALE THE BRIGAND
The most striking supernatural foe is
Nightingale the Brigand (shown above in
a traditional tile design), a creature half
bird, half human, who lives in a tree
blockading the road to Kiev. He can
summon up a howling, whistling wind
which flattens trees and flowers and kills
mortals. Ilia of Murom, a famed *bogatyr*
(epic hero), urging his horse to ignore the
terrifying noise, shoots Nightingale in the
right temple and takes him to Kiev tied to
his stirrup.

Reached only after a long journey, undertaken by the hero to gain the
object of his quest, the Other World may lie beyond an impenetrable forest on the other side of a fiery river, or beyond or below the sea, or above
or below the earth. To gain access it may be necessary to scale a precipi-
tous mountain or descend into a cave or a hole in the ground. But wherever situated, the "thrice tenth kingdom" (as it is termed in the East
Slavonic folktale) is closely connected with the sun. The objects of the
hero's efforts are almost always golden (golden apples in one Bulgarian
tale, while another story revolves around a magical Fire Bird with fiery
golden feathers, sitting in a golden cage). Palaces are adorned with gold
and silver.

The remote golden kingdom recalls the ancient Slav belief that the
earth is an island floating in water, and that beneath the water lies another world into which the sun sinks at night. It is also possible that the concept of worlds above and below distantly reflects shamanistic notions of
the World Tree with roots plunging down and branches reaching up to
the heavens. In his trance, the soul of the shaman was believed to fly to
the world above or descend to accompany the soul of a dead person.
Thus, the journey of the hero represents the shaman's magical journey to
the land of the dead and his return as a wiser and more powerful man.
Another theory sees the source of journeys to the Other World in initiation rites in which the initiate was believed to die before being reborn into
a new stage of his existence. Certainly, the hero must face terrifying danger before emerging from the Other World. Furthermore, the belief in
death as a journey involving a climb seems to have been preserved in parts
of Russia in the custom of saving one's nail clippings so that they would
turn into talons after death.

Dragons

The dragon or serpent features in folktales as well as
in Serbian and Russian folk epic. Known as the Fiery
Serpent, it is connected with fire, water and mountains, all boundaries of the Other World. In pre-
Christian Russia jagged flashes of lightning were
believed to be dragons, as well as being associated
with the god of thunder, Perun. This may explain the
folk epic Dobrynia and the Dragon which depicts in
allegorical form the conversion of Russia (late
10th century) through the victory of
Dobrynia over a dragon symbolic of paganism and its
chief god Perun.
Typically, the Slavic
dragon appears as an

abductor of women – either a woman close to the hero
who is transported to the Other World, or maidens vic-
timized in a campaign of terror. The creature also commonly acts as guardian of the aspen-wood bridge over
the fiery river leading to the Other World. In both
instances the hero must defeat the dragon and, where
appropriate, rescue the captive. Before he tries to decapitate the dragon, he must ignore taunts that he will be
swallowed and resist the overwhelming desire to sleep.

*The dragon appears on many
objects. On this carved
beam (Novgorod, 11th
century) the dragon forms
are in green, for clarity.*

THE BABA IAGA AND THE AMAZONS

Female creatures of folk tale

By far the best-known mythical figure in Slav folk tales is the witch, the Baba Iaga. She has power over birds and beasts and travels in a mortar, propelling herself along with a pestle and erasing her tracks with a broom. More often she is encountered in her hut, which stands on chicken legs in the midst of a dense forest. To enter, the hero or heroine must utter a magic formula, upon which the hut will turn to reveal the door. The Baba Iaga fills the interior, a hideous aged crone whose long nose presses the ceiling, while her legs straddle the entire room. She is so scrawny that she resembles a skeleton with sharp teeth. She is known as "Bonyleg", and her garden fence is made of bones. The house's remote location implies guardianship of the gateway to the Other World; certainly, entry into her hut may mean death. There is a clear link with prehistoric initiation rites: initiation into manhood in many cultures is enacted in a special building outside the village, and initiates are believed to die before being reborn. Day and Night obey the Baba Iaga's commands, suggesting that her origins may lie in a once-powerful goddess of the Other World. This theory is supported by the occasionally positive role she plays in helping the hero in his quest, a relic of a time before her cult was overthrown.

Vestiges of a belief in powerful women of a different type also exist among the Slavs. An 11th-century legendary tale from Bohemia tells of a group of Amazons who fight like men and take the initiative sexually. These warrior-maidens, led by the bravest of them, Vlasta, live in a castle on the banks of the River Vltava. Battle with men ends ultimately in peace and marriage. In Russian folk epic, the *polenitsa*, as Amazons are termed, are figures riding alone. In the tale of Dobrynia and the Dragon, the hero, coming upon such a woman, attempts to overcome her. She seizes him by his yellow curls, wrenches him from his horse and drops him in her pocket. Eventually, she agrees to release him on condition that he marries her – usually, Amazons are either killed in the end, or tamed by marriage.

THE BABA IAGA AND MARIA MOREVNA
In one folk tale, Prince Ivan, whose wife Maria Morevna has been abducted by the monster Kashchei, seeks her out but discovers that he can rescue her only if he acquires a horse at least as swift as his foe's. From Kashchei, Maria learns that the Baba Iaga, who lives beyond the fiery river, owns a herd of such horses. When her husband finds her, Maria gives him the power to cross the river. Before acceding to his request for a horse, the Baba Iaga sets the prince the impossible task of guarding her herd of brood mares for three nights. Each night, following her instructions, the mares gallop away but are herded together again by animals and insects which Ivan has treated kindly. Finally, they advise him steal the mangy colt lying on the dung heap in the stable, and make his getaway. He does so and, hotly pusued by the Baba Iaga in her mortar and pestle, escapes back across the fiery river. With the colt, now miraculously able to outrun Kashchei's steed, Ivan rescues his beloved.

The Baba Iaga, mounted on a pig, confronts a "crocodile" in this early 18th-century woodcut. She waves a pestle, normally her means of propelling herself when she travels inside her mortar.

ANCESTORS AND HEARTH SPIRITS

Ivan the Fool and the *domovoi*

SPIRITS OF THE FARMSTEAD
Closely related to the *domovoi* were various farmstead spirits – the *dvorovoi*, the *ovinnik* and the *bannik*. The activities of the *dvorovoi* were confined to the farmyard but otherwise he behaved and looked much like the *domovoi*. The *ovinnik* (spirit of the threshing barn) was much more hostile to mankind, in keeping with the dangerous nature of the threshing floor. Also hostile was the *bannik* (spirit of the bathhouse, a place for divination and magic). Belief in the *domovoi* and the *bannik* survives in Russian villages in Siberia today.

Elaborate ceremonies commemorating the dead were practised by all Slav groups (although by the 19th century they survived only among those Slavs who were Orthodox Christians). Three or four times a year on fixed days the memory of dead ancestors was celebrated with food and drink beside the grave, a portion of the food being left out for the ancestor to consume.

Ancestor worship is also reflected in Russian folk tales in the figure of Ivan the Fool, whose place in the house is on the stove and who may even have a sooty appearance. It is Ivan, rather than his elder brothers, who is close to his ancestors; and it is he who receives a reward for observing the wishes of his dead father. The widespread Slav belief in household spirits is witnessed by the *dedushka domovoi* ("grandfather house-spirit": this is the Russian, and there are variant forms in other languages). The *domovoi*, who is active at night, needs to be treated with respect by the family, who avoid sleeping in his path, and leave regular supplies of his favourite food out for him every evening. If such things are not done, the *domovoi* is prone to behave badly, smashing crockery or tormenting the animals. Mostly he was invisible, but those who caught sight of him described him as a grey-bearded old man, sometimes suggesting that his body was covered with hair. Certainly his touch presaged good fortune if it was furry, ill fortune or death if it was cold and hard. New farm animals were introduced to him, and efforts made to keep only animals of the colour he was believed to like. Domestic prosperity depended upon his happiness, and extra efforts had to be made to please him if things went badly. Elaborate rites ensured that if the family had to move house the domovoi went too. Often he was enticed by some coals from the old fire – further evidence of the link with an ancient cult of ancestors.

Silver Roan

A saddle ornament from southern Russia.

The Russian tale of Silver Roan describes how a guardian of the hearth and family traditions is rewarded by the gift of a magic horse. An old man's instructions to his three sons to guard his grave for three nights after his death are ignored by the two well-dressed elder sons. In their place they send Ivan the Fool, who spends his days lying on the stove, dirty. At midnight on the third night, the dead father appears, rewarding Ivan with the gift of Silver Roan, a horse whose eyes spark fire and nostrils breathe smoke.

When the tsar declares that any man who can snatch his daughter's veil at a great height will wed her, Ivan utters a spell to summon Silver Roan, climbs into his ear and changes into a handsome youth. He wins the contest on the third occasion, and then, unrecognized, reverts to his squalid existence. The tsar arranges feasts in the hope of finding the handsome youth. Ivan, sitting behind the stove in the banqueting hall, wipes his beer mug with the veil and is recognized. He gains his just reward, to the chagrin of his brothers.

SPIRIT SOULS OF THE DEPARTED

The *rusalka*, *vila* and other visitors

The idea that the soul is separable from the body and can emerge during sleep as well as death is found among all Slavs. Called Zduhach by the Serbs, souls gather on mountain tops and do battle with each other. Victory in these battles brings prosperity to the sleeping owner, but if his soul perishes he will never awake. In Russia souls can take on the form of the *kikimora*, a small female being with flowing hair who, like the domovoi, dwells in houses, but whose role as an oracle of disaster makes her a less welcome presence. After death the windows and doors of a peasant hut were left open to enable the soul in the form of a bird to flutter in and out unseen. The souls of those who die unbaptized, as the result of a violent death or after being cursed by their parents, take various forms.

A *nava* is the soul of an unbaptized or stillborn infant. Among the Macedonians it is believed to take the form of a bird which flies around seeking its mother and attacking women in childbirth. It can be set free by conducting the baptism service. Much better known is the *rusalka*. In Southern Russia and the Ukraine, the *rusalka* were commonly believed to be the souls of infants or drowned maidens. They loved singing, and men who drowned were believed to have been lured by the song of the *rusalka*: taking the form of attractive maidens dressed in leaves, they were believed to entice village lads away to their underwater homes. In late spring during Rusalnaia Week (the seventh week after Easter) they were believed to emerge from the water into the fields and forest to fall on victims from behind and tickle them to death. In particular they disliked women, and there are accounts of them trying to steal the souls of unwary girls; and they would punish women for indulging, for example, in domestic activities during Rusalnaia Week. Although the Russian *rusalka* in the 19th century was connected with the dead, this may be a later development; the original association may be with fertility, and particularly with the pagan festival of Rusalii known in 11th-century Kiev (which has links with the Roman festival of roses, or Rosalia).

THE *SIRIN*
The *sirin* is a bird of paradise with the face of a young girl. Unlike other mythical creatures, which emerge from Slav folk tradition, it is of Greek origin, arriving with Orthodox Christianity. Clearly related to the Greek Siren (see p.147), it was particularly popular in Russia where its image acquired Christian and folk overtones. Like its Greek prototype, it is believed to sing exquisitely, but is more commonly known not as a creature who lures sailors to a watery death but as a bird of happiness and beauty, which flies down to earth from heaven as a reward for a good life. He who listens to the song forgets everything and then dies.

The *vila*

*L*ike the rusalka, *the vila is seen as an eternally young and beautiful woman with long fair hair. She too is associated with the souls of the departed – either girls who have died unbaptized (a Bulgarian belief), or frivolous girls whose souls now float between heaven and earth (a Polish belief).*

The *vila* has a close, sometimes friendly relationship with mankind. In South Slav countries she is the best-known mythic figure, absorbing features from other spirits whose identity has elsewhere been kept distinct.

The epic songs of the South Slavs frequently feature the *vila*. In one song, the hero Marko spies a *vila* group dancing. He sends his falcon to capture the wings and headdress of Nadanojla, their leader, and then sets off home followed by the distressed *vila*. Explaining her as a shepherdess, Marko marries her. But when he foolishly boasts one day that his wife is a *vila*, she takes up her wings and flies away. Only after being recaptured by Marko, does she accept her role as Marko's wife.

MALEVOLENT SPIRITS

Forest creatures, werewolves and vampires

WEREWOLVES

Those born with a birthmark, wolfish tufts of hair or a caul on their head were believed to be werewolves. The caul was usually rolled up and kept as an amulet or sewn into the clothes. This was everywhere believed to bring luck. Among both the Serbs and the Slovenes, and in the north of the area in Poland and among the Kashubs, such a child, as well as those born with hair or a birthmark, were supposed to possess magical powers of second sight and metamorphosis. Though they could turn into various animals, it was the bold and bloodthirsty wolf that they were believed to prefer, shown in the 16th-century print illustrated here (right) by Lucas Cranach. In the 16th century the Church in Russia felt obliged to condemn beliefs in the power of the caul and its "wolfish" associations.

Werewolf beliefs are reflected in the various stories about Vseslav, the 11th-century prince of Polotsk (now in Belorus). Unlike the other princes of Rus who converted to Christianity in 988, Vseslav and his family remained pagans. Historical sources suggest that his birth, with a caul on his head, coincided with an eclipse of the sun. Born of a princess violated by a serpent, the prince-werewolf rapidly assimilated the magic arts and the skills of hunting and warfare. As an adult he enjoyed miraculous success as a warrior "coursing as a wild beast, at midnight, shrouded in blue mist", as one 12th-century text puts it.

The *vila* (see p.211) is often well-disposed towards mortals, but the other spirits believed by the Slavs to dwell outside the immediate vicinity of the house are at best prone to play tricks on mankind and at worst actively hostile. Among the East Slavs, the most fearsome is the *leshii* or forest spirit. He is master of the forest and guardian of the animals that live within it. Thus, in 1859 a great migration of squirrels across the Urals was explained in terms of Siberian forest spirits, who having lost at cards to their fellow spirits in European Russia were driving their animals over to them as payment for their debts. Anthropomorphic in character, the *leshii* appears as a peasant, but varying in size according to habitat — from the height of the tallest tree to that of a grass-blade. He possesses the power of metamorphosis into various animals but, in order to deceive, could appear in the guise of a relative. Woe betide the peasant who failed to take precautions when entering the forest, especially on certain days, whether by uttering a protective prayer or by turning his clothes inside out. The *leshii* led people astray, sometimes right to the edge of a precipice, and carried off maidens and even children, usually after a mother had exclaimed impatiently to the child, "May the *leshii* take you".

Belief in forest spirits still survives in remote areas in Russia, whereas the notion of a threatening male water spirit has been on the decline for over a century. The *vodianoi* differs from the *rusalka* in being not only male but ugly, covered in slime, shaggy with claws or possibly bloated and white. He takes pleasure in drowning those who have offended him. In one village in Southern Russia, the story was told of a peasant who liked to dive for carp in a deep water hole where the *vodianoi* was believed to live. When, after numerous successes, he boasted that he would bring up the water-devil himself, he drowned.

The whole Slav area from ancient times was permeated by beliefs about werewolves (lycanthropy: see margin, opposite), which in time merged with the idea of the vampire. Serbian and Bosnian songs about Zmaj Ognjeni Vuk (Fiery Dragon Wolf) have attached the idea of a werewolf hero to a later 15th-century ruler, Despot Vuk. The songs depict him as born with a birthmark (red to the shoulder of his fighting arm, or in the shape of a sabre), tufted with wolf hair, and breathing fire. Growing up with miraculous speed, he becomes a warrior, and is the only person able to defeat the dragon (who may have fathered him).

Vampires

Of all the mythical creatures familiar to the Slavs and their neighbours, none is better known than the vampire. The word comes from the South Slav vampir, *with its variant forms in other languages (*upir, upyr, upior *and so on).*

By the 19th century, vampire beliefs were more prevalent among Ukrainians and Belorussians than among their East Slavic neighbours the Russians, but vampire lore had its greatest hold among the West Slavs (particularly the Kashubs who live at the mouth of the River Vistula) and the South Slavs. In South Slav countries the concept of the vampire has become entwined with the werewolf, to such a degree that the modern word for vampires is *vukodlak* (wolf's hair). However, unlike werewolves, vampires are essentially manifestations of the revenant unclean dead. Certain categories of people become vampires after death, including werewolves as well as sorcerers, witches, sinners and the godless (which in Russia included heretics). In some places (for example, Bulgaria) murderers, robbers, prostitutes and other socially undesirable people are also believed to turn into vampires. Even non-miscreants who die normally may turn into vampires, particularly when burial rites have not been read over them, or when they have met an untimely death (for example, by suicide). People

conceived or born on a holy day, the stillborn, and those born with a bony growth at the bottom of their backbone or with teeth, are marked out as vampires.

Vampires remain in the grave undecayed and often bloated, and there may be signs of movement of the corpse in the coffin (Macedonians believed that the corpse would turn face down). At midnight they visit houses to suck the blood of or have sex with the sleeping, often their own relations, who then waste away and die. They may also suck the flesh of their own breast or their funeral garments, both of which cause their relatives to die. Vampires are also found at crossroads or in cemeteries seeking their victims, often with a shroud over their shoulder. Methods of combating vampires are numerous. Some are designed to allow the vampire to rest in peace, such as placing in the grave small crosses of poplar wood, or flax or millet grains to keep them busy counting (a Macedonian and Kashubian belief). Of the sterner measures, best known is the sharpened hawthorn or aspen stake driven into the body, or a stake or nail into the head. Alternatively, the body was decapitated (West Slavs), dismembered (West and South Slavs), or the heels or ankles were maimed to inhibit movement (Croatia).

Belief in vampires still exists in remote areas and among the Kashub communities in Canada.

THE ARCTIC REGIONS

*This photograph shows walrus-stalking in Greenland.
Many Arctic peoples believe, even today, that game animals
are in the gift of the Spirit of the Sea who in winter supplies them
through holes in the ice.*

The mythology of the Arctic regions reflects a harsh, dangerous environment – a lonely landscape with a thinly spread population. Against this bleak backdrop, the threat of starvation is a common mythic theme. Agriculture is impossible, and all food must come from animals, which feature in myths as helpers and tricksters. Crucial to survival, animals are regarded throughout the Arctic as having souls of their own, and are respected accordingly: it is common for the hunter to apologize to the animal he has just brought down. Some Inuit throw back into the sea the bladder of a hunted seal, so that the seal will be reborn and in its next incarnation will offer itself as prey to the same hunter.

The seasons, the health and fertility of humans and animals, the kindness and harshness of the elements, are all believed to come from the world of spirits. The role of helping people in the community to achieve success and avoid misfortune falls to the spirit-medium, or shaman, whose calling is attained only by a few (usually, though not always, men). By beating a special drum in a ritual performance of dramatic intensity, the shaman enters a trance to communicate with the world of spirits. While he is unconscious, his soul travels among the spirits, to find out the whereabouts of game animals (or a particular lost reindeer or dangerous bear), to discover which spirit is causing sickness, or to rescue the stolen soul of a sick person, and thus save a life.

Accounts of shamanic healing in Inuit cultures describe a process of relentless interrogation, as the shaman attempts to find out from the sick person why the spirits are offended. Perhaps the sufferer smoked a forbidden pipe, or split a meat bone that should not have been touched, or ate a piece of raw, frozen caribou steak that was taboo for that individual. If the sufferer is a woman, perhaps she combed her hair after giving birth to a child. The shaman asks about such possible transgressions, and the whole community, gathered in the winter snow-house, clamours for the patient's release.

THE INUIT

The Eskimo-speaking peoples of the Arctic New World and Greenland are divided into a number of linguistic and political groups, the chief of which are the Kalaallit, Inuit, Inupiat and Yupik. The term Inuit ("genuine people"), which the Canadian groups apply to themselves, is nowadays widely used to cover all these peoples. Except in south Alaska and Labrador, the Inuit live beyond the northern limit of trees, traditionally pursuing a nomadic or semi-nomadic hunting and fishing lifestyle, in groups seldom numbering more than a few hundred people. In winter and spring, on the coast, they would pursue sea mammals (particularly seal, walrus and, where available, whales); in summer and autumn they would sometimes live inland, and their quarry would be caribou (the North American reindeer), fish and birds. Since contact with Europeans, a vigorous commercial trapping economy has been grafted on to this subsistence pattern.

THE PEOPLES OF THE RUSSIAN NORTH

This huge region stretches between Finland and the Pacific, and from south to north straddles two main types of landscape: virtually unbroken coniferous forest (taiga), with a belt of treeless tundra near the Arctic Ocean shore. The numerous native peoples belong to several language families, some in the west (including Saami, or Lapp) related to Finnish, others in the east related to the Turkic and Tungus-Manchu families. The Ket language cannot be related to any other in the world; while the Eskimo and Aleut are related to the other Eskimo languages of Alaska, Canada and Greenland.

Traditionally leading a nomadic life of hunting, fishing and reindeer herding, these peoples have been radically affected by Russian settlement, especially since the 1917 Revolution. All except the Komi, Karelians and Yakut are considered vulnerable, on account of their small population, and are afforded special protection.

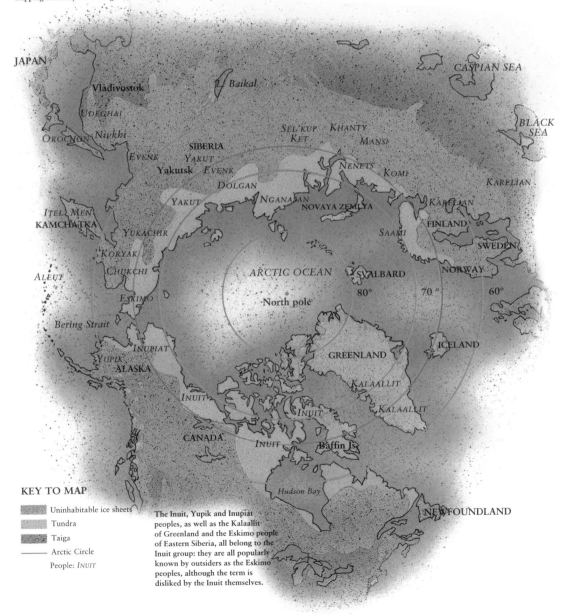

KEY TO MAP

- Uninhabitable ice sheets
- Tundra
- Taiga
- —— Arctic Circle
- People: *INUIT*

The Inuit, Yupik and Inupiat peoples, as well as the Kalaallit of Greenland and the Eskimo people of Eastern Siberia, all belong to the Inuit group: they are all popularly known by outsiders as the Eskimo peoples, although the term is disliked by the Inuit themselves.

MYTHS OF THE INUIT

Spirits of sea and sky

THE MOON SPIRIT
One of the major spirits of the Inuit is the Moon Spirit (Tarqeq), whose concerns are with fertility, moral propriety and, in the case of the Alaskan Inuit, the control of animals. The Moon Spirit is male, a mighty hunter, whose abode is the land in the sky. Illustrated here (right) is a Moon Spirit mask from West Alaska. The white border around the face symbolizes air, the hoops denote the levels of the cosmos, and the feathers signify stars.

THE SOULS OF ANIMALS
This illustration shows an effigy of a bowhead whale, which would have been lashed to a boat. The Inuit believe that prey is not "taken" by a hunter, but permits itself to be killed. When the animal dies, the hunter performs a brief ceremony to ensure that its soul is returned to the non-earthly world to rejoin the society of animals – in readiness for being sent out again as hunter's quarry. Over much of Alaska, Inuit hold important festivals to acknowledge and influence the animals' appearance on earth. For example, the Bladder Festival is a five-day winter event at whose climax the inflated bladders of all sea mammals caught by the community's hunters during the year are pushed through holes in the ice, thus returning the animals' souls to the spirit world.

Spiritual powers, of lesser or greater import, dominate Inuit life. The most famous is the Sea Spirit of the Canadian and Greenlandic Inuit. Known as Sedna (also Nuliajuk, among other names), the Sea Spirit exercises suzerainty over all animals which provide food for humans. In her residence at the bottom of the sea, from where she sends out the animals for hunting, she takes on the form of a woman. Even shamans fear her. Another major spirit is the Spirit of the Air, known in many parts as Sila ("weather", "intelligence"). This spirit, acknowledged in virtually every Inuit region, controls rain, snow, wind and sea from a domain far above the earth. Though conceived of as a person, the Air Spirit does not take embodied form. The Moon Spirit is the third of these major spiritual forces. All are inherently benevolent, yet humans perceive them, perhaps especially the Sea Spirit, as threatening, because they are highly sensitive to human misdemeanour, responding to it by sending foul weather, failure in hunting and sickness. To fend off such visitations, people incant magical words, don masks and amulets (the extremities of animals are favoured) and mobilize their shamans.

Among the plethora of other, lesser spirits, both benign and powerfully evil, the most interesting are the "helping spirits" – spirits of animals, objects or dead persons, which shamans encounter during their long apprenticeships: by possessing a shaman, a helping spirit can lend vital assistance to all shamanic endeavour.

The Inuit belief in lands in the sky and under the world's surface, each realm defined by a major spirit who dwelt there, facilitates the concept of "souls" and the notion that these are recycled. An important idea is that animals have souls (see margin, left), which leads to a special respect for prey. The spiritual essence of the human being is more complex. On physical death, a part of this essence enters, perhaps for ever, either the underworld or the land in the sky, depending on how the person died. A further part, embodied in the person's name, will come to be reincorporated in a newly born relative: naming an infant after someone recently deceased means that certain personal qualities will be transferred from ancestor to child.

In the present day, virtually all Inuit profess Christianity, which they have readily grasped in the light of their traditional beliefs. Traditional Inuit myth recognizes no omnipotent creator deity, yet the Inuit have associated the Christian God with the chief spiritual powers, and missionaries with shamans. In parts of southwest Alaska, Inuit profess the Russian Orthodox faith and engage in a Christmas ceremony which they call Selaviq. This ceremony, which for the Inuit incorporates both Christian and traditional meanings, starts and ends with a church service. It can last as long as ten days, and involves a house-to-house procession headed by large representations of stars announcing Christ's birth. As each house is visited, there is hymn singing and an enormous distribution of gifts.

House-to-house processions were important in traditional religious practice among these Alaskan peoples. For example, before the Bladder Festival (see margin, opposite) the human community would be opened up to the spiritual world by leading boys from house to house around the village. The distribution of gifts in Selaviq is a modern version of the traditional distribution of food in the Inuit community, reflecting the Inuit ethic of generosity.

THE RAVEN

The Raven Father, a key figure in the mythology of Alaskan Inuit (as also among neighbouring Indian and Siberian societies), is the only clear Inuit manifestation of a personified creator.

Descending from the sky, the Raven first created dry ground, then a man and various species of animals and plants; eventually he created a woman as the man's companion. In human guise, the Raven was also a teacher. Having made the man and woman, he instructed them in the use of animals, how to care for children, how to make fire, and so on.

An interesting feature of the myth is that the man is believed to have sprung from a vine pod which the Raven had made. Later, more men emerged from this pod – a simple explanation of the evolution of the race.

After these "first times", the Raven subsequently came to exercise only rather narrow powers. In his abode in the sky he can be propitiated to send good weather; and should anyone kill a raven, foul weather may certainly be expected.

The origin of the Sea Spirit

A Canadian Inuit myth tells of the origins of the Sea Spirit and of the animals of the sea.

The story begins with a young girl, forced by her father to marry a dog. In fact, the marriage begins well, but after the birth of several children things turn sour. The father drowns the dog, and the children try to exact revenge: they are sent away after failing in the attempt. Then a bird (a stormy petrel), in the guise of an ugly man, appears, and the girl goes with him, as his wife, in his kayak. Her father manages to retrieve her, but the bird catches them and starts a storm which threatens to capsize their boat. The terrified father tries to throw the girl to the

bird, but she clings to the boat's side. So the father successively hacks off her fingers at the joints until eventually she slips into the sea. This is how the beasts of the sea were created – the smaller seals from the girl's fingertips, the bearded seals from the middle joints, and the walruses from the last joints.

The seal originated from the severed finger of the young woman who became the Sea Spirit. This storage box represents a seal lying on its back. The human-like face on the lid is the seal's soul.

The girl herself drops to the bottom of the sea where she becomes the great Sea Spirit, with the animals (possibly including the land animals) seated beside her. There she is rejoined by her father, who has been swept out to sea in his grief, and by her first husband, the dog.

The dog takes up his role as her guardian, while her father remains the irascible tormenter of humans who transgress against the rules of life.

MYTHS OF SIBERIA

Animals, trees and shamans

All Siberian peoples traditionally practised hunting and fishing, and many of them herded reindeer. The Yakut and Buryat peoples are migrants into the area who introduced horse and cattle herding from further south, as well as a style of central Asian mythological epic.

It is in hunting that the special relationship with animals is clearest. In Siberian belief, animals are thought to give themselves of their own free will to a hunter who respects them. Animals are equal in status to their hunters, and in myths often change into humans or marry them. The brown bear, considered to be Lord of the Forest, has a soul-force of immense power which can be dangerous, but can also be used for healing. Even today, injuries are healed by stroking the affected part with a bear's paw or rubbing it with bear's fat. A bear hunt is surrounded by taboos, and in many areas the soul of a killed bear must be appeased by an elaborate rite. For example, the eyes are sewn up to prevent the bear from pursuing the hunter.

The Yukaghir tell of an ancestral hero who is half human, half bear. One version of the story tells of a man who took refuge in the den of a female bear. In spring she gave birth to a child, who later wanted to see his human father's village. But the child could not endure the village, and fled back to the forest. Later, after defeating various magical enemies underground, where he found a wife for himself, the bear-man returned once more to the human world, riding on an eagle and bringing a bride for his brother.

It is not only living animals that feature in myth. In Evenk mythology the mammoth, whose remains are often discovered in the ground, is one of the masters of the lower world. It used its tusks to draw up mud from the water and make the land. Wherever the mammoth walked, it created rivers in its wake; and wherever it lay down, it created lakes.

Throughout Siberia, people traditionally believed in several worlds, usually three, five or seven, stacked on top of each other. Our world is the middle one. The upper worlds are usually the realms of good spirits, while the lower worlds often contain evil spirits. The path between these worlds is usually seen as a tree with its roots in the lower world and its branches in the upper world. During a trance, the shaman climbs or flies to these other worlds in order to negotiate or fight with the spirits. In a performance, a shaman may sometimes climb step by step up notches cut in a tree trunk, at each step singing about his journey through the different layers and his encounters with spirits in each of them.

This tree features again and again in myth. According to the Nivkh, there were originally two moons and two suns, making the world too cold at night and too hot by day. Nothing remained alive except two titmouse brothers. These brothers came to a huge larch tree reaching up to the sky, and ate food left there by an old man who was the tree's master. Two birds, one silver and the other gold, appeared and challenged the titmouse brothers to a fight. The golden bird rose into the sky, and one of the brothers followed her. To escape him the bird changed in turn into a bear, a seal, a fish and a human, but the pursuer also changed into these animals, and caught her every time. In her human form, she was the daughter of an old man, whom the hero (formerly one of the titmouse brothers) asked for permission to marry her. The old man agreed, on condition that the hero would first kill the extra sun and moon. In this the hero was helped by the master of the sea, who shut him up inside an iron

A Tungus shaman in ritual dress, with shamanic drum, in an early photograph. The details of the costume had ritual significance.

kettle and boiled him; then he scraped up the remants and moulded them together into a new person. Thus, the hero was transformed into the iron man. Equipped with an iron bow, iron arrows and a flying horse, he shot the second sun and moon and the earth became habitable again.

The cooking and reconstitution of the hero are the unmistakable sign of shamanic initiation. The initiate is taken apart in a cooking pot by the spirits and then put together, bone by bone, as a reborn person with shamanic powers. Such is the power of iron that the blacksmith is the only person whom the shaman must fear as being stronger than himself.

Siberian origin myths include the Evenk story attributing the succession of day and night to a mighty elk dwelling in the upper world. One day the elk ran out of the forest and up to the crest of a hill, where he impaled the sun on his antlers, and carried it back down to the forest with him. The humans in the middle world were plunged into darkness. A hero called Main put on a pair of winged skis and rose to the upper world where he pursued the elk. At midnight, Main caught up with the creature and shot it with an arrow. Daylight returned to the the middle world. Main, however, did not return to his own world, but was turned into a spirit who guarded over the sun. Ever since, in the middle world, the episode has been repeated: each evening the elk captures the sun on his antlers, and each night Main recaptures it and returns it to his people by morning.

A double-headed bird, carved in wood, representing the shaman's ability to travel to the upper world.

The shaman and the police chief

Shamans were often attached to a particular group or clan, protecting that clan's territory and ensuring the rebirth of their souls. Wars between clans led to extraordinary battles of magic between rival shamans. After the Russian revolution of 1917, shamans were persecuted by the Communists, and older myths about conflicts between rival shamans were recast as contests between a shaman and the Commissar who arrests him. The following Yakut tale falls into this category of modernized myth.

A young police chief threatened a shaman with his revolver. The shaman warned him not to wave his revolver around: "My son, don't do that, you will hurt yourself!" The policeman then shot off his own thumb. Furious, he put the shaman into prison, but the shaman escaped. Several times the policeman imprisoned him again, each time putting him in a cell more secure than the last, but each time the prisoner got out and came walking back in through the front door.

Finally, the shaman was sentenced to hard labour in the forest, cutting down trees for firewood. An inspection team visited him there in the summer and saw the axe flying magically around the clearing, felling trees and stacking up the wood in neat piles.

At the beginning of the winter, when the authorities came again, both the shaman and the firewood had disappeared. The wood had joined together again to make living trees, standing just as they had before the shaman had begun his work.

Some children of shamans have in modern times become poets or surgeons, and it is believed that this is a continuation of the shaman's gift. In the post-Communist era there are movements to revive shamanism.

A shaman's helmet with reindeer antlers, made in iron. This would have been fashioned for the shaman by a blacksmith, after he had proved his powers. The reindeer was associated with the upper world.

NORTH AMERICA

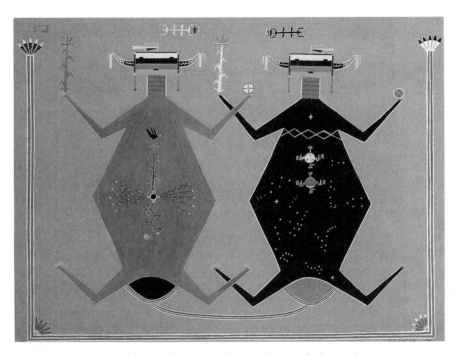

*A reproduction of a Navajo sandpainting depicting the figures of
Mother Earth (left) and Father Sky, two of the most widespread
creator gods in Native American mythology (see p.222).*

Since the arrival of their ancestors in North America – variously estimated to have happened between 12,000 and 60,000 years ago – the continent's aboriginal inhabitants have developed a wide range of small-scale, oral cultures, many of which survive on the reservations where most Native Americans live today. Traditionally, depending to a large extent on the terrain, their societies have ranged from nomadic hunting tribes to settled agriculturalists. For Native Americans, religion permeates all aspects of life and nature. Myths are regarded as sacred: they help to explain the cosmic and social order as well as the relationship between humans and the gods. Spiritually, the most important are those myths which detail the activities of the gods, especially creation myths and myths explaining the basic structure of the universe and

the origins of humans, death, maize and game. Such myths can often be told only under certain circumstances or at certain times of year. Also important are "institutional" myths, which relate how human institutions and culture came into being, usually through the activities of a primordial culture hero who gave the first instructions to human ancestors. "Ritual" myths are the basis for sacred ceremonies at which stories are re-enacted under prescribed ritual circumstances, for example the Hopi ceremonies re-enacting parts of the emergence story (see p.223). Such myths are most prominent in settled agrarian societies. "Entertainment" myths, told for pleasure and gentle moral instruction, are open to greater freedom of interpretation on the part of the storyteller. The most prevalent of these involve tricksters (see p.227).

LANGUAGES AND PEOPLES

Out of around 300 languages flourishing in North America before the arrival of Europeans, about 200 survive, spoken by perhaps three-quarters of a million people. They range from Navajo, with 160,000 speakers, to endangered languages such as Chinookan, with just 30. The map shows the broad cultural regions of North America (these do not correspond strictly with geographical areas) and the historic locations of some of its many aboriginal peoples. Since the 19th century, most Native Americans in the USA have lived on reservations; the largest of these are shown.

TIME CHART

60,000-12,000 years ago First people arrive in North America across land or ice bridge from northeast Asia

10,000-8000 years ago First distinct cultures emerge

C.AD 1000-1300 Speakers of Athabascan languages (Apache, Navajo) migrate southward from Canada to the Southwest

C.1600-1750 Peoples such as the Cheyenne and Dakota move to the Plains. Horses, introduced by the Spanish, revolutionize Plains warfare and hunting

1830-40 US expels westward most Native Americans living east of the Mississippi River

1890 Massacre by US cavalry of 200 Dakota at Wounded Knee Creek, South Dakota, ends armed resistance to white expansion

KEY TO MAP
Cultural regions:

West and Northwest

Plains

Southwest

Woodlands and Southeast

Reservation (USA)

People: CHEROKEE

Present-day country: **CANADA**

NORTHWEST

The peoples of the Northwest coastal culture live in villages of large wooden houses. Enjoying a mild climate and abundant food supplies (especially salmon), they have been able to devote much time to ceremonies and the production of ceremonial materials. Each clan has a mythical animal founder, represented on totem poles and other artefacts. Raven, Thunderbird and Cannibal Spirit are significant mythic figures.

PLAINS

The classic culture of the Great Plains, home to formerly nomadic buffalo hunters, developed only after the introduction of the horse and the influx of migrant Woodland peoples. Personal relationships with spirits are important, and myths reflect the importance of gods of the elements as well as the notion of a supreme being. Prominent are animal myths and myths relating to important institutions such as the sacred pipe (see p.231).

SOUTHWEST

This desert culture area includes the various Pueblo peoples, so called because of their settled existence in villages (*pueblos* in Spanish). They share ideas derived from "emergence" mythology (see p.223) and agriculture, and masked impersonators of mythic spirits are important to Pueblo religious practice. The Navajo and Apache arrived in this area in *c.*AD1400 and adopted, in varying degrees, elements of the local mythology and ritual.

WOODLANDS & SOUTHEAST

Stretching across much of northern and eastern North America are dense forests, broken by lakes and rivers. The region's mythology reflects the terrain, with many accounts of forest spirits, demons and monsters. There are also elemental gods, a supreme being and the idea of an upper and a lower world. Largely under the pressure of European settlement, some Woodland peoples migrated onto the Plains, but retained much of their mythology.

CREATION MYTHS

Great Spirit and Earth Diver

This mask (right), collected in 1913, represents a creator-ancestor who, in the myths of the Bella Coola of the Northwest, came to earth as an eagle.

Despite the enormous diversity of cultures in North America, there are relatively few types of myth about the creation of the world. Most Native American peoples attribute the conception, if not the making, of the universe to a supreme divinity or "Great Spirit". This being, known for example as Gitchi Manitou to the Algonquians of the Northeast Woodlands and as Wakan Tanka to the Lakota of the Plains (see p.230), is greatly revered, but is too passive and vaguely defined to be regarded as a distinct personality. Often its role in myths is only to create more definite figures, such as the widespread deities Mother Earth and Father Sky, or the Sun and the Moon, who are charged with further acts of creation while the supreme god withdraws to heaven. These figures may also be instrumental in the creation of humans (see opposite).

In most creation stories the active deities include animal figures: for example, in scattered parts of the West, the Spider is said to have woven a web which eventually formed the earth. But by far the most prevalent creation myth is that of the Earth Diver, an often lowly creature which goes to the bottom of the primeval sea and retrieves mud which then expands to form the earth. The world is often said to rest on the back of a turtle, a common character in the mythology of the Woodlands (see margin, left). Like accounts of a great flood, which occur in some versions of the creation story, this type of myth has its parallels in Eurasia, suggesting that it may have migrated eastward.

THE EARTH DIVER
The turtle, depicted in this detail from a 19th-century Cheyenne shield (right), plays an important role in the Earth Diver myths of many peoples. The Cheyenne account contains all the essential elements of this story. Maheo, "All Spirit," created the Great Water together with water creatures and birds. The birds grew tired of flying and took turns to dive to look for land. They failed, until finally the coot tried. When he returned, the coot dropped a little ball of mud from his beak into Maheo's hand. As Maheo rolled the mud in his palms it expanded and soon there was so much only old Grandmother Turtle could carry it. On her back the mud continued to grow; in this way the first land was created.

THE ORIGINS OF HUMANITY

The first human ancestors

The creation of the first people is typically attributed to one or more of the divinities involved in the creation of the world. For example, the Pawnee relate how Tirawa ("Arch of Heaven"), their primordial divinity, ordered the Sun and Moon deities to unite and produce the first man, while the Morning Star and Evening Star were told to produce the first woman. Among some peoples of the Southwest, the supreme divinity is said to have created the gods Mother Earth and Father Sky (see p.220), who in turn mated to create the first living beings, including people. The Hopi tell how twin deities first created the animals and then moulded humans from clay, bringing them to life with a ritual chant.

According to the Iroquois and Huron of the Woodlands, the first human ancestor was a woman, Ataensic, the offspring of the Sky People, divinities who came down to earth. The Navajo also believe that humans are descended from a female progenitor.

The Pueblo peoples and some peoples of the Plains possess, in their "emergence" myths, some of the most distinctive accounts of how people arrived in the present world. Reflecting the concerns of an agricultural society, the myths portray the earth as a fertile mother and all-powerful nurturer which gives birth to humans, animals and plants (see the Hopi example, right). The narratives contain implicit moral guidance, as humans are often forced to move on upward as a result of their own misbehaviour. In some versions, this delinquency causes the destruction of the lower worlds, leaving few survivors. From the point of emergence, humans spread out to their present habitats.

According to where the myths are told, the people may be led on their upward journey by Corn Mother or Spider Woman (divinities representing the earth), twin gods, or sometimes a hero figure.

THE FOUR WINDS
The emergence myth told by the Hopi people of Arizona relates how, when the world was created, there were four worlds: this world and three cave worlds beneath. The first creatures lived in the lowest cave. When it grew overcrowded and dirty, twin brothers came from heaven with all the plants of the world, hoping that one would prove tall and strong enough to allow every being to climb to the world above. The cane proved ideal. After a time, the second cave also became full and the creatures climbed the cane into the third cave. There, the two brother gods found fire and, by its light, people built houses and could travel. But a time of evil came upon them, and the people climbed up out into this, the fourth world, led by the two brothers.

The Sun Dance

The role of the sun as a creator deity and source of power in Plains mythology was formerly reflected in the Sun Dance, the most important of Plains rituals. It still persists, in modified form, among some peoples.

Every year, normally in early summer, a tribe would gather to celebrate its beliefs in a series of ceremonies, chants and other devotional practices. At the heart of this festival lay the Sun Dance itself, at which those who wished

The Lakota Sun Dance, drawn on bison hide. The cross suggests a christianized ritual: most Lakota are now Christians.

to draw spirit power to themselves performed a ritual dance before the tribe. The tribe would assemble in a wide ring around a pole which symbolically linked the world above the earth with the world below. Around this pole the dancers would perform, often for days on end, until they collapsed in a frenzied trance or from sheer exhaustion. Sometimes the participants inflicted injuries upon themselves, the tearing of flesh symbolizing a release from the bonds of ignorance.

GODS AND HEROES

Shapers and controllers of the world

THE ORIGIN OF DEATH

Myths of the origin of death often involve an argument between two beings, as in the following account related by the Shoshoni people of the western Plains.

In ancient times, the two most important figures were Wolf and Coyote, who always tried to go against Wolf's wishes. Wolf said that when a person died he could be brought back to life by shooting an arrow into the earth beneath him. But Coyote said that it was a bad idea to bring people back to life, because then there would be too many people. Wolf agreed, but decided secretly that Coyote's son would be the first to die, and by this very wish brought about the boy's death. Soon the grieving Coyote came and told Wolf that his son had died. He recalled Wolf's words: that people could live again if an arrow was shot underneath them. But Wolf countered with what Coyote himself had said: that man should die. Since then it has always been so.

A Kwakiutl mask representing the sun and bearing the face of an eagle. It is used in dance rituals.

While the Great Spirit reigns over all creation, the day-to-day running of the world is believed by Native Americans to be in the hands of the powerful deities and culture heroes who brought the world out of chaos and gave humans the objects and skills needed for survival. The origin of the stars and planets, seasons, death, fire and corn are regularly ascribed to personified divine or superhuman beings, such as Coyote in the Southwest, Nanabush, Glooskap, Great Hare, Wisakedjak (anglicized as "Whiskey Jack") in the Woodlands, and Raven in the Northwest. These culture heroes may also be mischievous tricksters (see p.227).

Myths about the origin and ordering of the heavens occur throughout North America, often incorporated into other myths. Some peoples tell of the haphazard scattering of the stars by a culture hero or trickster (for example, the Tsimshian of the Northwest coast say that the heavenly bodies were kept by a greedy chief until stolen by Raven, who threw them into the sky), while others say that the heavens were more carefully and systematically arranged. The Pawnee relate in detail how the supreme spirit Tirawa assigned a position and part of his power to each celestial body. Shakuru (the Sun) was sent to live in the east, whence he rises each day to give light and heat, and Pah (the Moon) went to the west, to give light by night. Likewise, positions were allotted to the Morning Star,

Evening Star, a Star of Death, and four stars which hold up the sky.

The Spider frequently plays an important part in creating the world (see p.222), and may also be a culture hero, as in the Cherokee myth of the theft of fire. Originally there was no fire, but then the Thunder God sent lightning to put fire in the bottom of a hollow sycamore tree on an island. Water Spider span a thread into the shape of a small bowl, which she fastened onto her back. She crossed to the tree, put one small ember in her bowl and brought this ember back for all the other creatures.

Most accounts of the origin of death accept the logic that space is limited on earth and death makes room for life (see opposite). Myths describing the afterlife are few, because Native Americans are generally more concerned with the present world than with the next. On the whole the afterlife is regarded as a place much like this world but with more game. The best-known example – it has passed into the English language – is the "Happy Hunting-ground" of the Plains peoples.

Native Americans believe that the forces of nature are controlled by elemental gods and spirits to whom the various powers of the Great Spirit are delegated; these include the Sun, the Earth, Summer, Winter, Rain, Lightning and the Four Winds. One of the mightiest forces is Thunder (see panel, below). Many Plains peoples think in terms of spirits of Earth, Fire, Water or Air (Thunder is an Air god). The Woodland peoples divide their gods and spirits into those living above the earth and the waters (such as Thunderbird) and those living below. The underworld spirits, headed by dragon-like deities usually represented as panthers or horned serpents, are generally regarded as malevolent. The divinities of the Pueblo peoples also fall into two divisions: elemental gods on the one hand and, on the other hand, ancestral spirits called *kachinas*, intermediaries between humans and the gods who are represented at rituals by masked impersonators.

A Thunderbird mask of the Haida people (above and below) which opens to reveal a human face, symbolizing the close kinship between animals and humans. It is believed that in primordial times there was no distinction between them and that they could change shape at will (see p.232).

The Thunderbird, king of the skies

The spirit of Thunder is believed to manifest itself on earth in the form of the Thunderbird. The beak or eyes of this huge, eagle-like beast flash lightning, while the beating of its wings is heard as thunderclaps. It is credited with awesome powers of creation and destruction.

Among the Lakota, the Thunderbird, Wakinyan, is an assistant god, a manifestation of the supreme being: there is a strong cult associated with personal experience of meeting him. For the Iroquois he takes on human form as Hino, the Thunder Spirit, guardian of the sky. On the Northwest coast, the Thunderbird is among the chief gods of the sky and is large enough to carry off whales, upon which it preys. Peoples of the West believe that there are four Thunderbirds, one in each quarter of the world. In this region and elsewhere the Thunderbird is engaged in a continual battle with the malevolent spirits or serpents of the underworld, such as the underwater panther. Their clashes are believed to be the cause of the most violent natural phenomena, such as earthquakes, floods and great thunderstorms.

Anything struck by the Thunderbird's lightning is held by Native Americans to exert a particular spiritual power, either to be avoided or venerated depending on local tradition.

THE ORIGINS OF CORN

Corn (maize) is the most important crop in the diet of Native Americans, and there are many accounts of its origin. The corn myth of the Mikasuki of Florida brings together two common ideas: the important role of two brothers or heroes and the creation of something from part of another being. Two brothers lived with their grandmother, and one day, tired of meat, they asked her for something new to eat. From then on, when they returned from hunting, she served up some corn, which they found delicious. Their grandmother would not say where it came from, so the younger brother spied on her when she went to the storehouse. To his horror he saw her rub corn from the sides of her own body. That night the brothers refused the corn, and the old woman could tell that they knew her secret. She announced to the brothers that she would have to leave them forever, but would live on as the corn growing from her grave.

SHAMANS

Vision quests and guardian spirits

The drumskin below was painted with a design representing a shamanistic horned spirit. Its artist belonged to the Assiniboine people, a group living on the US-Canadian border west of Lake Winnipeg.

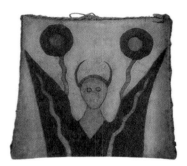

Direct contact with the world of the gods and spirits is of great importance in most traditional Native American cultures. It is achieved principally through the "vision quest", a process of solitary fasting and prayer in a remote place, by means of which a person hopes to attain a vision of a guardian spirit, which generally appears in the form of an animal, bird or one of the elements. Those to whom such a visionary experience occurs most spontaneously may go on to become shamans, healer-priests who are the chief intermediaries between human beings and the sacred world. While many individuals may acquire power from guardian spirits and visionary experiences, only the most powerful will become full shamans. (Those who do not possess the full range of shamanistic attributes are usually termed "medicine men".) The path to shaman status typically begins when the individual (usually male) falls ill at an early age and undergoes a visionary death and rebirth, during which he or she meets spirits and acquires sacred knowledge (see panel, below).

The relationship between a shaman and the spirit world amounts almost to a personal religion, while the account of the first meeting with the spirits becomes the shaman's personal myth. The power of this myth is important for establishing the shaman's credentials with the tribe, on behalf of which his or her skills are used to locate game, find lost objects and, above all, treat the sick. Shamans can enter a trance at will and journey to the sacred world, the land of the dead. Visible representations of the spirits are found in the shaman's "medicine bundle", a collection of artefacts of spiritual significance used in curing rituals. Symbols of the spirits are also depicted on clothing and on ritual and personal objects.

A shaman receives his calling

*I*n this shortened account, a shaman of the Kwakiutl people of British Columbia relates his personal myth, the visionary encounter which resulted in his acquisition of shaman powers.

"All of us were sick with the smallpox. Presently I thought I was dead. I awoke because of all the wolves coming into the tent, whining and howling. Two were licking my body, vomiting foam and trying to put it all over me, taking off all the scabs and sores. Evening fell and the two wolves rested. I crawled into a shelter of spruce, where I lay all night. I was cold. The two wolves lay down on either side of me and, when morning came, licked me again all over. A figure from an earlier dream, Harpooner-Body, vomited foam and pressed his nose against my breastbone. He was vomiting magic power into me, and in a dream he laughed and said: 'Friend, take care of the shaman power that has gone into you. Now you can cure the sick and make sick those in your tribe whom you wish to die. They will all fear you.' "

A "soul-catcher", used by a shaman to "rescue" a sick person's soul. It was made of bone and shell by a Tlingit artist of the Northwest, where shamanism is particularly common.

TRICKSTERS

Entertainers and mischief-makers

The superhuman culture heroes of North American mythology (see p.224) may also behave as tricksters, using cunning and stealth to steal fire, outwit monsters or play tricks on others. Many peoples have developed these trickster tales into a separate body of myth, and in some areas, such as the Northwest coast, the culture hero and trickster are sometimes regarded as separate beings. The trickster myths allow great scope for elaboration by storytellers and are undoubtedly the most widespread and popular tales among Native Americans. One character, the Rabbit trickster of the Southeast, passed into modern American folklore as Brer Rabbit after West African slaves fused him with their own Hare trickster (see p.276).

Because the trickster is usually the same as the culture hero, he is usually called by the same name: Great Hare, Nanabush or Glooskap in the Woodlands, Rabbit in the Southeast, Coyote on the Plains and in the West, Spider on parts of the Plains, and Raven, Blue Jay or Mink on the Northwest coast. Despite his different guises, he exhibits similar characteristics across the continent, the same tales occurring in widely separated areas. He can be a crafty joker and a bungler, who is usually undone by his own horseplay or trickery, ending up injured or even dead – only to rise again, seemingly none the wiser for his experience. At times utterly irreverent and idiotic, the trickster's doings highlight, in an entertaining context, the importance of moral rules and boundaries. Many trickster myths are extremely vulgar (see margin, right, below).

At times the character's dual roles as culture hero and trickster are combined in one tale, as in the myth of how Raven stole the heavenly bodies (see p.224). An Algonquian myth relates how Glooskap first brought the summer to the frozen northern lands. The hero-trickster wandered south from the country of the icy giant Winter and used his cunning to kidnap the beautiful Summer, the chief of the little people. He took her to the *tipi* of Winter, who melted away in the presence of her warmth. Glooskap then let Summer return home.

RAVEN
The figure of Raven as a trickster or culture hero features prominently in the mythology of the far Northwest and along the Pacific seaboard. Some peoples, such as the Tlingit of southern Alaska, distinguish two Ravens, the culture hero and the trickster. The mid-19th century whalebone knife handle (above), from the Haida people of Alaska, depicts the head of Raven. He is also represented on totem poles and, especially, in masks used during long winter rituals.

GREAT HARE'S PAINFUL LESSON
The following story, told by the Winnebago people of Wisconsin, is a good illustration both of the bungling personality of the trickster (in this case Great Hare) and of the vulgarity of many trickster stories.

Great Hare killed some ducks and put them in the fire to roast while he had a snooze, telling his anus to keep watch. But foxes stole all the meat, and when he awoke and saw that the food had gone, Great Hare turned to his anus angrily: "Didn't I tell you to watch the fire? I'll teach you a lesson!" He took a firebrand and burnt the mouth of his anus, yelling in pain as he did so.

Moaning at his own stupidity, Great Hare hobbled off. He found a piece of fat in the road and began to eat it. It was delicious, but he soon realized that he was eating parts of his own intestines which had fallen out of his burnt anus. "People are right to call me the fool!" he cried, and tied his intestines back in place. In doing so, he pulled the string tight to form ridges and wrinkles, which is why the human anus has its present wrinkled shape.

A chest of soft grey shale (argillite) carved by a Haida craftsman. It bears various human and animal trickster images and motifs.

NAVAJO MYTHS

Curing ceremonies and Coyote tales

Crossed snakes, a detail from a Navajo sandpainting. Snakes are associated with the soil and fertility, which obviously are of particular importance to farming peoples in a desert environment.

THE YEI GODS

In Navajo mythology there is a class of gods called Yei, who are prominent in the creation of the world and are impersonated during certain curing ceremonies. The masks used in these ceremonies are created from deer that have been suffocated by having corn pollen placed in the nostrils, ensuring that the deer skin is unwounded. These masks are made during a performance of the Night Chant ceremony, when young Navajos are traditionally initiated into the secrets of the Yei. The masks are ritually consecrated and "brought to life" by having cornmeal "fed" to them and smoke blown over them. Talking God is the leader of the Yei, who manifest themselves either singly (during ceremonies) or in groups (during dances outside the ceremonial house or *hogan*).

RITUAL SANDPAINTINGS

This copy of a Navajo sandpainting (right) represents one of about 600 designs used in curing ceremonies such as Coyoteway (see margin, opposite). The "paintings" are drawn on clean sand using coloured powders, such as charcoal and pollen, and depict stylized scenes from myths. They are entered from the east (on the left in the illustration) by participants in the ceremony and after use are swept away. Each curing ceremony has its own myth. Because the number of ceremonies has declined during this century, many of the myths have been lost.

The Navajo of Arizona, New Mexico and parts of Utah are the most numerous of present-day Native American people, with a current population of more than 160,000. Like their cousins and near neighbours, the Apache, they were originally immigrants from Canada, arriving in the region probably before 1300. Apart from some hunting myths, dating from before this time and now on the decline, Navajo mythology shows the influence of the agrarian Pueblo peoples, such as the Hopi, from whom they adopted the emergence myth and much of its symbolism (see p.223). Most Navajo mythology can be said to derive from the creation-emergence myth and the various ceremonial myths which branch off it. Ceremonial myths describe how one or more heroic figures become injured or lost and travel in search of the gods in order to be cured. After being cured, and having learned the curing ceremony in the process, the hero returns home to pass on the ceremony and then departs to live with the gods.

One typical ceremonial myth tells of twin boys who were the offspring of a Navajo girl and the Yei deity known as Talking God (see margin, left). The boys are always wandering away from home and one day they are crushed by a rockfall. The accident leaves the elder son blind and the younger one crippled. They become a burden to their poor family and are asked to leave home. They go in search of the gods. Talking God helps them and eventually reveals himself as their father, upon which the gods greet the boys as kin and prepare a curing ceremony in the sweat-lodge (a form of sauna). As the cure takes effect, they cry out in joy, breaking a taboo on talking in the sweat-lodge. Everything vanishes and the boys are left blind and lame as before. They make a gift to appease the gods, who finally cure them and make them as beautiful as their brothers. The twins return home and pass on the curing ceremony before departing to become spirit guardians of the thunderstorm and of animals.

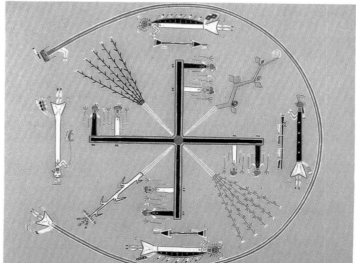

Coyote and the giant

*C*oyote is among the most popular of all Native American mythological characters. He appears in the Southwest and West and on the central Plains in a wide range of roles, including that of creator, culture hero, trickster, sorceror and lover. Coyote's prominence as spirit and trickster reflects the nature of the coyote itself, a member of the dog family found from Alaska to Costa Rica. It is crafty and swift, and eats almost every kind of animal or plant. One of its tricks is to pretend to be dead in order to attract scavengers, which it then catches and eats. Coyote's cunning is well illustrated by the following Navajo myth.

Long ago the earth was roamed by giants who were especially fond of catching and eating little children. Coyote was crossing a rocky place one day when he encountered one of the giants and decided to teach him a lesson for his cruelty. He persuaded the monster, who was very stupid, to help him build a lodge for a sweat-bath, claiming it would make him as agile as Coyote himself. When the dark interior had filled with steam, Coyote said he would perform a miracle by breaking his own leg and mending it again. He took a rock and pounded an unskinned leg of deer, which he had secretly pushed into the sweat-lodge, until it broke with a loud crack. The giant felt the broken leg and, completely fooled, listened as Coyote spat on it and chanted: "Leg, become whole!" The giant reached over, felt Coyote's real leg and was astonished to find it uninjured. Coyote offered to repeat the miracle on the giant's leg, and the monster agreed, screaming in pain as his companion started pounding it with the rock.

Soon the giant's leg broke and Coyote told him that to mend it all he had to do was to spit on it. The giant spat until his mouth was dry, but the pain became no more bearable and the leg refused to mend. Eventually the giant begged for help. "Just keep spitting," said Coyote, reassuringly. Coyote then slipped out of the sweat-lodge, leaving the child-eater with his agony.

Other myths ascribe great creative powers to Coyote. For example, in the Navajo version of the Pueblo emergence myth there are three creator figures, First Man, First Woman and Coyote. The myth relates how, when they emerged from four underground worlds into this world, Coyote brought seeds with him from the fourth world. He gave them to the different tribes as they were created.

Coyote has long been popular in the mythology of the Southwest. This coyote figure was painted on a plate made c.1050-1200 by people of the Mogollon culture, which flourished in the region from c.200BC-c.AD1200. It has been suggested that the holes commonly found in such plates were made to release the spirits of the painted figures.

COYOTEWAY

Coyote is the tutelary spirit of "Coyoteway", one of the Navajo curing ceremonies which feature masked impersonators of divinities. The ceremony is necessary if someone in the tribe catches "coyote illness", which can result from killing a coyote or even seeing its dead body. During the ritual, the patient takes the part of the hero of a ceremonial myth and sits on a sandpainting depicting an episode from the myth. He or she "meets" Coyote, who appears in the form of a masked impersonator. The ceremony restores the patient's harmonious relationship with Coyote and the world and thus ensures a return to good health.

MYTHS OF THE PLAINS

Wakan Tanka and the sacred pipe

THE LAKOTA CREATION MYTH

The Lakota account of the creation begins with the supreme being, Wakan Tanka (Great Mystery), whose spirit was in the first god, Inyan (Rock). Nothing else existed except Han (Black of Darkness). Inyan desired to show his powers, but there was nothing to exercise them upon, so out of his blood he created the goddess Maka (Earth) and the blue waters. From the waters the great blue dome of Skan (the Sky) was created, his edge forming the earth's boundary. Skan used his energy to create earthly darkness from Han, and then created Wi (the Sun) from Inyan, Maka, the waters and himself. He ordered Wi to shine and the world became hot.

The four gods, Skan, Inyan, Maka and Wi, assembled. Skan, the most powerful, addressed them: "Although we are four we have one source, Wakan Tanka, which no one, not even the gods themselves, can understand. He is God of Gods."

The peoples of the Plains have given the world its classic image of the traditional Native American way of life. Nomadic and warlike, they lived in encampments of *tipis* (also spelled "tepees") and depended for their livelihood on hunting big game, especially the huge herds of buffalo which used to migrate across the great expanse of grassland stretching from Canada to southern Texas. This lifestyle, which flourished in the two centuries after the Spanish introduced horses c.1600, came to an end in the 19th century as European settlers pushed relentlessly westward and the buffalo was hunted nearly to extinction.

Some Plains mythology resembles that of the Woodlands, because a number of peoples, such as the Cheyenne, migrated from the east under pressure from the first European colonists. As in the Woodlands, the belief in an all-powerful and remote Great Spirit is widespread. He has various names, for example Wakan Tanka among the Lakota and Tirawa among the Pawnee. His powers are manifested through a range of elemental deities, especially Sun, Moon, Morning Star, Wind and Thunderbird (see also pp.224-5).

Plains mythology reflects the character of a featureless landscape dominated by the expanse of the heavens. The power of the sun was acknowledged through the Sun Dance (see p.223). The Morning Star is particularly powerful, represented as a young man responsible for spreading life on earth. Many myths describe encounters of human ancestors with spirits who passed on information vital to hunting and survival. Some stories account for the origin of important ceremonial objects, such as "medicine bundles" and sacred pipes (see panel, opposite). Trickster tales are also common: the trickster is often referred to as Old Man Coyote or, among the Lakota, the Spider (Inktomi).

The aspects of Wakan Tanka

Wakan Tanka, the "Great Mystery", is the supreme being of the Lakota. Their creation myth relates how the Superior Gods (see diagram), each of which is an aspect of Wakan Tanka, grew lonely and created other manifestations of the god. In prayer, the Lakota use the term "Father" to address any of these individual aspects. The transcendent deity is addressed as "Grandfather".

The Superior Gods first created the Associate Gods (Moon, Wind, Falling Star and

Thunderbird). They then caused the creation of the Kindred Gods: Two-Legged (humans and bears, which are seen as relatives of humans), Buffalo, Four-Winds and Whirlwind. The fourth group, the God-Like, relate to the soul, spiritual essence and sacred powers: *Nagi* (shade or ghost of the dead), *Nagila* (shade-like), *Niya* (life or breath) and *Sicun* (spiritual power). These four groups of four aspects, or *Tob Tob* ("Four-Four"), make up Wakan Tanka, who is manifested through his sixteen aspects but is greater than their sum.

WAKAN TANKA

Superior Gods	Associate Gods	Kindred Gods	God-Like
Sun	Moon	Two-Legged	*Nagi*
Sky	Wind	Buffalo	*Nagila*
Earth	Falling Star	Four-Winds	*Niya*
Rock	Thunderbird	Whirlwind	*Sicun*

The sacred pipe

The smoking of a sacred pipe is one of the most widespread and ancient rituals among the peoples of the Plains and elsewhere. Communal smoking confirms the bonds linking family, tribe and universe, and the pipe itself, which is often decorated with feathers and designs reflecting the owner's personal spirits and visions, symbolizes creation. The following myth explains the origin of the sacred pipe of the Lakota. Unlike the sacred stone, the pipe is believed still to exist. Very few people outside the Lakota have ever seen it.

One morning, many winters ago, a mysterious and beautiful woman, dressed in white buckskin and bearing a bundle on her back, approached two Lakota hunters. One desired her and was instantly reduced to bones. The woman spoke: "I wish to talk with your chief. Return to him and tell him to prepare a large *tipi*." The hunter obeyed.

When the woman entered the *tipi*, she presented her bundle to the chief, saying: "I am the White Buffalo woman. This is very sacred, and no impure man should ever be allowed to see it. With this, during the winters to come, you will send your voices to Wakan Tanka." She took a pipe and a small round stone from the bundle and placed them on the ground. Then, holding the pipe with its stem to the sky, she said: "With this sacred pipe you will walk upon the earth; for the earth is your grandmother and mother, and she is sacred. The bowl of the pipe is made of red stone; it represents the earth. Carved in the stone is a buffalo calf, which represents all four-legged creatures. The stem of the pipe is made of wood and represents everything that grows. The twelve feathers hanging from the pipe are from the Spotted Eagle and represent all creatures of the air. The seven circles on the stone represent the seven rites in which the pipe will be used [see margin, right]." After talking of the first rite, White Buffalo woman announced her departure, saying that she would return one day, before which the other rites would be revealed. As she walked away from the people, White Buffalo woman became first a young red and brown buffalo calf, then a black buffalo. The buffalo bowed to each of the four quarters of the universe, then disappeared over the hill.

A 19th-century slate sacred pipe made by a member of the Santee (Eastern Sioux). It depicts a couple and a horse, perhaps spirits associated with pipe rituals.

THE RITES OF THE LAKOTA PIPE
According to the Lakota pipe myth, the round stone left by the White Buffalo woman (reconstructed above) was engraved with seven circles representing the seven rites associated with the pipe. The first rite, the Keeping and Releasing of the Soul, is used to "keep" the soul of a dead person for a number of years until it is properly released, ensuring a proper return to the spirit world. The second ritual is the Sweat-Lodge, a purification rite used before any other major ritual. The third, Crying for a Vision, lays down the ritual pattern of the Lakota vision quest, when an individual goes out alone to seek a sacred vision.

The fourth ritual is the communal recreation ceremony known as the Sun Dance (see p.223). The fifth is the Making of Relatives, a ritual joining of two friends into a sacred bond. The sixth is the girl's puberty ceremony. The final ritual is called "Throwing the Ball", a game representing Wakan Tanka and the attaining of wisdom.

ANIMAL MYTHS

The relatives of humankind

A Tlingit house partition screen in the form of a squatting bear. The oval opening provided access to the sacred room at the rear of the house of Chief Shakes of Wrangell, Alaska.

TOTEM POLES
Representations of mythic beings have attained a particular richness of expression on the Northwest coast, and nowhere more so than on totem poles, whose carved images represent the animal beings which founded and assisted the clan and gave it its power. Totem poles are basically heraldic emblems, representing status, wealth or ownership. "Memorial poles" are erected on the waterfront of lakeside villages (where they can be seen by anyone approaching by water) by a chief's heir as part of the procedure of inheriting the chief's title and prerogatives. Another type is the "mortuary pole", which is set alongside the grave of a deceased chief. The third type is the house "portal pole", erected on the front of the clan house and bearing clan symbols. It has a large opening forming the gateway, which represents the symbolic entrance to the supernatural world. The illustration (below), shows the top of a totem pole from Alert Bay in British Columbia. The carved figure represents an eagle ancestor.

Animals play a major part in Native American mythology because they are believed to possess a close kinship with humans. In ancient times, it is said, before some break occurred which fixed them in their present identities, people and animals were indistinguishable and could change appearance at will. For example, some peoples of the Northwest coast believe that their ancestors were animals which landed on the beaches and took off their animal guises, becoming human and establishing the various clans. Numerous myths of marriages between humans and beasts describe how people and animals came to be separated.

No animals, it is believed, are closer to people than bears, which sometimes walk on two legs and have skeletons like those of a human, only larger. In many myths bears are depicted as a race which have human form but always wear their bear coats in public. One Northwestern myth relates how Rhpisunt, a chief's daughter, was out collecting berries one day when she came across two young men, who led her to a house in the village which was the home of the bear people. Inside sat a huge man, the bear-chief, and bear coats hung everywhere. Rhpisunt married the chief's son and bore twin cubs.

Some time later, Rhpisunt's brothers found the den in which she and her new family lived. With her cubs she returned with them to her father's village, where the twins took off their bear coats to reveal two handsome boys, who grew up to be successful hunters. Eventually Rhpisunt grew old and died, and her sons returned to the bears. Afterwards Rhpisunt's descendants had good luck while hunting whenever they reminded the bears of their kinship with Rhpisunt.

The hunting and killing of beasts is carried out in accordance with numerous important rituals and myths. In the tribe there may be a master or mistress of animals, who possesses the authority to withhold captured game if the relevant ritual is observed incorrectly by the hunters. Animals are regarded as an important source of spirit power and Native American shamans often rely on animal helpers, who pass on their powers during visionary encounters (see panel, p.226).

How game was released

There are many accounts of how game was released before the arrival of humans. The following version is told by the Navajo people, who were primarily hunters before migrating to the Southwest from Canada (see p.228).

Before humans were created, the Holy People met in the sweat-lodge to discuss how to locate all the game animals, which had disappeared. A mysterious black figure entered the lodge: no one knew who he was. Two of the Holy People hid and saw him put on the coat of a crow and fly away.

The assembled company decided on a ploy to retrieve the game animals. They would transform one of their number into a puppy dog and allow him to be carried away by the black crow. Crow came and picked up Puppy and carried him to a place called Rim

Hill, which was the home of Black God, to whom all the game animals belong.

The gatekeeper of Black God's house was Porcupine, who had a turquoise rod for stirring the fire and opening the gate. Puppy knocked him out and opened the gate with the turquoise rod. Inside, he saw game everywhere: they had all been herded inside by Crow, who was really Black God in disguise. Seeing the open gate, all the animals quickly escaped into the wild.

The myth goes on to relate how, as the first four deer ran through the gate, Puppy touched them between their legs to create odours. As all the other animals came through, Puppy touched their noses with the wind to make them sensitive to these smells. That is the origin of an animal's ability to sense what is approaching before it appears.

Crows and ravens are common throughout North America and figure in the mythology of most Native American peoples. Two ravens are depicted in the stylized animal design on this Tlingit blanket (bottom left and bottom right). The other creatures are whales or porpoises.

MESOAMERICA

*The flat-topped stepped pyramid is the ubiquitous form
of sacred architecture in Mesoamerica. In some
cultures it symbolized the heavens, visualized as a series
of layers, each occupied by a deity. Pictured here is a
Toltec-Maya pyramid at Chichen Itza in the Yucatan.*

Historians and anthropologists use the term
"Mesoamerica" to denote the part of central
America (principally Mexico) that was civilized
before the Spanish conquest in the early 16th century. Underlying the variety of nations, tongues
and artistic styles of this region, there is a surprising unity of culture and religion. One shared
feature was the use of a complex calendar based
upon a 260-day sacred cycle combined with a
solar year of 365 days. Equally widespread were
a sophisticated knowledge of astronomy, hieroglyphic writing, a ball game resembling basket-
ball played in a special court with a solid rubber
ball, and a pantheon of remarkable complexity,
incorporating gods of wind, rain and corn.

The region is a mosaic of contrasting landscapes, from the deserts in the north to the rain
forests of the south. There was either too much
or too little rain, dry riverbeds would turn into
raging torrents overnight, earthquakes shook the
ground. This background of instability may help
to explain the Aztec myth of the five suns: each

sun was a cosmic world or era, and each era
ended in a cataclysm (see pp.237-8).

The Aztecs were not the first to appease the
gods by human sacrifice. The religion of the
Toltecs (whose capital Tula was established
toward the end of the 11th century) was similarly
bloodthirsty, as evidenced by their *chacmool*
sculptures – reclining figures with dishes held out
to receive sacrificial offerings (in the middle
ground of the photograph above). Aztec practices,
however, are the best documented. To help the
god Huitzilopochtli, as the sun, in his daily battle
against the forces of night, it was necessary to
nourish him with human hearts and blood. The
need for sacrificial victims was supplied by prisoners taken on military campaigns.

In a sense the Aztecs can be said to have captured
their pantheon in the same way, adopting the gods
of earlier peoples, such as the rain god Tlaloc
and the fire god Huehueteotl. However,
Huitzilopochtli was the tribal god of the Aztecs,
and not known elsewhere.

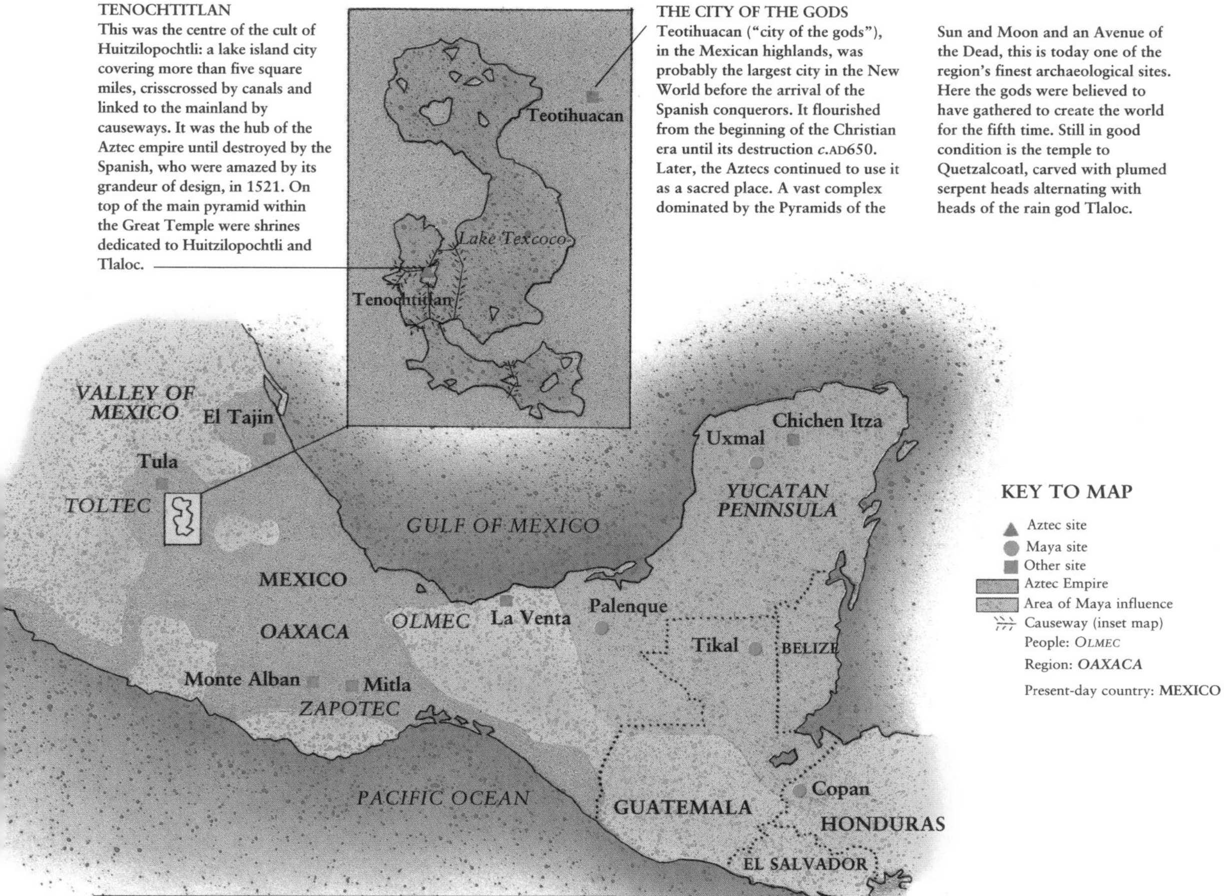

TENOCHTITLAN

This was the centre of the cult of Huitzilopochtli: a lake island city covering more than five square miles, crisscrossed by canals and linked to the mainland by causeways. It was the hub of the Aztec empire until destroyed by the Spanish, who were amazed by its grandeur of design, in 1521. On top of the main pyramid within the Great Temple were shrines dedicated to Huitzilopochtli and Tlaloc.

THE CITY OF THE GODS

Teotihuacan ("city of the gods"), in the Mexican highlands, was probably the largest city in the New World before the arrival of the Spanish conquerors. It flourished from the beginning of the Christian era until its destruction *c.*AD650. Later, the Aztecs continued to use it as a sacred place. A vast complex dominated by the Pyramids of the Sun and Moon and an Avenue of the Dead, this is today one of the region's finest archaeological sites. Here the gods were believed to have gathered to create the world for the fifth time. Still in good condition is the temple to Quetzalcoatl, carved with plumed serpent heads alternating with heads of the rain god Tlaloc.

[Map of Mesoamerica with inset map of Lake Texcoco showing Teotihuacan and Tenochtitlan. Map labels:]

Teotihuacan
Lake Texcoco
Tenochtitlan

VALLEY OF MEXICO
El Tajin
Tula
TOLTEC
MEXICO
OAXACA
OLMEC
La Venta
Monte Alban
Mitla
ZAPOTEC
PACIFIC OCEAN
GULF OF MEXICO
Chichen Itza
Uxmal
YUCATAN PENINSULA
Palenque
Tikal
BELIZE
Copan
GUATEMALA
HONDURAS
EL SALVADOR

KEY TO MAP

▲ Aztec site
● Maya site
■ Other site

  Aztec Empire
  Area of Maya influence
  Causeway (inset map)
People: *OLMEC*
Region: *OAXACA*
Present-day country: MEXICO

MAIN MESOAMERICAN CIVILIZATIONS

People	Civilization flourished	Principal centres
Olmecs	*c.*1500-400 BC	San Lorenzo, La Venta
Zapotecs	*c.*AD 300-600	Monte Alban, Mitla
Maya	*c.*AD 300-900	Tikal, Palenque, Copan
Toltecs	*c.*AD 900-1180	Tula
Aztecs	*c.*AD 1325-1521	Tenochtitlan

PRONUNCIATION GUIDE

Most Mesoamerican peoples of the highland regions spoke a language they called Nahuatl; the accent usually falls on the next to last syllable. The Mayans had their own language.

Pronounce

qua, quo (Etzalqualitzli) as *kw*   *x* (Xipe Totec) as *sh*
que, qui (Quetzalcoatl) as *k*   *z* as the *s* in sat
tl as in the English *atlas*   *cht* (Tenochtitlan) as *sht*

THE GODS OF THE AZTECS

The Aztecs worshipped individually (every house had an altar) and collectively, on sacred festivals. Each god was associated with a point of the compass, or with the central axis of a disc-shaped world surrounded by water. Among the principal deities were:

CHALCHIUHTLICUE (Jade Skirt). Kinswoman of Tlaloc, goddess of rivers and lakes.

CHICOMECOATL (Goddess of Sustenance). A fertility deity.
COATLICUE (Snake Skirt). Earth goddess and mother of Huitzilopochtli.
HUEHUETEOTL (Old God). God of fire, the oldest deity.
HUITZILOPOCHTLI (Hummingbird of the South). Tribal god of the Aztecs, both warrior god and sun god. (See pp.242-3.)
MICHLANTECUHTLI (Lord of the

Dead). With Mictlancihuatl, ruled over Mictlan, the underworld.
QUETZALCOATL (Feathered Serpent). One of the four creator gods. God of the morning and evening star. Also, as Ehecatl, god of the wind. (See pp. 240-41.)
TEZCATLIPOCA (Smoking Mirror). One of the four creator gods. Associated with the night sky, the moon and forces of evil and destruction. Often portrayed

as a jaguar. (See p.239.)
TLALOC (He Who Makes Things Grow). God of water and rain, assisted by the four Tlaloques. Known as Chac among the Maya, Cojico among the Zapotecs. (See pp.244-5.)
XIPE TOTEC (Flayed Lord). God of planting, spring and jewellers. In his honour victims were flayed and their skins worn by priests.

THE OLD GODS

The jaguar and the fire deity

The earliest Mesoamerican deities represented in art are those of the Olmec civilization, which flourished in the swamplands of eastern Mexico between *c*.1500 and *c*.400BC. Representations in stone, ceramic, jade and cave paintings all attest to the precocious nature of Olmec society, the creative genius of its craftsmen, and the guiding influence of its priests and rulers.

The Olmec legacy to later Mesoamerican religious traditions is extensive, but perhaps most clearly seen in the continuing preoccupation with jaguar imagery. "Were-jaguar" figures appear linked to myths from both Central and South America which testify to shamans magically transforming into felines. Such jaguar-shamans were especially feared as powerful sorcerers who conjured up the dangerous forces of the spirit world — an ancient and widespread idea that had a profound and enduring effect on Mesoamerican religious beliefs. Olmec were-jaguars are often depicted snarling, with an open mouth. Associated with royalty, fertility and the earth, the jaguar theme is found in Maya, Zapotec and Teotihuacan art, and recurs most dramatically in the jaguar manifestation of Tezcatlipoca, the supreme Aztec deity (see p.239). However, other influences were also felt in the Olmec world: birds, crocodiles, serpents and anthropomorphic beings all figure prominently in the artefacts of the culture. Some of these beings are strange hybrids, combining aspects of the jaguar with a bird or a serpent.

The Olmec preoccupation with anthropomorphic jaguar imagery is seen in this jadeite votive axe, representing a half-human, half-feline supernatural being.

It was once thought that the Olmecs worshipped only one deity, a rain god, but this idea has been discredited. Among the many Mesoamerican gods who have been tentatively identified in the Olmec pantheon are prototypical forms of Tlaloc (the rain deity), a maize god, Quetzalcoatl (the feathered serpent, another hybrid animal deity), Tezcatlipoca, and a fire deity, known in later times as Huehueteotl or Xiuhtecuhtli (see panel, below). Under a variety of names these god recur throughout the whole of the Mesoamerican region.

Huehueteotl

The Fire God, Huehueteotl, was seen by the Aztecs as the Old God, and the first companion of mankind.

One Aztec festival involved boys hunting small creatures of the wetlands, such as snakes, lizards, frogs, and even dragonfly larvae, to present to old men who served as custodians of the Fire God, and receiving food from the priests in return for these offerings.

On such occasions, the god was ceremonially shown in his young aspect, with turquoise and quetzal plumes. Later in the month he was shown as aging and weary, bedecked in gold, black and red, the colours of embers.

Typically, Huehueteotl is shown as a toothless, bent-backed old man, with a brazier on his head – a form found in art from c.500 BC.

CREATIONS AND CATACLYSMS

The myth of the suns

Mesoamerican cosmology conceived of the universe in five parts – four cardinal directions and the centre. A page from the Mixtec Codex Fejervary-Mayer illustrates this distinctive worldview by assigning world directions to the offspring of Ometecuhtli. Each cardinal direction encompassed important symbolic values. For example, east (at the top of the page) was regarded as the bright region of fertility and life whose sacred colour was red; whereas north symbolized a cold black region associated with death. The all-important centre is here occupied by the god Xiuhtecuhtli.

In the beginning was Ometecuhtli, self-created Lord of Duality, who appeared also in his male and female aspects as Ometeotl and Omecihuatl. The offspring of this cosmic pair were the four Tezcatlipocas. The Red Tezcatlipoca, otherwise Xipe Totec (the flayed god), was associated with the east, the Blue Tezcatlipoca or Huitzilopochtli with the south, the White Tezcatlipoca or Quetzalcoatl with the west, and the Black Tezcatlipoca (Lord of the Night Sky) with the north. To these four were added Tlaloc the rain god, and his consort Chalchiuhtlicue, goddess of water.

The confrontations between these deities, engaged in a cosmic struggle for supremacy, led to the creation and destruction of five successive world eras or "suns" – each identified by the particular forms of cataclysm that engulfed it. The first sun was ruled by Tezcatlipoca and was known as "Four-Jaguar". After 676 years, Quetzalcoatl knocked Tezcatlipoca into the water, and the earth was consumed by jaguars. Quetzalcoatl then presided over the second sun, known as "Four-Wind", and this era ended when Tezcatlipoca took his revenge and threw Quetzalcoatl off his throne, whereupon he was carried off by a great hurricane. The third sun, "Four-Rain", was dominated by fire and ruled over by the rain god Tlaloc. It ended when Quetzalcoatl sent a fiery rain to consume the earth. Then followed the fourth sun, "Four-Water", identified with Chalchiuhtlicue the water goddess. This in turn ended when the world was engulfed by a flood and the people turned into fish. In the wake of these imperfect worlds came the most portentous creation of all – the fifth sun (see p.238).

OMETECUHTLI
In Aztec thought the concept of duality was all-pervasive and was personified in Ometecuhtli (below) – the primordial dual-natured cosmic being, who sustains all life from his position at the "navel of the earth". He had both male and female aspects (Ometeotl and Omecihuatl), enabling him to give birth to the four Tezcatlipocas as both mother and father.

The fifth sun

The calamities which engulfed the previous four suns (see p.237) left a void in the cosmic order. By creating and sustaining the fifth sun (our current era), the gods offered the peoples of Mesoamerica a last fleeting chance for life.

The fifth sun was created at Teotihuacan when the god Nanahuatzin hurled himself into a blazing fire and was mystically transformed into the rising sun. However, at first he was motionless, and so the other gods sacrificed their blood to provide the energy for his celestial movement. Thus, the fifth world era is known as "Four-Movement". Its unique genesis set a mythic precedent for the Aztec idea that only through sacrifice could the life of the universe be extended. However, this was only a temporary concession by the gods, as even the fifth sun would eventually be destroyed by earthquakes.

The sign "Four-Movement" embodied the concept of human sacrifice which permeated the Aztecs' religion and found physical expression in the great Aztec Calendar Stone – a carved stone disc some 12 feet (4m) wide whose central image was the face

of the sun god Tonatiuh enclosed by the sign "Four-Movement". Discovered in 1790 near the site of El Templo Mayor in downtown Mexico City, the elaborately carved artefact portrays the main elements of the fifth creation. Tonatiuh was conceived by the Aztecs as a manifestation of their tribal war deity Huitzilopochtli (see p.242). In this complex symbolism we see the Aztec manipulation of myth to provide a justification for war and sacrifice, and to express these aspects of life in cosmological terms. The face of Tonatiuh is flanked on either side by two giant claws which grasp human hearts as nourishment. This theme is elaborated further by the tongue of the deity which is an image of the sacrificial flint or obsidian knife with which Aztec priests cut out the hearts of their victims. According to Aztec belief, human blood contained the precious liquid essence known as *chalchihuatl*, regarded as the only suitable nourishment for the gods. Around the image of the sun god are four boxed figures representing the four previous suns – those dedicated to the jaguar, wind, fire, and water. Surrounding these are the glyphs (emblems) of the twenty day signs from the sacred calendar or *tonalpohualli*, and symbolic representations of Tezcatlipoca, Quetzalcoatl and Tlaloc.

The elaborately carved Calendar Stone, which may also have served as a sacrificial stone, enshrines a distinctively Aztec view of life and death in a fragile universe maintained by a continuous supply of blood to the gods.

The Calendar Stone, a sculptural masterpiece, is not a true calendar but rather a stone representation of Aztec cosmogony, depicting features of the fifth world era.

TEZCATLIPOCA

Lord of the Smoking Mirror

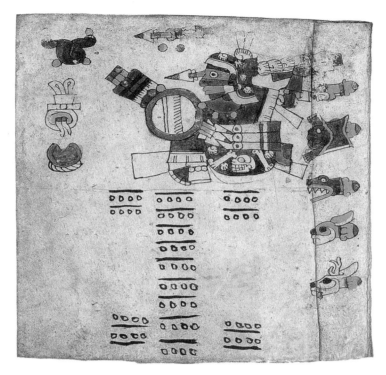

Tezcatlipoca is shown in his black aspect in this codex illustration. The skull and bones signify his association with death. Armed and dressed as a warrior, he is surrounded by calendrical symbols.

Tezcatlipoca, whose name means "Lord of the Smoking Mirror", is widely regarded as the supreme god of the Mesoamerican pantheon. All other creator deities were but aspects of this omnipotent and omniscient being. His cult was brought to central Mexico by the Toltecs around the end of the 10th century AD. In myth he is described as corrupting the virtuous god of the Toltecs, Quetzalcoatl, the Feathered Serpent, initiating him in drunkenness and carnality. By the Aztec period Tezcatlipoca had acquired more guises and names than any other deity. For example, his identification as Yaotl (Warrior) and Yoalli Ehecatl (Night Wind) reveals his association with death, warfare and the realm of darkness. He was believed to appear at crossroads at night to challenge warriors.

The Aztecs revered him as the patron of royalty and sorcerers. His preeminent status was reflected in his symbolic association with jaguar imagery, and especially in his manifestation as Tepeyollotli, the jaguar "heart of the mountain". Conceived as an invisible, ever-present god, Tezcatlipoca was the lord of shadows, who wielded a magical mirror with which he was able to divine the future and see into the hearts of men. The Aztecs feared and respected his capricious nature, which led him to dispense misery and death as well as wealth, valour, and good fortune. They employed a telling epithet for the god: Titlacauan ("We are his slaves"). He presided over the first era of creation (see p.237), brought to a cataclysmic end by his cosmic struggle with Quetzalcoatl.

Tezcatlipoca can see through darkness, like his alter ego the jaguar. In this decorated Aztec skull, eyes of polished stone equate with the god's all-seeing mirror.

QUETZALCOATL

The feathered serpent

A carved head of Quetzalcoatl as the feathered serpent on a wall of the temple dedicated to the god in Teotihuacan, the City of the Gods. At this time Quetzalcoatl was still associated with fertility: accordingly the feathered serpent heads on the temple alternate with those of the rain god Tlaloc. Traces of blue, red, yellow and green paint show that such sculpture would originally have been brightly coloured.

SERPENT IMAGES
The serpent – coiled or undulating – is the most frequent of all animal motifs in Aztec art. In addition to the feathered serpent, there are plentiful depictions of the fire-serpents, the *xiuhcoatl*, who helped Huitzilopochtli vanquish his brother and sister (see p.242). Below is a feathered serpent sculpture, with plumes covering the body, and a forked tongue drooping from half-open mouth. In other depictions the feathered serpent has the tail of a rattlesnake.

Quetzalcoatl (the name means "feathered serpent", but also "precious twin") was a major god of the Aztec pantheon, with origins in earlier Mesoamerican civilizations. As one of the four creator gods, he has a key role in the myth of the five suns (see p.237). He also appears in various other guises, notably as the wind god Ehecatl, the benevolent god of learning and crafts, the god of twins and, most famously, the feathered or plumed serpent.

The idea of the feathered serpent dates back at least to the civilization of Teotihuacan (3rd-8th centuries AD), the great city on the central Mexican plateau. At that period Quetzalcoatl was probably seen as a vegetation god, closely linked with the rain god Tlaloc. The Toltecs (9th-12th centuries) perceived him as god of the morning and evening star, and it was in this form that he was worshipped at the Toltecs' chief city, Tula.

The Aztecs assimilated Quetzalcoatl and revered him as patron of priests, inventor of the calendar, and protector of craftsmen. With his twin the dog-headed god Xolotl he was said to have penetrated to the underworld (Mictlan) and there collected the bones of a man and woman who had died in the four cosmic upheavals. In flight from the Death Lord's wrath, he dropped the bones, which shattered. Picking up the

Ehecatl, the wind god

Ehecatl was associated with all four points of the compass, because the wind blows in all directions. His temples were built on a cylindrical plan, in order to offer less wind resistance. He was sometimes depicted as wearing a pair of protruding masks, through which the wind blew.

After the destruction of the fourth sun in the Aztec creation myth, the gods gathered at Teotihuacan, and here Nanahuatzin and Tecciztecatl jumped into the sacrificial fire and became the sun and moon. They were motionless until Ehecatl blew upon them fiercely. Only the sun moved at first, but when the sun came to set, the moon moved also.

An image based on the Codex Magliabechiano *showing Quetzalcoatl as Ehecatl, with symbols of giant shell, wind trumpet mask and quetzal bird – famous for its iridescent green tail feathers.*

pieces, he escaped with them to the earth goddess Cihuacoatl (Snake Woman), who ground them into meal, which Quetzalcoatl sprinkled with blood from his penis. In this way the human race was created anew.

The mythical Quetzalcoatl is difficult to separate from a real Toltec priest-king, Topiltzin-Quetzalcoatl, who was also associated with the feathered serpent. This confusion is marked in the story of the rivalry with Tezcatlipoca, god of the night and of the north.

Whereas Quetzalcoatl demanded of his subjects peaceful sacrifices (offerings of jade, birds, snakes, butterflies), Tezcatlipoca wished to impose more bloodthirsty rituals. There was a clash between them, resulting in Quetzalcoatl's explusion from Tula in AD987. With his entourage he travelled to the Gulf of Mexico, immolated himself on a pyre, and was reborn as the planet Venus.

Another version has Quetzalcoatl embarking on a raft of serpents and disappearing over the eastern horizon. It was foretold that he would one day return – a prophecy exploited by the Spanish conqueror Hernán Cortés who, when he landed in Mexico in 1519, was thought by the Aztec ruler Moctezuma to be Quetzalcoatl come home to take possession of his kingdom.

QUETZALCOATL AS VENUS
In the myth of the feathered serpent, Quetzalcoatl wanders down to the "divine water" (that is, the Gulf of Mexico), fasts for four days, and then bedecks himself in his finest garments. Then, as he immolates himself on the funeral pyre, birds fly out of the flames, and in the midst of them his heart is seen, ascending to the skies where it becomes Venus, the morning star. As Venus, the god symbolized death and resurrection.

HUITZILOPOCHTLI

God of sun and war

THE DEFEAT OF THE MOON AND STARS

At Coatepec (the Serpent Hill) near Tula, Huitzilopochtli was magically conceived by Coatlicue (Snake Skirt), who was impregnated by a ball of down which descended from heaven. Forewarned of an attempt to kill his mother by his sister Coyolxauhqui and his four hundred brothers, Huitzilopochtli sprang from the womb fully formed and painted blue, wielding his flaming fire-serpent, or *xiuhcoatl*. Cutting off Coyolxauhqui's head, and hurling her body down the mountainside, Huitzilopochtli then routed his brothers.

Shown above is a carved image of the dismembered Coyolxauhqui at the foot of the stairway leading to Huitzilopochtli's Templo Mayor shrine at Tenochtitlan.

This event is usually interpreted symbolically: Huitzilopochtli as the sun defeated Coyolxauhqui the moon, and his four hundred brothers the stars, thereby creating the fifth "sun" or world era.

Huitzilopochtli ("the Hummingbird of the South") was a uniquely Aztec deity, with no identifiable predecessors in other Mesoamerican cultures. The tribal war and sun god of the Aztecs, he was the principal deity of their imperial capital Tenochtitlan. In codex imagery his divinity is shown by his blue-painted limbs, hummingbird feathers on his left leg, arrows tipped with feather down, and a serpent-shaped *atl-atl* or spearthrower. His ritual association with war and death is reflected in his name: hummingbirds were seen as the souls of fallen warriors who accompanied their patron's solar image as it made its daily journey across the sky.

As with Quetzalcoatl, myth and history are intertwined in differing accounts of Huitzilopochtli's origins. Whether he was originally perceived as a god, or whether he was a hero figure who was subsequently deified, is unclear. He is most commonly regarded as having initiated and led the wanderings of the Aztec people from a homeland near Aztlan in northwest Mexico. The events surrounding the god's birth at Coatepec (see margin, left) may be seen as a form of mythical rebirth – the transformation of a man into a prophetic, all-powerful guiding deity.

During the course of their great southward migration to the Valley of Mexico, the Aztecs were led by four priest-rulers who carried a great idol of Huitzilopochtli before them. This magical image divined future events, advised a change of name from Aztec to Mexica, and talked to them secretly regarding the route to be taken. According to their migration myths, Huitzilopochtli inspired his followers with promises that they would conquer all peoples and become masters of the known world, and would receive tribute of precious stones, quetzal feathers, coral, and gold.

Huitzilopochtli's elevation by the Aztecs to the same status as other, more established creator deities is reflected in his mythic identification as the blue Tezcatlipoca, whose sacred direction was the "south".

The founding of Tenochtitlan

In the 12th century the Aztecs' ancestors set off on a journey south as part of the general migration that followed the collapse of Toltec rule. A quasi-historical myth describes the various stages of the trek, including the guidance given to them by Huitzilopochtli, whom they carried before them in a medicine bundle. At critical moments he would speak to them in a high-pitched, twittering voice with advice and instructions.

A low point in the Aztecs's fortunes was reached when they found themselves, after a 200-year journey, lacking all faith or purpose on a swampy island in Lake Texcoco. Here they saw a huge eagle perched on a cactus which bore red fruit (a symbol of the human heart). The eagle was an emblem of the sun – that is, of Huitzilopochtli himself. The god chose this moment to call out to the people, "O Mexica, it shall be here!". This was the future site of Tenochtitlan ("place of the cactus fruit").

Sacrifice at the Great Temple

Huitzilopochtli's role as the embodiment of the Aztec ideology of sacrifice was luridly exemplified by the actions of the emperor Ahuitzotl, who in 1486 dedicated to the god the great Templo Mayor (Great Temple) in the island city of Tenochtitlan, sanctifying the occasion by the ritual execution of perhaps as many as 60,000 victims.

Revered as a cosmological warrior identified with the sun god Tonatiuh, Huitzilopochtli was at the centre of the Aztec cult of sacrifice. The Aztecs regarded themselves as his chosen people: their divine mission was to wage war and offer the blood of their captives to feed Tonatiuh, thereby keeping the fifth sun in motion. Adorned with white skulls on a red background, Huitzilopochtli's shrine atop El Templo Mayor was the site where countless sacrificial victims had their hearts cut out with a flint or obsidian knife. The hearts were offered to the sun and burned in the *quauhxicalli* ("eagle's vase"). The lifeless bodies were then thrown down onto the image of Coyolxauhqui, thereby re-enacting Huitzilopochtli's heroic victory at Coatepec (see margin, opposite).

Warriors who lost their lives in battle or on the sacrificial altar were described as *quauhteca* ("the eagle's people"). The Aztecs believed that such warriors posthumously formed part of the sun's dazzling retinue for four years, after which they lived forever inside the bodies of hummingbirds.

The Aztec preoccupation with blood is also seen in the behaviour of priests, who performed frequent acts of sacrifice on themselves, as a penance, by blood-letting using barbed cords passed through their tongues and ears. Huitzilopochtli's high priest, Quetzalcoatl Totec Tlamacacazqui (Feathered Serpent, Priest of Our Lord), together with the high priest of Tlaloc, provided double leadership over the Aztec priesthood.

A Spanish view of human sacrifice, from the mid 16th-century Codex Magliabechiano. *The victim is arched over a stone to facilitate the removal of the heart.*

TLALOC AND FERTILITY

Aztec gods of rain and corn

In this detail from an illustration in the Codex Borbonicus, *showing a temple rite during the festival of Ochpaniztli, a priest wearing the great bannered headdress of Chicomecoatl the maize goddess is flanked by priests wearing Tlaloc headdresses.*

Xipe Totec, the flayed god of springtime, seeds, and planting, was commonly represented wearing the flayed skin of a sacrificial victim, as in this sculpture. In this guise he symbolized the appearance of new life emerging from the old. Tied into Aztec mythology, Xipe Totec was also identified as the Red Tezcatlipoca who had ruled over the first "sun" – whose cataclysmic end paved the way for subsequent creations.

Dominating the Aztec pantheon by sheer numbers were the many gods of moisture, agriculture and fertility. In a valley region of erratic rains, seeing crops wither before they sprouted was all too common. In the reign of Moctezoma I, late rains combined with autumn frosts destroyed the harvest three years in succession, leading to threat of famine. In this context, the Aztecs' complex spiritual foundation for farming is unsurprising. Chief among the fertility gods was Tlaloc, an ancient rain deity (see panel, opposite), who was worshipped throughout Mesoamerica under a variety of names – for example, Cocijo among the Zapotecs, and Chac among the Maya. As lord of the rains, Tlaloc presided over a host of related fertility deities, and it was to these (despite the prominence in myth of such major gods as Huitzilopochtli and Tezcatlipoca) that most sacrificial rites were dedicated. Like a thread binding together the complex web of Aztec beliefs, the symbolic equation of blood, water, human sacrifice and fertility was all-pervasive. Maize stalks and ears, brought in from the fields and venerated in the households as gods, were also used as ritual adornments for warriors, along with quetzal plumes.

Chalchiuhtlicue, the wife of Tlaloc, had presided over the fourth "sun" and was regarded as a sister of the rain god's helpers, the Tlaloque. Her epithets "Lady of the Jade Skirt" and "Lady of the Sea and Lakes" denote some of her distinctive qualities. She had the power of conjuring up hurricanes and whirlwinds, and of causing death by drowning. She is usually represented wearing a necklace of precious stones and a blue skirt adorned with sea shells, and as having turquoise mosaic covering her ears.

Closely identified with her were the two gods of maize, Chicomecoatl (the female aspect) and Cinteotl (the male aspect). Chicomecoatl represented sustenance in general, while Cinteotl was specifically associated with maize, as his name "maize cob lord" attests. Related to both was yet another deity, Xilonen, the goddess of the tender young ear of corn.

The cosmological connection between fertility and human sacrifice is graphically embodied in the figure of Xipe Totec – "the flayed lord".

Conceived as the god of vegetation and springtime renewal, this deity was honoured in the festival of Tlacaxipeualitztli: victims sacrificed in his honour were flayed, and their skins worn by the god's priests. For the Aztecs this act symbolized the regeneration of plant life, as dried human skin when worn by a priest was considered analogous to a husk enclosing a living plant. In pre-Aztec times, Xipe Totec was a god of the Zapotec and Yopi peoples, and among the Zapotec was regarded as a vegetation deity associated with Quetzalcoatl.

Other gods recognized as manifestations of fertility included Xochiquetzal, the goddess of flowers (originally the consort of Tlaloc, but later abducted by Tezcatlipoca), and Xochipilli, prince of flowers and symbol of summer. In addition there were the Tlaloques – lesser deities who inhabited the paradise of Tlalocan. It was they who presaged the rains by creating thunder from the smashing of their water jars. One of these deities, Opochtli, was said to have invented fishing nets and the *leister* (fish spear). Another, Napatecuhtli, gave life to rushes and reeds and so was credited with inventing the important skill of mat-making.

Also associated with fertility are a group of little corn gods, collectively known as the "Four Hundred Rabbits" (Centzon Totochtin). Among these are Ometochtli (god of a fermented drink called octli) and the god of drunkenness, Tepoztecatl.

Tlaloc, the rain god

Tlaloc in a Mixtec representation, shown with characteristic goggle eyes.

*I*mages of Tlaloc date from at least as early as the culture of Teotihuacan (3rd-8th centuries), but it was in the Aztec period, in the 14th to 16th centuries, that he became supremely important. His cult spread throughout the whole of Mexico. The bringer of death as well as agricultural prosperity, he could bring two types of rain – the rain that fructified the land, or the rain that laid waste. Tlaloc was associated with mountains, where rain clouds gathered, mists lingered, and rivers had their sources. He kept four great jars (representing each of the sacred world directions). From the jar associated with the east he dispensed fertilizing rain: from the others he poured out disease, frost and drought.

Pre-eminent in Aztec cult, though less so in myth, Tlaloc was a major god particularly honoured in the ritual festivities celebrated during the months of Atlcahualo and Tozoztontli when young children were sacrificed on mountain tops. If the victims cried, this was seen as an especially good sign, as their tears symbolized rain and moisture.

A carved symbol of Tlaloc with four giant teeth. In this form he resembles Chac, the Mayan god of rain, with whom he has great affinities.

The god's high status is indicated by his shrine, which shared the sacred summit of El Templo Mayor alongside that of Huitzilopochtli, the Aztec war and solar deity (see pp.242-3). Tlaloc's shrine was painted white and blue, the war god's white and red. Their high priests were regarded as equal in rank.

As lord of fertility, Tlaloc gave his name to the Aztec heaven – Tlalocan, which was conceived as an earthly paradise where food, water and flowers were found in abundance. Only those who had died at Tlaloc's hands by drowning or by being struck by lightning were permitted to enter. The Aztec dead were normally cremated, but those killed in one of these ways, or by certain water-related illnesses particularly associated with the god (such as dropsy) were buried with a piece of dried wood alongside their body, which would sprout with leaves and blossom profusely in Tlalocan.

GODS OF THE SACRED CALENDAR

Sacred and solar cycles

THE NEW FIRE CEREMONY

For the Aztecs, the end of the old 52-year cycle and the beginning of the new was marked by the New Fire Ceremony (right). In the dying hours of the old year all fires were extinguished, effigies of the gods were thrown into water, children and women were hidden away. In costumes impersonating the gods, the priests walked to the top of the "Hill of the Star" above Ixtapalapa and waited for the passage of the Pleiades star group through the zenith. This was the time when the world was believed to be in imminent danger of destruction, and to avert the catastrophe a human sacrifice was made by cutting the heart from a well-born victim. In the chest cavity, a fire-drill sparked into life a new fire, and, by analogy, a new 52-year cycle. Torches were cast into the human fire and taken back to El Templo Mayor, Tenochtitlan. From here the torches were carried to the temples and cities which dotted the shore-line of the ancient lake which surrounded the island capital.

A detail from a book of days in the Codex Borbonicus, *showing gods associated with the hours of the day and their sacred birds.*

Mesoamerican peoples attached a ritual significance to the gods, signs and numbers used to mark the passage of time.

The solar calendar, called Haab by the Maya, and Xihuitl by the Aztecs, comprised eighteen months each of twenty days, to which were added five unlucky days to make a total of 365. This calendar was used to count the years. For the Aztecs, years were denoted by numbers from 1 to 13 combined with four of the twenty day signs (that is, House, Rabbit, Reed, and Flint) – One Reed Year, and so on. No date would repeat itself until 52 (13 x 4) years had elapsed.

Running in parallel with the solar year, and dovetailed into it, was the sacred calendar, known as Tzolkin by the Maya and Tonalpohualli by the Aztecs. This was made up of 260 days divided into twenty "weeks" of thirteen days. Each of these "weeks" was presided over by a particular deity or deities, and every day also had its own god or goddess (see table, above right). Thus, for the Aztecs, the first week of the cycle started with "One Crocodile" and ended thirteen days later on "Thirteen Reed"; the second week began on "One Jaguar" and ended on "Thirteen Death". For the same day-sign to recur, 260 days would have to elapse. The importance of the Tonalpohualli was its use in divination – a person's destiny depended on the good or bad qualities attached to the date of birth. For example, "Seven Rain" was favourable, but "Two Rabbit" was unlucky. For both the Maya and the Aztec peoples, the intermeshing of the two calendars produced a "Calendar Round" of 52 years. Time, and the fates of individuals and of society, were conceived as cyclical: at the end of every 52-year period, time and the world were symbolically reborn in the "New Fire Ceremony": in the illustration from the *Codex Borbonicus* (above) four priests are feeding the new fire with bundles of the old years.

DAY GODS OF THE AZTEC SACRED CALENDAR *(Tonalpohualli)*

Day	Symbol	God
1	Crocodile (*cipactli*)	Tonacatecuhtli, the Lord of Sustenance
2	Wind (*ehecatl*)	Quetzalcoatl, the Feathered Serpent
3	House (*calli*)	Tepeyollotli, the Heart of the Mountain
4	Lizard (*cuetzepalin*)	Hueyhuecoyotl, the Old Coyote
5	Serpent (*coatl*)	Chalchiuhtlicue, the goddess of water
6	Death (*miquiztli*)	Tecciztecatl, the moon god
7	Deer (*mazatl*)	Tlaloc, the rain god
8	Rabbit (*tochtli*)	Mayahuel, the goddess of pulque
9	Water (*atl*)	Xiuhtecuhtli, the Fire God
10	Dog (*itzcuintli*)	Mictlantecuhtli, Lord of the Underworld
11	Monkey (*ozomatli*)	Xochipilli, Prince of Flowers
12	Grass (*malinalli*)	Patecatl, the god of medicine
13	Reed (*acatl*)	Tezcatlipoca, Lord of the Smoking Mirror
14	Jaguar (*ocelotl*)	Tlazolteotl, goddess of love and filth
15	Eagle (*cuauhtli*)	Xipe Totec, the Flayed Lord
16	Vulture (*cozcaquauhtli*)	Itzpapalotl, the Obsidian Butterfly
17	Motion (*ollin*)	Xolotl
18	Flint (*tecpatl*)	Tezcatlipoca, Lord of the Smoking Mirror
19	Rain (*quiauitl*)	Chantico, goddess of the hearth
20	Flower (*xochitl*)	Xochiquetzal, goddess of flowers

The Maya calendar

Like two interlocking cog-wheels, the 260 days of the sacred calendar intermeshed with the 365 days of the solar calendar to produce the "Calendar Round". The example here is from the Maya calendar, and shows how every day for a total of 18,980 days (that is, 52 years) was assigned a unique date.

This dual calendar was a sophisticated system, both for measuring time and for divination: each day and month had its own patron deity believed to exert an influence over people and events. In the solar calendar there were 18 months of 20 days each, plus 5 unlucky days (uayeb). The last (20th) day of each solar month was regarded as a time when the influence of the next month was already being felt. The Maya, therefore, would designate "day 20" as either the last day of the current month or the "seating of" the next month. Thus, for example, the "seating of Pop" came before "One Pop", and the 20th day of Pop was the "seating of Uo".

In addition to measuring cyclical time, the Maya possessed a "Long Count" of years by which they fixed a date in linear fashion from a mythical starting point – 4 Ahau 8 Cumku, or 3113BC. This notion of historical time was based on units of 360-day years, or tuns. The cyclical calendar was ancient when the Maya adopted it. It is possible that an agricultural calendar developed in prehistoric times, based on a basic unit of 20 – the number of fingers and toes in the human body. Certainly, priests were using a 260-day cycle in the Olmec period, and the Maya took over this system and refined it. Perhaps 260 days reflected some important timespan in Maya life. The average human gestation period is 266 days, about the same amount of time as the agricultural cycle in the Yucatan. Thus, the calendar may connect with two key fertility cycles.

The solar calendar: 18 months, each of 20 days.

The sacred calendar: outer wheel has 20 day names; inner wheel has 13 day numbers.

GODS OF THE MAYA

The three-layered cosmos

THE MAYA PANTHEON
No less than 166 Maya deities are named in the 18th-century document known as the "Ritual of the Bacabs", and more than thirty can be recognized in the surviving Maya codices of the Pre-Columbian period. Our picture of the Maya pantheon is far from clear however, as there are differences between the names, signs and attributes accorded to these deities in the Classic, Postclassic and Colonial periods of Maya culture. This page (right) from the *Codex Tro-Cortesianus* shows numerous gods and dignitaries.

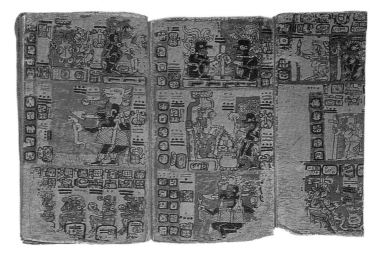

Itzamna, lord of the heaven and supreme god of the Maya pantheon, was shown as a toothless old man with a hooked nose. He was also depicted as a giant serpent of the sky.

The Maya pantheon is made bewilderingly complex by the many guises and titles which each deity could adopt. Each god was associated by colour with the four cardinal directions, many had a counterpart of the opposite sex, and some also possessed underworld manifestations. The universe they inhabited was conceived in three levels – a nine-layered underworld (Xibalba), a middle world inhabited by humans, and a heavenly upper world, supported by four Atlantean gods, the Bacabs. Connecting these three levels was the *axis mundi* – a great Ceiba tree, along which the souls of the dead as well as the gods could travel.

The Maya, like many Mesoamerican civilizations, believed that the natural world was infused with spiritual essence. Gods or spirits were believed to be manifest in mountains, rivers and the sky, and could also be embodied as blood, maize and the favoured waterlily. Most deities, however, were more readily identifiable in their anthropomorphic, zoomorphic or animal form. The chief god of the Maya pantheon was Itzamna ("Lizard House"). Conceived as supreme creator deity, Itzamna was the patron of writing and learning, and is usually represented as an old man with a prominent Roman nose. His consort was Ix Chel ("Lady Rainbow"), goddess of medicine, weaving and childbirth; she may also have been the moon goddess. The sun god, Ahau Kin, could appear in youthful or aged aspects, and between sunset and sunrise he journeyed through the underworld as the Jaguar God. Other supernatural denizens of the underworld included God L, usually seen wearing an elaborate Muan Bird headdress and sitting on a jaguar throne, and God N or Pauahtun, often associated with the conch or turtle shell. Also important were Gucumatz or Kukulkan, the Maya equivalent of Quetzalcoatl, the feathered serpent (see pp.240-41); a maize deity, Ah Mun; and God K, who wore a smoking mirror device on his forehead. The four benevolent rain gods, or Chacs, advertised their presence by thunder and lightning.

The Maya believed in a succession of previous worlds before the creation of the present universe. Lengthy debates took place among the gods concerning the right material for human flesh. The first people were made of earth, but were destroyed because they were mindless. The next race was one of wood, and these people too were destroyed (by a flood, or eaten by demons), this time because they lacked souls and were ungrateful toward their creators.

The last race, the Maya's ancestors, were made of white and yellow maize blended together. Because these maize people had divine understanding, the gods decided to "chip their eyes": this ensured that the people would be fired by the urge to reproduce themselves.

There is a Mayan myth telling of the sun's courtship of the moon. Sun falls for a weaving girl, whom he tries to impress by carrying a deer by her hut every day. Her grandfather tries to sabotage the relationship, whereupon Sun changes into a hummingbird who flits among the tobacco flowers in the girl's garden. Asking her grandfather to shoot the bird, she nurses Sun back to human form, she herself becomes the moon, and they elope together.

As they flee in a canoe, the rain god hurls a thunderbolt at the lovers. Sun changes into a turtle, Moon into a crab, but Moon dies despite the transformation. Aided by dragonflies, Sun collects her remains in thirteen hollow logs. Thirteen days later, twelve of the logs are opened, setting free venomous snakes and insects which have been in the world ever since. In the thirteenth log is Moon. A deer tramples on the log and makes a vagina with its hoof. Sun makes love to his wife – the first act of sexual intercourse.

In one tradition Sun and Moon are transferred from earth to heaven as a result of Moon's carnality. Lunar light is duller than solar light because Sun blinded Moon in one eye as punishment for unfaithfulness.

In Mayan sculpture, the maize god Ah Mun is typically represented with a maize cob sprouting from his head.

The hero twins and the ball game

The mythical narrative of the Hero twins was preserved in the Popol Vuh *– the sacred book of the Quiche Maya.*

Annoying the lords of the underworld by constantly playing the ball game, the twins Hunahpu and Xbalanque were invited to play against the gods, in their own infernal realm. By magic they passed safely through the House of Knives and lit fires to survive the House of Cold. In the House of the Jaguars they tamed the animals by feeding them bones rather than themselves, and then went on to survive the House of Fire. In the House of Bats, Hunahpu was decapitated by one of the creatures. Charming the animals, Xbalanque convinced a turtle to pose as the head of his twin. The boys then pretended to play ball with the gods, with

Hunahpu's head suspended over the court. The gods threw the ball at the head, but it bounced away, and as it did so a rabbit ran out of its hole, distracting the gods and allowing Xbalanque to swap the turtle head for the real head. Finally, the twins tricked the gods by demonstrating their ability to cut themselves up and repair themselves. When the gods asked for this trick to be performed on them too, the boys dismembered them as requested, but left them in pieces. This was the Hero Twins' final victory. They were reborn as the sun and moon. The myth reflected the belief that on death a Maya ruler should be prepared to confront and outwit the gods, and be reborn as a celestial body.

The "Headband Twins" may have been an earlier manifestation of the Hero twins. They are often shown shooting blowguns.

Scenes of human sacrifice decorate the ball-court at Chichen Itza, in which the winning players decapitate the losers.

SOUTH AMERICA

The spectacularly sited Inca city of Machu Picchu, in the Andes, is one of Pre-Columbian South America's most impressive architectural achievements – and one of the best preserved, as it was never found by the Spanish.

Civilization in Pre-Columbian South America was essentially an Andean phenomenon. While diverse ancient cultures flourished along the length of the cordillera, it was in the central Andes of Peru, the adjacent coast and northern Bolivia that they were most concentrated. By contrast, Amerindian tribal societies occupied the whole continent, from the highlands, through Amazonia, to the southernmost reaches of Tierra del Fuego. For both prehistoric and more recent Amerindian peoples, the environment was the focal point of spiritual belief: many myths concern the gods who created the dramatically fractured Andean landscape, and spirit beings who inhabited or personified mountains, or brought rain and controlled fertility.

The concentration of ancient civilizations in the central Andes was due partly to geography: a relatively small area accommodates contrasting landscapes of Pacific coast, high Andes and Amazonian rainforest, which led to economic specialization and trading contacts. From the earliest times the myths and beliefs of Amazonian societies influenced their technologically more advanced highland neighbours. This influence manifested itself primarily in the art of pre-Inca civilizations, in which rainforest animals and anthropomorphic beings are a recurring theme.

Despite their differences, Andean civilizations shared many traits, such as ancestor worship and the belief in an animated landscape, as well as the sophisticated use of gold, silver and textiles – all of which had a deep religious significance. While no South American culture developed a writing system, the wealth of ethnographic information on recent Amerindian peoples, together with historical documentation on Inca culture, provides plentiful evidence for the myths.

THE INCA EMPIRE

At the time of the Spanish conquest in 1532, the Incas ruled an empire that extended along the Andes and Pacific coast from the northern border of present-day Ecuador in the north to central Chile in the south. Cuzco was established as the Inca capital in the 12th century. The emperor ruled his subject peoples through an aristocratic bureaucracy designed to exact manual service from the populace. The vast road system which threaded the empire (used for military and government purposes only) facilitated the process of conquest by the Spanish. Despite the power of state religion, the beliefs of subject peoples were tolerated. The modern descendants of the Inca are the Quechua-speaking peoples of the Andes, who make up almost half the population of Peru; they practise Catholicism infused with a belief in various native gods and spirits.

CUZCO

The great city of Cuzco in the southern Peruvian Andes dominated imperial Inca civilization. Here, the emperor Pachacuti built the great temple of the Coricancha, the centre of the state cult of the sun god Inti. Laid out (according to some accounts), in the form of a great puma, Cuzco was the physical and cosmological centre of the Inca empire of Tawantinsuyu – the "land of the four quarters" – and the focus of political and religious activity. From a ceremonial plaza flanked by the palaces of earlier emperors ran four great roads, one to each corner of the empire. Following an ancient Andean tradition, the city, and its royal lineages, were divided into two halves or moieties: upper or *hanan* Cuzco, and lower or *hurin* Cuzco.

BELIEFS OF THE FOREST PEOPLES

The tribal cultures of South America form a complex mosaic of beliefs and social systems, expressed in hundreds of languages. Life in the tropical forest depends heavily on various magical measures and precautions. For example, perforating the lips or earlobes, and painting the body, are thought to preserve health and fertility. A stick piercing the nasal septum is believed to keep illness at bay. Both shamans and ordinary tribespeople use various drugs in ritual practices, although in some cultures hallucinogens are reserved for shamanistic use. Almost all tribes acknowledge a creator god, who after creating the cosmos and mankind took little interest in earthly matters. Social institutions, agricultural skills and the like are often the gift of one or more culture heroes (sometimes the sun and moon, represented as brothers).

KEY TO MAP

- ● Centre of Chavin culture
- ◆ Centre of Mochica culture
- ▲ Centre of Nazca culture
- ■ Centre of Tiwanaku culture
- ● Centre of Chimu culture
- ■ Centre of Inca culture
- —— Frontier of the Inca Empire, c.AD1500
- ▒ Amazon rainforest region
- ▓ Andes mountains
- present-day country: **BOLIVIA**

TIME CHART: SOUTH AMERICAN CIVILIZATIONS

People	Civilization flourished	Principal centre
Chavin	*c.*800-200 BC	Chavin de Huantar
Mochica	*c.*AD 1-750	Moche
Nazca	*c.*AD 1-650	Cahuachi
Tiwanaku	*c.*AD 200-1000	Tiwanaku
Chimu	*c.*1000-1475	Chan Chan
Inca	1438-1532	Cuzco

ANCIENT RELIGIONS

Spirits, sacrifice and sacred journeys

CHAVIN ART AND MYTH
The influence of Amazonian myth and symbolism in the highland art of the Chavin culture is shown in its repertoire of naturalistic and anthropomorphic tropical forest creatures, such as the jaguar, cayman and harpy eagle. Above is a sculpted jaguar being on the Old Temple, with typical "thick-lipped", fanged appearance.

From the earliest times, the ancient South American civilizations shared common features in their religious outlook and mythic beliefs. Supernatural significance was attributed to plants, animals, rivers and mountains. Although there were local and regional differences (such as the early importance of fire rituals in some cultures), worship of a supreme creator deity, the reverence of ancestors and semi-divine rulers, human sacrifice (notably head-hunting) and sacred pilgrimage were universal.

These ancient civilizations expressed their religious and mythic beliefs in textiles, gold, silver, pottery and stone. One of the most influential cultures in this respect was that based at Chavin de Huantar in the Andes (800-200BC). Here, mythical fanged beings dominated the sophisticated Chavin art style, notable for such startling images as the "Smiling God" and the "Staff God". The supernatural figures depicted in Chavin artefacts had an enduring effect on many later civilizations, and may be regarded as the prototypes of later mythical beings, such as Ai apaec, the fanged deity of the Mochica culture of Peru's arid north coast, and the "Weeping God" carved into a solid block of lava onto the Gateway of the Sun at the ceremonial centre of Tiwanaku (see p.254). Dating from *c.*AD500, Tiwanaku was in ruins by the time of the Incas. However, the myths and cultures of the various tribes that fell under the domination of the Inca empire were assimilated into Inca beliefs, and the Weeping God is generally equated with Viracocha, the Creator, who became central to Inca mythology (see panel, p.257).

Sacred journeys to mountains, springs and temple-pyramid shrines were evidently important in prehistoric times, and indeed continue to be so today. The most famous ancient pilgrimage site was the shrine of Pachacamac on Peru's central coast. Here, a priesthood administered the worship of an earth and creator deity, whose devotees enriched the shrine with gold, made human and animal sacrifices, and received oracular predictions in return. Pachacamac was considered to be the supreme god by the coastal peoples and his influence was so great that when the Incas conquered the area they acknowledged his importance by permitting his shrine to continue functioning alongside a temple to their sun god, Inti.

A pot from the Mochica culture of Peru, depicting a fanged deity confronting a sea-demon – possibly an acknowledgment of the importance of Pacific Ocean animals in everyday life as well as in the supernatural beliefs of this coastal civilization.

MYTHS OF THE ANDES

The Incas and their predecessors

Dominated by snow-capped mountain peaks, volcanoes, fast-flowing rivers and high *puna* grasslands, the Andean cordillera was home to a diversity of Pre-Columbian cultures. This dramatic landscape was infused with spiritual power: high peaks were regarded as the abode of deities and spirits, and mythical significance was attached to rivers, lakes, caves and rain. This tradition still survives today: prominent peaks such as Ausangate are venerated as Apu, or "Lord", and are thought to exert influence over animal and crop fertility. Throughout much of the Andes, sacred pilgrimages to prominent mountains continue to be a central feature of traditional religion, harking back to Pre-Columbian times. This aspect of the Andean world-view is also associated with the concept of *huacas*, holy places dotted across the landscape, where in pre-Inca and Inca times offerings were made to local deities (see p.257, margin) – and still are.

The ancient Andean societies believed in a variety of local origin myths. The advent of the Incas, however, led to political and religious realignments which were reflected in the reshaping of local myths to conform to a new and imperialistic Inca ideology, in which the role of the creator deity Viracocha was pre-eminent.

For the Incas, as well as for their predecessors, the place of mythical origins lay to the southeast of Cuzco, in the vicinity of Lake Titicaca. Here,

The origin myth of the Incas

The mythical ancestors of the Incas emerged from three caves at Pacariqtambo ("the place of origin"), near Cuzco. They were three brothers and three sisters, dressed in blankets and shirts of fine wool and carrying a number of gold vessels.

One of the brothers, Ayar Cachi, incurred the wrath of his siblings by performing feats of strength, hurling his slingstones to shape the landscape. Jealous of such prowess, his brothers tricked him into returning to Pacariqtambo to retrieve a golden goblet and the sacred llama, whereupon they sealed up the cave behind him. However, Ayar Cachi escaped and appeared to his brothers, telling them that they should henceforth wear golden earrings as a sign of their royal status, and that they would find him residing on the summit of a mountain called Huanacauri. His brothers and sisters made their way to the mountain, where Ayar Cachi reappeared once more, only to turn to stone, along with another brother. The third brother, naming himself Manco Capac, went on to found the city of Cuzco (in some versions, with the aid of a golden staff) on the site where Coricancha, the Temple of the Sun, was later built. The various forms of this myth unite in establishing the prerogatives of the Inca ruling dynasty, such as sister-marriage by the emperor, the accoutrements of the nobility, and the origins of shrines and pilgrimages to sacred mountains.

A Spanish illustration of c.1560 (part of an imaginary coat of arms), showing the three caves at Pacariqtambo from which the Inca ancestors emerged.

THE GATEWAY OF THE SUN

At the great pre-Inca city of Tiwanaku, situated on the southern shores of Lake Titicaca, stands the monolithic "Gateway of the Sun", onto which has been incised an elaborate anthropomorphic figure with "weeping eyes" (see detail, above). This figure wears a sun-ray headdress, holds two condor-head staffs, and is surrounded by rows of smaller winged figures also bearing staffs. The importance of Tiwanaku in Inca creation myths suggests that the figure may have represented an earlier version of Viracocha, the Creator.

according to one version, Viracocha first created a world of darkness, populated by a race of giants whom he had fashioned out of stone. However, these first people disobeyed their creator and were punished either by being turned back to stone at places such as Tiwanaku and Pukara, or by being engulfed in a great flood sent by Viracocha. The only survivors were a man and a woman who were magically borne away to the god's abode at Tiwanaku. On his second attempt, Viracocha fashioned humans out of clay, painting on them the clothes that distinguished each nation and bestowing on them their distinctive customs, languages and songs, and the seeds which they would cultivate.

After he had breathed life into his creations, Viracocha commanded them to descend into the earth and to emerge from caves, lakes and hills; this they did, each nation establishing shrines in the god's honour at the places where they had re-entered the world. To bring light into the world, Viracocha now ordered the sun, moon and stars to emerge from the Island of the Sun in Lake Titicaca, from where they ascended to the heavens. As the sun rose into the sky, Viracocha called out to the Incas and their leader Manco Capac, prophesying that they would be lords and conquerors of many nations. On Manco Capac he bestowed a headdress and a battle-axe as the insignia and weapon of royalty. This newly made king then led his brothers and sisters down into the earth, from where they emerged at the cave at Pacariqtambo (see panel, p.253). This central creation myth not only represents an Inca reworking of ancient Andean beliefs, but also probably preserves Christian influence. Stories of a great flood, the first man and woman, the description of Viracocha as a white man, and the journeys undertaken by Viracocha as a hero figure all suggest the teachings of the Catholic priesthood in their efforts to suppress native paganism.

According to a contemporary myth of the Q'ero community near Cuzco, there was a time before the sun existed when the world was populated by powerful primeval men. Roal, the creator deity, offered these men his own power, but they replied that they had no need of it. To punish them, Roal created the sun. They were blinded and their bodies dried up, but they did not die, and still sometimes come out of hiding at sunset and the new moon. The Apus (mountain spirits) then created a man and woman, Inkari and Collari. Inkari was given a golden crowbar and told to found a city where the crowbar fell upright when thrown. The first time he threw the crowbar it landed badly. The second time it fell at an angle, and here Inkari built the town of Q'ero, whereupon the Apus, angered by his disobedience, resurrected the primeval men, who rolled blocks of stone at him in an attempt to kill him. Inkari then fled to the region of Titicaca for a time. On his return he threw the crowbar again: it fell straight, and he founded Cuzco on the site. Inkari then sent his eldest son to establish a population at Q'ero, and the rest of his descendants became the first Incas. With Collari, Inkari travelled throughout the land, dispensing his knowledge to the people, and finally disappeared into the jungle.

El Dorado

The ceremonial imagery of the El Dorado legend is captured in this goldwork artefact from the Muisca tribe of the Lake Guatavita region. Essentially a votive offering, or tunjo, it shows a chief or shaman on a gold raft, attended by several smaller figures holding lime gourd containers and dippers, rattles and masks.

*O*ne of the enduring features of South American mythology is the legend of El Dorado – a name which conjures up fantastical images in Western minds, but which simply means "The Gilded Man". Gold was a sacred medium for many Pre-Columbian civilizations, such as the Mochica, Chimu and most famously the Inca, owing partly to its brilliant incorruptible sheen, as well as its ritual and mythological associations with the sun, the spirit world and fertility. The gold and silver treasures from Inca Peru fired the imagination and greed of the Spanish conquistadors. Gonzalo Pizarro, brother of the conqueror of Peru, launched an expedition with Francisco de Orellana to find the land of the king whose riches were so vast that every day he was annointed with precious resins to fix the gold dust ornamenting his body. In fact, however, the El Dorado legend originated north of Peru, among the chiefdoms of Colombia, where several distinct goldworking styles have been identified. Concerning these ancient Colombian societies, the Spaniard Juan de Castellanos noted in 1589 that gold was the substance which gave the native inhabitants the breath of life, and for which they lived and died.

The El Dorado legend was grounded in historical reality, deriving from Amerindian rites which originally took place at Lake Guatavita in the Colombian highlands. There, a ceremony was held to mark the accession to power of a new ruler who, after a period of seclusion in a cave, made a pilgrimage to the lake in order to make offerings to the chief deity.

Upon arriving at the lakeside, the ruler-to-be was stripped of his finery and his body was covered with a sticky resin, onto which was applied a shimmering layer of fine gold dust. Thus prepared, he set out into the lake accompanied by his attendants (who were four principal subject chiefs) decked out in elaborate accoutrements of gold. The raft itself was richly adorned, and from four braziers the smoke of sacred incense rose into the air. As they journeyed across the water, the air reverberated with the sound of flutes, trumpets and singing from the shore. When they reached the centre of the lake, the sounds were silenced, and the new chief and his companions threw his pile of gold into the lake. They then made their way back to the shore, where the new ruler was ceremonially greeted.

This ceremony made a powerful impression on the Europeans who witnessed it. "He went about all covered with powdered gold, as casually as if it were powdered salt", wrote Gonzalo Fernandez de Oviedo in the mid-16th century. An engraving of 1599 shows two men preparing a new Muisca chief for his glittering accession to office. One individual smears resin onto the chief's body, while the second blows gold dust over him through a tube. European influence is readily apparent in this depiction, as the artist (Theodor de Bry) himself never visited the Americas, and took his inspiration from second-hand reports. Nevertheless, the image is a potent symbol of the power exerted by Amerindian myth and ritual over the European imagination, and of the fascination that gold has always exerted.

Fashioned in the classic "Quimbaya style", this golden image of a seated person probably served as a lime-container for a chief or shaman who would have used a removal dipper to apply lime from the container to his mouth, where it would have activated the trance-inducing wad of sacred coca which was either sucked or chewed on important occasions.

THE INCA PANTHEON

Viracocha, Inti, Mama Kilya, Ilyap'a

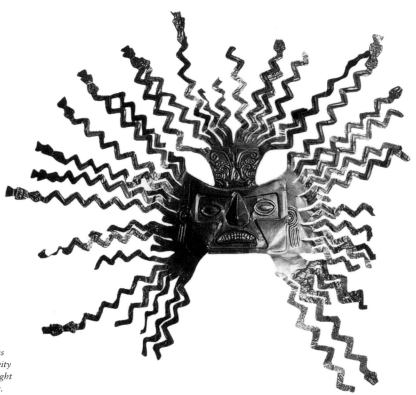

A Pre-Columbian sun mask. The Incas and their predecessors held the sun deity in great awe. Solar eclipses were thought to be the result of the sun god's anger.

VIRGINS OF THE SUN
A special place in Inca religion was reserved for the Acllas, or "chosen women", sometimes referred to as the "Virgins of the Sun". Supervised by elder women called Mama Cunas, these young Inca maidens served the cult of Inti and attended the royal family. Cloistered in convents (called Acllahuasi) from the age of eight, they prepared clothing, food and maize beer for state occasions and guarded the sacred fire for Inti Raymi – the festival of the sun held at the June solstice. The Acllas were also concubines for the emperor and, on occasion, for foreign dignitaries with whom he wished to cement political marriage alliances.

Inca religion was dominated by a host of powerful sky gods, of whom the most important, if somewhat remote, was Viracocha (see panel, opposite). More active in everyday life were three major deities – Inti, the sun god; Mama Kilya, the moon goddess; and Ilyap'a, the god of thunder and weather. These deities, and others, acted out their mythological roles within a typically Amerindian landscape, infused with supernatural power and sacred essence.

Conceived as a divine ancestor of the Inca royal family, Inti was a uniquely Inca deity and the cult focus of many state rituals: in Inca ideology the emperor was regarded as the "son of the sun". Inti himself was usually represented as a great golden disk surrounded by sun-rays and possessed of a human face. Reverence for this deity centred on the great Sun Temple or Coricancha at Cuzco, where Inti's shimmering solar image was flanked by the elaborately garbed mummies of dead emperors and surrounded by walls covered in sheets of sacred gold – the "sweat of the sun". The mythological connection between gold and Inca ideology was particularly apparent in the Coricancha's temple-garden, where metalsmiths cast gold and silver representations of every form of life known to them, from a butterfly to a llama.

Despite the pre-eminence of sun worship as the official state religion,

Inti was not the only major deity revered within the Coricancha temple compound. Also important was Ilyap'a, a male god to whom prayers for fertilizing rain were addressed. In Inca thought, Ilyap'a drew water from the heavens, in particular from the Milky Way, regarded as a celestial river flowing across the night sky (see pp.258-9). Rain was kept in a jug owned by Ilyap'a's sister, and was released only when Ilyap'a shattered the vessel with a slingshot in the form of a lightning-bolt. Thunder was the crack of his sling, lightning the flash of his clothing as he moved.

Mama Kilya, goddess of the moon, and consort and sister of Inti, was widely revered as the mother of the Inca race. She was responsible for marking the passage of time and thereby regulating the religious festivals of the Inca ritual calendar. The Incas believed that during a lunar eclipse a great serpent or mountain lion was attempting to eat Mama Kilya's celestial image, and so they would scare the creature away by making as much noise as possible. Mama Kilya's image in the Coricancha was flanked by mummies of previous Inca queens (*coyas*), and the shrine itself was covered in silver, the colour of the moon in the night sky.

A number of lesser gods also figured prominently in Inca religious thought. Among these was Cuichu, the rainbow, and a group of female supernatural beings – most notably Pacha Mama the earth mother, and Mama Coca the sea mother.

An early 17th-century drawing of Incas offering a child sacrifice to the mummy of an ancestor. The text identifies the mountain cave as one of the huacas, or sacred places (see below).

Viracocha, the supreme creator

*V*iracocha was the omnipresent but incomprehensible creator deity, who animated the universe by bestowing life on humans, animals, plants, and lesser gods. A somewhat distant supernatural being, he delegated the affairs of everyday life to more active deities such as Inti and Ilyap'a. He was represented in the Cuzco shrine, where the Spanish conquerors first observed him, as a golden statue about the height of a ten-year-old boy, depicting a bearded white man wearing a long tunic.

For the Incas, this immanent deity had no name, but instead was referred to by a number of titles befitting his primordial status. Ilya-Tiqsi Wiraqoca Pacayacaciq ("Ancient Foundation, Lord, Instructor of the World") was the most common, usually rendered in Spanish as Viracocha. The ultimate source of all divine power, Viracocha was also conceived as a culture hero who, after creating the world (see p.253-4), travelled through his dominions instructing people how to live and shaping the landscape. Myths about his magical journeys relate how, on reaching Manta in Ecuador, he set off across the Pacific Ocean, either on a raft or by walking on his cape (the latter story may owe a debt to Christian influence). When the Spanish arrived by sea to discover Peru in 1532, they were seen as the returning emissaries of the creator deity and were referred to as *viracochas* – a term of respect still used by Quechua speakers.

In the most important sacrifices, which accompanied only the most solemn occasions such as the coronation of an emperor, humans were offered to Viracocha and other major deities. Child sacrifices called *capacochas* were especially prized, and the Inca priests would recite a prayer to Viracocha before such offerings were made. Sacrifices (often of children) have been found preserved by the cold on snow-capped Andean peaks and volcanoes – the mythical abode of gods and spirits.

HUACAS: THE SACRED PLACES
In Inca religious thought, *huacas* were features of the Andean landscape imbued with mythic significance and supernatural power. Such spirit-laden places were usually stones and springs, but could also be mountains, caves, and the tombs of ancestors. Of particular importance were *apachetas* – piles of stones located at the tops of mountain passes or at crossroads. Here, travellers made offerings to local deities of coca, pieces of clothing or an additional stone before continuing their journey. The relationship between *huacas* and myth is shown in the legend of the stones which turned briefly into men in order to help the Inca emperor Pachacuti defeat his enemies.

THE SACRED SKIES
Animal constellations and sacred lines

The "Hitching-post of the Sun", or intihuatana, *at Macchu Picchu. Priests symbolically tied the sun to the pillar with a mystical cord to prevent its disappearance.*

THE INCA CALENDAR
Like other ancient civilizations, the Incas created and used their calendar as a religious and political instrument which derived its sacredness from mythic tradition. Correlated with the first appearance of the Pleiades before sunrise, the sidereal lunar calendar began on the night of June 8-9 and ended on the night of May 3-4. In the month of Ayrihua (April), ceremonies honouring royal insignia were held, and a pure white llama, dressed in a red shirt, was taught to eat coca and drink *chicha* (maize beer), thus symbolizing the first llama which appeared on earth after the great flood.

The sacred power of celestial phenomena in the Inca world-view manifested itself in a rich tapestry of beliefs which correlated earthly events with those in the night sky. In typically Amerindian fashion, astronomical phenomena were imbued with spiritual and mythic significance. In part, this is reflected in the celestial nature of such major deities as Inti (the sun god), Mama Kilya (the moon goddess), and Ilyap'a (the thunder and weather deity). However, the Milky Way was also considered important, and the stars themselves were regarded as lesser deities and as the patrons of certain earthly activities.

Particularly prominent in this respect were the Pleiades, known as Collca ("the granary"), and considered to be the celestial guardians of seeds and agriculture. Together with several other constellations, they were used to construct a sidereal lunar calendar. The Pleiades were also important for prognostication of agricultural fertility and animal husbandry. The star group known as Orqo-Cilay ("the multicoloured llama"), was thought to protect the royal llama flocks from harm, and Chaska-Qoylor ("the shaggy star") was identified with Venus as the morning star.

While far from being astronomers in the modern sense, the Incas made precise observations of such celestial events as sunrise and sunset, and correlated these with the phases and movements of the moon. Inca astronomer-priests observed the movements of the sun to calculate the dates of the two most important ritual celebrations held at Cuzco – the December and June solstices. The December solstice period included the great festival of Capac Raymi, the royal feast, centring on the initiation rituals of young boys of royal descent. At this important time, the sun was observed at sunset from the Coricancha (Sun Temple) at Cuzco.

Myth, religion, astronomy, architecture and the unique *ceque* system (see margin, right) were all woven together in the Inca belief system. For example, the Incas observed sunset on April 26 from the same location they used for watching the setting Pleiades around April 15 – that is, a place in Cuzco's central plaza called Ushnuo. The sunset was viewed between two pillars set up on a nearby mountain to the west of the city, and these pillars were themselves regarded as a sacred *huaca*, situated on a *ceque* along which (beyond the horizon) there was a sacred spring called Catachillay – an alternative name for the Pleiades.

Arguably, the most distinctive feature of Inca astronomy concerns the Milky Way and its adjacent "dark cloud" constellations made up of opaque patches of interstellar dust (see panel, below). Such constellations include Yacana (the Llama) and Yutu-yutu (the Tinamou, a partridge-like bird). According to myth, when the celestial llama disappears at midnight it is believed to be drinking water from the earth and thereby preventing flooding. Llamas were among the most prized sacrificial animals, and were offered on mountaintops at the new moon. Black llamas were starved during October in order to make them weep and thereby sympathetically petition the deities for rain.

SACRED LINES
The concept of *ceques* – straight "lines" radiating out from the Coricancha – was unique to Inca myth, astronomy and religion. Each line was conceived as having sacred *huacas* distributed along its length: there were some 41 *ceques* organizing 328 *huacas* within the environs of Cuzco. In 1551 the Spanish chronicler Juan de Betanzos described the sixth *huaca* lying on the sixth *ceque* of Antisuyu as "the house of the puma", where the mummy of Inca Emperor Yupanqui's wife was offered young children as sacrifices.

The skies above Misminay

In the Quechua-speaking Andean village of Misminay, some 16 miles (25km) from Cuzco, animal constellations and the Milky Way continue to this day to exert a profound influence on mythological and cosmological thought.

At Misminay, the Vilcanota River is regarded not only as the terrestrial reflection of the Milky Way, or Mayu, but also as an integral part of the cosmic recycling of water from earth to sky, whence it eventually falls back to earth again as rain. Seen also as the pivot of the celestial sphere, the Milky Way moves over a 24-hour period in such a way as to appear to form two intersecting axes which create a four-part division of the heavens. Each quarter is called a *suyu*. Together the four quarters make up a celestial grid which enables Misminay's inhabitants to plot and characterize astronomical phenomena as they travel across the sky.

This four-part division of the heavens is not an isolated phenomenon, but is integrated into the wider world, as a celestial counterpart of the four-part division of Misminay itself. The village is divided into quarters by the intersection of two major footpaths and the two largest irrigation canals which parallel them. These footpaths and canals meet at a chapel called Crucero (the cross), and the same name is given to the point in the sky where the two celestial axes meet.

In 1571 the Spanish chronicler Polo de Ondegardo wrote that in Inca thought all animals and birds had their likenesses in the sky, and that these likenesses were responsible for the procreation and sustenance of their equivalents on earth. Characteristic of Misminay astronomy, and recalling earlier Inca beliefs, is the recognition of "dark cloud" constellations, such as the Adult Llama, Baby Llama, Fox, Toad, Tinamou and Serpent. These constellations are referred to collectively as Pachatira, reflecting their association with Pachamama the earth mother and concepts of earthly fertility. Thus, when alpha and beta Centaurii ("the eyes of the llama") rise before dawn in late November and December, earthly llamas give birth.

"Dark cloud" constellations are also important for their relationship with the rainy season, and with the weather generally. The constellation of the Serpent, for example, is visible in the sky during the rainy season, but is "below ground" (actually, below the horizon) during the dry season. In Quechua thought, this corresponds with the apparent emergence of rainbows (regarded as multicoloured serpents) from the ground following a rain shower.

SPIRIT WORLDS
The universe transformed

A ceremonial dance performed by one of the peoples of the Xingu River area, Brazil. Rainforest peoples perform complex puberty, fertility and funerary rites. Male initiation rites can be painful: for example, in the Guianas, boys are subjected to poisonous ants and hornet stings. In some societies, girls have all their hair pulled out: its regrowth symbolizes the coming of adulthood.

The vast expanses of the Amazon basin contain an extraordinary variety of Amerindian societies which, while technologically simple, possess social, economic, ritual and mythic systems that reveal an intimate understanding of their surroundings. They also show great sophistication in accounting for their humanity and way of life. Although sharing a dependence on hunting, gathering, fishing and horticulture, these cultures have no common set of deities or beliefs. Nevertheless, their local myths demonstrate an underlying unity and coherence in that the myths belonging to one group appear to be developments of those belonging to another group, thereby illustrating common concerns conceived and dealt with by a common logic.

To the Western mind, the Amerindian universe is a "magical" world, defined partly by the capricious actions of powerful but ambivalent spirits, and partly by the activities of the shaman who intercedes with them on behalf of his society (see panel, opposite). In this world-view, where people change into animals and animals into people, the boundaries between humankind and animal kind, nature and supernature, are not only permeable but can be constantly reinterpreted.

Amerindian myths depict a universe of transformations, where social life is believed to be the result of a controlled mingling between otherwise mutually hostile and dangerous categories of beings – men and women, kin and in-laws, jaguars and humans. In primordial times the world order was inverted, and it was men who menstruated and jaguars who owned fire and hunted with bows and arrows. The myths recount how these first relationships were overturned and the current order established. For society to endure, the rules of social behaviour and ritual observance as laid down by the mythic ancestors must be adhered to if disorder and ultimately disaster are to be avoided.

The ceremonial houses of tropical forest peoples are deeply symbolic in design: many were conceived as microcosms of the tribes' cosmic and social universes. For example, the roundhouses of the Venezuelan Yekuana are designed as imitations of the primordial structure built by an incarnation of the sun god Wanadi. Architectural details reflect features of the celestial sphere and mythical geography. Thus, the central house-post (topped by a sculpture of a crimson-crested woodpecker, the animal form of Wanadi's incarnation) symbolically links the netherworld of lost souls with the middle earth of men and the vault of the heavens; the two cross-beams are orientated north-south to mirror the appearance of the Milky Way in the night sky; and the main entrance faces east, permitting the rising equinoctial sun to shine onto the central post.

HEAD-HUNTING AND SOUL CAPTURE

For some Amerindian tribes, head-hunting was an activity charged with supernatural and ritual significance. Among the Jivaro of Ecuador, where head-hunting persisted until the 1960s, the privilege of taking human heads was restricted to a coterie of feared warriors who had established reputations as killers. In Jivaro thought, killing and head-hunting were intimately associated with the possession of two kinds of souls, the Arutam and the Muisak. While the former allowed its owner to join a head-hunting expedition, the purpose of the latter was to avenge its owner's death. However, if a corpse's head was shrunk, the Muisak soul was irresistibly drawn into it and was powerless to escape.

Shamans of South America

In the world-view of tropical forest societies, everything that happens has a spirit-world cause or consequence. All-powerful spirits are dangerously ambivalent, and the shaman thus has a key role as an intermediary with the supernatural world.

By virtue of his ability to persuade or cajole dangerous spirits on equal terms, the shaman acts as sorcerer, curer, diviner, dispenser of justice and upholder of the moral code. He often conducts his spirit world activities in nocturnal seance. Those shamans who identify with, or magically transform into, a jaguar – South America's largest, most powerful predator – are the most feared and respected of all. They dress in jaguar skins, wear necklaces of jaguar teeth, and may even growl like the jaguar in ceremonies where they divine the future, cure magical illness, ensure hunting success, or act as "supernatural warriors" by sending death and disease to enemy villages.

Hallucinatory visions, such

An Andean shaman in Colombia. A shaman's visions are usually experienced through hallucinogenic plants.

as those produced by *ayahuasca*, or *vihoo* snuff, are the shaman's window onto the spirit world, permitting him to see and understand the true nature of things, explain events and suggest courses of action. In the northwest Amazon region, some of the drugs needed for ceremonies used to be described as the jaguar's drug or the jaguar's sperm, and were sometimes kept in a hollow jaguar bone.

The shaman's vision quests are often imbued with mythological significance, representing the primordial activities of ancestor spirits.

In some societies, the shaman's powers remain effective after his death, continuing to protect his community from malevolent spirits or from shamans from other villages.

Often, however, the dead shaman's soul is thought to change into his dangerous alter ego the jaguar, and is greatly feared by the people. A jaguar seen roaming near a village or a graveyard at night is believed to be the transformed essence of the dead shaman.

THE ANCESTRAL FOREST

Origin myths of the forest peoples

Myths of the Amerindian forest peoples are primarily concerned with explaining the origins of humanity and culture, in opposition to nature. Reflecting this underlying aim, individual myths are multilayered, embracing a variety of themes, such as the origins of horticulture, the relations between kin and in-laws, and notions of knowledge and ignorance.

The origin of human beings is the subject of many myths in which animals, stones and clay can all play equally important roles. According to the Chibcha of Colombia, the Sun and Moon created the first man from clay and the first woman from reeds. Further south, the tribes of the Choco region speak of a first race of men destroyed by the gods because they were cannibals, a second generation who were changed into animals, and a third fashioned out of clay. Many peoples, such as the Warao of the Orinoco and the Toba of the Gran Chaco, consider that humans once dwelt in the sky but descended to earth to steal game, whereupon they became trapped and had to remain here forever.

The nature of Amerindian myth as a kind of sacred charter, preserving the current social order, is particularly evident in myths which relate to the differences between men and women. Women tend to be associated with natural fertility, chaos and ignorance, men with cultural fertility, order and sacred knowledge. A widespread myth, told with variations from the Amazon to Tierra del Fuego, explains how originally the world was dominated by women, not men. According to the Tupi of the Brazilian Amazon, the Sun became so angered by women's rule over the world that he decided to reverse the situation, and eventually to take a perfect woman as his own companion. First, he caused a virgin called Ceucy to become pregnant by the sap of the cucura tree, and subsequently to give birth to a child named Jurupari. This child stripped women of their rule and transferred it to men, instructing the men to hold regular feasts to celebrate their monopoly of knowledge and power; all women would be barred from attending these feasts on pain of death. Setting a precedent for such punishment, Jurupari arranged for the death of his own mother. According to the Tupi, he wanders still in search of a perfect woman worthy to be the Sun's wife.

Amazonian cosmology often features various themes associated with fire. Untamed, fire was seen as having massive potential for destruction, and some myths tell of whole regions and many communities ravaged by conflagration. Fire is also linked with sex, birth and the menstrual cycle. The acquisition of fire as a key stage in the evolution of society is sometimes brought about by trickery, in which case the event is linked with loss of innocence.

In the beginning, according to the Kayapo of central Brazil, people did not possess fire, and so ate their vegetables raw, warming pieces of meat on rocks in the sun. One day a man and his younger brother-in-law, Botoque, spotted a macaw's nest high on a cliff. Botoque climbed up a makeshift ladder and threw two eggs down to his companion. The eggs turned into stones, however, and broke the man's hand, whereupon he became so angry that he pushed away the ladder, leaving Botoque stranded up on the cliff.

After several days, Botoque saw a jaguar carrying a bow and arrow and all kinds of game. The jaguar pounced on Botoque's shadow, but on realizing his mistake, the animal spoke to the boy, promising not to eat

These men of the Kamiura tribe of the Xingu River, Brazil, are playing flutes in a sacred ritual (their music is thought to be the voices of spirits). The yellow headdresses symbolize the sun perceived as the source of male potency.

The world of the Yanomami

The Yanomami people of southern Venezuela have made a sustained attempt to protect their traditional life and beliefs against incursions from the outside world.

Regarding themselves as "the fierce people", the Yanomami explain that the blood of Periboriwa (the Moon Spirit) spilled over the earth, changing into men as it hit the ground. Born of blood, the Yanomami for this reason conceive of themselves as naturally fierce, and continually make war on each other. Later, one of Periboriwa's descendants gave birth to more docile men and women. According to one of the four Yanomami groups, the origins

The Yanomami practise an elaborately graded system of inter-group violence, related to their mythical origins as the blood of the Moon Spirit.

of everything are due to the beneficent creator deity, Omam. At first there were two layers in the world, but now there are three. The third appeared when the upper layer became worn and shed a large chunk of itself, on which there were two men: one was Omam. One day, while fishing, Omam pulled out of the stream a woman who had no genitalia, only a hole the size of a hummingbird's anus. With the piranha teeth, Omam fashioned sexual organs, and proceeded to father many children by her – the ancestors of the Yanomami. Other races were made from river mist or foam, manipulated by a large bird to form men of different colours.

him, and saying that he would adopt him as a son and hunting companion. He then replaced the ladder so that Botoque could descend.

Despite his wife's hostility, the jaguar took Botoque into his home, where the boy saw fire and ate cooked meat for the first time. However, when the jaguar went hunting, his wife refused Botoque's requests for roasted tapir meat, and bared her claws threateningly so that he took refuge up a tree. Although the jaguar scolded his wife on his return, she ignored his warnings to leave the child alone. Eventually the jaguar showed Botoque how to make a bow and arrow to defend himself. When the wife threatened him again, the boy killed her with an arrow and, gathering up some cooked meat, his weapons and a burning ember, returned to his village.

On seeing Botoque's gifts the men went to the jaguar's house, where they stole not only fire but also cooked meat, cotton string, and bows and arrows. The jaguar was incensed at his adopted son's ingratitude, and now eats its food raw and hunts with its claws and fangs, whereas humans eat grilled meat and hunt with bows and arrows. Today, the reflection of the jaguar's lost fire can be seen in its mirror-like eyes. In some versions of this myth, as the villagers were carrying the stolen fire through the forest, many birds picked up the flying sparks in an attempt to prevent a blaze in the jungle. Some of the birds were burned as they did so, which is why some species have flame-coloured beaks, legs and feet.

According to the Barasana people of Colombia, it is Yurupary, or the Manioc Stick Anaconda, who obtains fire from the underworld. Anaconda uses the fires to murder his brother Macaw. When he himself is burned to death, his bones become the charred logs of a manioc garden, in which the first cultivated plants are grown, using his body as nourishment.

CANNIBALISM AND POWER
Cannibalism was a widespread feature of Amerindian ritual belief, and various forms are historically well attested throughout South America. Intimately associated with notions of warfare, death and regeneration, cannibalism had less to do with eating people for food than with concepts of social identity, kinship, and the transference of soul essence from one person to another.

"Exocannibalism" involved the actual or symbolic eating of an enemy's flesh as an expression of martial ferocity and as the ultimate humiliation and revenge. Cannibal tribes were greatly feared as their warriors were believed to be possessed by a fierce jaguar-spirit, which encouraged them to savage and then devour their prey. "Endocannibalism" had a more respectful motivation: it involved grinding to powder a dead person's bones, which were then added to manioc beer and drunk by family relatives. The deceased's bones were thought to retain vital elements of the person's spirit, which could be perpetuated in the lives of those who took part in the ritual consumption of the dead.

AFRICA

Great Zimbabwe, which gives its name to the country in which it stands, is the most monumental structure in sub-Saharan Africa. It was probably built from the 8th century by ancestors of the Shona people. As is commonly the case with similar royal enclosures throughout southern Africa, the ovoid shape of the Great Enclosure (above) very likely refers to the myth of the cosmic egg (see p.266). Zimbabwe means "stone dwelling".

Africa is home to an enormous diversity of cultures and its peoples speak more than 1,000 languages, many of them still inadequately recorded or studied. However, African mythologies display a broad unity: for example, myths of a cosmic serpent (see p.277) and of a great tower (see p.273) are found from the Sahara to the Cape; also widespread are the concept of a remote, usually asexual creator god and the motif of twinship.

Every local indigenous African belief system has a myth which tells of the origins and early wanderings of the people. This reflects the great internal migrations which were a feature of African history up to colonial times. For example, the Khoisan (a term covering the Khoi or "Hottentots" of southwestern Africa and the San or "Bushmen" of the Kalahari Desert) appear to be the remnants of a people who emerged in the once fertile Sahara before it became largely desert about 7,000 years ago. About 2,000 years ago, the ancestors of today's Bantu-speaking peoples began to move southeast from the Cameroon highlands, reaching the Cape as late as the 17th century. The Bantu languages form part of the Niger-Congo family, which includes at least 890 tongues. The often relatively rapid migrations of peoples and the wide spread of language families help to explain the common threads running through African mythology.

With the spread of Islam and Christianity, and modern economic developments, Africa's indigenous religions have declined. But many peoples, such as the Yoruba, have tenaciously preserved their beliefs and the myths that go with them.

PEOPLES, LANGUAGES AND MYTHS

The map shows the main indigenous language families of the African mainland (see key) and the location of some of the continent's many peoples. The principal rivers and certain important geographical features appear for reference, but modern political frontiers have been omitted for the sake of clarity. There follows a brief outline of the character of the mythology in each of the main language areas.

HAMITO-SEMITIC
The mythology of this largely Muslim area retains many pre-Islamic features, including the concept of a cosmic serpent whose body serves as the material of the universe (see also p.266). Another idea is the division of the world into an upper world of divinities, a middle region for humans and an underworld of departed spirits.

NILO-SAHARAN
The speakers of the Nilo-Saharan languages demonstrate little concern in their mythology for the origin of the world or in the fate of the soul after death. Their myths are mainly about the origins of clan and lineage groups, which are often associated with animals. For example, one Nuer myth traces a clan to a woman who bears sets of twins consisting of a human son and a wild animal.

NIGER-CONGO (BANTU)
The mythology of Bantu-speaking Africa, like that of the Nilo-Saharan area, shows relatively little interest in the creation of the universe, which is typically attributed to a High God now withdrawn from the world. More important is the origin of the social order, especially kingship and its relationship to other authorities such as priesthood. Myths may associate such institutions with natural phenomena such as the sun, moon or rainbow (see p.271), and with animals such as the lion. Many peoples maintain elaborate ancestor cults.

NIGER-CONGO (NON-BANTU)
The non-Bantu region of the Niger-Congo language area contains some of the world's most complex myths, with the Dogon, Bambara and Yoruba cosmologies rivalling those of India and Mesoamerica in grandeur and subtlety (see p.266). One key idea is that all life is animated by a duality which is perfectly symbolized in the relationship between twins of the opposite sex.

KHOISAN
The name Khoisan combines the virtually extinct Khoi or "Hottentots" with the San or "Bushmen". The fragmentary remains of their mythology indicate a richly imaginative philosophy of life conveyed in terms of personified wild creatures, the most important of which is the mantis (see p.276).

KEY TO MAP

African language families:

- Hamito-Semitic
- Nilo-Saharan
- Niger-Congo (non-Bantu)
- Niger-Congo (Bantu)
- Khoisan
- Mixed Hamito-Semitic/Nilo-Saharan
- Mixed Nilo-Saharan/Niger-Congo
- Mixed Niger-Congo/Khoisan
- ● Site or town: **Great Zimbabwe**
- People: _YORUBA_

TIME CHART

20,000 years ago Mongoloid peoples migrate into northeastern Africa and the Sahara
10,000 years ago Ancestral Negroid peoples emerge in western Sudan
7,000 years ago Ancestral Khoi and San peoples migrate southward through eastern savannah regions, eventually reaching southern Africa _c._5,000 years ago

2,000 years ago Ancestral Bantu-speakers from the Cameroon highlands migrate through tropical forest to the savannah of the Shaba region of southeast Zaïre
1,000 years ago Secondary dispersal of Bantu, probably in association with spread of iron-making, occurs from southeast Zaïre into most of sub-Saharan Africa

ORIGINS OF THE WORLD

Africa's creation myths

The vibrations of the cosmic egg at the beginning of creation are represented by the spirals on this brass box, used for storing gold dust by the Ashanti of Ghana.

THE COSMIC EGG

The Dogon of Mali believe that creation began with a being called Amma, an egg which was the seed of the cosmos. It vibrated seven times, then burst open, to reveal a Nommo creator spirit. This fell to earth and was followed by a female twin, then four more Nommo pairs. The Nommos created and organized the sky and earth, the succession of day and night, the seasons and human society. The idea of a "cosmic egg" as the source of the universe is widespread throughout Africa.

The Dogon cave painting (right) probably depicts a Nommo falling to earth. Two Nommos (with raised arms) feature on the stool below, which was used by a Dogon spiritual leader. The base of the stool represents the earth and the seat the sky.

African peoples have many different ideas about origins, from the belief of the Akan of Ghana that the universe was produced by Nyame, a mother goddess identified with the moon, to the widespread image of a vast serpent, often identified with the rainbow, as the origin of the cosmos. In southern Africa this primal serpent is commonly called Chinaweji and is thought of as a great python. From southern Algeria to Timbuktu, the first created object in the universe is said to have been a vast serpent, Minia, out of whose body the world and all life were made (see also p.277).

Peoples as far apart as the Dogon of Mali and the Lungu of Zambia speak of creation in terms of vibrations from a "cosmic egg" (see left). In the Dogon myth, the origin of the world is the seed of the universe, a star which they call by their name for *Digitaria exilis*, their smallest cultivated grainseed. For them, this star is the "twin" of Sirius, the Dog Star, and is the smallest and heaviest of all the stars; it is so dense, they say, that all the people on earth together could not lift a small part of it. Its movement around Sirius, which is said to last fifty years, upholds all creation in space. Curiously enough, modern astronomy has discovered that Sirius does indeed have a companion, Sirius B, visible only to the most powerful telescopes, which orbits Sirius every fifty years and is also extremely dense, what astronomers call a "collapsed white dwarf". This has led one American scholar, Roger Temple, to claim that the Dogon myth is a remnant of knowledge brought to earth by intelligent beings from the

Sirius star system. However, the American astronomer and cosmologist Carl Sagan suggests, less fancifully, that the Dogon account could have derived from information passed on by some Western scientist before the myth was first recorded by a French anthropologist in the 1930s.

One of the most complex myths of creation is told by the Bambara, near neighbours of the Dogon. They relate how in the beginning emptiness, *fu*, brought forth knowing, *gla gla zo*. This knowing, full of its emptiness and its emptiness full of itself, was the prime creative force of the universe, setting in train a mystical process of releasing and retracting energy which in turn led to the creation of human consciousness, the "seed" or principle of the universe. (In every human being, because of the fundamental law of twinness which, the Bambara believe, rules all creation, there is both male and female, in body and in spirit.) Then the spirit called Pemba made the earth and the spirit Faro made the sky and each established the four cardinal directions in space. Then life appeared on earth. Faro produced twins in the desert and the first grass grew. Then the first waters appeared and with them a fish which took Faro and his children to the sea, where he created all the aquatic animals. Faro named all the creatures and things on earth, determined the seasons and, in place of the primal darkness, installed the alternation of night and day. Then he ordered all living beings. Human beings were also named and classified, the races and tribes divided according to the qualities of their blood, in which Faro inscribed their destiny. Then he returned to the sky.

Many African mythologies do not concern themselves unduly with speculation on the creation of the cosmos, taking as their starting point the emergence of humans in an already constituted universe. The Fipa of southwest Tanzania and the Tutsi of Ruanda say that semi-divine ancestors fell from the sky at the beginning of time to found humankind, while the Maasai pastoralists of Tanzania and Kenya say that in the beginning earth and sky were connected by a rope, by which the High God sent down cattle for the people below. The Yoruba people of West Africa say that the original earth was water and uninhabited marsh until divinity came down from the sky and made solid ground. Human beings were then created in heaven and sent down on a spider's web to earth.

THE SAN CREATION MYTH

In the following story the San hunter-gatherers of the Kalahari attribute the creation to a being called Dxui:

"Dxui was Dxui, the first spirit of creation. His works were many. When the sun rose Dxui was a flower and at night he was a man. When day came he was another flower and at sunset he was a man again. The following day he was a tree bearing abundant fruit. Again the sun set and he was Dxui, a man. When Dxui awoke he saw the sun for the first time and found he was alone. Then he became a tree that bore fruit but was also covered with thorns. Then the first woman appeared and tried to take the fruit, but the tree vanished and the woman cried and lay down on the earth and died.

"Dxui became a fly, and then water, then another flower, a bird, then the snarer of the bird, and then the one who ate the bird. Again he became a man and was hunted by other men and so Dxui became a great bird and flew to his father and mother. When his father recognized him, Dxui became a man. He died and became a lizard, the oldest creature of all."

The heavenly blacksmith

In African mythology a divine blacksmith often plays a crucial role in preparing the new universe for humanity. He is commonly described as descending from the sky.

According to the Fon people of Benin in West Africa the eldest son of Mawu-Lisa, the twin creator divinities, was Gu, the heavenly blacksmith. He was brought down to earth by Lisa, the male twin, in the form of a ceremonial iron sword which Lisa held in his hand. It is said that Gu was then charged with making the earth habitable for humans, a task he has never given up. Gu taught ironworking

A Dogon wrought-iron equestrian figure, probably the blacksmith who stole fire. His image is common in shrines.

and showed people how to fashion tools so that they could obtain food, cover their bodies and build shelters.

Amma, the creator god of the Dogon (see The Cosmic Egg, opposite), made the first spirit blacksmith from the placenta of a Nommo. But this spirit had no fire, so he stole a piece of the sun from the heavenly Nommo twins and came down from heaven to earth in a celestial ark. Other myths of the Sahara region relate how the first blacksmith made a hoe from the skull of a heavenly antelope called Bintu, then descended to earth with it in order to teach the newly created human race how to cultivate.

THE UPSIDE-DOWN WORLD

Realms of the living and the dead

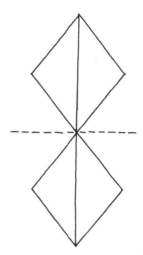

An oasis dweller in the Tidikelt region of southern Algeria drew this representation of the upper and lower worlds and the cosmic tree in its three manifestations. The diamond shapes probably represent the four cardinal directions in each world.

The newly created universe is commonly said to consist of two parts: an upper part for the living and an underworld for the dead. For the peoples on the southern shores of Lake Tanganyika the world of the dead is an upside-down version of the world of the living, where people sleep during the day and come out at night by moonlight. It can be reached through the burrow of a porcupine. Across the Sahara and Sahel regions of North Africa the upper and lower regions of the universe are thought of as opposed aspects of a "cosmic tree", which has the form of a vine in the world above and a fig tree in the world below. On earth, which is between heaven and the underworld, the tree appears as a grenadine tree. In the oases of the Sahara, people plant representatives of the three levels of the cosmic tree: a vine in the east, referring to heaven, a grenadine tree in the middle of the cultivated area, representing the earth, and a fig tree on the western margin, for the underworld.

In other parts of Africa the world of the dead is pictured as being a sky world rather than an underworld, but again it resembles the world of the living. The Thonga people of Mozambique tell of a girl who broke her pot on the way to the river. She cried out and a rope appeared, hanging from the sky. The girl climbed the rope and found a village, where the dead people lived. An old woman told her to keep walking and to listen to the advice of an ant which had crawled into the young visitor's ear. She reached another village, and the elders gave her work to do. The next morning, pleased with her labours, the elders showed her some babies, some wrapped in red and others in white cloths. The woman was about to choose one in red when the ant whispered in her ear to take a white one, which she did. When the young woman returned home, she was well received by her family. However, her sister was jealous and went up to heaven to get a baby for herself. However, she was rude to the old woman and refused to listen to the ant. She chose a red baby and was immediately transformed into a skeleton. Her white bones fell to earth.

The Kongo cosmos

*T*he Kongo people of western Zaïre say the universe has two regions, separated by an ocean. The upper region, the world of the living, is like a mountain. The underworld, the world of the dead, is similar, but faces downwards. Each world has villages, waters and hills.

Heaven is white, but the earth below is black, on account of evil and disobedience to the High God's will.

This wood and raffia mask of Zaïre's Pende people may represent the sun, and opposites such as day and night.

Between heaven and earth is the rainbow, represented as red. Beneath the black earth is the water barrier, the origin of all life, which is also red, and beneath that is the underworld, which is white. Like the universe, the alternation of night and day and the stages of human life are red, white and black. The red dawn is like birth, the white noonday sun is maturity and justice, and sunset heralds the blackness of death.

DEATH AND SEX

The loss of immortality

According to many African peoples there was originally no death, and its arrival is widely attributed to the transgression either of human beings or of some animal. The Nuer pastoralists of the southern Sudan relate how there was once a rope joining heaven and earth, and anyone who grew old climbed up the rope and was made young again by the High God before returning to earth. But one day a hyena and a weaverbird climbed up the rope and entered heaven, so the High God gave instructions that these visitors were to be closely watched and not allowed to return to earth where they would certainly cause trouble. One night they escaped and climbed down, and when they were near the ground the hyena cut the rope. When the part above the cut was drawn up to heaven, there was no way that human beings could get there, and now when they grow old they die.

The Kuba people of Zaire account for the beginning of death in a version of their creation myth. The creator god Mboom, or "Original Water", had nine children, all called Woot, who each took turns to assist in creating the world. Woot the inventor of all prickly things such as fish and thorns quarrelled with Woot the sharpener, who made the first sharp blades. Death came to the world when Woot the inventor of prickly things was killed by a sharpened blade.

Among the Ganda people who live along the northern shore of Lake Victoria it is said that Kintu, an immigrant stranger who founded the royal dynasty of Buganda, went to heaven to find a wife. The High God gave Kintu his daughter Nambi, but warned his new son-in-law to hurry back to earth with his wife. Otherwise, Nambi's brother Walumbe, meaning Death, would accompany them. Kintu left with Nambi as requested, but along the way she realized that she had forgotten to bring grain to feed the chicken given to them as a present from the High God. Kintu tried in vain to dissuade her from going back, and when Nambi caught up with Kintu after obtaining the grain she was followed by her brother Death, who took up residence beside the couple. Since that time all people on earth have been mortal.

A woman is also blamed for the arrival of death on earth in a myth of the Dinka, cattle keepers of the southern Sudan. In the beginning, they say, the High God gave a grain of millet a day to a certain couple called Garang and Abuk, and this satisfied their needs. But Abuk greedily decided to plant more grain and in doing so accidentally hit the High God with the end of her hoe. The deity was so angry that he withdrew to his present great distance from humanity and sent a bluebird to sever the rope which at that time linked heaven and earth.

Since that time, the Dinka believe, humans have had to work hard in order to procure food and have suffered from sicknesses and death.

A wooden Yoruba shrine carving with an erotic fertility theme, from Northern Yorubaland, Nigeria.

THE ORIGINS OF SEXUALITY

A story which exists in many versions in Africa tells how the High God originally made people without sexual organs. They lived together quite happily for a while but then became discontented and asked the High God if he could send them a different type of people. So the divinity sent the male and female sexual organs, which at first went around just like people, on their own. One day the original people decided to divide themselves into two camps, the better to perform the work of everyday life. They invited the sexual organs to join one or other camp, and the male organs attached themselves to the people in one camp, and the female organs to the people in the other camp. From that time the two lots of people became men and women saw that they were different and there has been division and conflict between them ever since.

A painted wooden spirit mask by a Dan craftsman of Liberia. The characteristic slitted eyes are said to restrict the power emanating from the world of the dead spirits.

MYTHS OF KINGSHIP

The divine lineage of earthly rulers

COLOURS OF LIFE AND SOCIETY
The colours red, white and black have a profound significance for many African peoples, for example as representations of the universe (see panel, p.268). On the above winnowing tray from northern Zambia they have a dual significance. On the one hand they evoke the mythological origins of the society of the Lungu people: red is associated with kingship, white with spiritual power and priesthood, and black with the common people. At the same time, the red refers to the blood of first menstruation, the white to semen and the black to pubic hair. Such winnowing trays are presented to marriageable young women after ritual initiation.

Among the most important African myths are those dealing with the origins of royal rulers, in which, typically, kings are described as being descended from divine beings. For example, the Zulus of South Africa relate how a young man, the High God's son, was expelled from heaven because he had stolen the god's favourite white cow. He was thrown through a hole in the sky and descended to earth by a magical umbilical cord which was tied around his waist. After a month had gone by, the High God took pity on his son and sent him a wife by the same means, afterwards drawing up the cord and closing the hole in the sky. That young man became the first king of the Zulus. Because of their heavenly origin, the Zulu rulers have power over rain. Kingship and the weather are also associated in Yoruba mythology, according to which the greatest Yoruba warrior-king, Shango, became god of thunder and rain after hanging himself on a tree and ascending to heaven. His wife was a lake called Oja, which after Shango's death became the river Niger.

A similar story about the origin of kingship is told in Ruanda in East Africa. There it is said that the master of heaven, Nkuba the Lightning, had a sterile wife. One day, in the absence of her husband, this wife stole one of her husband's cows and killed it, extracting the heart and hiding it in a pot. For nine months she fed the heart with milk and then a male infant appeared in the pot. Called Kigwa, this child grew up in heaven, eventually falling from the sky to become the first king in Ruanda.

In many cases the myths of the origin of kings are also myths of human origin. The *reth* (king) of the Shilluk of the southern Sudan was identified in myth and royal ritual with Nyikang, the ancestor of the royal line and founder of the Shilluk nation. Nyikang's father was the son of a heavenly being and his mother, Nyakaya, was a crocodile. Nyikang left his homeland after quarrelling with his half-brother, and on his journey he fought and won a battle with the sun and divided

In Africa, as elsewhere, the lion symbolizes royal authority. As king of beasts it appears in many myths, although it is often outwitted by smaller and more cunning animals such as the hare. This carved wooden figure of a lion comes from the royal palace of the Fon people of Benin (formerly Dahomey) in West Africa.

the waters of the White Nile so that he and his followers could cross. The praise-names of Nyikang and all subsequent kings of the Shilluk – all held to be his incarnations – honour his association with sky, river and earth, the Shilluk universe. He is god, demi-god and man, on whose health that of the land depends. In pre-colonial times (and it is rumoured still to happen today), when he began to lose physical strength, he was ritually killed to make way for a suitably vigorous successor.

Another account of ritual regicide is the myth of King Mwetsi, which explains the ritual slaying of the *Mambo* (king) of Monomotapa in medieval Zimbabwe, believed to have occurred every four years. According to the myth, the first man created by Mwari, the High God, lived at first beneath the waters. He was called Mwetsi (Moon) and he wanted to live on earth, which was at that time a complete desert. Mwetsi began to lament and Mwari sent him a wife, the Morning Star, who bore all the grass, shrubs and trees. The trees grew until their tops touched the sky and it began to rain. In their new state of abundance Mwetsi built a house, made hoes and cultivated the earth. But after two years Mwari took Morning Star away. Mwetsi lamented for eight days until Mwari brought him a new wife, the Evening Star, at the same time warning Mwetsi that he was heading for disaster. When night came Evening Star ordered him to her bed. As a result of their coupling she gave birth to chickens, sheep, goats, cattle and antelopes and then boys and girls, who grew to adults in one day. On the evening of the fourth day there was a violent storm and Evening Star warned her husband that he was in danger of death. Nonetheless he made love with her and the next day she bore lions, leopards, snakes and scorpions. On the evening of the fifth day Evening Star refused to lie down with her husband. Instead she suggested that he take his daughters. He did this and his daughters bore children in the morning who had grown to adulthood by the evening.

Mwetsi thus became king of a numerous people and Evening Star lay down with a serpent and became sterile. Mwetsi wanted her back, but as he lay down, the serpent bit him. The health of the land depended on Mwetsi's

A MYTH-TELLER'S MEMORY DEVICE

At the Luba royal court a class of elders is entrusted with the telling and recording of the myths related to the Rainbow King and the history of the Luba kings (see panel, below, and p.272). The elders use a remarkable device, the *Lukasa* or "long hand", to record the essential features of the stories. It consists of a board studded with coloured beads and incised with symbolic patterns. For example, a blue bead might stand for Mbidi Kiluwe and a large red bead surrounded by smaller yellow ones for Nkongolo and his followers. The storyteller holds the *Lukasa* to remind him of the story as he goes along.

Kalala Ilunga and the Rainbow King

The Luba of Zaïre believe that a founder of one of their kingdoms was Kalala Ilunga. He spent his early life at the court of the Rainbow King, Nkongolo, who features in many myths of the central savannah.

One day a prince from the east, Mbidi Kiluwe, came hunting in the land of Nkongolo, who did his best to please his guest. He lent him his twin sisters and both became pregnant, Bulanda bearing a son, Kalala Ilunga, while Mabela had twins, a boy and a girl. Nkongolo claimed Kalala Ilunga as his own son and Mbidi Kiluwe had to return home. The boy grew up to be the country's best runner and dancer. Nkongolo resented his fame and decided to kill him. He had a hidden pit full of sharpened stakes dug in the dancing ground, and then invited Kalala to take part in a dancing contest. Warned of the danger by his drummer,

Kalala fled across the Lualaba River to his real father. Mbidi gave him an army to beat Nkongolo, who fled with his sisters to Kaii mountain in the west. But the sisters betrayed him to Kalala's men, who cut off his head. Nkongolo's spirit lives on as a serpent, which sometimes appears as a rainbow.

A Luba wooden neckrest in the form of twin sisters. Twins play an important role in the story of Kalala Ilunga (the king is betrayed by his twin sisters) and in many other myths.

A mask representing the ancestral hero Woot and worn during Kuba initiation rituals. Only men of royal lineage are permitted to wear the mask, which is decorated with beads and shells.

own health, and as he grew sick with the snake venom the rain ceased to fall, the waters dried up, and death visited the people. To end their woes Mwetsi's children decided to kill their father. They strangled Mwetsi and buried him, then chose another king to rule the land.

According to the Kuba people of Zaïre, the first two gods were also kings, Mboom and Ngaan, who each ruled one half of a world which was dark and covered in water. But they quarrelled and left the place they had created, Mboom going to heaven and Ngaan sinking beneath the waters. One day Mboom vomited the sun, the moon and the stars. Under the sun, the waters began to dry up and expose the land. Mboom vomited again and brought up all the animals. Then he vomited human beings, including Woot, the ancestor of the Kuba kings and people, who lived in a village with the other humans and the animals. They all got on well together, speaking the same language. Then Woot fell in love with his sister Mweel. He took her into the forest and as a result of their liaison she bore a son, Nyimi Lele, who was to found the nearby Lele tribe.

When the people heard of Woot's incest they were angry and expelled him from the village. In revenge, Woot uttered a curse. The millet began to rot, most of the animals became wild and the sun did not rise. Mweel sent messengers to beg his forgiveness and eventually Woot relented, allowing the birds of morning to summon the sun to return. He then led his followers into exile. As Woot went he created the landscape, plants and animals and left more sons, the founders of the various tribes. Woot twisted their tongues, so that from that time they spoke different languages.

Chibinda Ilunga

A myth told by the Mbangala people of Angola continues the story of the Luba dynasty founded by Kalala Ilunga (see p.271). The protagonist, Chibinda Ilunga, is one of the most highly revered figures in the mythology of the region.

There once came to the Lunda kingdom a young prince, a hunter called Chibinda Ilunga, the grandson of Mbidi Kiluwe, who was the forefather of the Luba kings. His face was shining and white like the moon. This prince had left the Luba country because the king, jealous of his hunting prowess, had insulted him by alleging that he had never made war. One day the Lunda queen, Lueji, who was descended from the primordial serpent Chinawezi, mother of all things (see pp.266 and 277), went to a river in the forest and met the hunter prince. She was immediately captivated by his charming manners and invited him to stay with her. In due course they married and one day Lueji made a speech to the elders and told them that from that day on Chibinda Ilunga would rule in her place. The prince also spoke to them and said that he was a hunter and would never shed the blood of men, only of animals. After Lueji had handed him her royal bracelet of office, she began her menstruation and went into seclusion. This lasted a long time and became known as Nkula ("the tree with red sap"), the name of the ritual that, ever since, has been applied to women with menstrual disorders. Because of her prolonged flow of blood, Lueji was never able to bear children. In the end she gave Chibinda Ilunga another wife, Kamonga, who was fertile.

A wooden figurine from Zaïre representing the Luba king Chibinda Ilunga.

TOWER MYTHS

The folly of human presumptuousness

Stories of the building and ultimate destruction of huge towers abound throughout southern Africa from Mozambique to Angola and usually serve as a warning of the perils of overambitiousness. For example, a story told among the Luba people of the Kasai province of Zaïre relates how at the beginning of time, human beings lived in the same village as the High God. But tiring of their noisy quarrels, the creator dispatched his human neighbours to earth, where they suffered from hunger and cold and came to know sickness and death. A diviner advised them to return to the sky to acquire immortality again, so they began to build an enormous tower of wood. After many months the builders arrived at the sky, beating a drum and playing a flute to announce their success to those who remained on earth and encourage them to follow. But the people below were too far away to hear. When he heard the noise the High God became angry and destroyed the tower, killing the musical builders.

A tower myth also occurs as part of the Luba story of the struggle between Nkongolo, the cruel and despotic Rainbow King, and Prince Kalala Ilunga (see p.271). It is said that Nkongolo tried various ways to force or lure his enemy back into his power after Kalala's escape from the pit trap the king had set for him. First Nkongolo sent parties of his men in boats across the Lualaba river with orders to kidnap the fugitive prince, but the waters rose up and drowned them before they could reach the shore. Then Nkongolo tried to build a stone causeway across the river, but the stone resisted his iron implements. Finally the king ordered the building of a great tower from which it would be possible to see right into his enemy's country. When the tower had been built, Nkongolo commanded the diviner Majibu and another man called Mungedi to climb to the top and call the fugitive back. But Majibu, using his magical powers, leapt into space and landed on Kalala's side of the river, where he joined the prince and helped him in his successful war against his enemy. The tower collapsed, killing Mungedi and many other followers of the Rainbow King.

THE TOWER OF CHITIMUKULU
According to the origin myth of the Bemba people of Zambia, their first king, Chitimukulu, tried with his two brothers to build a tall tower in the royal village of their mother Mumbi Mukasa, who was a niece of the High God. The tower collapsed, killing many people, and their father Mukulumpe ordered the three to be put to death. Chitimukulu and his brothers fled to what is now Zambia.

The conical tower (centre, left) is the most prominent feature of the ruins of Great Zimbabwe. Standing more than 30 feet (9 metres) high, it is one of a string of similar towers across southern Africa, which are believed to be connected with the widespread tower myths.

ESHU THE TRICKSTER

Cunning mediator between heaven and earth

These figures from a 19th-century Yoruba shrine represent the popular trickster god Eshu in various guises.

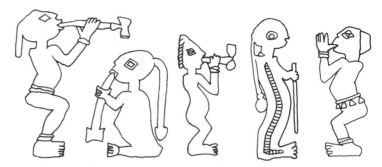

THE SONG OF ESHU

There are a great number of entertaining songs about the trickster Eshu, many of them with deliberately absurd words. The following is a Yoruba example:

"Eshu slept in the house, but the house was too small for him.

Eshu slept on the veranda, but the veranda was too small for him.

Eshu slept in a nut – at last he could stretch himself.

Eshu walked through a groundnut farm – the tuft of his hair was just visible.

If it had not been for his huge size, he would not have been seen at all.

Having thrown a stone yesterday, he kills a bird today.

Lying down, his head hits the roof.

Standing up, he cannot see into the cooking pot.

Eshu turns right into wrong,

Wrong into right."

The most famous trickster figure in African mythology is the West African character known as Eshu to the Yoruba and as Elegba or Legba in Benin (only the name Eshu is used here). He is said to be responsible for all quarrels between human beings, and between humans and gods. The most cunning of all divinities, he is described as a homeless, wandering spirit, who inhabits the marketplace, the crossroads, and the thresholds of houses. He is also in attendance wherever there is change and transition. In one myth Eshu entices the sun and moon to exchange houses, thus reversing the order of things. But the best-known story is one in which he manages to break up a lifelong friendship between two men. These men farm adjoining plots of land and their friendship is so close that they are always seen together and even dress alike. Eshu decides to walk down the path which divides their farms wearing a hat which is black on one side and white on the other. He puts his pipe at the back of his head and hooks his club over one shoulder so that it hangs down his back. After the god has passed by, the two friends quarrel about the direction the stranger has taken and the colour of his hat. The quarrel becomes so heated that the king himself takes notice of it and summons the two men.

While each accuses the other of lying, Eshu comes and tells the king that neither is a liar but that both are fools. When he confesses to his trick the enraged king sends his men after him, but the god outruns them all. In his flight Eshu sets fire to many houses, and as the occupants run out carrying their possessions he offers to take care of them, but instead gives each bundle to a passer-by. The belongings of the victims of the fire are sent off in every direction.

In another story Eshu tells the High God that thieves are planning to raid his yam garden. During the night he creeps into the High God's house and steals his sandals, then goes into the garden in them and steals all the yams. It had rained the day before and the footprints are plain to see. In the morning Eshu reports the theft, saying it would be easy to identify the thief from the footprints. All the people are called but nobody's feet fits such big prints. When Eshu suggests that perhaps the High God himself took the yams in his sleep, the divinity denies it. But the High God's foot matches the prints exactly. He accuses Eshu of tricking him and by way of retribution he announces his immediate withdrawal from the world, telling Eshu to come to the sky every night to report on what has happened below during the day. This is how Eshu became the messenger between human beings and the High God.

Eshu and Ifa

*A*ccording to the Yoruba, Ifa was a god who came to earth to tell humans the secrets of medicine and prophecy. The following myth shows how the trickster Eshu and Ifa, the god of order and control, work together in the world.

Eshu and Ifa were travelling through the world. Eshu boasted that one day he would bring ruin to his companion. Ifa just laughed and said: "If you transform yourself, I shall do the same, and if I die, you will die, for so it has been ordained in heaven."

One evening Eshu disappeared. He stole a cock from a neighbouring house and cut off its head, then hid the pieces of the fowl in his garment, returned to Ifa and cried: "Wake up! Death is coming!" The approach of villagers, angry at the loss of the cock, could be heard in the distance. Ifa and Eshu fled, and as they went the trickster god slyly sprinkled drops of blood from the dead cock on the ground to mark their trail. Ifa looked back and saw that the villagers were carrying hatchets and clubs. Eshu then climbed a tall white cotton tree. Ifa changed into a bird and flew up and perched alongside the trickster, who said: "Did I not tell you? Have I not brought death to you?" Ifa replied: "Whatever happens to me, happens to you!" The villagers chopped down the mighty tree and ran to where they thought the bodies had fallen. But in place of Eshu and Ifa they found only a large stone and a pool of clear, cool water. Staring at the stone, their heads filled with agony and heat; only when they turned to the pool did the terrible heat disappear. The village chief recognized that a miracle had occurred and prostrated himself, saying: "We of the world bow down and worship you!"

Whenever people offer sacrifice to Ifa, they must also present Eshu with the first taste to make sure that their work will turn out well.

A wand or tapper used during the Ifa divination process (see margin, right, above).

THE IFA ORACLE

The most famous African system of divination is the Ifa of the Yoruba people. The Yoruba diviner takes 16 palmnuts from a tree which has not been used for the making of palm wine. He (the diviner is always male) sits before a divining tray and divides the nuts equally between his right and left hands, eight in each. The nuts are shaken together, then most of those in the left hand are transferred to the right, a process repeated until either one or two nuts remain in the left hand. If one nut remains, two marks are made in the dust in the divining tray, and if two remain only one mark is made. The procedure is repeated until there are eight sets of marks on the round divining tray. This constitutes a figure called *odu*, which in turn refers the diviner to a set of symbolic tales which the diviner proceeds to recite from memory to his client. He goes on reciting until the client intuitively recognizes the story whose message applies to him or her. There are said to be 256 (that is, 16 squared) permutations within the Ifa system. A basically similar though less elaborate system is used in southern Africa, where four pieces of carved ivory or bone are thrown to yield 16 possible combinations of symbolic meaning.

The Fon of Benin have adopted the Ifa divinatory system under the name of Fa. They say that the destiny of each human being is determined by the creator High God, Mawu, and can be revealed through the Fa oracle. But Elegba has tricks and stratagems to evade the strict government of the world laid down by Mawu, so everyone must make equal offerings to the High God and to the trickster deity.

A wooden bowl with the base in the form of a crouching figure. It is used for holding the palmnuts used in Ifa divination.

ANIMAL MYTHS

Tricksters, inventors and transformers

The hare is among the most popular animal tricksters in African myth. It is depicted here on a Yoruba mask.

Animal characters figure prominently in African myth in a wide variety of guises and roles. Among the most popular of these characters is the trickster figure represented in West and Central Africa by a spider and in the savannah regions of eastern and southern Africa as a hare. These tricksters, unlike divine ones like Eshu (see p.274) are relatively insignificant and powerless in themselves, but typically use their cunning to outwit more powerful beasts such as the lion, the hyena or the elephant. In a story told by the Zande people of Central Africa, Ture the Spider meets a man-eating monster with a double-sided gong which he uses to trap people. To gain the creature's confidence Ture offers to climb into the gong but leaves his arm sticking out so that the monster as unable to close it. "Show me how to do it properly," Ture asks. The monster obliges, whereupon Ture slams the gong shut and kills him.

In another myth known over much of the continent, the trickster Hare (a character, incidentally, which went to America with West African slaves and ultimately became Brer Rabbit) decides to get married, but is too lazy to cultivate the field of millet needed to support a wife. So he thinks of a better way of getting the work done and goes into the bush with a long rope to look for Hippopotamus.

"My uncle," Hare says, "I want to tie this rope to you and see if I can pull you. When you see the rope move, just pull like mad!" Hippo replies: "All right, if you want to do it, I will. But you'll certainly be done for if we have a tug-of-war and then you'll be sorry!" Hare ties the rope around Hippo's neck, and goes off with the other end until he meets Elephant, to whom he tells a similar story. Then he goes to the middle of the rope and

The bringers of fire

*I*n Africa animals are often credited with the acquisi-tion of fire. The Pygmies attribute its arrival to a dog or to the chimpanzees, while the Ila people of Zambia say that a mason wasp brought fire from the High God to the earth. The San (Bushmen), in the following myth, say that fire was stolen by the praying mantis, a crea-ture widely regarded by Africans as sacred.

One day Mantis noticed something strange: the place where Ostrich ate his food always smelt good. Mantis crept close to Ostrich while he was eating and saw that he was roasting food on a fire. When he had finished eating, Ostrich carefully tucked the fire under his wing.

Then Mantis thought of a trick by which he could get that fire for himself. He went to Ostrich and told him: "I have found a wonderful tree with delicious fruit. Follow me and I will show it to you!" Ostrich followed

Mantis to a tree that was covered with yellow plums. As Ostrich began to eat Mantis told him: "Reach up, the best fruit is at the top!" As Ostrich stood on tiptoe, opening his wings wide to balance himself as he tried to get the fruit, Mantis stole the fire from under his wing. From that time Ostrich never attempted to fly again but always kept his wings close to his body.

Afterwards, the story continues, Mantis was destroyed in his own fire, and out of his ashes and bones two dif-ferent Mantises were made: one reserved and thought-ful, the other bold and enterprising. One day the baboons killed the son of bold Mantis and took out his eye. The spirit of Mantis saw what happened in a dream and did battle with the baboons, defeating them and retrieving the eye. He immersed it in water and it grew into a new being.

jerks it on both sides. Hippo and Elephant begin pulling and their struggle lasts until sundown, by which time they have cleared and churned up a large patch of the bush – which Hare then uses to sow a large crop of millet.

In many African mythologies sacred animals assist in the creation of the world and help to mould human culture. Prime examples are the widespread "cosmic serpent" (see The Great Serpent, right) and the mantis spirit of the Khoisan peoples of southwestern Africa. The Khoisan attribute the invention of words to the praying mantis, which, they claim, also brought fire to people after stealing it from the ostrich (see panel on opposite page).

Other famous animal transformers include the Pale Fox, who appears in the creation myth of the largely agricultural Dogon of Mali (see also p.266). Pale Fox is said to have invented agriculture by stealing seeds from Amma, the creator god, and sowing them in the body of the Earth, who was his mother. The main result of Pale Fox's act of theft was that it became necessary to purify the soil, which had dried up as a result of what amounted to incest. To make the soil pure, men sowed it with seed which had not been stolen, but which had been given to them by Amma for the purpose.

An outcast, Pale Fox fled and took refuge in the wilderness, which became his home, but men followed him, and cultivated and planted new fields. In this way, it is believed, the wanderings of the fox led to the expansion of human civilization and it is said that Amma made the fox to introduce both disorder and order into the world. Driven out from human society, the fox now communicates with humanity through the sand oracle, on which, it is said, he leaves his paw marks to show people the way to the future.

Elsewhere in Mali, the Bambara people attribute the invention of agriculture to a different animal, a primordial Antelope culture hero which was sent down from heaven by the creator god Faro to teach them the skills of farming. Representations of this divine Antelope hero are very common throughout the region (see illustration, right).

A wooden Bambara sculpture representing the divine Antelope culture hero who brought the secrets of agriculture from heaven.

THE GREAT SERPENT

The snake or serpent is one of the most widespread creatures encountered in African mythology. The concept of a "cosmic serpent" as a prime force of creation is particularly important. For example, the Fon people of Benin believe that the twin bisexual divinity Mawu-Lisa constructed the world with a creative power which flows like a huge snake and has the name of Da Ayido Hwedo. This power also appears in the rainbow and in all waters. In the beginning, the serpent power coiled itself around the unshaped earth, holding it together, and it still has this function. It moves constantly, its spiral flow setting the heavenly bodies in motion.

In Southern and Central Africa a similar role is ascribed to the primordial serpent Chinaweji or Chinawezi, which appears in the mythology of southeastern Zaïre as Nkongolo, the Rainbow King (see p.271). In Northern Africa a common myth relates how the first thing that the creator god made was the cosmic serpent Minia, whose head is in the sky and whose tail is in the waters below the earth. Its body was divided into seven parts, from which the god made the world (see p.266).

The bronze head of a serpent from the West African kingdom of Benin, which flourished from the 15th to the 18th centuries.

AUSTRALIA

*Ayers Rock, a solid sandstone outcrop also known by its
Aboriginal name of Uluru, is one of Australia's most sacred sites.
It is the location of many myths, such as the story of the
Bell Bird Brothers (see p.286).*

It is now thought that Australia has been inhabited for at least 50,000 years, the ancestors of present-day Aboriginal peoples arriving by boat from Southeast Asia during the last Ice Age. The subsequent rise in sea level is believed to have covered the oldest camp sites in the north.

Until European colonization began in the late 18th century, the people of Australia were almost exclusively hunter-gatherers. Aboriginal society was egalitarian, uncentralized and divided into independent clans, each consisting of 50 to 500 members related by common descent. This system persists today in the outback and, in a modified form, in the cities.

Although linked to an area of land over which it had pre-eminent rights, a clan would frequently join forces with its neighbours to forage over a wider area. Clans relied on access to each other's land to exploit temporary or seasonal abundances of foods, and intermarriage further strengthened clan ties. A mosaic of mythic elements common to different clans mirrored this economic and social interdependence.

Despite these interrelations, no individual myths are told throughout the continent. Typically, a narrative recounts the adventures in a particular clan's area of a wandering ancestral culture hero. The neighbouring clan relates what this figure did in its own area, and so on in a chain of myths stretching for perhaps hundreds of miles. Any one clan is unlikely to know where the hero's journey began or ended: for example, it was only when Central Australian men went to Port Augusta as cattle drovers that they discovered that this was where the Seven Sisters ended up (see p.287 and map, opposite). One theory suggests that the paths of these heroes represent routes by which religious cults were transmitted.

DREAM TIME

The roots of all Australian Aboriginal mythology lie in the Creation Period or Dream Time, which is called *Laliya* by the Worora of the Kimberleys, *Wongar* by the Yolngu of Arnhem Land and *Jukurpa* by the Pitjantjatjara of the Western Desert. Dream Time (or the Dreaming) is both a period of time and a state of being. As a period of time, it refers to the primordial epoch in which the ancestors travelled across Australia, shaping the landscape (see pp.286-7), determining the form of society, and depositing the spirits of unborn children. As a state of being, the Dreaming remains accessible to participants in ritual, who briefly *become* the ancestors whose journeys they recreate, or whose power they can liberate by striking sacred sites.

Aboriginal people commonly distinguish between the present, the past within living memory, and the distant past when the ancestors were active. However, the edges of these periods are blurred, and the lifetimes of the recently deceased merge imperceptibly into those of their ancestral prototypes, a process which may begin even before a person's death.

MYTH AND RITUAL

There are two main types of Aboriginal ritual. The first is public and commemorative, involving the re-enactment of episodes from the Dream Time, which give shape to important events such as initiation ceremonies and funerals. Typically, individual clans own the songs and body paintings used at various stages during these ceremonies.

The second type is the "increase" ritual, which often involves only a few people. It takes place at a sacred site, such as a rock, which is infused with the creative power of an ancestor. Dust from the site is thrown into the air, or the sacred rock is struck, or smoke from a fire is driven against the rock. Whatever the method, the aim is to release the ancestor's creative power and propagate the animal species with which he or she is totemically linked.

MYTH AND ART

Aboriginal society was non-literate until modern times, so art is the chief non-oral source for Australian mythology. In the north, humans, animals and other beings are depicted in the outline or silhouette style (see illustrations on pp.280, 281, 284 and 285), which is thought to be at least 15,000 years old. In central Australia people and animals are depicted according to the marks they leave in the sand: animals by their footprints, and humans often by the impression left by a person sitting cross-legged (see illustration on p.287). This tradition is between 10,000 and 30,000 years old. The themes of myth are also depicted on rock, body, ground and bark paintings. Rock art, which has endured for thousands of years, testifies to the antiquity of Aboriginal cultural traditions.

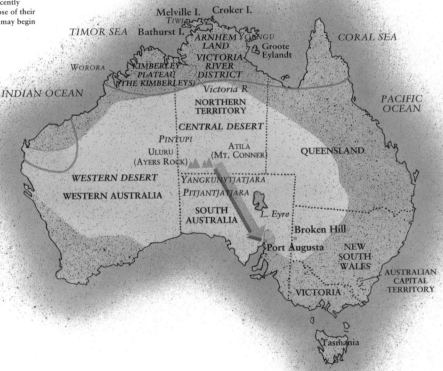

A bark painting from the Kimberleys of a wandjina, *an ancestral spirit being from the Aboriginal Dream Time. Every clan has a* wandjina, *who is associated with a particular animal, as its guardian ancestor.*

THE TELLING OF MYTH

Aboriginal narratives have traditionally been transmitted by word of mouth. No single, orthodox version exists of any myth, as each teller introduces variations for effect. Which incidents are related depends on the status of the audience (because many myths include details known only to initiates) or of the teller (for example, young people should not display their knowledge in the presence of their elders). An Aboriginal "myth" in the sense of a prose narrative is often merely a summary of a much more detailed story told in song cycles running to hundreds of verses and normally performed only during a ceremony (see p.281).

The future of this oral culture is uncertain as Aboriginal languages decline. Of perhaps 200 languages spoken before colonial times, only about 50 survive, spoken by a quarter of the present-day Aboriginal population of 160,000. The most flourishing tongues are those of the centre and north, where European settlement was least dense.

KEY TO MAP

— Southern limit of "silhouette" art style

▲ Sacred mountain

Aboriginal people: *TIWI*

Australian federal state: QUEENSLAND

Region: *ARNHEM LAND*

▓ Route of the Seven Sisters

░ Desert area

THE BIG FLOOD

Myths of origin

A rock painting from the Victoria River District, depicting a snake (possibly the great flood serpent), together with a kangaroo, a dingo and various other designs.

Aboriginal myths about the beginning of the world deal not with the creation of the cosmos out of nothing, but with the origin and shaping of present-day environments and societies in a world which has always existed. Several peoples, especially in the tropical northern coastal region of Australia, ascribe their origins to a great flood which swept away the previous landscape and society. These myths may be rooted in fact, as there is archaeological evidence to suggest that the rising sea level that followed the last Ice Age had a massive effect on the societies of northern Australia, reflected in changes both to patterns of camping and to rock art. Western Arnhem Land rock paintings of the giant flood serpent are thought to have originated at about the time that the post-glacial sea level stabilized to create the present northern Australian shore line.

The primordial flood is ascribed to various beings, both human and animal. According to the Worora of the Kimberleys of northwestern Australia, ancestral heroes known as the *wandjina* (see p.279), caused a flood which wiped out the previous social order. The *wandjina* then dispersed, each to their own country, where they put up their paintings in rock shelters and created the new order of society. The Tiwi people of Melville and Bathurst Islands, which lie off Australia's northern coast, describe how their islands were separated from the mainland during the Creation Period or Dream Time by a blind old woman called Mudungkala, who emerged from the ground at the southeastern end of Melville Island carrying three infant children. These children were the first people, who populated the islands. As the old woman crawled across the featureless landscape, water bubbled up in her track, cutting off the islands from the mainland.

In the origin myths of a number of peoples, a great serpent associated with the rainbow is held responsible for the flood. This creature, which is believed still to exist (living in deep pools of water or in coastal whirlpools), occurs in the story of the Wawilak Sisters told by the Yolngu people of northeastern Arnhem Land. The story is typical of those in which particular ancestors are said to have travelled during the Creation Period across the land whose ownership is now divided among many clans. As is usual with such myths, the Yolngu know only that part of the journey of the Wawilak Sisters which took place in their own area. Each clan on the route possesses certain totemic animals, plants and other objects associated with the sisters and their adventures. For example, the morning star is said to rise from the place where the sisters' travels began, while the mosquito, a creature which marks the onset of the season of rain and floods, is associated with Yurlunggur, the serpent who causes a great flood in the myth.

The sisters set out from somewhere in the distant interior and travelled toward the northern coast of Arnhem Land. The younger sister was pregnant, while the elder had a child which she carried in a paper bark cradle under her arm. As they travelled, they hunted lizard, possum and bandicoot, and gathered plants to eat. They named each species of plant and animal, as well as the places through which they walked. One day they met two men with whom they had intercourse, even though they all belonged to the same division of society (see p.284). When the younger woman was ready to bear a son, her sister collected soft bark to make a bed. Unwittingly, the elder sister allowed her menstrual blood to fall into a waterhole, angering Yurlunggur, a semi-human python who lived there. Yurlunggur created a storm and a great flood. The sisters sang songs in an attempt to drive the snake away, but he swallowed them and their sons as a punishment for polluting the well.

When the flood had subsided, Yurlunggur, who had reared up above the waters, came down to earth, creating the first Yolngu initiation ground at the spot where he landed. The serpent then regurgitated the sisters and their sons, who became the first Yolngu initiates. Two other men, who had heard the storm, came to see what was happening. After learning the songs which the sisters had sung, they carried out the first Yolngu initiation ceremonies (see panel, below).

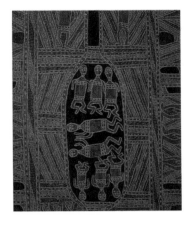

Men re-enact a Dream Time myth in song and dance. An Arnhem Land bark painting.

Reliving the Wawilak myth

The swallowing of the Wawilak Sisters and their sons is re-enacted during the initiation ceremony for adolescent Yolngu boys. Each episode of the rite, which represents a symbolic death before rebirth as an adult, is accompanied by songs which describe, in great detail, the relevant part of the myth as it unfolds. The songs form part of an extended cycle which runs to many hundreds of verses in the course of the ceremony.

Yolngu women take the role of the travelling sisters, and the accompanying songs commemorate what happened at each of the landmarks on the sisters' journey, such as waterholes and rocks.

Later in the ceremony, the men, taking the part of the serpent Yurlunggur, "swallow" the boys by sweeping them up and carry them off to the seclusion of the

sacred initiation ground, which women are forbidden from entering. When the boys return after initiation, they are regarded as having been "regurgitated" by the snake.

Although the story of the Wawilak Sisters has been the subject of extensive study by anthropologists, it is only one of a large body of myths which are of great spiritual and ritual importance to the Yolngu.

The serpent Yurlunggur, from a modern Aboriginal bark painting by Paddy Dhatangu. Yurlunggur is coiled around the Wawilak Sisters and their sons, who stand among the footprints made by the sisters in their attempts to escape from the creature.

DEATH AND MOURNING

The origins of mortality

The bark painting (above) from northeastern Arnhem Land, shows a funerary rite for three people, who are depicted lying in their graves. The circles represent the waterholes from which the spirits of children emerge, and to which the spirits of the dead return in boats which are represented by the shape of the graves. One man (in the upper right of the picture) beats a pair of clapsticks in time to the ceremonial songs which accompany the ritual. Other mourners carry paperbark baskets on their heads. The background design identifies the clan of the deceased.

Aboriginal myth treats death as the consequence of human misdeeds. It was not inevitable, and the heroic ancestral beings in the Creation Period (see p.279) had the opportunity to live for ever. However, through spite, foolishness or greed, the gift of immortality slipped beyond the grasp of humankind and was retained only by the moon, which waxes and wanes every month, and by the crab, which casts its old, battered shell to grow a new one.

According to the Worora of the Western Kimberleys, a certain Widjingara was the first person to die, killed in a battle against some *wandjina* beings (see p.279). They had wanted to steal a woman who had been promised in marriage to someone else, and Widjingara had fought to ensure that the marriage rules established by Wodoy and Djunggun (see p.284) were upheld. His body was wrapped in a bark coffin and his wife, the Black-Headed Python, began to mourn. She shaved off her hair and rubbed ashes over her head and body, thereby founding the traditional Aboriginal way of showing mourning.

When Widjingara returned from the grave, his body renewed, the Black-Headed Python was angry: "Why have you come back?" she asked. "Look at me, I've already shaved my head and made it black with ashes!" Widjingara, angry in his turn at this poor welcome from his wife, indignantly returned to the grave: he was later transformed into the native cat (*Dasyurus*), a nocturnal Australian marsupial which resembles a domestic cat. Since then, the possibility of rejuvenation has been lost. Everyone has to die, and the python perpetually has the appearance of mourning. It was Worora custom, until stopped by missionaries early in the 20th century, to lay a dead person's body on a burial platform until the flesh had decayed, whereupon the bones would be placed in a cave in the person's own region. If the burial platform was not carefully constructed, the native cat, which is the living manifestation of Widjingara, could sometimes be seen scavenging on the decaying corpse.

The Murinbata people of the northeastern Victoria River District relate how Crow and Crab argued about the best way to die. Crab said that she knew a good way, and told Crow to wait in their camp until she returned. She found a hole in the ground and, casting off her wrinkled old shell, went into the hole to wait while a new one formed. Crow grew impatient, and after a while went to see what was happening. When Crab saw him peering down the hole she told him to wait a while longer. Eventually she returned to the camp in her new shell, but Crow exclaimed: "That way takes too long. I know a quicker way to die!" He promptly rolled back his eyes and fell over backwards. "Poor Crow!" said Crab. She fetched some water and splashed it over Crow, but could not revive him, because he was dead. The Murinbata compare the different types of death chosen by Crow and Crab to the dances chosen by two dancers at a secular dance. Each dancer opts for the dance to which they are best suited, and in the same way the best way for people to die was Crow's way.

Another myth about the origin of death is found among the Tiwi of the Melville and Bathurst Islands, which lie just off the coast of Northern Territory. Although living only 15 miles (25 km) from the mainland, the Tiwi are thought to have been isolated from other Aboriginal societies for several thousands of years. According to their myth, the island was populated by the offspring of an old blind woman, Mudungkala (see p.280). Her son, Purukupali, later married (it is not clear where his wife came from) and fathered a son. Purukupali shared his camp with Tjapara, the Moon Man, an unmarried man bent on seducing Purukupali's wife. One very hot day she went with Tjapara into the forest, leaving her young son asleep in the shade of a tree. While she was away, the sun moved across the sky, exposing the infant to its rays and killing him. Purukupali was very angry, and declared that from now everyone should die. Tjapara pleaded with him, saying that if he were allowed to take the boy's body for three days he would restore him to life. Purukupali refused and, after a struggle with Tjapara, snatched up the boy's body and walked into the sea, leaving a powerful whirlpool at the place where he sank below the surface. Tjapara changed himself into the moon and rose into the sky, still bearing the scars inflicted by Purukupali as they had fought over the corpse. The rest of the original inhabitants came together to perform the first mortuary ceremony, preparing the large decorated poles now used at all Tiwi funerals (see panel, below).

Aboriginal origin myths often present first beings as the creations or offspring of a single progenitor, which makes them brothers and sisters. How, once they have lost their immortality, they can marry to beget future generations, is dealt with in various ways. Sometimes it is suggested that siblings were free to mate with each other at that time because the idea of incest was invented only later. In other myths, the primordial hero or heroine couples with another primordial being whose origin is simply unaccounted for, for example Purukupali's wife. In such cases it is not thought necessary to explain the existence of more than one first being, because the myth is deemed to be taking place in a world which is in a state of flux and therefore not bound by the conventions of the present world.

Tiwi funeral myths

The Tiwi are renowned for colourful funerary poles first erected, it is believed, following the conflict between Purukupali and Tjapara (see above).

When a Tiwi person dies, the body is buried immediately, but the funeral ritual is delayed for several months until the grief of family members has subsided. At the funeral, or *pukimani* ceremony, brightly decorated poles are erected to mark the grave, the number of poles varying with the age and status of the deceased. In an unspecific way, the poles symbolize the link between the worlds of the living and of the dead.

Ironwood pukimani *poles from a burial site on Bathurst Island. Carvers are paid according to the quality of their work.*

THE ORIGINS OF MARRIAGE

Eaglehawk and Crow; Wodoy and Djunggun

Various regional myths explain the origin of marriage. In the southeast, two men, Eaglehawk (Biljara) and Crow (Wagu), are said to have instituted marriage by specifiying the degrees of kinship within which a relationship was permissible. Crow often tried to trick Eaglehawk. In one tale, Eaglehawk was the guardian of two girls whom he forbade Crow to marry. In retaliation, Crow killed Eaglehawk's son and tried to blame someone else for the murder, but Eaglehawk knew the truth and buried Crow with his dead son. Crow escaped and the feud continued. In one account, Eaglehawk turned Crow into a crow by burning him black, and became a bird himself when Crow tricked him into soaring into the sky.

Aboriginal communities are usually divided into two halves or moieties, each associated with a participant in the original marriage myth, such as Eaglehawk or Crow. A person may marry only a member of the opposite moiety. Children belong either to the moiety of their father (as in the Kimberleys), or to that of their mother (as in the southeast).

Wodoy and Djunggun

This myth from the Western Kimberleys parallels the lowland South American myths of raw and cooked food which were interpreted by the French anthropologist Claude Lévi-Strauss (see p.13 and pp.262-3). He suggested that cooking honey is a metaphor for incest (some South American bees make such sweet honey that those who eat it wonder whether they are savouring a delicacy or burning with the fire of love).

In early times people lived without distinguishing between generations or families and incestuous relationships were commonplace. There was a man called Djunggun and another called Wodoy, who made the right way to marry, distinguishing sister from wife. They exchanged sacred wooden carvings as gifts and said, "Let us marry each other's daughters, so that we can respect each other and get along together." (In the Kimberleys to this

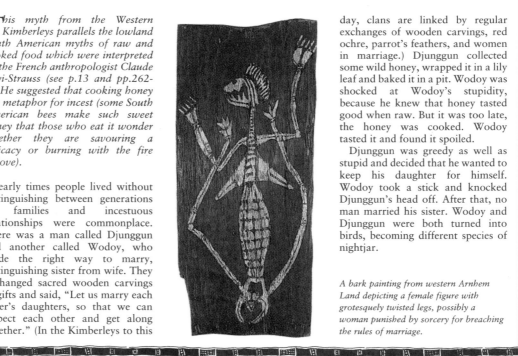

day, clans are linked by regular exchanges of wooden carvings, red ochre, parrot's feathers, and women in marriage.) Djunggun collected some wild honey, wrapped it in a lily leaf and baked it in a pit. Wodoy was shocked at Wodoy's stupidity, because he knew that honey tasted good when raw. But it was too late, the honey was cooked. Wodoy tasted it and found it spoiled.

Djunggun was greedy as well as stupid and decided that he wanted to keep his daughter for himself. Wodoy took a stick and knocked Djunggun's head off. After that, no man married his sister. Wodoy and Djunggun were both turned into birds, becoming different species of nightjar.

A bark painting from western Arnhem Land depicting a female figure with grotesquely twisted legs, possibly a woman punished by sorcery for breaching the rules of marriage.

TRICKSTERS

The ancestral order disrupted

In many parts of Australia, myths tell of trickster beings who cause unpredictable events. They may be benign, but more often they subvert the ancestral order by stealing wild foods or by leading people to steal, fight or otherwise renege upon social obligations. Some writers argue that these tricksters represent an early stratum in Aboriginal mythology, pre-dating the ancestral heroes associated with the division of society into clans.

In the Western Kimberleys, races of tricksters known as the Ngandjala-Ngandjala and Wurulu-Wurulu are said to wander through the bush looking for mischief, spoiling the caves where the ancestral heroes left paintings of themselves by putting their own paintings on top. In Aboriginal art these tricksters closely resemble one another. The Ngandjala-Ngandjala are not necessarily malevolent, because although some people claim that they spoil the harvest, others believe that they enhance it and ripen edible fruits by cooking them. During the monsoon season they can sometimes be seen in the clouds, and columns of mist rising from the bush after rain mark the camp fires where they cook their fruit. They are themselves the victims of another trickster, Unguramu, who steals edible roots as they roast in the Ngandjala-Ngandjala's fires. The Ngandjala-Ngandjala retaliate by grabbing Unguramu's tail and pulling it until he reveals where he has hidden the cooked food.

The Wurulu-Wurulu disrupt the ancestral order by finding banksia (bottle-brush) flowers and tying them to slender sticks, which they use as a tool to extract honey from wild bees' nests. If someone finds a nest empty, they know the Wurulu-Wurulu have been there first.

Another trickster of the Western Kimberleys, Argula, is associated with sorcery. In this area, anti-social behaviour may be punished by painting a distorted human figure in a rock shelter and singing insulting songs at it which, it is believed, will inflict disability or death upon the evil-doer. Sometimes these paintings are thought to be the work of Argula. Similarly, Aboriginal people attribute the ancient rock paintings of western Arnhem Land, which are thought by archaeologists to pre-date the rise in sea level after the last Ice Age, to a class of tricksters known as the *mimi*. The graceful, agile figures which appear in the paintings are said to represent these beings, who live in the cracks of the cliff face along the Arnhem Land escarpment. The *mimi* are angered if suddenly surprised by the presence of an unfamiliar person wandering through the bush. To avoid antagonizing the *mimi*, people foraging through rocky country call out to the tricksters to make them continually aware of the presence of humans. The *mimi* punish people who appear without warning by inflicting sickness upon them. Otherwise they are generally benign: for example, they taught people how to hunt. However, if a hunter comes across a wallaby that acts as if it is tame, the animal should be left well alone: it may be a pet of the *mimi*, who will kill anyone who harms it.

Other tricksters are more sinister figures. The Namorodo of western Arnhem Land, who are so thin that they consist only of skin and bones held together by sinew, are particularly feared. They travel at night, making a swishing sound as they fly through the air, and may kill with one of their long claws anyone they hear. The sick and injured are particularly vulnerable. If a dead person's spirit is captured by the Namorodo, it cannot rejoin the totemic ancestors but becomes itself a malevolent being wandering through the bush. The Namorodo are associated with shooting stars and, in bark paintings, with sorcery.

A bark painting from Arnhem Land of a group of male and female spirit beings, probably a representation of mimi *tricksters. They can sometimes be heard at night, singing or beating the rhythm of a song with clapsticks within the rocks where they dwell.*

SHAPING THE LANDSCAPE

Myths of ancestral wanderings

Central Australia is crisscrossed by the routes of many ancestral heroes, who are often said to have journeyed for hundreds of miles, some of them in human form, others travelling in the shape of kangaroos, wallabies, lizards, snakes or birds. Some, such as the Bell Bird Brothers (see panel, below), travelled no more than sixty miles (almost 100 km), and are of primarily local significance. Others, such as Malu the Red Kangaroo, who journeyed from the Kimberleys to the centre of the continent, or the Seven Sisters (see opposite), travelled for hundreds of miles, through the lands of many clans. These heroes left caves, rocks and creeks to mark the places where they camped, hunted or fought. Such landmarks are regarded as sacred and are infused with the ancestors' creative energy.

It is believed that the energy of a primordial being can be released by rubbing or striking the spot where he or she left the world and went into the ground. The ancestral being associated with a particular place is said to be reincarnated in anyone who is born there, who becomes the guardian of the sacred site.

Legends of ancestral travel often underpin regional ceremonies and strengthen the bonds between peoples speaking different languages who may need to camp together during long droughts.

The Bell Bird Brothers

The emphasis of a myth can vary according to where the story is told. The following versions of the myth of the ancestral heroes known as the Bell Bird Brothers were related in 1976, the first by Pompy Wanampi and Pompy Douglas at Wangka Arkal, the second by Paddy Uluru at Uluru (Ayers Rock).

The two Bell Bird Brothers were stalking an emu at Antalanya, a rock pool where emus still come to drink. Unknown to them, a young woman was searching for grubs nearby, at Wangka Arkal. The dome of rock is her forehead. When you call out, your voice echoes from the rock as if the girl were responding. On her head she carried a collecting dish, supported on a ring made of human hair. While feeding on the grubs, the load slipped from her head, disturb-

Transformed into this boulder, the body of Lungkata lies at the foot of Uluru, his head raised.

ing the emu, who ran north toward Uluru, chased by the brothers. At the foot of the rock, a semi-circular indentation is the girl's head pad, lying where it fell. A little further on is the pool where the emu drank.

In Paddy Uluru's version, the Blue Tongue Lizard, Lungkata, stole a fat emu from the brothers at Antalanya. Lungkata hid the meat by burying it at Uluru – it became slabs of rock – and gave the two hunters a skinny emu to eat instead. Angered at this trick, one brother set fire to Lungkata's hut, burning him alive. The smoke from the fire can be seen on the face of Uluru and Lungkata himself is a boulder (left). Paddy Uluru's father was believed to be the incarnation of Lungkata. He looked after the boulder by keeping it free of weeds and telling the myth to his own sons and other young men.

The Seven Sisters

The following story pieces together the incidents related at a few of the places along the route through central and southern Australia (see map, p.279) of the ancestral heroines known simply as Kungarankalpa, the Seven Sisters.

The Seven Sisters fled south to escape a lustful man named Nyiru, who was planning to rape the oldest of them. East of Uluru their route is marked by a string of claypans and rock pools. At Witapula, west of Atila (Mount Conner), they stopped to camp for the night and built a windbreak, which is now a low cliff.

Next morning they dived into the ground, re-emerging at Tjuntalitja, a well. A sandhill nearby records the place from which Nyiru watched them. From Tjuntalitja the girls walked to Wanukula, a rock hole (a depression in rock where water collects), and on to Walinya, a hill, where they built a hut and camped again. Their hut is now a cave in a grove of

wild fig trees, one of which, standing apart, is the oldest sister. Where they sat is recorded by swirling lines in the rock. Nyiru watched them from a pile of boulders and, when he thought they were asleep, burst into their shelter, gouging the rock as he did so. A low opening at the back of the cave marks where the sisters broke through the wall to continue their flight.

Finally, when they reached the coast (near Port Augusta), the girls plunged into the sea. The shock of the cold water caused them to leap into the sky, becoming the constellation Kurialya, the Pleiades. Nyiru chases them still, and his footprint can be seen in the sky: his toes are the "belt" in the constellation others call Orion, his heel the tip of Orion's "sword".

Bush Potato Dreaming, a modern bark painting by Victor Jupurrulla Ross. It depicts marks left in the landscape by ancestral heroes. Arcs represent people sitting on the ground, and circles are sites imbued with the power of the ancestors.

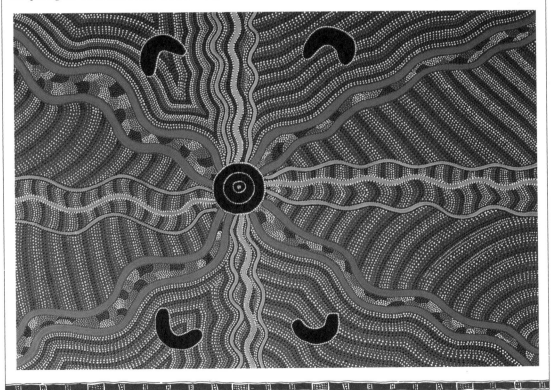

OCEANIA

*A reconstruction of a cult house built to commemorate fourteen
ancestors in the village of Medina on the island of New Ireland,
Papua New Guinea. The figures are carved in a style called*
malanggan *after the local mortuary rituals in which they are used.
The style is noted for its technical skill, range of colours,
and mythological motifs.*

Oceania comprises three distinct regions – Melanesia, Micronesia and Polynesia – which are home to an extraordinary diversity of languages and cultures. Before contact with Europeans, societies ranged from the small populations of Papua, numbering as few as 300 and grouped into patriarchal clans with no institutionalized leadership or social ranking, to the large, complex societies of New Zealand and Hawaii, with elaborate political and religious hierarchies and divine lineages of ruling chiefs.

In Melanesia there is no distinct and recurring hierarchy of gods, unlike in Polynesia, where something closer to a pantheon can be said to exist (see p.294). It would be inaccurate to label as "gods" the important culture heroes who are said to have journeyed around the southern part of New Guinea bringing the customs of mortality, sex, mourning and warfare to humans (see p.290). Secret cosmogonic myths, known only to initiates, feature in the societies of coastal Melanesian peoples such as those of the Massim

area of New Guinea. Myths told in the interior of New Guinea serve principally as examples of moral and cosmological dilemmas, expressed in allegorical, otherworldly terms.

Several important themes recur in mythology throughout the entire region: for example, the idea that the actions of ancestral culture heroes remain alive and effective among their living human descendants.

The context in which myths are told varies throughout Oceania. Traditionally, they have found their most vivid and meaningful expression in ritual, through which the "work of the gods" is celebrated. This is particularly the case in Polynesia, especially among the Hawaiians and Maori: the rituals of sacrifice to the gods Lono and Ku in pre-colonial Hawaii (see p.296) are the best examples. Micronesian myths are usually related for entertainment, outside a ritual context. Melanesia is a mixed area in this respect: myths generally have a more serious purpose in coastal regions than in the interior.

TIME CHART

*c.*2000 BC Immigrants from Indonesia begin to settle Melanesia

*c.*1300 BC Settlers reach Fiji, later spreading to western Polynesia via Tonga and Samoa

*c.*300 BC Eastern Polynesia settled

*c.*850 AD First settlers reach New Zealand from eastern Polynesia

*c.*1000-1300 All major Polynesian island groups are settled

1513 First sighting of the Pacific by a European, the Spanish explorer Vasco Nunez de Balboa

1768-79 Three voyages of the English explorer Captain James Cook (1768-71, 1772-5 and 1776-9) complete the main work of European discovery in the Oceanic region

A detail (right) of a malanggan *carving from a vertical frieze found in New Ireland. Such objects were grouped on a decorated platform to honour the dead. The carvings were sometimes made by members of the dead person's clan.*

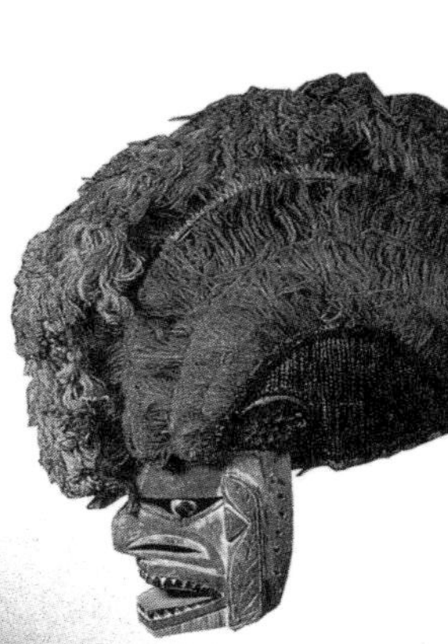

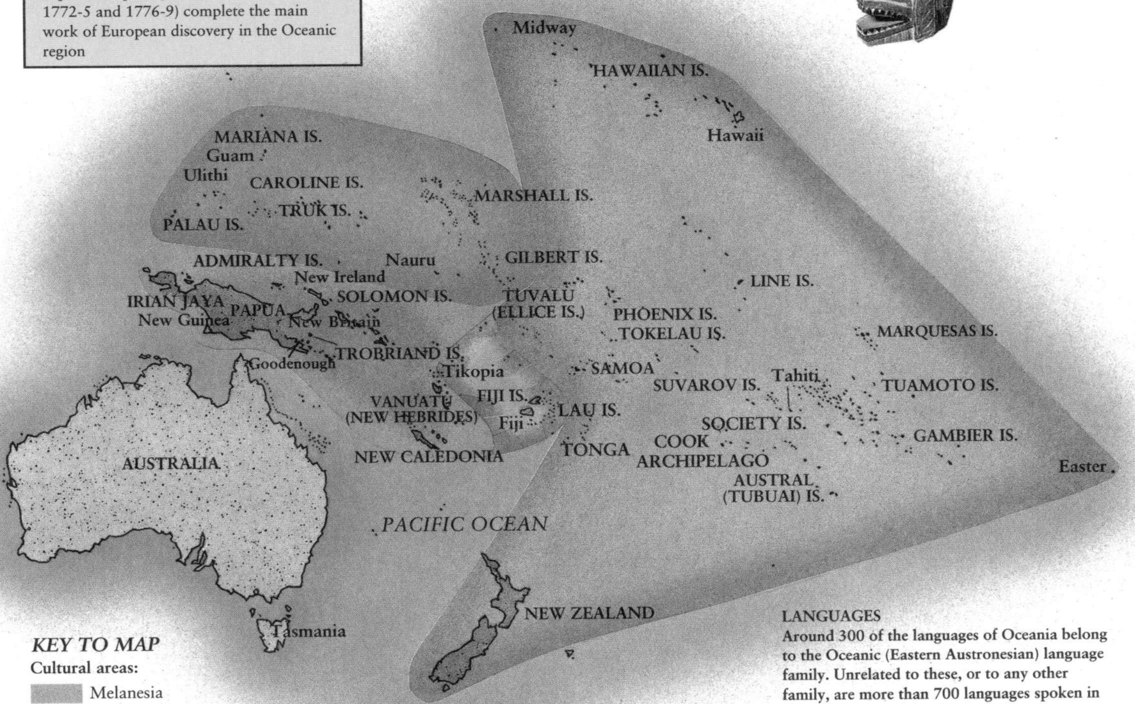

KEY TO MAP

Cultural areas:

Melanesia

Micronesia

Polynesia

Area of mixed Melanesian-Polynesian culture

Island group: VANUATU (NEW HEBRIDES)

Island: Tahiti

LANGUAGES

Around 300 of the languages of Oceania belong to the Oceanic (Eastern Austronesian) language family. Unrelated to these, or to any other family, are more than 700 languages spoken in Papua New Guinea – nearly a quarter of all the world's known tongues. Oceania's languages range from those with hundreds of thousands of speakers, such as Fijian (260,000 speakers), Samoan (200,000) and Maori (100,000), to those with just a few hundred, such as many Papuan languages and Hawaiian, which was once spoken by around 100,000 people.

MICRONESIA

Micronesia, which has the smallest population of Oceania's three regions, includes the Caroline, Marshall and Mariana Islands, and Kiribati (principally the Gilbert and Phoenix Islands). Many Micronesian societies have important myths which recount the arrival of foreigners from across the sea who defeat the indigenous inhabitants and become the ruling élite. These stories explain the present-day division of societies into ruling and commoner lineages.

MELANESIA

This region includes Papua New Guinea and the islands of the southwest Pacific as far east as Fiji. Melanesian myths sometimes relate the origin of humanity, from an animal or plant or a feature of the landscape. However, more often they take as their starting point the unstated assumption that humanity has always existed and has no origin: the present order was established by ancestral culture heroes as they wandered through the landscape (see p.290).

POLYNESIA

Polynesia is the largest region of Oceania and includes, most importantly, the island groups of Hawaii and New Zealand. To a much greater extent than Micronesia and Melanesia, the region furnishes a rich fund of cosmological myths, of which the Maori stories of the male Sky (Rangi) and female Earth (Papa) are perhaps the best known (see pp.294-5). As in Micronesian societies, myths of the arrival of strangers from the sea are also important.

MYTHS OF ORIGIN

Creator gods and culture heroes

A painted wooden ritual mask from the Torres Strait Islands. It represents an ancestral culture hero, probably Sida.

The most important Oceanic myths relating the creation or origin of the world occur mainly in Polynesia and Micronesia. Of the many myths from these regions describing the primordial separation of the heavens and the earth, the most widely known is the mainly Polynesian account of the forcing apart of the deities Sky and Earth to release their children (see p.294). This theme also occurs in Micronesia, for example in the Gilbert Islands, Kiribati, where the primordial deity Nareau is said to have persuaded an eel to separate the sky and earth. In nearby Nauru the primordial Spider, Areop-enap, found a clamshell and asked a shellfish to prise it open. The shellfish only partly succeeded, so Areop-enap asked a caterpillar to help. The caterpillar opened the shell but exerted itself so much that its salty sweat formed a pool in the bottom of the clamshell and it died from exhaustion. The raised top part of the shell became the sky and the dead caterpillar became the sun. Its sweat is the sea, while the shellfish became the moon.

Melanesian origin myths rarely deal with the creation of the world and humanity by primal deities. More characteristic are myths about how the landscape and the original conditions for society were established by ancestral culture heroes who wandered the earth. Similar myths are told in Australia (see p.286), and they may have been brought from here to Papua New Guinea. On the south coast of Papua, along the Fly and Purari Rivers, and in the mountainous interior, many myths relate the wanderings of a male culture hero called variously Sido, Sosom, Soido, Souw and other related names. Each local community claims this hero as its own, but also recognizes that he left its territory behind and had further adventures among other peoples. His journey can be traced in a series of geographical features which he made as he travelled through the landscape: in one place he cut a pass through a ridge, in another he urinated and left a small lake, and so on.

In most places, the hero's adventures are part of a secret male cult and are disclosed only to initiates on ceremonial occasions. He is portrayed as exaggeratedly male, with a very long penis, and the stories told of him all describe how he was shamed by women as a result of his desire for sexual intercourse. This shame caused him to curse humankind, which had been immortal until that time, with death. The Daribi relate how a young woman comes across a snake which turns out to be Souw's penis. It tries to enter her but she cries out in fear and it withdraws. Angry at being shamed in this way, Souw visits death, warfare and sorcery upon humanity. Afterwards, however, he travels into the highlands and leaves hairs which became dogs and pigs, so that the people there have many domestic animals. In many areas the hero is also said to have given people stocks of fish and the first vegetable crops.

A culture hero, carved in one of the many distinctive styles of the Sepik River region of New Guinea. Brightly painted decoration is believed to enhance a sculpture's magical power.

Voices of the spirits

All over Oceania, sound-producing instruments figure prominently in traditional religion and mythology. The sounds they create are often believed to be the voices of the beings or gods who were responsible for creation and the current order of society.

In Hawaii the most sacred inner part of many temple complexes is the drum house, containing the "god's drums". These are employed to summon people to the temple, to send messages, to signal changes in posture during ceremonies, and, formerly, to consecrate human sacrifices. In Melanesia, a variety of sound-producing instruments is central to most traditional secret male rituals and their associated myths. These instruments include the bullroarer, an elliptical piece of wood with a hole in one end through which string is threaded: it is whirled around the head to produce a very loud whining drone, believed to be the voice of the spirit. The bullroarer and its mythology probably travelled from central Australia through Northern Territory, across the Torres Strait and into the interior of Papua New Guinea. They were said to have been brought by the same culture heroes described on the opposite page.

In male initiation rituals, the sound of the bullroarer is used to frighten the young initiates, and its phallic appearance makes it an appropriate symbol for the assertion of male identity. Indeed, among the Kiwai of southern Papua, the word for the bullroarer is *madubu*, which means "I am a man". Among the Marind-anim and, further east, the people of the Trans-Fly area, the bullroarer was formerly associated with homosexual initiation, carried out to give boys the extra amounts of semen they were thought to need in order to grow into proper adult men. The name of the Trans-Fly bullroarer being is Tokijenjeni, which connects the instrument to another adult male activity: it also denotes the war club used on head-hunting raids. According to local myth, Tokijenjeni was the son of Tiv'r, the Trans-Fly culture hero. Tiv'r heard a faint roaring from something in his wife's belly and

sent different birds to try to extract it. They all failed, until one bird managed to seize the object while Tiv'r's wife was bending over with her legs apart. It turned out to be the first bullroarer.

The bullroarer appears as far north as Lake Kutubu in the southern highlands of Papua New Guinea. Further north still, in the central highlands, the traditional phallic ritual instrument is the flute. Transverse flutes are associated with male initiation all over the central highlands, especially in the east, where the cult achieved its greatest elaboration. They were blown only by men on specific ritual occasions and always in seclusion. The existence of the flutes and their identity was the men's most closely guarded secret. However, many myths of these societies recount how the flutes were originally the property of women. The men either stole them or tricked women into giving them up, after which women were forbidden all knowledge of the sacred instruments. In former times, it is said, men would kill a woman who so much as looked upon one of the sacred flutes.

Not all myths about sacred instruments are serious in tone. Throughout Melanesia, humorous stories are told of an ugly man who becomes handsome only when he plays the flute or jew's harp at public ceremonies, which he does with great skill. He attracts young women from all around, one of whom eventually discovers his secret.

This elaborately decorated drum, from the Sepik River region, bears the image of an ancestral spirit who is manifested in both human and bird forms.

MYTHS OF THE SKY

Human and heavenly realms

THE SUN AND THE MOON

In many parts of the world the moon is associated with femininity and the menstrual cycle, but in Oceania it is more common for the moon to be represented as male and the sun as female. The moon and the sun are looked on as brother and sister in much of inland New Guinea, because the moon allows men to hunt by night with their dogs, while women's work takes place chiefly during the day. The moon is also male in Maori mythology. In one story, a male deity, Rona, goes to the moon to look for his wife, who has gone missing. When he arrives he starts a fight with the moon which has never ended: the two spend the entire time attacking and eating each other, which is why the moon wanes every month. When it waxes, the two combatants are said to be recovering their strength for the next bout of fighting.

Stories of traffic between the earth and the sky are an important part of Oceanic mythology, particularly in Micronesia and Melanesia. In Melanesia, myths involving sky beings are common, especially in the central Papuan highlands. The Kewa believe that sky beings are usually detached from the affairs of earthly mortals, but that sky women sometimes come to earth to dig up red ochre for body decoration. Thunder, mist, cloud and lightning herald the descent of these beings to earth, and Kewa people avoid venturing into the forest in such circumstances.

Birds of magical or spiritual significance often feature in sky myths. In one Melanesian story, a young man shoots a bird of paradise, which flies away with his arrow. He follows it and discovers a path to a village in the sky, where, on the veranda of the village longhouse, a man is extracting a thorn from his foot. The hunter realizes that this man is the bird he has shot. In other myths, a man thinks he has killed a brightly coloured bird, only to discover that it is really a young woman, whom he then marries.

Iolofath or Olifat, Micronesia's most renowned trickster, features prominently in the region's sky myths. On Ulithi Atoll, a story is told about a woman who bears a child, Thilefial, by a man from Lang, the sky realm. He is mistreated on earth by his mother's elder sister, and returns to the sky, where Iolofath, the sun, adopts him. Thilefial makes one last visit to earth, in order to take his revenge on his mother's sister. He kills her with a spear and goes back to Iolofath.

A painted wood malanggan *carving of a mythical sky being in the form of a bird, from northwestern New Ireland.*

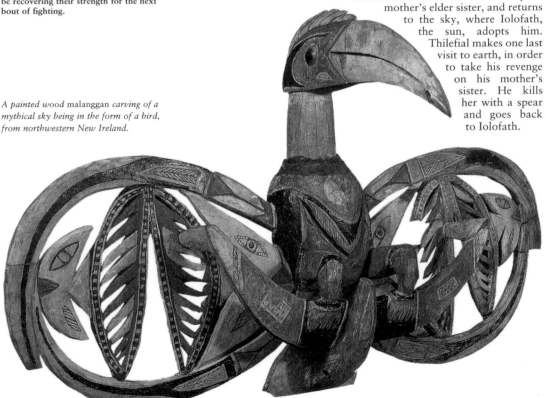

FOOD AND FERTILITY

Sex and the origins of horticulture

In most Oceanic societies the sexual and domestic relations between men and women underlie many myths about the origins of food and gardening. A myth sung at the Tongan *kava* ceremony (a ritual performed on important occasions, during which the euphoria-inducing drink *kava* is consumed) relates how an eel has intercourse with Hina, a noblewoman whose virginity is revered and protected by the community. When she becomes pregnant and tells her people what has happened, they capture the eel, cut it into pieces and eat it all except for the head, which Hina keeps and buries. From the head sprouts the first coconut.

Melanesian myths often relate how plants grow from ground made fertile by semen or menstrual blood. In one story, Soido, the culture hero of Kiwai Island off southern Papua, tries to have sex with a woman, but his penis is so large that he kills her in the attempt. He then ejaculates and shakes semen over the island. Where it lands, all the different vegetables grow. The people of Kiwai also tell of a man who makes a hole in the ground and copulates with it, unwittingly impregnating an underground spirit woman. She gives birth to the first yams (see also panel, below).

The origin of yams

The sweet potato or yam is one of the most common staple foods of the Oceanic region. The following myths give two very different accounts of its origin.

The Maori relate how the god Rongo-maui went up to heaven to his brother Wahnui, who was the keeper of the sweet potato or yam. Rongo-maui hid it in his loincloth and then returned to earth and made his wife, Pani, pregnant. She later gave birth to the first earthly yam, which was given to humans.

A myth which is widespread over a large area of the interior of New Guinea tells how once, when there were no foodstuffs on earth, a young woman and an old woman saw a man defecate in a creek. After he had left, they examined his excrement and found that there were sweet potatoes in it, which they took home with them and planted.

A Maori stone figure of a god in yam form, probably Rongo-maui. Its imagery is both phallic and uterine, reflecting the sexual element in the yam origin myth.

MYTHS OF THE MAORI

Rangi, Papa and the Polynesian pantheon

A sculpture in volcanic rock from northern Taranaki on New Zealand's North Island. It probably represents the god Maui.

A distinctive feature of Maori and other outer Polynesian mythology is the grouping of gods into something resembling a pantheon. At its head are the two supreme creator beings, Rangi, the male sky, and Papa, the female earth, who in the beginning, according to Maori cosmology, were locked together in the primordial void in a static embrace. Between them were trapped their offspring, the gods Tane, Tangaroa, Tu, Rongo, Haumia and Tawhiri, who sought a means of escape and debated killing their parents to achieve this. But Tane, the god of the forests and trees, suggested that it was better to pull the sky and earth apart. Accordingly, each god attempted to separate Rangi and Papa. Rongo, the god of cultivated foods, tried but failed, as did Tangaroa, the god of the sea, fish and reptiles. Haumia, the god of wild vegetables and plants, Tu, the god of war, and Tawhiri, the god of the winds and other elements, also failed, until only Tane had yet to try. Putting his head against the mother earth and his feet against the father sky, he strained and pushed and gradually separated the two, who assumed their present positions.

Tane's success caused jealousy and anger among his siblings. Tawhiri caused the winds to blow and created storms and hurricanes which brought down the trees of Tane's forest. The fish, who used to live not in the sea but in the forest, fled in confusion to the ocean of Tangaroa. Tane became angry at losing his progeny in this way. Tane and Tangaroa have continued to quarrel to this day – Tangaroa of the sea seeks to overwhelm the forests of the land, while Tane's trees provide the canoes with which men can tame the sea and sail upon it.

Later, Tane sought a mate for himself. He first approached his mother, Papa, who refused him, and then mated with various beings to produce a

Maori myth and architecture

*I*n Maori myth the sky realm has twelve terraces, on the highest of which stands the divine dwelling-house, Rangi-atea. It is the model for the dwellings of the Maori ruling chiefs. The carved panels on these houses have great ritual and mythological significance.

The Maoris believe that a god called Rua was the first to attempt decorative carving. The figures on Maori carved panels have characteristically staring eyes like those of an owl: Rongo, the craftsman who is said to have originated this architectural feature, sacrificed an owl to the gods and planted it under the back wall of the house. The figures also have protruding tongues and heavily incised, tattooed bodies. The tongues draw attention to the power of speech, and the tattoo patterns indicate the figure's social rank.

The carving of panels such as this lintel from the house of a Maori chief involves magical formulas and techniques vouchsafed only to the class of architects who serve the chiefs.

diversity of offspring, such as animals, stones, grass and creeks. But Tane desired a mate in human form, like himself, so he took Papa's advice and fashioned the first human, a woman, from the sand of Hawaiki Island. He breathed life into her and she became Hine-hau-one, the "Earth-created maiden", who bore a daughter called Hine-titama, "Dawn maiden", whom he also took as a wife. Hine-titama did not know that Tane was her father, and when she discovered the truth she fled to the dark underworld realm. Tane pursued her, but she called out to him that he had severed the cord of the world. Henceforth, she would remain in the dark underworld and pull his children down to death: this is how humankind became mortal. Hine-hau-one thus has a dual nature as the source of the first human birth and the first human death.

Tu had originally suggested killing Rangi and Papa rather than separating them. Called Ku in Hawaii (see p.296), Tu is the god of war to whom human sacrifices were once made in New Zealand and throughout the other Polynesian kingdoms. Tawhiri now turned his anger towards Tu, who nevertheless withstood the wrath of his brother. Tu in turn sought revenge against all his brothers, who refused to aid him in his struggle against Tawhiri. To this end, Tu created animal and fish traps to snare the progeny of Tangaroa and Tane; and he uprooted the plants which were the offspring of Haumia and Rongo and ate them. Tu learned many magical spells and incantations in order to control his brothers' offspring, who were the weather, plants, animals, wealth and other possessions.

In Maori myth there are also human heroes, the best known of whom are Tawhaki and Rata, whose exploits are part of the mythology of New Zealand, Tuomotu, Rarotonga, Tahiti and Hawaii.

Hema – the son of a sky goddess, Kaintangata, and a cannibal chief, Whaitiri – marries a goddess who gives birth to two brothers, Tawhaki and Kariki. Hema is killed by ogres and Tawhaki journeys to where his father was slain in order to avenge his killing. The episodes surrounding this adventure form the main part of the myth cycle. Many of them contrast the noble and successful Tawhaki with the awkward and foolish Kariki, and the theme of contrasting brothers is common throughout Oceanic myth. Along the way, Tawhaki finds a wife and fathers Wahieroa, who in turn sires Rata. Rata is destined to search for his father, who in the end is killed out of jealousy by the lizard guards of his enemy, Puna.

Rata is courageous and strong like Whaitiri, but lacks his grandfather's balanced judgment, and his impetuousness causes trouble for Tawhaki. Eventually Rata recovers his father's head from the belly of Matuku, the great shark, and the rest of his body from the lizard monsters who had played their part in his death. Returning home, Rata meets the same fate: he is hacked to death by Puna's lizard guards.

A wooden carving of the god Tangaroa, from the Austral or Tubuai Islands, where he is known as A'a. He is depicted in the act of creating other deities.

The open mouth of this statue on a meeting-house in Rotorua, North Island, reflects its role as a place of discussion.

The Maori pantheon

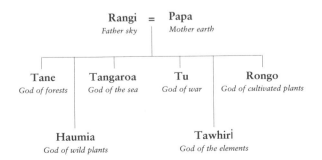

Rangi = Papa
Father sky   *Mother earth*

Tane	Tangaroa	Tu	Rongo
God of forests	*God of the sea*	*God of war*	*God of cultivated plants*

Haumia
God of wild plants

Tawhiri
God of the elements

KU AND LONO

The Hawaiian ritual cycle

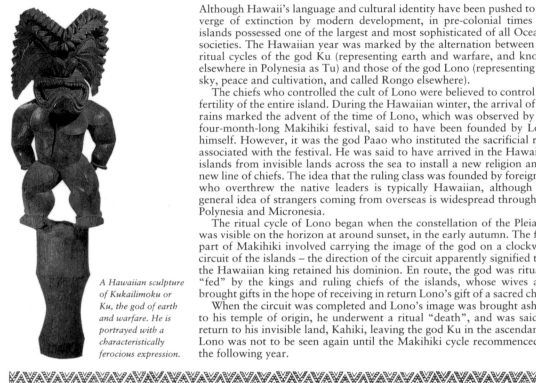

A Hawaiian sculpture of Kukailimoku or Ku, the god of earth and warfare. He is portrayed with a characteristically ferocious expression.

Although Hawaii's language and cultural identity have been pushed to the verge of extinction by modern development, in pre-colonial times the islands possessed one of the largest and most sophisticated of all Oceanic societies. The Hawaiian year was marked by the alternation between the ritual cycles of the god Ku (representing earth and warfare, and known elsewhere in Polynesia as Tu) and those of the god Lono (representing the sky, peace and cultivation, and called Rongo elsewhere).

The chiefs who controlled the cult of Lono were believed to control the fertility of the entire island. During the Hawaiian winter, the arrival of the rains marked the advent of the time of Lono, which was observed by the four-month-long Makihiki festival, said to have been founded by Lono himself. However, it was the god Paao who instituted the sacrificial rites associated with the festival. He was said to have arrived in the Hawaiian islands from invisible lands across the sea to install a new religion and a new line of chiefs. The idea that the ruling class was founded by foreigners who overthrew the native leaders is typically Hawaiian, although the general idea of strangers coming from overseas is widespread throughout Polynesia and Micronesia.

The ritual cycle of Lono began when the constellation of the Pleiades was visible on the horizon at around sunset, in the early autumn. The first part of Makihiki involved carrying the image of the god on a clockwise circuit of the islands – the direction of the circuit apparently signified that the Hawaiian king retained his dominion. En route, the god was ritually "fed" by the kings and ruling chiefs of the islands, whose wives also brought gifts in the hope of receiving in return Lono's gift of a sacred child.

When the circuit was completed and Lono's image was brought ashore to his temple of origin, he underwent a ritual "death", and was said to return to his invisible land, Kahiki, leaving the god Ku in the ascendancy. Lono was not to be seen again until the Makihiki cycle recommenced in the following year.

Lono and the death of Captain Cook

It has been suggested by some scholars that the Lono myth was behind the death of the English navigator Captain James Cook, who was the first European to visit the Hawaiian islands.

Cook arrived off the islands in November 1778, just as Lono's circuit was due to begin, and circumnavigated Hawaii Island in a clockwise direction. The Hawaiians assumed that this year Lono had come in person, and when Cook came ashore at Kealakekua he was immediately escorted to the main temple of Lono. Cook went along with his hosts' efforts to teach him certain ritual responses, unaware that they represented the words of Lono and confirmed the belief that he was the god. When Lono was due to "die" and depart for Kahiki, the chiefs were reassured when Cook communicated that his departure was imminent. However, shortly after leaving, Cook decided to return to Kealakekua to repair one of his ships. He arrived on February 11, 1779, to find the Hawaiians first bewildered, then angry and abusive, because Lono was supposed to be dead. One hundred chiefs, all anxious to ensure that their god died as he should do, killed "Lono" with the iron daggers that he had given them just a few months earlier.

MAUI

Oceania's trickster hero

Perhaps the best known of Oceanic mythological beings is Maui, a Polynesian trickster and culture hero whose actions, accidentally or otherwise, undo the efforts of others and lead to the present-day state of things. He is a rebel, a seducer and a toppler of established hierarchies. Maui flouted the conventions of the strict social order and the customs of tapu (taboo); he represented the power of the weak over the mighty, and of the commoner and outcast over the privileged.

Maui was born prematurely. In the version of the myth told on Arawa atoll, his mother wrapped him in a lock of her hair and threw him into the surf, but he was saved by the sun, or Tama of the Sky, and was eventually reunited with his mother. One of Maui's first feats was to slow down the journey of the sun by beating it with the enchanted jawbone of his dead grandmother, in order to give his mother more daylight to make tapa (bark) cloth. Elsewhere in Polynesia, people say that Maui did this to give people more time to cook their food.

Like Souw and Sosom in Melanesia, Maui is involved in humanity's loss of immortality, which revolves around an incident of sexual shaming. Maui travels to the underworld and comes upon Hine-Nui-Te-Po, the giant goddess of the underworld and of death, as she sleeps. He orders his companions, the birds, to be silent as he strips off his clothes and attempts to force himself inside the goddess, certain that this way he will defeat death. However, one of the birds is unable to refrain from laughing at the sight of Maui half-trapped within the giant deity, who wakes up and kills him. The version of this story told on Arawa relates how Maui's own father tricks him into believing that if he enters the sleeping goddess through her vagina and emerges from her mouth he will attain immortality. Again, a bird laughs while Maui is forcing his way into the goddess, who wakes up and kills him, crushing him inside her body. In both accounts the result is the same: because of Maui's transgression, humans are never able to achieve immortality.

Maui is not always a subversive character. He is also said to have created the land (that is, islands), which he hauled up from beneath the ocean with his fishing line. In a version of this story told in the Tuomotuan archipelago, Maui joined his brothers on a deep-sea expedition. They fished for a long time without success and decided to go to sleep, and as they dozed Maui let out his fishing line.

When the brothers awoke, they hauled in Maui's line, only to discover that it had caught a fish so huge that they cried out in astonishment: "It is not a fish, but an island!" With that, the fish broke the line and was lost. The same thing happened once again, but the next time Maui was able to grab part of the fish's body, which became Hawaiki island, or Te-ika-a-Maui, the Fish of Maui (the island is said to be shaped like a stingray). The canoe used in this exploit is believed to be beached on the top of the highest mountain of the island, Mount Hikurangi. Maui's fish-hook became the Bay of Hawke.

One of Maui's other accomplishments was to steal fire for humans from its keeper, the ancestor-heroine Mahui-ike, who lived in the underworld. He tricked her into relinquishing her burning fingernails, the source of fire, one by one, until she had only one left, which she flung to the ground, starting a blaze. Maui called upon the rain to put the fire out, but Mahui-ike saved a few sparks by throwing them onto the trees. As a result of this action, people knew that they could use wood to make fire.

This Maori carving of Maui, the great trickster and culture hero of Oceanic mythology, depicts him pulling up the land, represented by a fish, from the sea for humans to live on.

CARGO CULTS

The European impact

Souvenir objects bearing the portrait of Prince Philip, the Duke of Edinburgh, husband of Queen Elizabeth II. They come from Tanna Island in Vanuatu, where the prince is the focus of a cargo cult.

Contact with Europeans and their civilization led in Oceania to the spontaneous creation of new myths and the alteration of existing ones to account for the Europeans' place in the cosmos. What most impressed Melanesians and others about the newcomers from overseas was the staggering amount of material goods they brought with them in their ships. New Guineans and others concluded that Europeans were fated to carry their culture around with them, and "cargo" became the pidgin word *kago*, meaning "goods", "belongings" or "wealth".

Melanesians believed that Westerners must possess particularly effective magic and ritual to acquire such wealth, and started "cargo cults" in an attempt to acquire this lore for themselves. Typically, it was believed that the *kago* would be brought by an ancestor, god or other revered figure (sometimes even the European or American masters of the local colonial overlord), whose arrival would herald a new age of plenty, justice and, some hoped, freedom from foreign control. Consequently, cargo cults were generally persecuted by colonial authorities.

During the Second World War, many believed that the Japanese had been sent by God to help defeat the Europeans, so that the indigenous peoples could take control of the secret sources of *kago*. The people of Vanuatu, who were converted to Christianity before the war, had formerly believed in a being named Karaperamun, from whom everything in life derived. In 1940 they began withdrawing from church and reviving traditional customs, because they had heard that a man named "John Frum", an incarnation of Karaperamun, had come to bring a new age of *kago*. One night, a man stood up during a traditional ceremony and announced he was a manifestation of John Frum. He claimed that there would be a natural disaster, following which a powerful kingdom would emerge, the land would flatten out and become more fruitful, sickness and old age would disappear, and toil cease. The Europeans would leave and John Frum would give money to everyone according to their needs.

An unexploded Second World War bomb, hanging up in a hut in the Solomon Islands as a cargo cult object. Wartime air raids were believed by many islanders to presage the new age of kago.

Many aeroplanes flew over Vanuatu in the following year as the war in the Pacific intensified; it was widely believed that these were the vessels bringing the *kago* and the promised new age. Since that time individuals have regularly claimed to be John Frum, bearer of the secrets of *kago*. However, modern development has gradually led Melanesians to realize that people can gain access to *kago* goods only through labouring for them on the Europeans' own economic terms.

MYTH AND MAGIC

Living myth on Goodenough Island

The Kalauna of Goodenough Island in Papua New Guinea possess a class of myths, *neineya*, which contain their most important magical formulas, necessary for weather control, crop fertility, gardening prowess, and the suppression of hunger. *Neineya* stories can be narrated publicly only if the speaker omits the secret names, spells and other information of magical significance.

Such myths are the property of individual men, the pre-eminent magicians of the different Kalauna clans, who pass them on to their heirs. These men, the *toitavealata* ("those who look after the village"), take on the personalities of the mythical characters themselves. But in addition to using their sorcery to promote the collective welfare of the community, they also use it against their enemies by invoking the dark magic of gluttony (*tufo'a*) and famine (*loka*). The origin of these evils is attributed to a mythical serpent deity called Honoyeta. He would send his two wives off to work each day and, while they were gone, he would shed his skin and become a handsome young man. One of the wives discovered Honoyeta's secret and destroyed his snake's skin. In revenge the serpent deity brought humans drought, hunger and death.

Cannibalism

The competitive abutu *exchanges, in which modern Goodenough Islanders challenge each other to present the largest gifts of garden produce, began as a ritual to satisfy the appetite of Malaveyoyo, a voracious cannibal who is said to have roamed the interior of the island. The islanders believed that if they gave Malaveyovo enough vegetables to eat, he would not need to eat humans. Cannibalism occurs in mythology throughout Oceania and is characterized by a strong theme of intersexual hostility.*

In Papua New Guinea, many stories revolve around the male hero pursuing a woman, or a game animal, to a region beyond that of human habitation, only to find himself in a land of cannibals. His

successful attempts to extricate himself from the clutches of such cannibals constitute the heart of these myths. In Polynesia, tales of cannibalistic women are known from Tahiti and the Chatham Islands just east of New Zealand. One Tahitian myth recounts the story of the female ancestress "Rona long-teeth", whose daughter Hina grew into a lovely young woman and fell in love with a man called Monoi. Rona, however, trapped Monoi and ate him. Hina then enlisted the aid of the "hairy chief" No'ahuruhuru to put an end to the rapacious cannibal.

A basket once used to present a Fijian chief with cooked human flesh. Cannibalism persisted until modern times in Melanesia and Polynesia.

SOUTHEAST ASIA

*The Pura Beji temple at Sangsit on the island of Bali. The Balinese
practise a version of Hinduism which is mixed with Buddhist
and indigenous Malay beliefs.*

Southeast Asia is one of the most culturally diverse regions of the world, and its mythology reflects many layers of cultural heritage. Hinduism, disseminated throughout the region since ancient times, was overlaid in Laos, Thailand, Vietnam and Kampuchea (Cambodia) from the 14th century by the doctrines of Theravada Buddhism. After its arrival in Java in about 1600, Islam became the predominant religion of insular Southeast Asia, where it has been strongly influenced by Hinduism and Buddhism, and by the older animistic beliefs still practised in the region's more isolated inland areas.

In spite of this religious diversity, certain recurrent ideas give Southeast Asian mythology its distinctive character. The most general is the concept that the universe has many layers, usually seven above this world and seven below it (see p.303). The layers of society are often said to be modelled on the structure of the universe, an idea developed most elaborately in eastern Indonesia. The concept of the unity of all forms of life is present in some degree throughout the region, most explicitly in the beliefs of the aboriginal peoples of Borneo and Malaya (see p.305). Underlying the world of appearances is said to be an all-pervasive spirit force, which permits metamorphoses from human form to animal or even plant form, and vice versa.

For many aboriginal peoples, the human head is a special repository of spiritual power. Head-hunting is frequently practised in these cultures: it is believed that warriors who capture the heads of their enemies substantially augment their own spirit power.

Apart from city dwellers, scattered groups of nomadic cultivators and remote forest-dwelling hunter-gatherers in Malaysia, Thailand, Borneo and the Philippines, the vast majority of people live in villages and depend on wet-rice cultivation. This fact is reflected in the widespread myths about rice (see p.307).

PEOPLE AND LANGUAGES

The earliest inhabitants of Southeast Asia appear to have been Negrito groups which migrated into the region from further north by *c.*23000BC, and are related to Australia's aboriginal peoples. Their descendants live as hunter-gatherers in remote forest areas in the interior of Malaysia, Thailand, Borneo and the Philippines. Much later, from *c.*2500BC, further waves of immigrants from the north spread through mainland Southeast Asia and into the islands, where their language group, the western branch of the Austronesian (formerly called Malayo-Polynesian) family, is now dominant. As a result of further migrations speakers of Austronesian, Austro-Asiatic, Tai and Sino-Tibetan languages are in the majority on the mainland (see map below). In modern times there has been substantial immigration of Chinese-speakers into Malaysia, Borneo and the Philippines.

KEY TO MAP

Main language groups:

- Predominantly Austro-Asiatic (including Vietnamese, Khmer)
- Predominantly Austronesian (including Malay, Indonesian, Pilipino)
- Tai (including Thai, Lao)
- Sino-Tibetan (including Chinese, Burmese)
- Mixed Austro-Asiatic/Tai
- ········· Present-day frontier
- Region, island or island group: *JAVA*
- Present-day country: LAOS
- People: *DUSUN*

MYTH AND PERFORMANCE

The dramatization of myths has been most highly developed on the islands of Bali and Java in Indonesia. On Bali, masked dancers regularly enact the struggle between the good demon king, Barong, and the evil queen of the witches, Rangda (see p.306). A form of ritual drama which is particularly important on Java is the *wayang* or shadow theatre, in which elaborately fashioned puppets are manipulated behind an illuminated screen. Although shadow theatre is found in many parts of Southeast Asia, it is only on Java that it has become an important medium for expressing religious or mystical ideas. The technique is believed to have originated in India in the 10th century, which probably explains why the favourite subjects of Javanese shadow plays are drawn from the great epics of Hindu mythology, the *Ramayana* and *Mahabharata*, although Java has long been a predominantly Muslim island. The adventures of the five heroic Pandava brothers are especially popular. Performances last all night and may be watched from either side of the screen. Conventionally, the shadow figures representing the forces of good appear on the right (viewed from the front as shadows), those representing evil on the left. *Wayang* plays are customarily presented to mark important celebrations or anniversaries.

TIME CHART			
50,000-25,000 years ago	Southward migration of aboriginal Negrito peoples into Southeast Asia	15th century	Islamic influence expands throughout the region
4,500 years ago	Beginning of southward migration of Austronesian peoples into Southeast Asia	1509	Arrival of Portuguese explorer Vasco da Gama in Malacca in Malaysia marks beginnings of European influence and colonization
3rd century AD	Hindu kingdoms founded in Kampuchea, Malaysia and Indonesia	*c.*1600	Islamicization of Java complete
1100-1200	Theravada Buddhism reaches Laos and Kampuchea from Sri Lanka via Burma	1945-57	Colonial powers (Netherlands, USA, France and Britain) withdraw from most of Southeast Asia

MYTHS OF ORIGIN

The creation of the world and humanity

A detail of an embroidered robe from Indonesia depicting a stylized hornbill, a manifestation of celestial spirits. Fabulous birds play an important part in creation myths in many parts of Southeast Asia.

Southeast Asian myths commonly ascribe the creation of the world to some creator deity, who is often a bird or other animal with creator powers. For example, in Sumatra it is said that in primordial times God possessed a fabulous blue chicken, Manuk Manuk, instead of a wife. Manuk Manuk laid three huge eggs, out of which emerged the three gods who created the three levels of the universe: the upper world (heaven), the middle world (earth) and the underworld.

At this time the middle world contained only a limitless sea. Boru Deak Parudjar, daughter of the god Batara Guru, sprang from the upper world into the sea below to avoid the unwelcome courtship of another god, Mangalabulan. When a swallow told Batara Guru what had happened, and how his daughter was now languishing in the ocean, he sent the bird back with a handful of soil to lay on the waters. The soil expanded on the sea until it became the land, upon which Batara Guru scattered seeds, and from these sprang all the varieties of animals. The god then sent a heroic human incarnation of himself to make the earth safe by fighting Naga Padoha, serpent ruler of the underworld (a figure of Hindu origin), and confining him to the lower depths of the cosmos.

A powerful serpent, and the idea of the upper and lower worlds, also occur in the creation myth of the Dayak, the indigenous non-Muslim peoples of the interior of southern and western Borneo. These tell of a primordial time "when everything was still enclosed in the mouth of the coiled Watersnake". There then arose Gold Mountain, seat of the supreme deity of the lower region of the cosmos, and Jewel Mountain, seat of the supreme deity of the upper region. These mountains clashed together several times, on each occasion bringing part of the universe into existence, beginning with the clouds. Afterwards came the vault of the heavens; the mountains and cliffs; the sun and moon; the Hawk of Heaven and the great fish Ila-Ilai Langit; two fabulous beasts, Rowang Riwo with the golden saliva and Didis Mahendera with the jewel eyes; and, finally, the golden headdress of the god Mahatala, which was crowned with a perpendicular jewel. This was the first epoch of creation. In the second epoch, rivers appeared and Jata, the divine maiden, created land and hills. In the third epoch, the Tree of Life appeared, with golden leaves and ivory fruit, uniting the upper and lower worlds.

The creation myth of the Dusun people

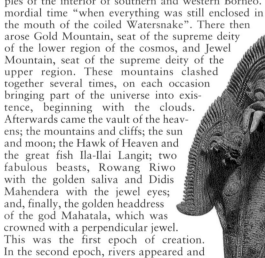

A bronze figure of a naga, *a serpent being of Hindu provenance common in Southeast Asian mythology. This one comes from Angkor Wat in Kampuchea.*

CREATION MYTHS OF THE IBAN
The Iban, one of the Dayak peoples of Borneo, say that the world began with two spirits, Ara and Irik, who floated in the form of birds above a limitless expanse of water. The birds swooped down and gathered from the water two great eggs, from one of which Ara formed the sky, while Irik formed the earth from the other. But the earth was too big to fit the sky, so the two creator spirits compressed the earth until it was the right size, causing great upheavals on the surface as they did so, and producing rivers and streams to water the valleys and the plains. As soon as these had been created, trees and plants began to appear.

Finally, seeing that there was no one to inhabit this new world, the two bird-spirits decided to create humankind. First, they tried to make people from the white and red sap of trees, but they could not give this material life and so turned to the earth itself. They moulded the first humans from soil, and brought them to life with their bird-spirit cries.

of Sabah in northern Borneo is based on a related theme. According to them, in the beginning there was only a great rock amid the waters of the universe. The rock split to release a male divinity, who was an ironsmith, and a female deity, who made the heavens and the earth. The male god created the vault of the sky with ribs like an umbrella, and the female shaped the earth from the dirt on her own body and on the body of her companion.

Often the creation of humans follows on directly from the creation of the world. For example, in the Sumatran creation story, the divine hero who defeated Naga Padoha was rewarded with the gift of Boru Deak Parudjar, the daughter of Batara Guru, as his female companion, and together the couple produced the first humans. In the Dusun creation myth, after the sky and the earth were formed, the two divinities turned to the creation of humans, making them first of stone. However, this stone race could not talk, so the two gods tried again, this time making people of wood. The wood decayed too quickly, so a third race was fashioned from the earth of a termite mound. This attempt was successful, and humanity is descended from the third race. Several other peoples in the region also relate how humans were created from the soil, sometimes after more than one previous attempt.

The myth of human origins told by the Carabaulo people of Timor, in eastern Indonesia, serves to explain the social order. According to this account, there were originally no humans, just the sea. Two pieces of land emerged from the waters to become the entire island of Timor. Then a huge vagina appeared in the ground, out of which came the ancestors of the present population: the first to emerge became the landowing aristocrats, and those who followed were their commoners and tenants. To climb out of the vagina, the first people hauled themselves up by the creepers of a tree. It is said that the place of emergence is still to be seen today, but no one is allowed to penetrate the tunnel which descends from it.

THE MANY-LAYERED COSMOS

The idea that the universe is made up of several layers is widespread in the creation myths of Southeast Asia. For example, the Kédang of Lembata island in Indonesia believe that there are seven levels above the earth and five below. Anyone who dies is reborn on the next earth down, ultimately returning to the top level as a fish to recommence the cycle of rebirth and death.

The Chewong people of the Malayan rainforest say that the underside of one layer of the universe forms the sky of the layer below; the sky of this earth, Earth Seven, is thus the underside of Earth Six. It is made of stone and touches the earth at two points, where the sun rises and sets. When our sun sets, it becomes the sun of Earth Eight, which lies beneath this one.

For the Ma'Betisék, another Malaysian people, the universe is like a seven-layered onion, floating in water. This earth is the sixth layer, with the seventh layer as its overworld, populated by the transparent ancestral spirits of humans. Malevolent creatures such as cannibals live in the layers below the earth.

The serpent and the turtle

*T*he Balinese, in their creation myth, relate that in the beginning there was neither heaven nor earth. Then, through meditation, the World Serpent Antaboga created the World Turtle, Bedawang.

On the World Turtle lay two coiled snakes and the Black Stone, the lid of a cave which is the underworld, where there is neither sun nor moon. The underworld cave is ruled by the god Batara Kala and the goddess Setesuyara, and is the home of the great serpent Basuki. Kala created the light and Mother Earth, over which extends a layer of water, and over the water a series of domes or skies. There is the middle sky, and above it the floating sky, where Semara, the god of love, sits. Above that is the dark blue sky with the sun and moon, and above that the perfumed sky, beautiful and full of rare flowers, the

A shadow puppet of c.1800 representing the World Serpent Antaboga of the Balinese creation myth. It comes from Klung-klung, Bali.

home of Tjak, the bird with a human face, the serpent Taksaka, who has legs and wings, and the awan snakes, which are the falling stars. Higher still is the flame-filled heaven of the ancestors, and above that lies the highest layer of all, the abode of the gods, watched over by Tintiya, the male supreme being.

The gods created Bali as a flat, barren place. But when neighbouring Java fell to the Muslims (in fact a long process lasting from *c*.1250 to *c*.1600), the disgusted Hindu gods moved to Bali and, at each of the four cardinal points, built mountains high enough for their exalted rank. In the middle they created the volcano Gunung Agung ("Great Mountain"), also called the "Cosmic Mountain" and "Navel of the World".

HUMANS, GODS AND SPIRITS

The origins of civilization

THE ORIGIN OF NIGHT AND FIRE
According to the Chewong of Malaysia, there was originally no night or fire on this earth, which is the seventh layer of the eight-layered universe. If people wanted to cook tapioca, they just put it on the ground and it cooked itself. One day a boy lost his knife through a hole in the earth and in trying to retrieve it fell through to the eighth earth below, where the people gave him some food to eat. When it grew dark, the boy was frightened, so the people lit a fire; but this was also new to him, and again he was frightened. The kind people gave him both night and fire for his own earth, putting them into a piece of bamboo. Then they showed him how to cook food before helping him to climb back into this world with his gifts.

Many Southeast Asian myths explain how the rules and means of civilized behaviour are revealed to or discovered by an ancestral culture hero, after being in the possession of a divinity or spirit. The Chewong, a Malayan hunter-gatherer people, explain *maro*, their custom of sharing food, in the story of the hunter Bujaegn Yed. He was cooking and eating his catch one day when he saw Yinlugen Bud, the Ghost of the Tree-trunk and a spirit older than all humans. He warned Bujaegn Yed that by not sharing his food he had entered a dangerous and possibly fatal state of transgression. Bujaegn Yed took his meat home and gave it to his pregnant wife. When she was due to give birth, the hunter took out a knife and was about to slit her belly open, as was then the custom, when Yinlugen Bud showed him how to deliver a child properly. He also told the couple all the birth spells and rules of childbirth, and how to breastfeed a baby. From that time women did not die when their children were born and people always shared the game they had caught.

The Iban of Borneo tell how a man called Surong Gunting travels to see his grandfather, the spirit Sengalong Burong. On the way, he learns about the annual farming cycle from the stars, and his grandfather then teaches him certain rituals and tells him about bird omens for farming and headhunting (the Iban believe that birds transmit spirit messages). When Surong Gunting impregnates his aunt, Dara Chempaka Tempurong, he is expelled from his grandfather's longhouse after being taught that it is a serious transgression for people of adjacent generations to couple, spelling possible disaster for the harvest. He returns to his own longhouse and passes on his new wisdom to the Iban.

Stone figures, representing divine ancestral culture heroes, at the sacrificial site of the Toba-Batak people, at Ambarita on the island of Samosi in eastern Indonesia.

THE HUNTER AND THE MOON
The Ma' Betisék of Malaysia recount how, in the beginning, humans had no rules and were constantly committing murder, incest and cannibalism. At this period, the rules of behaviour were kept secret by a spirit called Moyang Melur, who was half human and half tiger, and lived on the moon. One night, fascinated by the disarray on earth below, he leaned out of the moon too far and fell to earth, where he met a hunter, Moyang Kapir, to whom he swore that he would kill every human unless he got back to the moon at once. Moyang Kapir flung a rope to the moon and they both ascended. Moyang Melur secretly prepared to kill and eat Moyang Kapir, but he escaped down the rope back to earth, taking the secret bag containing the rules of human behaviour, which he had found under a mat. Moyang Kapir then gave out the rules to his kinsfolk.

The Thens and the three great men

In Laos and northern Thailand the origins of human society, practical skills and culture are attributed to three divine ancestors, the Thens, and three earthly ancestors, who are sometimes known simply as the three great men.

A long time ago, there were the earth, the sky and the plants. Above the world, in the upper kingdom, lived the Thens, and the masters of the lower world were three great men, Pu Lang Seung, Khun K'an and Khun K'et, who made a living from fishing and growing rice. At this time the upper and lower worlds were joined by a huge rattan bridge.

One day, the Thens announced to the world that before eating any meal, people should give them a part of their food as a sign of respect. However, the people refused, and in a rage the Thens created a flood which devastated the world. Pu Lang Seung, Khun K'an and Khun K'et built a raft, on top of which they made a small house. Taking women and children with them, they voyaged to the upper kingdom, where they went to pay homage to the king of the Thens, who asked them what business they had in his kingdom.

After hearing their account of what had happened, the king told them to go and live in heaven with one of his relatives, Grandfather Then Lo. At the same time the waters down below began to recede, and on seeing this, the three great men went to the king and told him: "We cannot walk or run in this insubstantial world. We want to go back and live in the lower world, where the ground is flat and solid." The king gave them a buffalo and sent them back to live on earth.

Three years later the buffalo died, and soon afterwards a creeper grew from its nostrils and produced three gourds, from which a strange noise was heard. Pu Lang Seung heated a drill and bored a hole in each gourd, out of which came people. They were the aboriginal slave people, and were taught by Pu Lang Seung to cultivate in the primitive slash-and-burn fashion. Still many people remained inside each gourd until Khun K'an made a second opening with scissors. For three days and three nights the people poured out, until finally the gourds were empty. Those who emerged from the second opening were the Thai peoples, who were taught by the three great men how to cultivate fields and how to weave. (In fact, the Thais migrated into the region from China in the 10th century.) Later, the divine ancestors sent Then Teng, the builder, and Pitsanukukan, the designer. Then Teng instructed the people how to reckon time and the correct order in which they should cultivate their plots, fields, orchards and gardens. Pitsanukukan taught the people how to work metals and to fashion all kinds of tools, and also gave instruction in weaving cotton and silk, making dresses and preparing food.

After this, the king of heaven sent Sik'ant'apatewada, lord of the Gandharva, the divine musicians. He taught the people how to make and play the gongs, flutes, drums and all the instruments of the orchestra, and how to sing and dance.

When Sik'ant'apatewada had finished his task and returned to heaven, the rattan bridge was demolished. Since then the divine ancestors and human beings have been unable to visit each other.

THE ONENESS OF LIFE

Southeast Asian myths of the origin of civilization carry the implication that all things in the world have one source or are otherwise closely connected to each other. For example, the Dayak of Borneo believe that humans, animals and plants are all descended from the same spirit and are therefore related. Also widespread, especially among the more ancient indigenous peoples, is the idea that any form of life can readily change into another. The Chewong of Malaysia suppose that children are metamorphosed flowers. The Bagobo of Mindanao in the Philippines say that monkeys once looked and behaved like humans: they assumed their present form only when humans were created as a separate race by the god Pamalak Bagobo. The affinity between the two species is reflected in the fact that some people can change at will into monkeys.

The Ma' Betisék express their sense of the interrelationship of all forms of life in a belief in reincarnation. Good people are rewarded by being reborn as humans, but because they have to be free from greed, ambition, violence and jealousy, such people are rare. Most human souls are reborn as animals, or occasionally as plants. The Ma' Betisék also relate how, at one stage in their history, they became so numerous that there was a catastrophic shortage of land. With the consent of the people, God solved the problem by changing half the population into trees.

ENCOUNTERS WITH MAGIC

Barbarians, demons and witches

A statue of the witch queen Rangda, represented as a character in Balinese dance.

A common theme in mythology throughout Southeast Asia is the encounter with some magic power, often a representative of the dark forces of evil or barbarity which stand in opposition to civilized society. These forces usually take human or near-human form and can be either male, such as the half-human and half-tiger spirit Moyang Melur (see p.304), or female, like Bota Ili (see below).

The ferocious Balinese female folk demon Rangda figures as the leader of a band of evil witches whose immortal antagonist is the spirit king, Barong. She is commonly depicted nearly naked, with long hair, and clawlike fingernails and toenails. The combat of these two magical powers, in which Rangda is customarily defeated, is re-enacted on Bali by masked dancers (see p.301). The name *rangda*

A Balinese dance mask representing Barong, the opponent of evil and adversary of Rangda.

means widow, and some scholars believe that she derives from an 11th-century Balinese queen, Mahendradatta, who was exiled from court by her husband, King Dharmodayana, for allegedly practising sorcery against his second wife. After Dharmodayana died, the widowed Mahendradatta is said to have persecuted Erlangga, their son and Dharmodayana's successor as king, for not having dissuaded his father from taking another wife. She is said to have tried to destroy the kingdom with black magic. Half the population had died of plague as a result of her sorcery by the time she was vanquished by the superior magic of a holy man.

Bota Ili

The Kédang of eastern Indonesia relate how the wild woman Bota Ili was turned to civilized ways.

Bota Ili lived at the top of a mountain. Her body was covered with hair and she had extremely long fingernails and toenails. She ate reptiles, and to cook them she would strike her backside on a rock to make a fire. A man called Wata Rian lived on the beach. One day he noticed smoke on the mountain and decided to find out who lived there. Early one morning he set off, taking fish to eat and palm wine. He reached the summit at noon and found a hearth. Wata Rian climbed a tree and waited until Bota Ili returned from hunting with a

heavy catch of snakes and lizards. After she had rested, Bota Ili struck her backside on a rock to make fire, but without success. Then she spotted Wata Rian. She cried out in anger: "You stopped my fire from lighting – come down so I can bite you to bits!" Wata Rian replied: "Don't make trouble or my dog will bite you!" Bota Ili relented and Wata Rian came down. Bota Ili now succeeded in lighting the fire, and they cooked their food. He poured Bota Ili a lot of palm wine and eventually she fell down drunk. He shaved her all over as she slept and saw that she was a woman. Later, after Bota Ili learned to wear clothes, she and Wata Rian lived together and were married.

THE GIVER OF LIFE

Myths about rice

Throughout Southeast Asia a close association is recognized between the "life force" of rice, the staple food of the entire region, and that of human beings. The Dayak of Borneo say that the souls of the dead in the underworld dissolve into dew, which is absorbed into the ears of rice and, in turn, becomes part of living people as food. When people die, the cycle recommences. One Dayak people, the Iban, make offerings to Pulang Gana, the earth spirit, in order to ensure that the rice grows. They say that a long time ago people began to clear jungle for the first rice farm but found the next morning that the trees were all back in place. After this had happened three times, they decided to clear the field again and keep watch that night. From their vantage point they saw that Pulang Gana caused the trees to come back to life and root themselves firmly in the soil again. When they tried to catch the spirit, he told them who he was and explained that the earth and everything growing in it belonged to him, and only he had the power to make the rice grow. The people asked what they should do before making a field, and Pulang Gana said that if they offered him such gifts as jars, beads and ornamental shells they would be allowed to cultivate rice.

In northern Thailand there are long recitations in village temples to encourage the growth of rice and to accumulate spiritual merit for the Buddhist monks and the entire village. On Bali, before the rice harvest begins, each family makes a figure called the Rice Mother out of one long sheaf of rice known as the Rice Husband, and one shorter sheaf known as the Rice Wife. It is tied to a tree on the edge of the paddy-field to encourage a good rice crop.

After the harvest, all the Rice Mothers in a village are taken in procession to the local temple to be blessed by a priest, after which each Rice Mother is set on a wooden throne in the family granary to protect the crop. No one must enter the granary if they have sinned, and it is forbidden to eat any of the grains of rice on the Rice Mother itself.

A northern Balinese figure representing a rice-goddess, c.1800. Such figures are kept in temples, and during certain festivals the rice deities are invited to enter them and bring them to "life".

Sujata and the Buddha

A popular Thai story relates how Sujata, the daughter of a wealthy landowner, offers the god of the bo or fig tree (Ficus religiosa) a gift of rice enriched with milk in gratitude for bearing a son.

Sujata ordered a thousand cows to be driven into a meadow of rich grass. With their milk she fed another five hundred cows, and with the milk of the five hundred cows she fed another two hundred and fifty cows, and so she went on until she had eight cows that produced a very rich milk. Sujata added this to some rice and went to make her offering to the bo tree. She saw a figure sitting under a bo whom she assumed was the god of the tree, but in fact it was the Buddha himself, on the very day of his enlightenment. Sujata, filled with joy, presented her gift of rice and milk. The wonderful food sustained the Buddha into enlightenment, lasting him for 49 days.

FURTHER READING

General

Campbell, Joseph, *The Masks of God* (Penguin, Harmondsworth, 1982)

The Inner Reaches of Outer Space (Harper and Row, New York, 1988)

Dundes, Alan (ed.), *The Sacred Narrative: readings in the theory of myth* (University of California Press, Berkeley,1984)

Eliade, Mircea, *Cosmos and History: the Myth of the Eternal Return* (Harper and Row, New York, 1959, rep. 1985)

Lévi-Strauss, Claude, *Myth and Meaning* (Routledge, London, 1978)

Maranda, Pierre, *Mythology: selected readings* (Penguin, Harmondsworth, 1972)

Propp, Vladimir, *Morphology of the Folktale* (University of Texas, Austin, 1968)

Egypt

Faulkner, R.O. (ed. C. Andrews), *The Ancient Egyptian Book of the Dead* (British Museum, London, 1985)

Hart, G., *Egyptian Myths* (British Museum, London, 1990)

A Dictionary of Egyptian Gods and Goddesses (Routledge, London, 1986)

The Valley of the Kings (Timken, 1990)

Lichtheim, M., *Ancient Egyptian Literature,* 3 vols (University of California Press, Berkeley, 1973, 1976, 1980)

Lurker, M., *The Gods and Symbols of Ancient Egypt* (Thames and Hudson, London, 1980)

Quirke, S., *Ancient Egyptian Religion* (British Museum, London, 1992)

Rundle Clark, R.T., *Myth and Symbol in Ancient Egypt* (Thames and Hudson, London, 1959)

Shafer, B. (ed.), *Religion in Ancient Egypt: gods, myths and personal practice* (Routledge, London, 1991)

Spencer, A.J., *Death in Ancient Egypt* (Penguin, Harmond –sworth, 1982)

Thomas, A.P., *Egyptian Gods and Myths* (Shire, 1986)

Middle East

Brandon, S.G.F., *Creation Legends of the Ancient Near East* (Hodder, London, 1963)

Dalley, S., *Myths from Mesopotamia: Creation, The Flood, Gilgamesh and Others* (Oxford University Press, Oxford/New York, 1989)

Gray, J., *Near Eastern Mythology* (Hamlyn, London, 1969)

Gurney, O., *Some Aspects of Hittite Religion* (Oxford University Press, 1977)

Hinnells, J.R., *Persian Mythology* (Hamlyn, London, 1973)

Hooke, S.H., *Middle Eastern Mythology* (Penguin, London, 1963)

Kramer, S.N., *Sumerian Mythology* (revised edn) (Harper and Brothers, New York, 1961)

Leick, G., *A Dictionary of Ancient Near Eastern Mythology* (Routledge, London/New York, 1991)

Pritchard, J.B., *Ancient Near Eastern Texts Relating to the Old Testament* (Princeton University Press, 1950)

Ringgren, H., *Religions of the Ancient Near East* (S.P.C.K., London/Westminster Press, Philadelphia, 1973)

Saggs, H.W.F., *The Greatness that was Babylon* (Sidgwick and Jackson, London, 1962)

India

Daniélou, Alain, *Hindu Polytheism* (Routledge, London, 1964)

Dimmitt, Cornelia, and J.A.B. van Buitenen, *Classical Hindu Mythology: A Reader in the Sanskrit Puranas* (Temple University Press, Philadelphia, 1978)

Ions, Veronica, *Indian Mythology* (Hamlyn, London, 1967)

Kinsley, David, *The Sword and the Flute: Kali and Krishna* (California University Press, Berkeley, 1975)

Hindu Goddesses: Visions of the Divine Feminine in the Hindu Religious Tradition (University of California Press, Berkeley, 1986)

Kuiper, F.B.J., *Ancient Indian Cosmogony* (Vikas Publications, New Delhi, 1983)

Mahabharata, trans. and ed. J.A.B. van Buitenen, vols 1-3 (University of Chicago Press, Chicago, 1973-78)

O'Flaherty, Wendy Doniger (trans.), *Hindu Myths, A Sourcebook* (Penguin, Harmondsworth, 1975)

The Origins of Evil in Hindu Mythology (University of California Press, Berkeley, 1976)

Puhvel, Jaan, *Comparative Mythology* (Johns Hopkins University Press, Baltimore, 1987)

Shulman, David Dean, *Tamil Temple Myths* (Princeton University Press, 1980)

Stutley, Margaret and James, *A Dictionary of Hinduism: Its Mythology, Folklore and Development, 1500BC- AD1500* (Routledge, 1977)

Zimmer, Heinrich, *Myths and Symbols in Indian Art and Civilization* (ed. Joseph Campbell) (Pantheon Books, Washington D.C., 1946)

China

Birch, C., *Chinese Myths and Fantasies* (Oxford University Press, 1961)

Bodde, Derk, "Myths of Ancient China", in Samuel N. Kramer: *Mythologies of the Ancient World,* pp. 367-408 (Doubleday, NewYork, 1961)

Chang, K.C., *Art, Myth and Ritual* (Harvard University Press, Cambridge, Mass./London, 1983)

Christie, A.H., *Chinese Mythology,* (Hamlyn, 1968)

Waley, Arthur, *Ballads and Stories from Tun-huang* (Allen and Unwin, London, 1960)

Werner, E.T.C., *Myths and Legends of China* (Harrap, London, 1922)

A Dictionary of Chinese Mythology (Kelly and Walsh, Shanghai, 1932)

Tibet and Mongolia

Altangerel, D., *How Did the Great Bear Originate? Folktales from Mongolia* (State Publishing House, Ulaanbaattar, 1988)

Campbell, Joseph, *The Way of the Animal Powers: Historical Atlas of World Mythology,* vol. 1 (Times, London, 1983)

Eliade, Mircea, *Shamanism: Archaic Techniques of Ecstasy* (trans. from the French Willard R. Trask) (Princeton University Press, Princeton, 1971)

Norbu, Namkhai, *The Necklace of Gzi, a Cultural History of Tibet* (Information Office of H.H. Dalai Lama, Dharamsala, 1981)

Stein, R.A., *Tibetan Civilisation* (Faber, London, 1972)

Tucci, Giuseppe, *The Religions of Tibet* (Routledge, London, 1980)

Yeshe De Project, *Ancient Tibet* (Dharma Publishing, Berkeley, 1986)

Japan

Aston, W.G. (trans.) *Nihongi (= Nihonshoki)* (Charles E. Tuttle Co., Tokyo, 1972)

Jensen, Adolf E., *Myth and Cult among Primitive Peoples* (trans. Marianna Tax Choldin and Wolfgang Weissleder) (University of Chicago Press, Chicago, 1963)

Littleton, C. Scott, "Some Possible Arthurian Themes in Japanese Mythology and Folklore", *Journal of Folklore Research 20,* pp. 67-81, 1983

"Susa-nö-wo Versus Ya-mata no Woröchi: An Indo-European Theme in Japanese Mythology", *History of Religions 20,* pp. 269-80, 1981

Philippi, Donald L. (trans.), *Kojiki* (University of Tokyo Press,1968)

Saunders, E. Dale, "Japanese Mythology", *Mythologies of the Ancient World* (ed. Samuel Noah Kramer), pp. 409-442

(Doubleday, New York, 1961)

Greece

Blake Tyrrell, W., and Frieda Brown, *Athenian Myths and Institutions* (Oxford University Press, 1991)

Carpenter, T.H., *Art and Myth in Ancient Greece*(Thames and Hudson, London, 1991)

Dodds, E.R., *The Greeks and the Irrational* (University of California Press, Berkeley, 1951)

Easterling, P.E. and J.V. Muir (eds.) *Greek Religion and Society* (Cambridge University Press, 1985)

Gordon, R.L. (ed.), *Myth, Religion and Society* (Cambridge University Press, 1991)

Kerenyi, C., *The Heroes of the Greeks* (Thames and Hudson, London, 1991)

Morford, Mark, and Robert Lenardon, *Classical Mythology* (Longman, New York, 1991)

Stanford, W.B., *The Ulysses Theme* (Oxford University Press, 1963)

Vernant, J-P., *Myth and Society in Ancient Greece* (trans. Janet Lloyd) (Zone Books, New York, 1990)

Rome

Donaldson, I., *The Rapes of Lucretia: a myth and its transformations* (Clarendon Press, Oxford, 1982)

Dowden, K., *Religion and the Romans* (Bristol Classical Press, London, 1992)

Gransden, K.W., *Virgil, the Aeneid* (Cambridge University Press, 1990)

Ogilvie, R.M., *The Romans and their Gods* (Chatto, London, 1969)

Perowne, S., *Roman Mythology* (Newnes, Twickenham, 1983)

Scullard, H.H., *Festivals and Ceremonies of the Roman Republic* (Thames and Hudson, London, 1981)

Wardman, A., *Religion and Statecraft at Rome* (Granada, London, 1982)

Celtic World

Green, Miranda J., *Dictionary of Celtic Myth and Legend* (Thames and Hudson, London, 1992)

Jarman, A.O.H., *The Legend of Merlin* (University of Wales Press, Cardiff, 1960)

Loomis, R.S. (ed.), *Arthurian Literature in the Middle Ages. A Collective History* (Oxford University Press, 1959)

MacCana, Proinsias, *Celtic Mythology* (Hamlyn, London/ NewYork/Sydney/Toronto, 1970; 3rd impression 1975)

McCone, Kim, *Pagan Past and Christian Present in Early Irish Literature* (Maynooth

Monographs 3, 1990, rep. 1991)
Nagy, Joseph Falaky, *The Wisdom of the Outlaw. The Boyhood Deeds of Finn in Gaelic Narrative Tradition* (University of California Press, Berkeley and Los Angeles/London, 1985)
Ross, Anne, *Pagan Celtic Britain. Studies in Iconography and Tradition* (Routledge, London, 1967)

Northern Europe
Davidson, H.R.Ellis, *Gods and Myths of Northern Europe* (Penguin, Harmondsworth, 1964)
Pagan Scandinavia (Hamlyn, London, 1984)
Lost Beliefs of Northern Europe (Routledge, London, 1993)
Hutton, R., *The Pagan Religions of the Ancient British Isles: Their Nature and Legacy* (Blackwell, Oxford, 1991)
Jones, G., *A History of the Vikings* (Oxford University Press,1984)
Owen, G.R., *Rites and Religions of the Anglo-Saxons* (David and Charles, Newton Abbot, 1981)
Simek, R., *Dictionary of Northern Mythology* (Boydell and Brewer, Woodbridge, 1993)
Todd, M., *The Early Germans* (Blackwell, Oxford, 1992)
Turville-Petre, E.O.G., *Myth and Religion of the North* (Weidenfeld, London, 1964)

Central and Eastern Europe
Chadwick, H. Munro, and N. Kershaw Chadwick, *The Growth of Literature*, vol.II, pt. i "Russian Oral Literature", pt. ii "Yugoslav Oral Poetry" (Cambridge University Press, 1936)
Ivanits, Linda J., *Russian Folk Belief* (M.E. Sharpe Inc., Armonk, New York/London, 1989)
Jakobson, Roman, "Slavic Mythology", *Funk and Wagnalls Standard Dictionary of Folklore, Mythology and Legend*, vol. II pp. 1025-28, ed. M. Leach and J. Fried (Funk and Wagnalls, New York, 1949-50)
Oinas, Felix J., *Essays on Russian Folklore and Mythology* (Slavica, Columbus, Ohio, 1985)
Perkowski, Jan L., *Vampires of the Slavs* (Slavica, Cambridge, Mass., 1976)
The Darkling: Essays on Slavic Vampirism (Slavica, Columbus, Ohio, 1989)
Popovic, Tatyana, *Prince Marko. The Hero of South Slavic Epic* (Syracuse University Press, Syracuse, N.Y., 1988)
Warner, Elizabeth, *Heroes, Monsters and Other Worlds from Russian Mythology* (Peter Lowe, London, 1985)

Arctic Regions
Damar, D., *Handbook of North American Indians: Arctic* (Smithsonian Institution, Washington, 1984)

Fienup-Riordan, Ann, *Eskimo Essays* (Rutgers University Press, London, 1990)
Nelson, Edward, *The Eskimo about Bering Strait* (Smithsonian Institution, Washington, 1983)
Rasmussen, Knud, *Intellectual Culture of the Hudson Bay Eskimos* (Nordisk Forlag, Copenhagen, 1929)
Ray, Dorothy Jean, *Eskimo Masks: Art and Ceremony* (University of Washington Press, Seattle, 1967)
Spencer, Robert, *The North Alaskan Eskimo* (Bureau of American Ethnology, Washington, 1959)
Weyer, Edward, *The Eskimos* (Yale University Press, New Haven, 1932)

North America
Boas, F., *Tsimshian Mythology* (Johnson, New York, 1970)
Burland, C.A. and M. Wood, *North American Indian Mythology* (Newnes, London, 1985)
Brown, J.E., *The Sacred Pipe* (Penguin, Harmondsworth, 1971)
Campbell, J., *The Way of the Animal Powers* (Times, London, 1984)
Curtin, J., *Seneca Indian Myths* (E.P. Dutton, New York, 1923)
Dooling, D.M. (ed.), *The Sons of the Wind* (Harper, San Francisco, 1992)
Erdoes R. and A. Ortiz (eds.), *American Indian Myths and Legends* (Pantheon, New York, 1988)
Haile, B., *Navajo Coyote Tales* (University of Nebraska, Lincoln, 1984)
Mariott A. and C.K. Rachlin, *American Indian Mythology* (Mentor, New York, 1968)
Plains Indian Mythology (Thomas Crowell, New York, 1975)
Parsons E.C., *Pueblo Indian Religion* (University of Chicago, Chicago, 1939)
Radin, P., *The Trickster* (Philosophical Library, New York, 1956)
Tooker, E., *Native American Spirituality of the Eastern Woodlands* (Paulist Press, New York, 1979)
Turner, F.W., III, (ed.), *Portable North American Indian Reader* (Penguin, Harmondsworth, 1977)
Walker, J.R., *Lakota Myth* (University of Nebraska, Lincoln, 1983)

Mesoamerica
Carrasco, David, *Ancient Mesoamerican Religions* (Holt, Rinehart and Winston, New York, 1990)
Coe, Michael D., *The Maya* (Thames and Hudson, London, 1987)
Coe, Michael D., Elizabeth P. Benson and Dean Snow, *Atlas of*

Ancient America (Facts on File, Oxford, 1985)
Fagan, Brian, *Kingdoms of Jade, Kingdoms of Gold* (Thames and Hudson, London, 1991)
Pasztory, Esther, *Aztec Art* (Abrams, New York, 1983))
Schele, Linda, and Mary E. Miller, *The Blood of Kings* (Kimbell Art Museum, Forth Worth, 1986)
Tedlock, Dennis, *Popol Vuh* (Simon and Schuster, New York, 1985)
Townsend, Richard, *The Aztecs* (Thames and Hudson, London, 1992)

South America
Bray, Warwick, *The Gold of El Dorado* (Times, London, 1978)
British Museum, *The Hidden Peoples of the Amazon* (British Museum Publications, London, 1985)
Chagnon, Napoleon A., *Yanomamo: The Fierce People* (Holt, Rinehart and Winston, New York, 1977)
Coe, Michael D., and Elizabeth P. Benson and Dean Snow, *Atlas of Ancient America* (Facts on File, Oxford, 1985)
Fagan, Brian, *Kingdoms of Jade, Kingdoms of Gold* (Thames and Hudson, London, 1991)
Hadingham, Evan, *Lines to the Mountain Gods* (Heinemann, London, 1987)
Harner, Michael, *The Jivaro* (Robert Hale, London, 1973)
Moseley, Michael E., *The Incas and Their Ancestors* (Thames and Hudson, London, 1992)
Saunders, Nicholas J., *People of the Jaguar* (Souvenir Press, London, 1989)

Africa
Cosentino, Donald, *Defiant Maids and Stubborn Farmers: tradition and invention in Mende story performance* (Cambridge University Press, 1982)
Davidson, Basil, *Old Africa Rediscovered* (Gollanz, London, 1959)
Finnegan, Ruth, *Oral Literature in Africa* (Clarendon Press, Oxford, 1970, rep. 1976)
Forde, Daryll (ed.,), *African Worlds: studies in the cosmological ideas and social values of African peoples* (Oxford University Press, London, 1991)
Mbiti, John S., *African Religions and Philosophy* (Heinemann, London, 1969)
Okpewho, Isidore, *Myth in Africa: a study of its aesthetic and cultural relevance* (Cambridge University Press, 1983)
Willis, Roy, *There Was A Certain Man: spoken art of the Fipa* (Clarendon Press, Oxford, 1978)

Australia
Layton, R., *Uluru: an Aboriginal history of Ayers Rock* (Aboriginal Studies Press, Canberra, 1986)

Australian rock art (Cambridge University Press, 1992)
Morphy, H., *Journey to the crocodile's nest* (Aboriginal Studies Press, Canberra, 1984)
Neidjie, B, *Kakadu Man* (Mybrook/Allan Fox Associates, Sydney, 1985)
O'Brien, M., *The Legend of the Seven Sisters* (Aboriginal Studies Press, Canberra, 1990)
Sutton., P., (ed.), *Dreamings: the art of Aboriginal Australia* (Braziller, New York)
Utemorra, D., and others, *Visions of Mowanjum* (Rigby, Adelaide, 1980)
Warlukurlangu Artists, *Kuruwarri: Yuendumu Doors* (Aboriginal Studies Press, Canberra, 1987)
Western Region Aboriginal Land Council, *The story of the falling star* (Aboriginal Studies Press, Canberra, 1989)

Oceania
Gifford, E. W., *Tongan Myths and Tales*, Bulletin No. 8 (Bernice P. Bishop Museum, 1924)
Grey, Sir George, *Polynesian Mythology* (Whitcombe and Tombs, London and Christchurch, 1965)
Handy, E.S.C., *Marquesan Legends*, Bulletin 69 (Bernice P. Bishop Museum, 1930)
Landtman, G., *Folktales of the Kiwai Papuans* (Finnish Society of Literature, Helsinki, 1917)
Lawrence, P., *Road Belong Cargo* (Manchester University Press, Manchester, 1964)
Lawrie, M., *Myths and Legends of Torres Strait* (University of Queensland Press, 1970)
Lessa, W.A., *Tales from Ulithi Atoll*, Folklore Studies 13 (University of California Press, Berkeley, 1961)
Luomola, K., *Maui-of-a-thousand-tricks*, Bulletin 198 (Bernice P. Bishop Museum, 1949)
Malinowski, B., *Magic, Science and Religion* (Anchor Books, 1954)
Powdermaker, H., *Life in Lesu* (Williams and Norgate, 1933)
Young, M., *Magicians of Manumanua* (University of California Press, Berkeley, 1983)

Southeast Asia
Coedès, G., and C. Archaimbault, Davids, T.W.R., (ed.) *Buddhist Birth Stories; or, Jataka Tales* (Trubner and Co., London, 1980) (ed.) *Buddhist Suttas* (Clarendon Press, Oxford, 1981)
Davis, R.B., *Muang Metaphysics. A Study of Northern Thai Myth and Ritual* (Pandora, Bangkok, 1984)
Izikowitz, K.-G., *Fastening the Soul. Some Religious Traits among the Lamet* (Göteborgs Högskolas Arsskrift, 47, 1941)
Trankell, I.-B., *Cooking, Care and Domestication. A Culinary Ethnography of the Tai Yong, Northern Thailand* (Almqvist & Wiksell, Uppsala)

PICTURE CREDITS

MH: Michael Holford
BM: British Museum, London
BAL: Bridgeman Art Library
JG: Japanese Gallery:
  66D Kensington Church Street, London
V&A: Victoria and Albert Museum, London
WFA: Werner Forman Archive:
T: Top B: Bottom C: Centre
L: Left R: Right

1 WFA/National Museum of Anthropology, Mexico City
2 MH/BM 3 Zefa/Damm
Introduction to Myth
11 Zefa/Damm 12T Scala/Rome, Museo Arte Orientale
12B MH/BM 15 BAL/BL
17 Hutchison Library
Great Themes of Myth
18 MH/BM 20 National Museum of Copenhagen/Kit Weiss
21 DBP/Private Collection
23 BAL/Musée Condé, Chantilly
24 ET/Christie's Images
25 BAL/BL 27 BAL/V&A
28 Axel Poignant Collection
29 MH 30 BM 31 BAL/National Museum of Delhi 32 WFA/ Eugene Chestow Trust 33 BAL/ Giraudon 34 MH 35 BAL/Private Collection
Egypt
36 Zefa/Damm 38B MH
39L BAL 39R MH/BM
39B MH/BM 40 MH 41 MH
42T BAL 42B MH/BM 43 BAL/ Louvre 44T MH/BM 44B BAL/ BL 45 WFA/Cairo Museum
46T BAL/Giraudon 46B BAL/ Giraudon/Egyptian National Museum 47 Zefa 48T MH/BM
48B BAL/Louvre 49 BM
50L Zefa/Damm 50R MH/BM
51 WFA/Cairo Museum
52T Scala/Museo Archeologico, Florence 52B WFA/Cairo Museum 54 BM 55 BAL/BM
56 BAL/Louvre/Giraudon
Middle East
58 E T Archive 59T BAL/BM
59B Pierpont Morgan Library, NY
60T BM 60B BM 61 MH/ Louvre 62 BM 63 DBP 64 DBP
65 MH/Louvre 66T DBP
66B, 67T Mansell Collection
67B DBP
India
68 BAL/National Museum of India, New Delhi 70 WFA/ National Gallery, Prague 71 MH
72 BAL/V&A 73 BAL/V&A
74 V&A 75T BAL/National Museum of India 75B V&A
76 BAL/V&A 77 V&A 79 MH
80 V&A 81T Rajasthan Institute of Oriental Studies 81B MH
82T BAL/National Museum of India 82B MH 83 MH
84T BAL/V&A 84B V&A
85 MH 86 MH 87B BAL/ National Museum of India
87T BAL/BM
China
88 Zefa/Scholz 90 MH/Wellcome Collection 91 DBP 92T Zefa/

Damm 92B Robert Harding Library 93 DBP 94 BAL/BM
95 DBP 96 E T Archive/Nelson Gallery of Art, Kansas City
97 MH/Horniman Museum
98T and BL DBP 98BR Christie's Images 99 T and B DBP 100 Christie's Images 101 E T Archive
Tibet and Mongolia
102 DBP/Private Collection
103 MH 104/5,106 DBP/Private Collection 107L DBP/Private Collection 107R Courtesy of Richard Williamson 108/9 DBP/Private Collection
Japan
110 Spectrum/DJH 112 JG
115 JG 116 JG 118 JG
120 JG 121 Christie's Images 122 JG 123T BAL/BL 123B MH
Greece
124 Scala 126T BM 126B Louvre/Réunion des Musées Nationaux 127 MH/BM
128 Istanbul Archaeological Museum 130 Scala/Museo Gregoriano Etrusco 131 Ashmolean Museum, Oxford
132 Scala/National Museum of Athens 133B Virginia Museum of Fine Arts 133T Scala/Olympia Museum 135 MH 136T Louvre/ Réunion des Musées Nationaux
136B BM 137T National Museum of Copenhagen/Kit Weiss 137B Bildarchiv Preussischer Kulturbesitz 138T MH
138B Bildarchiv Preussischer Kulturbesitz/Laurentius
140 Munich Antikensammlungen/Studio Koppermann
141T Bildarchiv Preussischer Kulturbesitz 141B Scala/Museo Nazionale, Naples 142 Scala/ Acropolis Museum 143 MH
144 DBP 145 BM 146 Munich Antikensammlungen/Studio Koppermann 147 Ny Carlsberg Glyptothek 148 Metropolitan Museum, NY/Joseph Pulitzer Bequest 149 MH 150T Louvre/ Réunion des Musées Nationaux
150B BM 151 BM
153 Scala/ Ruvo di Puglia, Jatta
154 BM 156T MH 156B Bildarchiv Preussischer Kulturbesitz/ Laurentius 157T BM 157B Scala/ Museo Clementino, Vatican
158 BM 159 Scala/Museo Gregoriano Etrusco 160 MH
161 Boston Museum of Fine Arts/Wm Frances Warden Fund
163T University of Tübingen
163B Scala/Museo Gregoriano Etrusco 164 BM 165 Martin von Wagner Museum, Würzburg
Rome
166 Spectrum 168 Scala
169T MH/BM 169B Scala/Museo Nazionale, Naples 170 Scala/Città del Vaticano 171T WFA/Museo Nazionale, Rome 171B Scala/ Milano Soprintendenza Antichità Silva 172 Scala/Museo Nazionale, Naples 173T Somerset County Museum Service 173B BAL

174T Leeds Leisure Services
175 Spink & Son
The Celtic World
176 WFA 178T National Museum, Copenhagen/Kit Weiss
178BL Corinium Museum/Rex Knight 178BR WFA/Musée de Rennes 179 National Museum, Copenhagen/Kit Weiss 181 National Museum, Copenhagen/Kit Weiss 182 City of Bristol Museum & Art Gallery 184 Réunion des Musées Nationaux 186T Musée d'Alesia 186B WFA/ Musée de Rennes 187 WFA/ National Museum of Ireland
198 BAL/BM, Ms Add10294
Northern Europe
190 Universitetets Oldsaksammling, Oslo/Foto Johnsen
192T MH/Musée de Bayeux
192B WFA 193T WFA
193B Gotlands Fornsal Museum/ Raymond Hejdstrom 194 WFA/ Arhus Kunst Museum 196 WFA/ Statens Historiska Museum, Stockholm 197T WFA 197B, 198T, 198B WFA/Statens Historiska Museum, Stockholm
199 WFA 200T, 200B WFA/ Statens Historiska Museum, Stockholm 201T WFA/Viking Ship Museum 201B, 202 WFA/ Statens Historiska Museum, Stockholm 204L WFA/ Universitetets Oldsaksammling, Oslo 204R WFA/Universitetets Oldsaksammling, Oslo 205 WFA
Central and Eastern Europe
206 DBP 208T/B DBP 209 DBP
210/11 DBP 212 Metropolitan Museum of Art, New York
The Arctic Regions
214 Robert Harding Library 216T WFA/Smithsonian Institute 216B WFA/Museum of Natural History, Chicago 217 WFA/ Smithsonian Institute
218 American Museum of Natural History
North America
220 Wheelwright Museum of the American Indian 222T WFA/Provincial Museum of British Columbia 222B WFA/Field Museum of Natural History, Chicago 223 WFA/Haffenreffern Museum of Anthropology, RI
224 WFA/BM 225T and 225B WFA/Centennial Museum, Vancouver 226L WFA/Chandler Point Collection 226R, 227T WFA/James Hooper Collection, Watersfield 227B WFA/Provincial Museum of British Columbia
228 Wheelwright Museum of Indian Art 231 WFA/Museum of the American Indian 232T WFA/ Denver Art Museum 232B Zefa/ Paolo Koch 233 WFA/BM
Mesoamerica
234 WFA 236T E T Archive
236B St Louis Museum of Art, Gift of Morton B. Day
237T WFA/Liverpool Museum
237B WFA/Museum für Völkerkünde, Basle 238 WFA/National

Museum of Anthropology, Mexico
239T WFA/Biblioteca Università, Bologna 239B WFA/BM
240T WFA/artwork based on *Codex Magliabechiano*
241B WFA/Museum für Völkerkünde, Basle 243 E T Archive 244T Bibliothèque Nationale de l'Assemblée
244B WFA/Museum für Völkerkünde, Basle 245L WFA/Philip Goldman, London 245R WFA/ National Museum of Anthropology, Mexico 246T and B Bibliothèque Nationale de l'Assemblée 248T MH/BM
249T E T Archive
South America
250 Zefa/Presho 252T South American Pictures 252B E T Archive 253 South American Pictures 254 South American Pictures 255B BAL/BM
256 South American Pictures
258 Zefa/Luz 260 Robert Harding Picture Library
261 Hutchison Picture Library 262 Robert Harding Picture Library 263 South American Pictures
Africa
264 Dr Georg Gerster/John Hilleson Agency 266BL WFA/ Museum of Art, Dallas
266BR WFA 267 WFA/Museum of Art, Dallas 268 WFA/MRAC Terveuren 269T WFA/Private Collection 269B WFA/Robert Sainsbury Collection 270B WFA/Allan Brandt Collection 272B WFA 273 WFA/Robert Aberman
275L WFA/Entwistle Gallery, London 275R WFA/ Freide Collection, New York
276 MH 277L WFA 277R BAL/BM
Australia
278 WFA/Tambaran Collection, New York 280 Zefa/Bagli
281T Robert Harding Picture Library 281B National Gallery of Australia © Paddy Dhatangu
282 Rebecca Hossack Gallery
283 National Gallery of Australia
284 WFA/Auckland Gallery of Art 285 WFA 286 Professor Robert Layton 287 BM
Oceania
288 Color Photo Hans Hinz
289 BAL/Bonhams 290L MH/BM
290R MH/BM 291 MH/BM
292 MH/BM 293 Axel Poignant Collection 294T WFA/National Museum of New Zealand
294B MH/BM 295T MH/BM
295B Robert Harding Picture Library/Israel Tabley 296 BAL/ BM 297 Hamburgisches Museum für Völkerkünde
Southeast Asia
300 Spectrum 302 MH/Musée Guimet 303 WFA/Klung-klung, Bali 304 Zefa 306L MH/BM
306R WFA 307 WFA/Private Collection

INDEX